flying visits
SCANDINAVIA

CADOGANguides

Contents

Authors' acknowledgements

Joan Gannij: My appreciation goes to the following individuals and organizations for their support: Helge Gjellestad of SAS and Partners, Annette Saether, Ellen Frisvold, Gunhild Vevik, Svein Jakob, Siri Gill, Inger Foyn Hermansen, Egil Fjellhaug, Harald Hansen, Ann Helen Eriksen, Audun Stene, Ingrid Nernas at Norwegian Railways, Flyggruten, National Car Rental, Johan Hjelmaas, Torill Torsvik, Per Husby, Helene Winsents and Norwegian Coastal Voyage, and the countless others who showed me Norwegian hospitality at its best. *Tusen takk!*

Antonia Cunningham would like to thank the following for their help and hospitality: Marie Ravn Jürgensen at the London Danish Tourist Board for being so helpful, Henrik Thierlein at Wonderful Copenhagen, Vibeke Wiboe and Kenn Andersen in Helsingør, Lise Retboell in Esbjerg, Birgit Iversen, Birgit and Niels Steen Sørensen and Unika Cykler on Fanø, Sanne Stamrose, Richard Kværnø and the Hotel Dagmar in Ribe, Cecilie Mortensen at Hotel Guldsmeden, Villa Provence, Anne Hübner and Bjarne Bækgaard in Århus, Anne Marie Jensen and the Hotel Chagall in Aalborg, Lene Kappelborg and Finn Bredahl Jørgensen in Skagen; Enda O'Toole at Hertz; Paul Fitzsimmons and Aoife McGlynne at Ryanair and Lucy Walton at easyJet. And finally, I would like to thank Susan Hazledine for her peerless skills in drawing up military campaigns, laughing a lot, being such a fabulous friend and searching out delicious food; Duncan Robertson, without whom I wouldn't have got very far – both of whom made this project lots of fun; Ali Qassim, whose 'essay crisis' was just as bad as mine, and Alex Brown – to all of them my love and thanks.

About the authors

Ali Qassim (Sweden) is of British birth but is half-Swedish on his mother's side and has grandparents living in Sweden. He graduated from Cambridge University in 1987 and went on to follow a successful career in journalism. He has contributed articles to travel books on Latin America, but this is the first time he has been able to use his fluent Swedish on an assignment.

Joan Gannij (Norway) was born in New York City and raised in Los Angeles. She began her career as a photojournalist documenting pop culture. Born on Amsterdam Avenue, she decided to explore her European roots by relocating to Amsterdam in 1987. She has written and edited various travel guides in the last fifteen years, with a focus on Scandinavia. She has her own editorial office in Amsterdam and is currently studying astronomy.

Antonia Cunningham (Denmark), born in the not-so-exotic London suburb of Hampton Hill, thoroughly enjoys hopping on and off aeroplanes and has found her degree in French, Italian and art history surprisingly handy. She lives in London and, in between planning her next jaunt, she writes and edits both adults' and children's books.
(*For my parents and Nick, Tim, Giles, Francesca et al, with love.*)

Cadogan Guides
Network House, 1 Ariel Way
London W12 7SL, UK
info@cadoganguides.co.uk
www.cadoganguides.com

The Globe Pequot Press
246 Goose Lane, PO Box 480, Guilford,
Connecticut 06437–0480, USA

Copyright © Ali Qassim, Joan Gannij and
   Antonia Cunningham 2004

Cover design by Sarah Gardner
Book design by Andrew Barker
Cover photographs: (front) © CORBIS, © Bo
   Zaunders/CORBIS, © Walter Bibikow/Jon Arnold,
   © Doug Pearson/Jon Arnold; (back) © Antonia
   Cunningham, © Gavin Hellier/Jon Arnold
Maps © Cadogan Guides,
   drawn by Map Creation Ltd
Managing Editor: Natalie Pomier
Series Editor: Linda McQueen
Editing: Rhonda Carrier, Dominique Shead
Design: Sarah Gardner
Proofreading: Joss Waterfall
Indexing: Isobel McLean
Production: Navigator Guides

Printed in Italy by Legoprint
A catalogue record for this book is available
   from the British Library
ISBN 1-86011-137-8

The author and publishers have made every effort to ensure the accuracy of the information in this book at the time of going to press. However, they cannot accept any responsibility for any loss, injury or inconvenience resulting from the use of information contained in this guide.

Please help us to keep this guide up to date. We have done our best to ensure that the information in this guide is correct at the time of going to press. But places and facilities are constantly changing, and standards and prices in hotels and restaurants fluctuate. We would be delighted to receive any comments concerning existing entries or omissions. Authors of the best letters will receive a copy of the Cadogan Guide of their choice.

Getting There

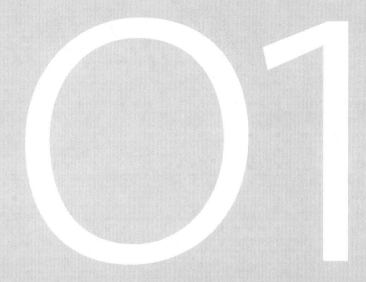

By Air

In the last few years the airline industry has undergone a revolution. Inspired by the success of Stelios Haji-Ioannou's easyJet company, other airlines flocked to join him in breaking all the conventions of air travel to offer fares at rock-bottom prices. After September 11th 2001, while long-haul carriers hit the ropes in a big way, these budget airlines experienced unprecedented sales, and responded by expanding their list of destinations throughout Europe.

Whereas in their first years no-frills airlines had an undoubted 'backpackerish' feel, this has become an increasingly mainstream way to travel. New airlines are still starting up all the time – and, most importantly, larger national airlines such as British Airways and SAS have got in on the act, copying some of the more attractive aspects of budget travel, such as internet booking with discounts, and one-way fares.

The ways in which low prices are achieved can sometimes have a negative effect on the experience of travellers, but can sometimes be a bonus too. First, these airlines often use smaller regional airports, where landing fees and tarmac-time charges are at a minimum. In the UK this means you may be able to find a flight from nearer your home town. At the other end, you are often taken direct to small, uncongested airports that are right in the heart of the countryside, not just the capital cities. This may mean a longer journey to your destination city from the airport.

The **planes** tend to be all one class and with the maximum seating configuration.

Fares are one-way – so there is no need to stay over on a Saturday night to qualify for the lowest fares – and can vary enormously on the same route, according to when you travel and how far in advance you book: the most widely advertised, rock-bottom deals are generally for seats on very early-morning, early-in-the-week flights; on the most popular routes, while you might get a price of £40 for a 6am Monday flight, the same route can cost you £140 on a Friday evening. Because of this constantly changing price system it is important to note that **no-frills airlines are not always the cheapest**, above all on the very popular routes at peak times. One of the benefits of the no-frills revolution that is not

Who Goes Where?

	Page	Ryanair	easyJet	SAS	British Airways	British Midland (BMI)	SAS Braathens	Norwegian Air Shuttle	Wideroe	Maersk	Finnair	Skyways	Snowflake	Varig	American Airlines	Continental	SAS (USA)	DFDS Seaways	Fjordline	Smyril
Stockholm (S)	22	●		●	●						●	●	●		●		●			
Västerås (S)	58	●																			
Gothenburg (S)	71	●		●															●		
Malmö (S)	99	●	★	●																	
Oslo (N)	141	●		●	●			●	●							●	●				
Stavanger (N)	175			●			●		●											●	
Haugesund (N)	184	●																		●	
Bergen (N)	200						●	●	●											●	●
Copenhagen (D)	231	★	●	●	●	●				●			●			●					
Esbjerg (D)	267	●				●													●		
Århus (D)	286	●						★													

S = Sweden, N = Norway, D = Denmark   ★ not direct, but an easy connection

Airlines

UK and Ireland

BMI British Midland, t 0870 607 0555, *www. flybmi. com*. From Glasgow and Edinburgh to Copenhagen; and from Aberdeen to Esbjerg.

British Airways, t 0870 850 9850, *www.ba.com*. London Heathrow and Manchester to Copenhagen and Oslo; Heathrow to Stockholm.

easyJet, t 08717 500 100, *www.easyjet.com*. From Bristol, London Stansted and Newcastle to Copenhagen, which is also convenient for Malmö in Sweden.

EUjet, t 0870 414 1414, *www.eujet.com*. From Kent International Airport to Stockholm.

Finnair, t 0870 241 4411/**t** 0800 583 1888, *www.finnair.com*. Manchester to Stockholm.

Maersk, t (020) 7333 0066, *www.maersk-air. com*. From London Gatwick to Copenhagen. Also to Billund Airport in Jutland, from where there is a dedicated coach link with Århus and Odense.

Norwegian Air Shuttle, t (020) 7839 3300, *www.norwegian.no*. From London Stansted to Oslo and Bergen.

Ryanair, Irish Republic **t** 0818 30 30 30, UK **t** 0871 246 0000 (10p/min), *www.ryanair. com*. From London Stansted to Stockholm, Västerås, Malmö, Gothenburg, Oslo (Torp), Haugesund, Esbjerg, Århus. London Luton to Västerås and Esbjerg; Glasgow to Stockholm, Gothenburg and Oslo. There is a coach service from Malmö to Copenhagen.

SAS, t 0870 60 727 727/**t** (020) 8990 7159, *www.scandinavian.net*. From London Heathrow to Stockholm, Gothenburg, Oslo, Stavanger and Copenhagen. From Edinburgh to Stockholm. From Manchester to Stockholm and Copenhagen, and from Birmingham to Copenhagen. From Dublin to Copenhagen. Sometimes also Bergen.

SAS Braathens, t 00 47 815 20 000, *www. sasbraathens.no*. London Gatwick, Aberdeen to Bergen and Stavanger; Newcastle to Stavanger; Manchester to Bergen.

Skyways, *www.skyways.se*. From Birmingham to Stockholm.

Snowflake, t 00 45 77 66 10 05, *www.flysnow flake.com*. From Inverness to Stockholm.

Varig, t 0845 603 7601, *www.varig.com*. London Heathrow to Copenhagen.

Wideroe, t 00 47 810 00 1200, *www.wideroe. no*. From Manchester and Aberdeen to Bergen, Newcastle to Stavanger, and the Shetlands to Oslo.

USA and Canada

Air Canada, t 1 888 247 2262, *www.aircanada. ca*. From Toronto and Vancouver. Connections to Oslo.

American Airlines, t 800 433 7300, *www. aa.com*. From Chicago direct to Stockholm, and connecting flights to Oslo.

British Airways, t 1 800 AIRWAYS, *www.ba. com*. To London and Manchester with connecting onward flights.

Continental Airlines, USA **t** 1 800 525 0280, *www. continental.com*. Direct from Newark to Oslo; flights to London with connections.

Delta Airlines, t 1 800 241 4141, *www.delta.com*. To London with connecting onward flights.

Lufthansa, t (USA) 800 399 5838/800 645 3880; (Canada) **t** 800 563 5954, *www. lufthansa-usa.com*. From major cities to Scandinavian cities via Frankfurt.

NWA/KLM, t 800 447 4747/800 225 2525, *www.nwa.com*; *www.klm.com*. Via Amsterdam.

United Airlines, t 1 800 247 3663, *www.united airlines.com*. To London.

SAS (Scandinavian Airlines), t 800 221 2350, *www.scandinavian.net*. Direct from Newark to Oslo, Stockholm and Copenhagen; from Chicago to Stockholm and Copenhagen, and Washington and Seattle to Copenhagen.

Virgin Atlantic Airways, t 800 862 8621, *www.virgin-atlantic.com*. No direct flights. To London from Las Vegas, LA, Washington, New York, San Francisco and Orlando, with onward connections.

always appreciated is not so much their own prices as the concessions they have forced on the older, mainstream carriers. It is **always** worth comparing no-frills prices with those of the main airlines, and checking out what special offers are going.

No-frills airline tickets are only sold direct, by phone or on-line, not through travel agents. To get the lowest prices you must book on-line, not by phone. You may not be issued with an actual **ticket** when you book, but given a reference number to show with

To Scandinavia by Air from North America via London

You can fly directly to a few of the bigger cities in this guide from North America. But it is also possible for North Americans to take advantage of the explosion of cheap inter-European flights, by taking a charter to London, and booking a UK–Scandinavia budget flight in advance on a budget airline's website (*see* p.3). This will need careful planning: you're looking at an 8–14hr flight followed by a 3hr journey across London and another 2–3hr hop to Scandinavia; it can be done, especially if you are a person who is able to sleep on a night flight, but you may prefer to spend a night or two in London.

Direct to Scandinavia

The main airports for transatlantic flights are the three capital cities of **Stockholm**, **Oslo** and **Copenhagen**. The main carriers flying direct to these cities are SAS and Continental; *see* the boxes on pp.2 and 3 for details.

Since **prices** are constantly changing and there are numerous kinds of deals on offer, the first thing to do is find yourself a travel agent who is capable of laying the current options before you. The time of year can make a great difference to the price and availability; prices can range from around $500 for the best bargain deals to well over $1,000.

A number of companies offer cheaper charter flights to Scandinavia – look in the Sunday travel sections of *The New York Times*, *Los Angeles Times*, *Chicago Tribune*, *Toronto Star* or other big-city papers.

Via London

Start by finding a charter or discounted scheduled flight to London: try the main airlines, but also check Sunday-paper travel sections for the latest deals, and look on *www.priceline.com*, *www.expedia.com*, *www.hotwire.com*, *www.bestfares.com*, *www.cheaptrips.com*, *www.cheaptickets.com*, *www.onetravel.com*.

When you have the availability and arrival times for London flights, match up a convenient flight time on the website of the budget airline that flies to your chosen Scandinavian city. *If you are flying to London, be careful to choose only flights from the airports near London: Luton, Gatwick, Heathrow, London City and Stansted.*

You will most likely be arriving at Heathrow terminals 3 or 4 (possibly Gatwick), and may be flying out from Stansted, Luton, London City or Gatwick, all of which are in different directions and will mean travelling through central London, so leaving enough time is essential. Add together the journey times and prices for Heathrow into central London and back out again to your departure airport. You could mix and match – the Tube to Victoria and the Gatwick Express, or a taxi from Heathrow to King's Cross Thameslink and a train to Luton – but don't even think of using a bus or taxi at rush hours (7–10am and 4–7pm); train and/or Underground (Tube) are the only sensible choices. Always add on waiting times and delays in London's notoriously creaky transport system; and finally, although the cheapest airline fares are early morning and late at night, make sure your chosen transport is still operating at that time (*see* below).

For train, bus and tube information within London, call **t** (020) 7222 1234, *www.transportforlondon.gov.uk*.

Airport to Airport Taxis

A taxi directly between airports might avoid central London, but is an expensive option: Heathrow–Gatwick: 1hr 30mins, £85–£100. Heathrow–Stansted: 2hrs 15mins, £140–£160. Heathrow–Luton: 1hr 15mins, £80–£90.

Heathrow

Heathrow is about 15 miles west of the centre. **Airport information: t** 0870 0000 123.
By Tube: Heathrow is on the Piccadilly Line. Tube trains depart every 5–9 minutes from 6am to midnight and the journey time to

your passport at check-in. With some airlines you are not issued with an **assigned seat** at check-in either, but will board on a first-come, first-served basis. There are no 'air miles' schemes, and no **meal** will be included, though there will be (fairly expensive) snacks for sale on-board. There are no **refunds** if you miss your flight for any reason, although some of the airlines will allow you to **change** your destination, date of travel or the named the centre is 55mins. Single fare into the centre: £3.80.

By bus: The Airbus A2 (**t** 08705 80 80 80, *www.nationalexpress.com*) departs from all terminals every 30mins and makes several stops before terminating at King's Cross or Russell Square; the National Express 403 or 500 terminates at Victoria. £10 single, £15 return. It's a long ride: at least 1hr 45mins.

By train: The Heathrow Express (**t** 0845 600 1515) is the fastest option: trains every 15mins between 5.10am and 11.40pm to Paddington Station, which is on the Tube's Bakerloo, Circle and District Lines, taking 15mins. £13 single, £25 return.

By taxi: There are taxi ranks at all terminals. Fares into central London are about £35–£50.

Gatwick

Gatwick is about 20 miles south of London. There are two terminals, North and South, linked by a fast shuttle service. **Airport information: t** 0870 000 2468.

By train: The fastest service is the Gatwick Express (**t** 08457 48 49 50), which runs from Victoria Station to the South Terminal every 15 minutes and takes about 30mins. £11 single, £21.50 return. There are two other slower train services: another from Victoria, and one from London Bridge.

By taxi: Fares from central London with a black cab are about £40–£60.

Luton

30 miles north of London. **Airport information: t** (01582) 405 100.

By bus: Greenline bus 757 (**t** 0870 608 7261) runs roughly every half-hour between Luton Airport and stop 6 in Buckingham Palace Road, Victoria, via Finchley Rd, Baker St and Marble Arch. £8.50 single. The journey takes 1hr 15mins.

By train: Between 8am and 10pm, Thameslink (**t** 08457 48 49 50) run frequent trains from King's Cross Thameslink Station (10mins' walk from the King's Cross Station), via

Blackfriars, London Bridge and Farringdon, to Luton Airport Parkway. Tickets cost £10.40 single. At Luton a free shuttle bus takes you on to the airport; the journey takes 55mins.

By taxi: A black cab will cost you around £40–£60 from central London.

Stansted

Stansted is the furthest from London, about 35 miles to the northeast. **Airport information: t** 0870 000 0303.

By bus: Airbus A6 (**t** 08705 757 747) runs every 30mins from Victoria Station, Marble Arch and Hyde Park Corner, taking 1hr 30mins or more in traffic. There are less frequent services through the night. Tickets cost £10 single or £16 return.

By train: The Stansted Express (**t** 08457 48 49 50) runs every 30mins (15mins during peak times) between 5am and 11pm to and from Liverpool Street Station, in the City, taking 45mins. Tickets cost £13.80 single.

By taxi: A black cab from central London will cost £45–£65.

Sample Journeys

Heathrow–Luton: get to Heathrow Express from terminal 15mins; wait for train 10mins; journey 15mins; go from Paddington Station down into Tube 10mins; Tube to Farringdon 15mins; go up and buy Thameslink ticket 10mins including queueing; train and shuttle to Luton 55mins. **Total journey time** 2hrs 10mins, plus 45mins for delays and hitches, so 3hrs would be safest.

Heathrow–Stansted: get to Tube station from terminal 10mins, wait for Tube 5mins, Piccadilly Line to King's Cross 1hr 10mins, change to Circle Line and continue to Liverpool Street Tube Station 15mins, up into main line station and buy Stansted Express ticket 10mins, wait for train 20mins, train journey 45mins. **Total journey time** 2hrs 55mins, plus 45mins for delays and hitches, so 3hrs 40mins would be safest.

traveller for a fee. There are also charges for any **excess baggage**. Another way in which prices are kept down is by keeping **staffing levels** very low, especially on the ground. This means that check-in can take a lot longer.

Essentially, with no-frills flights, you're supposed to get what you pay for. If you pay a really low fare and get to your destination without a hitch, you think, hey, this is great. It's when a problem does arise, though, that you

Making it Work for You: 10 Tips to Remember

1 Whichever airline you travel with, the earlier you book, the cheaper seats will be.

2 Book on-line for the best prices, as there are often discounts of £2.50 to £5 per journey for on-line sales. Always compare the no-frills airlines' prices with those of main carriers

3 Be ready to travel at less convenient times. But be sure to check there is a means of getting from your destination airport if you arrive at night, allowing for at least an hour's delay – if you have to fork out for a taxi rather than a shuttle bus or local bus service, this could eat up the saving.

4 Think hard whether you want to book by credit card. You will have the consumer protection that that offers, but there is likely to be a supplement of anything up to £5. Consider using a debit card instead.

5 If you intend to travel often and can go at short notice, sign up for airlines' e-mail mailing lists to hear news of special offers.

6 Check whether airport taxes are included in the quoted price; they are usually extra.

7 Check the baggage allowance and don't take any excess. If you can travel light, take hand baggage only to avoid a long wait.

8 Take your own food and drink, to avoid paying for airport or on-board snacks.

9 Make sure you take your booking reference and confirmation with you to check in (this will have been emailed or posted to you).

10 Never ignore the advised check-in times, which are generally two hours. Don't be tempted to cut it fine, as check-in takes longer with budget airlines than with traditional carriers. If you are tall and want an aisle seat, or are travelling in a group, check in even earlier or get to the departure gate as early as possible.

start to notice the downside of no-frills operations. Since every plane is used to the limit, there are no 'spare' aircraft, so if one has a technical problem somewhere the day's schedules can collapse like a house of cards. And all the budget operators accept far fewer obligations towards customers in the event of lost bags, delays and so on than main carriers traditionally have; this is stated in the small print of their terms and conditions (all there, on the websites), but many people don't read this until after their problem has come up.

Disasters, of course, can always happen, but an awareness of the way the system works and why fares are cheap can go a good way to avoiding being caught out – *see* the tips in the box above. Finally, while corners are cut in many ways, there has been no evidence that those corners involve safety issues.

By Sea

You can take overnight ferries to some of the cities in this guide which are on the eastern coasts of Denmark, Norway and Sweden. Fast it is not, however; the crossing takes 17–22 hours, and passengers are required to book at least a reclining seat. However, if time is on your side and touring is on the itinerary, it can be cheaper than the combined cost of flights and car hire.

Ferry Operators

DFDS Seaways, t 08705 333 000 (booking)/ **t** 08705 333 000 (information); *www. dfdsseaways.co.uk*. Newcastle–Kristiansand–Gothenburg; Harwich–Esbjerg; Copenhagen–Oslo. There are also a selection of inclusive holidays and packages available in their main cruise holiday programme.

Fjordline, t (0191) 296 1313, *www.fjordline.co.uk*. Newcastle–Stavanger–Haugesund–Bergen. Also a wide range of holidays and cruises.

Northlink Ferries, t 0845 600 0449, *www.northlinkferries.co.uk*. In partnership with Fjordline and Smyril Line, offers a round-trip ticket linking Newcastle–Bergen–Lerwick–Kirkwall–Stromness–Scrabster–Aberdeen.

Smyril, t (01595) 690845, *www.smyril-line.com*. Lerwick (Shetlands)–Bergen via the Faroes.

See also *www.ferrybookers.com*.

Sweden: Introduction

02

Picture a small wooden house, painted a deep red with white trimmings around the bright yellow door and windows, set amid a deep spruce forest and close to a pristine lake. The only building in the vicinity is an outdoor toilet (also painted deep red) and maybe a tree house, and the noisiest neighbour an inquisitive passing deer. It sounds like a dreamy idyll, but this simple rural retreat is an affordable reality for many Swedes who, during the short and intensive Nordic summers, drop their deeply ingrained Lutheran work ethic and escape to their *stugas* (cottages) that dot the countryside to envelop themselves in the fleeting delights of nature. Embracing nature (and, with a population the size of Belgium – nine million inhabitants – in a country nearly the size of France, there's a lot of it) is almost a religion in Sweden. It is as if one of the world's most modern and highly sophisticated societies has to remind itself periodically that, only a few generations ago, most of its inhabitants eked a rather humble living out of farming.

Unravelling some of Sweden's surprising list of contradictions is one of the biggest pleasures of a visit to Scandinavia's largest country. Just a century ago, social and economic inequalities were extremely high in what was essentially a backward agrarian society, yet Sweden today is a shining example of a country that protects its citizens from cradle to grave but also practises successful capitalism – witness its diverse global brands such as Volvo, Ericsson, Electrolux, Absolut vodka, SKF, IKEA and Hennes & Mauritz. Swedes acquired international fame thanks to the devastation and death spread by the Vikings on the British Isles and the coasts of the Continent, a warrior-like mentality that continued through to the 16th and 17th centuries when the descendants of Gustav Vasa captured vast territories in Scandinavia and the Baltics. However, Sweden managed to remain neutral during the two 20th-century world wars and is today one of the leading promoters of world peace (though its domestic arms industry is dependent on exports for its survival). The extravagance of past Swedish monarchs is visible in the many splendid palaces located in some spectacular settings, yet the current royal family is low-key and modest (certainly by British standards), even if the romantic adventures of the two princesses, Victoria and Madeleine, are assiduously followed by the more scandalous elements of the Swedish press (there's another surprise – Swedes' sense of propriety and respect for privacy does not make them immune to gossip).

Proud of and enthusiastic about their own traditions, such as heading to the mountains to ski in February, lighting up community bonfires to mark the arrival of spring, or dancing around the maypole on Midsummer's Eve, Swedes are at the same time tolerant of other cultures, not least given the high number of immigrants that have entered the country (now representing about 15% of the total population). They are also highly considerate. Note how, during the summer exodus to their *stugas*, Swedes empty their main towns to allow tourists to make the most of the considerable cultural and gastronomical amenities on offer, at considerably deflated prices! On the other hand, you could always join the locals and hire your own small wooden house...

Sweden: Travel and Practical A–Z

Travel

Entry Formalities

A valid passport is required. Entry visas for temporary visits are not required for citizens of the UK, USA or Canada. Citizens who do not need visas for a temporary stay may remain in Sweden for up to 90 days.

Customs

Alcohol: The amount of tax-free alcohol allowed into Sweden is equivalent to 1 litre of spirits (i.e. an alcoholic beverage with an alcoholic content exceeding 22% by volume) or 2 litres of fortified wine (i.e. an alcoholic beverage with an alcoholic content exceeding 15 but not 22% by volume), or sparkling wine, or two litres of wine (i.e. other wine than fortified as well as other alcoholic beverages with an alcoholic content exceeding 3.5 but not 15 per cent by volume, which does not include strong beer). People under 20 are not allowed to bring in alcohol.

Tobacco: The amount of tobacco exempt from taxes is the equivalent of 200 cigarettes or 100 cheroots, or 50 cigars or 250 grams of tobacco, or a proportional selection of these tobacco products. People under 18 are not allowed to bring in tobacco products.

Firearms and ammunition may not be brought into or taken out of Sweden without a permit.

Getting Around

By Train

Sweden's national rail network is highly efficient and extensive, with pleasant, modern trains. The fastest and most comfortable option is the high-speed **X2000**, which reaches speeds of 200kph (125mph) on all the major routes. Services include radio and music outlets in all the seats, and meals served in seats in first class compartments and in the bistro coach in second class. Only slightly slower are the **Intercity** services. For longer routes, the **Nordpilen** (Northern Arrow) provides sleeping compartments, couchettes and sometimes even a bistro/cinema coach.

For lengthy travel, go-as-you-please tickets such as the **Sweden Rail Pass** or **ScanRail Pass**

(includes supplement for the X2000) are recommended. Call SJ national train information, **t** 0771 75 75 75, *www.swedenbooking.com*.

By Coach and Bus

Inter-city **coach** travel is well serviced and inexpensive. The largest bus operator is Swebus Express, **t** (020) 0218 218 (toll free within Sweden), *www.swebusexpress.se*, which has 300 destinations.

City buses are generally efficient, though in Stockholm the islands make the underground a faster alternative, and in Gothenburg the excellent tram system is quicker.

By Plane

Although Sweden's four biggest cities are well connected by train and coach, air travel can be an affordable option if you make use of Scandinavian Airlines (SAS)' special **Air Pass** fares for domestic travel, **t** (08) 797 2202.

By Car

While virtually all the day trips that we propose in this guide are easily accessible by public transport, you may decide to hire a car if you plan to follow the touring itineraries suggested in this guide. *See* pp.127 and 217 for car hire addresses in the UK and USA; local addresses are also given in each city chapter.

Driving in Sweden is a real pleasure given the country's huge open spaces and sparsely populated countryside. Motorways also have numerous natural and man-made roadside stops to enjoy the scenery. It is best to avoid city centres, particularly Stockholm.

Rules and Regulations

If you are over 18 and have a driver's licence from your home country, you can use it in Sweden for a maximum period of one year. Vehicles not registered in Sweden must display their nationality.

Swedes are generally safe drivers, though like their continental counterparts drivers may exceed **speed limits** on motorways. Officially though, speed limits are 50kph in urban areas, 70kph outside urban areas and 110kph on motorways. Cars with caravans may not drive over 80kph and should be fitted with special mirrors.

For extra precaution, cars must always use a **dipped beam** at all times, even, rather inexplicably, during the intense sunlight of the never-ending summer days. **Safety belts** must be used in both front and back seats and children under 7 must use special equipment such as a baby protector, child seat, pad with belt or a chair with belt.

Drink-driving is even more frowned upon here than elsewhere in Europe, with the alcohol limit for drink driving at 0.2 grams per litre of blood.

For emergency car repairs call the emergency services on **t** (020) 91 00 40.

Main roads and motorways are never far from nature and extra caution should be used at dawn and dusk with **wild animals**, particularly moose, roe deer and reindeer, who cause half of all accidents in Sweden. For all unattended, signposted **pedestrian crossings**, vehicles are obliged to give way to pedestrians who are on or about to use the crossing, which means that the vehicle must stop and let the pedestrian cross. **Mobile phones** may currently be used when driving, but there are serious moves afoot to prohibit hand-held mobile phones in the future. **Snow tyres** are a must for travel during winter.

Most **petrol stations** are self-service and you can usually pay by credit card. Many have card/cash-operated fuel pumps (which take SEK20, 50 and 100 notes) that are open round the clock.

Swedish National Road Administration, Röda Vägen, SE 781 87 Borlänge, **t** (0243) 750 00.

By Taxi

Following the deregulation of the Swedish taxi industry, prices can vary by time of day and week, so it is a good idea to confirm the taxi fare before setting off. Credit cards are usually accepted.

By Bike

The country's relative flatness, and the concerted state effort to create bike paths, encourage cycling and make Sweden an ideal country for cyclists. Two cycle paths traverse the whole country: **Sverigeleden** (the National Route) takes you from south to north and from east to west; and **Cykelspåret** (the Bike Path) follows the southern coast from Ystad. Unlike cars, bikes don't need to have lights on during daylight. The average price for a day's hire is SEK70.

Practical A–Z
Alcohol

Alcoholic beverages can only be bought in state-owned monopoly stores called '*Systembolaget*'. You must be 20 years old and prepared to show some ID. In pubs, you can buy a drink from the age of 18.

Allemansrätten

In theory, every Swedish citizen is entitled to the right of public access across the countryside. Effectively, this means tourists are allowed to walk, cycle, horse-ride, ski, and stay in country areas providing they do not damage crops (and ask permission first). You are also allowed to camp for one night on land not used for agriculture that is located away from someone's dwelling-house, pick flowers, berries and mushrooms in the countryside (though certain plants like orchids are protected species), and to light a fire providing it is safe and never on bare rocks as this might cause permanent damage due to cracking. Like all model Swedish citizens, don't leave any litter. Call the **Swedish Environmental Protection Agency, t** (08) 698 10 00.

Climate and When to Go

Despite its northern position, the warm Gulf Stream has blessed Sweden with a relatively mild climate and sea temperatures that are slightly higher than in the English Channel or the Baltic Sea. **Winters** are certainly severe in the northernmost part of the country, but coastal towns like Gothenburg in the southwest, and Malmö in the southernmost tip of Sweden, escape much of the icy conditions that can block much of the archipelago

	temp (°C/°F)	hours' daylight
January		
Stockholm	−2.8/27.0	6
Malmö	−0.2/31.6	7
July		
Stockholm	17.2/63.0	18
Malmö	16.8/62.2	17

around Stockholm. The majority of summer resorts and castles, however, are closed outside May–Sept. **Summer** is the best time to visit, not only because of the relatively warm (if slightly wetter in August) weather, but also thanks to the virtually endless days during the peak midsummer days. Even in summer, though, weather is changeable.

Consulates and Embassies

Swedish Embassies Abroad

UK: 11 Montagu Place, London, **t** (020) 7917 6400/**t** (020) 7917 6410/6411, **f** (020) 7917 6475 (*open Mon–Fri 9–12*).
Canada: 377 Dalhousie St, Ottawa, **t** (613) 241 8553, **f** (613) 241 2277 (*open Mon–Fri 9–12*).
USA: 1501 M Street NW, Suite 900, Washington DC, **t** (202) 467 2600, **f** (202) 467 2699 (*open Mon–Fri 10–5*).

In Stockholm

UK: Skarpögatan 6–8, **t** (08) 671 3000, **f** (08) 671 9989 (*open Mon–Fri 9–5*).
Canada: Tegelbacken 4, **t** (08) 453 3000, **f** (08) 453 3016 (*open Mon–Fri 8.30–12 and 1–5*).
USA: Dag Hammarskjölds Väg 31, **t** (08) 783 53 00, **f** (08) 661 19 64 (*open Mon–Fri 8–4.30*).

Crime and the Police

In spite of a couple of high profile political murders in the last two decades, Sweden has a relatively low crime rate, with most crimes involving the theft of personal property from cars or residences or in public areas, particularly the centre of major towns. **Police, fire and ambulance** can be reached by dialling **t** 112. If you call from a phone booth you can call free.

Disabled Travellers

Sweden is generally regarded as a leading country with respect to service and adapting facilities for the disabled. Call **DHR** (Swedish Federation for Disabled Persons), Katrinebergsvägen 6, Stockholm, **t** (08) 685 80 00.

Electricity

220V AC current is used in Sweden.

Festivals

Walpurgis Night (Valborg): A large fire is lit on the night of April 30, around which people gather to sing out the winter and sing in the spring.
Midsummer: A maypole is raised in most people's gardens and public parks and people dance to folk music, followed by a meal consisting primarily of herring, new potatoes, schnapps and strawberries.
August: Popular for crayfish parties and for fermented Baltic herring, an acquired taste as it can be foul-smelling (*see* p.20).
December 13 (Santa Lucia): In remembrance of the Sicilian Saint Lucia, Swedish girls dress up in white with candles in their hair and boys put on wizard-like hats and wake their parents up with breakfast in bed.
Christmas: A special time of the year in Sweden, with most windows lit by candles and special market stalls in central squares.

Fishing

The plethora of lakes and rivers offer ideal locations for spinning, fly-fishing, sea-fishing, angling and trolling. Fishing using hand tackle is free along the Swedish coast and in the five largest lakes, Vänern, Vättern, Mälaren, Hjälmaren and Storsjön. It is also free to fish using hand tackle in the middle of Stockholm city, where even salmon can be caught. A fishing permit (starting at SEK45 per day) is required for freshwater fishing in all other areas in Sweden. A permit for fish such as salmon, salmon trout and char costs SEK200 per day. Ask at the local tourist office.

Health and Insurance

Before arriving in Sweden, you need to ensure that you have adequate health insurance coverage, as medical treatment is very expensive without any form of insurance. Citizens of any of the Nordic or EU/EEA countries have access to public medical services for immediate necessary care, but they should make sure to bring a stamped E128 or E111 form, available from post offices.

A local primary health clinic, **Vårdcentralen**, listed in the blue pages of the telephone directory, charges about SEK120 for a consultation. Hospital casualty departments are ready to take care of acute illnesses or accidents.

For emergency care for EU members you can contact **Stockholm Care AB, t** (08) 672 24 00.

Chemists are generally open Mon–Fri 9–6, Sat 10–2. Prescription drugs and over-the-counter medicines are sold only in chemists.

There are no **vaccination** requirements for any international traveller entering Sweden.

Money and Banks

Sweden is one of the few EU member states not to use the euro; the currency is the Swedish krona (crowns/SEK), which is divided into 100 öre. The following notes are available: 20, 50, 100, 500, 1000; the coins are 50 öre, 1, 5, and 10 krona. 1 krona = 100 öre.

Sweden's central bank is the **Riksbank**, *www.riksbanken.se*. The service charge for exchanging **foreign currency** is SEK20–35 irrespective of how much money you exchange. Currency specialists do not charge. The service charge for **traveller's cheques** is as follows: FOREX SEK15 per cheque; post office SEK50 for up to 10 cheques. FOREX branches are centrally located at railway stations, airports and ferry terminals.

Most **credit cards** are accepted in Sweden, including American Express, Diners Club, Visa and Eurocard. Credit cards are used even for small amounts, including taxi fares. You can also use them in **ATMs** for cash withdrawals.

Opening Hours, Museums and National Holidays

Banks: Open Mon–Fri 9.30–3. Many offices have additional opening hours in the late afternoons at least once a week (in larger cities until 6). Closed at weekends.

Shops: Regular opening hours are Mon–Fri 9.30–6, Sat until 2 or 4. In the big cities, opening hours can be longer – until 8 on weekdays and 10–4 on Sundays. Many supermarkets are open from early in the morning until the evening. Look out for special offer signs: *Rea* (sale), *Extrapris* (special offer) or *Fynd* (bargain).

National Holidays

1 Jan New Year's Day
6 Jan Epiphany
Mar/April Good Friday/Easter Sunday/ Easter Monday
1 May May Day
May Ascension Day
May/June Whit Sunday/Whit Monday
June Midsummer Day
I Nov All Saints Day
25 Dec Christmas Day
26 Dec Boxing Day

Post offices: Open Mon–Fri 9–6, Sat 10–1, with some local variations.

Museums: The best of Sweden's museums are located in the three main cities covered in this guide, and are almost always closed on Mondays.

Churches (Roman Catholic, Romanian Orthodox, Finnish Lutheran, Estonian Lutheran, Syrian Orthodox, Methodist, Pentecostal, Islamic, Hindu and the Swedish Church): Open every day.

Post and Telephones

Postal and parcel services are provided by Posten. For information on postage and the service network, see *www.posten.se*.

Stamps are also sold at retail outlets including newspaper kiosks, local supermarkets and hotels.

For post office opening hours, *see* above.

Telephones

When you call abroad from Sweden, first dial 00 and then the country number and wait for the tone. Then dial the area code without the 0 and finally the subscriber's number. To order collect call service, ring **t** (020) 0018.

When calling Sweden from the UK or USA, dial 46 for Sweden and then drop the first zero of the relevant city code (Stockholm 08, Gothenburg 031, Malmö 040, Vasterås 021).

If you are already in Sweden, and dialling from within a city to a number in the same city, you drop the city code.

Telephone cards are common and can be bought from kiosks, shops, hotels or at telephone stores. All kiosks accept credit cards.

Hotel Price Categories
luxury SEK2,000
very expensive SEK1,550–2,000
expensive SEK1,050–1,550
moderate SEK800–1,050
inexpensive below SEK800

Restaurant Price Categories
very expensive over SEK950
expensive SEK400–950
moderate SEK135–400
inexpensive below SEK135

Price Categories

The hotels and restaurants in this guide have been assigned categories reflecting a range of prices (*see* box, above). Restaurant categories are for set menus or a two-course meal for one without wine. Hotel prices are for a double room with bath/shower in high season.

SHR, the Swedish Hotel and Restaurant Association, launched a national classification scheme for hotels in Sweden in 2000, but the system is still not consolidated.

Tax Refunds

Non-EU residents are entitled to a tax refund of up to 15–18% on every purchase exceeding SEK200 in shops affiliated with **Global Refund Sverige**, *www.global refund.com/sweden*.

When you make your purchase, show your passport and ask for a Global Refund Cheque. Your goods will be sealed and must not be opened until you have received an export validation. The goods must be exported no later than three months after the date of purchase. On leaving Sweden, present your passport, your sealed purchases and your Global Refund Cheques for export validation (stamp). You can cash your Global Refund Cheques at any refund office.

Tipping

Tips are always included in the price, but it is customary to leave at least a 10% tip at restaurants and bars, and when taking a taxi.

Tourist Information

Sweden's excellent tourism information is serviced by 325 authorized tourist offices that were classified into two levels in 2000: Level 2 with green 'i' signs, and the more professional tourist offices, Level 1, with blue and yellow signs. The national office updates its own database, and the information is available for other tourist offices on *www.sweden.se*.
Swedish Travel & Tourism Council, t 00 46 620 150 10 (from outside Sweden), *www. visit-sweden.com*.
UK: Swedish Travel & Tourism Council, 5 Upper Montagu Street London, **t** (020) 7870 5602/4/5/9, **f** (020) 7724 5872.
North America (Canada and USA): Swedish Travel & Tourism Council, Grand Central Station, New York, NY, **t** (212) 885 9700/62/ 20, **f** (212) 885 9764.

Where to Stay

Sweden offers a wide variety of accommodation to suit all tastes and budgets. Hotels are of generally high standard and invariably include a lavish buffet breakfast in the room rate. Look out in particular for summer and weekend rates and special travel pass and accommodation packages (check the main city tourist offices), which are available even at the higher end of the market.

For those with more eclectic tastes or in search of special experiences, there are charming manor houses, elegant country houses, renovated sailing ships, former prisons and even the odd tree house (*see* p.60).

Also available are earthy red cabins (or cottages) that dot the Swedish countryside and are synonymous with Sweden. Varying considerably in quality, cabins represent an individual and economical type of holiday housing, as they can be rented from SEK2,000 per week. Most cabins have a modern kitchen with cooker, fridge, plates, a large living room with colour TV and bedrooms with comfortable beds.

Sweden:
Food and Drink

04

The most common introduction to Swedish food today is likely to be a pile of meatballs and boiled potatoes soaked in cream sauce, with a spoonful of lingonberry jelly, at one of the ever-growing number of IKEA stores mushrooming around the world. No offence to the meals offered by the Swedish furniture giant, but this does rather a disservice to the culinary revolution that has gripped Sweden in the last decade.

Certainly, there is a modicum of truth in past associations of the run-of-the-mill Swedish restaurant with dull and starchy cafeteria-style food, but this is now as outdated a perception as the image of Sweden as an expensive place to dine. Two main trends have transformed Swedish dining: the popularity of eating out in the style of southern Europeans, accompanied by a growing taste for a wide range of international cuisines that Swedes have become accustomed to sampling during frequent trips abroad; and the rapid rise of locally grown, mostly organic products that cater to the brigade of travellers who demand healthy and fresh food.

Leading the trend for imaginative cooking is Sweden's second city, Gothenburg, which has proudly run off in the last decade with the largest number of Swedish Chef of the Year awards. The ingredients for this success are fine basic ingredients (typically fresh fish and seafood, fruits and fungi, game and whitefish roe) and a herd of young, inventive chefs. In recent years, the Swedish National Cooking Team has won three of the world's most prestigious gastronomic competitions: the 1999 World Cup in Basel, the 2000 Olympics in Erfurt, and the 2002 Expogast in Luxembourg. As the explosion of designer-conscious eateries in Sweden's top cities and their environs testifies, this dining bonanza has also boosted Swedish design and architecture. By extension, exciting food-related experiences such as a lobster safari, oyster-catching and moose-spotting trips are now becoming integral to holidays in Sweden.

In the wake of international food scares like BSE and dioxin poisoning of chicken and egg products, travellers to Sweden are also being lured by the country's reputation for safe meat and poultry, untainted dairy products and ecologically grown vegetables, potatoes and grain. Sweden established in 1985 an inspection body for certification accredited to both the Swedish Board of Agriculture and the National Food Administration, called KRAV, which today claims to be the biggest certifying organization of its kind in the world. And, with its 435 shops, the consumer-owned Green Konsum chain touts itself as the biggest ecological food retailer in Europe.

Classic and Typical Dishes

Although the fusion of two or more culinary traditions is now *de rigueur* in many trendy eating establishments, there is still an opportunity for travellers to sample

Dagens Rätt

Stiff competition and a weaker Swedish krona may have helped to bring down the cost of dining out in general, but you should still make the most of the *'dagens rätt'* ('daily special') that restaurants and cafeterias offer every day at lunchtime (rather early by European standards – from 11–2). A special (which may include a beverage, salad and coffee) might cost from SEK50 up to SEK150–200, depending on the courses and the type of restaurant.

Swedish Menu Reader

Traditional Hot Dishes

årtsoppa pea soup
blodpudding black pudding
fläsk och bruna bönor pork rinds and
  brown beans
falukorv traditional Swedish sausage
Jansson's fretelse Jansson's temptation
  (anchovy and potato pie)
kåldolmar stuffed cabbage rolls
köttbullar meatballs
pölsa hash
pytt i panna hash of fried diced meat with
  onions and potatoes

General

frukost breakfast
lunch lunch
middag dinner
skål! cheers!
kan jag få bestallä? can I order?
kan jag få notan? can I have the bill?

Förrätter (Starters) and Soppor (Soups)

sparrissoppa asparagus soup
blandat salad mixed salad
blomkålsoppa cauliflower soup
dagens soppa soup of the day
ärt soppa pea soup
fisksoppa fish soup
gravadlax marinated salmon
grönsaksoppa vegetable soup
moröttersoppa carrot soup
hönssoppa chicken soup
kålsoppa cabbage soup
krabbcoctail crab cocktail
laxsoppa salmon soup
linssoppa lentil soup
löksoppa onion soup
melon melon
oxsvanssoppa oxtail soup
paj filled pastry

potatissoppa potato soup
spinatsoppa spinach soup
tomatsoppa tomato soup

Köt (Meat)

anka duck
biff beef steak
rådjur venison
elg elk
fasan pheasant
gås goose
hare hare
hjort deer
kalkun turkey
kanin rabbit
köttbullar meatballs
kyckling chicken
kalvkött veal
lammkött lamb
stuvadbiff beef stew
lever liver
rost biff beef
korv sausage
renstek reindeer meat
skinka ham
stek steak
flask pork

Fisk (Fish) and Skaldjur (Shellfish)

ål eel
ansjovis anchovies
helgeflundra halibut
musslor mussels
fiskbullar fishballs
fiskkakor fishcakes
flyndra sole
gravadlax marinated salmon
hummer lobster
inlagd sill salted herring
forell trout
krabba crab
kräftor crayfish
lax salmon
makrill mackerel

husmankost ('home cooking'), even if it sometimes has been tempered by the gentle influence of French, Italian or Far Eastern cuisines.

The most traditional of offerings is likely to be **smörgåsbord**, a buffet-style table in a restaurant, prepared with a wide assortment of cold and hot dishes that you can spend a long time admiring. The word *smörgås* means something like 'open sandwich', and *bord* is the Swedish word for 'table', but actually a *smörgåsbord* is not a table full of sandwiches. Typically, it will comprise a number of herring dishes (sweet-

östron oysters
piggvar turbot
räkor shrimp
rödspätta plaice
röklax smoked salmon
sardiner sardines
sill herring
surströmming fermented Baltic herring
marinerad sill marinated herring
torsk cod
tonfisk tuna

Grönsaker (Vegetables)
råa grönsaker raw vegetables
gurka cucumber
aubergine aubergine/eggplant
kronärtskokor artichoke
blomkål cauliflower
bönner beans
broccoli broccoli
ärtor peas
morötter carrots
sallad lettuce, salad
kål cabbage
mais corn
paprika green/red/yellow pepper
purjolök leek
rödbetor beetroots
rosenkål Brussels sprout
selleri celery
sikori chicory
sjamp/champignon mushroom
potatis potatoes
spinat spinach
tomat tomato

Kryddor (Spices) and Urter (Herbs)
anis anis
basilika basil
dill dill
fennel fennel
grässlök chives
vitlök garlic
ingefära ginger

kanel cinnamon
muskat nutmeg
paprika paprika
peppar pepper
pepparot horse radish
persilja parsley
rosmarin rosemary
salt salt
timian thyme

Frukt, Bär, Nötter (Fruit, Berries, Nuts)
ananas pineapple
apelsin orange
aprikos apricot
banan banana
vindruvor grapes
äpple apple
persika peach
fikon fig
grapefrukt grapefruit
hasselnöt hazelnut
jordgubbar strawberry
korsbär cherry
kokosnöt coconut
mandel almond
mango mango
melon melon
hallon raspberry
hjorton cloudberry
nektarin nectarine
päron pear
jordnötter peanuts
citron lemon
valnötter walnuts
lingon lingonberry

Bread, Cakes and Snacks
kex biscuit
bröd bread
knackebröd crispbread
knäck traditional Swedish toffee
pepparkakor ginger snaps
palt blood bread
semlor cream bun with almond paste

pickled herring, pickled herring with onions, mustard and dill), *köttbullar* (meatballs of fried minced ground veal or beef, as opposed to the more traditional pork); salmon, pies, salads, 'Jansson´s temptation' (sliced anchovy, potatoes and onions baked in cream), eggs, bread, and boiled and fried potatoes. *Smörgåsbord* was already being served in the 18th century, when it was used as an appetizer before the main course. Gradually, however, it has become a meal in itself, and in many hotels the experience can be appreciated for breakfast. Christmas Eve and Midsummer's Eve are two special

tårta cake
tunnbröd thin, flat unleavened bread
ost cheese
getost goat's milk cheese
ostfat cheese platter

Efterätter (Desserts)
äppelkaka apple cake
grädde cream
vispgrädde whipped cream
fruktsallad fruit salad
glass ice cream
yoghurt yoghurt
kaka cake
crème caramel flan
pannkaka pancakes
pepparkakor cookies with pepper
risgrynsgröt rice porridge
chokladkaka chocolate cake
chokladmousse chocolate mousse
våfflor waffles
vaniljsås vanilla sauce

Drinkar (Drinks)
apelsinjus orange juice
champis soft drink like sparkling wine
fruktsoda traditional lemon-lime soft drink
julmust Christmas soft drink
lingonjus lingonberry juice
filmjölk soured milk
mjölk milk
vatten water
pommac soft drink like sparkling wine
sockerdricka sugar drink
kaffe coffee
kakao cocoa
saft juice
te tea
vatten (kolysrad) mineral water (fizzy)

Spirits
glögg sweet, mulled red wine
öl beer
starköl strong beer

mellanöl medium beer
lättöl light beer
alkoholfritt alcohol-free
vin wine
röd vin red wine
vitt vin white wine
rosé rosé

Miscellaneous
smörgåsbord open sandwich table
korvkiosk hot dog stand
snapsvisor Swedish drinking songs
apelsinmarmelad orange marmalade
vinäger vinegar
ägg egg
ägg roar scrambled egg
ägg stekta fried egg
kokta cooked
gröt porridge
pommes frites French fries/chips
pastej paté
potatischips crisps/potato chips
ris rice
senap mustard
smör butter
socker sugar

Preparation
varm hot
kall cold
okokt/blodig rare/underdone
medium/lagom medium
genomstekt well done
ångkokt steamed
flamberad flambéed
friterad deep-fried
gravad cured
gratinerad gratinated
grillat grilled
grytestekt braised
hemlagat (based on a) home recipe
kokt boiled
bakad baked/roasted
pocherad poached

occasions when *smörgåsbord* emerges in its most extravagant guises and when the bountiful banquet is interrupted with endless songs and speeches and invitations to chase the accompanying *öl* (beer) with a variety of vodka-based schnapps.

For a taste of some other homely Swedish fare, the national dish is **årt soppa**, a thick soup of dried yellow peas, onion, pork and herbs that used to be served on a Thursday – a relic from medieval times when Friday was a meatless or fast day. Another popular dish, useful to make the most of leftovers, is **pytt i panna**, a hash of fried diced meat with onions and potatoes, served with fried eggs and slices of pickled red beets. **Kåldolmar**, or stuffed cabbage rolls, is an unusual third option, a dish brought to Sweden by King Karl XII after an involuntary residence in Turkey, nearly 300 years ago. Another throwback to the days when Swedes had to fill up with warm, filling dishes is pork rinds and brown beans. A popular weekly dessert, often following a plate of pea soup, is pancakes (the thin variety as opposed to the North American waffle version) laced with jam and whipped cream.

A rather more simple national snack is the **korv** (hot dog), which you can try at one of the many *korvkiosks* scattered around towns and the countryside. The choice is normally between fried and boiled hot dogs, served with French fries or mashed potatoes. You will almost certainly be asked by the vendor *'Senap eller ketchup?'* ('Mustard or ketchup?').

A rather more delicate operation is the peeling of crayfish (**kräftor**), an August tradition. The crayfish are boiled with dill, sugar and salt, and you eat them using your hands, picking out the delicious meat around the claws and in the tail.

By far the most traumatic culinary experience, and only for the bravest of epicureans, is **surströmming** (fermented Baltic herring that, please note, has absolutely nothing to do with the pickled herring served at a typical *smörgåsbord*). Definitely an acquired taste, the dish is initially offensive because there is such a strong, foul smell emitted when the herring is released from the can, where it is nearly rotten. The experience is made more palatable when the *surströmming* is served with boiled potatoes and onions and maybe rolled into a slice of *tunnbröd*, a type of thin, flat unleavened bread.

Coffee and Pastries

Swedes are reputed to be the second-heaviest coffee-drinkers in the world (per capita) and there are certainly an impressive number of traditional and modern cafés in most Swedish towns, almost always accompanied by a mouthwatering selection of home-made buns and cakes. One cream bun with almond paste to watch out for is **semlor**, which is typically only served around Easter time.

Drink

While the consumption of wine is becoming more commonplace in Sweden, the local drinking culture is still associated with heavy spirits, which miraculously seem to transform reserved, cautious Swedes into boisterous imitations of their more aggressive Viking forefathers. The most traditional spirit is schnapps (**brännvin**), a grain-based spirit not unlike vodka that comes in a variety of flavours depending on whether it has been heavily sweetened or had native herbs and spices (aniseed, caraway, fennel, coriander or wormwood) added. Schnapps is served in dainty glasses and during feasts, and is downed to a *snapvisa* ('schnapps ditty'). Another local spirit beverage, **punsch** (sweet arrack), is said to be Sweden's most unique contribution to drinking culture in the West, and harks back to the 18th century, the heyday of Sweden's trade dominance in the Far East (large quantities of arrack came from Java).

Sweden: Stockholm and Västerås

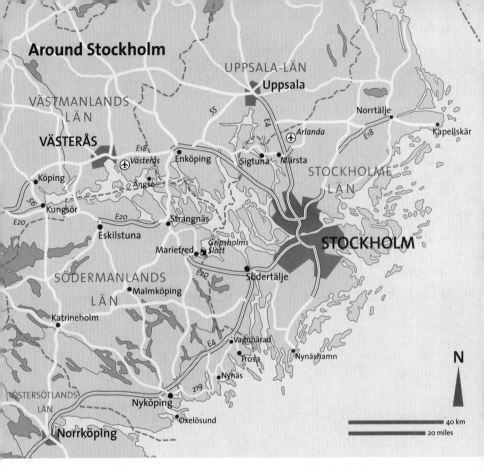

Stockholm

Sweden's capital has often been named the 'Venice of the North', and certainly, anyone fortunate enough to enjoy a hot-air balloon journey across the city (a trip Swedes treat each other to on very special anniversaries) would get the perfect snapshot of a city almost literally floating on water. Even without the benefit of a distinguished vantage point, of which Stockholm has many, it's impossible to escape the corridors of water that zigzag around 14 islands set between the fresh waters of Lake Mälaren and the salty Baltic Sea. Promenades across endless bridges, ferry crossings in the long midsummer days, invigorating skating across the lake in the icy winter may be taken for granted by the 1.4 million people who live in Greater Stockholm, but for the visitor these waterways are a major part of the capital's appeal. And that's not counting the 20,000-odd forest-laden islands to the east of the city where residents escape every spring when the solid ice bays begin to break, ushering in a massive fleet of passenger ferries and private sailboats that scuttle off to thousands of summer and weekend getaways.

The 'Venice' tag has its limitations, though. Not only because it fails to reflect how a third of Stockholm is made up of woodlands and parks (Djurgården, the largest and a former 17th-century royal hunting ground, is the verdant setting for the impressive Skansen Open-air Museum), but because it suggests a city mired in the past and struggling to keep afloat. While Stockholm's pride in its history is amply reflected in the formidable quality and quantity of museums extolling past ways of life, and the beautifully restored medieval Gamla Stan, the city is also one of Europe's most modern. Sweden's fame for clean design permeates most aspects of city life, from its efficient transport system, through its no-nonsense approach to furniture and clothes, to its plethora of design-conscious restaurants and bars that exude the ultimate in 'cool' (literally, in the case of the famous Absolut Icebar made of ice brought from Lapland, *see* p.31). The irony is not lost on Stockholmers that the country's most famous and blatant design mistake – the impeccably restored 17th-century royal *Vasa* warship, which sank as it was leaving Stockholm harbour for being too top-heavy – is now the city's top tourist attraction.

Stockholm may have garnered an unfair reputation for adopting the rather disdainful air of an *'isdrottning'* ('ice queen'). Tellingly, this is the view of the beholder – most often the rest of the country – reflecting a mixture of pride, envy and sheer awe. Stockholm would probably win a European city beauty contest hands down, but as the capital of the world's most famous social democratic state she is the informal glamour queen who makes sure the spoils are equally shared, whether it's promoting outdoor exercise in one of the many parks or allowing her citizens to freely cast a fishing rod right outside the Royal Palace and the Riksdag (parliament).

History

For a city dominated by water, it is fitting that one of the legends surrounding Stockholm's birth involves a humble fisherman who, in the service of the Bishop of Strängnäs, one late June day in the 13th century, caught an enormous salmon. It was his duty to offer the fish up but, too proud to let go of his prized catch, the fisherman decided to flee across the islands of Lake Mälaren and ended up on an island at the outlet of the salty Baltic; thus Stockholm got her first inhabitant. Another story goes that when Sweden's oldest town, Sigtuna (*see* p.52), was attacked by invading Estonians, the citizens hid their most valuable possession in a hollow log and threw it into Lake Mälaren. The log ('*stock*' in Swedish) floated ashore at a certain island ('*holm*') and the homeless Sigtuna citizens decided this was an ideal place to settle.

A rather more scholastic version, which emanates from the *Erikskrönikan*, the oldest depiction of medieval Sweden written between 1322 and 1332, narrates that the city was founded in 1252 by Birger Jarl, a leading member of the Folkunga dynasty, who in association with the powerful German merchants in the Hanseatic League chose to turn the small islands between Mälaren and Saltsjön into a city that would protect the growing trade of iron, copper, tar and fur from the interior with the Baltic states. As trade prospered, older settlements in the area, such as Birka, Helgö and Sigtuna, saw an exodus of citizens towards Gamla Stan island with its impeccably restored medieval quarter. Made of rather simple wood, the city houses were stacked close together and frequently burnt down, and there was so much overcrowding that even the stone houses that replaced them were built in similar narrow fashion.

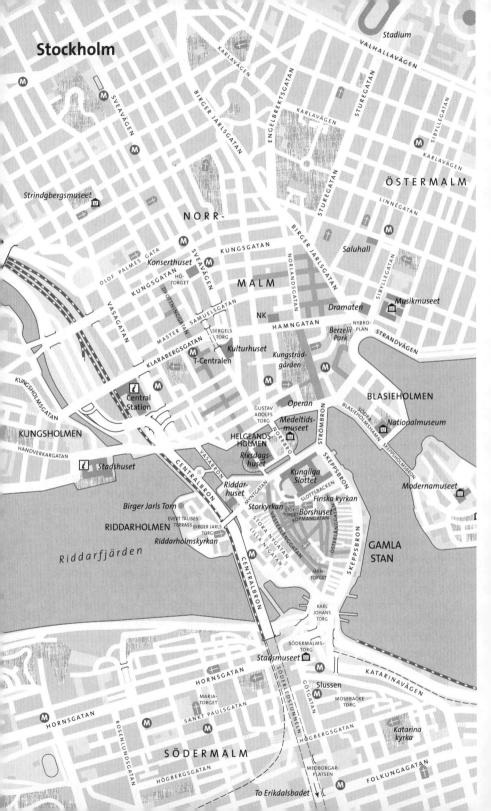

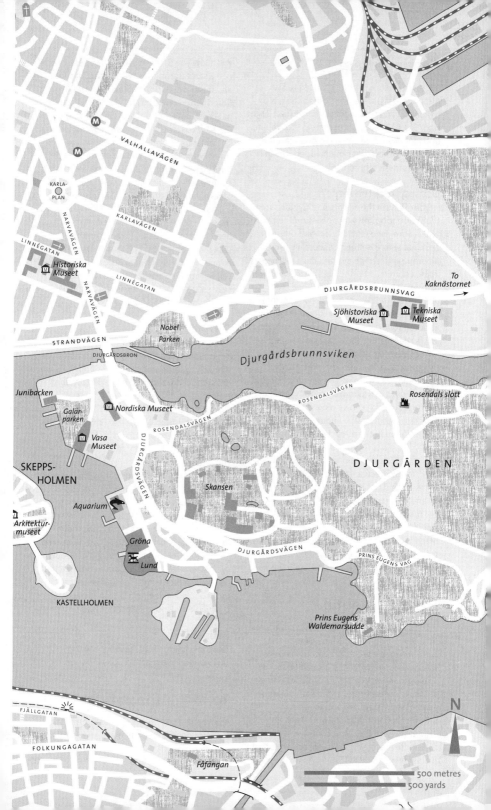

VALHALLAVÄGEN

M

M

KARLA-
PLAN

NÄRVAVÄGEN

KARLAVÄGEN

LINNÉGATAN

LINNÉGATAN

NÄRVAVÄGEN

Historiska
Museet

DJURGÅRDSBRUNNSVAG

To
Kaknästornet

Sjöhistoriska
Museet

Tekniska
Museet

STRANDVÄGEN

Nobel
Parken

DJURGÅRDSBRON

Djurgårdsbrunnsviken

Junibacken

Galär-
parken

Nordiska Museet

ROSENDALSVÄGEN

Rosendals slott

ROSENDALSVÄGEN

DJURGÅRDSVÄGEN

Vasa
Museet

SKEPPS-
HOLMEN

Skansen

DJURGÅRDEN

Aquarium

Arkitektur-
museet

PRINS EUGENS VÄG

DJURGÅRDSVÄGEN

Gröna
Lund

KASTELLHOLMEN

Prins Eugens
Waldemarsudde

FJÄLLGATAN

FOLKUNGAGATAN

Fåfängan

N

500 metres

500 yards

Getting There

Ryanair flies daily from Stansted to Skavsta Airport, t (0155) 280 400 (close to the city of Nyköping) and to Västerås airport t (021) 805 600/610, both about 100km from Stockholm. British Airways and SAS fly to Arlanda, t (08) 797 6000, Stockholm's main airport which is 40km from the city centre.

Getting from the Airport

From **Skavsta** the airport bus, **flygbussarna**, t (08) 600 1000, *www.flyggbussarna.se*, takes about 80mins to reach Stockholm City terminal and may stop at Södertalje Syd (approx 45mins). The airport coach will depart approx 30mins after the flight arrival but will wait for delayed flights. Tickets (one-way SEK130, return SEK199) can be bought from the bus driver or at the ticket counter at the airports. **Södertalje Taxi AB**, t (08) 550 30 000, offers special rates to Ryanair passengers.

From **Västerås** non-stop coaches run by **flyggbussarna** take about 75mins to reach Stockholm City terminal. Details and prices as above. **Trains** leave from a train station near the airport which can be reached by bus no.41. The train journey takes about 60mins.

From **Arlanda** the **airport coach**, t (08) 600 1000, departs to Cityterminalen every 5–10mins. The 35min journey costs SEK60 one-way. An airport coach ticket plus SL bus or underground ticket in zone 1 costs SEK80. The **Arlanda Express rail link**, t (08) 588 890 00, is the more expensive option at SEK160 for a single ticket, but is faster, taking 20mins to reach the Central Station. Trains leave every 15mins. From Arlanda, you can also take the **commuter train** to Märsta and catch bus 583.

Getting Around

The capital's well connected islands are best appreciated on foot, but **ferry** rides in the summer are a scenic and sometimes faster alternative. The excellent **Tunnelbanen** (the underground system) is a warmer option in the icy winters (it runs until 2am), while the city **buses** are frequent and reliable.

By far the most practical option (as the minimum price for a single journey is SEK14) is to acquire one of several transport cards that will allow you to make use of the integrated network of trams, commuter trains, metros and buses run by **Stockholms Lokaltrafik** (information office inside T-Centralen station at Sergels Torg, t 660 10 00, *www.sl.se; open Mon-Sat 6.30am–11.15pm, Sun 7am–11.15pm*). The most basic cards, valid for unlimited transport in Greater Stockholm, are the 24hr pass (SEK95) and 72hr pass (SEK180). The most comprehensive package however is the Stockholm Card, **Stockholmskortet**, which includes free public transport, admission to 70 museums, street parking in the centre and boat sightseeing: 24hrs (SEK220), 48hrs (SEK380), 72 hrs (SEK540). Cards can be bought at one of the main tourist offices, at the many yellow-fronted *Pressbyråer* (press kiosks) scattered around the city or on-line at *www.stockholm.com/stockholmcard*.

Car Hire

Unless you are using Stockholm as a base, negotiating your way around the complicated one-way systems and numerous bridges is not recommended, and parking, especially downtown, is difficult and costly.

Hertz, Vasagatan 26, t (08) 454 62 50.
Avis, Vasagatan 10 B, t (08) 202 060.
Budget, Klarabergsviadukten 92, t (08) 411 15 00.

Bicycle Hire

Cycling is rather less frustrating than driving a car, though not as leisurely as in other Swedish cities, despite politicians trying to encourage citizens to use bikes more often by filling the city with cycle paths. **Stockholm Visitors' Board**, Kulturhuset, Sergels Torg, t (08) 789 2490, has an excellent pamphlet about cycling etiquette. Helmets are recommended. For general bicycle and scooter rental, call t (08) 660 7959. To hire a bike in the verdant Djurgården island, try **Sjöcafé**, t (08) 660 57 57.

Taxis

Taxi Stockholm, t (08) 150 000.
Taxi Kurir, t (08)30 00 00.

Tourist Information

Stockholm: Stockholm's tourist information offices provide free city maps and can also help with booking hotels, excursions and theatre tickets. They also sell the Stockholm Card, and sightseeing tickets.

Tourist Centre, Kulturhuset Cultural Center, Sergels Torg, **t** (08) 780 2490 (*open Mon–Fri 9–6, Sat and Sun 10–3*).

Stockholm Information Service, Hamngatan 27, **t** (08) 789 2400; *www.stoinfo.se* (*open Mon–Fri 9–5, Sat and Sun 10–3*).

Hotellcentralen, Centralstationen, **t** (08) 789 2490 (*open Sept–May Mon–Sat 9–6, Sun 12–4; June–Aug Mon–Sun 8–8*).

Stockholm's official tourist website, available in nine languages, is available at *www.stockholmtown.com*.

Stockholm Visitors Board AB/Guide Booking, **t** (08) 789 2490, offers more than 400 guides who master around 30 languages.

Post office: inside the Centralstation (*open Mon–Fri 7am–10pm, Sat 10–7*). Stamps can also be bought in most news stands and kiosks.

24hr pharmacy: C.W. Scheele, Klarabergsgatan 64, close to the central train station. Pharmacies are marked '*Apotek*'. In case of **emergency**, call **t** 112. If you get acute toothache, contact **t** (08) 654 1117.

City Tours

Tickets for coach and boat tours (many only available in the summer) are available from the tourist centre, Sergels Torg. Also visit *www.citysightseeing.com*.

A novel (and expensive) way of discovering Stockholm from above is by hot-air balloon. Try **City Ballong**, **t** (08) 345 464 or **Upp & Ner**, **t** (08) 42 0380.

Festivals

Check *www.stockholmtown.com/events*.
Jan: Antiques Fair.
Feb: **Stockholm International Furniture Fair**; **Sweden Hockey Games**.
March: **Stockholm Art Fair**.
April: **Valborg Festival** is held on the last day in April to celebrate the arrival of spring, a tradition that dates back to the Viking Age.
May: **Elitlopped** (trotting race).
June: **Restaurant Festival**; **Stockholm Marathon**; **Ulriksdal Palace Gala** (outdoor classical concerts).

July: **Stockholm Jazz Festival**; **DN Galan** (international athletics); **Stockholm summer concerts**; **Tjejmilen** (the world's biggest race for women).
Sept: **Stockholm Beer Festival**; **Lidingöloppet** (the world's biggest cross-country race).
Oct: **Stockholm Open** (tennis tournament).
Nov: **Stockholm International Film Festival**; **Stockholm International Horse Show**.
Dec: **Nobel Day**; **Santa Lucia** Festival of Light; Christmas markets and Christmas concerts.

Shopping

Normal shopping hours are 10–6 weekdays and 10–3 on Sat, although many stores are now open on Sun, particularly the big department stores like NK, Åhléns, PUB, Debenhams, Gallerian or Sturegallerian, all located near each other in Norrmalm and Kungsholmen. The main shopping areas stretch from Hötorget to Gamla Stan, via Drottninggatan, and from Hamngatan, Kungsgatan and Biblioteksgatan down to Stureplan.

Streets to watch out for are: **Biblioteksgatan**, touted as the equivalent of New York's Fifth Avenue – exclusive clothes, jewellery, furs and watches; and **Drottningatan**, the former royal street which leads straight from the Royal Palace to Observatorielunden, lined with the main high street brands. The middle of the pedestrianized street is popular with street vendors, most from the fast-growing immigrant community.

In Gamla Stan, **Västerlånggatan** has a vast number of small shops, many of which sell tourist wares (and a lot of kitsch) and postcards. **Österlånggatan** has a wide, more discreet selection of arts and crafts; **Sergels Torg**, the main business square, is surrounded by discount shoe and fashion stores.

Shopping malls and **department stores** include **Gallerian**, Hamngatan 37, Stockholm's first shopping mall. **Götgatsbacken** has many design stores like Filippa K, Tiogruppen, Ordning & Reda and Designtorget. **NK**, Hamngatan 18–20, is an exclusive department store; **PK-Huset**, Hamngatan 10, is a more conventional shopping mall; **Pub**, Drottninggatan/Hötorget, is housed in a department store where Greta Garbo once famously flogged hats; **Puckeln**, Hornsgatan, is a centre for art galleries featuring traditional and modern design; **Åhlens**, Klarabergsgatan 50, is a popular department store with a super-market in the basement.

Traditional outdoor and indoor **markets** include the rather exclusive **Östermalms-hallen** in Östermalm Torg and the more down-to-earth **Hötorgetshallen**.

For world-famous **Swedish glass**, try BodaNova-Höganäs Keramik AB, Västerlång-gatan 66, **t** (08) 228 545, or Nordiska Kristall, Kungsgatan 9, **t** (08) 104 372. **Design Torget** has branches at Sergelstorg, Kulturhuset, and Götgatan 31, Södermalm; **t** (08) 508 3 1520/ **t** 08 462 3520; *www.design torget.se (open Mon–Fri 10–7, Sat 10–5, Sun 12–5)*. For **porcelain**, **chandeliers** and **silverware**, try Afrodite Antik, Odengatan 92, or Mormors Spegal, Odengatan 84.

Select **food shops** include Pralinhuset, Drottninggatan 112, with a selection of 120 chocolates and truffles; and Osthuset Androquest, Sibyllegatan 19, for cheese.

The best **bookshop** is Akademibokhandeln, Mäster Samuelsgatan 32; and for **maps** go to Kartcentrum, Vasagatan 16. For information and books on Sweden, Sweden Book Shop at Slottsbacken 10 (close to the Royal Palace), is recommended.

Shopping at Christmas

Skansen, Djurgårdsslättan 49–51, **t** (08) 442 8000; *www.skansen.se (open daily 10–4)* has a Christmas fair on December weekends.

Tomtar & Troll, Österlånggatan 45, **t** (08) 10 56 29; *www.tomtar-troll.com (open Mon–Fri 11–6, Sat 10–4)*. For handmade Swedish Christmas men and trolls.

Where to Stay

Stockholm t (08) –

Summertime in Stockholm, when much of the country takes off to their country homes, is the best time for bargains, or at least when most hotels offer reductions of 30–50%.

The **Stockholm à la Carte** hotel package, consisting of bed and breakfast rates at 41 Stockholm hotels from SEK300 per person, unlimited free public transportation by buses, subway and commuter trains, six free boat tours, free admission at 60 sights and attrac-tions and a 156-page guide book, is a limited offer available at sharply discounted rates during off-peak periods, i.e. all weekends year-round, every day from mid-June to mid-Aug and all holidays, holiday eves and weekdays squeezed in between. The package is offered by **Destination Stockholm**, Nybrogatan 58, **t** 663 0080, **f** 664 1807, *info@destination-stockholm.com*.

Another hotel service that can help with accommodation is **Hotellcentralen**, Central Station, **t** 789 2490, **f** 791 8666, *www. svb. stockholm.se*; reservation fee SEK60.

Grand Hotel, S Blasieholmen 9, **t** 679 35 00, *www.grandhotel.se (luxury)*. With views of the Royal Palace and Gamla Stan across the waterfront, this magnificent turn-of-the-20th-century institution is the *grande dame* among the capital's premier hotels.

Berns Hotel, Nackstromsgatan 8, **t** 566 32200, *www.berns.se (luxury)*. An intimate offshoot of the Grand Hotel that has been remod-elled as a boutique hotel by Terence Conran. Guests who have tried the new cherrywood and marble rooms include Oasis, Prince, Bill Gates and Isabella Rossellini.

Lady Hamilton Hotel, Storkyrkobrinken 5, **t** 506 401 00, *www.lady-hamilton.se (luxury)*. A stone's throw away from the the Royal Palace, this hotel has rooms named after flowers and full of rustic antiques lovingly collected by its owners, the Bengtssons.

Hotel Birger Jarl, Tulegatan 8, **t** 674 1800; *www.birgerjarl.se (very expensive)*. Housed in a 1970s building in a lively shopping and entertainment area; the owners of the hotel recently recruited 20 Swedish designers to renovate the rooms to create a crisp and restful ambience that have earned it a place in the capital's *Hip Hotels* book series.

Rica City Hotel Gamla Stan, Lilla Nygatan 25, **t** 723 7250, *www.rica.se (very expensive)*. A short distance from Gamla Stan, this 17th-century building was recently reno-vated in Gustavian style.

Nordic Light, Vasaplan, **t** 505 63300, *www. nordichotels.se (very expensive)*. Opposite the drop-off point from the airport train. Rooms have special light effects, as you would expect from a hotel that is in the Design Hotel group. Houses the 'ice' bar (*see* p.31).

Hotel Rival, Mariatorget 3, **t** 545 789 00, *www. rival.se* (*expensive*). Originally built in 1937, this boutique hotel in the elegant square of Mariatorget in Söder has been renovated by Abba's Benny Andersson, alongside partners Christer Sandahl and Christer Hägglund. In keeping with the entertainment theme (the Rival complex includes a large cinema, a bakery, restaurant, café and Art Deco-style bar), the cherrywood panelled rooms have bold images of film stars such as Ingrid Bergman or Greta Garbo above each bed. Bathrooms are divided from the rest of the room by a glass window, allowing guests to wallow in a bath while watching a film on the plasma screen in the bedroom.

Lord Nelson Hotel, Västerlånggatan 22, **t** 506 401 20, *www.lord-nelson-se* (*expensive*). Naval antiquities fill this very narrow but cosy hotel in a tall 17th-century building along the liveliest street in the district.

Hotell Kung Carl, Birger Jarlsgatan 21, **t** 463 5000, *www.hkchotels.se* (*expensive*). A quiet and charming oasis close to the busy and lively Stureplan.

Pärlan Hotell, Skeppargatan 27, **t** 663 5070, *www.parlanhotell.com* (*expensive*). Located near the elegant Östermalmstorg, this stylish hotel has only nine rooms.

Hotel J, Ellensviksvägen 1, Nacka Strand, **t** 601 3000, *www.designhotels.com* (*expensive*). Converted summer house with a nautical theme – not surprising since it is located on the edge of sea, only a quarter of an hour by boat or car from the city centre.

Den Röda Båten Mälaren/Ran, Södermälarstrand, Kajplats 6, **t** 644 43 85, *www.roda baten.nu*, *www.theredboat.com* (*expensive*). Located in Söder, there are only four rooms in this former steamship, which has a floating cafeteria in the summer and spectacular views of the City Hall.

Art Hotel, Johannesgatan 12, **t** 402 3760, (*moderate*). Close to Stureplan, this is one of the best-priced group of cutting-edge design hotels that have sprouted in the capital, with carefully designed individual rooms.

Queen's Hotel, Drottningatan 71, **t** 249 460, *www.queenshotel.se* (*moderate*). This has been a reliable, family-run hotel for more than a century, with an excellent location right in the heart of the city.

Söder Höjder, Renstiernas Gata 15, **t** 615 21 35, *www.sodershojder.com* (*moderate*). Small, friendly hotel in Söder that is located near the fabulous viewpoint in Fjallgatan and the entertainment district around Nytorget.

Pensionat Oden, Odengatan 38, **t** 612 4349, *www.pensionat.nu* (*moderate*). Established in 1943, this guest house has retained the genteel atmosphere of the 19th century with discreetly updated conveniences.

Hotel tre små rum, Högbergsgatan **t** 641 2371, *www.tresmarum.se* (*moderate–inexpensive*) The hotel's name means 'three small rooms', but there are in fact seven rooms in the basement of this townhouse in Södermalm; they share impeccably clean bathrooms.

AF Chapman, Västra Brobanken, Skeppsholmen, **t** 463 2266 (*inexpensive*). A unique youth hostel, set in a huge ship that was originally built in 1888.

Eating Out

Stockholm **t** (08) –

Stockholm and Gothenburg vie strongly for top place in the restaurant stakes, although the capital has been losing out lately in the Chef of the Year competitions. The variety and quality of eateries has improved vastly in the last decade, with lavish attention now bestowed on food presentation as well as ambience and décor. The latest buzz word is 'crossover' cuisine – dishes that are served in intriguing and unusual combinations. Dining out is no longer as costly as it used to be, and lunch menus are always worth checking out.

Bon Lloc, Regeringsgatan 111, **t** 660 60 60 (*very expensive*). This is a 'good place' (the literal translation of '*Bon Lloc*' in Catalan) and the northeastern Spanish cuisine is well deserving of its Michelin *Guide Rouge* star.

Operakällaren and Opera Bar, Karl XII Torg, **t** 676 5800 (*very expensive*). Although the food is excellent, you are also paying for the magnificent surroundings – frescoes, gilt plasterwork, chandeliers and mirrors – and the venue's history: food has been served here since 1787. For a more affordable option, try the traditional food at the bar.

Berns, Berzelii Park, **t** 566 322 22 (*very expensive*). This is a classic restaurant from the

19th century, and was frequented by August Strindberg. Recently renovated by Terence Conran, and live jazz music is played here on special evenings.

F12, Fredsgatan 12, **t** 248 052 (*very expensive*). One of the capital's 'crossover cuisine' restaurants *par excellence*, frequented by food connoisseurs and the fashion-conscious.

Gondolen, Stadsgården 6, **t** 641 7090 (*very expensive*). The excellent food and popular bar match the excellent views over Gamla Stan from the 36m tower that you reach by lift from Slussen.

Pontus in the Greenhouse, Österlånggatan 17, **t** 238 500 (*very expensive*). Mingle with the local rich and famous in this trendy restaurant run by one of the many up-and-coming young Swedish chefs. For a more down-to-earth experience, there is a more affordable bar on the ground floor.

Den Glydene Freden, Österlånggatan 51, **t** 249 760 (*very expensive–expensive*). Sweden's most famous poet, Bellman, and much-loved troubadour Taube, as well as a host of other revellers, have dined in the capital's oldest restaurant; Swedish-French cuisine.

Restaurang Kaknästornet, Ladugårdsgärdet on Norra Djurgården **t** 667 21 05 (*expensive*). The views from the 28th floor are unrivalled, and the traditional Swedish home cooking doesn't disappoint either.

Nouveau Riche, 4 Birger Jarlsgatan, **t** 545 03 560 (*expensive*). Not quite as expensive as the name suggests, this restaurant is one of the favourites in the elegant Östermalm area. Leave room for dessert, a blackcurrant pannacotta with elderberry.

Stallmästargården, Norrtull, **t** 610 13 00 (*expensive*). Located in a building from 1600, this restaurant serves traditional Swedish cuisine that is complemented by stunning views over Brunnsviken.

Sturehof, Stureplan, **t** 440 57 30 (*expensive*). A former watering hole from the 1800s, this is an ideal place to be introduced to grilled Baltic herring or other Swedish seafood delicacies, including an excellent oyster bar.

Wedholms Fisk, Nybrokajen 17, **t** 611 7874 (*expensive*). For fish-lovers.

Folkhemmet, Renstiernas Gata 30, **t** 640 5595, *www.users.wineasy.se/folkhemmet* (*moderate*). Södermalm devotees flock here for the friendly service, the lively, laid-back atmosphere and the reasonably priced food which is international with a Swedish twist. Book to avoid disappointment at weekends.

Atrium, Södra Blasieholmshamnen, **t** 611 34 38 (*moderate*). There is no better way of appreciating fine art at the fine National Museum than a stop at its equally fine restaurant, set in an inner courtyard.

Kulturhuset, Sergels Torg, **t** 508 315 08, (*moderate*). Flamboyant theatrical types abound on Café Panorama at the top, with excellent city views, or at the Teaterbaren.

Anders Limpbar, Upplandsgatan 2, **t** 411 2720 (*moderate*). A former Swedish soccer player runs this American-style joint, which caters for meat-lovers who also enjoy watching sports on surrounding TV screens.

Peppar, Torsgatan 34, **t** 09 342 052 (*moderate*). Cajun food is served in colourful surroundings, with walls plastered with postcards.

Halv Grek Plus Turk, Jungfrugatan 33, **t** 665 94 22 (*moderate*). For those seeking a change from Swedish cuisine, this is a welcome (and unusual) mix of Greek and Turkish dishes.

Restaurang Lisa Elmqvist, Östermalms Saluhall, **t** 553 404 10 (*moderate*). Superb fish soups and other fish-based meals in this stylish indoor food hall.

La Famiglia, Alströmergatan 45, **t** 650 63 10 (*moderate*). It has been a long time since Frank Sinatra dined here, but the family-run restaurant still remains popular.

Shogun, Tyska Brinken 36, **t** 208 205 (*moderate–inexpensive*). In Gamla Stan, a reliable Japanese restaurant with friendly staff.

Kaffe Bönan, Humlegårdsgatan 9, **t** 662 4904 (*inexpensive*). Popular central café, serving a filling variety of quiches, pies, baked potatoes, sandwiches and cakes.

Hermans Höjdare, Fjällgatan 23, **t** 643 94 80 (*inexpensive*). Excellent vegetarian meals are served on an outside terrace with stunning views from the cliffs of southern Stockholm.

Frodo, Kungsgatan 3, **t** 611 5060 (*inexpensive*). Thin, crispy pizzas are served in this small, friendly restaurant.

India Gate, Tulegatan 10, **t** 673 50 30 (*inexpensive*). A spicy vegetarian option at highly reasonable prices. The garlic naan bread is an absolute must.

Cafés

Chokladkoppen and **Kaffekoppen** on Stortorget are classic Gamla Stan cafes that serve reasonably priced lasagne, quiches and sandwiches. Two classical coffee shops are **Wienkonditoriet**, Biblioteksgatan 6–8, and, for the long summers, **Rosendahls Trägårdenscafé**, Rosendalsterrassen 2, Djurgården. **Wayne's Coffee Bar** is located at Drottninggatan 31, Drottninggatan 82, Kungsgatan 14, and Vasagatan. For a more refined experience, try **Medelhavsmuseets Café**, Fredsgatan 2, with a beautiful view of the Royal Palace.

Internet cafes include **Arena**, Torkel Knutssonsgatan 35, **t** 429 98 28, **Dome-house**, Sveavägen 108, **t** 612 61 10, **Kulturhuset**, Sergels Torg 103, **t** 508 315 08; and **Sidewalk Express** at Centralstationen and at Arlanda airport.

Entertainment

Stockholm **t** (08) –

Stockholm's premier concert venue is **Stockholms Konserthus**, Hötorget 8, **t** 786 0200; the opera house is **Operan**, Gustav Adolfs Torg, **t** 791 43 00; and the doyenne of theatres is **Kungliga Dramatiska Teatern** (the Royal Dramatic Theatre, more commonly known as **Dramaten**), Nybroplan, **t** 665 6100.

Other main theatre and music venues include: **China Teatern**, Berzelii Park 9, **t** 566 323 50; **Cirkus**, Djurgårdsslätten 43, **t** 587 987 00; **Folkoperan**, Hornsgatan 72, **t** 616 07 50; **Glenn Miller Café**, Brunnsgatan 21, **t** 10 03 22; **Gröna Lunds Teatern**, Lilla Allmänna Gränd 9; **Jazzklubb Fasching**, Kungsgatan 63, **t** 534 829 60; **Lydmar Hotell**, Sturegatan 10, **t** 08 566 113 00; **Musikaliska Akademin**, Blasieholmstorg 8, **t** 407 18 00; **Mosebacke Etablissement**, Mosebacke Torg 3, **t** 556 098 90; **Theater in the Park**, Sergels Torg 1, **t** 506 201 00; **Regina**, Stockholms Operamathus, Drottninggatan 71, **t** 411 63 20; **Stampen**, Stora Nygatan 5, **t** 205 793; **Södra Teatern**, Mosebacke Torg 1, **t** 556 972 30.

Film-watching is easy for foreign visitors as, with the exception of a few children's movies, all films are shown in their original language (mainly English, given the Hollywood-dominated fare) and subtitled.

For info about sporting events and tickets, contact **Globen**, **t** 725 1010; **Råsunda** Fotbollsstadion, **t** 735 09 35; and **Stockholms Stadion**, **t** 219 456.

Nightlife

Nightlife has become significantly livelier and noisier in the last decade, and drinks are no longer as prohibitively expensive as in the past. For a general pointer, bars in **Gamla Stan** are the most traditional; the more preppy bars are in **Östermalm** (an area frequented by the so-called 'party princess' Madeleine, the king's youngest daughter); and the more laid-back haunts in **Söder**, especially around Götgatan.

Absolut Icebar at Nordic Light hotel in Vasaplan is the coolest place (literally, as it is made out of ice brought from the Arctic Circle). Warm clothing is provided as you sip iced vodka from specially made ice glasses in freezing temperatures.

Cadierbaren, located in the elegant Grand Hotel, Södra Blasieholmshamnen 2. A classic though rather pricy venue.

Gondolen, Stadsgården 6, at Slussen. Great cocktails and views over Gamla Stan.

El Cubanito, Scheelegatan 3. Offers vintage rum to a Latin beat.

Ett Liter Kak, Grev Turegatan 15. One of the smallest bars in town.

Guldapan, Åsögatan 140. Another cramped but trendy outlet in Söder.

Lydmar Hotel, Sturegatan 10. A posey lobby bar with live jazz music.

Operabaren, Operahouse, Kungsträdgården. Expensive drinks in a sumptuous Art Nouveau setting.

Soldaten Svejk, Östgötagatan 35. Czech beer.

Among the top clubs are: **Storecompaniet**, Stureplan, *www.sturecompaniet.se*, a nightclub with four floors, **Tech Noir** (*www.technoir.org*), a fusion between two well-known synth clubs 'Dieters Synthbar' and 'Necronomicon' that is located in Kolinborg, an underground concrete bunker with no street address about 200m north of Slussen underground station; **Mosebacke**, a centre located in a 19th-century venue in Söder Teatern/Kägelbanan, Mosebacke Torg, **t** 556 098 90, *www.mosebacke.se*. For jazz enthusiasts, **Fasching**, Kungsgatan 63, *www.fasching.se*, is an internationally known jazz club.

The early 16th century saw one of Stockholm's most bloody episodes, when King Kristian II of Denmark, nicknamed Kristian the Tryant, decided to hold his coronation in Stockholm, for which he invited all the local nobility to a three-day banquet. On the last day of celebrations, all doors were locked at the Tre Kronor castle (where the royal palace stands today) and more than 100 bishops and noblemen accused of treason beheaded in the main square. Known ever since as 'Stockholm's Bloodbath', the event sparked off nobleman Gustav Vasa's two-year revolt against the Danes which ended with his victorious march into the city in 1523 when he proclaimed himself Sweden's first king and dynasty-founder. As Gustav Vasa, and his sons after him, attempted to consolidate the new nation, Stockholm's importance as a military headquarters grew rapidly, as did its population, which by the time the city was formally established as the capital in 1634 had reached 60,000. Town planners began to map out a street grid north of Gamla Stan in Norrmalm, although the population growth was stymied after a harsh winter of 1696–7, also the year when the old royal castle was burned down. A bout of plague more than a decade later reduced the population further.

After a period of stagnation and Sweden's loss of its Baltic empire to a group of common enemies, Denmark, Saxony, Russia and Finland, in its defeat in the Great Northern War (1700–21), Stockholm was more than happy to indulge King Gustav III's penchant for the arts, and the latter half of the 18th century is remembered as a period where science and arts blossomed, as exemplified in the construction of the magnificent Royal Opera House. But Gustav's focus on his artistic protégés gave him a false sense of security, and it was at the Opera House he so adored that the party-loving monarch attended a masquerade evening in 1792 in spite of warnings that he might be assassinated. A group of masked men surrounded him, greeting him with the words, '*Bonjour, beau masque,*' before shooting him.

It's difficult to believe, walking around the pristine capital today, but in the 19th century Stockholm had a reputation as one of the dirtiest cities in Europe. The now highly desirable Södermalm was a veritable slum where children grew up with severe disfigurements and citizens were cooped up in tiny basements with no sunlight. In the northeast of the city, however, the aristocracy was able to finance the elegant Östermalm with its intricate mansion blocks that mimicked Haussmann's Paris. But for the majority, despite the construction of the railways and incipient industrialization in the late 19th century, this was a period of mass poverty and of vast population flight to the United States. A growing intolerance of social injustice led to the rise of strong popular movements that included the labour movement, free churches movement and women's movement, paving the way for the leadership of the city council by the more progressive Social Democrats and Liberals by the 1920s.

The architectural style known as 'National Romanticism' emerged at the turn of the 20th century, of which the highly original and '*faux*' Renaissance town hall – a stellar attraction – has become its most typical exponent. Also during this period, and a further instance of a resurgence in national pride, was the still-intact stadium built for the city's hosting of the 1912 Olympic Games. The overblown style was followed by the so-called 'Swedish Grace' style which attracted international attention between 1900 and 1930 for its emphasis on the detail in gates, door handles and banisters.

With Stockholm suffering none of the ravages of world war faced by other European cities, the centre did not experience any major transformations until the 1960s, when many old buildings around the 19th-century Klara district were razed to give way to functional, grey concrete blocks that now make up a large part of the main (often underground) shopping precinct. Stockholm today faces a shortage of housing, not surprising given the respect for green space, the keen preservation of older buildings and the plentiful surrounding water. Brownfield sites are now being developed and a few formidable Marbella-style developments, rather un-Swedish in their flashy brilliance, are sprouting along lakesides not far from the centre.

Gamla Stan

Stockholm's picturesque old town is a combination of churches and meandering cobbled streets lined with antiques stalls, designer linen shops, touristy trinket and souvenir outlets and cosy cafés, but its central location straddling three islands – Stadsholmen, Helgeandsholmen and Riddarholmen – also lends a practical air to the medieval centre as a thoroughfare between the business and transport hub around T-Centralen to the north and the more fashionably laid-back atmosphere just south around Slussen. The shenanigans of politics in Riksdagshuset (Parliament), at the north end of these closely connected islands, also helps to inject a dose of everyday reality to the centuries of history in the immaculately restored buildings.

Stortorget

The compact medieval square in the heart of Stadsholmen provides a breathing space amid the narrow alleyways that fan out of it. In summer there's room to sit and sip coffee peacefully, and in winter, more vigorous shopping at its Christmas stalls. The pastel tones of the pristine tall stone buildings, and the cobbled square's benches, create a tranquil atmosphere that belies the square's violent past. At the so-called 'Stockholm's Bloodbath' in 1520, the square's cobbles ran with blood from the noble-men murdered in a surprise attack on the orders of tyrannical Danish king Kristian II during a three-day feast. The square was also a site for public pillory until 1770.

Dominating the north side of the square is the **Börshuset**, the former exchange building that dates from 1778 and continued to be used for stock exchange trading as recently as 1990. Today it houses the **Nobel Museet, t** (08) 0 232 506 (*open mid-May–mid-Sept Wed–Mon 10–6, Tues 10–8; mid-Sept–mid-May Wed–Sun 11–5, Tues 11–8, closed Mon*) with displays on many former winners of the Nobel Peace prize as well as an exhibit devoted to Albert Nobel himself.

Almost rubbing backs with the square is **Storkyrkan**, Trångsund 1, **t** (08) 0 723 3016 (*open May–Sept daily 9–6; Oct–April daily 9–4*), Stockholm's 700-year-old cathedral, originally built as a village church by the city's founder Birger Jarl. Inside the opulent, brick-columned interior, don't overlook amid the eclectic art collection: the silver altar donated by Councillor Johan Adler Salvius and his wife; the seven-branched candle-stick, a bronze candelabra made in Germany in the 15th century; or the light globe at the left of the entrance that since its creation in 1972 has been an assembly point for the lighting of candles and prayers for the world. The cathedral's most famous sculpture, though, is of *Sankt Göran och Draken* (St George and the Dragon). Sten Sture the Elder commissioned the ensemble, carved in oak, gilt metal and elk horn, in 1489, as a token to St George for helping him successfully defend the city from King Kristian of Denmark when the 'Danish dragon' attempted to occupy Brunkeberg.

Behind the cathedral is the wide and long space called **Slottsbacken**, its south side flanked by the yellow-coloured **Finska kyrkan** (Finnish Church), erected between 1648 and 1653, at the back of which is a small park, **Bollhustäpan**, with the smallest statue in Stockholm, a young boy called the 'Iron Boy' whom caring citizens are constantly offering garments to wear, depending on the season. After the Finnish church is **Tessinska Palatset**, built in 1697 by the Swedish architect Nicodemus Tessin the Younger to accommodate him while he was building the Royal Palace. Today, the house that was once considered the most beautiful private building north of Paris is the residence of the county governor. Adjacent to the palace is **Svenska Institutet**, Skeppsbron 2, **t** (08) 453 7800, *www.swedenbookshop.com*, an excellent reference point.

It is impossible to ignore, on the north side, **Kungliga Slottet**, **t** (08) 402 61 30, *www.royalcourt.se*, the Italian Baroque-style Royal Palace that dominates the Old Town. Built on the site of the old Tre Kronor (Three Crowns) Palace that burnt down in 1697, it is the official residence of Carl XVI Gustaf and Sylvia, although the couple and their three grown-up children live in the more intimate Drottningholm (*see* p.44). To discover how former regents whiled the time away inside, or even how visting dignitaries are today put up, you can visit specific sections of the palace including: the **Livrustkammaren** (Royal Armoury; *open June–Aug daily 10–5; Sept–May Tues–Sun 11–5, Thurs 11–8; adm*), exhibiting the armour, coaches, coronation regalia and even Gustav II Adolf's stuffed horse; the **Guest Apartments**, the **Hall of State**, the **Apartments of the Chivalry Offices**, the **Treasury**, and Gustav III´s **Museum of Antiquities** (*open Sept–April Tues–Sun 12–3; May–Aug 10–4; adm*); and the **Tre Kronor Museet** (*open Feb–mid-May Tues–Sun 12–3; mid-May–end June 10–4; end June–mid-Aug 10–5; mid-Aug–end Aug 10–4; Sept–Dec 12–3; adm*), which provides an insight into daily life in the original castle between the 13th century and 1697. It is also entertaining to watch the **changing of the guard** (don't be surprised by the number of young women parading), in summer Mon–Fri 12.15, Sat and Sun 1.30.

North of the palace across the Norrbro bridge is a chance to experience some of the ambience of the original medieval town at **Medeltidsmuseet**, Strömparterren, Norrbro, **t** (08) 508 31 808, *www.medeltidsmuseet.stockholm.se* (*open Sept–June Tues–Sun 11–4, Wed 11–6, closed Mon; July–Aug Thurs–Tues 11–4, Wed 11–6; guided tours 2pm; adm*). Relating the experiences of medieval Stockholm through imaginative recon-structions of its brick houses, the harbour, and – always a popular attraction – its gallows, the museum was built around several ancient monuments, including part of the city wall, that were excavated in an extensive archaeological dig as recently as the late 1970s. Across the Riksplan is the modern **Riksdagshuset** (parliament).

Riddarhuset and Riddarholmen

West of the Royal Palace, on the north side of Myntgatan is **Riddarhuset**, Riddarhus-torget 7, **t** (08) 723 39 99, *www.riddarhuset.se* (*open Mon–Fri 11.30am–12.30pm; adm*), the House of Nobility that was built in the Dutch Renaissance style to demonstrate the grandeur of the Swedish empire in the 17th century. It was built between 1641 and 1674 by four different architects for meetings in parliament of the Swedish nobility; the two pavilions that look out across the water were added 200 years later.

Across the tiny bridge to Riddarholmen island, you step into **Birger Jarls Torg**, the square that bears a statue of the city's founder, Birger Jarl. On the south side of the square is **Riddarholmskyrkan**, Birger Jarls Torg, **t** (08) 402 6130 (*open mid-May–Aug 10–4; Sept Sat and Sun 12 12–3*), the eldest church in Stockholm (built 1280–1310) and the burial place of kings from Gustav II Adolf to Gustav V. Also flanking the square is **Svea Hovrätt Wrangelska Palatset**, which, as the largest private palace in Stockholm during the 17th century, housed the royal family while the new palace was being built. Today, the building is used by the Court of Appeal.

Behind the palace, overlooking the water is **Birger Jarls Torn**, a tower that is the only building left of Gustav Vasa's defensive works. It overlooks **Evert Taubes Terrass**, a square named after Sweden's much-loved troubadour who died in 1976, which offers an excellent vantage point for viewing the City Hall over the water in Kungsholmen.

South of Stortorget

The atmospheric winding alleys south of Stortorget are a maze to get lost in. The two main streets that cross a large part of Gamla Stan – **Österlånggatan** and **Västerlånggatan** – act as a reference point as well as providing ample scope for shopping and eating. Don't miss however, **Brända Tomten** ('Burnt Site'), a small, pretty square resembling an Italian piazza that survived rebuilding after a house fire in 1728 when it became a turning area for carriages; **Köpmangatan**, the oldest merchant street; and **Mårten Trotsigs gränd**, the city's narrowest lane at less than a metre wide, named after a German merchant who married the mayor's daughter. If you manage to squeeze down the cobblestoned lane you reach **Järntorget** where at No.84 you can see the site of the National Bank from 1686 to 1906, with its third floor bridge connecting it to the building next door where the bank notes were printed.

Kungsholmen and the Stadshuset

Diagonally across from Gamla Stan over Centralbron or Vasabron bridges, or a few minutes' walk southwest of the central station at Vasagatan, is the building that has dominated the Stockholm skyline south of Lake Mälaren for almost a hundred years and has since become the capital's irrefutable symbol. Located on the eastern fringes of Kungsholmen island, **Stadshuset** (City Hall), Handverkargatan 1, **t** (08) 508 290 58 (*entrance only possible with daily tours: Sept–May 10 and 12, June–Aug 10, 11, 12, 2 and 3; tower open May–Sept daily, April Sat and Sun; adm*) is like no other city hall. It's not just the magnificent position on Ridderfjärden's waterfront but the architect Ragnar Östberg's unique and remarkable conception of the building that plays homage to Venice's Doge's Palace, not slavishly but rather irreverently, full of imaginative twists. Together with Vasa Museet in Djurgården (*see pp.41–2*), this is a must-see.

It took more than 12 years (1911–23) and 8 million bricks to complete the red brick building that is built around two piazzas, Borgargården and the Blue Hall, with a massive square tower rising from the corner topped by an observation tower, above which gleam Tre Kronor, the three golden crowns, symbol of Stockholm. The excellent (compulsory) tour guides point out intricate and playful details inside the building that the rather formidable Östberg so painstakingly included to make the early-20th-century example of the Swedish National Romantic style appear much older.

The building is full of surprises, with no room preparing the visitor for the style of the next. The tour starts with the **Blue Hall**, the building's largest space, which looks like the setting for a medieval pageant, and in spite of its name is not blue, since Östberg decided the red bricks were too beautiful to be concealed by blue plaster. The **Council Chamber**, where the city council meets on alternate Monday evenings, has a ceiling with an imitation opening, creating the impression of entering a Viking long-house, while the **Ovale**, the antechamber to the banqueting halls, has a late-17th-century feel with its Tureholm tapestries, woven in Beauvais, France. Civil weddings take place in this tiny chamber, with two choices of ceremony, the longest taking just over three minutes and the second only 45 seconds. City receptions take place in the adjoining and more traditional-looking **Gallery of the Prince**, which has a splendid view of Riddarfjärden, a panorama reflected on the opposite wall in Prince Eugene's *al fresco* painting *The Shores of Stockholm* (Swedish artists of the period were encouraged to take part in the interior decoration of the Stadshuset). Most unexpected of all is the wildly extravagant **Golden Hall**, which contains over 18 million mosaic pieces, made of glass and gold to create a glistening backdrop for the 700 banqueters who can be seated here. It's difficult to miss the Romanesque-looking *Queen of the Lake Mälaren* which dominates the northern wall.

Most of the **Kungsholmen** island west of Stadshuset is mainly residential and of limited interest, although for fitness fanatics **Rålambshovsparken** stages, in summer, entertaining outdoor aerobics courtesy of the '*Friskis och Svettis*' keep-fit association.

Norrmalm

East of the Stadshuset begins a criss-cross grid of modern office blocks rather grandly called 'City' that eventually lead to the heart of modern Stockholm, **Sergels Torg**, a square laid out on two levels, the upper for cars and the lower for pedestrians and a shopping mall. For the visitor who has only been exposed to the old city or the beautifully preserved waterfronts, a stroll through this central plaza and surrounding grey blocks may come as a jolt: former 19th-century houses were torn down from the 1950s onwards to make way for functional buildings; but the shopping area and cinemas and eateries are lively. At the centre of Sergels Torg is Edvin Ohlstrom's 120ft-high glass obelisk known as **Pinnen** (Stick), a popular meeting place, and on the south side a glass building houses the **Kulturhuset, t** (08) 5083 1508, *www.kulturhuset. stockholm.se* (*open mid-Aug–mid-June Tues–Fri 10–7, Sat and Sun 11–5, closed Mon; mid-June–mid-Aug Tues–Fri 10–6, Sat–Mon 11–4*), a multicultural venue that was opened in 1974 and is visited by over three million Stockholmers a year. As well as its huge library with wide range of foreign-language newspapers, it exhibits art, photography, fashion and design by both local and international artists and is also the headquarters of Stockholm City Theater, one of the country's most influential theatres.

The pedestrian street that crosses the west side of the square is **Drottninggatan** (Queen's Street), named in honour of Queen Christina, and a busy thoroughfare since the 1640s. The long streets extend southwards towards Gamla Stan, passing **Gustav Adolfs Torg** where the star attraction of the elegant square that overlooks the Royal Palace is the **Royal Opera House (Operan)**, opened in 1777 and replaced by the present building in 1898. The busiest section of Drottninggatan, though, is north of Sergels Torg, where the popular pedestrian way is heralded with strings of multicoloured flags between the buildings, and is bursting with high street shops (*see* 'Shopping', p.27) and street vendors until you hit **Hötorget**, an outdoor fruit and flower market. On one side of the cobbled square is the **Hötorgshallen**, an indoor market, and on the other is **Konserthuset**, **t** (08) 0 506 677 88, the concert hall designed in the 1920s with a Greek temple in mind, and the site for the Nobel prize-giving ceremony.

A couple of blocks up, across the wide shopping street of **Kungsgatan**, peer along **Olof Palmes Gata**, named after the former Swedish prime minister who in 1986 was shot dead nearby when he was walking home from the cinema with his wife. The first of Sweden's political murders in modern times, the assassination has never been resolved. Palme's body lies in **Adolf Fredriks kyrka** two blocks further north. For a respite from the surrounding shopping, **Centralbadet** at Drottingatan 88, **t** (08) 545 213 00 (*open Mon–Fri 6am–8.30pm, Sat and Sun 8am–8.30pm; adm*) offers the amenities of a modern spa in a sumptuous Art Nouveau environment.

Continue north to reach the **Strindbergsmuseet**, Drottninggatan 85, **t** (08) 411 5354, www.*strindbergsmuseet.se* (*open Sept–May Wed–Sun 12–4, Tues 12–7; June–Aug Tues–Sun 12–4; closed Mon; adm*), which shows how Sweden's most famous playwright, August Strindberg, lived between 1908 and 1912. Authors facing writing blocks in their garrets (Strindberg's apartment is more enticingly called the Blue Tower) may offer a limited range of visual stimulation, but celebrity-obsessed visitors may be partially satisfied by noting that Strindberg's flat enjoyed all the modern conveniences of its time but, peculiarly, had no kitchen. Instead, the author had his food sent down from the Falkner's family hotel on the fifth floor, and when the hotel was eventually shut down he had to resort to eating out.

A five-minute walk east of Sergels Torg past department store **NK**, another relief from the busy commercial beat of the modern centre is **Kungsträdgården**, formerly a royal garden that grew cabbages and carrots for the royal household until it was relaid in French Baroque style in the 19th century and opened to the public. In the summer, there are several cafés and plenty of benches to enjoy, and in the winter a popular ice-skating rink is laid out. At the north entrance to the park is the excellent **Sverigeshuset**, a tourist information centre covering the whole of Sweden.

Blasieholmen and Skeppsholmen

Southeast of Kungsträdgården, jutting out into the water, is the tiny grid of **Blasieholmen**, its exclusive tone set by the magnificent faded pink and green copper-roofed **Grand Hotel** that hogs the view across the water to the Royal Palace and Gamla Stan's Skeppsbron side. Outside the hotel at Strömkajen, **Waxholmsbolaget**, **t** (08) 679 5830, operates boat tours to the Stockholm archipelago.

At the far end of the waterfront is **Nationalmuseum**, Södra Blasieholmshamnen, **t** (08) 519 543, *www.nationalmuseum.se (open Tues and Thurs 11–8, Wed and Fri–Sun 11–5; closed Mon)*, Sweden's largest art museum, whose striking 1866 design was modelled on Florentine and Venetian Renaissance buildings. The pre-19th-century collections were originally at Nationalmuseum's predecessor, the Konglig Museum (Royal Museum), which in 1792 became one of the world's first public museums. Although there is a large number of international works including Rembrandt and Renoir, the rooms with Swedish art (and note the impressive frescoes painted by Carl Larsson in the entrance hall) are of particular interest.

Emblematic of the late-19th-century local artistic movement is *Midsummer Dance* by Anders Zorn, who belonged to the 'Opponents' movement headed by fellow painter and friend Ernst Josephson, which rebelled against the academic autocracy and conservative thinking at the Academy of Fine Arts in Stockholm. The magical Nordic light associated with the never-ending days of early summer is delicately captured in the 1897 painting that shows couples in folk costumes dancing on the lawn of a courtyard; the maypole of midsummer celebrations and the bright red country house in the background are a typical Swedish summer sight.

Of earlier vintage and one of the best known of Alexander Roslin's paintings is *The Lady with the Veil* (1768), a picture of Roslin's wife, Marie-Suzanne Giroust, herself a pastel-painter. Dressed in the fashion of Bologna in the time, the way the model gazes at the viewer behind her, half coyly, half coquettishly, is masterful. Among the more modern displays, the three stone prototypes of the *'Excent'* chair, designed by Jonas Palmius, is intriguing because for once it shows a Swedish designer indulging in creating an unusually shaped chair that eschews all the country's traditional consideration for comfort and practicality.

Across **Skeppsholmsbron**, a bridge consisting of five 30m-long spans of malleable iron – an innovative design for the 1860s when it was built – is **Skeppsholmen**. The island's splendid nautical past (it served as a naval base from the 17th century onwards) is immediately evident along Västra Brobänken (with stunning views of Gamla Stan) where the beautiful full-rigged ship **AF *Chapman*** is anchored. Built in England in 1888 and used as a British cargo ship until 1908, it was eventually sold to Sweden, becoming a popular youth hostel in 1949. Further south is **Konsthögskolan**, originally built as barracks for boatswains and now housing the Royal University College of Fine Arts. But the island's main attraction, smack in the centre, has to be **Moderna Museet**, Slupskjulsvägen 7–9, **t** (08) 5195 5200, *www.modernamuseet.se (open Tues–Wed 10–8, Thurs–Sun 10–6; adm free except for two temporary exhibitions)*, a museum of contemporary art first established in the early 1960s in a former naval drill hall and recently rebuilt by Spanish architect Rafael Moneo to hold more than 100 square metres of exhibition space. A generous government grant made possible the purchase of some classic modern paintings by Georges Braque, Pablo Picasso, Giorgio de Chirico and Salvador Dalí. Sharing the same space is the **Arkitekturmuseet**, **t** (08) 587 270 00, *www.arkitekturmuseet.se (open same hours; adm free)*, with displays on Swedish architecture. Rounding up the wealth of artistic display on the small island is **Östasiatiska Museet**, Tyghusplan, **t** (08) 519 557 50, *www.ostasiatiska.se,* the Museum of Far Eastern Antiquities with unique collections of Chinese stoneware and other pieces of art from Japan, India and Korea.

On the Östra Brobänken and Slupskjulsplan along the eastern fringes of the island, festivals such as the Stockholm International Jazz & Blues Festival are often held.

South of the island is the **Engelska** (English) **Parken**. It is worth crossing the small bridge south of Skeppsholmen to **Kastellholmen** to spot the 1848 **citadel** (the original one was built in 1660 to protect the entrance to Stockholm) where the Swedish naval flag is hoisted every morning and from which salutes are fired at noon every weekday and at 1pm on weekends. It was also along the shores of this steep cliff that the warship *Vasa* sank during its maiden voyage in 1628 (*see* 'Vasa Museet', pp.41–2).

Östermalm

The area north of the pretty square of Blaseiholmstorg and east of the modern shopping centre of Norrmalm marks the beginning of the Östermalm district, the capital's most exclusive district composed of Paris-style boulevards, grandiose stone mansion blocks with intricate iron balconies and star-shaped squares that emerged from the 1870s to replace an original mishmash of wooden houses and herb gardens.

At its western fringes, proudly squatting over Nybroplan and Berzelii Park, is the **Kungliga Dramatiska Teatern** (Royal Dramatic Theatre, more commonly known as **Dramaten**), Nybroplan, t (08) 665 6100, *www.dramaten.se* (*guided tours in summer, 3 and 5.30*). Opened in 1908, the theatre's beautiful Art Nouveau exterior is matched by a lavish interior which has been the setting of many Ingmar Bergman-directed plays long after the renowned film director retired from the cinema. Swedes are passionate about their theatre and prefer to attend performances in comfortable clothes, eschewing the formality of their European counterparts. The original Dramaten, on the exact same site, was built in 1788 by the artistically inclined King Gustav III.

In front of Dramaten, apart from offering a peaceful stopping place, the leafy **Raoul Wallenberg Torg** is worth pausing at, if only to learn about Raoul Wallenberg, the Swedish citizen who rescued thousands of Jews from Nazi deportation in Hungary. A sculpture in his honour was put up in 2000 by Danish artist Kirsten Ortwed. For pure entertainment, head behind Dramaten to **Musikemuseet**, Sibyllegatan 2, t (08) 519 554 90, *www.musikmuseet.se* (*open Tues 11–7, Wed–Sun 11–4; adm*). Founded in 1899, two years after the city's successful art and industrial exhibition, the music museum began as a rather literal display of 200 instruments and musical and theatrical archive material but has since metamorphosed into a highly interactive tour of more than 6,000 musical instruments, many which can be banged, strummed and tinkled to varying effect. Housed in a former Crown Bakery that used to supply the Swedish armed forces with bread, the museum also includes a concert hall with excellent acoustics and seating capacity of 300 – check with the museum for the latest programmes. Sweden's success in the pop world in the last 30 years is also charted.

A couple of blocks north of Musikemuseet is **Östermalms Saluhall**, a turn-of-the-20th-century indoor food hall that is worth a visit to watch the immaculately groomed residents select their vegetables and fish from pristine market stalls, or even to join them for lunch in one of the charming side restaurants where a delicious creamy fish soup won't break the bank. The neat and elegant grid that fans beyond the food hall up to **Valhallavägen** – along which the 1912 **Olympic Stadium**, still intact, was built – is mostly of interest for enthusiasts of rather exclusive shops and some fine restaurants. The one exception is the **Historiska Museet**, Narvavägen 13–17, **t** (08) 519 556 00, *www.historiska.se* (*open mid-May–mid-Sept daily 11–5; mid-Sept–mid-May Tues–Sun 11–5, Thurs 11–8, guided tours in English June–Aug daily at 2; adm*), which narrates the history of Sweden from the Stone Age until the 16th century with a particular focus on the Vikings. Of particular interest is the Gold Room, which houses an unusual number of Sweden's oldest gold objects from the Bronze Age to the 16th century including the Dune Treasure, the largest medieval treasure in Europe.

Östermalm's most magnificent sight is along **Strandvägen**, the wide avenue along the waterfront that served as a promenade to the World Exhibition event hosted by the capital in 1897. The sternness of the imposing stone buildings is softened by the bobbing, classy yachts along the quay and the tranquil views over the leafy Djurgården. It's a good walk (*an alternative is the 69 bus that starts at Sergels Torg*) along the venerable avenue, across Nobel Parken and on to Ekoparken, the site of a cluster of museums that include: **Tekniska Museet**, Muselvägen 7, **t** (08) 450 5600 (*open Mon–Fri 10–5, Sat and Sun 11– 5*), featuring the history of Swedish technology and industry; **Sjöhistoriska Museet**, Djurgårdsbrunnsvägen 24, **t** (08) 519 549 00 (*open Wed–Mon 10–3, Tues 10–8.30; adm*), of interest for maritime historians; **Etnografiska Museet**, Djurgårdsbrunnsvägen, **t** (08) 519 550 00 (*open Tues–Sun 11–5, Wed 11–8*), an exhibition that reveals how Sweden's attitude to the outside world has changed over the centuries; and the **Thielska galleriet**, Sjötullsbacken 6, **t** (08) 1 662 5882 (*open Mon–Sat 12–4, Sun 1–4*), a splendid villa that houses the great art collection of wealthy banker Ernest Thiel, whose venerable list of artist friends at the turn of the 20th century included Edvard Munch, Carl Larsson, Anders Zorn and Bruno Liljefors.

The star attraction of this easterly neck of the capital, primarily for its sweeping vantage point, has to be **Kaknästornet**, Ladugårdsgärdet on Norra Djurgården, **t** (08) 667 21 05 (*open Sept–April daily 10–9; May–Aug 9am–10pm; adm*). The TV and telegraph tower, one of the tallest buildings in northern Europe and owned and operated by Teracom which provides TV and radio transmissions in Sweden, has two viewing platforms on levels 30 and 31 as well as a restaurant and café. The panorama is outstanding as well as informative; hire a set of headphones in the lobby at the ground floor to help identify the different sights that can be spotted from up high.

Djurgården and the Vasa Museet

It's not difficult to appreciate why Djurgården is Stockholmers' favourite play-ground. The verdant island that King Karl XI converted into a royal hunting ground in the 17th century is home to the capital's outdoor museum, Skansen, a giant park scattered with historic buildings from all over the country, the fascinating *Vasa* ship museum, and the impressive Nordiska Museum; plus it has ample open spaces for walking, picnicking or leisurely coffee-sipping, and, for thrill-seekers, a rather old-fash-ioned fairground. The short ferry trip to the island is a pleasure itself, the bows of the Djurgårds-ferry providing some of the best vistas of Stockholm. **Ferries** leave from

Räntmästar-trappan in Slussen all year 8am–midnight, and from Nybroplan between May and August 10am–8pm (a much shorter hop). A more prosaic route is the 44 or 47 **bus** from Sergels Torg, while the healthier option is a half-hour **walk** from the modern city centre (less from Karlaplan underground station) through the elegant waterfront of Östermalm. For those with a historical bent, try the **Museispårvagnen** (*runs June–Aug 11–6; April–Dec Sat and Sun 11–5*), an old-fashioned tram driven by enthusiastic members of the Swedish Tram Association (from Norrmalmstorg).

Approaching the island from Strandvägen across the cast-iron **Djurgårdsbron** (bridge), the splendid Nordic Renaissance castle that houses **Nordiska Museet**, Djurgårdsvägen 6–16, **t** (08) 519 560 00 (*open Sept–May Mon–Fri 10–4, Sat and Sun 10–5; June–Aug daily 10–5; adm*) looms ahead. Inside the monumental building, designed in the so-called Vasa Renaissance style in 1907, is a fascinating collection of more than 1.5 million objects that aims to paint a picture of Sweden's cultural history from 1520 to the present. The idea came from a man and a woollen skirt, specifically Artur Hazelius, who, when travelling in the province of Dalarna in 1872, became obsessed with saving the province's rustic culture. A typical Dalarna woollen skirt became the first item in the museum that opened in 1873 in central Stockholm and today includes a whole range of fashion items up to the punk era, plus furnished rooms from 1870 to 2004, table settings from 1500 to 1900, three centuries of doll's houses and a particularly impressive exhibition on the Sami people, a Nomadic minority group in the north of Sweden who are still fighting for total inclusion.

West of Nordiska Museet, overlooking the waters, is **Galärparken**, at the edge of which sits **Junibacken**, **t** (08) 587 230 00 (*open June–Aug daily 10–8; Sept–May Tues–Sun 10–5; adm*), a children's theme park with a fairy train ride through a miniature world featuring Astrid Lindgren's best known fictional creation, Pippi Longstocking, and other characters from popular children's writers in Sweden. Further along the waterfront is the **Estonia Minnesvården**, a granite-walled memorial honouring the hundreds of victims who died on board the *Estonia* ferry which sank inexplicably in the Baltic Sea on its journey to Stockholm, in September 1994.

Past victims of the sea are also remembered in the rather different kind of memorial at the adjacent **Vasa Museet**, **t** (08) 519 548 00, *www.vasamuseet.se* (*open Aug 21–June 9 Thurs–Tues 10–5, Wed 10–8, June 10–Aug 20 daily 9.30–7; adm*), which tells the story of the battleship that set out on its maiden voyage in 1628, only to sink in front of the incredulous eyes of King Gustav II Adolf's subjects as it was leaving Stockholm harbour. The fascinating story of how this mighty warship sank, and how, equally astonishingly, it was raised almost intact from the sea bed in 1961, explains why this custom-built space that holds the original 17th-century vessel and an array of side exhibits has become the most visited tourist attraction in Sweden.

Armed with 64 guns on two gun decks, the *Vasa* was commissioned in the 1620s at the request of Gustav Adolf as a showpiece for the Swedish navy, which was at war with Poland. On the fateful Sunday, August 10, the beaches around Stockholm were teeming with proud citizens and admiring foreign diplomats as the vessel, created by experienced Dutch shipbuilder Henrik Hybertsson, set sail with a resounding salute. Yet within minutes the ship began to keel over, righting herself slightly before keeling again, the second time unable to prevent the gushing water pouring in through the gun ports, flooding the ship and drowning about a third of the 150 people on board.

When the king, busy heading the troops in Poland, heard of the disaster, he demanded an immediate inquiry. Heading the list of blamed parties was Admiral Klas Fleming, who didn't act on a failed stability test before *Vasa* undertook her maiden voyage. Henrik Hybertsson was then accused of designing too narrow a hull, a charge complicated by the fact that he had died a year before the vessel was completed. Captain Söfring Hansson was also held a prime suspect, for sailing with open gun ports that allowed the water to gush in so quickly. Indirectly, the king himself was blamed for having approved the *Vasa*'s dimensions and for insisting on the ship's carrying as many heavy guns as possible. Typical of Swedish consensual tradition, no single party ended up being blamed and the verdict rather inconclusively held that the *Vasa* was a well-built ship but badly proportioned. The museum tour includes a visual and aural reinterpretation of the inquiry, reconstructions of life on deck and an external tour of the vessel, which has had its lower rig rebuilt, complete with masts, stays and shrouds. Equally fascinating are the exhibits showing how the wreck was salvaged in 1961 and how the subsequent restoration work was carried out.

East of Vasa and making up the central part of the island is **Skansen, t** (08) 442 8000 (*open May daily 10–8; June–Aug daily 10–10; Sept daily 10–5; Oct–April daily 10–4*), the world's oldest open-air museum, founded in 1891 as an extension of the Nordiska Museet. For history-lovers there are at least 150 buildings from different parts of the country and eras that to life with the help of performers acting out roles of their inhabitants. Walk for instance into a Skåne farmstead from the 1920s, or a 19th-century farm from the north of Sweden showing how an entire family huddled together in one room during the severe winters, or watch how craftsmen lived and worked in a stroll through Djurgårdsstaden, a small, picturesque residential area made of some tiny 18th-century wooden houses. For animal-lovers, Skansen's **zoo** includes bear, wolves, elks and lynx as well as traditional Swedish livestock and more exotic animals in the **aquarium**. Music-lovers are rewarded with a wide range of classical, jazz and pop concerts throughout the summer, while **Gröna Lund** (*open end April–mid-Sept*) offers the traditional joys of an amusement park. Skansen also comes alive with bazaars in the pre-Christmas festive season (*see* 'Shopping', p.28).

Those with more reclusive or artistic tastes can give themselves a treat, with a walk along the island's shores to **Waldermasudde**, Prins Eugens Väg 6, **t** (08) 662 4740, *www.waldermasudde.com* (*open Tues, Wed and Fri–Sun 11–5, Thurs 11–8, closed Mon*), the former home of the painter prince Eugene. The large villa, built in a mixture of Art Nouveau and Swedish manor-house styles, was designed by Ferninand Boberg and houses a collection of the prince's own works, his first-class collection of Swedish art from 1880 to 1945, sculptures and temporary exhibits. Romantics are also rewarded by the leafy walk towards the northeastern part of the island to **Rosendal Slott**, Rosendalsvägen, **t** (08) 402 6130 (*open June–Aug; guided tours at 1, 2 and 3*), a splendid country house in Empire style, and the best example of the architectural style that emerged during the reign of Karl XIV Johan, who reigned from 1818 to 1844. The palace gardens are a beautiful spot for coffee, sandwiches and cakes. Amid all the flora it is difficult to imagine that **Bellmans Bysten** (located further south) once upon a time marked the city boundary, outside which lawlessness and tax exemption prevailed as favourite pastimes.

Södermalm

Traditionally a working class district and now one of the city's highly sought-after residential hot spots and night-time haunts for trendy urbanites, Södermalm, or **'Söder'** as it is more fashionably known, is easily reached a few minutes' walk south of Gamla Stan or via Slussen underground station. From Slussen ('sluice gates') take the Katarina Hissen lift (*Mon–Fri 7.30am–10pm, Sat and Sun 10–10; adm*) to the heights of **Fjällgatan** with its picturesque 300-year-old wooden shacks (No.34 is thought to be the oldest), offering a magnificent panorama of the capital that explains why this was a popular promenade back in the 17th century. (A more morbid reason is that nearby open ground Stigberget was the site for executions.) For those with a distaste for giddy lift rides, buses 46 and 53 go to Fjällgatan and bus 404 to **Fåfängan**, another spot further west with a former late-18th-century gazebo that overlooks the old city to the west, Djurgården straight ahead and the sea approach to Stockholm to the east. Fåfängan was the name given to land that was no good for agriculture, making it an ideal place for the gazebo built by merchant Frederik Lundlin in 1770, and now serving as a **coffee house** (*open May, Aug and Sept daily 11–9; June and July 11–10*).

Behind the scenic viewpoints and worth a short detour are the pleasant 19th-century **Mosebacke Torg**, where there are several eateries and the classical Södra Teatern, and, a few blocks down, **Katarina kyrka**, Högbergsgatan 13, t (08) 743 6840 (*open Mon–Fri 11–5, Sat and Sun 10–5*), the first of Stockholm's three dome-shaped churches to be built, in 1690. Apart from the outer walls, the splendidly restored interior only dates back to 1995 after a fire destroyed the church that had previously been burnt down a first time in 1723. Further southeast in **Vita Bergen** park, outdoor plays are staged in summer.

Not content with its splendid eastern shores, Söder provides further options for beautiful viewing points west of Slussen at **Monteliusvägen**, of the City Hall and the western side of the old city. If you don't get that far, just outside Slussen station is the informative and entertaining **Stadsmuseet**, Ryssgården, t (08) 508 31 600, *www.stads museum.stockholm.se* (*open Tues, Wed and Fri–Sun 11–5, Thurs 11–9, closed Mon*), which traces the origins and development of the city and life of Stockholmers from the Middle Ages to the present day.

Southwest of Södermalmstorg is the most informal and buzzing nightlife in town, with a couple of popular haunts in the beautiful Art Deco square of **Mariatorget** (*see* 'Rival' in 'Where to Stay', p.29) and an eclectic line of traditional cafés, designer bars and restaurants that flank Götgatan and don't seem to end till **Medborgarplatsen**. This modern square is flanked to the west by the curved **Bofills Båge** building and by **Söder Torn**, whose large and rather severe designs (created by venerable Spanish and Danish architects Ricardo Bofill and Henning Larsen respectively) caused rather a lot of un-Swedish controversy. An ingenious use of space was made on the eastern side of the square when a former power station, designed in 1903 in Andalucian-

Moroccan style, was converted in 2000 into a **Mosken** (mosque), **t** (08) 509 109 00 (*open daily 12–5*), in a nod to the growing influx of Muslim immigrants.

A robust walk (or take the tube to Skannstull) to the south side of the island is rewarded with the calm green space of **Eriksdalsbadet** (a popular swimming pool in the summer) and a walk through former allotments where poorer city-dwellers had a chance to grow their own vegetables.

Millesgården

*Herserudsvägen 32, Lidingö, **t** (08) 446 7590, www.millesgarden.se;*
Ropsten underground station and then a direct bus 207, or a bus to Torsvik
from where it is a 300m walk to the park. Open mid-May–Aug daily 10–5;
Sept–mid-May Tues–Fri 12–4, Sat and Sun 11–5, closed Mon; adm.

The creations of Sweden's best known 20th-century sculptor, Carl Milles, set in beautiful gardens, make for a most pleasant excursion to the shores of Lidingö island in the northeast of Stockholm. Carl Milles, whose statues grace many public squares and museum entrances in major Swedish cities, bought a plot of land on Lidingö island in 1906 where, together with his wife Olga, he built a house and studio. After the couple left their home in 1931, they created the generous Carl and Olga Milles Lidingöhem Foundation, which opened the park to the general public towards the end of that decade. The monumental statues that seem to soar energetically into this sky, and the natural island-side setting, make this a popular year-round destination.

Day Trips from Stockholm

Drottningholm and Birka

Drottningholm Palace and the former Viking settlement of Birka, both on the UNESCO World Heritage list, are west of the capital on Lake Mälaren.

Drottningholm Palace, **t** (08) 402 62 80, **f** (08) 402 62 81 (*open May–Aug daily 10–4.30; Sept daily 12–3.30; Oct–April Sat and Sun 12–3.30*) has been the home of the royal family since 1981. The original palace in Drottningholm (literally 'Queen's Island') was built in the late 16th century by King Johan III for his consort, Queen Katarina Jagellonika, but was destroyed by fire on 30th December 1661. After the fire, Nicodemus Tessin the Elder, the architect who worked on the original plans of the Royal Palace in Stockholm, was commissioned to build the new palace by the Queen Dowager, Hedvig Eleonora. The most impressive elements of the resulting mixture of Italian and French Baroque design are the monumental staircase, the Ehrenstrahl Drawing Room, and Hedvig Eleonora's State Bedchamber. Large parts of the exclusive French Baroque park still remain, including bronze sculptures by Adrian de Vries, one of the most eminent sculptors of the northern European Renaissance.

The period following 1744, when the palace was given as a wedding present to Princess Lovisa Ulrika of Prussia on her marriage to the Swedish heir apparent Adolf Fredrik, heralded some impressive additions, including Lovisa Ulrika's Green Antechamber, redecorated in a French rococo style; the fabulous Drottningholm Court

Getting There

Drottningholm Palace: From Stadshuskajen outside the City Hall, **boats** take about 50mins. A less scenic route is the **underground** to Brommaplan, after which the 300 **bus** takes 30mins to the palace.

Birka: Boats depart in the summer from Stadshusbron by the City Hall and take 2hrs 45mins.

For more info and tickets for both Birka and Drottningholm, call the tourist centre at Sergels Torg, **t** (08) 789 24 90.

Eating Out

Drottningholmspaviljongen, t (08) 759 0425 (*expensive–moderate*). Located in the Royal Garden; the spectacular views of the palace and Lake Mälaren make this turn-of-the-20th-century pavilion the first choice for lunch. There are prices to suit all tastes, from the daily lunch offer (*Mon–Fri 11–2.30*) to the more lavish dining aimed at the business clientele. There is seating inside the pavilion and outside in the garden.

Lunch on board: M/S *Prins Carl Philip* and S/S *Drottningholm*, boats belonging to Strömmakanalbolaget, **t** (08) 587 140 00, *www.strommkanalbolaget.com* (*moderate*). For those travelling only to Drottningholm, there are lunch round-trips on two newly renovated boats (dating back to around 1900) where finely presented meals consisting of local produce can be enjoyed alongside views of Lake Mälaren. Meals are also available on boats returning from Birka to Stockholm.

Theatre (1766) that includes a stage with moving waves, trapdoors, cloud cars and wind and thunder apparatus; and the delightful Chinese Pavilion in the grounds.

Birka is further west, the former centre of the wealthy Mälar valley in the Viking Age which at its peak had more than 700 inhabitants composed of craftsmen like bronze-casters, bead-makers, weavers and comb-makers, and merchants who used the island as a trading spot for precious commodities. Many of the townspeople were baptised after AD 840 when the young Benedictine monk Ansgar came to Birka to bring the Christian gospel to the pagan Swedes. But Birka never became a Christian community, and by the end of the 10th century Sigtuna (*see* 'Touring from Stockholm', p.52) took over Birka's role. Much of the former Viking town has yet to be excavated.

Archipelago Tours

Stretching for 80km east of the capital towards the Baltic Sea are more than 24,000 islands, islets and rocks that make up the spectacular Stockholm archipelago.

Vaxholm, the capital of the archipelago and a meeting point for the surrounding boat traffic since the 19th century, hosts the Day of the Archipelago Boats (June 4), and the Archipelago Market (Aug 16). Arts and crafts are sold in the market stalls in the harbour all year round and the fortress built in 1647 includes a museum.

Grinda's excellent sand beaches, forests and cliffs make it one of the more popular resorts. Rowing boats can also be rented. **Utö** was an iron mine in the 12th century, but today the shafts are filled with water and the workers' houses are part of the small mining museum. Located far out in the southern archipelago, the island is inhabited all year. Aside from the obvious waterside attractions like fishing and bathing, there are arts and crafts stalls and horse and carriage trips and a famous windmill built in 1791.

Sandhamn in **Sandön** has an impressive harbour which has served as a natural meeting point for seafarers since the 18th century and today is the starting point for

Getting There

Waxholmsbolaget, t (08) 679 58 30, *www.waxholmsbolaget.se*, located at Strömkajen outside Grand Hotel, is the shipping company, founded in 1869, that operates about 40 boats across the archipelago. **Tickets** vary according to the length of the journey, with a standard ticket to Vaxholm, the most popular destination, costing about SEK55 one-way. Most vessels have a cafeteria. with vintage steamers S/S *Storskär* and S/S *Norrskär* offering a full meal service. If you intend to do a lot of island-hopping, the **Båtluffarkort** is a boat pass that lasts for 16 days and costs SEK420. The card can be bought at the Waxholm terminals at Strömkajen, in Vaxholm, at Utflyktsbutiken in Kulturhuset (Sergels Torg) and at many tourist offices. The pass comes with a map, the company's brochure on archipelago tours, the Skärgårdsstiftelsen's yearbook *Skärgårdsnatur*, schedules, and a brochure on accommodation.

the famous sailing race, Gotland Runt (29 June) and the Sandhamn Regatta (23–6 July). Bathing places abound, along Trouville's sandy beaches and on the island's northern part. **Finnhamn**, on the border between the outer and the intermediary archipelago, is made up of three islands, Idholmen, Stora Jolplan and Lilla Jolplan, from which rowing boats can be hired for excursions to the surrounding islets.

Overnighters from Stockholm or Västerås

Mariefred

Of all the pretty villages dotted around Stockholm's archipelago, Mariefred is one of the most charming, its rather exclusive picturesque wooden houses enhanced by the fairytale castle that dominates Lake Mälaren. The main sights can easily be appreciated in a day, but the peaceful, intimate setting is more than tempting enough for an overnight stay, especially in the summer when swimming or sailing are inexpensive.

After a stroll in the main square, the obvious magnet for the traveller is **Gripsholms Slott** (Gripsholm Castle), **t** (0159) 101 94, *www.royalcourt.se* (*open mid-May–mid-Sept daily 10–4; mid-Sept–mid-May Sat and Sun 12–3; adm; guided tours mid-May–mid-Sept at 1pm*). Slottsholmen (the castle islet) was already inhabited from the 9th century, apparently popular as a sacrificial site. The first lavishly decorated castle to appear was in 1380 on the orders of Bo Jonsson Grip, then Lord Treasurer of the Realm, but only six years later, after his death, a group of farmers vented their frustration about their ill-treatment on the castle, which they tore down.

A hundred years later, two Carthusian monks visited Bishop Rogge in nearby Strängnäs to ask for land to build a monastery. They were granted the piece of land where the **church** in Mariefred ('Mary's Peace', named after Carthusian monastery Pax Mariae) now stands. For a while, the monks lived peacefully, each one digging his own well to avoid the temptation of breaking the monastic rule of silence; but their days were numbered after Gustav Vasa was elected king of Sweden at nearby Strängnäs cathedral: the king's growing sympathies with Protestantism led to an assault on monks and nuns and the monastery was torn down, its stones used in 1547 to build a keep on the islet with four round towers mounted by cannons, to defend the harbour.

Getting There

By train: From **Västerås**, take the train to Eskilstuna, from which you take another train to Läggesta (approx 28mins). From **Stockholm**, take the train direct to Läggesta (approx 37mins). From Läggesta, in the summer, walk 150m to its museum railway station, where there is a connecting steam train to Mariefred. In the winter, there is a bus connection/feeder bus to Mariefred/Gripsholm Castle.

By boat: Arriving in Mariefred is a real treat, although possible only after mid–late-April, when the ice around the harbour has finally thawed. From **Stockholm**'s City Hall, S/S *Mariefred*, the last coal-burning steamer in original condition, sails Tues–Sun during the summer season to Mariefred. The journey takes 3½ hours. For more info, call the shipping line on **t** (08) 669 88 50 or go to Gripsholm Mariefred Ångfartygs AB. From **Västerås**, the Strömma Kanalbolag (*www.strommakanalbolaget.com*) company's M/S *August Lindholm* leaves the East Harbour to go to Mariefred.

Regional train/bus information services: **TiM**, **t** (0771) 846 846, *www.tim-trafik.se*. **SJ**, **t** (0771) 757 575, *www.sj.se*.

Getting Around

The town is small and the castle is only a short walk away.

Tourist Information

Mariefred: Rådhuset (main square), **t** (0159) 297 90, **f** (0159) 297 95. Attentive, knowledgeable staff in the beautiful town hall.

Where to Stay

Mariefred t (0159) –

Also check at the tourist office for summer cottages; online booking, *www.strangnas.se*.

Gripsholms Värdhus/hotel, Kyrkoplan 1, **t** 347 50, **f** 347 77, *www.gripsholms-vardhus.se* (luxury). The inn is steeped in history and that's partly what you are paying for when you stay here. In the early 17th century, Karl IX used to visit Gripsholm frequently, putting a huge burden on the town, which was forced to feed all his court employees as a form of tax payment. Following protests, a letter of privilege was issued to a German tavern keeper in Stockholm, Jochim, who became the first in a long row of innkeepers. The 'Smockska' room is named after him.

In my Garden, Strandvägen 17, **t** 133 53, *www. inmygarden.se* (*expensive*). This rather magnificent house converted into an intimate, personal hotel rather coyly calls itself a bed and breakfast, but the owners have evidently spent a lot of time and attention creating the differently decorated rooms in a traditional old-world Swedish style.

Röda Korsets Idé- och Utbildningscenter, **t** 367 00, *www.redcross.se/gripsholm* (*moderate*). This as good-priced a bed as you are going to find in this rather chichi town. Check with the tourist office about availability of rooms, as the Red Cross sometimes has to use the large building for conferences.

Eating Out

Mariefred t (0159) –

When Gustav III invited poet and entertainer Carl Michael Bellman to Mariefred, the latter complained that, apart from the women being too ugly and the castle too old-fashioned, the town was simply too provincial. In those days however, there were 14 taverns to choose from, considerably more than today.

Gripsholms Värdhus/hotel, Kyrkoplan 1, **t** 347 50, **f** 347 77 (*very expensive–expensive*). As the oldest inn in Sweden, used to serving well-heeled customers, the restaurant is pricy. Traditional fare won't disappoint.

Strandrestaurangen, Strandvägen, **t** 133 88 (*expensive*). The setting for this restaurant is almost as spectacular as that of the nearby Gripsholms, and the food is of similar standard although more affordable.

Mariefreds Bistro, Storgatan 16, **t** 100 19 (*expensive–moderate*). Given the competition at the lakeside, this option appears rather more mundane.

Gripsholms Grill & Pizzeria, Gripsholmsvägen 1, **t** 211 51 (*moderate*). Standard grills and pizzas served close to the castle.

Konditori Fredman, Kyrkogatan 11. Nice cakes and a pleasant view of the square.

Presumably unintended by Gustav Vasa, the castle ended up being used as a prison after his death, rather shockingly, for his son Johan and his wife Katarina Jagellonica at the hands of his eldest son Erik XIV. Johan spent six years in captivity plotting his revenge, during which his son Sigismund was born, and it was the later-deposed Erik who was to spend the rest of his life imprisoned in several castles. Fortunately Gustav Vasa's third son, Karl IX, was able to see beyond fratricide and realized the potential of the keep as a castle, so extensive renovations ensued – arrow loops were elevated, real windows fitted and a primitive central heating, crucial during the icy winters, installed. By the late 18th century, perhaps captured by the royal intrigue that had surrounded the castle's birth, the theatrical monarch Gustav III loved to visit Gripsholm, where he could re-enact historical fantasies. The splendid theatre constructed in one of the round towers is a remnant from this period, kept intact since 1792 when Gustav was shot at the Stockholm Opera House. A walk through a hotch-potch of centuries (furniture and art objects were transferred randomly from various royal residences during the 19th century) is made to seem that much longer by the seemingly never-ending collection of portraits that feature prominent Swedes from Gustav Vasa to present-day pop stars, soccer players and politicians.

A relaxing antidote to these regal excesses is **Grafikens Hus**, Gripsholms Kungsladu-gård, Mariefred, **t** (0159) 231 60, *www.grafikenhus.se* (*open May–Aug Tues–Sun 11–5; closed Mon; guided tours Sat and Sun 1pm; adm*), a well laid-out and well-lit interna-tional centre for fine art printmaking in one of the former royal stables.

Uppsala

The hues of ruby-red, yellow and orange on the grand stone houses flanking the twisting, cobbled streets of central Uppsala were beautifully shot in celluloid in Ingmar Bergman's Oscar-winning *Fanny and Alexander*, and a walk down Tragårdsgatan, where the famous director spent his first year as a child, does not disappoint. Sweden's fourth-largest city is a lovely place to get lost for a day or two. Befitting its status as the religious and educational centre of the country, Uppsala has a magnificent Gothic cathedral, the largest in Scandinavia, imposing edifices that belong to the region's oldest university, a domed, blood-red-washed castle, magnifi-cent botanical gardens, a river that runs through the city and a large student population to liven up the evenings. Enthusiasts of the pre-Christian era won't be let down either. On the outskirts of the town are three royal burial mounds, believed to be the site of ancient sacrificial rites.

At the centre of the medieval town, a 15-minute walk from the train station, is the **Domkyrkan**, Domkyrkoplan 2, **t** (018) 187 201, *www.uppsaladomkyrka.se* (*open daily 8–6; guided tours Sept–May Sun 12.30; June–Aug daily 12.30*). King (or St) Erik, who was killed in Uppsala in 1160 by a Danish pretender to the throne and subsequently became a patron saint of Sweden, has a prominent place in the twin-spired cathedral that was completed in 1435. St Erik's bones are kept in a silver basket, while the legend of his life is narrated in a set of restored 14th-century paintings that hang in one of the tiny side chapels off the French Gothic ambulatory. Tombs of other illustrious figures include King Gustav Vasa, who ushered in the Reformation, his son Johan III, whose regalia was later taken to Västerås cathedral to honour the brother he deposed (King Erik XIV), and famous home-grown scientist Carl Linnaeus (*see* below).

Opposite the main entrance of the cathedral is **Gustavianum**, Akademigatan 3, **t** (018) 471 57 060, *www.gustavianum.uu.se* (*open daily 11–4; adm*), the university museum, which tells the history of the university since it was founded in 1477, partly to satisfy the need to train priests. There are five permanent exhibitions, which include the university collections of Nordic, Classical and Egyptian antiquities, students' notes made in the mid-15th century, and unique objects like a Celsius thermometer and the intricate ebony Augsburg Art Cabinet, a museum in miniature. The high spot has to be the atmospheric anatomy theatre, where it's not difficult to imagine students watching a public dissection of executed criminals.

Modern students hurtle around for lectures during term-time (or graduation in May) at the nearby **University Hall, t** (018) 471 1715 (*open Mon–Fri 8–4*), a 19th-century Renaissance-style building, or hang around outside **Carolina Rediviva** (Uppsala university library), Dag Hammarskjölds Väg, **t** (018) 471 3900, *www.ub.uu.se*, which boasts a silver bible from the 6th century among its five million books.

Head down Övre Slottsgatan past the students' union buildings and towards **Uppsala Slott, t** (018) 727 2485, *www.uppsala/se/konstmuseum* (*group tours all year round, art and architectural tours in English June–Aug 3pm*). The castle, which affords sweeping views of the town, was first built in the 16th century by Gustav Vasa, the first king of a united Sweden, primarily as a defence structure, although much of it was destroyed in a fire that devastated three-quarters of the city in 1702.

From the castle, you can wander down to the relaxing **Uppsala University Botanical Garden**, Villavägen 8, **t** (018) 471 2838, **f** (018) 471 2831, *www.botan.uu.se* (*open May–Sept 7am–8.30pm; Oct–April 7–7*). The garden is the oldest botanical garden in Sweden, and was first laid out in 1655 by Olof Rudbeck the elder, professor of medicine. The same fire that destroyed much of the castle also ravaged the garden, which came under strict supervision again in 1741 by Carl Linnaeus, a scientist who had already made a name for himself in the botanical world when he discovered a hundred botanical species during an expedition by foot to the Arctic Ocean. More notoriously, Linnaeus had published a classification of plants based on their sexual parts. His home between 1743 and 1778, north of the river, where much of his research and teaching took place, is also open to the public at **Linnémuseet** (Linnaeus Museum), Svartbäcksgatan 27, **t** (018) 471 2576, *www.linnaeus.uu.se* (*open May–Aug 9–9; Sept daily 9–7; closed Oct–April; adm*). Near the museum, the **Linnaeus Garden** is a reconstruction of the Uppsala University Botanical Garden the way it looked during Linnaeus' days.

Gamla Uppsala (Old Uppsala)

A visit to Uppsala would be incomplete without a visit to the three **royal burial mounds** in Gamla Uppsala, 5km north of Uppsala, which point to the original city's pagan past. To get there, take buses 2, 20, 24 and on Sundays 54 from Stora Torget

Getting There

From Stockholm: Trains take 40mins and buses slightly longer.

From Västerås: Trains and buses take slightly over an hour and leave frequently during the day. For more info, contact **Upplands Lokaltrafik**, St Persgatan 16, **t** (018) 141 450, www.upplandslokaltrafik.se.

Uppsala's train and bus stations are adjacent to one another, off Kungsgatan.

Getting Around

Walking or cycling is the best way to appreciate the river-cut town and the many gardens and parks. A bus is only necessary to visit Gamla Uppsala.

Tourist Information

Uppsala: Fyristorg 8, **t** (018) 727 4800, **f** (018) 132 2895, www.uppsalatourism.se (open Mon–Fri 10–6, Sat 10–3). The tourist office hands out an English guide with a map inside. Ask for the **Uppsalakortet** (Uppsala Card), which includes free admission to museums and Fyrishov outdoor swimming area, parking in specified municipal parking areas, and half-price fares on local buses. Available June–Aug only, a one-day card costs SEK100 and covers one adult and two children. The card is also sold at museums and hotels.

Where to Stay

Uppsala t (018) –

First Hotel Linné, Skolgatan 45, **t** 102 000, www.firsthotels.com (very expensive–expensive). Small but homely rooms overlooking the former home and gardens of revered 18th-century botanist Carl Linnaeus.

Grand Hotel Hornan, Bangardsgatan 1, **t** 139 380, www.grandhotelhornan.com (expensive). Newly renovated and large rooms, some which look out on the River Fyrisån. Breakfast is served in the elegant turn-of-the-20th-century dining room.

Hotel Uppsala, Kungsgatan 27, **t** 327 000, www.profithotels.se (moderate). Rooms have been refurbished in birchwood in Uppsala's biggest hotel, close to the train station and the airport buses. About 40 of the rooms have their own microwave oven, kettle and refrigerator.

Hotell Muttern, St Johannesgatan 31, **t** 510 414, **f** 510 415 (moderate). This new hotel is rather out of the way behind the Observatorieparken, but it is very good value and even cheaper at the weekends.

Hotell Wittullsberg, Vittullsberg, Gamla Uppsala, **t** 327 000 (moderate). One of the few hotels (and reasonably priced) in Old Uppsala, useful if you want to wander around the three huge royal burial mounds before the crowds descend.

Akademihotellet, Övre Slottsgatan 5, **t** 102 000 (inexpensive). As the name suggests, this is close to the university and other

(Uppsalabuss info, **t** (018) 727 3702). Established in the 6th century AD, the burial mounds have fired up a series of legends across different generations. In the 11th century a German clergyman, Adam of Bremen, wrote about the barbaric sacrificial rites in Uppsala to the three Aesir gods, Thor, Odin and Frej, a version which was discredited later when it transpired that Adam of Bremen never set foot in Uppsala. The plot was thickened two centuries later by an Icelandic storyteller, Snorre Strulasson, who recounted that the Scandinavian Yngling royal dynasty was descended from the Nordic god Frej. In the 19th century, when Scandinavian nationalism became the vogue, students from Norway, Sweden and Denmark would make pilgrimages to Uppsala to drink mead from horns and sing songs celebrating their shared past glories (a local mead of sorts is available at the nearby Odinsborg restaurant.) This pan-nationalism led a respected professor in Uppsala to claim that the historic buildings, which more than compensates for the simple, clean rooms.

Samariterhemmet Guest House, Samaritergrand 2, t 103 400 (*inexpensive*). This is a no-frills option, but the main building is an attractive turn-of-the-20th-century house with a garden, centrally located.

Eating Out

Uppsala t (018) –

Svenssons krog/bakficka, Sysslomansgatan 15, t 553 310 (*expensive*). One of the best places for fish dishes and meatballs, although pasta is also served.

Hambergs Fisk o kräft, Fyristorg 8, t 710 050 (*expensive–moderate*). Next to the tourist office, this is highly recommended for smoked salmon dishes and other fish specialities.

Domtrappkalleren, St Eriksgrand 15, t 130 955 (*expensive–moderate*). The buzzing atmosphere and excellent, traditional Swedish fare quickly dispels any reminders that the atmospheric, vaulted cellars at the foot of the cathedral were formerly a prison.

Sten Sture & Co., Nedre Slottsgatan 3 (*expensive–moderate*). This wooden house at the foot of the castle offers meaty dishes, outdoor tables in the summer and live jazz in the evenings.

Odinsborg Restaurant, Gamla Uppsala, t 323 525 (*expensive–moderate*). Close to the royal burial mounds, this turn-of-the-20th-

century mansion converted into a restaurant and entertainment venue for weddings and parties provides a filling, traditional-style buffet in elegant yet homely surroundings. This is also the place to try the local mead.

Svenssons I saluhallen och åkanten, St Eriks Torg, t 150 150 (*moderate*). The river location and outdoor café attracts huge crowds in the summer.

Pub Nutton, 19 Svartbäcksgatan, t 122 680 (*moderate*). An excellent and reasonable lunch menu is served here.

The Saluhallen, St Eriks Torg (*inexpensive*). Fresh fish soup doesn't come more reasonably priced than in this reopened covered market on the river, which suffered a fire in 2002.

Cafés

Ofvandahls, Sysslomsgatan 3–5. The Viennese-style décor makes the oldest café in town ever-popular with students.

Café Katalin and all that jazz, Godsmagasinet, Östra Station, t 019 140 680. This old railway goods shed serves up live jazz or blues in the evenings, mainly to locals in the know.

Güntherska, Östra Ågatan 31, Another favourite, and strictly non-smoking.

Wayne's Coffee, Smedgränd 4, t 018 710 012. This is a local, sophisticated and roomy coffee chain.

Café Linne, Svartbäcksgatan. A lovely spot opposite the Linnaeus Museum to sip a coffee and accompany it with a delicious cinnamon bun.

legendary 'Atlantis' must have referred to Sweden, with Gamla Uppsala as its centre. So it was somewhat disappointing when, in the summer of 1846, excavations began at **Odin's Mound** (or the **East Mound**) and a cairn was found that contained only a couple of burned bones and some burial gifts. Later excavations in the **West Mound**, however, unearthed gold objects and a goshawk, a type of fowl common only among the upper classes. At least it was confirmed that the settlement had been inhabited by a prosperous people.

An exploration of the myths, in an exhibit called 'Myth, Might and Man', can be viewed at the **Old Uppsala Museum**, Disavägen, t (018) 239 399, *www.raa.se/gamla uppsala.se* (*open May–Aug 11–5; Sept–April 10–4; adm*), which has some great views of the mounds. And at the original site of a pagan temple stands a beautiful 12th-century church, **Gamla Uppsala kyrka**.

Touring from Stockholm

Day 1: Sweden's Oldest Town

Morning: Take the E4 north of Stockholm towards Uppsala and turn east at Märsta, taking the 263 to **Sigtuna**, Sweden's oldest town. Walk down Stora Gatan, the city's high street for 1,000 years, lined with pretty wooden houses, garden cafés and small arts and handicrafts workshops, and pop into the Rådhuset (*open June–Aug Tues–Sun 12–4*), Scandinavia's smallest town hall, built in 1744. The city was founded considerably earlier in 980 by King Erik Segersäll, whose son Olof Skötkonung minted Sweden's first coin. In 1100, Sigtuna became the bishop's seat when nearby Uppsala was still a pagan town, and seven stone churches were erected during the Middle Ages, although the ruins of only three remain. For a visual history, visit the **Sigtuna Museum** (*open Sept–May Tues–Sun 12–4, June–Aug daily 12–4; adm*), on the site of the old royal hall built by King Eric Segersäll towards the end of the first millennium, in the middle of the town where the first Swedish coins were minted.

Lunch: In Sigtuna, *see* below.

Afternoon: Visit **Steninge Slott Kulturcenter**, Stenladugården, **t** (08) 592 595 00, *www.steningeslott.com* (*open April–Dec Mon–Sat 10–5, Sun 11–5*), a stunning palace by Lake Mälaren, 15mins from Sigtuna, designed by renowned architect Nicodemus Tessin in the late 17th century and widely considered Sweden´s most beautiful Baroque building. The cultural centre within houses Swedish and Nordic crafts.

Dinner and Sleeping: In Uppsala, *see* below.

Day 1

Lunch in Sigtuna

Sigtuna Stads Hotell, Stora Nygatan 3, **t** (08) 592 501 00 (*expensive*). In an elegant hotel, this is the finest dining place in town and only uses local ingredients.

Glasmästarfruns kök, Steningeslott, **t** (08) 592 595 00 (*moderate*). In the Steninge Palace Cultural Centre, the restaurant offers pickled herring as starter to a five-course banquet.

Tant Bruns Kaffestuga, Lauräntii gränd 3, **t** (08) 592 509 34 (*moderate*). Undoubtedly Sigtuna's favourite café.

Sigtuna Museum Café, Stora Gatan 55, **t** (08) 597 838 70 (*moderate*). Serves filling sandwiches and home-made cakes.

Kopparkitteln, Stora Gatan 31, **t** (08) 592 510 95 (*moderate*). Traditional Swedish food is served in this centrally located eatery, which has a summer terrace with views of the lake.

Dinner and Sleeping in Uppsala

Also *see* pp.50–51.

Grand Hotel Hornan, Bangardsgatan 1, **t** (018) 139 380, *www.grandhotelhornan.com* (*expensive*). Newly renovated with large rooms, some which look out on the River Fyrisån. Breakfast is served in the elegant turn-of-the-20th-century dining room.

Hotel Uppsala, Kungsgatan 27, **t** (018) 327 000, *www.profithotels.se* (*moderate*). Rooms have been refurbished in birchwood in Uppsala's biggest hotel. About 40 rooms have their own microwave oven, kettle and refrigerator.

Akademihotellet, Övre Slottsgatan 5, **t** (018) 102 000 (*inexpensive*). Close to the university and other historic sights, which more than compensates for the simple, clean rooms.

Svenssons krog/bakficka, Sysslomansgatan 15, **t** (018) 553 310 (*expensive*). One of the best places for fish dishes and meatballs.

Domtrappkalleren, St Eriksgrand 15, **t** (018) 130 955 (*expensive–moderate*). The buzzing atmosphere and excellent, traditional Swedish fare quickly dispels any reminders that the atmospheric, vaulted cellars at the foot of the cathedral were formerly a prison.

Day 2: Uppsala Cathedral and a Haunted Castle

Morning: Head to the university heart of **Uppsala**, Sweden's fourth largest town, which is dominated by Domkyrkan, Domkyrkoplan 2 (*open daily 8–6; tours Sept–May Sun 12.30, June–Aug daily 12.30*), Scandinavia's largest cathedral. The bones of King Erik, who became Sweden's patron saint after being killed in Uppsala's main square by a Danish pretender to the throne, are kept in a silver basket inside. Opposite the cathedral is Gustavianum, Akademigatan 3 (*open daily 11–4; adm*), the university museum that tells the history of the Sweden's oldest university, founded in 1477. South of the main university area is the domed, blood-red-washed castle built in the 16th century by Gustav Vasa, the first king of a united Sweden, although a major part of the edifice was destroyed by a massive city fire in 1702.

Lunch: In Uppsala, *see* below.

Afternoon: Take the 55 route south towards Enköping. At Annelund, just before Enköping, switch to the E18 route to Västerås and look out for signs veering off to **Engsö Slott**, **t** (0171) 44 40 12, *www.engsoslott.se* (*open May–Aug Sat and Sun 12–5; July–mid-Aug Sat–Thurs 12–5; call for out of season viewings*). The austere fortified building is infamous for its ghost stories, related with gusto by Catherina Piper, the descendant of the 18th-century Count Carl Frederik Piper, who lives nearby and manages the castle. The eeriest tale is of Sophie von Fersen's beloved dog, Cottilion, whose claws are supposed to be heard scratching against the stone floor of the dining room. If you get spooked, it's only 25mins west along the E18 to **Västerås**.

Dinner and Sleeping: In Västerås, *see* below.

Day 2

Lunch in Uppsala
Also *see* p.51.
Odinsborg Restaurant, Gamla Uppsala, **t** (018) 323 525 (*expensive–moderate*). Close to the royal burial mounds in Old Uppsala, a 15-minute car drive from the Uppsala. Filling, traditional-style buffet in elegant yet homely surroundings.

Dinner and Sleeping in Västerås
Also *see* pp.60–61.
Elite, Stora Torget, **t** (021) 102 800, **f** (021) 102 810, *www.vasteras.elite.se* (*expensive*). This is the oldest-established hotel, located in a beautiful Art Deco shell that was originally meant to include the town hall.
Hotell Hackspett, Vasaparken, or **Hotell Utter Inn**, Västerås Fjärden/Amundsgrund, **t** 073 998 7326 *www.mickaelgenberg.com* (*moderate*). Two highly original accommodation alternatives (up on a tree house or on a little floating hotel on the lake), the creation of local artist Mickael Genberg; they are popular, so book early.
Hem till Gården, Boställevägen 8, **t** 070 228 7518, *www.hemtillgarden.nu* (*moderate*). Tina, the owner, likes to call this bed and breakfast 'the house in the middle of the city'. The décor is old-fashioned but unfussy, creating a homely, relaxing atmosphere.
Ibis Hotel, Slånbärsgatan 1, **t** (021) 120 220, *www.ibishotel.com* (*inexpensive*). A no-frills option with generous buffet breakfast.
Karlsson på Taket, Radisson SAS Plaza, **t** (021) 101 010, *www.karlssonpataket.nu* (*expensive*). Inspired by French cuisine, this elegant restaurant has unbeatable views from the 23rd floor and a cocktail bar.
Å, Slottsgatan 6, **t** (021) 417 270, *www.aresto bar.nu* (*expensive*). This is the sort of design-conscious, gourmet-style restaurant that wouldn't look out of place in Gothenburg.
Bill och Bob, Stora Torget 5, **t** (021) 101 010 (*moderate*). A safe option if you are interested in eating amid a buzzing crowd with a good view of the central market square.

Day 3: A Wooden Enclave and Stone Reconstruction

Morning: To explore Kyrkbacken ('Church Green'), the oldest quarter of Västmanland's otherwise rather modern capital **Västerås**, start at the cathedral (*open Mon–Fri 8–5, Sat and Sun 9.30–5*), where the disgraced King Eric XIV's body lies. The 18th-century district north of the cathedral is a delight to wander around: the enclave of pristine wooden houses was rather shunned 200 years ago, not least as it was close to the home of the dreaded city executioner. Promenade along the banks of the River Svartån towards the old fish market (Fiskartorget) where a former 1860-built court-house now houses the Västerås Konstförening (Art Museum), Fiskartorget 2 (*closed Mon*). For more on Västerås, *see* pp.58–65.

Lunch: In Västerås, *see* below.

Afternoon: Take the E18 for about half an hour to **Köping**, which surprises with its handsome late-19th-century stone buildings, designed by Theodor Dahl after a fire destroyed most of the wooden town in 1889. Dahl's elegant creations are concentrated around Stora Torget and adjoining Östra Långgatan and Västra Långgatan, but don't miss his courthouse across the river or the splendid mansion west of the railway station. The town's other historical heroes include chemist Carl Wilhelm Scheele and Richard Dybeck, an archaeologist. A more contemporary native, the wealthy Bertil Lindblad, left a unique car collection at the excellent Bil & Teknikhistoriska Samlingarna (Car and Technical History Collections), Glasgatan 19, *www.autosite.se* (*open 10–6; adm*). For more on Köping, *see* pp.65–7.

Dinner and Sleeping: In Köping, *see* below.

Day 3

Lunch in Västerås

Also *see* pp.60–61.

Restaurang Bellman, Stora Torget 6, t (021) 413 355, *www.bellman.lunchinfo.com* (*expensive*). One of the most elegant restaurants in town, with 18th-century décor. The food is traditional Swedish and international.

Kalle pa Spången, Kungsgatan 2, t (021) 129 129 (*moderate*). Bordering the river, this café looks more like an antique shop with its eclectic tables and chairs. Kalles's specialities include toasties with various fillings.

Café Falkenbergska kvarnen, Skultunavägen (*moderate*). The park setting is a good reason to visit this café/restaurant, especially in the summer as the tables are by the rapids. The daily soups and salad buffet are excellent.

Dinner and Sleeping in Köping

Also *see* p.67.

Kohlswa Herrgård, Herrgårdsallen 14, Kolsva, t (0221) 509 00, f (0221) 511 80, *www. kohlswa-herrgard.se* (*expensive*). This manor house is about 10km northwest of Köping between Kohlswa and Fagersta (follow road 250 from Köping). The mansion house has a lovely 17th-century stucco ceiling), and is surrounded by beautiful grounds.

Hotell Gillet, Östra Långgatan, t (0221) 212 90, f (0221) 100 47, *www.gilletkoping.se* (*moderate*). Given the setting near the old town and not far from the river, this comfortable enough hotel offers a highly reasonable rate.

Restaurang H, Östra Långgatan 1, t (0221) 760 000, *www.restaurangh.se* (*moderate*). New and trendy restaurant just off the central square that offers excellently priced and tasty lunch buffets and slightly pricier *à la carte* dishes.

Athos Café & Matsalar, Hamnplan 5, t (0221) 150 70 (*moderate*). You can't miss this converted railway station which is a favourite with locals for its good-value, traditional food and location near the water. *Closed winter*.

Day 4: Dragons and Castles

Morning: Take the 56 route towards Kungsör where you take the E20 straight to **Eskilstuna**. Head west of the centre along route 230 towards Parken Zoo (*open May–Sept Mon–Fri 10–4, Sat and Sun 10–6; Oct–Easter weekends only 10–3; adm*) to admire the rather unique Komodo dragon as well as a pack of white tigers. Closer to the town centre is a dark red wooden complex called the Rademacher Forges (*open May–Sept Tues–Sun 11–4; adm*), the birthplace of Sweden's steel industry, which includes an art gallery, workshops and small museums plus the local tourist information office. A more refined kind of craftsmanship can be admired at Tingsgården, Rådhustorget, a handicrafts complex where craftsmen make handblown glass.

Lunch: In Eskilstuna, *see* below.

Afternoon: Follow the E20 towards Södertälje and veer off at road 223 for signs to **Mariefred**, the pretty lakeside town that is dominated by **Gripsholm Castle** (*open mid-May–mid-Sept daily 10–4; mid-Sept–mid-May Sat and Sun 12–3; adm*). Gustav Vasa's castle was built in 1547 with the stones of a torn-down monastery close to the site, primarily as a defensive keep on the islet. It wasn't until the late 18th century that the artistic Gustav III saw the theatrical potential of the castle; a splendid stage-set was built and the monarchy began to use the castle as an occasional residence. Scattered across the castle is a hotch-potch of furniture and art objects that have been added since that period, alongside what must be the largest portrait gallery in Sweden. For more on Mariefred, *see* pp.46–8.

Dinner and Sleeping: In Mariefred, see below.

Day 4

Lunch in Eskilstuna

Sundbyholms Slott & Konferenshotell, t (016) 42 84 00, *www.sundbyholms-slott.se* (*expensive*). Traditional Swedish or international dishes in a lakeside castle 9km north of Eskilstuna, where you can work up an appetite by renting a raft in the summer or ice skates in the winter.

Restaurang Tingsgården, Rådhustorget 2, t (016) 51 66 20, *www.tingsgarden.se* (*expensive–moderate*). The waterside restaurant with views over the River Eskilstuna is rather more elegant than its working surroundings with prices to match. There is also a café which serves exquisite pies and salads.

Restaurant Jernbergksa, Rademacher Forges, Rademachergatan (*moderate*). This restaurant is set picturesquely in the Rademacher Forges complex, the cluster of 20 wooded houses that were erected in the latter half of the 17th century by King Carl X Gustav's French architect Jean de la Vallée.

Dinner and Sleeping in Mariefred

Also *see* p.47.

Gripsholms Värdhus/hotel, Kyrkoplan 1, t (0159) 347 50, *www.gripsholms-vardhus.se* (*luxury*). The inn is steeped in history and that's partly what you are paying for when you stay here. The restaurant is also pricy.

In my Garden, Strandvägen 17, t (0159) 133 53, *www.inmygarden.se* (*expensive*). This rather magnificent house converted into an intimate, personal hotel rather coyly calls itself a bed and breakfast, but the owners have evidently spent a lot of time and attention creating the differently decorated rooms in a traditional olde-worlde Swedish style.

Röda Korsets Idé- och Utbildningscenter, t (0159) 367 00, *www.redcross.se/gripsholm* (*moderate*). This as well-priced a bed as you are going to find in this rather chichi town.

Strandrestaurangen, Strandvägen, t (0159) 133 88 (*expensive*). The setting for this restaurant is almost as spectacular as that of the nearby Gripsholms and the food is of similar standard, although more affordable.

Day 5: Nyköping: Castle Complex and River Stroll

Morning: From Mariefred, take the E20 east to Södertälje and then switch to the E4 south to **Nyköping**, the charming waterfront capital of Sörmland. Visit the fascinating Nyköpingshus (*open mid-Aug–mid-June Tues–Sun 11–5; mid-June–mid Aug daily 10–6; adm*), the castle complex by Nyköpingsån river, built by King Magnus Ladulås as a fortress in the 13th century, when the first parliament was held. In 1317, Magnus Ladulås's son, Birger, invited his brothers Erik and Valdemar to a banquet in the castle only to throw them down into the dungeon and hurl the key into the river. The dungeon where the brothers died a lonely death still exists today, alongside some atmospherically created smaller-scale models of the dungeon and the feast. The tragic events are also re-enacted every year in a play, *Gästabudsspelet*, performed in the inner courtyard. Prince Karl (1550–1611) converted the fortress into an extravagant Renaissance palace in the late 16th century, but in 1665 a fire destroyed the whole town including the castle when a maid knocked over a candle.

Lunch: In Nyköping, *see* below.

Afternoon: Wander along the banks of the river which is supposed to mark Sweden's longest civic museum, since information boards along the route describe Nyköping's history; in the 16th and 17th centuries, glassworks, blast furnaces, rolling mills, iron and brass foundries and mints mushroomed along the town's water artery. The town centre is neat and compact, the result of the grid system of streets built on the site of the old medieval settlement after the fire.

Dinner and Sleeping: In Nyköping, *see* below.

Day 5

Lunch and Dinner in Nyköping

Restaurant Forsen, Forsgränd 14, **t** (0155) 215 600 (*expensive*). Housed in an 18th-century building picturesquely poised on the edge of the river Nyköpingstån, this is one of the more popular, upmarket eateries in town.

Café Hellmans, Hellmanska gården, V Trädgårdsgatan 24, **t** (0155) 210 525 (*moderate*). This café's pretty back garden is always buzzing in the summer as people flock for a late breakfast, lunch buffet or cakes.

Café Aktersnurran, Skeppsbron 7, The Harbour, **t** (0155) 281 370 (*moderate*). Locals flock to this café in summer, both for its large outdoor area on the quay front as well as for its 30 varieties of ice-cream.

Anna's Restaurant, Forsgränd 3, **t** (0155) 202 010 (*moderate*). Good, old-fashioned home cooking is served in this popular restaurant, which has an idyllic spot by the river, not far from the main market square.

Tzatziki, Östra Storgatan 23, **t** (0155) 214 320 (*moderate*). For a break from Swedish food, this is a genuine Greek restaurant that stays open reasonably late.

Cafékrogen Smått & Gott-boden, Skeppsbron 3, **t** (0155) 219600 (*inexpensive*). Buy picnic food or have a coffee over the harbour.

Sleeping in Nyköping

Comfort Home Hotel Kompaniet, Folkungavägen 1, **t** (0155) 288 020, *www.choicehotels. se* (*expensive*). The location – close to Nyköpinghus and towards the harbour – is excellent, and there are exhibitions of Swedish furniture and the local car industry.

IBIS Hotel, Gumsbackevägen 2, **t** (0155) 289 000, *www.ibishotel.com* (*moderate*). This is a reasonably priced if unexciting option characteristic of this modern chain located 1.5km from the town centre, close to Kolmården Zoo and Jönåker's beautiful 18-hole course.

Hotell Wiktoria, Fruängsgatan 21, **t** (0155) 217 580, *www.hotelwiktoria.com* (*inexpensive*). Close to Nyköping's theatre, regarded as one of Sweden's best 19th-century examples, and the main shops; no-frills but friendly.

Day 6: Nynäs Manor, a Nature Reserve and Harbour

Morning: From Nyköping, take the scenic 219 route for about 25mins, and look for a sign on the right towards **Nynäs Manor**. The route passes through the **Stendörren Nature Reserve**, which is well worth at least a half-hour stop to capture a fleeting glance at the beauty of the archipelago and maybe take a short walk on a series of rope bridges that connect islets at the entrance of the reserve. Nynäs Manor, **t** (0155) 261 505, *www.landstinget.sormland.se/nynas* (*open May–Sept; other times by appt*) is a yellow manor house that was transformed into its present elegant state from a dilapidated Baroque palace in the late 18th century and further modernized in the 1860s. The estate includes huge barns, white-plastered cowsheds and stables and red barracks, and the surrounding nature reserve provides excellent walking country, with part of the popular marked hiking trail *Sörmlandsleden*.

Lunch: At Nynäs Manor, *see* below.

Afternoon: Continue northwards on the 219 route towards Vagnhärad and swing right towards **Trosa**, an idyllic, intimate 17th-century town divided by a river, with charming walks to the open harbour and the spectacular archipelago. The harbour is ideal for sailing and swimming in the summer and ice-skating in the winter. Garvaregården (*for hours call* **t** *(0156) 122 20*), a cluster of typical deep-red wooden houses from the 17th century that used to be a tannery, now includes the restored home of the old master tanner, a museum on Trosa history and a handicrafts shop.

Dinner and Sleeping: In Trosa, *see* below. In the morning, the 216 route past Vagnhärad joins the fast E4 north to Stockholm.

Day 6

Lunch at Nynäs Manor

Orangeriet (The Orangery), **t** (0155) 261 505 (*moderate*). Built in 1907, the pretty orangery contains a restaurant with a terrace that serves local produce in picturesque surroundings. Although the Orangery is closed Oct–April, the heated winter garden can be pre-booked for up to 40 guests; contact Mia Andersson, **t** (0155) 261 510.

Dinner and Sleeping in Trosa

Bomans Hotell & Restaurant, Hamnen, **t** (0156) 525 00, **f** (0156) 525 10, *www.bomans.se* (*very expensive–expensive*). This lovely turn-of-the-20th-century inn has been run by four generations of Boman women who pride themselves on their home cooking (it helps that the latest Boman matriarch is married to an excellent chef). The rooms range from comfortable, cosy (if rather flowery) rooms to more private and luxurious suites in adjoining buildings definitely worth splashing out the extra for. Added attractions are the open-air café in the central garden, and the harbour location.

Trosa Stadshotell, Stortorget, **t** (0156) 170 70, **f** (0156) 166 96, *www.trosastadshotell.se* (*expensive*). Located in the pretty main square a 5min walk from the harbour, this is a charming alternative to Bomans and is also family-run; the chef-owner is Swiss.

Svalins Spis, Mamsells Trosa, Torget 6, **t** (0156) 126 80, **f** (0156) 22042 (*moderate*). This is a lively and popular place not far from the Trosa River, with a wide selection of well-priced, hearty dishes. It fills up in the evenings when musicians come and play.

Tre Små Rum, Östra Långgatan 8, **t** (0156) 121 51, *www.tresmarum.com* (*moderate*). This 18th-century establishment provides an atmospheric setting for delicious home-made sandwiches and cakes. *Closed weekdays Sept–May*.

Café Garvaregården, **t** (0156) 122 20 (*moderate*). Scenic café in the former tannery and adjoining 17th-century wooden houses.

Västerås

Västerås refuses to be pinned down. The lakeside town may be close to the country's largest royal burial ground, dating from the sixth century, but it has also produced the world's fastest robot, which can sort out 150 chocolates a minute in a factory line. The capital of Västmanland boasts the province's only glass and concrete 'skyscraper', but also one of the most meticulously preserved clusters of 18th-century wooden houses in the region. And a history of Viking markets and 16th-century royal intrigue somehow fuses naturally with its role as a site of the world's largest electro-technical company. Sweden's sixth-largest city (although its inhabitants still hover in the 130,000 range) appears as unconcerned about flogging its tourist wares to the world as it is about being less than an hour's train ride from desirable Stockholm, and that is a great part of its charm. It may also explain why so many of the capital's residents are choosing to lay down commuter roots in a small town that has much of a big city's amenities without the queues and traffic, and which is a hop away from primeval forests, wetlands teeming with fauna, great boat connections and fabulous beaches.

The Svartån river looks innocuous enough as it trickles through the centre of town, but upstream it widens considerably, and with so many waterways using it to empty into Lake Mälaren it has played a pivotal role in the city's long history. An early trading settlement was founded on the river's estuary at the time of the Vikings, when it was called Västra Aros ('river delta'). The lake harbour, Sweden's largest, was by the end of the Middle Ages a major port for exporting copper, silver and iron from the Bergslagen district. In 1527, a special honour was bestowed on the city when King Gustav Vasa held the Riksdag (parliament) here to support the Lutherans' cause to hand over Church lands to the Crown, a move that ushered in the Reformation and considerably consolidated the king's control over government and trade. A hereditary law of accession to the throne was adopted in Västerås, but that didn't help Gustav Vasa's eldest son and successor Erik XIV, who, deposed by his brother Johan III, ended up getting locked up in Västerås Castle (now a museum and residence of the county governor) in 1573 for more than a year, separated from his consort Karin Månsdotter and their children. He was later transferred to Örbyhus Castle, where he was poisoned by pea soup laced with arsenic. His body now lies buried in the imposing Västerås cathedral.

As well as its good connections by water, Västerås was also strategically situated along the old 'King's Road' that linked Oslo to St Petersburg, and so the city continued to prosper right up until the Industrial Revolution, but it wasn't until the end of the 19th century that it was catapulted into a new economic sphere, once again because of the Svartån river. A visit to the city in 1891 by Jonas Wenström, an electrical engineer from electro-technical company ASEA in the neighbouring medieval town of Arboga, proved crucial. The company had developed a dynamo for generating electric power but needed larger facilities and a ready source of water. Västerås was happy to oblige, and the original turbine house, now a power station museum, was built in the heart of the town. From that time onwards, ASEA (now ABB) became the city's main source of employment and built some of the turn-of-the-20th-century 'National Romantic'-style buildings near the station. Eventually, the city grew so rapidly after

Getting There

Ryanair flies from London Stansted. From Stockholm a direct train takes 50mins.

Getting from the Airport

Stockholm/Västerås Airport, **t** 021 805 600, *www.vasterasflygplats.se*, is 5km southeast of Västerås city centre in an area called Hässlö. Local bus 941 runs all day to the city centre. A direct train runs to Stockholm in 50mins.

Getting Around

With the largest lake harbour in Sweden and strategically situated along the old 'King's Road' (now route E18) that linked Oslo to St Petersburg, Västerås has fast connections in all directions. The county rail traffic is comprehensive and is well supplemented by bus lines. For rail info, contact **TIM**, Mälarbanan/Svealandsbanan, **t** (020) 846 846, *www.tim-trafik.se* or **SJ**, **t** (020) 757 575, *www.sj.se*. For the slightly cheaper but often more long-winded bus traffic, try Västmanlands Lokaltrafik, **t** (020) 255 075, or *www.vl.se* or Swebus, **t** (020) 640 640. The **train station** is on Södra Ringvägen, 10mins' walk from the tourist office through Vasaparken. The **bus station** is next to the train station.

Västerås is so compact that you shouldn't have to get on one single bus to enjoy the sights. Walking along the river Svartån is recommended for its scenic value and to get your bearings as it crosses most of the centre. Bicycles are highly recommended, since the city is criss-crossed by cycle paths that are conveniently marked on a special city map available at the helpful tourist office, which also hires out the actual bikes.

Car Hire

Avis, Centralstationen, **t** (021) 800 188, *www.avis.se*.
Hertz, Tegnér, Reaktorgränd 12, **t** (021) 328 680, *www.hertz.se*.

Europcar, Kopparbergsvägen 47, **t** (021) 124 143, *www.europcar.se*.
Statoil, Klockartorpet, Knektgatan 2, **t** (021) 135 933, *www.statoil.se*.

Taxis

Taxi 021 HB, **t** (021) 203 040.
Taxi Kurir, **t** (021) 122 222.
Taxi Västerås, **t** (021) 185 000.
Taxi Västmanland, **t** (021) 140 140.

Tourist Information

Västerås: Stora Gatan 40, **t** (021) 103 830, **f** (021) 103 850, *www.vasterasturism.se* (open Mon–Fri 10–7, Sat 10–3, Sun 10–2). Ask about the informative and entertaining **guided city walks** that start at the tourist bureau during the June–Aug summer season. If you are into hiking, also ask for maps, descriptions and information on the **Bruksleden Trail**, which starts at Lake Mälaren and winds its way northwards to cover up to 230km. The walk through forests and mine areas of the Bergslagen district can be done in daily stages or in sections. Simple buildings and windbreaks offer overnight stays. Enquire too about bicycle and canoe trails.
Central post office, Sturegatan 18.

Festivals

The **spring market** is held in the Rocklunda area (the parkland in the very north of the city) in the last weekend in May.

In celebration of the town's medieval roots, **Arosfestivalen** is held in June with music parades, **t** (021) 127 730.

The **Power Meet**, the largest car meet in Europe, attracting up to 50,000 car enthusiasts worldwide, is held in the Johannisberg airfield in early July and includes a car procession through the city centre.

The **Västerås market** is the last weekend in August in Rocklunda, **t** (021) 136 211.

the Second World War that workers from southern Europe were recruited to work in the local factories, giving pockets of the city a noticeably cosmopolitan feel.

The globalization of recent years has indirectly helped Västerås reclaim its cultural and tourist heritage. With so much of ABB's attention today on overseas operations,

Shopping

As the main shopping centre in the county, Västerås has no lack of shops, with most high-street chains and brands available in the city centre and big shopping malls outside at Hälla, Stenby and Erikslund och Bäckby. Shopping hours are Mon–Fri 10–7, Sat 10–4.

For timeless jewellery, try the Västmanlands Läns Museum in Västerås (see p.63), where you can buy a bronze ornament, a gold ring or bronze pendant, all modern replicas of the golden jewellery from the Roman Iron Age that was found in Badelunda parish.

Where to Stay

Västerås t (021) –

Comfort Hotel Etage, Stora Gatan 32, t 151 220, f 151 221, www.choicehotels.se (expensive). Don't be put off by the rather bland modern exterior, as the rooms are tastefully decorated and comfortable. Ask about the special three-day package.

Elite, Stora Torget, t 102 800, f 102 810, www.vasteras.elite.se (expensive). This is the oldest-established hotel, located in a beautiful Art Deco shell that was originally going to include the town hall. When it was built at the turn of the 20th century, it was the first building with modern bathrooms.

Radisson SAS Plaza Hotel, Karlsgatan 9A, t 101 010, f 101 091, www.radisson.com (expensive). This hotel sits in the unlikely skyscraper that looms over the city and the lake. There is a solarium and sauna on the 25th floor as well as the popular **Sky Bar** in the evenings.

Hotell Arkad, Östermalmsgatan 25, t 12 04 80, f 830 050, www.arkad-hotell.se (expensive). One of the smaller hotels in town, with one family suite with room for six people and seven rooms with their own pantry and fridge. Billiards, darts and a sauna.

Hotell Hackspett, Vasaparken t 070 775 5393/ t 073 998 7326, www.mikaelgenberg.com (moderate). For anyone who has ever wanted to live in a tree house, this is a fairly inexpensive option (unless you order food on a rope and forget your sleeping bag). Bring a video or tape recorder if you want to share the experience, because there is only room for one sleeper. Open April–mid-Oct; book early.

Hotell Utter Inn, Västerås Fjärden/Amundsgrund, t 070 775 5393 / t 073 998 7326, www.mikaelgenberg.com (moderate). If the experience of living in a tree is not enough, local maverick Mikael Genberg has also created a little floating hotel on the lake. This seems less claustrophobic than the tree option because you can sunbathe on the floating platform and go off for a swim if you like, but you could get short of breath when you discover the room is underwater, with a panoramic window. At least there's room for two of you. Open April–Oct, and it's essential to book early.

Park Inn Västerås, Vallbyinstitutet, Svalgången 1, t 303 800, f 303 888, www.parkinn.com, www.winnhotels.se (moderate). A surprisingly reasonable package that includes a swimming pool and sauna. An even better price for people travelling with under-18s.

Hem till Gården, Boställevägen 8, t 070 228 7518, www.hemtillgarden.nu (moderate). Tina, the owner, likes to call this bed and breakfast 'the house in the middle of the city'. The décor is old-fashioned but unfussy to create a homely, relaxing atmosphere.

Ibis Hotel, Slånbärsgatan 1, t 120 220, f 120 255, www.ibishotel.com (inexpensive). This is a no-frills option but the price includes a generous buffet breakfast.

Eating Out

Västerås t (021) –

The culinary explosion that has hit Stockholm, Gothenburg and Malmö in the last decade hasn't quite reached Vasterås yet, but there are a couple of restaurants that are setting the trend. There is a fair number of kebab, pizza and Far East outlets around the

the town has started to focus on other resources such as its expanding university, which is drawing in a greater number of young people who demand new eating and drinking venues. It is also reclaiming its marvellous but slightly neglected lake, ideal for swimming, fishing, sailing, canoeing, water-skiing, long-distance skating and centre (often quite good), as well as a handful of more upmarket, established restaurants and a few excellent coffee shops.

Karlsson på Taket, Radisson SAS Plaza, t 101 010, *www.karlssonpataket.nu* (*expensive*). Inspired by French cuisines, this is one of the more elegant dining places in Västerås and the view from the 23rd floor is unmatchable. Enjoy a cocktail in the **Sky Bar** above.

Restaurang Bellman, Stora Torget 6, t 413 355, *www.bellman.lunchinfo.com* (*expensive*). In the main square, this is one of the most elegant restaurants in town, with 18th-century décor. Traditional Swedish and international cuisine.

Stadskällaren, Stora Torget, t 102 800, *www.vasteras.elite.se* (*expensive*). Part of the Elite Stadshotellet, a refined dining choice with views of the central square.

Å, Slottsgatan 6, t 417 270, *www.arestobar.nu* (*expensive*). This is the sort of design-conscious, gourmet-style restaurant that wouldn't look out of place in culinary-conscious Gothenberg.

Bill och Bob, Stora Torget 5, t 101 010 (*moderate*). A safe option if you are interested in eating among a buzzing crowd, with a good view of the central market square.

Kalle pa Spången, Kungsgatan 2, t 129 129 (*moderate*). Bordering the river, this café looks more like an antique shop with its eclectic tables and chairs, no two of which match. Kalle's specialities include toasties with various fillings and grilled baguettes.

Café Falkenbergska kvarnen, Skultunavägen (*moderate*). The beautiful park setting is a good enough reason to visit this café-restaurant, especially in the summer as the outdoor tables are by the rapids. The daily soups and salad buffet are excellent. There is also a shop with art and craft items.

Piazza di Spagna, Vasagatan 26, t 124 210, *www.lunchinfo.com* (*moderate*). One of the better Italian restaurants, in a central location.

La Tapita, Stora Torget 3, t 12 10 44, f 12 1044, *www.latapita.nu* (*moderate*). The emergence of this trendy tapas bar is one of the signs that the locals are demanding a more imaginative choice of cuisines.

Kungsbyn-Bygdens mat, Bistron, Kungsbyn (village), t 212 50 (*moderate*). It's well worth the 15min car ride (or 20mins on the 804 bus) to this charmingly converted farmhouse where you can stock up on a selection of locally grown farm produce or even sample some home prepared food (don't miss the moose stew) at the cosy, informal restaurant. For a full-on organic experience, you can visit the farm animals behind the main building. A lunch visit can be combined with a trip to Engsö Castle (*see* p.53) further along the E18. *Open Tues–Fri 11–6, Sat 11–4; closed Sun and Mon.*

K&K, Kopparbergsvägen, t 182 020 (*inexpensive*). Coffee place where you sit in a combined café and kitchen to feel at home (except the dishes are being washed up).

Piece of Cake Excelsior, Timmermansgatan 10, t 180 800 (*inexpensive*). The name says it all. Every imaginable cake is baked on the premises. A clear winner are the marzipan prints.

Nightlife

Stadskällaren, Stadshotellet, Stora Torget, t 102 800. One of the quieter places for a drink in the main square. In winter, sit at the bar under the brick vaults; in summer, go out on to the veranda.

Klippan, Kungsgatan 4, t 120 180. Techno dancing in a venue established in 1751, with a casino for serious gamblers.

The Bishop's Arms, Kykrogatan, t 187 440. A smart British-style pub with wide selection of beer, single malt whisky and cigars.

Village, Sigurdsgatan 25, t 418 822. Check the schedule for this harbourside venue's live jazz, blues and folk music events.

Extremes, Kopparbergsvägen. Nightclub with bar, disco and games tables.

Konrad, Kopparbergsvägen. Disco and bar.

even, as one creative entrepreneur has discovered, a setting for an underwater hotel. A shortage of housing space in Stockholm is propelling the drive to build around 4,000 state-of-the-art apartment blocks along the water's edge over the next decade, to be accompanied by a series of waterfront walks, a marina, restaurants and parks.

Västerås Cathedral and Kyrkbacken

A fair distance back from the forward-looking water shore, the lugubrious cathedral and Kyrkbacken ('Church Green' or Old City), north of the two main squares, are fitting places to trace the steps of the city's venerable past. On the Cathedral Square, it is difficult to miss the statue of the 17th-century bishop of Västerås, Johannes Rudbeckius, sculpted by the highly prolific Carl Milles.

The **cathedral** (*open daily 8–5*), which dates back to the 13th century when the original church was built, although the bulk of the structure was shaped some two centuries later, is famous as the resting place of King Erik XIV, who died in disgrace as a prisoner of his brother Johan. In the 18th century, King Gustav III decided that his ancestor deserved a worthy resting-place, so he ordered the regalia from the sarcophagus in Uppsala of brother Johan (who imprisoned Erik) to be brought over to bury the unfortunate Erik with some honour (like all other churches used for royal burial, the gilded spire carries a crown). The gesture came with a price, as was discovered in the 1950s when the grave was opened: Erik was rather taller than his brother so his feet had been cut off and placed alongside his legs.

Of particular curiosity in the cathedral, which is often called the Church of the Sepulchral Tablets (notice the great works of Baroque and rococo art on the tablets from the 18th century), is the baptismal font in the Virgin's Chapel. It is a copy of an original late-14th-century font that for as-yet unexplained reasons was never delivered, a detail not discovered until the 1950s when a Västerås immigrant was holidaying in his old home town of Burg in northern Germany. On a chance visit to Burg Church, he noticed an inscription on the baptismal font that read 'Gift to the Västerås Cathedral from its Bishop Korp, 1391'. A generous donor ensured a copy was made and, after a 564-year-long wait, the Virgin's Chapel finally got its baptismal font. Another oddity, by the high altar, is a black and white marble monument crowned by three figures in alabaster and created in 1637–41 by Danish sculptor Jost Henne. In a crypt under the floor rests Count Magnus Brahe, the Lord Chancellor, in an arrangement that was presumably impossible during his lifetime: both his wives lie beside him.

North of the cathedral is **Rudbeckianska Gymnasiet**, Sweden's first school, founded in 1623, next to which are the **botanical gardens** containing rarities such as Chinese Sequoia, primitive conifers that are supposed to be living fossils from the dinosaur age. Further up begin the narrow, winding streets flanked by low houses and plank fences, sometimes in irregular lots, that make up **Kyrkbacken**, the oldest part of Västerås. Shunned as a poor district during the 18th century, the small neighbourhood is now highly sought-after and, although the mostly pristine homes shine inside and out, it is still easy to imagine what life must have once been like in the harsh alleyways. Down Rektorsgatan, one of the main alleyways, you might notice a small circular window on Långlasses Gård. In the 17th century, a bell-ringer created the opening so that his bedridden wife, a true believer, would be able to see the church spire from her bedroom. Stop too at the Lars Westholm Cottage.

The most evocative house at the northern end of the pretty district must be on Brunnsgränd alley, the ominously grey-coloured **Mästermansgården**, the former home of the city's executioner until 1830. At Vasagatan you may notice an old well which the executioner reputedly used exclusively for himself, as ordinary citizens refused to get water from the same well as the hated man.

South of Stora Gatan

From Kyrkbacken, it's a lovely walk down Västra Kyrkogatan, parallel to the river, until you reach **Stora Torget**, the market square, which is dominated by the impressive Art Nouveau building erected at the turn of the 20th century when ASEA's arrival as a mass employer heralded a spate of new construction. Originally, the building was going to serve as a town hall as well as a hotel, restaurant, banquet hall and hair salon. Today it is one of Västerås's premier hotels, the **Elite hotel** (see 'Where to Stay'), whose inspiring presence is not matched by the rather drab grey 1970s blocks around.

The light pink **tourist office** at Stora Gatan, with views of Stadsparken, marks a cheery return to a more monumental part of town. Head down Slottsgatan until you pass the small **Slottsbron** (bridge) where on the left is the renowned **Turbine House** (*tours by arrangement, call County Museum, t (021) 156 100, or Energi och Vatten, t (021) 161 211*), a fully operative power station museum.

Opposite is the **Västmanlands Läns Museum** (county museum), Slottsgatan, **t** (021) 156 100 (*closed for renovation in 2004; afterwards, check with tourist office; adm*). Highlights of the cultural and historical artefacts from ancient and modern times are the large silver treasure which was discovered under Stora Torget, and gold jewellery from the Iron Age. The gold ornaments were only discovered in 1952, when a future house-owner in the provincial Badelunda parish was digging out his new foundation and happened to come across a casket grave from around AD 200. Archaeologists unearthed what was believed to be the richest grave treasure in the country, consisting of gold rings, silver spoons and bronze vessels belonging to a woman of high rank. What continues to stump experts to this day is that, while the men's graves only had a few personal weapons, the women's graves were all generously supplied with jewellery, pointing to their possible role as religious functionaries or even priest-esses. Or perhaps the women were simply running a matriarchy. The mystery deepens with the fact that the women weren't cremated, a standard practice of the time as it was believed that smoke made for a speedier trip to the kingdom of the dead.

West towards Vasaparken, at the old fish market, is a former 1860-built courthouse, now the **Västerås Konstförening** (Art Museum), Fiskartorget 2, **t** (021) 123 801 (*open mid-Aug–mid-May Tues–Fri 10–5, Sat and Sun 11–5; mid-May–mid-Aug Tues–Fri 11–4, Sat and Sun 12–4; adm*). The displays are a mixture of rolling exhibitions, mainly of contemporary Swedish art, and an older collection that dates back to the foundation of the Västerås Art Association in 1919. Almost more compelling, though, is some of the **public art** scattered around the city, one example of which is outside the adjacent City Hall: a gilded bull (1963) who looks poised to leap from high on his black mast pole. And don't miss the workers on their bikes in the main square. A recent addition to public art displays is also close by: a small, traditional Swedish summer house that is rather less traditionally poised in the tree tops in the middle of **Vasaparken**. Created by local maverick Mikael Genberg, this is meant to be experiential art, since you can actually stay in the hut hotels.

Outside the Centre

Vallby Friluftsmuseum

*t (021) 398 078. Gardens open all year 8–5, museum building open
21 June–31 Aug Tues–Sat 11–4, Sun 12–5.*

For a glimpse into older ways of life in the Västmanland area, a visit to Vallby Open-
air museum is worth the trouble of the 15–20min scenic river walk towards Aroslund
and across Vallbybron (a slightly shorter journey if you start from Kyrkbacken).
Founded in 1921 and one of the largest open-air museums in Sweden, it has around
40 different buildings moved from different parts of the county and reflecting
different periods between the 17th and 20th centuries. A popular exhibit is **Anund's
House**, showing how a Viking family lived.

Anundshög Burial Fields

*By car, take route E18 to Enköping until Ullvi and then veer off;
by bus, take the no.12 to Bjurhovda and then walk for around 20mins.*

The long Badeluna moraine attracted settlers as early as the Stone Age and the area
is teeming with ancient monuments and artefacts from around AD 500 to 1050, of
which Anundshög, Sweden's largest royal mound (14m high and 60m in diameter), is
the highlight. The actual grave at Anundshög has never been excavated, but folk
tradition has it that King Bröt-Anund rests in the mound, near which there are five
large stone ships from the year 1000 which may belong to graves of local magnates
who owned ships. An intriguing tumulus from the late Iron Age (400–1500) is at
Gryta Hög where, according to legend, two young lovers were buried by their parents
after the girl committed suicide.

An Elk Safari in Bergslagen Forests

*Skogens Konung, Ankargatan 25, t 070 400 7053 (ask for Marcus),
www.skogenskonung.se; runs April–mid-Oct.*

It's debatable whether any trip to Sweden can be considered complete without
spotting an elk. There are 300,000 roaming the forests of Sweden – though a third
are shot every year during the annual hunting season – but elk are notoriously shy
creatures and expert at camouflaging themselves, whether they are mating in
September–October or in the spring, when the elk cows keep the calves well hidden.
In fact, the most likely place to spot this largest of deer is when the 800kg creature
appears unexpectedly in front of your car on a dark night. Elks probably cause more
accidents on Swedish roads than drunk-drivers.

Northeast of Västerås, however, in the Bergslagen forests, there is an opportunity to
sight the 'king of the forest' courtesy of Skogens Konung, a new service recommended
by the Västerås tourist office. Marcus and fellow guides offer two moose safari packages with guarantees of spotting at least one of the proud woodland animals (if not,
you get offered an Elk Safari Evening free of charge). The inexpensive evening option

costs SEK390 with an SEK125 surcharge for an elk-meat barbecue, and includes elk-tracking in the forest, a visit to the elk feeding grounds, learning how to call like an elk, and twilight elk-spotting. The overnight trip (SEK895), which lasts from 4pm to 10am, includes lodging in traditional forest huts, a Swedish breakfast and a swim.

Lakeside Trips on Lake Mälaren

Lake Mälaren was once the natural route for trade and business between Västerås and Stockholm, but now many of the boats traversing this beautiful lake in the summer months are for strictly recreational purposes. Recommended trips include cruises with Strömma Kanalbolag (*www.strommakanalbolaget.com*) and its M/S *August Lindholm* boat that leaves Västerås East Harbour to visit picturesque lakeside stops like Strängnäs, Mariefred (*see* pp.46–8), Björkö (the island of birches) and the Viking town of Birka, founded in AD 750 (*see* p.45). From Birka, it's possible to continue on to Stockholm. The M/S *Silvertärnan* makes trips to the islands of Almö-Lindö, Skåpholmen, Strömskär and Ridön Nature Reserve, which has a café. For more information and tickets, ask at the tourist office.

Overnighter from Västerås

See also **Mariefred**, pp.46–8, and **Uppsala**, pp.48–51.

Köping

If it hadn't been for a devastating fire in 1889, Köping might have passed off inconspicuously as another pretty wooden town on Lake Mälaren's shores with a medieval past, when it was known as '*Kaupinga*' ('trading site'), and a city charter dating back to 1474. Instead, a visitor to Köping encounters magnificent late-19th-century stone buildings that could have come straight out of any middle-European town from the period. The lethal fire was said to have been started on 4 July, 1889 by 10-year-old Malakias Andersson, when he was forbidden by his stepmother to watch a fire burning in the harbour. When almost 50 city complexes were destroyed, leaving 650 inhabitants homeless, architect Theodor Dahl, who had been commissioned to build a new pharmacy in the main square, was given *carte blanche* to create a new, contemporary city that would share the latest elegant styles from the continent.

The first building designed by Dahl after the fire is only a couple of minutes' walk west of the railway station, the obvious starting point if you have arrived on public transport. Immediately across the bridge is **Köping Museum**, Östra Långgatan 37, t (0221) 253 87 (*open Mon–Thurs 1–4, Sat and Sun 1–4*), which tells the history of the town going back 10,000 years. On the second storey of the slanting 18th-century building earlier used as a crown distillery is a reconstruction of a chemist's shop from 1900, designed to honour one of Sweden's most famous scientists and Köping native Carl Wilhelm Scheele, also known as the discoverer of nitrogen and oxygen. Another of the town's historical heroes was Richard Dybeck, an archaeologist who became famous for unknowingly writing the text for Swedish national anthem, 'Du Gamla Du Fria' ('You old, you free'). Originally words from a Västmanland folk song that starts, 'As I ride through the twelve-mile forest...', these were rewritten and performed for the first time on November 13 1844 by a prominent opera singer at a musical evening arranged by Dybeck in Stockholm. Dybeck sat on the stage wearing a wolfskin-fur coat which he suddenly threw off during the last verse as he got up to join the singer. The public responded with a standing ovation, but, although the song was later printed in 1865, it did not become the national anthem until several years later.

Other exhibitions run by the Köping Museum and celebrating Köping's past are spread across the town and include, a few blocks down at No.26, **Nyströmska Gården**, an early-20th-century joinery workshop owned by five generations of Nyströms. Since the shop was closed down in 1970, a Friends' Association gives tour of the workshop by arrangement (**t** (0221) 253 51). The other outbuildings include **KUJ-Museet** by the small harbour and **Gammelgården Open-air Museum** (*see* below).

From the Köping Museum, past the few wooden houses that escaped the fire in Gamla Stan, stick to the picturesque river and walk up Västra Åpromenaden until Torggatan where you turn left into **Stora Torget**, the town's main square. This imposing square is flanked by **Köping City Hall**, actually built a decade before Dahl's arrival in the neo-Renaissance style. At No.2 Stora Torget is Dahl's first commission, the old brick **chemist's shop** that replaced the venerable Scheele's original 'apotek'. Notice the entablatures over the windows on the second storey, decorated with medallions illustrating Scheele and another famous Swedish chemist, Jöns Jacob Berzelius (Scheele is further commemorated with a statue by famous sculptor Carl Milles in the nearby Scheele Parken). Next to the pharmacy is the impressive **Jönsson House**, a commercial and residential complex built by Dahl in 1893–4. South of the square are another cluster of Dahl buildings that give this part of town its well-planned, coherent aspect: four commercial and residential complexes at **Östra Långgatan**, No.1 (Arpi House), 4 (Rosen property), No.6 (Watternström) and No.9 (Bergendahl). In the parallel **Västra Långgatan**, at Nos.9 and 11 are the former Bärgslagsbladet offices, originally built as residences, shops and a bakery.

Dahl has also left his elegant mark across the river south of Nygatan, at Esplanaden, where the **Court House**, built in 1893, is possibly the most grandiose of all his creations; and with some of the additional buildings at the **Köping Mechanical Workshop**, a set of handsome industrial buildings erected in 1856. Dahl creations outside Köping include court houses in Kolbäck, Lindesberg and Västerås, a savings bank in Arboga and the former train station, known nowadays as 'Galleri Astley', in Uttersberg. Sadly, Dahl was never able to long enjoy the fruits of his town planning, as he died in 1897 in Köping where he was still working.

On this side of town, there are also the excellent **Bil & Teknikhistoriska Samlingarna** (Car and Technical History Collections), Glasgatan 19, **t** (0221) 206 00, **f** (0221) 206 00, *www.autosite.se* (*open 10–6; adm*). You don't have to be a car enthusiast to enjoy Bertil Lindblad's unique collection, which includes rarities like a 1929 35 B Grand Prix, a 1931 Bentley and a 1929 Mercedes SSK, an old car repair shop, and a gasoline station from 1920; the displays are all put into an entertaining social and historical context.

Getting There

Köping is easily reached from Västerås, with both buses and trains leaving from the central station several times a day. The **trains** make the journey in about 20mins, while **buses** are rather more leisurely, taking almost an hour. Information from Västmanlands Lokaltrafik, Retortgatan 7, **t** (021) 470 1800, **t** (0200) 255 075, *www.vl.se.*

Tourist Information

Köping: Barnhemsgatan 2, **t** (0221) 256 55, *www.koping.se (open Mon–Fri 9–5).*

Where to Stay

Köping **t** (0221) –

Nya Star Hotel Scheele, Hultgrensgatan, **t** 181 20, **f** 107 03, *www.swedenhotels.se (expensive).* The name of the famous chemist Carl Wilhelm Scheele may conjure up pretty, late-18th-century dwellings, but this hotel has a modern, rather bland exterior. The rooms are of high standard, though, and some even have their own Jacuzzi and sauna.

Kohlswa Herrgård, Herrgårdsallen 14, Kolsva, **t** 509 00, **f** 511 80, *www.kohlswa-herrgard.se (expensive).* This manor house is about 10km northwest of Köping between Kohlswa and Fagersta (follow road 250 from Köping). The mansion house has a lovely 17th-century stucco ceiling) and is surrounded by beautiful grounds, perfect for a semi-luxurious long weekend. Activities offered include riding, shooting and canoeing. After strenuous activity, there is a choice of beer-, whisky- and wine-tastings.

Hotell Gillet, Östra Långgatan, **t** 212 90, **f** 100 47, *www.gilletkoping.se (moderate)* Given the setting near the old town and not far from the river, this comfortable enough hotel offers a highly reasonable rate. Couples should book early as there are only five double rooms.

Eating Out

Köping **t** (0221) –

Restaurang Glada Gösen Klassisk, Malmön, **t** 20082, *www.glada-gosen.nu (expensive).* A car is preferable to get to Malmön on the E18 route from Köping, but it is well worth the trip to this old-fashioned restaurant built by two brothers in 1932 with a splendid outdoor balcony that has views of the lake. *Between Sept and Nov, phone to book. Closed Jan–May.*

Pub & Restaurang Hantverkaren, Torggatan 12, **t** 100 36, *www.hantis.com (expensive–moderate).* A wide-ranging menu in a lively pub-restaurant that is a popular gathering point in the evening for sports nights, after work Friday evening specials and late nights during the weekend, with a disco. *Closed Sun.*

Restaurang H, Östra Långgatan 1 (*Arpi huset*), **t** 760 000, *www.restaurangh.se (moderate).* New and trendy restaurant just off the central square that offers excellently priced and tasty lunch buffets and slightly pricier *à la carte* dishes.

Café Gammelgården, Friluftsmuseet Gammelgården, **t** 253 51 (*moderate*). A great summer lunch location in a converted old building that belongs to the open-air museum. The freshly baked waffles served with raspberry jam and whipped cream are particularly good. *Open June–mid-Aug Mon–Fri 12–4.*

Athos Café & Matsalar, Hamnplan 5, **t** 150 70 (*moderate*). You can't miss this converted railway station, which is a favourite with locals for its good-value, traditional food and location near the water. *Closed winter.*

West of the museum at the Karlbergsskogen woods at the end of Otto Hallström's Road is another section of Köping Museum, **Friluftsmuseet Gammelgården**, **t** (0221) 253 51 (*open June–mid-Aug Mon–Fri 12–4*), an open-air living museum. Another part of the museum is in the idyllic spot by the harbour, the **KUJ-Järnvägsmuseum** (Railway Museum), **t** (0221) 253 51, which houses a handsome steam engine, several cars and the history of iron transport by rail from the Bergslagen district to Köping's harbour.

Touring from Västerås

You can follow the Stockholm tour, see pp.52–7, by starting on Day 3 in nearby Köping, then Day 4, Day 5 and Day 6. On your 5th day, visit Stockholm, below, then head off to Sigtuna (Stockholm tour Day 1) and then finally Day 2, ending back in Västerås.

Day 5: A Whirlwind Tour of Stockholm

Morning: Head off early from Trosa on the 216 past Vagnhärad to join the fast E4 north to Stockholm and aim to join one of the excellent hourly tours at **Stadshuset** (City Hall), Hantverkargatan 1 (Kungsholmen island) (*tours Sept–May 10 and 12; June–Aug 10, 11, 12, 2 and 3; tower open May–Sept daily 10–5, April Sat and Sun 12–4; adm*). Built between 1911 and 1923, the red brick building is an inventive homage to Venice's Doge's Palace. From the nearby T-Centralen, take a tube to Karlaplan (or a ferry from Nybroplan) to Östermalm and cross the Djurgårdsbron (bridge) to Djurgården. In this former royal hunting ground is the fascinating **Vasa Museet**, Djurgården (*open Aug 21–June 9 Thurs–Tues 10–5, Wed 10–8; June 10–Aug 20 9.30–7; adm*), the battleship that sank outside the harbour on its maiden voyage in 1628.
Lunch: In Stockholm, see below and also pp.29–31.
Afternoon: Take a ferry to Slussen or the 44 or 47 bus to the modern Sergels Torg and walk down Drottningatan to **Gamla Stan**, the immaculately preserved medieval city that is dominated by **Kungliga Slottet**, the Italian Baroque-style royal palace. Next door is **Strokyrkan**, Trångsund 1 (*open May–Sept daily 9–6; Oct–April daily 9–4*), Stockholm's 700-year-old cathedral, originally built as a village church by the city's founder Birger Jarl. Have a coffee break in **Stortorget**, Gamla Stan's cobbled main square, before exploring the surrounding winding alleys and shopping streets; don't miss the impossibly narrow lane at **Mårten Trotsigs gränd**. It's then only a short walk to Slussen ('sluice gates') where the Katarina Hissen lift (*Mon–Fri 7.30am–10pm, Sat and Sun 10–10; adm*) takes you to the heights of **Fjällgatan** and its sweeping views. Kick off the evening in one of the many bars and restaurants in Götgatan at the heart of the trendy **'Söder'** (Södermalm) district.
Dinner and Sleeping: In Stockholm, see below and pp.28–31.

Lunch or Dinner in Stockholm
Gondolen, Stadsgården 6, t (08) 641 7090 (*very expensive*). The excellent food and bar match the views over Gamla Stan from the 36m tower reached by lift from Slussen.
Berns, Berzelii Park, t (08) 566 322 22 (*very expensive*). A classic 19th-century eatery recently renovated by Terence Conran. Live jazz music on special evenings.
Den Glydene Freden, Österlånggatan 51, t (08) 249 760 (*very expensive–expensive*). Sweden's most famous revellers have dined here, in one of Stockholm's oldest restaurants; delicious Swedish-French cuisine.

Dinner and Sleeping in Stockholm
Nordic Light, Vasaplan, t (08) 505 63300, *www.nordichotels.se* (*very expensive*). Close to the train terminal, a hip option for designer fans. Don't miss the bar made out of real ice.
Hotel Rival, Mariatorget 3, t (08) 545 789 00, *www.rival.se* (*expensive*). A bright and arty boutique hotel in 'Söder', partly owned by ex-Abba member Benny Andersson, who sometimes plays in the bar.
Queen's Hotel, Drottningatan 71, t (08) 249 460, *www.queenshotel.se* (*moderate*). This has been a reliable, family-run hotel for more than a century, with a central location.

Sweden: Gothenburg and Around

06

Gothenburg (Göteborg)

Attention-seeking and fierce competitiveness are traits frequently associated with second cities, and Gothenburg is no exception, even if it masks its ambitions with a carefree, laid-back air. Fortunately for this vibrant city of 474,000 inhabitants (858,000 if you include the whole Gothenburg region), it enjoys an impressive range of attributes to back its grand pretensions.

The city's happy situation at the mouth of the Göta River in West Sweden has graced it with Scandinavia's largest port, and that superlative seems to have set the tone for the city's subsequent man-made achievements: Nordstan shopping centre, at the heart of the city, is the largest in Northern Europe; Liseberg Amusement Park is Scandinavia's most extensive; the central park blooms with the Nordic region's most abundant rose gardens; the art museum boasts the most complete collection of Nordic art; Sahlgrenska University Hospital is northern Europe's vastest hospital; Heden football stadium hosts the Gothia Cup, the world's biggest football competition; the newly built 23-storey Hotel Gothia Towers is Scandinavia's most enormous hotel; in a nod to Stockholm-based Abba, home-grown pop group Ace of Base scored the best-selling debut album ever in the 1990s...there is no end to the records that Gothenburg likes to show off. The city is even proud to point out that it has the largest waste incineration plant in northern Europe.

Size obviously matters to Gothenburg, and it does for the visitor too, but not necessarily for the same reason. The compact city centre brimming with first-class museums and a wealth of culinary choices, the easy and fast tram system, the proximity to the beautiful archipelago in the west and to the lakes in the east – in short, Gothenburg's small, manageable proportions are precisely what makes the city such an attractive tourist destination. Added to this is an open, friendly response to visitors, less quantifiable than the size of a building but definitely palpable after only a day or two's visit. This tolerant attitude probably owes a lot to the city's traditionally international outlook: the city's first town council was made up of Scotsmen, Dutchmen, Germans and Swedes. Later, a meteoric maritime development led to significant contact with the Far East, and to this day a continuing curiosity for foreign cultures accounts for the recent success of home-grown cuisine, where the wealth of West Swedish ingredients are suffused with far-flung influences picked up from globe-trotting chefs.

History

Although the remains of an early Stone Age settlement show that there were settlers in the Kungsladugård district near the river in the year 7000 BC, the present city had a relatively late birth by European standards in 1621 when King Gustaf II Adolf, still in his twenties, gave the city its charter. The decision to build a town that would act as a well-defended gateway to the burgeoning Atlantic trade proved considerably far-sighted and contributed to Sweden's rise as a European power during Gustaf's reign. The shifting, flaky top bed of clay underneath the city

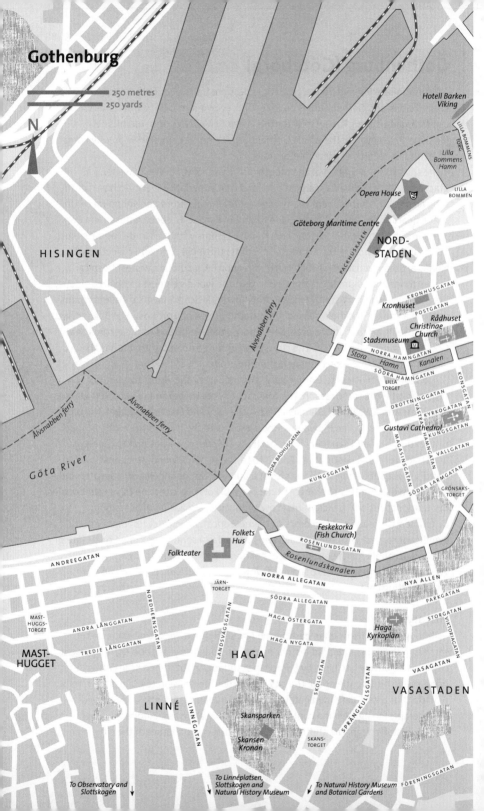

Gothenburg

250 metres
250 yards

N

HISINGEN

Göta River

Älvsnabben ferry

Älvsnabben ferry

Älvsnabben ferry

Hotell Barken Viking

LILLA BOMMENS TORG

Lilla Bommens Hamn

Opera House

LILLA BOMMEN

Göteborg Maritime Centre

NORD-STADEN

PACKHUSKAJEN

KRONHUSGATAN

Kronhuset

POSTGATAN

Rådhuset

Christinae Church

Stadsmuseum

NORRA HAMNGATAN

Stora Hamn

Kanalen

SÖDRA HAMNGATAN

LILLA TORGET

KONSGATAN

DROTTNINGGATAN

VÄSTRA HAMNGATAN

KYRKOGATAN

KUNGSGATAN

Gustavi Cathedral

MAGASINSGATAN

VALLGATAN

STORA BADHUSGATAN

KUNGSGATAN

SÖDRA LARMGATAN

GRÖNSAKS-TORGET

Feskekorka (Fish Church)

ROSENLUNDSGATAN

Rosenlundskanalen

Folkets Hus

Folkteater

ANDREEGATAN

NORRA ALLEGATAN

NYA ALLEN

JÄRN-TORGET

SÖDRA ALLEGATAN

PARKGATAN

NORDHERNSGATAN

MAST-HUGGS-TORGET

ANDRA LÅNGGATAN

TREDJE LÅNGGATAN

LANDSVÄGSGATAN

HAGA ÖSTERGATA

HAGA NYGATA

HAGA

Haga Kyrkoplan

STORGATAN

VIKTORIAGATAN

VASAGATAN

VASASTADEN

MAST-HUGGET

LINNÉ

LINNÉGATAN

SKOLGATAN

SPRÄNGKULLSGATAN

Skansparken

Skansen Kronan

SKANS-TORGET

FÖRENINGSGATAN

To Observatory and Slottskogen

To Linnéplatsen, Slottskogen and Natural History Museum

To Natural History Museum and Botanical Gardens

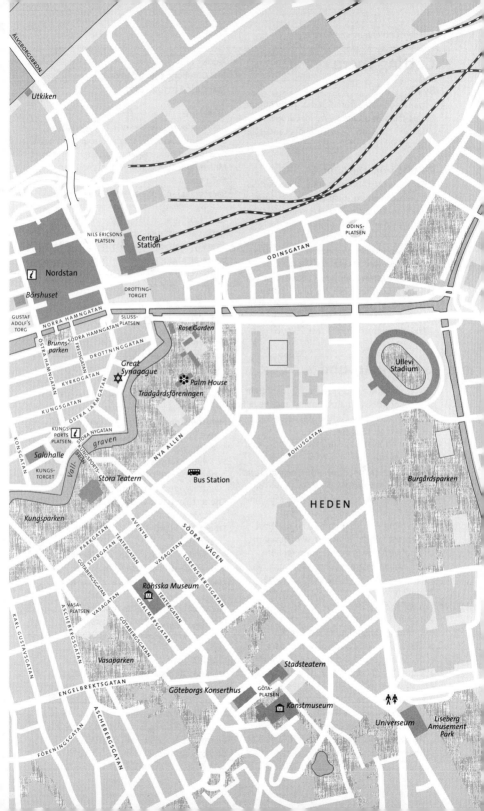

Getting There

By Air

Ryanair operates from Göteborg City Airport, t (031) 926 060, and other major European airlines such as SAS fly to Göteborg Landvetter International Airport, t (031) 941 000.

Getting from the Airport

Göteborg City Airport is about 15km north-west of Gothenburg, near the Volvo factory. Buses from the airport leave 30mins after the flight arrival and to the airport leave the Nils Ericson terminal, t (031) 926 060, at the Central Station complex, 90mins before the flight. A one-way ticket costs SEK30.

Göteborg Landvetter Airport is 22km east of Göteborg. Coaches leave every 15mins from Nils Ericson via Kungsportsplatsen, Parkgatan, Korsvägen and Liseberg, 25mins, SEK60.

Taxis from both airports cost SEK300.

Getting Around

Swedish Railways (SJ) provide frequent train connections between Gothenburg and the rest of Sweden from Central Station on Drottningtorget square.

SJ Information and bookings, t 0771 757 575, www.tagplus.se.

The city centre's pedestrian-friendly grid and wide avenues make it easy to get around on foot. Beyond the canal and for some museums around Götaplatsen and for Liseberg Amusement Park, trams are by far the most convenient form of transport, with buses an alternative if slower option. Fares for both trams and buses are coupons which can either by bought from the driver or at the Tidpunkten centres (t 0771 414 300, www.vasttrafik.se), located at the Nils Ericson terminal at Central Station and in the middle of Drottningtorget Square, outside the station. Tidpunkten also sells a 24hr pass allowing access to tram, bus and ferry. Tram and bus stops have electronic signs showing exactly when your next tram or bus is due.

An attractive travel option, and often necessary for commuters, is the Älvsnabben ferry that crosses the Göta river.

The best deal covering travel in the city is a Gothenburg Pass, see opposite.

Taxis

Taxi Göteborg, t (031) 650 000.
Taxi Kurir, t (031) 27 27 27.

Bike Hire

Gothenburg is well served by cycle paths. Cycling maps can be bought at tourist offices.
Cykelnova, Chalmersgatan 19, t (031) 778 1570.
Millennium Cykel, Chalmersgatan 19, t (031) 184 300.
Sportskällaren, Bohusgatan 2, t 070 727 5682.

Car Hire

Hertz, Centralstationen, t (031) 803 730; Landvetter Flygplats, t (031) 946 020, www.hertz.se.
Europcar, Stampgatan 22D, t (031) 805 390, Landvetter Flygplats, t (031) 947 100, www.europcar.se.

Tourist Information

Gothenburg: To book hotels, call t (020) 838 485.
Kungsportsplatsen 2, t (031) 612 500, www.goteborg.com (open June–23 July daily 9–6; 24 June–11 Aug daily 9–8; 12–30 Aug daily 9–6, Sept–Dec Mon–Fri 9–5, Sat 10–2). Five minutes' walk from the station.
Nordstadstorget, Nordstan shopping mall, near Central Station, t (031) 612 500 (open all year, Mon–Fri 10–6, Sat 10–4, Sun 12–3).
W. Sweden Tourist Board, Kungsportsavenyn 31–5, t (031) 818 300, f (031) 818 301, www.vastsverige.com, www.west-sweden.com.
Chemist: Apoteket Vasen, Nordstan, t (031) 802 0532 (open daily 8am–10pm).
Emergency health care: Axess Akuten, t (031) 725 0000.

As well as free city travel, a Gothenburg Pass gives free entrance to most museums and even certain gyms, as well as discounts in shops and restaurants, and a boat trip to Elfsborg Fortress. You can buy it in hotels and kiosks and online at www.goteborg.com. Adults pay SEK175 for one day, SEK295 for two.

Guided Tours

Guided sightseeing tours by bus run daily between June and September. For more info or to buy tickets, call the Kungsportsplatsen tourist office on t (031) 612 500. Buses depart from Stora Teatern, Götaplatsen. A scenic alternative is the 'Paddan' boat (t (031) 609 670, www. borjessons.com, a highly recommended tour along the old moat, the canals and into the harbour, lasting 50 mins. The boat departs May–Sept from Kungsportsbron from 10am, up to four times an hour.

'Ringlilnien', *www.ringlilnien.org*, a vintage tram, runs from the Central Station to Liseberg daily in July and weekends April–Sept. Or you can try touring from Kungsports-platsen by **horse and cart** at weekends in May and June and daily July–Aug, **t** 070 8925 764.

You can also book an **authorized guide** at **t** (031) 615 250. Highly recommended is **Göteborg Guideklubb**, Sveagatan, **t** (031) 711 0658, *www.goteborgsguideklubb.org*. One of the guides, Christina Buisman, gives an energetic and fluent account of the city.

Festivals

Note: in 2006, the European Championships in Athletics will be held at the Ullevi Stadium in central Gothenburg, 7–13 August.

Another important event is the **Art Biennal**, when urban spaces and the Göteborg Art Museum are open for special exhibitions. The next Art Biennial is scheduled for 2005.

Feb: **Gothenburg Film Festival**, which bills itself as Scandinavia's biggest public film festival, over about 10 days.

July: **Gothia Cup**, the world's biggest youth football tournament, *www.gothiacup.se*.

Aug: **Göteborg Party**, comprising music and general entertainment. **Jazz Festival**, a weekend where about 30 bands play in Vasastan and along Avenyn. **Dance and Theatre Festival**, Sweden's international festival for the modern performing arts.

Shopping

Avenyn, Gothenburg's longest and most fashionable street, advertises itself as 'the most famous street in Sweden'. It even has its own website, *www.avenyn.se*.

Nordstan, Northern Europe's biggest shopping mall, has 150 shops under one roof.

Fredsgatan is home to several small complexes like Arkaden, Citypassagen, Kompassen and upmarket department store NK; and Kungsgatan, teeming with mainstream clothes chain stores and shoe shops.

Haga Nygata, the old artists' quarter, has many second-hand goods from 1950s butter dishes made of Rörstrand porcelain to large 19th century cut-glass chandeliers. A few shops to look out for include: A.A Antik, Haga Nygata 36, Fåfängans Antik, Haga Nygata 16 and Bebop Antik, Kaponjärgatan 4. **Linnégatan**, just off Haga, is the place for trendy little boutiques.

Kronhusbodarna, Gustav Adolfs Torg, has craft shops built in the 18th century.

Saluhallen indoor market, Kungstorget square. An indoor food market built in 1889, selling spices, coffee, cheeses, fruit, cold meat and fish delicacies. *Open Mon–Thurs 9–6, Fri 8–6, Sat 8–3*.

Feskekôrka (literally means 'fish church'). Shopping for fish has never been so special.

The Antique Halls, Västra Hamngatan 6, **t** (031) 774 1525. Scandinavia's biggest permanent antique and collectors' market. About 20 shops sell furniture, porcelain, coins, art and stamps. *Open Aug–May Mon–Fri 10–5, Sat 10–2; closed June and July*.

Göteborg Auction House, Tredje Långgatan 9. Even if you don't actually buy anything, these auction rooms provide an entertaining half-hour. *Open Mon 10–7, Tues–Fri 10–5, closed Sat and Sun*.

Where to Stay

Gothenburg t (031) –

Most of the luxury and mid–upper range of hotels lower their prices considerably at weekends and in summer (*mid-June–mid-Aug*). The **Göteborg Package** is highly recommended, as it includes accommodation at 30 selected hotels, buffet breakfast and a Gothenburg Pass. Prices start at SEK485 per person; ask at the tourist office.

Hotel Eggers, Drottningtorget, **t** 806 070, **f** 154 243, *www.hotel.eggers.com* (*very expensive*). Originally the railway hotel, dating back to 1859, this is the *grande dame* of hotels. Under its chandeliers, the renowned turn-of-the-20th- century painters Anders Zorn, Bruno Liljefors and Carl Larsson signed the rules of their famous alliance. The hotel offers 'cultural' weekend packages.

Elite Plaza Hotel Göteborg, Västra Hamngatan 3, **t** 720 4000, **f** 720 4010, *www. designhotels.*

com (*very expensive*). Opened in 2000 in a palatial insurance building close to the canal and not far from the port. The reception of this 1889 building is a tourist attraction in itself, with its beautiful stucco ceilings and English mosaic floors. It contains the Bishop's Arms pub and the classic Restaurant Swea Hof – *see* below.

Hotel Gothia Towers, Mässans Gata, **t** 750 8800, **f** 750 8882, *www.gothiatowers.com* (*very expensive*). It's difficult to miss the two white towers located near the busy Göteborg Convention Centre, the popular Liseberg Amusement Park and the new science centre Universeum. A member of the SRS World Hotels, the hotel has 704 rooms and boasts one of the best views of the city from its Heaven 23 Restaurant & Bar.

Hotel Riverton, Stora Badhusgatan 26, **t** 750 1000, **f** 750 1001, *www.riverton.se* (*very expensive*). Few rooms come as sleek and high-tech as at the Riverton, all light wood panelling, plasma TV screens and glass washbasins. Although it's technically on the waterfront, you risk craning your neck for river views from some of the rooms unless you go up to the lively top-floor bar.

Quality Hotel 11, Maskingatan, **t** 779 1111, *www.hotel11.se* (*very expensive–expensive*). The main feature of this top-range hotel is that it has retained the open space and high ceilings of the former shipbuilding machine yard it is housed in. It also has the buzzing **Kök & Bar 67** restaurant and bar.

Hotel Vanilj, Kyrkogatan 38, **t** 711 6220, **f** 711 6230, *www.vaniljhotel.entersol.se* (*expensive*). Apart from the pleasant 1865 building and newly renovated rooms, one attraction of this fetching hotel is that some of the rooms have a kitchenette. There is also a pleasant small café downstairs with outdoor space.

Hotel Odin Residence, Odinsgatan 6, **t** 745 2200, **f** 711 2460, *www.hotelodin.se* (*expensive–moderate*). Not far from the central station, this modern building with rooms that look as if they have come out of a Habitat catalogue provides dining and kitchen facilities in some rooms.

Hotel Robinson, Södra Hamngatan 2, **t** 802 521, **f** 159 291, *www.hotelrobinson.com* (*moderate*). Among the better bargains considering it forms part of an old palace, ideally located near the railway station and the shopping centre. The rooms are rather dated, however, behind the elegant façade.

Hotell Barken Viking, Gullbergs kajen, **t** 635 800, **f** 150 058, *www.liseberg.se* (*moderate*). As one of the few remaining four-master barques in the world, Barken *Viking*, now moored in the Göteborg Guest Harbour, provides a unique hotel experience where guests can chose between living in officers' cabins or the cheaper crew's quarters.

Hotel Vasa, Viktoriagatan 6, **t** 173 630, **f** 711 9597, *www.hotelvasa.com* (*moderate*). Although this turn-of-the-20th-century building was recently renovated, the hotel may not match the elegance of some of its surrounding apartment blocks but it is family-run and close to the main sights.

Hotel Lilton, Föreningsgatan 9, **t** 828 808, **f** 822 184, *www.hotellilton.se* (*moderate*). Very charming, Victorian-style hotel in quiet, leafy surroundings. Book early, as there are only 14 rooms, which accounts for its friendly, personal atmosphere.

Hotel Flora, Grönsakstorget 2, **t** 138 616, **f** 132 24, *www.hotelflora.se* (*moderate*). A cosy, family-run hotel with 53 rooms that can prove inexpensive if you choose a room without an ensuite bathroom. The more expensive rooms at the top floor have a picturesque view of the rooftops.

Apple Hotel & Konferens, Torpavallsgatan 6, **t** 251 100, **f** 251 707, *www.apple.se* (*moderate–inexpensive*). Contemporary hotel with business facilities, a spa area and an outdoor swimming pool. This is a well-priced option if you don't mind the 5min drive from the centre (off-street parking for guests available) or a 10min tram ride.

Eating Out

Gothenburg **t** (031) –

Eight of the past eleven winners of Sweden's Chef of the Year have hailed from Gothenburg. The main components of this culinary wave are West Sweden's natural ingredients like fresh fish, fruits, fungi and game, infused with international influences. Reflecting how seriously West Sweden is taking its emergent cuisine, in 2001 the regional tourist board launched a 'Västsvensk Mersmak' culinary certification body; so far, 26 restaurants have been accredited: *www.west-sweden.com*. The city is also proud of its three Michelin-starred restaurants:

Sjömagasinet, Kulturreservat, **t** 775 5929, **f** 245 539, *www.sjomagasinet.se* (*very expensive*). A fish and shellfish specialist located in an old seaside warehouse of the East India Company by the Klippan (the cliff). Guests sit on red, blue and gold sofas, admiring marine paintings in heavy gold frames and the light streaming from the sea through the curtainless windows. If you can't choose between delicately prepared sautéed sole in guinea hen vinaigrette or grilled halibut with scallops, there is a 'tasting menu' which features flavoured halibut or turbot fried in butter and served with beans. *Book early*.

Restaurang 28+, Götabergsgatan 28, **t** 202 161, **f** 189 757, *www.restaurangguiden.com* (*very expensive*). Ulf Johansson, who opened 28+ in 1985 with chef Ingemar Lyxell, has driven around Provence to decorate the succession of whitewashed rooms located in an inviting cellar with white vaults and candlesticks. Provence also inspires the cuisine, which includes a frothy *bouillabaisse*.

Fond Restaurange Bar & Café, Götaplatsen, **t** 812 580, *www.fondrestaurang.com* (*very expensive–expensive*). Stefan Karlsson, who created the main course at the Nobel Prize dinner in 1999, opened Fond (stock, *bouillon* in Swedish) that same year. A *Guide Rouge* star doesn't mean stuffiness – the open glass walls facing the city, bright yellow Venetian blinds and cosy wood panelling create a warm atmosphere.

Other restaurants striving to uphold Gothenburg's culinary reputation include:

Swea Hof, Västra Hamngatan 2, **t** 720 4040 (*very expensive*). International cuisine set in spacious premises that are part of the luxurious Elite Plaza Hotel.

Fiskekrogen, Lilla Torget 1, **t** 101 005, **f** 101 006 (*very expensive–expensive*). A classic, well-established fish restaurant with French influences complemented by Swedish starters like marinated herrings served with matured cheese, caviar and the delicious Fiskekrogens lobster salad. *Closed Sun*.

Herr Dahls, Kungstorget 14, **t** 134 555 (*expensive*). Mix of Swedish/international cuisine attractively presented in a bright, designer restaurant opposite the food market.

Hos Pelle, Djupedalsgatan 2, **t** 121 031 (*expensive*). Just off trendy Linnégatan, an urbane brasserie decorated with modern art.

Hemma Hos, Haga Nygatan 12, **t** 134 090 (*expensive*). Well-established Haga restaurant specializing in traditional Swedish food.

Cabaret Lorensberg, Kungsportsavenyn 36–8, **t** 206 058 (*expensive*). Inside the Radisson CSAS Park Avenue Hotel, this restaurant has an old tradition of serving up entertainment with fine dining. The cabaret artists are also waiters. After the show, the restaurant-cabaret metamorphoses into a nightclub.

Kometen, Vasagatan 58, **t** 137 988 (*expensive*). One of Gothenburg's oldest restaurants, with a colourful artistic past from the 1930s. Serves international food.

Pir 31, Kungsportsplatsen 1, **t** 203 131 (*expensive*). Fish and seafood specialities are served on a boat with a terrace strategically located on the moat close to Avenyn.

Thörnströms Kök, Teknologgatan 2, **t** 162 066 (*expensive–moderate*). If you want to imitate the fresh, light Swedish dishes at home, this restaurant arranges food and cooking classes on Mondays. *Closed for lunch every day, and Sun*.

Axel Engströms Vingard & Vaktmastare Karlsson Matsal, Hagabadet, Södra Allegatan, **t** 600 610 (*expensive–moderate*). The relaxed ambience of the former bathing house also permeates the restaurant which, as you'd expect, serves a healthy but delicious selection of hot and cold plates.

Sjöbaren, Haga Nygata 25, **t** 711 9780 (*moderate*). In the trendy former working class district, this serves fresh shrimps.

Smaka, Vasaplatsen 3, **t** 132 247, **f** 711 1279. (*moderate*). Heavenly meatballs front the traditional Swedish home cooking, with a popular bar among a young, lively crowd.

Hamngatans Restaurang & Bar, Norra Hamngatan 12, **t** 135 270, **f** 315 271 (*moderate*). Next to the excellent city museum, this restaurant serves fresh, varied menu in minimalist, milky-white interior.

Café Kronhuset, Kronhusbodarna, Postgatan 6–8, **t** 711 0832 (*moderate*). You can't beat eating outside the city's oldest secular building for atmosphere, and the pies are hearty, good-value fare.

Röhsska Café, Vasagatan 37–9, **t** 613 850 (*moderate–inexpensive*). The daily lunch buffet is varied, filling and particularly good value for the elegant Vasastaden district. *Closed Mon.*

Saluhallen, Kungstorget (*inexpensive*). The late-19th-century food hall is an atmospheric place to eat a filling fish soup or hot plate of the day at very reasonable prices. *Closed eves.*

Rosenkaféet/Coffea Rosarium, Slussgatan 1, t 802 970, f 809 781, *www.coffearosarium.se* (*inexpensive*). With a view of thousands of roses, it's difficult to beat the setting, and the lunch selection of sandwiches, pies and salad is excellent.

Café & Restaurang Nicolina, Stora Nygatan 3, t 159 595 (*inexpensive*). Excellent, hearty choice of four set menus every day, plus a pasta and salad buffet. Located along the moat path close to the central station.

Cafés

'*Fika*' is the word for the old Swedish tradition of having a coffee and cake. Gothenburg is spoilt for choice for coffee bars, traditional and trendy alike. The best cafés are along Vasagatan, Haga, Linnégatan, the shopping areas, most museums and some of the parks.

At Vasagatan, a haunt for university students, **Café Garbo, Rosa Pantern, Kafé Vasa** and **Kafé Java** are popular.

In Haga, the cafés have homelier interiors with a trend for second-hand furniture and porcelain. Massive cinnamon and sugar-filled buns are served at **Kafé Husaren** and **Haga Kafé och Hembageri** in the main street, Haga Nygata, while at **Café Efva** and **Jacob's Café** you can sip coffee amid antique furniture that's also for sale. Around the corner at Linnégatan, **Solsidan** and its neighbour **Bönor & Bagels** are popular for its outdoor seating. **Coffee House, Karlssons Garage** and **Titt Olle** are also frequented.

In the café-filled Avenyn, **Ljunggrens Kafé** stands out for its history as a meeting place for artists and other cultural personalities, some of whose portraits are on the wall.

At the shopping district around Fredsgatan, **Mauritz Kaffehus** is an old favourite as it was the first Italian-style coffee house with stand-up service and genuine espresso and cappuccino. Down the nearby Victoria-passagen is **Da Matte's**, which has picked up several international awards for its smooth lattes. Further down Västra Hamngatan is the elegant **Brogyllens**, which lures customers with its bread and pastries baked on the premises and its location in an old corner building with high ceilings and large windows.

Entertainment and Nightlife

Music and Theatre

Folkteatern, Olof Palmes Plats, Järntorget, t (031) 607 575.

Stadsteatern, Götaplatsen, t (031) 615 100.

Göteborgs Konserthus, Götaplatsen, t (031) 726 5300.

Göteborgs Operan, Lilla Brommen, t (031) 131 300.

Cinema

Biopalatset, Kungstorget, t 0 31 174 500. One of the city's bigger cinemas with 10 screens.

Royal, Kungsportsavenyn 45, t (031) 174 500. Royal first opened in 1940 and the cinema boasts magnificent interiors, including some fine paintings on the auditorium walls.

Bars

Avenyn is the city's most obvious and mainstream night scene. **Brasserie Lipp**, Kungsportavenyn, t (031) 138 555, is a popular eaterie with a nightclub, **Bubbles**, downstairs. At the corner of Vasagatan and Avenyn is legendary nightclub **Valand**, t (031) 183 093 with two dance floors and four bars.

Vasastan, especially around Viktoriagatan and Vasagatan, likes to think of itself as a slightly hipper alternative to Avenyn, with the Asian-influenced **Noon**, t (031) 138 800 bar at Viktoriagatan, and a popular student haunt, **Klara** t (031) 133 854, opposite.

More bohemian and relaxed are the watering holes in the Haga and Linee district – try **Gillestugan/Tullen**, one of the city's oldest beer halls on Järntorget square, or **Jazzå Bar & Restaurang**, a music bar at Andra Långgatan.

A night out is often rounded up with a 'Half Special', a hot dog with mashed potato, which you can grab at a hot dog stand. Try '**Lasse på Heden**' stand at the corner of Avenyn/Engelbrektsgatan or '**7:ans gatukök**' on Vasagatan.

compelled Sweden to turn to experienced Dutch architects and town planners, who followed the canal-grid model around a central square (Gustaf Adolf's Torg) employed in towns like Amsterdam. In return, the Dutch guest workers were offered religious freedom, exemption from duties and taxes and a place in the first so-called Magistrate, a local government, alongside other immigrant advisers – Germans and Scots – and the local Swedes.

Surrounded by walls, bastions and a moat, Gothenburg became one of Northern Europe's most well-defended fortresses, although only the remains of three bastions still stand: Nya Älvsborg Fort (New Älvsborg) on an island in the mouth of the river, Skansen Kronan in the old Haga district, and Skansen Lejonet, further away from the city centre. Of the canals, two disappeared under the major paved thoroughfares Östra Hamngatan and Västrahamngatan (although there is talk of their restoration), while the original town, mainly of wooden construction, was burned down in a succession of town fires. Two exceptions are Kronhuset, originally the town armoury, and Torstenson Palace, both within the confines of the Stora Hamn Kanalen (Grand Canal).

Propelling the 18th-century development of Gothenburg was the deep-water harbour with its natural dock surrounded by wide quay banks, which helped it to become the country's main port for Swedish exports of iron and wood to England, Holland and Germany. The city's maritime ambitions were furthered with the establishment in 1731 of Ostindiska Companiet, the Swedish East India Company, which catapulted Gothenburg into a European hub for China and Far East trade.

Combined with the flourishing fishing trade centred mainly around herring catches, the success of the city's international trade attracted a growing population, and by the beginning of the 19th century pressure was mounting to build on the land outside the overpopulated (and largely unsanitary) moat-enclosed centre. By the mid-19th century, Gothenburg's links with the world maritime power of Great Britain strengthened, and a new flux of guest workers – English industrialists and businessmen – built the impressive trading and merchant buildings that straddle the shoreline, as well as the some of the country's leading shipyards.

To cope with the chronic shortage of housing, a new self-government act was passed in 1862 giving the town council greater administrative powers, necessary to control the growing influx of workers who accounted for the dramatic doubling of the population between 1888 and 1919. At the elegant end of the building rage were the mansion blocks in Vasastaden outside the moat area. During this period, too, more for aesthetic than practical reasons and mimicking the tendency for open spaces in towns like Paris and London, parks like Kungsparken and Trägården were beautifully andscaped.

Industrialization reached its peak at the beginning of the 20th century when the shipping business dominated the port area and the ball bearing outfit SKF was born, followed a few decades later by two other well-known international brands, Volvo and Hasselblad. As in Malmö and other major European sea ports, Gothenburg is now gentrifying its industrial seafront, a transformation that travellers won't be able to appreciate in its full splendour, particularly with the massive road tunnel being dug along the central Skeppsbron waterfront, until considerably later in the current decade.

Nordstaden (The Old Town and Harbour)

As the central square and site of the copper statue of the city's founder, **Gustaf Adolf's Torg** is a fitting place to start a tour of the old town north of Stora Hamn Kanalen and the harbour. The story behind the statue of the young king is that, from across the river in Hisingen where an earlier attempt at constructing a major settlement was destroyed by the Danes, Gustaf II Adolf, standing on a hill in the marshlands, pointed towards this spot and proclaimed, 'This is where we will build the town.' Rather less dramatic are the historic buildings around the square: **Börshuset**, the former stock exchange, faces the canal in a building that dates back to 1849 and which now hosts city council meetings and official banquets. On the adjacent side is the subdued neoclassical **Rådhuset**, built as the town hall in 1673 but subsequently used as a court house. The edifice is enhanced by a 'Functionalist' extension by internationally renowned architect Gunnar Asplund built in 1937. Next to it are two 18th-century buildings, the **Stadshuset** (city hall) and **Wenngrenska Villa**, originally the home of city councillor Wenngren.

More impressive and providing a more tangible feeling of Gothenburg's influential past is **Ostindiska Huset** (East India House), built in 1750 to house the Swedish East India Company that monopolized all the country's trade with the Far East for almost 80 years. Located only a few blocks from the square, down Norra Hamngatan and past the Christinae church (also referred to as the 'German' church), the building now houses the **Stadsmuseum**, Norra Hamngatan 12, **t** (031) 612 770, **f** (031) 774 0358, *www.stadsmuseum.goteborg.se* (*open May–Aug daily 10–5; Sept–April Tues–Fri and Sun 10–5, Sat 10–8, closed Mon; adm*). A walk through the four floors of the museum is both an edifying and entertaining tour from prehistoric times through the Viking period (don't miss Sweden's only preserved Viking ship), the Middle Ages and the birth of the city in the early 17th century and up to the 1950s. The highlight, though, has to be the third floor, detailing the mid-18th-century heyday of trade with the East and its cultural and architectural legacy for the city. Even without the impressive display of Chinese furniture, porcelain and precious stones, the beautifully restored frescoes on the walls and ceilings and the carved stone pillars are a testament to the wealth accumulated from Sweden's links with China. The exhibition also serves as a salutary lesson on how golden periods can reach an abrupt end. By 1813, East India House had been sold at auction, and for the next century it metamorphosed several times into a library, a secondary school, a grain store and a natural history museum until its latest resurrection in the mid-1990s into a city museum. There is talk of restoring two of the main canals, so it's worth a glance at the photographs of Nordstaden in the 20th century, which reveal just how pretty the centre looked before the canals were filled to allow for car traffic.

Behind the museum, northwest at Kronhusgatan is the striking **Kronhuset** (*not open to the public except for concerts*), Gothenburg's oldest secular non-residential building, originally used as an armoury and then furnished as a Hall of State when Karl X Gustaf called representatives of the nation's various social classes to parliament in 1660, two years after the Danes formally gave up their claims to many territories in southern Sweden. The red brick construction, mounted in austere Dutch style with frontons and high pointed gables, ensured it was one of the few buildings not destroyed in the severe fires of 1746 and 1758. The glassworks, pottery and goldsmiths in the small surrounding 18th-century buildings, also known as **Kornhusbodarna** (*open Mon–Fri 11–4, Sat 11–2, closed Sun; café open Mon–Fri 10–7, Sat and Sun 11–6*) provide a tempting shopping break before a short walk to the ever-transforming river bank.

For boat enthusiasts or anyone who needs reassurance that living in a submarine is really only suitable for people who are comfortable in cramped spaces, there is the **Göteborg Maritime Centre**, Packhuskajen, t (031) 105 950, *www.goteborgsmaritima centrum.com* (*open Mar–April and Sept–Oct daily 10–4; May–Aug daily 10–6; adm*), which bills itself as the world's largest floating ship museum.

By Lilla Bommen – the departure point for ferries to the other side of the river and beyond – you can't miss the modern **Opera House**, whose massive size of two city blocks is meant to be able to store up to five assembled stage sets at any one time. To find out what happens backstage, learn the meaning of patination, see the work of a prompter and view other aspects of the building, which was completed in 1994, take a guided tour (*summer at 2pm; check with box office after 28 Aug; t (031) 108 203; adm*). Possibly an even more dramatic addition to the waterfront is **Utkiken**, an 86m-high office building whose shape has earned it the name 'Lipstick'. There is a café at the top with panoramic views of the harbour.

Head southwards down Östra Hamngatan, which is flanked to the east by **Nordstan**, Northern Europe's most sprawling shopping complex. You can negotiate your way through the maze of shopping avenues east towards the central station, but a more picturesque route is to hit Gustaf Adolf's Torg and continue eastwards parallel to the canal to Drottingtorget, where the stately Hotel Eggers (see 'Where to Stay') proudly stands. Even if you are not catching a train or bus, the **Central Station** is worth a visit for its grand 1856 façade and for a wander around the spruce, elegant interior, well served by cafés and restaurants of the quality more associated with an upmarket shopping mall than with a busy transport hub.

South of Stora Hamn Kanalen

From the station, with the massive post office building on your left, walk in a straight line south towards the **canal**, crossing it to reach Slussplatsen, and enjoy a stroll along the attractive, canalside stretch of Stora Nygatan with views of the beautifully landscaped Trädgårdsföreningen park with its Palm House (*see* 'City Parks', p.84) across the old moat. In the summer, you might spot, passing by, one of the popular 'Paddan' boats (*see* 'Guided Tours', pp.74–5) that depart from Kungsportsbron, which you reach at the end of the short stroll after passing the **Great Synagogue**, the oldest in mainland Sweden (*only open during services; times vary, contact the Jewish Community office, t (031) 77 245*).

Kungsportsplatsen is a good place to pause for a while, not only because the tourist office has its second office here but also for its convenient location in the middle of the **Avenyn**, the street Gothenburgers sometimes refer to as their Champs-Elysées. Southwards up the boulevard and across the canal is the beginning of the stylish 19th-century town leading up to the landmark statue of Poseidon (*see* 'Götaplatsen', p.84), while the view northwards is of Gustaf Adolfs Torg and the port beyond. You may be seduced into a detour, but if you continue on paralllel to the canal you come to Kungstorget, where the **Saluhallen**, the 1880s-built indoor market, provides food stalls and some reasonably priced restaurants.

Shopping is one of the main activities in the area north of Saluhallen and back up to Stora Hamn Kanalen – notably the pedestrianized **Kungsgatan**, popular for clothes and design shops, and the more stylish **Västra Hamngatan**, the site of Scandinavia's biggest permanent antique and collectors' market. A pot-pourri of architectural styles and periods makes up this central zone, and there is also a plethora of cafes, ideal for indulging in the generally excellent range of home-made cakes. Most of the cinemas are in this area too, mainly showing Hollywood or the more mainstream European films in their original languages.

Standing aloof from the surrounding focus on entertainment is **Gustavi Cathedral**, Västra Hamngatan (*open Mon–Fri 8–6, Sat 9–4, Sun 10–3*). Viewing it from the main street outside the cathedral drinking fountain, one of the town's oldest, it is noticeable that the cathedral is slightly inclined, victim of the city's shifting clay foundations. Gothenburg's cathedral has suffered from more fatal afflictions in the past, namely, two fierce fires, in 1721 and 1802. The third and present cathedral was built in neoclassical style in 1827, almost 200 years after the original church was erected on the site in honour of King Gustaf II Adolf when he died in the Battle of Lutzen. Inside, don't miss the idiosyncratic glassed-in areas before the font and the altar. Nicknamed the 'trams' by churchgoers, these spaces were originally reserved for private conversations between the bishop and the priests.

Back at Kungstorget and westwards along the Vallgraven canalside path, an idiosyncratic-looking church, with large windows, pointed gables and bays and a roof which almost reaches the ground, looms at Rosenlundsgatan. On closer inspection, the wafting sea aromas from within confirm that the building is actually an indoor fish and seamarket, **Feskekôrka**, or Fish Church (*open Tues–Thurs 9–5, Fri 9–6, Sat 9–2, closed Sun, Mon open summer only 9–5*). The experiment by Victor von Gegerfelt, a leading mid-19th-century architect, seems to have paid off handsomely, judging by the always crowded hall and popular fish restaurant in the upstairs gallery.

Haga

Immediately across the canal is Haga, the oldest-working-class suburb and now one of the most sought-after residential districts for young professionals attracted by the large apartment blocks and bohemian cafés and second-hand shops. A splendid remnant of the area's working class roots is **Hagabadet**, Södra Allegatan, **t** (031) 600 610 (*open Mon–Thurs 7am–9.30pm, Fri 7am–8.30pm, Sat 9–6, Sun 10–6; adm*). The customers of this splendidly renovated 1870-built bathhouse may be considerably more monied than its original users, but special prices are available for day visitors who want a massage after a busy day's walking, or to splash about in the beautifully restored old-fashioned pool.

You experience Haga proper two streets down at **Haga Nygata**, whose trendy cafés get very busy in the afternoon (try a *Hagabullen*, an enormous cinnamon bun, at Café Husaren) and pretty knick-knack shops (pop into Sintra arts and crafts gallery, Liten Karin and HagaHem). Many of these buzzing establishments are housed in what is referred to as 'Country Governor'- or Landshövdingehus-style blocks, which have a stone ground floor and two wooden upper storeys. These now highly desirable living quarters sprouted in the 1870s to replace the previous small, detached timber houses that had marked the city's first distinct workers' district in the 1840s. With the extreme shortage of housing in the second half of the 19th century, it was not unusual for up to 15 people to live in a single room of these blocks.

By the 1920s the population had begun to dwindle, the public baths were closed, and although the area remained a vibrant residential area it wasn't until 1962 that a redevelopment drive threatening to tear down many of the 19th-century buildings led to the 'Haga Group' campaigning for the district's restoration. The only other districts where these stone and wooden houses still survive are Majorna, Gårda and Kålltorp. To appreciate the mixture of red and green coppered roofs of Haga, as well as the stretch of city beyond towards the harbour, it is well worth traipsing the 193 steps from Bultekgatan up the steep **Skansparken hill**. A second reward is the sight of the gilded Skansen Kronan, one of the two 17th-century fortress towers that is still intact.

Linné and Beyond

At the bottom of Skansparken hill, Haga Östergata runs parallel with Haga Nygata, and a little way west along it is the piazza-like **Järntorget**, a lively meeting place close to the Folkteater (People's Theatre), with a beautiful fountain and lively pavement cafes such as Gillestugan and Cigarrkaféets. **Linnégatan** begins its climb southwards from here, the window fronts of its avenue increasingly taken over by offbeat boutiques and trendy night haunts for young people, an antidote in many ways to the more glitzy, established Avenyn over in Vasastaden. Don't miss **Saluhallen Briggen**, a market hall housed in the old fire station with charming little cafés and deli counters. Further west of Linnégatan, there are a couple of well-known sea navigation marks: **Masthugget Church**, Storebackegatan (*open Mon–Sat 9–6, Sun 1–6*), built in the National Romantic style, and the **Sailor's Tower** with the statue of the waiting woman. It's an energetic walk from Linnégaten; the less fit can take trams 9 or 11 to Stigbergstorget.

For park- and garden-lovers, the area south of Linné offers two impressive green spaces. From the top of Linnéplatsen (take trams 1 and 6 to avoid the hilly walk) begins the expansive **Slottsskogen** (Slottsforest) where activities and sights include a seal pond, penguins, flamingos and tropical birds, Sweden's oldest zoo, a special summer zoo where children can ride ponies and meet piglets, goats and chicks, an Observatory (*open all year, tour bookings t (031) 126 300*) and the **Natural History Museum**, Slottskogen vid Linnéplatsen, **t** (031) 775 2400, *www.gnm.se* (*open Jan–Mar and Sept–Dec Tues–Fri 9–4, Sat and Sun 11–5, closed Mon; May Mon–Fri 9–5, Sat and Sun 11–5, June–Aug Mon–Sun 11–5; adm*) featuring a huge blue whale.

South of the open park are the stunning **Botaniska Trädgården** (Botanical Gardens) at Carl Skottsberg Gata 22a, **t** (031) 741 1109, *www.gotbot.se*, tram 7, 8, 13 (*open 9–sunset*), Sweden's biggest botanical garden, opened in 1923. Amid the 12,000 species, try not to miss the 'Arboretum' section with trees from the four corners of the earth, the Japanese valley, and Klippträdgården, with a waterfall and rockery that has earned itself two stars in the Michelin Green Guide.

Vasastaden and City Parks

From Haga, Vasastaden is approached from the east of Haga Nygata that meets Hagaparken, at the north end of which is the 1859-built Haga Kyrkoplan church. A stroll through this elegant neighbourhood, which stretches east towards Vasaparken, the site of the distinguished main university building, reveals the self-confidence the merchant aristocracy must have felt at the turn of the 19th century. With their wrought-iron balconies, classical windows and intricately decorated façades, the l arge apartment blocks exude a discreet magnificence that spills over to the two parks just south of the canal, bordering the district. The closest park is **Kungsparken**, and further west is **Trädgårdsföreningen** (the Horticultural Society), founded in 1842 by Captain Henric von Norman. Highly popular with picnickers in long summer days, the rainbow-like profusions of flowers and well-tended flowerbeds of Trädgårds-föreningen are immediately impressive. That's before even reaching the far end of the park closest to Nordstaden where a magnificent Palm House containing a large collection of exotic plants was erected in 1876 as a copy of London's Crystal Palace. But the most dazzling spectacle at the right time of year is the Butterfly House in the park, and the Rose Garden, with the region's most comprehensive collection of roses.

One last deserving detour in Vasastaden is the **Röhsska Museum**, Vasagatan 37–9, **t** (031) 613 850, **f** (031) 184 692, *www.designmuseum.se* (*open Tues 12–9, Wed–Sun 12–5; closed Mon; adm*), Sweden's only museum for design and applied art. The exhibitions are far more accessible to a general public than the names of the displays (handicraft, commercial handicraft and industrial design) suggest. Particularly in these home-improvement-crazed times, the furniture and appliance designs of recent decades are fascinating. For more specialist tastes, there is a comprehensive catalogue of Egyptian textiles, Chinese silk cloth, clothes and carpets, Bohuslän Finnish cloth, Nordic long pile rugs, Far Eastern and Islamic ceramics and Swedish glass collections.

Götaplatsen and Around

At the hillier end of the famed Avenyn sits Götaplatsen, the square built for the World Expo in 1923, presided over by Carl Milles' bronze Poseidon statue of a naked young man whose gaze stretches along the 1km-long avenue down to the harbour. The square's cultural pedigree is undisputed: east of the statue is **Stadsteatern**, the city theatre, on the opposite site is **Göteborgs Konserthus**, home of the renowned Gothenburg Symphony Orchestra, and towering over the proceedings from a 1930s monolithic construction, behind the statue, is the doyenne of the group, **Göteborgs Konstmuseum** (Art Museum), **t** (031) 612 980, **f** (031) 184 119, *www.konstmuseum. goteborg.se* (*open Tues–Thurs 11–6, Wed 11–9, Fri–Sun 11–5; closed Mon; adm*). Appetizer to the visual feast spread across the six floors is the generally excellent, changing photographic exhibition on display at the Hasselblad Centre, *www. hasselbladcenter.se*, on the ground floor. For sculpture-lovers, the chequered-floored sculpture hall on the third and fourth floor shows works by Maillol, Bourdelle, Milles and other Nordic 20th-century artists; examples of more traditional European art from the 17th century to the 1880s, featuring some minor works by Rembrandt and Rubens, are found on the fifth floor, alongside examples of Nordic art from the beginning of the 19th century, which is generally regarded as the Golden Age of Danish painting.

The biggest treat, and not to be missed, is on the top floor, the Fürstenberg Gallery, created in 1925 from donations by Pontus Fürstenberg, a Jewish merchant who in 1880 married Göthilda Magnus, the city's richest heiress, and about the same time befriended a group of young Scandinavian artists who had severed their ties with the Royal Swedish Academy of Fine Arts. (Look out for Anders Zorn's portrait of the couple.) Fürstenberg ended up a patron of the group, which included Carl Larsson, Carl Wilhelmson, Anders Zorn, and Karl Nordström, when they founded the Artists' Unions. Several members of the group are shown enjoying breakfast together at Café Ledoyen in Paris in Hugo Birger's painting, hanging in the largest room of the gallery. Also in this room is a watercolour of Carl Larsson at work. Perhaps the most emblematic painting of the entire turn-of-the-19th-century movement is Richard Bergh's *Nordisk Sommarkvall* (*Nordic Summer Evening*), where a young couple meet in the exquisite twilight of a never-ending Scandinavian midsummer evening. A light of dramatically different luminosity is also beautifully captured by Karl Nordström in his painting *Vinterafton vid Rolagskull*, depicting a short Christmas afternoon in Stockholm. Also playing skilfully with light is the more modernist *Sol o ungdom* (*Sun and Youth*), a painting by Danish painter Jens Ferdinand Willumsen that sketches a group of young, carefree boys on the beach.

Universeum and Liseberg

Southeast of Götaplatsen, at the foot of the Liseberg Amusement Park, the largest of its kind in Scandinavia, is **Universeum**, Södra Vägen 50, **t** (031) 335 6450, **f** (031) 335 6451, *www.universeum.se* (*open Jan–May and mid-Aug–Dec Tues 11–6, Wed 11–8, Thurs–Sun 11–6; closed Mon; adm*), a museum about the environment of plants, animals and fish. Don't be put off by any school associations with the subjects; this is a compelling, often fascinating 3km walk through mountain streams, the ocean, rainforests, all painstakingly recreated with sound effects and real animals across various levels housed in a glass, wood and concrete building. Even if you never asked yourself questions about why grass snakes play dead, wondered how to tell the difference between a frog and a toad or interested yourself the feeding habits of leeches, it is guaranteed you will, once inside, be itching for answers (which are provided by well marked information points, or by one of the several enthusiastic animal or plant attendants inside).

If the sight of piranhas and sharks isn't thrilling enough, the region's biggest wooden rollercoaster, with a drop of 70 degrees and a speed of 90km per hour, may do the trick at **Liseberg Amusement Park**, **t** (031) 400 100, **f** (031) 7330 419, *www.liseberg.se* (*open May–Oct, times vary throughout the summer; July open 11–midnight; adm*). Other head-churning rides include Spinrock, Topspin and Wave Swinger.

Outside the Centre

Port Excursions

A pleasant hour or so can be spent on one of the ferries that depart frequently from Lilla Bommen (the harbour between Utkiken and the Opera House).

Hop on and off at your leisure at any of the stops including: **Klippan**, the former home port of the Swedish East India Company, with houses preserved from the city's trading heyday, and which is also the site of gourmet restaurant Sjömagasinet (*see* 'Eating Out'); **Novotel Hotel**, formely the Carnegie Porter Brewery; and **Elfsborg Fortress**, located at the mouth of the Göta River. For a guided tour of the fortress, tours depart from Lilla Bommen between May and September at weekends, *see www.borjessons.com*.

Hisingen and the Volvo Museum

Crossing Älvsborgsbron bridge, Gothenburg's 'Golden Gate', takes you to Hisingen, Sweden's fourth-largest island. On this side of the river, highlights include **Keiller Park**, a natural park with a magnificent view of the northern and southern archipelago; **Rya Skog** (Rya Woods), a nature reserve with footpaths through unspoiled nature; and **Krokängsparken**, dominated by oak and hazel woods and with a rich bird life.

Some way north of Hisingen, next to the Volvo factory, is the **Volvo Museum**, **t** (031) 664 814; take tram 5, 6 or 10 to Eketrägatan where you change to bus 32 towards Sörred; get off at Götaverken Arendal or Arendal Skans and follow the signs to the museum (*open Sept–May Tues–Fri 12–5, Sat and Sun 11–4; June–Aug Tues–Fri 10–5, Sat and Sun 11–4; adm*). The factory runs a Blue Train tour with Engligh commentary; a little way away, the museum contains classic cars and displays the history of the famous Swedish automobile from the summer day in 1924 when two engineers Gustaf Larson and Assar Gabrielsson were said to have conceived the 'Swedish Car' during a chance encounter over a plate of crayfish, two years after which the first Volvo prototype left Galco's premises in Stockholm.

The English Castle

Stiftelsen Tjolöholm, t (0300) 544 200, f (0300) 544 166; take a train from Gothenburg's central station to Kungsbacka and change to no.732 bus. Open April–mid-June Sat and Sun 11–4, mid-June–Aug daily 11–4; Sept Sat and Sun 11–4; Oct Sun 11–4; closed Nov–Mar; adm.

A good excuse for a short excursion south of Gothenburg is the delightful Elizabethan-style manor of Tjolöholm Castle. Wonderfully set by the water, the façade looks convincingly Tudor, so it is a shock to discover the Art Nouveau interior and the piped hot air system and shower-fitted bathrooms. The manor was in fact built between 1898 and 1904 and includes an estate workers' village and church located in a beautiful park.

Day Trips and Overnighters from Gothenburg

Gothenburg's Southern Archipelago

Hopping across the dozen islands that make up Gothenburg's southern archipelago must be one of the highlights of any trip to western Sweden, made all the more pleasurable because all you really need is a batch of skerry boat tickets and a picnic basket. It's not only a delight in the summer when the various sandy beaches are the most obvious attraction. Spring is perfect for bird-watching in Vrångo; for an appreciation of pastoral life in the westerly island of Galterö, autumn is recommended; while crab-fishing in Asperö continues until Christmas. For stauncher urbanites, there are also century-old mansions to admire, a few churches, and a couple of charming eateries. The beauty of a day tour is that the islands are close enough to each other and skerries so frequent (a normal summer day sees 50 departures from Saltholmen at the tip of Gothenburg's most westerly peninsula) that, if a particular island does not meet expectations, a hop to the next is simple.

Just 7mins from the mainland is **Asperö**, where the impatient can get off at Alberts Brygga and head straight to the nearby cliffs to sunbathe or take the few minutes' walk to Kvistevik beach for a swim. Evening visitors may be tempted to head to the old-fashioned dance-floor in the south towards Korshamn, frequented famously by boys who rowed out from the city.

Further west (and 18mins from Saltholmen) is **Bränno**, renowned for its musical traditions such as its jazz and song festivals and its dance floor at Bränno pier. For spectacular views of the archipelago, go to the Lookout, reached by walking straight along Rödstensvägen and Faggeliden to a little red house at the top. For a hint of past farming life – an anomaly in the fishing-dominated archipelago – stroll westwards to Galterö, where sheep graze on the heath and the sandy beaches are virtually empty.

Carpentry skills have always been highly sought-after in **Köpstadsö**, just south of Asperö (and 14mins from Saltholmen), evident in the highly ornamented white wooden houses and windowed verandas, relics of the island's golden age at the turn

Getting There

Take **Tramway** 4 (number 8 or 9 during the summer) or **express bus Ö-snabben** from the Nils Ericson terminal at Central Station or any tram stop with the numbers 8 or 9, direction Saltholmen, to Saltholmen harbour. You can either buy **ferry** tickets on board (SEK20 minimum for a single journey), or if you are going to island-hop furiously you can buy a **24hr regional ticket** (SEK220)at a Tidpunkten centre (Central Station or at Drottningtorget Square) or on board.,

For info on boat traffic, call Tidpunkten on **t** (031) 801 235 or Saltholmen ticket office on **t** (031) 297 599, *www.västtrafik.se*.

Where to Stay and Eat

Pensionat Styrsö, Skäretvägen 53, Styrsö, **t** (031) 973 239, **f** (031) 973 525, *www. pensionatskaret.se* (*expensive*). The beautifully converted beach mansion with huge verandas and sweeping views offers a rather pricy lunch, but the traditional Swedish food is tasty and a less expensive option is the day's fish soup laced with saffron and garlic. If you want to stay overnight, book early as there are only a dozen rooms, all tastefully decorated. Rooms are graded in price depending on whether they have a garden or harbour (*more expensive*) view.

of the 20th century when the elegant clubhouse Smutten, with pinnacles and towers, was built. In its heyday, the island boasted a school, post office and three shops. Today the hundred-odd permanent inhabitants wait expectantly for the arrival of the skerry boats with food boxes ordered from the supermarket on Styrsö island or the grocery on Donsö.

Literally the heart of the offshore islands, as it is the site of the archipelago's medical centre, the schools for older children and its only home for pensioners, is the island of **Styrsö** (20mins from Saltholmen). Getting off at the eastern port of Bratten, the famous merchant's house of one Mrs Öberg is a good place to start, less for the exhibits of handicrafts made by local artists than for the history of her popular inn, from where the lady ran a cunning smuggling operation, quite a common occupation, it turns out, among several islands during the 19th century. Tången in the west is worth visiting for its closely knit village houses that make up the charming old fishing community, as well as for the summer pier dance. Further south is Halsvik, the old village of cargo captains made up of impressive mansions, while on the opposite, eastern side of the island is Skäret, the site of the island's ancient monument, Stora Rös, a cairn that was once a bearing point for seafarers. A place to rest for a coffee or for a rather luxurious meal, and even for an overnight stay, is Pensionskaret – *see* box, above.

A bridge called 'Crow Jump' joins Styrsö to **Donsö**, although the latter is also a 35min skerry boat ride from Saltholmen. As the local population has almost tripled in the last 100 years, mainly from the unlikely mix of two bodies, the missionary society and the athletics association, the residential council has limited the summer houses in this most densely populated island to 40. The big and only grocery at Donsö harbour is a suitable place to stock up on picnic provisions.

To the west of Styrsö is the almost deserted island of **Vargö** (there are only two year-round inhabitants and 30 summer residents), perhaps partly due to the burning down of its beautiful bath-house in 1916. The sandy beach of Bälvik is attractive, with its high rocks that stand on each side of the rock and its view of the open sea.

Few bathers visit the tiny isle of **Källö** (25mins from Saltholmen), best known for its friendliness (it is so little that everyone knows everyone, especially in the summer when 70 people share the island's 25 houses) and for the fact that one family has owned most of it for almost 200 years.

South of Styrsö and a mere 14min trip on the direct ferry from Saltholmen is **Knarrholmen**, a throwback to an era of workers' solidarity as it is, unusually, owned by workers from the shipyard Götaverken and from Volvo, a legacy from the 1940s when ship-owner Axel Axson Johnson donated the island to shipyard workers. The main attraction is two beaches, one on the northern part of the island to the right of the waiting hall Sjappet and the Blue Lagoon in the south.

A collective spirit is said to endure in **Stora Förö** (40mins from Saltholmen) after a Motorboat Association started an economic co-operative in 1930 whereby members were divided into one of the island's seven road crews and had to fulfil 30 hours' duty each summer (today lowered to 10 hours per house). The result is a good road that circles the island, which is also known for its abundant pine trees, the planting efforts of an older generation.

Sweden's vaunted socialist model is also apparent in **Sjmansholmen**, once rented by Gothenburg's Communist Workers' Union in 1933 and then by the Worker Children's Island. Even today, when something has to be done on the island, a notice is set up for a work day. The collective spirit perhaps endures because the lack of toilet facilities keeps visitors away.

Kårholmen (40mins from Saltholmen) has fine bathing places and sweeping views from the peak of Höga Berget (High Mountain), but visitors seem to stay away, perhaps intimidated by the dense houses and their easy, inquisitive view of arriving skerry boats. The island is owned by an economic co-operative.

Far more popular, although furthest away, is **Vrångö** (52mins from Saltholmen). The attractions are plenty: a harbour teeming with fishermen who catch cod and herring in the Kattegat and the Baltic Sea, numerous fine beaches, a pilot lookout point above the harbour, and good strolling paths on the north side of the island, also the site of a nature reserve.

Marstrand

Of the chain of rocky islands linked by numerous bridges and short ferry crossings all the way up from the north side of Gothenburg to the Norwegian border, Marstrand is probably the most popular. Its attractions are numerous: it's only a short hop on a ferry or overland drive from the city; it has a colourful history symbolized by Carlsten Fortress and by a later reputation as a free-thinking (some said 'sinful') town; it has formidable beaches and an important sailing port that hosts summer regattas; and a stroll through the narrow streets of the town, flanked by pastel-coloured wooden houses, is delightful. Marstrand also aptly crystallizes the history of the Bohuslän county, a region that experienced a pre-Renaissance boom on the back of

Getting There

Bus 302 takes 70mins to Marstrand (via the town of Kungälv) and bus 312, an express bus, takes 55mins. Both buses start at Gothenburg's terminus at Nils Ericsonplatsen and end their journey in Arvidsvik, on Koön, only 50m from the ferry to Marstrand.

The Lasse-Maja **ferry** runs every 15mins and takes less than 5mins to get across. Buy the ferry tickets at the small booth right by the ferry, or on board. A car costs a whopping SEK500 on the ferry, which accounts for the lack of traffic on the island.

For a more leisurely and scenic route available in the summer (June to Aug), there is a daily Börjessons ferry, BM/S *St Erik* (built in 1881), from Lilla Bommen to Marstrand. The boat trip (there is a café and restaurant on board) itself takes about three hours one-way to Marstrand, and it stops by Öckerö Färjeläge and Rörö. Once you get to Marstrand, you have about 2hrs to see the island. The cruises depart at 9.30am and arrive at Marstrand three hours later. The return trips depart at 2.30pm and returns to Gothenburg at about 5.30pm.

Buy **tickets** at Kajskjul 207, Lilla Bommen; SEK160 for adults (return trip.) For more info, call Börjessons Restaurang & Utflyktsbåtar, Pusterviksgatan 13, **t** (031) 609 670.

Tourist Information

Marstrand: On the waterfront opposite the ferry arrival point, **t** (0303) 600 87, *www.marstrand.nu*. The island is also covered by Kungälv's tourist office at the foot of the fortress, **t** (0303) 992 00.

Where to Stay

Marstrand t (0303) –
Grand Hotell, Paradiset Park, **t** 603 22, **f** 600 53, *www.grandmarstrand.se (very expensive)*. The elegant turn-of-the-19th-century hotel was for many years used only as employee housing, but has recently been painstakingly restored in the lavish style of King Oscar II. The bathrooms stand out for their classic white shades and brass fittings and their old-fashioned bathtubs.

salt herring, which by the 19th century had virtually disappeared, forcing the so-called Golden Coast to reinvent itself as a fashionable spa resort.

The first glimpse of Marstrand is impressive, the short ferry ride from Koön literally forcing the visitor's attention to the waterfront lined by a pristine houses, above which peeps out the grey-stone guardian, **Carlsten Fästning** (Carlsten Fortress). From the ferry, turn left on to cobbled Kungsgatan and make the steep climb up to the fortress at Kommandantshuset, **t** (0303) 602 65, **f** (0303) 614 57, *www.carlsten.se (open Sept–June Sat and Sun 11–4; early June and late Aug daily 1–4; mid-June–mid-Aug 11–6; mid-end Aug 12–4; Sept–Dec Sat and Sun only 11–4)*. When Marstrand become Swedish for the first time in 1658, King Karl X decided to build a fortress on the highest point of the island to safeguard the city, but a shortage of labour to carry the rocks to the construction site led to a nationwide recruitment of prisoners – mainly murderers, rapists and thieves. They lived in stark conditions, each dragging a 2kg iron ball attached to a chain around their ankles, with the biggest troublemakers forced to wear a heavy iron crown.

The most illustrious prisoner was Lasse-Maja, a thief who for years managed to escape the law thanks to his clever female disguise. Eventually he was sentenced to Marstrand for life, but his culinary skills picked up as a 'woman' helped to land him a post as chef for the officers. He was reputedly such a good storyteller that people

Hotell Nautic, Långgatan 6, **t** 610 30, **f** 612 00, *www.hotellnautic.com* (*moderate*). Surprisingly reasonably priced option given its scenic setting by the water; the rooms are fresh if unspectacular.

Carlsten Fästning Kommandantshuset, t 602 65, **f** 614 57, *www.carlsten.se* (*inexpensive*). The rooms are no-frills and rather bland, but the point is spending the night within the walls of the fortress, specifically in the Southern Donjon, built in the 1840s, where thousands of soldiers have been quartered over the years. There are doubles, and larger rooms with up to ten beds.

Eating Out

Marstrand **t** (0303) –

Restaurant Tenan, Grand Hotel, Paradiset Parken, **t** 603 22 (*very expensive*). The high prices are justified by the splendid location in a gently sloping park with a view over the inlet and the delicious and inventive dishes such as half-and-half meatballs, made from ground beef and ground sea bird (although these have to be ordered well in advance) or Beef Africana that includes peanuts, bananas, mango chutney, cucumber, pearl onions, curry and rice.

Restaurang Oscar, Hamngatan 11, **t** 615 54 (*expensive*). With lovely, sheltered balconies for people-watching, this elegant dining place is set in former 19th-century spa hotel.

Restaurant Drott, Kungsplan, **t** 618 70 (*moderate*). The formidable setting, a former 19th-century bathhouse (now the youth hostel), is reason enough for a visit, but the fish dishes are reasonable too.

Societetshuset, t 606 00, *www.societets huset.se* (*expensive*). As the name suggests, this beautifully renovated green and white wooden seaside mansion was once high society's stomping ground and is now divided into two restaurants, a bar and casino.

Grenluns Etta Café au Mera, Drottningatan 4, **t** 611 77 (*moderate*). In the same street as the 12th-century church, this café has several advantages such as year-round opening, a wide selection of coffees, reasonably priced pies and sandwiches and a small art gallery with pictures of the town. *Closed eves.*

Arvidson Fisk, Kyrkogatan 25, **t** 600 40 (*inexpensive*). A wide selection of smoked fish for picnic enthusiasts.

came from Gothenburg in droves to hear him, tossing food to the prisoners in grati-tude. In 1839, after 26 years in prison, he was pardoned by Karl XIV Johan. A Swedish taste for historical re-enactments means that since 1982, the fortress has set up historical 'days' where tourists are escorted around by a commandant to meet the roughly treated prisoners wearing cuffs and shackles and even Lasse-Maja spinning yarns in his kitchen. For greater period authenticity, dozens of Karolian soldiers exercise in the central courtyard amid thunderous gunpowder cracks and smoke.

Leaving the fortress down Kungsgatan, the **Grand Hotell Marstrand** (*see* 'Where to Stay', above) squats elegantly over Paradis Parken square. Along with Societetshuset, today a restaurant and entertainment centre, and Marstrands Varmbadhus/Båtellet, now a youth hostel (both located at the end of Långgatan), the Grand Hotell, built in 1892, recalls the island's heyday as a fashionable spa resort at the turn of the 19th century. Setting the trend for holidaying in Marstrand was the music-loving King Oscar II who in 1887 spent one of 20 summers in the island. A party atmosphere is still evident today in the waterfront bars and restaurants and around the two squares close to Grand Hotell. For a quieter time, it isn't far to the **beaches** on the western side of the island behind the fortress, with a naturist bathing area marked on the Svarte Udde point.

Touring from Gothenburg

Day 1: A Medieval Fortress, and a Seaweed Spa

Morning: Take the E6 motorway north towards Oslo for about 20km to Kungälv where the 700-year-old ruins of **Bohus Fortress** (*open April Sat and Sun 11–4; May–Aug daily 10–9; Sept daily 11–5*) overlook the valley of Göta Älv and the cobbled streets and pastel wooden houses of the old village. The remaining colossal walls hint at the impregnability of a fortress originally built in 1308 by Norway to defend its southern border. Attacks on the bulwark that eventually enclosed a Renaissance palace culminated in its near-destruction in 1678 by a Norwegian onslaught; although Swedish troops staved off this final invasion, the stronghold was severely damaged, with restoration only beginning at the end of the 19th century.

Lunch: In Kungälv, *see* below.

Afternoon: Follow the E6 northwards and, before Uddevalla, turn off at **Ljungskile**, a former 19th-century seaside resort where, beside the small harbour, it's difficult to miss **Ljungskile Varmbadhus**, Strandvägen, **t** (0522) 20055 (*open Tues–Fri 11–7, Sat 11–4; adm*), a sunny yellow bathhouse that has been in use since 1924. Unwind for a couple of hours in a seaweed bath with warm seawater, or have a facial or massage. Then take a side road near the Lyckorna intersection at Ljungskile and follow sign-posts to **Villa Sjötorp**. Even if you don't stay, have a coffee at this *Hansel and Gretel* wooden house guest house with its unique three-high, deep Gothic revival vaults.

Dinner and Sleeping: In Ljungskile, *see* below.

Day 1

Lunch in Kungälv

Gourmetboden, Gamla Torget 4, **t** (0303) 183 90 (*moderate*). A delicatessen-restaurant conveniently located in the pretty, central old square, not far from the fortress. Select a picnic from a wide range of *charcuterie*, quiches, salads and cheeses to enjoy along the scenic river. Or eat in from a selection of home-made pasta, inventive hot and cold buffets and the delicious but rather pricy desserts.

Dinner and Sleeping in Ljungskile

Villa Sjötorp (*no street address, just follow the signs*), Ljungskile, **t/f** (0522) 201 74 (*expensive–moderate*). This calls itself a boarding house, but the name does no justice to the highly unusual wooden house that the owner Ellika Mogenfelt (granddaughter of its original architect) restored beautifully (10 bedrooms are individually decorated) with the help of artist friends, who were charged a low rent in exhange for fixing up the house over six summers in the 1990s. The idyllic setting close to a beach is matched by Ellika's culinary passion and strong belief in use of first-class ingredients from local fields and forests.

Ljungskile Turisthotell, Hälle Lider 9, **t** (0522) 200 39, **f** (0522) 200 30, *www.turisthotellet.nu* (*moderate*). The unfussy but clean rooms explain the good prices of this option, set in a former factory that was charmingly converted into a hotel in the spa heyday of the region in the 1920s.

Lyckorna Brygga, Strandvägen, **t** (0522) 222 55, **f** (0522) 222 54, *www.lyckornabrgga.com* (*moderate*). Relaxed waterside restaurant with imaginative use of local products, set in a former late-19th-century summer mansion.

Day 2: Herring and Watercolours

Morning: Take the E6 back south to Stenungsund, then turn right (west) on to route 169 and cross the bridge to the beautiful island of **Tjörn**, which together with Orust (across another fine bridge) is the largest of the islands in the Bohuslän archipelago (also known as the Golden Coast). In the southern corner of Tjörn, linked by yet another bridge, is the tiny island of **Klädesholmen**, where among the colourful hotch-potch of steeply inclined wooden houses is Sillebua, Sillgränd 8, t (0304) 673 308 (*open June–Aug 3–7*), a museum with displays on the history of the canned herring industry that was so vital to the region in the 19th century.

Lunch: On Klädesholmen or in Skärhamn, *see* below.

Afternoon: Back on Tjörn island, head to the small port of **Skärhamn**. The pink granite surroundings and natural pools of water are an unlikely setting for the conspicuously modern glass and new wood Nordiska Akvarellmuseet (Nordic Watercolour Museum), Södra Hamnen 6, t (0304) 600 080, *www.akvarellmuseet.org* (*open Sept–April Tues, Wed and Fri–Sun 12–5, Thurs 12–8; May–Sept Tues–Sun 11–6; closed Mon; adm*). Created to develop a forum for Nordic watercolour artists, the museum not only displays works of living painters but runs workshops for would-be artists. Then head north and cross the splendidly curved bridge, which has stunning views, to **Orust**, its indented coastline dotted with quaint fishing villages. The 178 route goes east to Ellös, from which a short car ferry takes you to a tiny island that despite its name, **Flatön**, is actually very hilly.

Dinner and Sleeping: In Flatön, *see* below.

Day 2

Lunch in Klädesholmen

Restaurang Salt & Sill Danmark, t (0304) 673 480, f (0304) 673 488 (*expensive*). Dainty dining right on the water. A starter of diced fillets of herring with Dijon mustard tartare is almost obligatory given that this is a canned herring island. Aquavit spirit helps you digest the fabulous chocolate truffles. *Closed Oct–mid-June.*

Lunch in Skärhamn

Restaurant Vatten & Café, Nordiska Akvarellmuseet, Södra Hamnen 6, t (0304) 670 087 (*moderate*). Spectacular setting over the water with outdoor seating on the museum jetty. Gourmet-style food at reasonable prices, prepared in an open-plan kitchen. The home-made vegetable soup is exquisite.

Dinner and Sleeping in Flatön

Handelsman Flink, Flatön, 474 91 Ellös, t (0304) 550 51, f (0304) 555 57 (*expensive*). If you have always wanted to live in a secluded, fir-tree-lined island with the benefits of the best of urban cuisine, this very special hotel, with a dozen simple but tasteful double rooms, is the place to go. The unique island setting means that competition for beds is virtually non-existent, though the hotel has 15 berths for sailing boats that want to spend the night in the tiny harbour. Much-loved folk singer Evert Taube famously spent his summers here composing some of his best-known songs just before the Second World War. Mementoes of his stay are apparent in the adjoining general store that still retains its 1912 furnishings and some old tin cans and brands that have long since disappeared. Activities include cycling, sailing, golf, paddling on a kayak, even axe-throwing. The charming family who run the hotel are also highly sophisticated chefs, rustling up delicacies like marinated haddock with seasonal vegetable ragout and *truffle vierge*, with speed and good humour. *Closed winter.*

Day 3: Seaquarium and Nordens Ark Zoo

Morning: After a morning swim and hearty breakfast at Handelmans Flink, it is a 10min drive to the shortest of ferry rides, to Fiskebäcksil, from where another ferry crosses the Gulmarn, Sweden's only genuine fjord, to the elegant and popular 19th-century summer resort of **Lysekil**, on the edge of the Stångenäset peninsula. Right in the middle of the town is the remarkable **Havets Hus** (House of the Sea), Strandvägen, *www.havetshus.com* (*open Feb–mid-June 10–4; mid-June–Aug 10–6; Aug–Nov 10–4; closed Dec and Jan; adm*). Here you can walk through a tunnel aquarium while all varieties of local fish, like Atlantic mackerel, herring, topknot, lemon sole and even the spotted dogfish, swim unheedingly above and around you. Then take road 162 north to Hallinden, turn off on to the 171, follow the Abyfjorden around to Aby and head across west for **Bovallstrand** on the coast for lunch.

Lunch: In Bovallstrand, *see below*.

Afternoon: Retrace your steps inland via Tossene to **Aby**, the site for **Nordens Ark**, Åby säteri (*open Jan–Mar and Nov–Dec 10–4; April–mid-June and mid-Aug–Oct 10–5; mid-June–mid-Aug 10–7; adm*), an animal sanctuary for endangered species. Depending on the season, it's possible to get a glimpse of a snow leopard, a white fox or a mini panda, especially at feeding times. Even if the animals are hiding, the surrounding forested mountains and green enclosures are spectacular, and for colder weather there is a café-restaurant and a souvenir shop. Afterwards, head back north via Hamburgsund along the coast of smooth pinkish granite rock to **Fjällbacka**.

Dinner and Sleeping: In Fjällbacka, see below.

Day 3

Lunch in Bovallstrand

Bryggcafet, Hamnen, Bovallstrand, **t** (0523) 510 65, **f** (0523) 510 41, *www.bryggcafet.com* (*expensive–moderate*). Ulrika and Bosse Ifver, who have run this harbourside restaurant since 1989, have lavished loving attention on both the fresh fish- and shellfish-dominated menus and on the décor, such as the window in the wooden floor of the restaurant through which fish can be viewed swimming past. *Closed Jan and Feb*.

Dinner and Sleeping in Fjällbacka

Stora Hotellet, Galärbacken, **t** (0523) 310 03, **f** (0523) 31093, *www.storahotellet-fjallbacka.se* (*very expensive–expensive*). A pricy choice that reflects the attention and imagination that has been bestowed on the 1997 refurbishment of this centrally located hotel. 'Around the world in twenty-three rooms' is the theme of the rooms, each of which tells through its décor a different story of a distant location or traveller like Casablanca, Marco Polo, Havanna, Buenos Aires or Sheba. The hotel's patron saint is appropriately the former globe-trotting Captain Klassen, whose favourite ports, explorers and lady-friends are also embedded in the décor. The **Galley Pub** serves up predominantly fish dishes, some from fishing trips arranged for seafaring guests.

Pensionat Oscar II, Ingrid Bergmans Torg 2, **t** (0523) 322 10, *www.oscar-2.com* (*moderate–inexpensive*). One of the best bargains along the Gold Coast, especially given the charming wooden construction, its central location, restaurant that specializes on fish and stunning views. It also has a lively bar.

Storm Kök & Nattclub, Allé gatan 1, **t** (0523) 324 25 (*inexpensive*). Thai-inspired meals for younger, more informal crowd. Bands sometimes play on the nightclub's stage.

Day 4: Ingrid Bergman, Vikings and Oysters

Morning: Meander through the twisting streets to admire some of the intricate carpentry of **Fjällbacka**'s white wooden houses that face the sea from a sheltered harbour. At the foot of a ravine called Kungskliftan (King's Cliff) is a small square with a vaguely recognizable bust of Ingrid Bergman, who chose this town in the last years of her life as a summer retreat; the town has toyed with the idea of creating a museum in honour of the actress. The church, built in 1882, is worth a visit both for its beautifully simple and tranquil interior and its sweeping views of the village. Afterwards, head along the winding road south to **Hamburgsund** for lunch.

Lunch: In Hamburgsund, *see* below.

Afternoon: Step back 1,000 years by visiting the **Viking Town** 2km south of Hamburgsund in Hornbore By, Rörvik 617, **t** (0525) 345 40, **f** (0525) 33530, *www.hornboreby.o.se*, which is being constructed as a joint project between the Archaeological Museum in Stavanger, Norway (*see* p.177), and professional experts from the University of Göteborg. So far there's a longhouse, a smithy, a harbour with a boathouse and a Viking ship. Then retrace your steps back through Fjällbacka and carry on north along route 163 to another pretty Golden Coast fishing village, **Grebbestad**, to take a stroll along the jetty, swim in the sea, catch the arrival of oysters or make an appointment (**t** (0525) 610 60) to tour the Grebbestad Brewery, located in an old canning factory where genuine Böhuslan beer is brewed in copper vats.

Dinner and sleeping: In Grebbestad, and the nearby town of Tanumshede (take the 163 route from Grebbestad), *see* below.

Day 4

Lunch in Hamburgsund

Skalhuset, Hamburgsund, **t** (0523) 339 44, *www.skalhuset.com* (*expensive–moderate*). Look out for the small pier named Skalhuset at the foot of an empty cliff called the Castle. Lunch is based on the day's catch of lobster, ocean crayfish or mussels. On the veranda right near the water, enjoy a Japanese-inspired meal with fish and vegetables arranged as a checkerboard.

Dinner in Grebbestad

Pelles Rökeri Restaurang & Café, Östra Kajen Grundstund, **t** (0523) 212 74, *www.pelles rokeri.se* (*moderate*). A well-priced evening eaterie in bright red wooden house with veranda overlooking the water. Fish and chips or a chilli hamburger.

Restaurang Cajutan, Strandvägen 5, **t** (0523) 610 20, *www.cajutan.com* (*moderate*). Much care has been taken in recreating the experience of eating in a wooden boat. The menu is unusually varied, from a fresh fish stew through seafood pasta to chicken wings.

Greby's, Strandvägen 1, **t** (0523) 140 00, **f** (0523) 102 60 (*moderate*). As you would expect from a former canning factory from 1901 that is now an informal, popular waterside restaurant. A bar and adjoining nightclub guarantees a lively atmosphere.

Dinner and Sleeping in Tanumshede

Restaurant & Hotel Tanums Gestgifveri, Apoteksvägen 7, **t** (0523) 290 10, **f** (0523) 295 71, *www.tanumsgestgifveri.com* (*expensive*). In two large houses built in rustic rococo style, and smaller annexes on the grounds, this inn has been serving travellers, including the current king, since 1663. The current owners, the Öster family, are no longer required, as were past innkeepers, to act as jurymen during the local trials that used to take place in the old court house, complete with prison cells, next to the inn. Fine cooking in the old-fashioned dining room is now their main focus.

Day 5: Ancient Rock Carvings and a Fairytale Ending

Morning: Down the road from Tanumshede is the fascinating **Vitlycke Museum**, Västerby, *www.vitlycke.bohusmus.se* (*open April–Sept 10–6; Oct–Dec Thurs–Sun 11–5; Jan–Mar by arrangement; adm*), a spacious wooden building opened in 1998 to try to explain the fascinating Bronze Age carvings located on the slope of smooth rock surfaces in the region that have recently been added to the UNESCO World Heritage List. Before scaling the rocks across the road to identify the scratched images that include the delicately called 'bridal couple', it is useful to gen up with a brief lecture, slideshow or exhibition in the museum. There is also an outdoor exhibition, which, with the assistance of some 'actors', aims to show life as it was in the Bronze Age.

Lunch: In Tanumshede, *see* below.

Afternoon: Take the E6 motorway south towards **Uddevalla**, the site of an ugly shopping mall complex just off the motorway. Once in Uddevalla, there's another chance to return to the past at the **Bohuslän Museum**, Museigatan 1, *www.bohusmus.se* (*open Tues–Thurs 10–8, Fri–Sun 10–4, closed Mon except May–end Aug*). This is an opportunity to get an overview of Bohuslän history and, honouring Swedish museums' penchant for interactive experiences, you can call in on the fisher-folk who moved in as the Ice Age ended, visit a traditional peasant cottage or peep into the skipper's galley. Afterwards, continue down the E6 until just after Ljungskile and take the 167 route east to Lilla Edet, where you look for signs for **Thorskogs Slott**, a beautiful setting for dinner even if you can't afford to stay over (*book in advance*).

Dinner and Sleeping: In Thorskogs Slott or Lilla Edet, *see* below.

Day 5

Lunch in Tanumshede

Restaurant & Hotel Tanums Gestgifveri (*see* Day 4).

Restaurant Skålgropen, Vitlycke Museum, Västerby, **t** (0525) 209 50, *www.vitlycke. bohusmus.se* (*moderate*). The restaurant in the museum prides itself on serving up 'Bronze Age' dishes, which basically means the emphasis is on organic products.

Dinner and Sleeping in Thorskogs Slott or Lilla Edet

Thorskogs Slott, Västerlanda, **t** (0520) 661 000, **f** (0520) 660 918, *www.thorskogsslott.se* (*very expensive–expensive*). If there is one place to splash out, this grand manor, resembling a mini-fairy castle, may be the place. Built in 1892 by shipyard magnate Petter Larson, the manor is not strictly open to the public since it was transformed into an elegant oasis for slow living (no TV sets in the individually designed rooms) by travel agents Lena and Tommy Johnson. Guests are asked to introduce themselves when they arrive, a bit intimidating given that past visitors include George and Barbara Bush, Bonaire Button, Mikhail Gorbachev and John Major. The procedure is made easier with a complimentary glass of champagne and a tour of the manor. Activities include fishing, rock-climbing, gold, croquet, swimming or simply sampling hot scones and freshly baked cakes in the elegant Orangery tea room. Gourmet-style dining is relaxed as guests can choose to eat in a variety of different rooms including the cellar, where they can help themselves to drinks at a bar (tabs are kept!).

Solveig Ekdahl, Uxås 20, Lilla Edet, **t** (0520) 650 053, *www.solveig.ekdahl.com* (*inexpensive*). If you can't afford to sleep in the manor, you could still dine there (book a week in advance) and disappear Cinderella-like at midnight to this enchanting and ridiculously low-priced bed and breakfast (as long as you don't mind sharing a bathroom).

Sweden: Malmö and Skåne

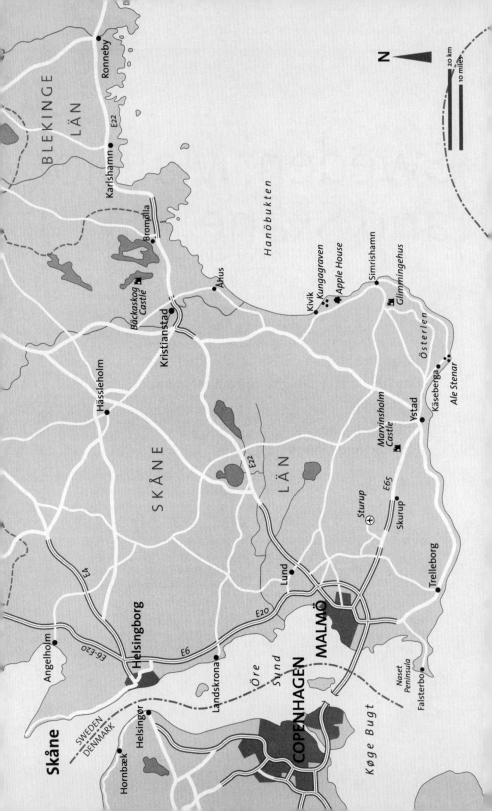

Malmö

Closer to the continental mainland than to the Swedish capital, Malmö has always been a city where European influences were distinctly palpable, and today even more so, following the opening in 2000 of the sensational 16km-long road and rail bridge over the Öresund Sound to Denmark, an architectural feat that has become a tourist attraction in itself. The locals never stop telling you what a difference the bridge has made, dramatically fast-forwarding the city's rather plodding progress of recent decades, creating a sudden burst of new bars, restaurants and revamped hotels. No longer a declining industrial hub, Malmö is discovering a new role as a welcoming leisure and shopping city, where travellers come to unwind at fairly reasonable prices. And Copenhagen is a mere half-hour train ride away.

The cobbled streets of the old town, the canals, the superb parks and the close sandy beaches were always there; the city simply needed a spurt of continental curiosity, particularly from its previously uninterested Danish cousins, to kick-start an urban regeneration that is most visible in the ongoing public projects around the harbour area. The new university has contributed to the new vibrant, upbeat feel of the city, while a recent wave of immigrants has added a cosmopolitan layer to areas like Möllevångstorget, with its bohemian bars and restaurants.

Links with Denmark were not always this friendly, particularly for a few hundred years after the Middle Ages, when political control of the Öresund Straits, and of the agriculturally rich counties that today form Skåne, Blekinge and Halland, was a paramount obsession for both Sweden and Denmark. Initially the Danes enjoyed the upper hand, overseeing the city's birth in the late 13th century when the abundance of silver herring along Skåne's coasts (the city's name comes from 'Malmhauger', which roughly translates as 'sand heaps') transformed it into Denmark's second most important city. Malmö's growth on the back of salted herring exports was consolidated by Eric of Pomerania, King of Denmark (1412–39), King Regent of the Kalmar Union in Norway (1412–42) and in Sweden (1396–1439), when he built the rather unprepossessing Renaissance castle today located west of the centre. He also gave Malmö the rather more attractive gold and red griffin of his own family crest, still the coat of arms for a city that proudly proclaims its independent spirit.

It wasn't until after several more bloody battles, and a fierce onslaught by Swedish king Karl X, that the Danes were finally forced to cede Malmö, along with surrounding counties, to Sweden under the 1658 Roskilde peace treaty. After a period of relative neglect from the distant capital, Malmö began a new period of revival in 1775 when local tobacco merchant Frans Suell had the foresight to develop a harbour that would take advantage of the city's location between the Baltic Sea and the Atlantic Ocean. The expansive Kockums Shipyard emerged, converting the Sound into one of the busiest waterways in the 19th century. There is a bronze likeness of Suell, to whom the city owes its late-19th-century opulence, opposite the station on Norra Vallgatan.

It took Malmö some time to come to terms with an inexorable industrial decline in the second half of the 20th century. The dramatic changes to the Kockums Shipyard today, much of which is being converted into commercial and residential property,

Malmö

N

Öresund

500 metres
500 yards

Kallbadhuset

JÖRGEN KOCKSGATAN

Central
Station

ÖSTRA PROMENADEN

DROTTNINGGATAN

KUNGSGATAN

CAROLI BRON

DROTTNING-TORGET

GRÖNEGATAN

STORA KVARNGATAN

Rooseum

RÖRSJÖGATAN

FÖRENINGSGATAN

ÖSTERGATAN

St Petri kyrka

Rådhus

GASVERKSG.

RUNDELSG.

SNAPPERSG.

DJÄKNEGATAN

BALTZARS-GATAN

STORA NYGATAN

STORA STUDENTG.

HADEGATAN

GAMLA
STADEN

KALENDE-GATAN

STRAUD. HAMBURGG.

SÖDRA VALLGATAN

SÖDERGATAN

FÖRSTA.

AMIRALSGATAN

Konserthuset

KUNGSGATAN

BERGSGATAN

MÖLLEVÅNGEN

Folketspark

AMIRALSGATAN

KRISTIANSTADSGATAN

MÖLLEVÅNGSGATAN

MÖLLEVÅNGS-TORGET

BERGSGATAN

HAMNG.

STORTORGET

MÄSTER
JOHANSGATAN

LILLA
TORG

PISKMAK.
NILSG.

JAKOB
NILSG.

GUSTAV
ADOLFS
TORG

Form/
Design
Centre

TORGGATAN

SÖDRA FÖRSTADSGATAN

Victoria
Theatre

KAPTENSGATAN

STORGATAN

TRIANGELN

St Johannes
kyrka

ST JOHANNESGATAN

Shopping
Centre

PILDAMMSVÄGEN

NORRA

GRÅBRÖDERSG.

ENGELBREKSG.

GRYNBOGATAN

SLOTTSGATAN

STORA NYGATAN

DROTTNINGGATAN

DAVIDSHALLSGATAN

HOLMGATAN

DAVIDS-HALLS-TORG

POL

City
Library

FERSENS VÄGEN

REGEMENTSGATAN

FÖRENINGSGATAN

Konsthall

CITADELLSVÄGEN

MALMÖHUSVÄGEN

Slottsmöllen

Malmöhus

Kungsparken

Slottsparken

KUNG OSCARS VÄGEN

REGEMENTSGATAN

ERIK DAHLBERGSGATAN

CARL GUSTAFS VÄGEN

KÖPENHAMNSVÄGEN

MARIEDALSVÄGEN

LIMHAMNSVÄGEN

RIBERSBORG

TESSINSVÄGEN

REGEMENTSGATAN

MAJOR NILSSONSGATAN

KÖPENHAMNSVÄGEN

JOHN ERICSSONSVÄGEN

ERIKSLUSTVÄGEN

St Andreas
kyrka

REGEMENTSGATAN

LIMHAMNSVÄGEN

ERIKSLUSTVÄGEN

Getting There

By Air

Malmö is served by two airports: **Ryanair** flies to Sturup, **t** 0771 777 777, *www.skane trafiken.com*, 30km south, and **easyJet** flies to Copenhagen Kastrup, **t** 00 45 324 747 47, *www.cph.dk*.

Getting from the Airport

From Sturup, the airport shuttle takes you to Malmö centre in 40mins. A one-way ticket costs SEK70. An airport shuttle taxi (**t** (040) 949 9494) costs SEK250–300. From Copenhagen Kastrup, the Öresund train to Malmö Central Station takes about 20mins and costs SEK80. Trains leave every 20mins from 6am to midnight, and once an hour during the night.

For train/bus info, contact Skånetrafiken, **t** 0771 777 777, *www.skanetrafiken.com*.

By Bus

Bus 999, **t** (046) 160 100, *www.linje999.se*, runs a daily service between Malmö and Copenhagen Central Station. The main bus terminal is outside the train station in Malmö.

By Train

Malmö has daily train connections with Copenhagen and Oslo. You can travel from Malmö to Stockholm in 4hrs on the high-speed X2000 train.

By Car

The 2000 opening of the Öresund Bridge (*www.oeresundsbron.com*), the 16km-long road link between Copenhagen and Malmö, has greatly facilitated car trips to Europe.
E22: to Kalmar or via Trelleborg to Rostock.
E20: to Copenhagen and other parts of Denmark.
E6: to Göteborg (Gothenburg) and Oslo.

Getting Around

Malmö's main attractions are all within walking distance of one another, so sightseeing on foot is the best option. The tourist office at Central Station provides maps. You are unlikely to hop on a **bus** in the main centre, but for longer journeys you can buy tickets on the bus. The best bet is to buy the Malmö Card (*see* 'Tourist Information', below). The bus station is behind the train station.

By Taxi

Some taxi companies run a set-price system within Malmö, but the tourist office recommends agreeing a price before getting into a cab. Trustworthy companies include:
Taxi Skåne, **t** (040) 330 330.
Taxi 97, **t** (040) 979 797.
Limhamns Taxi, **t** (040) 150 000.

By Bike

Numerous cycle paths and general flatness make the city ideal for cycling.
Cykelkliniken, Regementsgatan 12, **t** (040) 611 666. Bike hire.
Fridhems Cykelaffär, Tessins väg 13, **t** (040) 260 335. Bike hire.

Cards and Passes

Most places in the Skåne region around Malmö can be reached by train or bus within an hour; for information contact **t** 0771 777 777, *www.skanetrafiken.com*. The main bus station for regional buses is beside Central Station. The **Öresund Rundt ticket** (Around the Sound by Train) is a useful circular ticket that includes the train journey between Malmö and Copenhagen and across the Öresund bridge, and the ferry from Helsingborg to Helsingør. It also offers various discounts for museums, restaurants and hotels. The ticket costs SEK199 or SEK249, depending on how far you travel (children aged 6–16 travel for half-price). Contact Skånetrafiken, **t** 0771 777 777, *www.skanetrafiken.com*, or visit their office in Malmö, Helsingborg or Lund.

You can also buy a **Skåne Summer Card**, which covers bus and train travel in the region for 25 days between June 15 and Aug 15, with discounts to Dunkers Kulturhus, and concerts at Marvinsholm Castle. Buy it in Malmö Kund Center in Gustav Adolfs Torg, Lund station Kund Center, or Knutpunkten in Helsingborg.

Car Hire

Avis, at Sturup airport, **t** (040) 500 515; at Skeppsbron 13, **t** (040) 778 39.
Europcar, at Sturups airport, **t** (040) 500 260; at Nilsgatan 22, **t** (040) 716 40.

Hertz, at Sturups airport **t** (040) 500 257; at Jörgen Kocksgatan 1B, **t** (040) 330 770.
Sixt, at Sturups airport **t** (040) 405 000; at Thomssonsväg 1, **t** (040) 212 270.

Tourist Information

Malmö: Centralstationen 211, **t** (040) 341 200, *malmo.turism@malmo.se (open Oct–April Mon–Fri 9–5, Sat 10–2, closed Sun; May and Sept Mon–Fri 9–6, Sat and Sun 10–3; June–Aug Mon–Fri 9–7, Sat and Sun 10–5).* Stocks the handy *Malmö This Month* brochure, and sells the invaluable Malmö Card. You can also pick up a map suggesting a city walking tour. To book a hotel through Malmö Turism, call **t** (040) 109 210.

There is also a branch at **Skånegården**, a restored 19th-century farmhouse reached only from the road from Denmark, 800m on from the Öresund Bridge toll.

A **Malmö Card** is highly recommended, as it entitles you to free rides on local buses, free parking, and 20% discount on the train fare to Copenhagen. The card also includes free entry to Malmöhus Castle, Malmö museums and the Science and Maritime House and the casino, plus free sightseeing by bus. There are discounts on car (Hertz) and bike rental, pedal boats, a fishing tour, and selected concerts. 1 day SEK130, 2 days SEK160, 3 days SEK 190. Each card is valid for one adult and two children under 16 years of age.
Late pharmacy: Apoteket Gripen, Bergsgatan 48, **t** (040) 192 113 *(open 8am–12 midnight).*
Main post office: Skeppsbron 1 *(open Mon–Fri 11–2 and 3–5.30, Sat 10–1).*

Guided Tours

Guided sightseeing tours by bus *(5 June–5 Sept)*, lasting 90mins, depart daily at noon from Malmö Turism at Central Station. Adults SEK100, children SEK50. A scenic alternative is the 'Rundan' boat (**t** (040) 611 7488, *www. rundan.se*), a guided tour of the canals that circle the old city, lasting 45mins. The boat sails from the quay between the Savoy Hotel and Malmö Central Station on the hour.

Internet Cafes

Cyber Space, Engelbrektsgatan 13a. *Open daily 10–10; SEK44 per hour.*

Surfer's Paradise, Amiralsgatan 14. *Open Mon–Fri 10–midnight, Sat and Sun noon–midnight; SEK40 per hour.*
Library at Regementsgatan 3. *Open Mon–Thurs 10–7, Fri 10–6, Sat noon–4; free for 30mins.*

Festivals

The **Malmö Festival** takes place over a week in August, kicking off with an enormous traditional Swedish crayfish party, followed by music, dancing, poetry-reading, theatre performances and food-tastings.

Shopping

Shopping hours are Mon–Fri 10–6, Sat 10–3 (except for 'Long Saturday', every last Sat of the month, when the hours are 10–5). On Sundays most shops close all day except for department stores and shopping centres, which open roughly 12–4.

Sweden is famous for glassware, ceramics, arts and crafts, and the best place to get a taste for the latest designs is the **Form Design Centre**, Lilla Torg, **t** (040) 664 5150, *www. formdesigncenter.com*. Worth popping into in the same neighbourhood are **David Design**, **Designtorget**, **Filialaen** and **Olsson & Gerthel**.

For interesting gifts including miniatures, angels for doll's houses and replicas of ancient Nordic jewellery, try **Hökeriet**, Lilla Torg 9, or **Ålgamark**, Östra Rönneholmsvägen.

For more standard glassware and for all-in shopping, the biggest shopping centres are **Hansacompagniet**, **Gallerian** and **Triangeln**; the mid-level department chain **Åhléns** has two stores. These, along with boutiques, chain stores and sports stores, are mostly found in the pedestrianized area that runs from Stortorget, along Södergatan, across Gustav Adolfs Torg and across the canal, down Södra Förstadsgatan to Triangeln and Dalaplan. Antiques shops and second-hand bookshops are around Davidshalltorg and Davidshalls-gatan, next to Södra Förstadsgatan.

The most interesting food for picnics is found either at Saluhallen, the indoor food and delicacy market in Lilla Torg, or a bus ride or longer walk south to the bohemian district of Möllevångstorget, which has a lively fruit and vegetable market on the square.

Malmö **103**

Cheese-lovers should drop in at **Möllans Ost**, Bergsgatan 32, if only for a tasting.

Where to Stay

Malmö t (040) –

With a couple of exceptions, accommodation in central Malmö is on the expensive side, but don't be put off by the initial prices as even the top-flight hotels offer weekend packages, especially in summer when business travel is lowest. The tourist office also sells the useful Malmö Package, providing a double room in a central hotel, breakfast and Malmö Card, for SEK410 per person.

Scandic Kramer, Stortorget 7, t 693 5400, f 693 5411, www.scandic-hotels.com (very expensive). One of Malmö's stateliest hotels, carefully retaining its French manor exterior on the town's main square.

Hotel Mäster Johan, Mäster Johansgatan 13, t 664 6400, f 664 6401, www.masterjohan.se (very expensive). Classy hotel a block away from Lilla Torg, with an impressive Pillar Garden under a glass cupola.

Hilton Malmö City, Triangeln 2, t 693 4700, f 693 4711, www.hilton.com (very expensive). Towering, rather ugly complex in the less-historic downtown, with good views from the top. Popular for its late-night bar.

Mayfair Hotel, Adelgatan, t 101 620, f 101 625, www.mayfairtunneln.com (very expensive). Danish and Swedish royalty visited this building when it was the residence of the governor of Malmö. A taste of its medieval past can be sampled down in the medieval vaults of restaurant **Corfitz Källare**.

Clarion Hotel Malmö, Engelbreksgatan 16, t 710 29, f 304 406, www.choicehotels.se (expensive). Turn-of-the-20th-century hotel with new safari-themed interior. Fantastic breakfast spread that non-guests are recommended to visit.

First Hotel Garden, Baltzarsgatan 20, t 665 6200, f 665 6260, www.firsthotels.se (expensive–moderate). If it's not recommendation enough that Pele and the Brazilian national football team and the Beatles stayed here in the 1960s, guest rooms are in low-lying annexes surrounded by flowering gardens.

TeaterHotellet, Fersensväg, t 665 5800, f 665 5810, www.teaterhotellet.se (expensive–

moderate). Art-lovers will like this 44-room hotel, which has its own art gallery. Garners more artistic points by being close to the Malmö City Theatre and the City Art Hall.

First Hotel Jörgen Kock, Jörgen Kocksgatan 3, t 101 800, f 611 4433, www.firsthotels.com (expensive–moderate). A portside location behind the railway station, offering an alternative to the old city hotels but still a mere 10mins' walk from the heart of town.

Hotell Baltzar, Södergatan 20, t 665 5700, f 665 5710, www.baltzarhotel.se (expensive–moderate). Family-run, central, proud of its period furniture and chandeliers.

Hotel Astoria, Gråbrödersgatan 7, t 786 60, f 788 70, www.astoria.gs2.com (moderate). You get fewer frills in this family-run hotel than in its central neighbours, but the prices are also lower. Two apartments available.

Eating Out

Malmö t (040) –

'Lots of food, good food, and food at the right time,' goes an old Skåne saying, and that aptly describes the plethora of eateries that have multiplied in the region's capital to cater for the fast-growing taste for eating out in stylish surroundings. International cuisines have been taken up with relish, but visitors should try not to miss out on the rise of home-grown chefs who are getting maximum flavour out of Skåne's rich agricultural heritage and coast. Even the top end of the market offers good-value fixed lunch prices.

Gamla Staden

Nowhere is the eating out boom more visible than around Lilla Torg, where bars and restaurants jostle back to back. Saluhallen, the indoor market, offers a blend of world cuisine.

Johan P, Saluhallen, Lilla Torg, Landbygatan 3, t 971 818 (very expensive). If you can't afford to dine at one of Malmö's best fish restaurants, look out for fish soup specials at the indoor market end of the restaurant.

Årstiderna, Stortorget, Frans Suellsgatan 3, t 230 910 (very expensive). Exclusive dining in the vaulted cellars of famous 16th-century mayor Jörgen Kock's house. A French twist to traditional Swedish ingredients.

Spot, Stora Nygatan 33, **t** 120 203 (*expensive*). The best place to eat Italian. A choice of delicious takeaways for a picnic, too. *Closed eves.*

Victors, Lilla Torg 1, **t** 127 670, **f** 127 698 (*expensive–moderate*). A place for the hip lunch crowd. If in a hurry, you can slurp the excellent fish soup of the day at the bar. Lively venue in the evenings.

La Roche, Vin & Tapas, Lilla Torg, **t** 306 636, *www.laroche.se* (*expensive–moderate*). Slightly pricy tapas but well worth it for the atmosphere and the wine selection.

Rådhuskällaren, Stortorget, Kyrkogatan 6, **t** 790 20 (*expensive–moderate*). Also set in vaulted cellars (of the town hall) but a slightly more populist atmosphere and leaner prices, especially at lunchtime.

Trappaner, Långårdsgatan 8, **t** 579 750, *www.trappaner.se* (*expensive–moderate*). Intimate boutique dining in a quiet part of the old town. Emphasis on local ingredients served freshly without fuss. Very attentive service. Don't skip the intricate desserts.

Izakaya Koi, Lilla Torg 5, **t** 757 00 (*moderate*). If you ever tire of the wide selection of regional fish specialities, try the relatively inexpensive selection of sushi, nigiri, hand rolls, maki and sashimi by the piece or plate.

Indian Side, Lilla Torg 7, **t** 307 744 (*moderate*). For a more spicy option, this serves traditional Indian food. Has outdoor seating.

Short Stop, **t** 303 509, Saluhallen, Lilla Torg (*inexpensive*). Sit at the lively bar for better-than-average fast food and atmosphere.

Outside Gamla Staden

Atmosfär, Fersensväg 4, **t** 125 077 (*very expensive*). Close to the City Library, this tastefully decorated restaurant is just small enough to live up to its reputation as the most intimate gourmet dining experience in town. There's a fixed-price menu of three, five or seven dishes, and when he can, owner-chef Henrik comes out to chat to customers.

Hipp, Kalendegatan 12, **t** 974 030, **f** 974 031, *www.hipp.se* (*very expensive*). Visit this gourmet-style dining establishment if only to peep at the impeccably restored building that also houses the Malmö Theatre of Drama. The high elegance extends to a nightclub. *Closed Sun and Mon.*

Skeppsbron 2, Börshuset, **t** 306 202 (*expensive*). Another example of Sweden's modern, inventive cuisine in an attractive setting opposite the railway station, with views of the sea and canals. Busy on Saturdays.

Salt & Brygga, Sundspromenaden 7, **t** 611 5940 (*expensive*). Prides itself on its eco-friendly concept, from the modern furnishings to the cooking. One of the first restaurants in the new Western harbour area, and the view over the Öresund is stunning.

St Markus Vinkällare (Wine Cellar), Stadt Hamburgsgatan 2, **t** 306 820 (*expensive*). In the bar-packed Stadt Hamburg area, offering a luxurious buffet in a vaulted cellar. There's a dance hall above the restaurant.

Olgas, Pildammsvägen, **t** 125 526 (*expensive–moderate*). Open-air restaurant, well-known for its views of the lake in Pildammsparken. The traditional Swedish menu is also tasty.

Lemongrass, Grynbodgatan 9, **t** 306 979 (*expensive–moderate*). Brightening up a quiet part of the old town, the open-plan setting serves Asian fusion cooking nicely presented with friendly service. *Closed lunch.*

Brogatan Bar & Brasserie, Brogatan 12, **t** 307 717 (*expensive–moderate*). A lively meeting place popular for its international lunch menu, dinner or just a drink. *Closed July.*

Café Konsthallen, Malmö Konsthall (Malmö Art Gallery), St Johannesgatan 7 (*expensive–moderate*). A place to enjoy art and gastronomy in a wonderful garden setting. Specializes in vegetarian and fish dishes but carnivores also catered for. *Closed eves.*

Skogströms Kök Butik, Major Nilssonsgatan 6, **t** 917 601 (*moderate*). Off the tourist radar in a rather nondescript residential district, this excellent lunch place is run by a young, famous local chef. Great place for takeaway picnic food on the way to the town beach.

Tempo Bar & Kök, Södra Skolgatan 30, **t** 126 021 (*moderate–inexpensive*). Good value, quirky dishes in buzzing atmosphere.

Restaurant Hai, Davidshallstorg 5, **t** 505 005 (*moderate–inexpensive*). A stylish sushi bar close to a popular cinema.

Krua Thai, Möllevångstorget 14, **t** 122 287 (*moderate–inexpensive*). A family-owned Thai restaurant for the lower-end budget, in the bohemian Möllevångstorget area.

Cafés

Café Siesta, Hjorttackegatan 1. 1950s décor aimed at the arty crowd.

Aldo's, Saluhallen, Lilla Torg. Prides itself on its international award-winning coffee. A wide assortment of Italian cakes and ice-cream.

Café Rooseum, Gasverksgatan 22, Rooseum. Modern art and *panini*.

Coffee Maniac, Davidhalls Torg 3. A local favourite, in a quiet square.

Espresso House. A home-grown chain that is more personal (and serves better coffee) than its multinational rivals. Three main locations: Södra Förstadsgatan, Skomakaregatan (near Lilla Torg), and the Hansacompagniet shopping centre.

Restaurang & Café Gustav Adolf, Gustav Adolfs Torg 43. A venerable institution (established 1902). Try the home-made drinking chocolate.

Slottsträdgårdscaféet, Slottsparken, the Castle Park, behind Malmöhus Castle. An impossibly tiny café where you can enjoy home-made carrot cake surrounded by flowers, herbs and vegetables. *Summer only*.

Café Glassfabriken, Kristianstadsgatan 16. Student haunt in the trendy Möllevångstorget district. A serious hanging-out venue.

Entertainment and Nightlife

Music, Theatre and Dance

The **Malmö Theatre of Drama** has several stages: Hipp and Odromen at Kalendegatan 12, and Intiman at Östra Rönneholmsvägen 20. For tickets, call **t** (040) 208 610.

The **Malmö Symphony Orchestra** (MSO) is an orchestra of excellent repute. It plays about 70 concerts a year at the Konserthuset, Föreningsgatan 35, **t** (040) 343 500.

Malmö Music Theatre, Östra Rönneholmsvägen 20. Classic and contemporary opera, musicals, local and international. For tickets call **t** (040) 208 500, Mon–Fri 9–5. Ask about performances of the Skåne Dance Theatre (Skånes Dansteater).

Casino Cosmopol, Slottsgatan 33, **t** 664 1800, *www.casinocosmopol.se*.

Pubs and Bars

The Pickwick Pub and Gränden, Malmborgsgatan 5, **t** (040) 233 266. A more standard British pub with quiz nights on Wednesdays.

Paddy's Irish Pub and Restaurant, Kalendegatan 7, **t** (040) 786 00. Serves Guinness. Live music at weekends.

Mello Yello Bar and Restaurant, Lilla Torg, **t** (040) 304 525. Popular with over-25s. Be prepared to fight for space.

Moosehead Bar and Restaurant, Lilla Torg, **t** (040) 120 423. For a younger crowd. Thai-inspired food served.

Victor's Bar and Restaurant, Lilla Torg, **t** 12 76 70. Good for cocktails.

Scandic Hotel St Jörgen, Södergatan 20, **t** 693 4600. Two popular bars: the Times Bar, a popular post-work gathering place; and the Tahonga Bar Malmö, a cocktail bar.

Pubs and Restaurants with Live Music

Kulturbolaget, Bergsgatan 18. Rock club with a couple of live concerts every week: rock, pop, blues. Turns into a nightclub at weekends.

Jeriko, Spångatan 38. For music aficionados. Jazz concerts, world music and folk music concerts. Nightclub at weekends.

Mattsson's Musikpub. Göran Olsgatan 1, opposite St Petri kyrka. The oldest pub in Malmö, popular with over-30s. Thurs and Fri are traditional dance nights, Sat live rock 'n' roll.

Paddy's, Kalendegatan 7. Pub with live rock and blues concerts in weekends.

Nyhavn, Möllevångens Torget, a bar-pub in the trendy southern district.

Fyran, Snapperupsgatan 4, well-established gay club. *Open weekends 11–3.*

Nightclubs

Club Privé, Malmborgsgatan 7, near Gustav Adolfs Torg. Young, hip scene. Four floors. *Weekends only.*

Étage, Stortorget 6. A more relaxed crowd. Two dance floors – one for latest dance craze, one for 'classics'. *Open Mon and Thurs until 4am, Fri and Sat until 5 am.*

Harry's, Södergatan 14. A restaurant that turns into a nightclub at weekends. Mixed crowd.

Hipp, Kalendegatan 12. Beautifully restored venue for the 20s crowd. *Weekends only.*

Jörgen, Kocksgatan 7a, behind Central Station. Reputedly the biggest nightclub in Scandinavia. *Open weekends only.*

Restaurant Stadt, Stadt Hamburgsgatan 2, near Gustav Adolfs Torg. For the 30s crowd. Jacket and tie obligatory. *Open Thurs until 2am, Fri and Sat until 3am.*

show that the town has woken up to its enormous tourist potential as a gateway between Sweden and the continent, as well as the first stop *en route* to the beech-forested coastline that extends east and west, the wealth of châteaux and manor houses that dot the undulating hills of the farmland interior, and to nearby urban centres like the university town of Lund and the historic port of Helsingborg.

Gamla Staden

Visitors emerge from the weighty exuberance of the train station, where the tourist office is located, to be greeted by the canal that neatly encases Gamla Staden, the old city. It's only a five-minute walk across the canal down Hamngatan towards **Stortorget** (Central Square) where the medieval town once stood before it was torn down in the early 16th century to make way for it. The market square's rather vast size, the showy mix of architectural styles and the presence of two flashy hotels create rather a forbidding impression, not tempered by the statue of Swedish liberator Karl X on his horse in the middle of the square.

More welcoming and certainly eye-catching is the intricate exterior of the **Rådhuset** (town hall), with its red and gold flag flapping above it. Built in 1546 for the city's powerful mayor, Jörgen Kock, it is the oldest building in the square, although the fussy Dutch Renaissance design is the result of several revisions. The interior is better preserved (*for guided tours, check with the tourist office*). The reasonable lunch menu at the tavern in the cellars also gives you a taste of late-16th-century revelry. South of the town hall towards Södergatan, the principal pedestrianized shopping street that runs till it hits the other end of the canal, is the city's oldest pharmacy, **t Apoteket Lejonet**, with a splendid Art Nouveau interior; tours can be arranged inside the still-working chemist (**t** (040) 712 35).

East of Rådhus is **St Petri kyrka** (*open Mon–Fri 8–6, Sat 9–6, Sun 10–6*), its so-called Baltic Gothic style a reminder of the Germanic interest in the city during the 14th century. Not much of its pre-Reformation decorations are left: a whitewashing of the entire edifice in 1555, and the scraping away of all former frescoes in the 1850s, saw to that. The Merchant's Chapel on the side provides a hint of the riotous colour that must have originally lit up the church.

Slightly out of the way in this eastern quarter but a must for fans of contemporary art is the **Rooseum**, Gasverksgatan, **t** (040) 121 716, *www.rooseum.se* (*open Wed–Fri 2–8, Sat and Sun 12–6; closed Mon and Tues; adm*). If a VW Beetle turned upside down and converted into a swing proves too bizarre, you can always admire the remarkable restoration work of the 1900-built power station that houses the museum. This quarter of the city is mostly of interest for its shopping, but there is one other reason for lingering: **Ebbas Hus**, Snapperupsgatan 10, **t** (040) 344 423 (*open Wed and Sat only, 12–4*), the city's tiniest museum and a fascinating insight into a 100-year-old home.

Just visible southwestwards from Stortorget is the delightful **Lilla Torg** (Little Square). Added on to Stortorget in the late 16th century to accommodate the overspill of the crowded larger square, it is Lilla Torg, with its row of mid-19th-century brick and timber warehouses, that nowadays draws the multitudes. As one resident fondly remarks, it serves as everyone's living room, not just for its tightly packed bars and restaurants that jostle for outdoor space in the hot weather, but for the hive of activities it miraculously holds: outdoor skating in winter, volleyball in a transported sandpit in summer. At one end of the square is the **Saluhallen**, the sole remnant of the covered market that filled the square until the 1960s, and a good place to pick up delicate morsels for a picnic. At the other end is the **Hedman Estate**, made up of five buildings built between 1597 and 1894, all immaculately restored. Under an arch and into a courtyard entrance are several boutiques, a little café (Smaklöken) and the **Form Design Centre, t** (040) 664 5150, *www.formdesigncenter.com (open Tues–Fri 11–5, Thurs 11–6, Sat 10–4, Sun 12–4; closed Mon and Wed)*. Glance around the various temporary exhibits of design, arts and crafts and browse through the latest design magazines over a cup of coffee.

Malmöhus and Surroundings

Further west from Lilla Torg is **Kungsparken** (King's Park), the leafy setting of the Malmöhus castle and adjoining museums and site of the recently opened casino (Slottsparken 33, **t** (040) 664 1800). Rather than heading straight to the main entrance by the Restaurang Kungsparken, weave through the quiet, cobbled streets around Jakob Nilsgatan and peer discreetly through the windows of their low houses for a hint of cottage life in the heart of a city.

From there, the Citadellsvägen approach provides the most dramatic view of the low, fortified **Malmöhus, t** (040) 344 437, *www.malmö. se/museer (open daily 12–4; adm)*. With its two circular keeps, grassy ramparts and wide moat, Scandinavia's oldest surviving Renaissance castle is hardly inviting, and it's no wonder that for a while it served as a prison – Mary Queen of Scots' third husband, Bothwell, was one of its most notable inmates. Some of the castle's austere interior is still open for visitors, but since 1937 most of the complex is used for a hotch-potch of fairly standard exhibits covering natural and industrial history, science and technology, and arts and crafts. A more intriguing exhibition at the Sheriff's Apartment is 'Power Over People', which tells the story of how the people's fate has always been decided by those in power. The queues are longer for the flight simulator and the real submarine in the Science and Maritime House.

Just outside the castle, step straight into the living past along the short walkway off **Malmöhusvägen**, where traditional fishing shacks sell assorted fresh and smoked fish.

A stroll through the attractively landscaped Kungsparken, which spills into elegant Slottsparken, is a pleasure, and also the fastest route to the fabulous **Malmö City Library**, Kung Oscars Vägen, **t** (040) 440 8500, *www.stadsbibliotek.org (open Mon–Thurs 10–8, Fri 10–6, Sat and Sun 12–4)*. The old library, whose castle-like shape was used as barracks during the Second World War, is a fine specimen of the National Romantic style prevalent in Sweden at the turn of the 20th century. And, designed by renowned Danish architect in 1997, the library's recent extension, 'The Calendar of Light', with its clever, open-plan use of space and light, must be the envy of public libraries worldwide. It even has special music rooms where you can tinkle away at an electric piano with headphones on.

Further south down **Fersensvägen** are examples of the splendid mansion blocks and impressive secondary schools built on the back of late-19th-century industrial wealth; this is the scene for the city's cultural quarter, peppered with antiques and curiosity shops. In a straight line down from the library is the city theatre and further east is **Konsthall** (Art Hall), St Johannesgatan 7, **t** (040) 341 293, *www.malmokonsthall.malmo. se* (*open Thurs–Tues 11–5, Wed 11–9*). The single-storey concrete and glass structure shows vast contemporary paintings in temporary exhibitions. Further north as the crow flies, by shopping street Södra Förstadsgatan, is the Art Nouveau-style **Victoria Theatre**, and completing the imaginary artistic square further east beyond the Triangeln square is the **Konserthuset**, the concert hall on the corner of Förenings-gatan and Amiralsgatan.

South to Möllevångstorget

From Konserthuset, it's a 15-minute-long amble south down Amiralsgatan to Sweden's oldest existing public park, **Folketspark** (*open May–Aug daily; April and Sept weekends only; closed Oct–April*). Browse at the fleamarket stalls, take a ride on the huge Ferris wheel, or walk through the English-style gardens to the Möllevången exit, which paves the way to the vast **Möllevångstorget** square. This is the haunt of the city's growing Middle Eastern and Asian population and, increasingly, of trendy local university students attracted to the cheaper bars and restaurants, the less regi-mented atmosphere and the large, warehouse-style flats. One good place to drop in for a laid-back coffee and a changing menu of independent movie screenings is a former ice-cream factory, **Café Glassfabriken**, Kristianstadsgatan 16 (*open Tues–Sun 10–8; closed Mon*).

City of the Future in the Western Harbour

Locals and visitors used to rush past the industrial mass that composed the city's waterfront area to reach the long stretch of sandy beaches beyond, but the emerging apartment blocks of the so-called **Framtistaden** (City of the Future) in the Western Harbour are now reason enough for a stop. While the newness of the eco-friendly blocks have an inevitable unlived-in blandness about them, there is growing buzz about this new urban stretch, not least the **Turning Torso**, a spectacular 187m-high skyscraper designed by renowned Spanish architect Santiago Calatrava.

Further along, as the urban front gives way to a long sandy beach, dunes and grass-land, is the picturesque **Ribersborgs Kallbadhuset** bathing house (take bus 20 from the train station; *open May–Aug Mon–Fri 8.30–7, Sat and Sun 8.30–6; Sept–April Mon–Fri 12–7, Sat and Sun 9–4; adm*) Built in 1898, this is a popular destination for swimmers and naturists, and a favourite for its wood-fired sauna (*open May–Aug 11–7, Sat and Sun 9–4; adm*). In the colder months, it's still worth a visit for its cosy café (*open 10–4*), from which wafts a strong scent of home-made buns, and for the views of the sand dunes.

Outside the Centre

Foteviken Viking Museum

The guests, who do not follow the rules of Foteviken, will be sentenced to disgrace and expulsion from Foteviken.

Visitors approach **Foteviken Viking Museum**, Halörsvägen, **t** (040) 456 849, *www. fotoviken.se (open mid-May–Aug 10–4; Sept–April by appt; adm free)* at their peril, or at least by following some strict rules: no sunglasses, no make-up, no trainers, no cans (drinks must be consumed from horns or beakers), no mobile phones and, though there is a pagan sacrificial grove for the Norse gods, bloody offerings are strictly forbidden too. It's only a half-hour bus drive [100 from Central Station) from Malmö to Höllviken (the nearest town, 500m walk away), but the ancient coastal village, complete with longships, tents and clay ovens, has been so authentically reconstructed by a group of Viking scholars, antiquarians and costumed re-enactors that it feels more like a journey back to the 12th century. More than a museum (although there are guided tours), Foteviken is an experiment in recreating the atmosphere of a late Viking settlement. Key dates are mid–late June, when the traditional market week attracts 'Vikings' from 15 countries, all sporting bushy beards, long hair and the latest Viking attire; and the Swedish Viking Age archery championship in August.

Day Trips and Overnighters from Malmö

Lund

'...The town's gray stones/For ever appear in a youthful light...' famous poet Anders Sterling reminisces nostalgically in his frequently quoted poem (*Lund*, 1922) about his student days in Lund. Certainly, the thousand-year-old city with its emblematic charcoal-grey cathedral has a very distinctly youthful, upbeat feel to it, mainly due to its venerable university (founded in 1666 and often compared with Oxford and Cambridge), whose thousands of students can be seen whiling the hours away in the many laid-back cafes or cycling furiously on roads not built for modern traffic.

The relaxed atmosphere of its enchanting cobbled streets belies the town's ponderous birth as a royal and ecclesiastical centre for Harald Bluetooth's Danish kingdom at the end of the 10th century. When the town became formally Swedish in 1658, the Reformation had already seen to the destruction of dozens of its churches and monasteries. Locals gently point out that most of Danish Lund is now concealed in a massive rubbish tip underneath the present town centre.

The best place to start a tour is in the magnificent Romanesque cathedral or **Domkyrkan** (*open Mon–Sat 8–6, Sun 9–6; guided tours in summer Mon–Sat 12.15 and 2.50, Sun 1 and 2.50*). The imposing twin towers (rebuilt in the 1870s) are difficult to miss and in any case, the cathedral is only a couple of minutes' walk away from the train station and opposite the tourist office in Kyrkogatan – *see* below.

Getting There

Frequent **trains** from Malmö take 12mins to reach Lund's station (SJ, tickets and information, **t** 0771 757 575, *www.skanetrafiken. skane.se*), from which the centre is only a 2min walk. If you are travelling from Copenhagen airport Kastrup, take the Öresundståген train which stops in Malmö Central Station. Taking slightly longer than the train, the Linje 999 **bus** goes from Copenhagen and Malmö (Skånetrafiken, **t** 0771 777 777). From Malmö airport Sturup, take the 40min journey on the Flygbuss.

Getting Around

Walking is by far the best option around Lund's cobbled streets, but beware the horde of students on **bikes**. If you want to brave cycling, you can hire at Godsmagasinet, Bangatan, **t** (046) 355 742. For more distant university sites only, take a city **bus** (information at Stadstrafiken, **t** (046) 355 300. For a **taxi**, call Lunda Mini Taxi, **t** (046) 202 020, or Taxi M Lund, **t** (046) 012 12 12.

Car Hire

If you use Lund as a town base for regional travel, car hire can be found at:
Avis, Byggmästaregatan 11, **t** (046) 145 030.
Bilia, Fältspatsvägen 2, Lund, **t** (046) 181 800.
Europcar, Malmövägen Höjebro, **t** (046) 197 939.
Hertz, Västra Stationstorget 1, **t** (046) 306 012.

Tourist Information

Lund: Kyrkogatan 11, **t** (046) 355 040, **f** (046) 125 963, opposite the cathedral (*open Mon–Fri 10–6; Sat and Sun 10–2*). In the summer, city walks on offer include: Historic Houses; Ghosts and Other Strange Things in Lund; and 1,000 Years in 90 Minutes.

Where to Stay

Lund **t** (046) –

Grand Hotell, Bantorget 1, **t** 280 6100, **f** 280 6150, *www.grandilund.se* (*very expensive*). As its name suggests, this is a regal hotel proudly overlooking a stately square not far from the train station. If you can't afford a room or even a set meal, a visit to the splendid bar-restaurant is well worth it. Try the generously filled shrimp sandwich with a light local beer.

Petri Pumpa Hotel, St Petri Kyrkogata 7, **t** 135 519, **f** 135 671, *www.petripumpa.se* (*expensive–moderate*). Targeting business folk during the week, this 22-room hotel in a prime location offers good weekend rates and fine dining in its matsal dining room.

Concordia Hotel, Stålbrogatan 1, **t** 135 050, **f** 137 422, *www.concordia.se* (*expensive–moderate*). A recently renovated students' hostel. The two-storey corner building was also, in the 19th century, the home of well known scholar Henrik Schück, who from one of the windows is said to have spied famous dramatist August Strindberg trying to produce gold in the house across the street.

Hotel Oskar, Bytaregatan 3, **t** 188 085, **f** 373 030, *www.hotelloskar.com* (*expensive–moderate*). A 19th-century townhouse tastefully renovated by well known Swedish and Danish designers. Excellent central location.

Lilla Hotellet i Lund, Bankgatan 7, **t** 328 888, **f** 385 868, *www.lillahotelletilund.se* (*moderate*). 'Lilla' means 'small', which aptly describes this low, mid-19th-century house, recently renovated into a 19-room hotel

The official story states that the cathedral was commissioned in 1103 after Danish King Erik Ejegod convinced the Pope during a pilgrimage to Jerusalem that Lund, already important for its mint, should become the first archbishopric in Scandinavia. A more intriguing legend reveals that that it was a giant called Finn, who built the church for St Lawrence by carving mountains into beautiful ashlars. The giant's sole condition for his hard nocturnal work was that the saint had to guess his name before he completed the church or risk losing his eyes. When the saint eventually furnished in classically simple style. Includes a library to read and relax in.

Hotell Ahlström, Skomakareg 3, t 211 0174 (*moderate–inexpensive*). A bargain option reflected in the rather outdated décor and the shared bathrooms. The rooms are clean, though, and the hotel is a two-minute walk from the cathedral.

Hotell Gräddyllan, t 157 230, f 157 257, *www. graddhyllan.com* (*moderate–inexpensive*) Only four rooms, charming and inexpensive (shared bathrooms). Conveniently situated above a more elegant restaurant and café.

Eating Out

Lund t (046) –

Bantorget, Bantorget 9, t 320 200, f 320 213 (*expensive*). Elegant and traditional, the restaurant named after its street is set across three small 19th-century houses, the middle one of which used to be a bakery. After dinner, you are escorted to a separate room where you can enjoy a nice cognac and a Cuban cigar.

Godset, Bangatan 3–5, t 121 610, f 127 710, *www.godset.se* (*expensive–moderate*). Swedish food with an international twist in a converted railway building. Doubles as nightclub (including salsa) around midnight.

Spot, Klostergatan 14, t 124 331, f 125 393 (*expensive–moderate*). Clean, modern concept restaurant with two floors: good-value Italian luncheon and a takeaway delicatessen on the ground floor, with a gourmet Swedish restaurant on top. *Closed Sun.*

Restaurang Stäket, St. Södergatan 6, t 211 9367, f 148 320 (*expensive–moderate*). For steak-lovers. The setting is a late-16th-century step-gabled vaulted house.

Kulturen Restaurant, Tegnerplatsen (*expensive–moderate*). Apart from the entertaining 'period' dinners offered by the open-air museum, there is a relaxed café/restaurant that serves well priced local cuisine.

Saluhallens Fisk & Skaldjur, Saluhallen, Mårtenstorget, t 126 354 (*moderate*). Delicious fish soup in a traditional, local market environment. *Closed eves and weekends.*

Café Restaurang, Gräddyllan, t 157 230, f 157 257, *www.graddhyllan.com* (*moderate–inexpensive*). Cosy traditional Swedish décor, and intimate dining. The café is excellent for people-watching. Don't miss the home-made apple pie.

Brasserie at Hotel Lundia, Knut den Stores torg 2, t 280 6500, f 280 6510 (*moderate*). Smart surroundings for international influences on traditional Swedish produce.

Café Ariman, Kungsgatan 2, t 131 263 (*inexpensive*). Left-wing coffee house adjacent to the Nordic Law Department.

Café Credo, Krafts torg, t 211 16 83 (*inexpensive*). Sip a coffee in style in a 500-year-old refectory.

Conditori Lundagård, Kyrkogatan 17, t 211 1358 (*inexpensive*). The brilliant caricatures of professors on the walls signal this as a well established student hangout.

Pubs and Bars

The Bishop Arms, St Petri Kyrkogata 7, t 149 080. Traditional British-style pub.

The John Bull Pub, Bantorget 2, t 140 920. And another.

Gloria's, St Petri Kyrkogata 9, t 151 985. Lively, US-style bar that serves traditional American food. Bands play at weekends.

T-Bar, Sandgatan 2, t 131 333. Student bar, restaurant and nightclub next to the student union.

discovered the giant's name from a woman's lullaby, an enraged Finn crept into the crypt and grasped a pillar to try and tear the foundations down, but the first ray of the rising sun turned Finn to stone. Down at the crypt, the oldest part of the cathedral, is a pillar with a stone figure representing Finn hugged around it. A second pillar is similarly gripped by stone figures of a crouched woman and child – Finn's wife and son, it is presumed, though some chronicles say it is the wife and child of the cathedral's first architect Donatus. Another highlight, at the left of the entrance to the majestic interior, is a towering 14th-century astronomical clock. At the stroke of 3pm (midday on Sundays), puppet-like knights on horseback pop out to clash swords to the fanfare of trumpeters, and tiny doors open to admit small, mechanical replicas of the Three Holy Kings who shuffle towards the Virgin and Child.

North of the cathedral (turn right), up Kyrkogatan is the welcome open space of **Lundagård**, less a park than a wood with trees so ancient that they had to be filled with cement to restore them. The red-brick **Kungshuset** (King's House, built for Denmark's Frederic II), one of the town's few surviving Renaissance buildings, served as the main university building until 1882 when the nearby white classical building, Universitet, was built. Opposite is **Akademiska Föreningen**, the student union building, south of which emerges another open square, Tegnerplatsen, with its statue of celebrated poet Esias Tegner, also a former student and professor. This is the site of the open-air museum, **Kulturhistoriska Museet (Kulturen)** (*open April–Sept 11–5; park open summer 5–9pm; adm*), where up to 40 houses of all periods and styles, some gracing their original medieval sites, have been transported, complete with goats and geese. Complemented by collections of artefacts dating backing to the Vikings, this makes a fascinating walk, literally, through history. For period enthusiasts, the museum also offers a wide range of themed dinners called 'Glimpses of a Vanished World', which are preceded by guided tours and accompanied by light-hearted lectures (*for information, call **t** (046) 350 432 between 8 and 11pm*).

A stroll north of the Lundagård/Universitet area towards the Bishop's House and the University Library is rewarded by the **Skissernas Museum** (Museum of Sketches), Finngatan 2, **t** (046) 222 7285 (*the museum is being relaunched in December 2004, when times may change*). Viewers can trace artists' work in progress from preliminary sketches, rough outlines and plaster miniatures through to full-scale models.

West of Lundagård, walk up the pretty Adelgatan towards the **Botaniska Trägården** (Botanical Graden), Östra Vallgatan 20, **t** (046) 222 7320 (*open daily 6am–8pm, greenhouses 12–3*). Covering an area of eight hectares, the gardens are ideal for a rest – seek out exotic trees like the Central American chicly tree from which chewing gum is made, or the Madagascar ornamental tree that has wedge-shaped leaf sheaths containing sterile water.

For a hint of Lund away from the university world, a couple of minutes south of the cathedral is **Stortorget**, the main stamping ground for the townspeople and the busiest commercial shopping area. Past the town hall is the former market square **Mårtenstorget**, where the lively indoor market Saluhallen is worth a visit, especially for a filling bowl of fish soup. Check too the temporary modern art exhibitions at Lund's **Konsthall**, Mårtenstorget 3, **t** (046) 355 295 (*open Mon, Tues, Thurs and Sun 12–7, Wed 12–8, Sat 10–5*); it also shows films, concerts and plays.

Helsingborg

Strategically placed at the narrowest part of the strait between Sweden and Denmark, this port town oozes the cosmopolitan, open character so particular to the

Getting There

The fastest way of getting to Helsingborg from Malmö is on the Öresundståren train (39mins), which also stops at Lund and sometimes continues to Copenhagen (SJ trains, tickets and information, t 0771 757 575, *www.skanetrafiken.skane.se*). Trains arrive at the harbourside Knutspunkten, a glass travel terminal that also serves ferry travel to Denmark (HH-Ferries, t (042) 198 000, *www.hhferries.se*) and regional bus travel. For more info on the 'Around the Sound by Train' ticket, valid for two days and with lots of discounts, call t 0771 777 777.

Getting Around

The town's historical role as a fort means it is hilly, making cycling suitable only for the extra-fit (bike hire at the tourist office). For the rest, walking is best unless you are heading north towards the Royal Gardens of Sofiero, in which case take a bus from Knutspunkten. A favourite local pastime is 'tura', a word coined in Helsingborg that means to tour on a ferry that travels back and forth across the Sound while eating in the restaurant on board. Ferries leave every 10–20mins, 24hrs a day. You get a closer look at Hamlet's Elsinore Castle from the ferry (*see* pp.256–7).

Car Hire

If you are using Helsingborg as a travel base, car hire is available at:

Avis, Garnisonsgatan, t (042) 157 080, *www.avis-se.com*.

Europcar, Din Bil, Muskötg, Berga Industriområde, t (042) 170 115, *www.europcar.se*.

Hertz, Bildeve, Bergavägen 4, t (042) 172 540, *www.hertz.se*.

For **taxis**, call Taxi Helsingborg, t (042) 180 200.

Tourist Information

Helsingborg: Stortorget/Södra Storgatan 1, t (042) 104 350, f (042) 104 350, just off central Stortorget (*open Sept–April Mon–Fri 9–6, Sat 10–2; May Mon–Fri 9–6, Sat 10–2, Sun 10–2; June–Aug Mon–Fri 9–8, Sat and Sun 9–5*). For guided tours call t (042) 105 310. If you arrive from Denmark by ferry, visit **First Stop Sweden**, Bredgatan, t (042) 104 130, *www.firststopsweden.com* (*open Sept–May Mon–Fri 8–5; June–Aug daily 9–9*).

Where to Stay

Helsingborg t (042) –

Elite Hotel Mollberg, Stortorget 18, t 373 700, f 373 737, *www.mollberg.elite.se* (*very expensive*). Although sister hotel Elite Marina

continental-leaning south. The sweeping harbour, teeming with a growing number of bars and cafés and an impressive new waterfront museum, have helped to renew the town's historical rivalry with Helsingør, the Danish town only 4km across the Öresund Sound that likes to impose its superiority with its infamous Elsinore castle (*see* pp.256–7). The contest is mainly amicable, given that 14 million passengers take the short ferry ride between the two every year, and that both towns form stops in a special 'Around the Sound' ticket that includes Malmö and Copenhagen (*see* p.101).

Head straight for the **Kärnen** (Keep Tower), for a panoramic view of the town and the Öresund Sound beyond. From the Knutspunkten travel hub, it's only a short walk to the elongated central square, **Stortorget**, past the copper statue of Magnus Stenbock, under whose leadership in 1710 the town was seized from Denmark for the last time, and to the sloping far end of the square where a monumental spiral staircase greets you. The solid battlements and the 34m-high tower at the top of the hill were renovated at the end of the 19th century from the only remains of the castle buildings that were demolished in the Skåne War (1675–1679), one of the many bloody Swedish–Danish wars. There's a small admission fee to enter the tower, but more

Plaza (*www.marinaplaza.elite.se*) enjoys harbour views, Mollberg prides itself on its 14th-century roots, although Peter Mollberg tore down the original building in 1814. Overlooks the central Stortorget. Surprisingly good summer bargain prices.

Hotell Viking, Fågelsångsgatan 1, **t** 144 420, **f** 184 320, *www.hotell-linnea.se* (*expensive– moderate*). A charming little hotel set in elegant, turn-of-the-20th-century commercial hub. Ask about the 'romantic' weekend package that includes a four-course dinner at top gourmet restaurant **Niklas** (*see* below).

Hotel Sir James, Bruksgatan 40, **t** 219 292, **f** 212 584, *www.hotelsirjames.com* (*expen-sive– moderate*). Sparkling white rooms in another small, private hotel smack in the centre of town.

Hotell Linnéa, Prästgatan 2–4, **t** 372 400, **f** 372 429, *www.hotell-linnea.se* (*expensive– moderate*). This late 19th-century town house offers an intimate and affordable option, only a skip away from the harbour.

Alberga Herrgård, Långebergavägen 85, **t/f** 296 810, *www.albergherrgard.com* (*expensive–moderate*). An out-of-town option if you want to hide away in a family-owned mansion built in 1850. Set in a scenic park yet only 6mins' car drive from the town

centre. Book early, as it takes up to ten guests only.

Eating Out

Helsingborg **t** (042) –

Restaurang Niklas, Norra Storgatan 16, **t** 280 050, **f** 283 310 (*very expensive*). If money is no object, this is the place to splash out in the evening to sample the influence of Provence on Skåne's wealth of agricultural produce. Niklas, the young, award-winning chef, also runs a more financially palatable bistro and even a chef's table set in the kitchen where you watch the food prepared in front of you.

Mollberg's Matsal, Stortorget 18, **t** 373 750, **f** 373 737 (*very expensive*). An antidote to the up-and-coming sleek, minimalist venues, this is elegant, old-fashioned dining by candlelight and crystal chandeliers.

Råå Wärdshus, Kajgatan 1, **t** 262 250, **f** 263 419 (*expensive*). Fish is best in the nautical themed restaurant by the harbour. The buffet choice is nicely presented in a miniature wooden boat.

Sofiero Slott och Slottspark, Sofierovägen, **t** 140 440 (*expensive*). If you opt for lunch rather than dinner to eat in palatial surroundings, the prices are reasonable and

impressive (and free) is the surrounding parkland, particularly a nearby magnolia and rose garden from where there are further sweeping views. From this garden and down a rhododendron-lined path is the only other survivor of the war, **St Maria Kyrka**, a triple-nave brick church with an impressive interior – inspect the magnificent pulpit from 1615. Running north and south of the keep, Norra and Södra Storgatan are lined with old merchant homes.

Walk back to the Stortorget past the tourist office where the majestic **Rådhuset** (town hall) sits, its neo-Gothic towers and pinnacles and lavishly decorated façades bearing witness to Helsingborg's late-19th-century industrial boom. The daily guided tours (check times as these vary, **t** (042) 105 000) are well worth the money – look out for the stained glass windows narrating the town's history, particularly of Queen Margareta of Denmark releasing her foe Albert of Mecklenburg in 1395.

A few minutes away, overlooking the Sundstorget square is the outstanding new **Dunkers Kulturhus** (Henry Dunker Culture Centre), Kungsgatan 11, **t** (042) 107 400, *www.dunkerskulturhus.com* (*open Tues, Wed, Fri, Sat and Sun 10–5, Thurs 10–8, closed Mon; adm*). Named after benefactor Henry Dunker (1870–1962), the white brick the views of the rhododendrons, if in season, are unequalled.

Kajplats 10, Kajpromenaden 10, t 143 061, f 143 062 (*expensive*). Of all the fashionable eateries mushrooming along the waterfront, this has one of the best views.

Le Cardinal, S. Kyrkogatan 9, t 131 312, f 124 410 (*expensive*). The trendy crowd gravitates around this modern restaurant, particularly on Thursday to Saturday evenings where guests can enter the adjoining nightclub free. *Closed summer.*

Restaurangbåten S/S Swea, Kungstorget, t 131 516, f 131 020 (*expensive–moderate*). Taking the sea experience one step further, dining is on a luxury cruise liner (now stationary). A very good value weekend brunch menu sets up the day nicely.

Harrys, Järnvägsgatan 7, t 139 191 (*expensive–moderate*). Serves traditional, North American food in saloon-like surroundings. Lively bar in evenings.

Linnea Trädgård & Café, Paviljonggången 1 (*moderate–inexpensive*). Enjoy a light lunch or coffee and cakes surrounded by all variety of plants in the gardens, created in the 1930s. Located at the northern entrance to the Maria Park housing estate. *Closed eves.*

Möllebackens Våffelbruk, Södra Storgatan 31 (*moderate–inexpensive*). Climb the steep staircase for freshly baked waffles served in a late-18th-century farm building, moved to this spot, with good views of the town. Next to the café is a 19th-century windmill you can visit. *Open summer only.*

Ebba's Fik, Bruksgatan 20 (*moderate–inexpensive*). Every type of bric-a-brac from the 1950s and 1960s seems to have been squeezed into this entertaining café, which serves delicious cakes.

Wayne's, Stortorget 8 (*moderate–inexpensive*). A home-grown chain that is much better than its multinational counterparts. Great people-watching in this grand space overlooking the elongated central square.

Entertainment

Helsingborg t (042) –

Check listings at the tourist office, and pick up a copy of *Helsingborg This Month*.

Konserthuset, Drottningatan 19, t 104 350. Built in 1932, this fine example of Swedish functionalism is the home of Helsingborg's Symphony Orchestra. Seats more than 900.

Stadsteatern (Municipal Theatre), Karl Johansgatan 1, t 104 280. Next door.

Henry Dunker Culture Centre (Dunkers Kulturhus), home to the Helsingborg School of Music, t 107 400, *www.dunkerskulturhus.com*. Check for special performances.

building houses several temporary exhibitions, a concert hall and a theatre. If you only visit one exhibition in all your stay in southern Sweden, make it this centre's interactive journey through the history of Helsingborg. It starts in a forbiddingly dark tunnel which you enter and follow around as a cacophony of noises, visual images and objects flash around, slowly unveiling a compelling tale. Not to be missed.

Sofiero Castle and Gardens

219 bus from Knutpunkten; open April–mid-Sept 11–5; adm; park open all year; for guided tours call t (042) 137 400.

Four kilometres north of Helsingborg is Sofiero Castle and its splendid gardens. The real gem of this royal summer retreat, built in 1885 by Crown Prince Oscar and his wife Sofia, is the magnificent grounds, particularly in June when more than 300 varieties of 10,000 rhododendrons are in full bloom. The gardens were created by Crown Princess Marghareta, wife of Oscar's grandson and granddaughter of Queen Victoria, in the early 20th century. The park is also a venue for open-air concerts, garden shows and exhibitions.

Touring from Malmö

Day 1: Romantic Castles and a Night Bugler

Morning: Take the E65 (the Sturup airport road) from Malmö towards Ystad. Just before the turn-off to Skurup (not Sturup) is the sign to **Svaneholm Castle** (*open May, June, Aug Tues–Sun 10–5; July daily 10–5; April and Sept Wed–Sun 11–4, other times on request, t (0411) 400 12*). Built on an islet in 1530, as a wedding gift for chatelaine Elizabeth Trolle, the castle was named after the swans (*'svane'*) in the lake, which is ideal for walking around, a boat trip or fishing. Past illustrious owners include nobleman Axel Gyllenstierna (1653–1705) who imposed the Italian Baroque interior, and Baron Rutger Macklean (1742–1816). Less vaunted residents include a 'White Lady', once incarcerated in the dungeon, and a monk murdered in the cellars.

Lunch: In Svaneholm Castle, *see below*.

Afternoon: Continuing east on the E65 and just 10km before Ystad is the fairytale **Marsvinsholm Castle**. It's privately owned so the inside is out of bounds, but the Iacobaeus family open the park to the public all year round and the sight of the Renaissance manor house in the middle of a lake, and the impressively tall Marsvinsholm Church, is well worth it. See if you can spot the chestnut tree planted in the 18th century by Sweden's most revered scientist, Carl von Linné, with a circumference of more than 5m. Carry on to **Ystad** – and listen out for the night watchman who sounds a bugle every 15 minutes from 9.15pm to 3am.

Dinner and Sleeping: In Ystad, *see below*.

Day 1

Lunch in Svaneholm Castle

Svaneholm Castle, t (0411) 450 40, **f** (0411) 402 58. (*expensive–moderate*). Its Hall of the Knights and adjoining rooms make it a popular venue for business lunches, conferences and weddings, so ring Anneli or Christian beforehand.

Dinner and Sleeping in Ystad

Hotell Continental i Ystad, Hamngatan 13, **t** (0411) 13700, **f** (0411) 12570 (*very expensive*). Near the port, this is the *grande dame* of Ystad's hotels, as the lobby's grand staircase, wide pillars and crystal chandeliers testify.

Ystad Nyström Hotell & Restaurang, Saltsjöbadsvägen 6, **t** (0411) 136 30, **f** (0411) 555 835 (*very expensive–expensive*). More than 100 years old but newly refurbished, close to the sea. Weekend breaks with a 3-course meal.

Hotell Anno 1793 Sekelgården, Långgatan 18, **t** (0411) 739 00, **f** (0411) 189 97 (*expensive–moderate*). Family-owned hotel in a half-timbered house, proud of its old pear tree.

Hotell Bäckagården, Dammgatan 36, **t** (0411) 198 48, **f** (0411) 657 15 (*moderate*). Expect the hotel owner to give you personal, attentive service in this 17th-century house.

Hotel Tornväktaren, Stora Östergatan 33, **t** (0411) 784 80, **f** (0411) 729 27 (*moderate*). Located in the main walking street, where you can hear the night watchman's bugle.

Ystad Nyström Hotell & Restaurang, Saltsjöbadsvägen 6, **t** (0411) 136 30 (*very expensive*). Matching the excellent sea view is the *nouvelle cuisine* treatment of local, organic products like goose or eel.

Lottas Restaurang, Stortorget 11, **t** (0411) 788 00 (*expensive*). Atmospheric cellars in winter and a summer terrace. *Closed Sun.*

Bryggeriet, Långgatan 20, **t** (0411) 699 99 (*expensive–moderate*). Traditional Swedish menu in former 18th-century brewery that still produces fresh local beer Ysta Färsköl. Barbecues on cobbled courtyard in summer.

Ristorante La Bella Vita, Stora Östergatan 1, **t** (0411) 555 588 (*expensive–moderate*). Italian cuisine using only quality local products.

Day 2: Ystad, and Swedish Stonehenge

Morning: Get lost in **Ystad**'s cobbled lanes, lined with more than 300 half-timbered houses. The quaintest is Lilla Östergatan, off which, on Gäsergrän, is the delightful Book Café, with a cottage-like living room surrounded by English books. The grand old square is a short stroll away; peep into the Romanesque St Maria Kyrka (*open all year*), if only to try and pin down the little openings in the tower walls where the watchman blows his horn. To find out how priests fought for chastity, visit Klostret I Ystag, the Grey Friars Monastery at St Petri Kyrkoplan (*open Tues–Fri 12–5, Sat and Sun 12–4*) and, for a contrasting view of the underworld, the Ystad Police Museum, **t** (0411) 676 15 (*open by arrangement*). For strolling, there is the horse-chestnut-tree-lined Norra Promenaden northwest of the main square, go or down by the docks.

Lunch: In Ystad (*see* Day 1), or in the little fishing village of Kåseberga – *see* below.

Afternoon: **Österlen**'s white sandy beaches, lined with pine forests, are apparent as you continue east on the 9 coastal road towards Simrishamn. Stop at the little fishing village of **Kåseberga**, above which tower, on a flat hill, to paraphrase a local poet, a mighty ship of enchanted stones: **Ale Stenar**, Sweden's Stonehenge. What this 67m-long megalith monument of 58 stones, weighing 4–5-tonnes each, exactly is or represents is fiercely contested. Some say they are a prehistoric almanac, others a thousand-year-old ship barrow, but the most popular interpretation is that *Ale* was actually the name of a Viking chieftain who was buried among the stones. Continue east of the ridge through the Hagestad nature reserve to **Simrishamn**.

Dinner and Sleeping: In Simrishamn, *see* below

Day 2

Lunch in Kåseberga

Café Solståndet, Kasevägen 13, **t** (0411) 527 280 (*inexpensive*). Filled freshly baked baguettes. *Open summer daily 10–5, weekends in winter.*

Hammers Fisk, Kåseberga harbour, **t** (0411) 527 014 (*inexpensive*). Offers smoked fish and home-made pickled herring.

Johannasskafferi, Lejets Torg 2 Kåseberga, **t** (0411) 527426 (*moderate*). For a more upmarket spread of fish and other locally grown products, try this restaurant and deli in an old general store, which also has rooms. *Closed winter; closed Mon in summer.*

Dinner and Sleeping in Simrishamn

Maritim Krog & Hotel, Hamngatan 31, **t** (0414) 411 360, **f** (0414) 138 62, *www.maritim.nu* (*expensive–inexpensive*). You can't miss the bright blue exterior of this waterside hotel and restaurant; the individually designed rooms and wide range of painstakingly made food are excellent. Prices for all tastes, both for the rooms and for menus.

Hotel Svea, Strandvägen 3, **t** (0414) 411 720, **f** (0414) 143 41 (*expensive*). Traditional if dated rooms in a premier hotel with excellent harbour locations. Check for special weekend rates. Restaurant.

Kamskogs Krog Café and Logi, Storgatan 3, **t** (0414) 143 48, **f** (0414) 143 60 (*expensive-moderate*). With only three rooms, you don't get much more personal than this immaculate restaurant/inn, which serves excellent local food. Try the hearty saffron fish stew.

Hotel Turistgården, Storgatan 21, **t** (0414) 166 22, **f** (0414) 137 01 (*moderate*). The rooms in this converted farm shop are not the most aesthetic, but it's difficult to find much cheaper accommodation that is so central.

Strandpaviljongen, Småbåtshamnen, **t** (0414) 159 22, **f** (0414) 159 23 (*expensive*). Stunning pavilion setting on the water, and the gourmet fare matches the exquisite design. *Open Friday eves and all day weekends only.*

Modesty Nattclub and Restaurang, Djupadalsvägen 3, **t** (0414) 140 00 (*expensive*). The liveliest spot in this genteel, quiet town.

Day 3: Art in a Fishing Port, a Castle, and Apples

Morning: Plentiful fishing waters, smooth, sandy beaches and the small port have seamen of all sorts flocking to **Simrishamn**, but writers and artists also famously love this part of the southern coast. If the picture-perfect cottages in the medieval quarter are not enough of a visual feast, there is an ample choice of art and historical curiosities at Österlens Museum, Storgatan 24 *(open Jan–Feb Tues–Fri 10–2; Mar–May Tues–Fri 12–6, Sat 10–2; June–Aug Mon–Fri 10–6, Sat 10–2; Aug–Dec Tues–Fri 12–4, Sat 10–2)*. Gösta Werner Museum Konstmuseet, Strandvägen 5 *(open Easter and June–Aug 12–5; Sept 12–5)* specializes in life at and stories from the sea. At Easter, following a tradition that began in 1968, a handful of artists stage an Open Studio Week that allows visitors to witness an artist at work at first hand.

Lunch: In Simrishamn (*see* Day 2), or at Glimmingehus Castle, *see* below.

Afternoon: Take route 9 inland towards **Glimmingehus Castle**, Hammenhög, **t** (0414) 186 20, **f** (0414) 186 27, *www.raa.se/glimmingehus*. The austere, upright block shape of the medieval fortress with its steeply inclining roof is far removed from the fairy-tale image of a castle, but it strikes a menacing tone as it towers over the flat surrounding landscape, which was presumably the intention of the Danish nobleman who commissioned it in the Middle Ages. There is a museum, a kitchen and a museum shop *(open April–May daily 11–6; June–Aug 10–6; Sept 11–6; adm)*. Then drive back to the coast on route 9 and continue north towards the fruit farms and orchards that characterize the area around **Kivik**.

Dinner and Sleeping: In Kivik, *see* below.

Day 3

Lunch at Glimmingehus Castle

Glimmingehus Castle, Hammenhög, **t** (0414) 186 20, **f** (0414) 186 27, *www.raa.se/ glimmingehus* (*moderate*). The restaurant/ café serves staple foods and ingredients that were supposedly available in medieval times (they may cheat on the potatoes). *Open mid-April–May 11–4.30, June–Aug 11–6.*

Dinner and Sleeping in or around Kivik

Kiviks Hotell, Moriabacken, **t** (0414) 71070, **f** (0414) 714 40, *info@kivikshotell.se* (*expensive*). The views over the Kivik bay are stunning, the long sandy beach is only a few minutes' walking distance, and the rooms are charming. Look out for the special weekend package which includes accommodation and a three-course meal (including a pre-dinner aperitif) at the smart but cosy restaurant which prides itself on its use of local, organic ingredients: vegetables are hand picked from the hotel's own ecological garden, meat and game are provided by nearby farms, and fishing boats bring in daily catches of sole, cod, eel and herring. The package also entitles guests to free use of the sauna and Jacuzzi.

Logi Blåsingsborg, Blåsingsborg, **t** (0414) 70218, **f** (0414) 71422 (*moderate*). Two km from Kivik is this reasonably priced 17-room option housed in a typical Skåne mansion, recently rebuilt after a massive fire in 1998. Personal service by the owners Eva & Åke Gilck, who also provide home cooking at their ample, no frills restaurant. Icelandic horses are kept outside the hotel for tours of the surrounding apple orchards.

Agda Lund Bed & Breakfast, Kiviks stora väg 59 (Riksväg 9), **t** (0414) 701 75 (*moderate-inexpensive*). Fresh, simple rooms in a former fruit packing building. Highly reasonable prices made even better by the special bike and horse-riding packages arranged in-house. Book early as there are only nine rooms.

Day 4: A King's Grave, Cider Factory and Eel Coast

Morning: From Kivik's lovely stretch of unspoilt harbour, ideal for swimming, it's less than 500m to **Kungagraven** (King's Grave; *open mid May–Aug 10–6; adm*), a 75m-wide Bronze Age cairn discovered one summer's day in 1748 by a couple of farmers. From the grave, road signs point towards the cider factory 2km away past a wealth of apple trees, a spectacular sight when in blossom. Next to the factory is the **Apple House**, t (0414) 719 00 (*open April 10–5; July and Aug 9–6; Sept–Oct 10–4; Nov–Dec by appointment; Jan-Mar closed; adm*). A visit will tell you everything you ever wanted to about apples. If you've had enough of fruit, the entrance to **Stenshuvuds National Park**, a hill with fantastic views, is a couple of minutes' walk away.

Lunch: In Kivik, *see* below.

Afternoon: Follow the coastal road 9 which turns into 118 towards Åhus. Dotting the gently undulating sand dunes of the coast are eel huts, some from the 18th century, indicating that this is where in late summer, fully mature silver eels begin their 7,000km journey to the Sargasso Sea. **Åhus** is a picturesque port town, its waterfront and beaches providing a relaxing stroll, while inside the 14th-century walls is a beautiful square flanked by a 12th-century church (Mariakyrkan), a reminder that the town was once given to Lund's archbishop. The rise of nearby Kristianstad after the Reformation ushered in a decline that was not reversed until the railway and port boom in the late 19th century. Today's success story is Vin O Sprit, the makers of Absolut vodka, whose office has a colourful display of Absolut art in the foyer.

Dining and Sleeping: In Åhus.

Day 4

Lunch in Kivik

Apple House Café and Restaurang Kärnhuset (*moderate*). A wholesome setting in which to try all the apple derivatives you can imagine, washed down, naturally, by apple cider. There is more traditional Swedish food including a variety of wild fruits.

Dinner and Sleeping in Åhus

Åhus Gästgifvaregård, G Skeppsbron 1, t (044) 289 050, f (044) 289 250, *www.ahusgastis. com* (*expensive*). A traditional country inn and a sailor's tavern under one roof, this is a charming waterfront hotel with a small but exquisite dining area that puts a *nouvelle cuisine* twist on local produce. If you are put off by the idea of fresh eel, an aperitif of smoked eel in dill sauce is heavenly, matched only by the crème brûlée.

Åhus Strand, Kolonivägen, t (044) 289 300, f (044) 249 480, *www.ahusstrand.com* (*expensive–moderate*). The beach setting, tennis court, heated pool, wood-heated sauna facilities by the sea and nearby golf course make this conference-friendly hotel look more pricy than it is. It is definitely worth checking out the offers. Apart from the splendid views, the restaurant has a gourmet approach to local produce.

Paparazzi, G Skeppsbron 5, t (044) 289 300, *www.restpapa.com* (*expensive*). It's a wonder that such a small town should have a third top quality eatery open outside the summer tourist season, but this is the trendiest addition.

Gallericaféet Fina Fisken, Västra Hamngatan 4, t (044) 243 625 (*moderate*). A less pricy option in a central location. Herring sandwiches are the speciality but there is also a wide range of baguettes and toasties and the freshly baked waffles are delicious.

Handelsbaren, Åvägen, t (044) 247 330 (*inexpensive*). A popular summer spot that attracts a trendy crowd with an array of shish kebabs and a cool selection of vinyl records.

Day 5: Kristianstad and a Renaissance Fortress

Morning: Take the 118 inland to **Kristianstad**, founded by Danish King Christian IV in 1614 to defend the surrounding provinces from the Swedes. The large, open squares and neat grid of streets are a testament to the king's pains to make the fortress the most modern in Europe, but the revolutionary design did not prevent the Swedes from taking over the town just 44 years later. A bronze statue of Christian looks out from the niche of the Rådhus (town hall), built in 1891 to emulate the Danish king's original Renaissance design. An authentic late-17th-century building is Holy Trinity Church (*open daily 9–5*). More recent history was made at Östra Storgatan 53, east of Stortorget, Sweden's oldest film studio (1901–11) and now a film museum (*open all year Sun 12–5, plus June–Aug also Tues–Fri 1–6*). Also from that period is the Tivoli Park, where a former museum serves as a summer cafeteria.

Lunch: In Kristianstad, *see* below.

Afternoon: Take the E22 west from Kristianstad to Bromölla until you see signs to **Bäckaskog Castle**, a Renaissance fortress whose allure is a combination of royal residence, acres of gardens and parkland, the splendid location between two lakes and the surrounding forested hills. The strategic site attracted monks in 1250, Danes in the late 16th century and then King Karl XV of Sweden in the 1800s, who turned the fortress into a country retreat open to visitors all year around.

Dinner and Sleeping: In Bäckaskog Castle or Kristianstad. In the morning, take the E22 from either Kristianstad and Bäckaskog straight to Malmö.

Day 5

Lunch and Dinner in Kristianstad

Kippers, Ö Storgatan 9, t (044) 106 200, f (044) 106 290, *www.kippers.se* (*expensive*). Popular with locals, traditional Swedish food served in an atmospheric 17th-century vault.

Fredholms, Björkhemsvägen 15, t (044) 120 700 (*expensive–moderate*). Imaginative, eclectic mix of cuisines that is affordable for lunch, rather pricier in the evenings. *Closed lunch Thurs–Sat, and all day Sun.*

Bar-B-K, Tivoligatan 4, t (044) 213 355 (*moderate*). Meat-eaters will love this informal grill place in the Tivoli Park. *Closed Sun.*

Grafitti Café, Västra Storgatan 45, t (044) 125 990 (*moderate–inexpensive*). A light choice: baked potatoes with interesting choice of fillings, pies, salads and baguettes.

Sleeping in Kristianstad

Stadshotellet, Stora Torg, t (044) 100 255 (*expensive*) The old Freemasons' Hall that straddles the main square is a safe, central choice even if the conventional rooms don't match the opulence of the main hall.

First Hotel Christian IV, Västra Boulevarden 15, t (044) 203 850, f (044) 121 40 (*expensive*). Splendid central building, a former bank on one of the city's Parisian-style boulevards.

Hotel Turisten, Västra Storgatan 17, t (044) 126 150, f (044) 103 099 (*moderate*). Opposite the railway station and behind the church is this good-value, comfortable option located in a 16th-century town house that was rebuilt as a home for the county chief in 1890.

Dinner and Sleeping at Bäckaskog

Bäckaskog Castle, Barumsvägen 255, t (044) 53020, f (044) 53220 (*expensive–moderate*). A wide range of options to suit all wallets: the Castle (*expensive*), King Karl's Tavern and the Old Monastery (*expensive–moderate*), the Oast House and the Old Mill (*moderate*), the Gatekeepers Lodge and the Gunsmith's Cottage (*inexpensive*). Ask about the Castle package. The restaurant shows off the best of local produce, sometimes including deer.

Language

It's a frequent joke that Swedes speak better English than native English speakers and it's perfectly possible to get through an entire visit to Sweden without uttering a word of the language. The Swedes are so accepting that English is an integral tool for the success of its cultural (Abba, Ace of Base, Cardigans and other home-grown pop/rock music groups) and business (Ikea, Hennes & Mauritz, SKF, Volvo, Saab) interests around the world that with their customary tact and consideration they won't assume foreigners will attempt even some basic Swedish. All foreign-language films, predictably dominated by Hollywood, are shown in their original language and a significant number of imported drama and sitcoms on TV are aired in English. However, part of the fun of visiting a new country is to try and grapple with a new language even if you only manage a few basic words or idioms. Any attempt at a smattering of Swedish, at least to initiate a conversation with a local, is not only polite and respectful but will be greeted with enthusiasm and polite encouragement (even if the recipient then tactfully switches to English).

The Swedish language, which is best characterized by its singsong quality, is a member of the Indo-European family, to which almost all European languages belong, with its closest relatives being Danish and Norwegian (not surprising given the many centuries during which Scandinavian territory was disputed by the three nations.) It is the native tongue of some 90 per cent of the country's almost 9 million inhabitants and is also one of the two national languages of Finland (alongside Finnish), since its eastern neighbour was part of Sweden until 1809.

Until the 9th century, the languages of the Scandinavian countries were on the whole identical and jointly referred to as Proto-Norse, and during the Viking period (800–1050) described as the 'Danish tongue'. Distinguishing characteristics began to emerge more strongly during the Middle Ages and from the Renaissance, and so-called standard Swedish developed on the basis of the language spoken in the Lake Mälaren region of Central Sweden and around Stockholm. The Swedish spoken in the southernmost province of Skåne is particularly distinct for its more guttural sounds that it shares with its southern neighbour, Denmark.

For such a polite society, it is curious that there is no word for 'please', although it is not uncommon to stick the word for thank you ('tack') when you are making a request.

Pronunciation

The pronunciation of standard letters is close to their English equivalent. For a non-Swede, by far the most striking and unusual letters are Å,å, Ä,ä and Ö,ö which are considered extra vowels. Å is pronounced like the vowels in more and hot, ä like in care and best, and ö like in the French words *bleu* and *bœuf*. Ej is like 'a' in 'tape'.

J, dj, gj, lj as 'y' in 'yet'; qu is 'kv'; rs, sj, skj, stj and tj are similar to 'sh' but not exactly.

Useful Words and Phrases

yes *ja*
no *nej*
hello *hej*
goodbye *hej då*
good morning *god morgon*
goodnight *god natt*
good day *adjö*
How are you? *Hur mår du?*
I'm fine, thank you *Jag mår bra, tack*
See you later *Vi ses senare*
Excuse me *Ursäkta mig*
I am sorry *Förlåt*
I don't understand *Jag förstår inte*
I am lost *Jag har gått vilse*

Nice to meet [you] *Trevligt att råkas/träffas*
Thanks *Tack*
I am called... *Jag heter...*
What are you called? *Vad heter du?*
I am from... *Jag är från...*
Do you speak English? *Talar du engelska?*
I *jag*
you *du*
you (polite) *ni*
me *mig/mej*
we *vi*
us *oss*
they *dom*
them *dem*
he *han*
she *hon*
it *det/den*
man *män*
guest *gäst*
church *kyrka*
house *hus*

Days of the Week
Monday *måndag*
Tuesday *tisdag*
Wednesday *onsdag*
Thursday *torsdag*
Friday *fredag*
Saturday *lördag*
Sunday *söndag*

Months
January *januari*
February *februari*
March *mars*
April *april*
May *maj*
June *juni*
July *juli*
August *augusti*
September *september*
October *oktober*
November *november*
December *december*

Numbers
one *ett*
two/three/four *två/tre/fyra*
five/six/seven *fem/sex/sju*
eight/nine/ten *åtta/nio/tio*
eleven/twelve *elva/tolv*
thirteen/fourteen *tretton/fjorton*
fifteen/sixteen *femton/sexton*

seventeen/eighteen *sjutton/arton*
nineteen *nitton*
twenty *tjugo*
twenty-one/twenty-two *tjugoen/tjugotvå*
thirty *trettio*
forty *fyrtio*
fifty *femtio*
sixty *sextio*
seventy *sjuttio*
eighty *åttio*
ninety *nittio*
hundred *hundra*
thousand *tusen*

Transport/Travel Directions
aeroplane *flygplan*
airport *flygplats*
train *tåg*
train station *järnvägsstation*
ticket (to) *biljett (till)*
return ticket *tur och retur*
bus *buss*
bus stop *busshållplats*
tram *spårvagn*
How do I get to? *Hur kommer jag till?*
Where is? *Var är?*
What is the road to? *Vilken är vägen till?*
right/left *höger/vänster*
What time does it leave? *Hur dags går det?*
entrance/exit *ingång/utgång*
No Entry *Ingen ingång*

Shopping
shop *affär*
How much is this? *Vad kostar det?*
open/closed *öppen/stängt*
stamp *frimärke*
chemist *apotek*
doctor *doktor*
hospital *sjukhus*
police station *polisstation*
toilet *toalett*
ladies *damer*
gentlemen *herrar*

Useful Hotel Vocabulary
single room *enkelrum*
double room *dubbelrum*
Shower *dusch*
Can I leave the bags here? *Kan jag få lämna väskorna?*
morning *morgon*
evening *kväll*

Norway:
Introduction

Norway ('the way to the North') should never, at least according to one Norwegian journalist, have come into existence in the first place, because of its latitude and location – 'in fact, it could almost be the world's largest glacier!' he added. Outside the cities, Norwegians (who currently number 4.5 million) live far apart from one another, yet when you get a group together, talking about football or politics, say, the impressive sense of national pride seems stronger than in neighbouring Scandinavian countries and in Europe as a whole. This is a country where national costume still has an important role to play on name days, special occasions and national holidays.

Norway is one of the oldest nations in Europe, inhabited in prehistoric times and by the Vikings (c. AD 800–1050), who once controlled an extensive area from Russia to the British Isles where the common language was an Old Norse dialect. Yet, as a country that was only reconstituted in 1905, when the union with Sweden was dissolved, it can also be considered a relative youngster. Proud of its independent stance, it became financially secure in 1968 when it struck oil, and it can boast an excellent health care system, good housing and education, and a contented, well-paid workforce with good benefits and retirement plans. No wonder they keep voting to stay out of the European Union! As with other Scandinavian and European countries, immigration has become a controversial issue here in recent years, and Norway – a country known for its humanistic traditions – is often criticised for having some of the most severe immigration and asylum policies in Europe. That said, it does spend more per capita on foreign aid than other Western country.

They say that Norwegians are born with skis on their feet, and certainly the moment they have free time many of them take to the mountains, fjords and valleys to enjoy their changing climate and magnificent scenery – this is a country where people don't need to diet or go to the gym. Though many are rather shy and taciturn, when they do talk they can be direct and outspoken, and, rather than cold and distant as per the Scandinavian stereotype, they tend to be observant, dry-humoured and quite genial once they feel comfortable in a situation. Beer and *akavitt* lubricate many a social encounter, though some Norwegians still drink water or milk with their meals, sticking to traditional country values that are harder and harder to come by anywhere in the world.

Norway: Travel and Practical A–Z

10

Travel

Entry Formalities

Passports and Visas

Unlike Sweden and Denmark, Norway is not a member of the European Union. However, British, US and Canadian travellers need only a passport (valid for a minimum of three months after they enter the country) to get into Norway. Other visitors should check about visa requirements with their Norwegian Embassy (*see* p.128).

Customs

EU nationals may bring in or out 200 cigarettes, 2 litres of beer, one litre of wine and one litre of spirits. To and from North America the restrictions are 400 cigarettes and 2 litres of wine or spirits.

Getting Around

By Air

Domestic flights are relatively inexpensive and can save you time if you are making long trips between north and south.

The following airlines all offer a wide network of internal flights:

Braathens (a subsidiary of SAS), **t** 81 52 00 00, *www.sasbraathens.no*.

Norwegian Air Shuttle, t 81 52 18 15, *www.norwegian.no*.

Scandinavian Airlines System (SAS), **t** 81 52 00 00, *www.scandinavian.net*.

Widerøe, t 81 00 12 00, *www.wideroe.com*.

By Train

Norges Statsbaner (NSB), t 81 50 08 88, then dial 4 for English-speaking operator; www.nsb.no.

Norwegian State Railways trains are clean, comfy, punctual and fairly frequent – and surprisingly cheap for Norway. Additionally, **Minipris** discounts offer up to 50% off the price of long-distance journeys if you buy your ticket at least one day in advance and travel direct, with no stopover; the trains on which these are available are indicated by a green dot on timetables. There are also group and family reductions; students under 16 and

seniors over 67 pay half-fare; and children under 4 travel free if they do not take up a seat. If you buy a **Minipris** ticket once in Norway, a NOK50 administrative fee is added.

For those undertaking extensive travel, the **Norway Rail pass** (sold at major train stations in Norway, by Rail Europe and Eurostar in the UK, and by CIT Rail, Europrail and ScanTours in the USA) allows unlimited trips on nearly all of Norway's rail lines for a specific number of days within a specific period (i.e. 3, 4 or 5 days within one month). Children under 4 travel free, those aged 4–15 get a 50% discount, and seniors receive 20% off. The **ScanRail pass** (sold by the same agencies) covers all Scandinavia, either 1st or 2nd class, for 5 days' or 10 days' travel within 2 months, or 21 consecutive days.

Rail Europe UK, t 0870 584 8848, *www.raileurope.co.uk*. Agents for ScanRail passes, Inter-Rail and Eurostar.

Rail Europe USA: (USA) **t** 1 800 438 7245; (Canada) **t** 1 800 361 7245, *www.raileurope.com*. Official North American EurailPass agent. Sells ScanRail passes as well.

CIT Rail, (USA) **t** 1 800/223 7987 or **t** 212 730 2400; (Canada) **t** 1 800/361 7799, *www.cit-rail.com*. Sells Eurail and ScanRail passes.

Europrail International Canada, t 1 888/667 9734, *www.europrail.net*.

ScanTours, t 1 800 223 7226/**t** (310) 636 4656.

Trains tend to be busy, and queues to buy tickets can be quite long, so it is advisable to reserve on all main routes. Also note that all long-distance, overnight and international trains require an **advance seat reservation** (around NOK30), with or without a rail pass. Bookings can be made through the website.

Most stations have **Narvesen kiosks** selling sandwiches, hot dogs and a couple of hot dishes, as well as non-alcoholic drinks, newspapers (including international editions, in larger towns) and magazines, and basic sundries such as aspirin and dental floss.

By Ferry

Car and foot ferries are an excellent, economical way to travel around much of Norway, especially the western fjords, which they cover extensively. Most operate on a first-come, first-served basis, so it is advisable to arrive at least 20–30mins before departure in the busy spring and summer months.

Conductors generally collect the fares while you are parked in the queue, although some busier routes have a drive-by ticket booth.

Hurtigbåt Passenger Express Boats, high-speed catamarans concentrated around Bergen and its surrounding fjords, are quicker but more expensive than ferries (children, students and seniors over 67 get a 50% reduction), and you don't get to view the landscape. They are quite comfortable except in rough seas.

For the **Hurtigruten**, or Norwegian Coastal Voyage, *see* pp.208–209.

By Coach and Bus

Nor-Way Bussekspress, t 82 02 13 00 (NOK10 per min), www.nor-way.no; main information office at Oslo bus station.

Buses are a pleasant and reasonably priced way to travel beyond the extent of the train network, especially in the western fjords and in the far north, where, along with local ferries, they are often the only means of public transport.

Timetables for long-distance buses, which are linked to a network of local buses, are available at tourist offices and bus stations. Tickets can usually be bought on board, but you are advised to book ahead on the more popular long-distance routes to Bergen, Stavanger and Trondheim. There are student, group and family reductions, as well as 33% discounts for seniors over 67. Children aged under 4 travel free; those aged 4–15 pay half fare. All tolls and almost all ferry costs are included in the ticket price.

For those planning extensive bus travel, a **Nor-Way BussPass** (around NOK2,300) gives 21 days' unlimited trips on long-distance buses. It covers all toll and ferry costs, and guarantees a seat without advance booking. InterRail and ScanRail pass holders get a 50% discount on certain bus services, as well as certain boats, such as Hurtigbåt express boats.

By Car

While virtually all the day trips that we propose in this guide are easily accessible by public transport, you may decide to hire a car if you plan to follow the touring itineraries suggested in this guide.

Car Hire

In the UK
Avis, t 0870 606 0100, *www.avis.co.uk, www.avisworld.com.*
Budget, t (01442) 280181 or t 0800 181181, *www.budget.co.uk.*
Europcar, t 0870 607 5000, *www.europcar.com.*
Hertz, t 0870 599 6699, *www.hertz.co.uk.*
easyCar, *www.easyCar.com.*
National, t 0870 536 5365, *www.nationalcar.com.*
Thrifty, t (01494) 751600, *www.thrifty.co.uk.*

In the USA
AutoEurope, t 888 223 5555, *www.autoeurope.com.*
Avis, t 800 331 1084, *www.avis.com.*
Europcar, t 877 940 6900, *www.europcar.com.*
Hertz, t 800 654 3001, *www.hertz.com.*
National, t 800 227 7368, *www.nationalcar.com.*
Thrifty, t 800 367 2277, *www.thrifty.com.*

All major international rental companies (*bilutleie*) are represented in Norway, and it may be wiser to choose one of them rather than a local company, as contract details will be in Norwegian and English. To hire a car, you must be 21 or over and have been driving for at least a year, and a credit card is mandatory.

Rates are fairly high (about NOK3,600 per week for a small vehicle, with unlimited mileage, and a tank of petrol, which must be replaced). Collision damage waiver and vehicle insurance are provided, but not personal coverage and liability. Good weekend deals (often as little as NOK1,000) are usually available, and some packages include accommodation. The least expensive option is still to make rental arrangements before leaving home and pick up your car at the airport upon arrival.

Driving here is on the right, with dipped headlights required even in daylight. **Seatbelts** are compulsory.

Though main roads in Norway are excellent, when venturing towards lesser-travelled routes in the western fjords or in northern Norway, you should be prepared – take a spare can of fuel, stick to the main roads indicated on maps (*see* p.129), and check with locals about road changes due to storms, avalanches and other unpredictable situations.

Main highways are prefixed E, while secondary routes are numbered: the busier the route, the lower the number. Note that sometimes the numbers given on maps are wrong, due to frequent changes. The many tunnels you will encounter are well-lit.

Rules of the road are strict in Norway. The speed limit is 30kph in residential areas, 50kph in towns and cities, 80kph on open roads, and 90kph on motorways and some main roads. Watch out for the Automatisk Trafikk Kontroll warning signs – an extensive network of speed cameras. Fines are heavy (NOK700–3,000) and the rental car company will add a substantial extra charge to your credit card bill.

Absolutely **no alcohol** can be consumed before or while driving in Norway. Routine traffic checks often involve breath tests, and if you are over the limit your licence will be confiscated on the spot and you may face 28 days in prison.

If your hire car breaks down, roadside assistance will be provided by the garage that has been designated by the rental company. **Norges Automobil-Forbund** (NAF), the Norwegian automobile association, has a 24hr **breakdown service** (**t** 1 00 05 05; there are emergency telephones along many motorways) and patrols many mountain passes in spring and summer. **Viking Redningstjeneste** (**t** 80 03 29 00) also offers a 24hr breakdown service.

Petrol is relatively affordable by Norwegian standards, and there are many 24hr BP stations on main roads, with convenience shops selling food, drinks, maps and basic sundries. Road **toll stations** are sometimes unmanned and require coins to be inserted in order to pass through (generally NOK10).

Practical A–Z

Climate and When to Go

With the advent of global warming, Norway now experiences summer temperatures of 25°C (80°F) or higher, while the Gulf Stream contributes to pleasant weather conditions and especially mild winters in the southern and western regions covered by this guide. As is the case with many places in northern Europe, the weather here can change several times a day, however, so make sure that you come prepared (*see* 'Packing', p.130).

Oslo is one of the warmest places in the country during the winter: average January temperatures in the city range from about –2°C (28°F) to –7°C (19°F). Further north, temperatures hit sub-zero for months and many roads are closed over winter due to snowfall. For skiing, February and March are the best months, with Oslo an ideal spot for cross-country skiing. March, April and May are wet months with icy roads, though the temperature does start gradually rising from about 4°C (39°F) to 16°C (61°F).

In summer, when the midnight sun is in view, Oslo enjoys temperatures in the low to mid 20°Cs (about 74°F), which can also be experienced in the north. The rainy season begins earlier in the north, and by October autumn rains have caused a dip in temperatures to around 10°C (50°F) or lower. The first snow arrives around mid-October.

Most of the country's historical or cultural festivals are held in spring, summer and winter. *See* festival listings within each city, or ask at local tourist offices for a current schedule (or see their websites).

Consulates and Embassies

Norwegian Embassies Abroad
UK: 25 Belgravia Square, London SW1X 8QD, **t** (020) 7591 5500, *emb.london@mfa.no*.
USA: 2720 34th St NW, Washington D.C. 20008, **t** (202) 3 33 60 00, *www.norway.org*.
Canada: Royal Bank Center, 90 Sparks St, Suite 532, Ottawa, ON K1P 5B4, **t** 238 6571, *emb.ottawa@mfa.no*.

In Oslo
UK: 8 Thomas Heftyes Gate, **t** 23 13 27 00.
USA: 18 Drammensveien, **t** 22 44 85 50.
Canada, 7 Wergelandsveien **t** 22 99 53 00.

Crime and the Police

Police **t** *112*

Oslo is a great deal safer than other European capitals, and than North American capitals, and Bergen and other Norwegian cities are safer still. The **pickpocket** problem is universal, however, so be on your guard in crowded market areas, on buses and trams, and at outdoor public events. In Oslo you should be careful around the central train station, which attracts junkies, drunks and street types, and avoid the deserted streets around the harbour after dark.

The police generally keep a low profile here, and if there is a problem you should call **t** 112. **Women** can walk in most busy areas safely after dark but should always remain street-smart.

Drinking on the street is forbidden and calls for a fine of around NOK2,000 and time in jail. On the street, drunks tend to be more noisy than dangerous, but try to walk on the opposite side. Most bars have oversized bouncers to deal with drunks who get out of hand.

Disabled Travellers

A growing number of hotels and campsites are adapting their facilities for people with disabilities. **Euro Terra Nova**, 17 Rådhusgata, Oslo, **t** 22 99 23 99, *www.euroterranova.no*, recommended by the Norwegian tourist office, has information on hotels (including discounts), special deals with car rental agencies, and coach tours. The **Norges Handikapforbund**, 1 Schweigaardsgaten, Oslo, **t** 24 10 24 00, *www.nhf.no*, produces a variety of useful publications about accessibility for wheelchair users, throughout Norway, and has a good English-language website. Its English-language brochure, orientated towards people with disabilities, is available from the tourist office.

For information on special train carriages for the disabled, contact **Norwegian State Railways** (*see* p.126) or, in the UK, **Access Travel**, 6 The Hillock, Astley, Lancashire, M29 7GW, **t** (01942) 888 844, *www.access-travel. co.uk*, a specialist tour operator that can arrange flights, transfers and accommodation for disabled travellers.

The new generation of **Hurtigruten** ships (Norwegian Coastal Voyage; *see* pp.208–209) has very good facilities for wheelchair users, including elevators and a few specially adapted cabins.

Electricity

The Norwegian grid is set to 220 AC; you will need an **adapter** with two round-ended prongs. Water heating elements that can be powered by a car cigarette lighter are not allowed unless they have an automatic thermostat to cut them out.

Health and Emergencies

Ambulance and medical assistance **t** 113
Fire **t** 110

If you become ill, ask your hotel, tourist office or nearest pharmacy for the address of an **English-speaking doctor**. Private doctors are listed in the directory under *Leger*. In an emergency, call an ambulance or ask for the nearest **hospital** (*sykehus*).

Most large cities have a **24-hour pharmacy** (*apotek*). In smaller towns, ask at your hotel or look under *Legevakt* (doctor on duty) in the telephone directory.

There are reciprocal health care arrangements in place between Norway and EU countries; bring a stamped **E111** form with you (available from post offices). However, it is always advisable to take out travel insurance covering medical treatment, and for US/Canadian visitors this is essential.

Maps

Most tourist offices will provide free town plans and also sell various maps of the country. **Cappelens** publishes excellent road maps, covering the entire country, which can also be bought at bookstores and many Narvesen kiosks.

Media

City-centre, railway station and airport kiosks such as the **Narvesen** chain sell a variety of English-language newspapers, books and periodicals.

BBC radio stations 1, 2, 3 and 4 can sometimes be received on AM in winter. Radio 5 can be picked up on 909 and 693 MW. If atmospheric conditions are favourable, English-language broadcasts can also be heard on the short-wave frequency 9410.

Norway has three main **TV stations**: NRK, TV2 and TV Norge (TVN). Cable TV is also available, which means that you can get Sky, CNN and other English-speaking stations.

Suggested Reading

The History of Norway: From the Ice Age to Today, Øivind Stenersen, Ivar Libæk (Dinamo Forlag, 2003).

One Hundred Years of Norwegian Painting, Magne Malmanger (Nasjonalgalleriet Oslo, 2000).

A Journey Through Norway: Unique Places to Dine and Stay, Hans Martin Underdal, Espen Grønli, Cecilie F. Stang (Kom Forlag, 2001).

Money and Banks

The Norwegian **kroner** (NOK) is divided into 100 ore. Notes come in denominations of NOK50, 100, 200, 500 and 1,000; coins come in 50 ore and NOK1, 5, 10, and 20.

Currency can be changed at post offices, at Oslo's central train station, at international airports, at some hotels and at commercial banks. Airport and train station offices and banks offer slightly better rates than hotels . Most banks also have **ATM machines** where you can withdraw cash on your bank or credit card by punching in your normal PIN number.

Major **credit cards** are accepted in most hotels and restaurants.

Banking hours are summer Mon–Fri 8.15–3; rest of year Mon–Wed and Fri 8.15–3.30, Thurs 8.15–5.

Opening Hours

Shops are generally open Mon–Wed and Fri 10–4 or 5, Thurs 10–6 or 8; Sat 9–1, 2, or 3.

Most **supermarkets** are open Mon–Fri 9–8, Sat 9–6. The popular **Narvesen kiosks** are usually open until 9pm, and in recent years the USA-based **711** chain of 24hr stores has spread across Scandinavia, offering food, drink and various necessary sundries from aspirin to dental floss.

Museums are usually open May–Sept Tues–Fri 10–6, Sat and Sun 11–5; the rest of the year they tend to close at 4.

National Holidays

Most museums, banks and shops are closed.
1 Jan New Year's Day
Mar/April Palm Sunday, Maundy Thursday, Good Friday, Easter Sunday and Monday
1 May Labour Day
17 May National Independence Day
May Ascension Day 6th Thurs after Easter
May/June Whitsun and Whit Monday (7th Sun/Mon after Easter)
25 Dec Christmas Day
26 Dec Boxing Day

Churches, usually have Sunday morning services (times are listed on boards outside). If a service is not in progress, and the church is open, visitors are usually welcome. If you enter while a service is in progress, it is polite to stay.

For **banks**, *see* left; for **post offices**, *see* p.131.

Packing

Spring and autumn are quite rainy, and evenings can get quite chilly – bring a light raincoat or hooded windbreaker/anorak, a cardigan or sweater, gloves and an umbrella, and dress in layers. In winter, bring warm clothing you can also wear in layers, plus a hat, earmuffs and, if you are skiing, a face cover.

Good shoes are essential for exploring cities, and more serious shoes for hiking.

Price Categories

The **restaurant price** categories used throughout this guide (*see* box) are based on set menus or a 2-course meal for one person without wine. **Hotel prices** are for a double

Hotel Price Categories

luxury more than NOK1,800
very expensive NOK1,300–1,800
expensive NOK800–1,300
moderate NOK600–800
inexpensive less than NOK600

Restaurant Price Categories

very expensive more than NOK800
expensive NOK300–800
moderate NOK100–300
inexpensive less than NOK100

room with bath/shower in the high season (prices are considerably lower at weekends and in summer).

For general information on eating out in Norway, *see* **Food and Drink**, pp.133–8.

Shopping

Good Norwegian **souvenirs** include gold, silver and enamel jewellery, pewter, knitwear (especially classic pullovers) and wood carvings. Museums usually have good one-off shops selling unusual gifts and souvenirs. Among the famous native names are Porsgrund Porselen (china), Hadeland Glassverk (*see* pp.161–2) and Magnor Glassverk (crystal/glass), David Andersen (jewellery), Juhls (silver jewellery from Lapland) and Heimen (handicrafts). For unique handicrafts such as scarves and other textiles, ceramics and glass objects, **Husfliden** has branches in most cities and some small towns (this is the shop where Norwegians buy their national costumes). Other good buys are smoked salmon and trout, goat's milk cheese (*geitost*), caviar, candles, cheese slicers, trolls, schnapps glasses, and cloudberry, cranberry and blueberry preserves.

For **shop opening hours**, *see* p.130.

Telephones, Internet and Post

Hotels add a steep surcharge for phone calls made from your room to a foreign number; if you don't bring your mobile phone, it's better to find a **pay phone** (minimum charge NOK2; cheapest time 5pm–8am); they take NOK1, 5 and often 20 coins, or phonecards sold at Narvesen kiosks and at post offices; some also take credit cards.

The **international dialling code** when you call Norway from abroad is 47. When calling out of the country, dial 00, then the country code (UK 44; USA and Canada 1; Ireland 353), followed by the area code (minus the 0) and the number. When calling a number within Norway, dial 0 before the area code of the particular city (i.e. Oslo is 022/023).

Most chain and upmarket hotels offer **internet access** to guests, often free or for a reasonable fee (beware of the more expensive credit-card-accessed options in larger hotels). Larger cities have **internet cafés**, and public libraries offer free internet access (though there's generally a queue of locals waiting to get on). If you bring your laptop, don't forget a telephone adapter.

Post offices in cities are generally open Mon–Fri 8–4, Sat 8–1. The central post office in Oslo, at 15 Dronningens Gaten (entrance on corner of Prinsens Gate), is open Mon–Fri 8–8. **Stamps** are sold at post offices and occasionally in museum gift shops.

Time

Norway is on Central European Time, which is one hour ahead of Greenwich Mean Time and six hours ahead of Eastern Standard Time. At the end of March, the clock is set forward an hour to 'summer time', and set back an hour at the end of September.

Tipping

Hotel bills include a service charge and tipping is generally not expected. **Restaurants** usually include the service charge (though more and more are dropping it), and it is customary to tip 5–10% on top of that, although salaries are good and prices high, so don't feel you have to go overboard.

It is not necessary to tip **taxi** drivers, unless you have a lot of heavy luggage and they carry it some distance.

Toilets

There are public facilities in nearly every city and town. In train and bus stations, shopping centres and some hotels and restaurants, you may be expected to pay around NOK6; department stores are usually a better option.

Tourist Information

For tourist information within Norway, *see* the chapters on the respective cities and towns.
UK: Norwegian Tourist Board, 5th Floor, Charles House, 5 Lower Regent Street,

London SW1Y 4LR, **t** (020) 7839 2650, *www.visit norway.com/uk.*

USA and Canada: Norwegian Tourist Board, PO Box 4649, Grand Central Station, New York, NY 10163-4649, **t** (212) 885 9700, *www.visitnorway.com/usa.*

Where to Stay

There is a wide variety of places to stay in Norway, from luxury chains and historic hotels to simpler pensions, country cottages and farmhouses, and basic youth hostels (*vandrerhjem*). Hotel **prices** are considerably cheaper at weekends and, surprisingly, in summer (mid-June–mid-Aug, but especially July); this is because of the dearth of business travellers. Unlike many pensions, hotels include a copious **breakfast** buffet in the room price. For those travelling with children, family rooms are often available for little more than the cost of a double.

The **Fjord Pass** (**t** 55 55 76 60, *www.fjordpass. no*; NOK100; valid for families with children under 15) is Norway's biggest holiday and hotel discount card, offering substantial reductions on accommodation at some 200 hotels, inns, cottages and apartments throughout the country. It is valid for a year, though some establishments only accept it at certain times of the year.

The Rainbow and Norlandia hotels' **Scan+ Hotel Pass** (**t** 23 08 02 00, *www.scanplus.no*; around NOK95) offers discounts at 200 hotels around Scandinavia. The slightly more upmarket Rica Hotel group (**t** 67 85 45 00, *www.rica.no*) has a free **Feriepass** giving discounts on its room prices throughout Scandinavia (and a free 5th consecutive night). Nationwide **chains** such as Rica, Radisson SAS and Tulip Inn/Rainbow Hotels all maintain consistently high standards.

Norway:
Food and Drink

11

Restaurant Generalities

Don't be alarmed upon your arrival in Norway at the number of pizza parlours to be found both in big cities and tiny towns – an enterprising businessman brought back the idea nearly 40 years ago and it caught on quickly (pizza was considered exotic and was reasonably priced, enabling a family of four to get out for a meal every once in a while). Though there are a couple of reliable chains (Dolly Dimples and Peppes), however, you should try to be a bit more adventurous and seek out more traditional local offerings. In the last 10 years, Oslo, Bergen and Stavanger have developed quite a restaurant culture, with eateries now catering to more than just businessmen on expense accounts. In addition, with the arrival of so many immigrants in recent years, the variety of restaurants has widened a bit and now includes a range from Italian to Indian.

Most Norwegians have **dinner** early (around 6pm), though in the last few years cheaper prices have attracted a younger and more fashionable clientele who dine at 8 or 9, if not later. **Lunch** has traditionally been a sandwich in the work canteen (this probably goes back to the days of the Vikings, who had a hearty breakfast before setting out on a siege, returning for a multi-course banquet in the evening – perhaps a week later!). But though some upmarket hotels might still open only for dinner, these days most restaurants and cafés have lunch or all-day menus. The self-service lunch buffets offered at many larger hotels, consisting of a huge range of hot and cold dishes and small open sandwiches (*smørbrød*), are worth trying.

Norwegian Specialities

The Norwegian kitchen is known for its **fish** – depending on season, you can tuck into cod, pollack, mackerel, whitefish, monkfish, sea wolf and halibut. Fresh wild salmon (as opposed to farmed) is another speciality, as is marinated or smoked salmon and trout. Herring and shellfish, including crayfish, the summer delicacy, are quite popular; so too is dried cod, as well as clipfish, which is known as *bacalao* in the various southern countries from which it is imported (it's thanks to the Spaniards and Portuguese that it's now served in Norway with garlic, tomatoes and olive oil to pep it up). Fishballs with new potatoes is a traditional dish that you'll find served more in homes than in restaurants, though the fishcakes that are sold at fishmongers and in the fish section of supermarkets make a delicious snack, especially served warm. On a warm summer's day, you can't do much better than a plate of fresh shrimp and a glass of cold beer. And while it may not be considered politically correct, whale (from a non-endangered species; *see* box opposite) is worth trying, with its surprising steak-like flavour.

For **meat**-lovers, autumn is a time for indulging in game such as reindeer, elk or grouse, ideally served with tangy berries, wild mushrooms, potatoes and a hearty gravy and accompanied by a good red wine – unbeatable on a chilly evening. Lamb, though not found on many restaurant menus, forms the basis of several treasured

Whaling

Current international laws state that only whales that are not of an endangered species may be caught, and, unlike the Japanese, the Norwegians respect those rules. That said, they do find it absurd that other Europeans and North Americans have tried to impose what native writer Per Blissby described as 'Disneyfying standards to the creatures, in a kind of *"Free Willy* syndrome" that relies on emotions, when they don't think twice about slaughtering cows for hamburgers or torturing veal calves.'

It may therefore be a valid part of one's visit to Sandefjord, the former 'world capital' of whaling, to taste whale steak for yourself and to visit its whaling museum (*see* pp.173–4), which will teach you not only about the natural history of whales but also demonstrate what the industry meant to Norwegian culture in the early days, and the effects of its decline.

Norwegian dishes: *fenalå*, cured leg of mutton; *fårikål*, mutton slowly simmered with cabbage and peppercorns; and *pinnekjøtt*, a Christmas dish of salted, dried and sometimes smoked lamb or mutton spare ribs steamed and served with mashed *rutabaga*. Another holiday dish, which most Norwegians adore but which their guests are not always so sure about, is *lutefisk* or lye fish, made from cod soaked in water doctored with wood ash lye for many hours. Other Christmas specialities include marinated herrings, pork sausages or steak, and sheep's head.

One favourite that you will find at all hotel breakfast buffets is *geitost*, a caramel-coloured **cheese** made from goat's milk, slightly sweet in taste and virtually unknown beyond Norwegian borders. It comes under a multitude of names; the most common name for it is Norwegian *brunost* (brown cheese). Sour milk cheese, or *gammelost*, is another popular item, together with the filling sour cream porridge, *rømmegrøt*, which is served at summer lunches, accompanied by flatbread and dried, cured meat such as *spekemat*. This salty meat, which is also popular in summer, is best served with scrambled eggs and crisp flatbread accompanied by a chilled glass of aquavit (*see* p.138) and a beer chaser.

Finally, all year round there are delicious **cakes** to sample, often filled and frosted with whipped cream and jam. A lighter dessert is *karamellpudding*, very similar to Spanish *flan* or French *crème caramel*, or lighter still is the excellent **fruit** – apples, pears, berries, plums and morello cherries – grown on hillsides in the Hardangerfjorden, pesticide-free thanks to the cool climate and pure air.

Drinks

Norway, like the other Scandinavian countries, is a major coffee-drinking nation – **coffee** is jocularly described as the second national fuel, after oil. But before coffee was even introduced to the culture, those who could afford it drank **beer** – in the 19th century the daily beverage in rural areas, where around 90% of the Norwegian population lived, was *blande*, a mixture of water and sour whey. The tradition of home-brewed beer goes back to the Vikings, if not further. Depending on what

Norwegian Menu Reader

frokost breakfast
lunsj lunch
middag dinner
skål! cheers!
kan jeg få bestille? can I order?
kan jeg få regningen? can I have the bill?

Forretter (Starters) and Supper (Soups)

aspargessuppe asparagus soup
blandet salat mixed salad
blomkålsuppe cauliflower soup
dagens suppe soup of the day
erte- or betasuppe pea soup
fiskesuppe fish soup
gravlaks marinated salmon
grønnsakesuppe vegetable soup
gulrotsuppe carrot soup
hønsesuppe chicken soup
kålsuppe cabbage soup
krabbecoctail crab cocktail
laksesuppe salmon soup
linsesuppe lentil soup
løksuppe onion soup
melon melon
oksehalesuppe oxtail soup
pai filled pastry
potetsuppe potato soup
råkost crudités or raw vegetables
spinatsuppe spinach soup
tomatsuppe tomato soup

Kjøtt (Meat) and Vilt (Game)

and duck
biff beef steak
dyrestek venison
elg elk
fasan pheasant
gås goose
hare hare
hjort deer

kalkun turkey
kanin rabbit
kjøttboller/kjøttkaker meatballs
kylling chicken
lammekjøtt lamb
lapskaus beef stew
lever liver
oksekjøtt beef
pølse sausage (*varm pølse* hotdog sausage)
rapphøne partridge
reinsdyr reindeer
skinke ham
spekemat dried meat
stek steak
svinekjøtt pork

Fisk (Fish) and Skalldyr (Shellfish)

ål eel
ansjos anchovies
blåkveite halibut
blåskjell mussels
blekksprut octopus
breiflabb monkfish
fiskeboller fishballs (*fiskekaker* fishcakes)
flyndre sole
gravlaks marinated salmon
hummer lobster
hval whale
krabbe crab
laks salmon
lutefisk cod marinated in lye
makrell mackerel
østers oysters
piggvar turbot
plukkfisk fish stew in white sauce
reker shrimp
rødspette plaice
røkelaks smoked salmon
sardiner sardines
sei pollack
sild herring
steinbit catfish

part of Norway you find yourself in, you can try out various brands of beer, including the popular Ringnes in the south, or Mack in the north. Munkholm is a pleasant alcohol-free alternative.

Because it is very difficult to cultivate grapes so far north, wines are imported into Norway, and instead spirits such as **aquavit** (or *akevitt*) are produced. Distilled from potatoes, this vodka-like drink derives its intensely enjoyable flavour from caraway and tastes like distilled rye bread. Served chilled or at room temperature (Norwegians will go into endless discussions on the topic of the correct serving

sursild marinated herring
torsk cod
tunfisk tuna

Grønnsakker (Vegetables)

agurk cucumber
aubergine aubergine/eggplant
artisjokk artichoke
avocado avocado
blomkål cauliflower
bønner beans
broccoli broccoli
erter peas
gulrot (gulrøtter) carrot(s)
hodesalat/issalat lettuce
kål cabbage
mais corn
paprika green/red/yellow pepper
purre leek
rødbeter beetroots
rosenkål Brussels sprout
salat salad
selleri celery
sikori chicory
sjampinjong/champignon mushroom
sopp any edible fungus
poteter potatoes
spinat spinach
tomat tomato

Krydder (Spices) and Urter (Herbs)

anis anise
basilikum basil
dill dill
fennikel fennel
gressløk chives
hvitløk garlic
ingefær ginger
kanel cinnamon
karri curry
muskat nutmeg
oregano oregano

paprika paprika
pepper pepper
pepperrot horse radish
persille parsley
rosmarin rosemary
salt salt
timian thyme

Frukt, Bær, Nøtter (Fruit, Berries, Nuts)

ananas pineapple
appelsin orange
aprikos apricot
banan banana
druer grapes
eple apple
fersken peach
fiken fig
grapefrukt grapefruit
hasselnøtt hazelnut
jordbær strawberry
kirsebær cherry
kokosnøtt coconut
mandel almond
mango mango
melon melon
bringebær raspberry
multe cloudberry
nektarine nectarine
pære pear
peanøtt peanut
sitron lemon
valnøtt walnut

Ost (Cheese)

gammelost aged sour milk cheese
geitost a goat's milk cheese
ostefat cheese platter
Norzola Norwegian gorgonzola
pultost strong creamy cheese with caraway
brunost any one of a number of brown
cheeses made from regular or goat's milk,
or from a mixture of the two

temperature for their *akevitt*), along with a bottle of beer, it forms a traditional accompaniment to dishes such as *lutefisk* (*see* p.135) or mutton and cabbage, as well as many salted and smoked dishes. The production of '*linie akevitt*' or Linje is not considered complete until the liquor has been shipped in casks on Norwegian vessels on a round-trip to Australia (its name refers to the fact that it has passed the Equator, or Line).

Sadly, alcoholic beverages are extremely expensive in Norway, and, as in other Scandinavian countries, are highly taxed and legislated. A half-litre of beer, roughly

Desserter (Desserts)

eplekake apple cake
fløte cream
fruktkompott/salat fruit compôte/salad
is/iskrem ice cream
yoghurt yoghurt
kake cake
karamellpudding crème caramel/flan
kransekake an almond-based Norwegian
   holiday cake
krem whipped cream
lefse a traditional potato-based pancake
   eaten spread with sugar and butter, or
   geitost (see p.135).
pannekaker pancakes
pepperkaker cookies with pepper
risengrynsgrøt rice porridge
riskrem cold rice porridge mixed with
   whipped cream and flavoured with vanilla
sjokoladekake chocolate cake
sjokolademousse chocolate mousse
svele a local pancake made with baking
   soda (very popular and often served on
   fjord ferries)
vafler waffles
vaniljesaus vanilla sauce

Drikkevarer (Drinks)

kaffe coffee (koffeinfri decaffeinated)
kakao cocoa
melk milk (lettmelk low fat,
   skummet skimmed, kefir/surmelk sour)
mineralvann mineral water
   (med kullsyre sparkling; uten kullsyre still)
øl beer (fatøl on tap; lettøl low alcohol;
   alkoholfritt alcohol-free)
saft juice
te tea (krydderte herbal tea)
vann water
vin wine (rødvin red wine;
   hvitvin white wine; rosévin rosé)

Miscellaneous

appelsinmarmelade orange marmalade
brød bread
eddik vinegar
egg egg (eggerøre scrambled eggs)
flatbrød a flat, unleavened cracker
grøt porridge
kjeks biscuit
knekkebrød crisp bread
komler potato dumplings usually served with
   lamb or sausage
melk milk
postei pâté
potetchips/potetgull crisps/potato chips
ris rice
rømme sour cream
rundstykke bread roll
sennep mustard
smør butter
smørbrød open sandwich
sukker sugar

Preparation

rå rare/underdone, medium medium,
   gjennomstekt well done
dampet steamed
farsert filled
flambert flambéed
frityrstekt deep-fried (stekt fried) fish or meat
garnert garnished
gratinert gratinated
grillet grilled
grytestekt braised
hermetisert preserved
hjemmelaget (based on a) home recipe
kokt boiled
marinert marinated
ovnstekt baked/roasted
pochert poached
på spyd prepared on a spit
stuet in a sauce

equivalent to a British pint, costs between NOK45 and 60 in most bars or cafés (hotel bars, nightclubs and obvious tourist traps often serve smaller glasses without reducing the price accordingly), and beer that is sold in supermarkets (with a lower alcohol content) costs about NOK15–20 for a half-litre can, although strong beer, wine and spirits can only be bought at the government-operated **Vinmonopolet** ('wine monopoly', or polet to locals) in larger cities and towns. They open at 10 and close at 4, 5 or 6 during the week and at 2 or 3 on Saturdays.

Norway: Oslo and Around

12

Oslo

Oslo is a surprising capital, less hectic than the likes of London, Rome and Paris, except during rush hour in T-bane (underground) stations, when the normally mild-mannered locals turn into ersatz New Yorkers. This aura of relative calm may be down to the fact that most of the action takes place in its compact centre, while in the evenings locals retreat to their respective neighbourhoods – except in summer, that is, when the centre is like one big open-air gathering.

Romantically described as Scandinavia's 'City of Light', Oslo in spring and summer has a diamond-sharp luminosity that has long inspired painters, including Christian Krohg and Edvard Munch, while in late autumn and winter it is cloaked in a granite gravity. In recent years, immigration from Asia and the Middle East (Oslo's population is now just over 520,000) has led to the revitalization of many areas, including Grønland, a former industrial area parallel with the Akerselva river, with a number of Pakistani- and Turkish-run shops selling groceries and assorted wares, and eateries that have enhanced the city's constantly evolving restaurant scene.

History

The oldest Scandinavian capital, Oslo was founded in 1048 by Harald III, half-brother of Olaf II (later St Olav), nicknamed Hardrada or Harsh Ruler. Its name comes from the Nordic words Às (God) and Lo (field). By the early 14th century, the old town had a population of nearly 3,000 and two rulers, a bishop and a king, with separate palaces. Numerous fires over the years hampered the city's development, however, and in 1624, after Danish king Christian IV moved Norway's capital from Bergen (the major crossroads for trading and ship traffic) to Oslo to be closer to Denmark, he relocated the city centre to wider streets east of the original centre. He also, rather immodestly, changed its name to Christiania, the spelling of which was eventually changed to Kristiania to conform with the Norwegian. It was only in 1924, after many debates and arguments, that the Parliament (Storting) reinstated the name Oslo.

Perhaps best known as the home of the Nobel Prize and the 'City of Peace', Oslo also has an illustrious literary pedigree, thanks mainly to playwright Henrik Ibsen. A wealthy city, it was a shipbuilding centre until the mid 1800s. Its current prosperity is the result of both the growth in Norway's oil industry over the last few decades and the city's many IT businesses.

From the Nationaltheatret to the Harbourfront

The city's main pedestrian thoroughfare, Karl Johans Gate, leading from the Kongelige Slott (royal palace) down to the Domkirke (cathedral) and central train station, serves as a convenient dividing line between the harbour and downtown sector and the quarters leading up to the residential areas. Though Oslo's many fires destroyed most of the wooden buildings in the old city or Gamlebyen medieval quarter, there are still church ruins to be seen here, and in the centre itself there's a pleasant 19th-century ambience, with landmarks such as the Nationaltheatret and Grand Hotel recalling Norway's golden age of culture. The **Nationaltheatret**, known

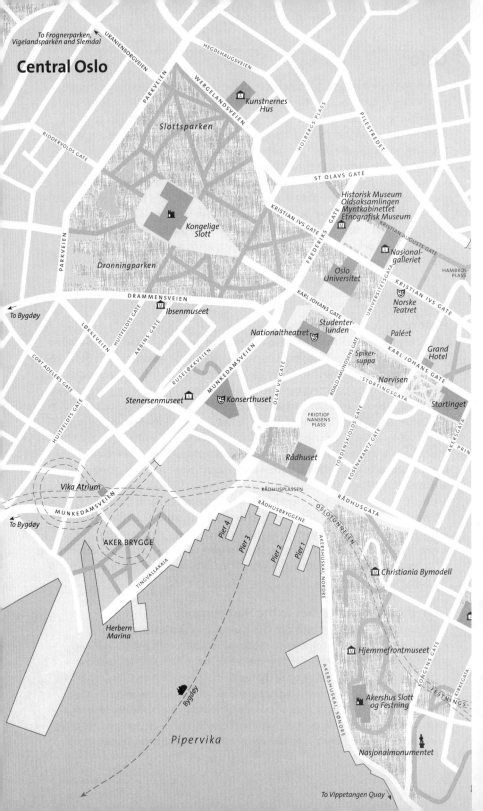

Central Oslo

To Frognerparken,
Vigelandsparken and Slemdal

URANIENBORGVEIEN

HEGDEHAUGSVEIEN

PARKVEIEN

WERGELANDSVEIEN

HOLBERGS PLASS

PILESTREDET

Slottsparken

Kunstnernes
Hus

RIDDERVOLDS GATE

St OLAVS GATE

Historisk Museum
Oldsaksamlingen
Myntkabinettet
Etnografisk Museum

KRISTIAN IVS GATE

FREDERIKS GATE

KRISTIAN AUGUSTS GATE

HAMBROS-
PLASS

Kongelige
Slott

Nasjonal-
galleriet

PARKVEIEN

Dronningparken

Oslo
Universitet

UNIVERSITETSGATA

KRISTIAN IVS GATE

To Bygdøy

DRAMMENSVEIEN

Ibsenmuseet

KARL JOHANS GATE

Norske
Teatret

HUITFELDTS GATE

ARBINS GATE

LØKKEVEIEN

Nationaltheatret

Studenter-
lunden

ROALD AMUNDSENS GATE

Paléet

Grand
Hotel

RUSELØKKVEIEN

MUNKEDAMSVEIEN

Spiker-
suppa

KARL JOHANS GATE

CORT ADELERS GATE

OLAV VS GATE

STORTINGSGATA

Narvisen

HUITFELDTS GATE

Stenersenmuseet

Konserthuset

Stortinget

FRIDTJOF
NANSENS
PLASS

TORDENSKJOLDS GATE

ROSENKRANTZ GATE

AKERSGATA

PRIN

Rådhuset

Vika Atrium

MUNKEDAMSVEIEN

RÅDHUSPLASSEN

RÅDHUSBRYGGENE

OSLOTUNNELEN

RÅDHUSGATA

To Bygdøy

AKER BRYGGE

Pier 4

Pier 3

Pier 2

Pier 1

AKERSHUSKAI NORDRE

TINGVALLAKAIA

Christiania Bymodell

Herbern
Marina

Bygdøy

AKERSHUSKAI, SØNDRE

Hjemmefrontmuseet

KONGENS GATE

FESTNINGS

KIRKEGATA

Akershus Slott
og Festning

Pipervika

Nasjonalmonumentet

To Vippetangen Quay

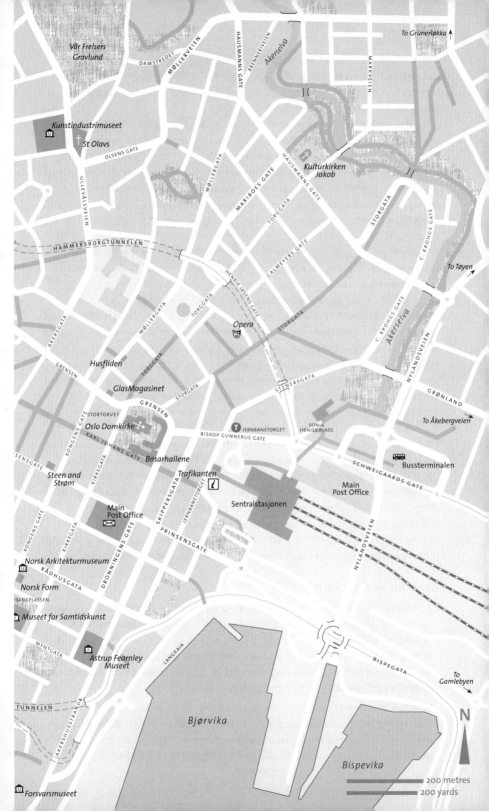

affectionately as 'Ibsen's Theatre', the **Opera House** on Storgata and the Oslo **Konserthus** (concert hall) have long dominated the cultural scene; in 2008 the 'old' opera house will be relocated to a sparkling new building in the Bjørvika quarter along the waterfront, near the main train station.

The Konserthus' terrace affords entry to the low-key, three-storey **Stenersenmuseet**, 15 Munkedamsveien, t 23 49 36 00, *www.stenersen.museum.no* (*open Tues and Thurs 11–7, Wed, Fri, Sat and Sun 11–5; closed Mon; adm*), part of the city's art collection, consisting of three private collections donated by the families of philanthropists and artists Rolf E. Stenersen, Amaldus Nielsen and Ludvig O. Ravensberg. Stenersen's 300-strong collection includes paintings, prints and watercolours by Edvard Munch and Norwegian Modernists such as Kai Fjell and Ludvig Karsten. Although Nielsen studied in Germany, he became known as the 'painter of the south' for his studies of southern Norway, many of which can be seen in the museum. Ravensberg, a relative of Munch, was known for his naïve, humorous portrayals of daily life in the capital, featuring well-known figures of the 19th century; there are some 160 in the museum, which also hosts changing exhibitions of contemporary Norwegian art.

A short walk from the Konserthus at Rådhusgata, the caramel-brown brick **Rådhuset** (city hall) was inaugurated in 1950 to celebrate Oslo's 900th anniversary. Designed by Arnstein Arneberg and Magnus Poulsson, this distinctive Modernist building was the subject of derision for 20 years before it opened its doors, though critics have had other contemporary structures to vent their wrath at in the intervening decades, and the controversial interior is now considered a fine tribute to Norwegian culture, with its main hall, or Rådhushallen, decorated with an impressive range of murals celebrating Norway's dramatic history. Outside, at the back of the Rådhuset is a row of powerful bronze sculptures representing the different tradesmen who worked on the building, while beyond are four massive female granite sculptures surrounding a fountain.

Just south of the Rådhuset is the quayside (from where you can catch a ferry to the Bygdøy peninsula; *see* p.158), southwest of which is the ultramodern **Aker Brygge** redeveloped docklands complex with its shops, waterside cafés and restaurants, and luxury housing. The harbourfront, now a popular pedestrian street thanks to the commuter ferry and cruise ship traffic, stretches round from here to historic Akershus fortress and castle with its magnificent views of the Oslofjorden and parts of the city.

Akershus Slott og Festning

*t 23 09 39 17; open **castle grounds** daily 6–9; **information centre** 17 June–18 Aug Mon–Fri 9–5, Sat and Sun 11–5; 19 Aug–16 June till 4; **Hjemmefrontmuseum** 15 April–14 June Mon–Sat 10–4, Sun 11–4; 15 June–Aug Mon–Sat 10–6, Sun 11–5; Oct–14 April Mon–Fri 10–3, Sat and Sun 11–4; **Forsvarsmuseet** June–Aug Mon–Fri 10–6, Sat and Sun 11–4; Sept–May Mon–Fri 10–3, Sat and Sun 11–4. **Guided tours of castle** summer daily 10, 12, 2 and 4; adm, grounds free.*

Strategically placed at the tip of the headland, the medieval Akershus Slott or castle, which withstood a number of sieges throughout the ages, is considered the nation's crown jewel. It is part of the Akershus fortress complex, the construction of which was initiated by King Haakon V Magnusson in 1299. Between 1637 and 48 it was

Getting to Oslo

Oslo's modern, efficient **Gardermoen airport** 45km north of the city has flights with British Airways from London Heathrow and Gatwick, with British Midland from Heathrow, with Scandinavian Airlines System (SAS) from London Heathrow (direct or via Copenhagen), with Norwegian Airlines from London Stansted, and with KLM from Amsterdam.

Torp airport 110km south of Oslo is served by Ryanair from London Stansted.

For airline contact details, *see* p.3.

Getting from the Airports

From Gardermoen airport there's an express **airport train** (t 81 50 07 77; *every 15mins daily 5.30am–12.30pm; c.* NOK140) to the Nationaltheatret stop in the centre, taking 25mins. The normal train (NOK72) takes 40mins.

The **Airport Flybussen** serving the Radisson SAS hotels at 3 Sonia Henies Plass and 30 Holbergs Gate and the central train station every 15mins (*Mon–Sat 5.30am–1am, Sun noon–midnight*; NOK100 one-way/150 return) takes 45mins. A **taxi** costs NOK545–600 and takes about 45mins (Airport Taxi, t 23 23 23 23).

From Torp airport, the **Oslo Torp Express Bus** (t 177 or t 815 00 176, *www.trafikanten.no*) leaves 30mins after each Ryanair arrival from London (if the flight is delayed, the bus waits), taking you to the Oslo bus terminal near the central train station in 2hrs (NOK100 each way, NOK49 children 3–15). To return, **Telemarkespressen** buses leave Oslo bus terminal for Torp about 3hrs before each flight departure, making several stops along the way. Seats are guaranteed for all passengers.

Getting Around

Aside from a few dicey areas on side streets near the harbour and around the train station, Oslo is a safe city to explore and one that is easily navigable by foot, tram, bus or T-bane (underground train). **Trafikanten** at 1 Jernbanetorget by the central train station (t 177 or t 81 50 01 76; *open daily 8am–11pm; office open Mon–Fri 7am–8pm, Sat and Sun 8–6*) provides information, maps and tickets for all public transport in and around Oslo, including local trains and ferries.

The **Oslo Pass** (*see* p.146) allows unlimited rides on buses, trams and T-banes in the metropolitan area. There is also a **day pass**, which can only be bought at Trafikanten; the date must be filled in when you begin use and it must be stamped in a little machine by the driver on the bus, in the middle of trams, and at T-bane stations. Don't risk riding 'black' (without a ticket): groups of agents patrol trams and T-banes (not buses) and a fine of around NOK750 will be imposed on the spot.

To let the conductor know you wish to get off a tram, you need to press a small knob to ring a bell. Doors do not open automatically – you need to press the knob by the door.

Taxis can be found at ranks around the city and in front of major hotels, or call Oslo Taxis, t 02 323, or Taxi, t 02 202.

By Ferry, and Ferry Excursions

Besides the Bygdøy ferry from behind the Rådhuset (*see* p.144), you can enjoy various **mini fjord cruises** by taking the ferries that run from from the city centre to inhabited islands within the Oslofjorden, including **Hovedøya** and **Lindøya** (year-round, ferry no.92) and **Langøyene** (June–Aug, ferry no.94). Boats leave from Vippetangen quay, at the end of the harbour past Akershus fortress. Hovedøya has a ruined Cistercian abbey built by English monks from Kirkstead, set in a landscaped park with a beach where you can swim. At Langøyene you can get off and have a pleasant walk around the island, stopping at the café for a lovely view of the Oslo skyline. Make sure you don't miss the last ferry, as the few water taxis are extremely dear. For camping information, call t 22 11 53 21.

For more on ferry trips, *see* pp.163–4.

Car Hire

Avis Bilutleie, t 23 23 92 00; Gardermoen airport, t 64 81 06 60.
Bislet Limousine/Carey Norway, t 22 57 00 57.
Hertz Bilutleie, t 22 21 00 00 or t 67 12 55 55; Gardermoen airport, t 64 81 05 50
Sixt Rent A Car, Gardermoen airport, t 07 050.

Bicycle Hire

The city has around 1,000 eye-catching white bicycles stored on prominent racks throughout the centre, accessed via a card sold at tourist information offices. The card costs NOK50 and is valid for a year, but you can only use a bike for 3hrs before returning it to any stand and exchanging it for a new one.

For longer rentals, try **Skiforeningen**, 5 Kongeveien (Holmenkollen), **t** 22 92 32 00, or **AS Skiservice** (by Voksenkollen station near Holmenkollen), **t** 22 13 95 00.

Tourist Information

Oslo: 5 Fridtjof Nansens Plass, by Rådhuset (entrance from Roald Amundsens Gate), **t** 23 11 78 80 or **t** 24 14 77 00, *www.visitoslo.com* (*open daily 9–7*). There's also a branch at the Oslo central train station at 2 Jernbanetorget (*open June–Aug daily 8am–11pm, shorter hours rest of year, closed public hols*).

The **Oslo Pass** allows free entry to various museums and attractions, free travel on public transport, parking at municipal car parks, discounts on sightseeing tours and more. It is stamped with the date and time when first used, and from then on is valid for the number of hours indicated on it (24/48/72; NOK200/290/380). There are reduced-rate children's passes (NOK80/100/130) and a 1-day Family Pass for 2 adults and 2 children (NOK400). Passes are sold at tourist offices, hotels, campsites, Trafikanten and some Narvesen kiosks, as well as *www.visitoslo.com*.

Guided Sightseeing

Båtservice Sightseeing (**t** 23 35 68 90, *www.boatsightseeing.com*) offers guided sightseeing tours by boat and/or bus, with daily summer departures from Pier 3 behind the Rådhuset. Fjord cruises last 1–2hrs, bus tours combined with cruises 4–7hrs.

H.M. Kristiansens Automobilbyrå (**t** 23 15 73 00, *www.hmk.no*) runs several bus tours lasting 2–4 hrs and taking in top attractions such as Akershus fortress, Vigelandparken and Holmenkollen. Buses depart every morning and afternoon from the main tourist office. Alternatively, you could try out the hop-on, hop-off **Oslo Pride** double-decker tours (*www.citysightseeing.com*), setting out from Karl Johans Gate opposite the university (9.30–4). Tickets, valid for 2 days, can be bought at tourist offices or on board.

The **Oslo Panorama Walking Tour** is a 75min tour of the city centre, held June–Aug Mon, Wed and Fri (*for details ask at tourist office*). During the Christmas season you can arrange horse sleigh tours (*kanefart*) in advance with Helge Torp, **t** 22 23 22 21 and Vangen Skistue, **t** 64 86 54 81. For **approved sightseeing guides**, contact **t** 22 42 70 20, *www.guideservice.no*.

For details of the scenic **Norway in a Nutshell** railway trip and fjord cruise between Oslo and Bergen, see p.160.

Festivals

Oslo hosts many festivals through the year but especially during the long summer nights. Music festivals include the **Norwegian Wood** rock festival in Frognerparken, around 18–20 June (*www.norwegianwood.no*), the **Oslo Chamber Music Festival** (**t** 23 10 07 30) around 21–31 Aug, the **Oslofjorden Opera Festival**, 14–22 June, the **Oslo Jazz Festival** (*www.oslo-jazz.no*) around 9–15 Aug, the **Øyafestivalen** (rock music; **t** 22 33 64 66) around 10–14 Aug, the **ULTIMA Oslo Contemporary Music Festival** around 7–17 Oct and the **Oslo World Music Festival** around 4–9 Nov.

Other major events include the **Holmenkollen Ski Marathon** (14 Feb), the **Holmenkollen Ski Festival** (6–9 Mar), Norway's **Constitution Day** and Children's Parade (17 May), the **Oslo Medieval Festival** (13–15 June), the **Norway Cup**, the world's largest football tournament (25–31 July), and the **Summer Parade** (31 July). For theatre buffs, the **Ibsen Festival**, held at the Nationaltheatret at the end of Aug every even-numbered year, hosts theatre companies from around the world, who come to perform well-known as well as more obscure works by the great scribe.

Shopping

Shop **opening hours** are generally Mon–Fri 10–5 and Sat 10–2.

Oslo has many shopping centres, speciality stores, stylish boutiques, fascinating antiques and bookshops and handicraft stores, plus one-off museum shops that are a good hunting ground for gifts and souvenirs (*see* p.131). Fashion-wise, you'll find everything from exclusive designers such as Denmark's Bitte Kai Rand to the ubiquitous H&M.

Good shopping areas include the harbourside **Aker Brygge** complex (*see* p.144), and **Hegdehaugsveien, Bogstadveien** and adjoining streets between the royal palace and Frognerparken. On the other side of the Slottsparken, just past the university, the restored turn-of-the-20th-century **Paléet** shopping centre has diverse shops and eateries, including the excellent Tanum bookstore, over several elegant floors.

The streets around the cathedral form a large pedestrian area where two of Oslo's top department stores, **Steen & Strøm** and **GlasMagasinet**, can be found. On Møllergata, **Husfliden** sells traditional handcrafted items such as wood carvings, rose-painted bowls, glassware and national costumes from all over Norway. At 8 Rosenkrantz Gate is Heimen, another authentic shop selling handicrafts.

For urban chic, try the dynamic **Grünerløkka** quarter northwest of the cathedral (tram no.12 or no.13), a former working-class area that has been massively gentrified over the past 5 years or so. Its main street, Markveien, and the parallel Thorvald Meyers Gate boast the most stylish assortment of shops and eating establishments. **Grønland** is another evolving working-class area with ethnic shops and eateries.

Markets

The main **flower market** is held daily in Stortorvet in front of the cathedral, and for a few weeks in autumn regional farmers come here to sell their **fruit and vegetables**. The rest of the year, fruit and vegetable stands are scattered throughout the city, on street corners or in neighbourhoods such as Grønland, Tøyen and Grünerløkka.

There's a **flea market** every Sat at Amaldus Nielsens Plass not far from the Frognerparken.

Sports

Oslo's wealth of alpine and downhill **ski areas** are well lit and open late in the evening, and also offer snowboarding, tobogganing and horse/dog sleigh rides. For ski information, contact the **Skiforeningen** (Association for the Promotion of Skiing) on **t** 22 92 32 00,

www.skiforeningen.no. For **Holmenkollen** with its famous ski jump, *see* pp.160–61.

Those who fancy a spot of **ice skating** should head for the floodlit Narvisen, Spikersuppa (next to Karl Johans Gate, **t** 22 30 30 33; Nov–Mar) or Frogner Stadion, 67 Frognerveien, at Frognerparken (**t** 22 55 89 94).

Where to Stay

The **Oslo Package** (**t** 47 23 10 62 62, *www.visitoslo.com*) includes hotel accommodation and breakfast, along with an Oslo Pass, and allows children under 16 to stay free in the same room as their parents. Prices start at NOK460 per person.

Hotel Continental, 24–6 Stortingsgata, **t** 22 82 40 00, *www.hotel-continental.no* (*luxury–very expensive*). An illustrious hotel owned and run by four generations of the Brochmann family since it opened in 1900, a year after the Nationaltheatret opposite. Rooms are very stylish and comfortable, and the **Theatercafeen** (*see* p.151) has been *the* place to see and be seen among Oslo's cultural cognoscenti since Munch and his friends gathered here. The **Annen Etage** is one of Oslo's most exclusive restaurants.

Bristol, 7 Kristian IVs Gate, **t** 22 82 60 00, *www.bristol.no* (*very expensive–expensive*). An elegant central hostelry that has been a favourite among discerning visitors since it opened in 1920. The rooms are tastefully decorated and there's a extensive spa facility. The **Grill**, **Lounge** and **Winter Garden** attract the city's movers and shakers, from politicians to publishers, while **Hambro's** café serves sandwiches, salads and daily specials in a more casual atmosphere.

Grand, 31 Karl Johans Gate, **t** 23 21 20 00, *www.grand.no* (*very expensive–expensive*). A chic address that has welcomed heads of state, Nobel Prize-winners and members of the entertainment world since it opened its doors on Oslo's main thoroughfare in 1874. The building is Louis XVI revival with touches of Nordic Art Nouveau and a distinctive 1913 clocktower. The welcome is warm, the rooms are elegantly furnished, and there's a rooftop pool. Among the various restaurants and bar are the well-known **Grand Café** (*see* p.151), which was frequented by Ibsen and friends, and an upstairs terrace bar with magnificent city views.

Holmenkollen Park Hotel Rica, 26 Kongeveien, t 22 92 20 00, *www.rica.no* (*expensive*). A classic spa hotel situated high above the city in the Holmenkollen area (*see* p.160), built in the neo-Gothic style more than 100 years ago but bearing a modern gloss. There are extensive fitness and spa facilities and two good restaurants (lunch in the main dining room comprises a buffet of delicious hot and cold Norwegian specialities), plus excellent hiking and skiing trails nearby.

Rica Bygdøy Allé, 53 Bygdøy Allé, t 23 08 58 00, *www.rica.no* (*expensive*). A stylish option in the fashionable west end quarter leading to the Bygdøy peninsula, renovated in 2002 and now under new management. There's a popular summer terrace and restaurant, **Magma** (*see* p.149).

Frogner House, 8 Skovveien, t 22 56 00 56, *www.frognerhouse.com* (*expensive–moderate*). A charming, antique-filled hotel that opened in a luxury apartment building just to the west of the Slottsparken in 1992, with 60 individually designed guest rooms, maritime paintings, chandeliers and even a resident dove of peace. Several of Oslo's best restaurants are within walking distance.

Rica Holberg, 1 Holbergs Plass, t 23 15 72 00, *www.rica.no* (*moderate*). A hotel extensively renovated in 2001, and conveniently located across from the SAS Hotel, where buses depart for the airport (*see* p.145). Rooms are comfortably furnished, although be warned that the air-conditioning is rather noisy.

Tulip Inn Rainbow Frogner, 33 Frederik Stangs Gate, t 23 27 51 50, *www.rainbow-hotels.no* (*moderate*). A no-frills hotel situated in the stylish west end on the way to the Bygdøy peninsula, with basic rooms and a decent breakfast buffet that can be enjoyed outdoors during the summer. Light meals are available from the bar.

Tulip Inn Rainbow Gyldenløve, 20 Bogstadveien, t 22 33 23 00, *www.rainbow-hotels.no* (*moderate*). A hotel that is popular with a wide variety of international visitors, set on a popular shopping street running between the Slottsparken and Frognerparken. The guest rooms are pleasant, the staff are helpful and the breakfast is excellent.

Bondeheimen, 8 Rosenkrantz Gate, t 23 21 41 00, *www.bondeheimen.com* (*moderate–inexpensive*). A unique hotel established in 1913 as a home from home for visitors from the Norwegian countryside, as well as artists and writers from Europe and America. Centrally located, it has friendly staff, a gift shop selling fine handicrafts and the popular **Kaffistova** café. A complimentary light supper of bread and soup is served in the lobby on weeknights.

Cochs Pensjonat, 25 Parkveien, t 23 33 24 00, *www.cochs.no* (*inexpensive*). A once-secret address right behind the Slottsparken, this family-run pension is now known to savvy travellers all over the world. A low-key Nordic version of New York's Chelsea Hotel, the chic Revival-style building houses many artists and musicians. Rooms are clean and cosy with TV but no phone. Breakfast is not served, but you're given a coupon for discounted meals at a nearby eatery.

Ellingsens Pensjonat, 25 Holtegata, t 22 60 03 59, *ep@tiscali.no* (*inexpensive*). A family-run, no-frills, spick-and-span pension in a rambling house just a few minutes from public transport along the busy shopping street of Bogstadveien.

MS Innvik, Langkaia, t 22 41 95 00, *www.msinnvik.no* (*inexpensive*). A boat-pension run by a Nordic theatre group, located just a few minutes from the central train station. Cabins have their own bathroom, breakfast is included, and there is a terrace. The views embrace sailing boats, cruise ships and the occasional killer whale taking a break in the harbour area.

Bogstad Camp & Turistsenter, 117 Ankerveien, t 22 51 08 00, *www.bogstadcamping.no* (*inexpensive*). A complex 9km northwest of the city centre in a scenic forest location by Bogstad lake on the edge of the Nordmarka (a 30min ride on bus no.32 from the central train station and Nationaltheatret). There's space for caravans or tents, as well as basic cabins with kitchens and deluxe cabins with kitchens, toilets and showers, televisions and telephone hookups. Besides swimming, you can hire watersports equipment, and the ski slopes are just 3km away. The site also has a grocery store, a pub, a laundry and a service station.

Eating Out

Bagatelle, 3 Bygdøy Allé, t 22 12 14 40 (*very expensive*). Innovative French cuisine in the fashionable west end by Eyvind Hellstrøm, holder of two Michelin stars, with daily 3-, 5- and 7-course menus based on market fare. Other menus can be arranged, and there are guest chefs throughout the year and special weeks featuring truffles and other delicacies. *Closed lunch and Sun.*

Oro, 6a Tordenskjolds Gate, t 23 01 02 40 (*very expensive*). An excellent restaurant near the Rådhuset, with an open kitchen in which internationally acclaimed chef Terje Ness displays his culinary skills. Depending on the season, you may be able to try dove, rabbit or trout prepared in unique ways and enhanced with unusual side dishes. The wine list is excellent. There's a 9-course speciality menu. *Closed Sun.*

Magma, 53 Bygdøy Allé, t 23 08 58 10 (*expensive*). A chic bistro in the Rica hotel (*see p.148*), attracting a seriously fashionable crowd. It's run by chef Sonja Lee and her husband Laurent-sur-Nille, who worked in Provence with Alain Ducasse before launching Damien Hirst's Pharmacy in London. There's dining outdoors in summer.

Mares, 12b Frognerveien, t 22 54 89 80 (*expensive*). An ultra-fashionable brasserie south of the Frognerparken, offering fish specialities according to season. The lobster bisque and oysters on the half shell are excellent ways to start off a meal, although the wine list, which has a separate list for white burgundies, is almost intimidating. An intimate wine bar is being opened next door. *Closed lunchtimes.*

Markveien Mat & Vinhus, 12 Torvbakkg, t 22 37 22 97 (*expensive*). An unpretentious but memorable restaurant in ultra-hip Grünerløkka, with a refined, seasonally changing menu. Service is attentive, with the staff highly knowledgeable about the fine wines on the extensive list. **Kneipp's** wine bar next door offers less expensive dishes to go with fine wines served by the glass or bottle. *Closed lunchtimes and Sun.*

Solsiden, 34 Akershuskai (søndre), t 22 33 36 30 30 (*expensive*). A popular, upmarket fish restaurant on the harbourfront by the castle, specializing in large seafood platters brimming with shellfish. The various catches of the day are prepared inventively, and the wine list is long. *Closed Oct–Mar.*

Statholdergaarden, 11 Rådhusgata, t 22 41 88 00 (*expensive*). A gourmet temple situated in an 18th-century Baroque building near the town hall, forming a fine backdrop to Bent Stiansen's award-winning cooking. There's a seasonal *à la carte* menu on offer, plus daily changing 4- and 6-course menus. *Closed Sun.*

Arcimboldo, 17 Wergelandsveien, t 22 69 44 22 (*expensive–moderate*). Located across from the Slottsparken in the Kunstnernes Hus gallery, home to the city's culturati, this is a large open room that serves as a café and lunchroom by day and a serious restaurant with candles and linen by night. There's friendly service and an excellent wine list. *Closed Sun and Mon eves.*

Bølgen & Moi Briskeby, 26 Løvenskiolds Gate, t 24 11 53 53 (*expensive–moderate*). What started out life as a serious gourmet canteen in the out-of-town Henie Onstad art centre (*see p.160*) has turned into a near industry, with branches in Bergen and Stavanger, as well as cookbooks and public appearances by the adventurous chef Trond Moi. The Oslo branch is situated in a former power station just behind the Slottsparken. Dishes can get precious – stick with the basics, which are as impressive to look at as they are to eat, or come for breakfast or lunch. The outdoor terrace is a popular posing and people-watching spot.

Arakataka, 7 Mariboes Gate, t 23 32 83 00 (*moderate*). A popular, noisy watering hole on a back street around the corner from the Rockefeller Music Hall (*see p.152*), in the Opera quarter, attracting a hip young crowd who enjoy the Mediterranean-inspired food. *Closed lunchtimes.*

Håndverkeren, 7 Rosenkrantz Gate, t 22 42 07 50 (*moderate*). A centrally located Oslo institution dating back to the 1880s, known for its bar and intimate atmosphere as well the popular restaurant serving a range of seasonal local dishes.

Kampen Bistro, 21 Bøgata, t 22 19 77 08 (*moderate*). An unselfconscious neighbourhood restaurant just a 15min walk uphill from the Munch-museet and botanical gardens. The service is as casual as the pine tables and 1950s-style lamps, but try to be patient – the simple Norwegian fare with gourmet embellishments is worth the wait. This is a good spot to head to for Sunday brunch. *Closed Mon–Fri lunch.*

Lanternen Kro, 2 Huk Aveny, t 22 43 78 38 (*moderate*). A popular restaurant on the Bygdøy peninsula, with an outdoor terrace and a good view of the Oslo skyline. Owned by an Italian, it offers fresh salads and delicious pasta dishes.

Lille Herbern Fjordkro, Herbernveien, Lille Herbern, t 22 44 97 00 (*moderate*). Probably Oslo's most romantically located eatery, set on a little island hideaway that is accessible only by ferry (25mins from Herbern Marina near Aker Brygge; around NOK25) and offering a variety of seafood. *Closed mid-Oct to mid-April.*

Lorry, 12 Parkveien, t 22 69 69 04 (*moderate*). A bohemian enclave right behind the Slottsparken, frequented by artists and writers, who come for the simple meals and enormous choice of beers. The laidback staff can communicate pretty well in English. The unique art and craft pieces on the walls have been contributed by regular customers, most likely in exchange for meals.

Pascal Konditori og Brasserie, 10 Drammensveien, t 22 55 00 20 (*moderate*). A charming spot opposite the Slottsparken, serving the best French pastry outside of Paris by day, as well as delicious lunches – try a quiche or a bowl of onion soup. In the evenings it's a brasserie offering a range of more gastronomically minded fare.

Sult, 26 Thorvald Meyers Gate, t 22 87 04 67 (*moderate*). A popular spot in fashionable Grünerløkka, attracting a trendy young crowd who seem oblivious to the noise, the tight spaces and the wait for tables. Blame it on the excellent fish dishes, prepared any way you like and served with a choice of tempting potato dishes. The name means hunger; there's a sister bar called **Dorst**, or thirst, nearby. *Closed lunchtimes Mon–Fri.*

Bambus, 57 Kirkeveien, t 22 85 07 00 (*moderate–inexpensive*). A restaurant near Frognerparken, serving all sorts of Asian fare, including Thai, Vietnamese, Chinese and Japanese dishes. The cheerful bar area is decorated with colourful fruit lampshades. *Closed lunchtimes.*

The Broker Café, 27 Bogstadveien, t 22 93 04 80 (*moderate–inexpensive*). A popular lunch spot by day (it's situated on one of Oslo's best shopping streets) and a 'powerbroking' place by night, where deals are made under a painted glass ceiling.

Curry & Ketchup, 51 Kirkeveien, t 22 69 05 22 (*inexpensive*). A restaurant offering cheap, basic but delicious fare such as chicken tikka masala and lamb karrai, with Indian décor, and live Indian or Irish music sesssions, in the heart of the bustling Majorstuen quarter close to the Frognerparken.

Georg Nilsen Fisk & Vilt, 39 Bogstadveien, t 22 46 50 16 (*inexpensive*). Excellent deli/fish and game shop selling fabulous picnic fare, including fishcakes, smoked salmon and smoked reindeer. *Closed Sun.*

Hai Cafe, 6 Calmeyers Gate, t 22 20 38 72 (*inexpensive*). A discreet venue located in Oslo's modest Chinatown district, close to the Opera, serving a number of delicious Vietnamese dishes at highly affordable prices. The spring rolls and the noodle soups are particularly excellent.

Kaffistova, 8 Rosenkrantz Gate, t 23 21 41 00 (*inexpensive*). A rural oasis set in the heart of the city, serving delicious traditional fare such as sour cream porridge, liver in cream sauce, and whale steak with potato balls, plus a selection of open sandwiches, soups and salads (but no alcohol). *Closed lunchtimes Sat and Sun, from 8pm Mon–Fri.*

Krishna Cuisine, 59b Kirkeveien, t 22 60 62 50 (*inexpensive*). A cheap and healthy vegetarian mainstay in the Majorstuen quarter to the northeast of the Frognerparken, serving up a variety of meals with an Indian bias. It's a non-smoking/no caffeine environment, but second portions are not discouraged. *Closed from 8pm.*

Paléet, 37–43 Karl Johans Gate, no phone (*inexpensive*). A good-quality international 'fast food' hall situated on the lower level of the exclusive shopping complex, including Japanese, Chinese and Italian cuisine. *Closed from 8pm Mon–Fri, from 6pm Sat, and all day Sun.*

Pizza da Mimmo, 2 Behrens Gate, t 22 44 40
20 (*inexpensive*). An authentic pizzeria set in
an unassuming cellar location in the chic
west end, drawing in many of the city's
chefs on their nights off, who come for its
wonderful thin-crust pizzas and tasty pasta
dishes. *Closed lunchtimes.*

Punjab Tandoori, 24 Grønland, t 22 17 20 86
(*inexpensive*). A no-frills Indian hole-in-the-
wall and takeaway located in the heart of
the colourful ethnic quarter to the northeast of the centre, with no-nonsense service
and a daily changing selection of curries.

Valkyrie Restaurant, 15 Valkyriegaten,
t 22 69 70 10 (*inexpensive*). An unpretentious
oasis located at the bustling Majorstuen
intersection, in which the city's poets,
playwrights and painters hang out to drink,
smoke, discuss and occasionally bolster
their energy levels with hearty Norwegian
dishes. *Closed Sat and Sun.*

Vegeta Verthus, 3B Munkedamsveien,
t 22 83 40 20 (*inexpensive*). A place near the
Konserthus, offering hot and cold buffets of
salads, curries, casseroles and pizza slices.
It's very popular among locals, so make sure
to get here early.

Cafés

Coffee bar culture has spread slowly
through Norway in the last few years, though
so far it has remained blessedly unscathed by
international chains.

Kaffebrenneriet and Kaffe & Krem are
popular Norwegian chains with outlets all
over Oslo, serving reasonably priced baguettes
along with their consistently good brews.
They are generally open from 9 to 7. Il Moro at
25 Thorvald Meyers Gate in the Grünerløkka,
and 36 Hegdehaugsveien to the north of the
Slottsparken is a real Italian coffee bar offering
tasty sandwiches.

Grand Café/Bar, 31 Karl Johans Gate, t 22 42 93
90 (*expensive–moderate*). The Grand's
colourful murals testify to the ghost of
Ibsen past, who used to come to this café
inside the Grand Hotel (*see* p.147) daily. The
ambience is still formal, but these days
there are more tourists than playwrights in
attendance, thanks to the reasonably priced,
excellent buffet and the *à la carte* lunch
options. The self-service rooftop café is a far

more pleasant option than the pavement
café with its passers-by and noisy traffic.

Theatercafeen, 24 Stortingsgata, t 22 82 40 50
(*expensive–moderate*). An elegant Art
Nouveau environment within the Hotel
Continental (*see* p.147) for dining or just
enjoying coffee and a pastry. Oslo's cultural
and political élite use it as their pre- and
post-theatre living room. The Lobby Bar has
authentic Munch works on its walls.

Café Amsterdam, 11 Universitetsgata,
entrance on Kristian Augusts Gate, no phone
(*inexpensive*). An authentic replica of a
traditional Amsterdam 'brown café',
drawing both students and staff from the
adjacent university. The range of simple,
cheap and tasty grub includes satay dishes,
sandwiches and lasagne.

Entertainment and Nightlife

Theatre

The glorious Nationaltheatret, which raised
its curtain for the first time in 1899, is
renowned for its Ibsen Festival (*see* p.146),
which includes a large number of English-
language performances. Even if you don't
attend a play, there are guided tours of the
theatre – ask at the box office (t 22 00 14 00).

Norske Teatret, 8 Kristian IV's Gate, t 22 42 43
44, *www.detnorsketeatret.no*. Hosts English-
language plays by touring companies.

Parkteateret, 11 Olaf Ryes Plass, t 22 38 12 62.
A recent addition to the burgeoning
Grünerløkka quarter, boasting a 250-seater
auditorium offering drama performances,
rock music and literary evenings, and a
stylish, 1930s-inspired bar.

Music and Opera

Music-wise, the choice is huge. Norske
Opera (t 81 54 44 88, *www.operaen.no*),
Norway's prestigious opera company, which is
moving from its Storgata location to new
harbour premises in 2008, has a popular
repertoire that includes works by the usual
suspects as well as modern operas. The Oslo
Konserthuset at 14 Munkedamsveien (t 23 11 31
11/00) is home to the Oslo Symphony and also
hosts many prominent international music

events, including the Oslo Filharmonien og Sommerkonserter (summer concerts; t 23 11 60 60, www.oslofilharmoniem.com), focusing on Scandinavian composers, and including, during Aug and Sept, free concerts at public venues such as the Vigeland sculpture park and the Domkirke.

There's also the **Kulturkirken Jakob**, a recently restored 18th-century church located at 14 Hausmanns Gate, to the north of the Opera quarter, and hosting classical, jazz, world music and other acoustic concerts (t 22 99 34 50), and the **Universitets Aula** (see p.154; check with tourist office).

Rockefeller Music Hall, 16 Torggata (entrance on Mariboes Gate), t 22 20 32 32. A laid-back concert venue in the Opera quarter above Storgata, with room for 1,500 people, featuring top international artists as well as regional talent, from folk and country to pop and post-punk. Other activities include film and literary debates.

Clubs and Bars

Drinking laws have been liberalized over the course of recent years, and you can now imbibe into the small hours. Snack bars offering *pølsar* (a type of sausage known for its hangover prevention) and pizzas are open until late, and many of the stylish bars serve snacks until the wee hours.

Blå, 9 Brenneriveien, t 22 20 91 81. A café set in a former storehouse in Grünerløkka, with a diverse musical menu that majors in jazz. In summer there is an outdoor café where you can enjoy delicious, cheap food on the bank of the Akerselva river.

Club Blue Monk, 23 St Olavs Gate, t 22 20 22 90. A pleasantly eclectic nightspot that is spread over two floors and located up near the Kunstindustrimuseet. The musical offerings range from blues to ska and from post-punk to Baltic funk.

Cosmopolitan, 14 Ruseløkkveien, t 22 01 70 90. A new hotspot in the modern Vika Atrium adjacent to Aker Brygge, attracting the financial mafia who work in surrounding buildings. There's dancing in the basement, a marble bar and a gourmet restaurant.

Herr Nilsen, Hambrosplass, t 22 33 54 05. A classic, cosy bar/traditional and bebop jazz venue not far from the Nasjonalgalleriet, with a constantly changing line-up of performers and an offbeat crowd.

John Dee, 16 Torggata (entrance on Henrik Ibsens Gate), t 22 20 32 32. A venue in the Opera quarter above Storgata, run by the Rockefeller Music Hall (see below) and featuring up-and-coming rock/pop music bands. The cosy cellar pub is the home of **Beat Basement**, a rhythm and soul club.

Last Train, 45 Karl Johans Gate (entrance on Universitetsgata), t 22 41 52 93. A small central bar where people come to seriously listen to music, as well as to check one another out. There's a charge for concerts.

Lille, 5 Bygdøy Allé, t 22 44 80 44. A west end disco/bar pulling a spirited, unpretentious crowd, some of whom like to take to the stage in its basement bar.

The Living Room, 1 Olav Vs Gate, no phone. A stylish lounge/bar that makes a good pitstop before or after a cultural event at the nearby Konserthus or Nationaltheatret.

Onkel Donald, 26 Universitetsgata, t 23 35 63 10. A lively city-centre café, bar and restaurant, the latter serving reasonably priced international fare. Beware that it can get unpleasantly crowded at weekends.

Original Nilsen, 11 Rosenkrantz Gate, t 22 72 12 21. A central jazz hole-in-the-wall.

Skansen, 25 Rådhusgata. A former urinal turned house music club. Things start to swing after midnight on Fri and Sat nights..

Smuget, 22 Rosenkrantz Gate, t 22 42 52 62. One of Oslo's largest entertainment halls, with 3 stages, 6 bars, a restaurant, a café and a nightclub. Music includes jazz, blues, rock and funk. Expect to have to queue for a fair while at weekends.

Stortorvets Gjæstgiveri, 1 Grensen, t 22 42 88 63. A pioneer jazz café near the Domkirke, showcasing traditional and modern jazz on Thurs evenings and Sat lunchtimes.

Teddy's Soft Bar, 3A Brugata, t 22 17 36 00. A 1950s mainstay with a Wurlitzer, one of many ultra-cool places to in the constantly evolving Grønland quarter.

Underwater, 4 Dalsbergstien, t 22 46 05 26. A quirky bar devoted to opera and decorated with large fish tanks, in an unfashionable artists' quarter near the Vår Frelsers Gravlund north of St Olavs church.

modernized into a Renaissance castle and royal residence by Christian IV, but during the 17th and 18th century it fell into decay and required considerable restoration work, completed in 1749. The castle's bountiful gardens, restored to their 19th-century glory and at their best in spring and summer, are one of the city's most romantic spots.

The drawbridge at Kongens Gate takes you back in time to Christiania's impressive legacy, including the castle's **church** and and **royal mausoleum** (1580s). Royal funerals have been held in the chapel within the church since 1938. There's also an **exhibition** on the castle's history, splendid banqueting halls and reception rooms with tapestries and other atmospheric décor, and a changing of the guard daily at 1.30.

During the Second World War, 40 members of the resistance were executed at the castle; there are displays on the five-year occupation under the narrow 17th-century arches of the **Hjemmefrontmuseum** (Resistance Museum), **t** 23 09 31 38. At the far end of the yard in two brick buildings is the **Forsvarsmuseet** (Armed Forces Museum), **t** 23 09 35 82, with models, dioramas and 80,000 books illustrating Norwegian defence history from Viking times through to the present day, including a Spitfire and a German tank. Next to the museum in the centre of the yard, the **Nasjonal-monumentet** (national war memorial) has a plaque listing the names of the patriots shot.

In a former hay barn just outside the castle walls, the **Christiania Bymodell** (*open June–Aug Tues–Sun 11–6*) charts the city's history from 1624 to 1840, through an hourly audio-visual presentation and an impressive 10 x 15m model of Christiania in 1840.

Kvadraturen (Quadrangle Area)

This area between the harbour and Karl Johans Gate has a good number of listed, well-preserved buildings, some housing important art collections. In 1990 the imposing granite and marble Art Nouveau building (1907) that once housed the Norges Bank (Central Bank of Norway) at 4 Bankplassen was transformed into the **Museet for Samtidskunst** (National Museum of Contemporary Art), **t** 22 85 22 10, *www.museet.no* (*open Tues, Wed and Fri 10–5, Thurs 10–8, Sat 11–4, Sun 11–5; closed Mon; adm, children free, all free Thurs*). *Shaft*, a sculpture by Richard Serra, has pride of place outside the main entrance. Containing more than 4,300 works of art, including paintings, drawings, sculpture, photography, graphics, video, objects and installations, this is Norway's largest museum of postwar Norwegian and international art. The basis of the permanent collection came from the Nasjonalgalleriet and Riksgalleriet, which were taken over when the museum became independent in 1988; artists include Nils Aas, Jakob Weidemann, Inger Sitter, Tony Cragg and and Christian Boltanski. There are also tempoary exhibitions throughout the year.

Just east, the **Astrup Fearnley Museet for Moderne Kunst**, 7 Dronningens Gate, **t** 22 93 60 60, *www.af-moma.no* (*open Tues, Wed and Fri 11–5, Thurs 11–7, Sat and Sun 12–5; closed Mon; adm, free Tues*), in a contemporary brick and glass building with 6m-high steel doors, displays various permanent private collections with an emphasis on postwar native artists, though there are also excellent works by British and German artists from the same period, including Francis Bacon, R.B. Kitaj and Sigmar Polke. In recent years, pieces by younger British artists like Damien Hirst and Sam Taylor-Wood have been acquired, and the museum often hosts prestigious temporary exhibitions.

Those interested in architecture and design with a focus on Norway should visit the **Norsk Arkitekturmuseum** (Norwegian Museum of Architecture), 4 Kongens Gate, **t** 22 42 40 80 (*open Mon, Tues, Thurs and Fri 11–4, Wed 11–6, Sat and Sun 12–4*), which, along with changing exhibitions dealing with the post-1900 period, features a permanent exhibition of 1,000 years of Norwegian architecture. In the same building, the **Norsk Form** centre, **t** 22 47 74 00 (*same opening hours*) holds exhibitions and lectures about design and architecture .

Along Karl Johans Gate to the University and Kongelige Slott

Oslo Domkirke (the cathedral, also known as Our Saviour's Church; *open daily 10–4*), consecrated in 1697, is still blessed with its original pulpit, altarpiece and organ front with distinctive carvings featuring acanthus leaves. It's an odd juxtaposition of Baroque and Modernist, with austere stained-glass windows created in 1910 by Emanuel Vigeland, brother of sculptor Gustav and a respected painter of local luminaries (*see* p.158), and vividly painted ceiling murals from 1936–50. Ask at the tourist office for details of the occasional services. The Domkirke is situated on the edge of the **Stortorvet**, which was once Oslo's main square and now hosts a flower market (*see* p.147). Just next door is the unique two-storeyed brick **Basarhallene** (19th-century food halls), which now house galleries and cafés. A few blocks along Karl Johans Gate is the rather unassuming **Stortinget**, **t** 23 31 35 96 (*guided visits in English 1 July–15 Aug daily 10 and 1; 15 Sept–15 June Sat 10, 11.30 and 3; Oct–May group visits by advance request*), the neo-Romanesque parliament building built in 1866.

Just opposite the Nationaltheatret, the university complex includes more than its busy academic buildings. Try to visit the **Universitets Aula**, especially if a concert is being performed (*see* p.152). This unexpected little gem, part of the main university building, is where the annual Nobel Peace Prize ceremony is held, and its walls are decorated with splendid, once-controversial murals by Edvard Munch, dating from 1916. After their completion, the artist explained, 'My aim was to have the decorations form a closed, independent, ideal world, whose pictorial expression should be at once peculiarly Norwegian and universally human.' The **Studenterlunden** (Student's Park) opposite the university buildings, with its outdoor cafés, is a popular meeting place.

At the top of Karl Johans Gate is the city's biggest green space, the **Slottsparken**, crowned by the **Kongelige Slott** or royal palace (*open 22 June–17 Aug, 1hr guided tours in English at 2 and 2.20; adm; tickets sold only at local post offices*). This royal residence was built in what was then Christiania between 1824–48 by Karl Johan XIV, whose equestrian statue stands proudly in front of his palace today. At 1.30 daily you can witness the changing of the guard; on special occasions in summer the royal guard gives more elaborate performances. The Slottsparken is open to the public year round, while the adjacent **Dronningparken** (Queen's Park) is open from May to Oct.

Those who admire the work of Ibsen – or would-be writers seeking inspiration – should hop across the road to the **Ibsenmuseet**, 1 Arbins Gate, **t** 22 55 20 09 (*open for tours only Tues–Sun 12, 1 and 2; adm*), a still-grand building in which the playwright lived from 1895 until his death in 1906. The apartment has been restored to its original appearance and hosts evening lectures and performances in spring and autumn.

North of Karl Johans Gate

Just to the east of the Slottsparken, the light-ochre building that dominates one side of Frederiks Gate houses the **Historisk Museum**, **Etnografisk Museum**, **Oldsaksamlingen** (Antiquities Collection) and **Myntkabinettet** (Collection of Coins and Medals); all **t** 22 85 99 12 (*open 15 May–14 Sept Tues–Sun 10–4; 15 Sept–14 May Tues–Sun 11–4*). Although the Historisk Museum tends to be overshadowed by the nearby Nasjonalgalleriet and the open-air exhibitions around the Bygdøy peninsula (*see* p.158), its well-preserved Viking tools, swords, costumes and jewellery are truly fascinating. Other displays of interest, in a collection ranging from the Stone Age to the Middle Ages, include medieval saints and items from rare stave churches, among them a painted ceiling with various scenes from the Creation. There are also ethnographic exhibitions from Africa, east Asia, south America, the Arctic and elsewhere.

The **Nasjonalgalleriet** (National Art Museum), 13 Universitetsgata, **t** 22 20 04 04, *www.nasjonalgalleriet.no* (*open Mon, Wed and Fri 10–6, Thurs 10–8, Sat 10–4, Sun 11–4; adm*) houses Norway's largest collection of Norwegian and international art up to 1945, including an excellent selection of major works from the national Romantic period – the golden age of Norwegian painting – with various pieces by Christian Krohg (who was also a journalist, novelist and all-round colourful personality of the period), Harriet Backer, Erik Werenskiold, Theodor Kittelsen (whose drawings of trolls and other folkloric characters brought him prominence), New Romantic landscape painters such as Frits Thaulow, Kitty L. Kielland and Halfdan Egedius, and Thomas Fearnley and his mentor Johan Christian Dahl (1788–1857), whose impressive career stimulated an interest in art in that period. Among the numerous works by Munch are versions of *The Scream*, *The Sick Child* and *Ashes*.

A 10-minute walk from the Nasjonalmuseet past **St Olavs church**, the **Damstredet**, a cobbled lane lined with early-19th-century wooden houses, offers a glimpse of how the city used to look. To see how Oslo's upper and lower classes actually lived then and in the following century, you should drop in at the nearby **Kunstindustrimuseet** (Museum of Applied Art), 1 St Olavs Gate, **t** 22 03 65 40, *www.kunstindustrimuseet.no* (*open Tues, Wed and Fri 11–3, Thurs 11–7, Sat and Sun 12–4; closed Mon; adm*), which was founded in 1876. The impressive building houses some outstanding reconstructions of period interiors and extensive collections of furniture, silver, glass, ceramics, porcelain and textiles, as well as some 16th- and 17th-century pictorial tapestries, including the rare, colourfully detailed 12th-century *Baldishol Tapestry*, which is considered one of the oldest examples of its type in Europe. The gift shop is a great hunting ground for interesting souvenirs.

Tøyen Quarter, Northeast of the Centre

A short underground ride from the Nationaltheatret (*T-bane lines 2, 3, 4 or 5*) then a five-minute walk brings you to the neighbourhood containing the Munch-museet, botanical gardens, and geographical and zoological museums, while nearby at Åkebergveien is Oslo's only purpose-built **mosque** (*not open to visitors*), completed in 1995, and just southeast is the **Kampen quarter**, with its tree-lined streets and charming wooden houses vividly painted in various hues.

The **Munch-museet**, 53 Tøyengaten, **t** 23 24 14 00, *www.munch.museum.no* (*open June–15 Sept daily 10–6; rest of year Tues–Fri 10–4, Sat and Sun 10–6; adm*), housed in a 1963 building, has, in addition to its impressive overview of Munch paintings and graphic works, a lecture/concert hall, gift shop and restaurant. Munch is the only Norwegian artist to have had a major influence on European art trends – his work paved the way for Expressionism in Germany and the Nordic countries. There are several examples of his most famous work, *Skrik* (*The Scream*), as well as many other equally powerful paintings depicting summer rituals, lovers' embraces, and the artist's friends and family. The collection of 100 paintings, 4,500 drawings and 18,000 prints bequeathed to the city by the artist on his death in 1944 is rotated, while the historical exhibition charting Munch's development is permanently on display.

After immersing yourself in the work of the tormented painter, you might want to take a break in the **Botanisk Hage** (Botanical Gardens), entrances at 1 Sars Gate and Monrads Gate, **t** 22 85 17 00, *www.nhm.uio.no* (*open April–Sept Mon–Fri 7am–8pm, Sat and Sun 10–8; Oct–Mar 7–5, Sat and Sun 10–5*). Part of the university, they boast more than 1,000 varieties of plants in a natural setting complete with waterfalls, greenhouses with tropical flora and a palmhouse with an exhibition about the evolution of palm trees. The grounds are also home to the **Mineralgeologisk**, **Zoologist** and **Botanisk Museums**, the university's natural history museum complex, **t** 22 85 17 00, *www.nhm.uio.no* (*open Tues and Thurs–Sun 11–4, Wed 11– 8; adm varies with exhibition*). **Tøyen manor house** near the greenhouses contains a pleasant café.

Northwest of the Centre

Although Gustav Vigeland's (1869–1943) international reputation as a sculptor might not equal that of Rodin (one of his inspirations), more than one million visitors come to see his work in the **Frognerparken** some way northwest of the city centre (*tram 12 or 15*) every year. It's here that you'll find the **Vigelandsparken** (*main entrance on Kirkeveien;* **t** 22 54 25 30), which was designed by the industrious artist as a site for more than 200 of his massive sculptures of humanity, 121 of which are depicted in a 14m-tall monolith, *The Wheel of Life*, carved out of a single block of granite around an obelisk and considered to be his masterpiece. Edvard Munch was supposedly furious at this gesture and, not to be outdone, eventually donated much of his own work to the city. The approach through the park to *The Wheel of Life* feels like a ritual, as one crosses the amazing Vigelandsbroen bridge, embellished with 58 lifelike bronze sculptures of men, women and newborn babies in poses celebrating the stages of life.

A short stroll away on the southern edge of the park, the **Vigelandmuseet**, 32 Nobels Gaten, **t** 22 54 25 30, *www.vigeland.museum.no* (*open Tues–Sun 12–6; adm*) has models of almost all the sculptor's monumental works, including dancing figures, intimidating bears and other beasts. The modest structure was built by the municipality of Oslo as a studio for the artist. If you have time, Café Vigeland (*open daily 9.30–7*) is a good place to reflect on what you have seen.

Other museums of interest in the Frogner area include the **Oslo Bymuseum** (City Museum), **t** 23 28 41 70 (*open 15 Jan–May and Sept–23 Dec Tues–Fri 10–4, Sat and Sun 11–4; June–Aug Tues–Thurs 10–6, Sat and Sun 11–5; guided tours in English, call for*

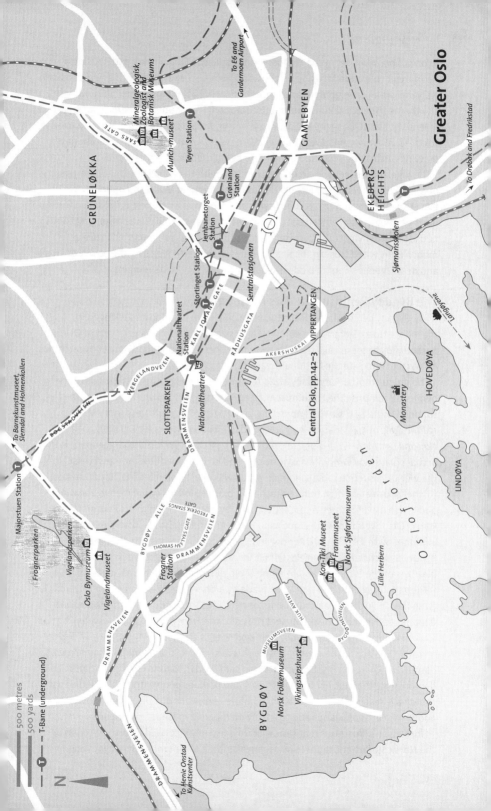

Greater Oslo

GRÜNELØKKA

GAMLEBYEN

SARS GATE

Mineralgeologisk, Zoologist and Botanisk Museums

Munch-museet

Tøyen Station

To E6 and Gardermoen Airport

To Drøbak and Fredrikstad

Grønland Station

EKEBERG HEIGHTS

Jernbanetorget Station

Sjømannskolen

Stortinget Station

Sentralstasjonen

KARL JOHANS GATE

RÅDHUSGATA

Nationaltheatret Station

VIPPETANGEN

AKERSHUSKAI

WERGELANDSVEIEN

SLOTTSPARKEN

Nationaltheatret

DRAMMENSVEIEN

Central Oslo, pp.142–3

To Barnekunstmuseet, Slemdal and Holmenkollen

BOGSTADVEIEN

Langøyene

Majorstuen Station

HOVEDØYA

Monastery

LINDØYA

DRAMMENSVEIEN

Frogner Station

FREDERIK STANGS GATE

THOMAS HEFTYES GATE

BYGDØY ALLE

Frognerparken

Vigelandsparken

Oslo Bymuseum

Vigelandsmuseet

DRAMMENSVEIEN

Kon-Tiki Museet

Frammuseet

Norsk Sjøfartsmuseum

Lille Herbern

BYGDØY

MUSEUMSVEIEN

HUK AVENY

BYGDØYNESVEIEN

Norsk Folkemuseum

Vikingskipshuset

To Henie Onstad Kunstsenter

DRAMMENSVEIEN

Oslofjorden

500 metres

500 yards

T-Bane (underground)

N

information; adm), set in the Frogner manor house in Frognerpark and housing a permanent collection focusing on the 1,000-year history of Oslo, with an emphasis on daily life, urban development and culture. There are also changing exhibitions with city themes. The **Barnekunstmuseet** (International Museum of Children's Art), 4 Lille Frøens Vei, **t** 22 46 85 73 (*open 20 Jan–25 June and 15 Sept–10 Dec Tues–Thurs 9.30–2, Sun 11–4; 26 June–9 Aug Tues, Thurs and Sun 11–4; adm*) has changing exhibitions of drawings, paintings, sculptures, and more by children from 180 countries.

The Vigelandmuseet should not be confused with the equally fascinating museum of the sculptor's younger brother, the **Emanuel Vigeland Museum**, Grimelundsveien, **t** 22 14 57 88 (*open Sun 12–4; guided tours at other times by request; adm*) much further northwest of the city at Slemdal (*T-bane line 1*). What started out as a building to house Emanuel Vigeland's paintings and sculptures was re-structured into a mausoleum, with Etruscan-inspired frescoes graphically depicting the power of Eros and death, genesis versus exodus, and an urn with Vigeland's remains.

The Bygdøy Peninsula and its Museums

The Bygdøy peninsula, home to the polar ship *Fram*, Kon-Tiki and Viking Ship museums, Norsk Sjøfartsmuseum and Norsk Folkemuseum, lies just west of Oslo's harbour. To get there, take the little ferry from Pier 3 behind the Rådhuset or catch bus no.30 from opposite the Nationaltheatret.

The unique mother- and baby-sized A-frame buildings on the eastern side of the peninsula comprise the **Frammuseet**, **t** 23 28 29 50 (*open Jan and Feb Mon–Fri 11–2.45, Sat and Sun 11–3.45; Mar and April daily 11–3.45; 1–16 May daily 10–4.45; 18 May–15 June daily 9–5.45; 16 June–Aug daily 9–6.45; Sept daily 10–4.45; Oct daily 10–3.45; Nov and Dec Mon–Fri 11–2.45, Sat and Sun 11–3.45; adm*). Within the larger space is the actual polar ship *Fram*, which is 39m long and is considered the strongest vessel in the world. This remarkable schooner, which was constructed in 1892, has advanced further south and north than any other ship of its kind. Its name means 'forward', and it was used for three Arctic expeditions by Norwegian explorers Fridtjof Nansen (1893), Otto Sverdrup (1898–1902) and Roald Amundsen (1910–1912). The ship is exhibited with its original interior , and there is a comprehensive display on the history of Arctic exploration. Best of all, you can actually go aboard to see the living quarters of the explorers and imagine their journey through rough seas and ice.

The various expeditions that were made by archaeologist/explorer Thor Heyerdahl (who died in 2002) to seek out prehistoric cultures from Peru to Polynesia are well documented in the **Kon-Tiki Museet** opposite the *Fram* at 36 Bygdøynesveien, **t** 23 08 67 67, *www.kon-tiki.no* (*open daily April and May 10.30–5; June–Aug 9.30–5.45; Sept 10.30–5; Oct–Mar 10.30–4; adm*). Besides his raft, *Kontiki*, the seemingly fragile reed barque the *RA II* is on display, which Heyerdahl used in 1970 to cross the Atlantic to demonstrate that ancient North Africans and perhaps people from the Middle East could have reached the Americas long before Europeans did. Displays on Easter Island and the Galapagos Islands add to a truly memorable museum experience.

Norwegian's illustrious maritime history is proudly displayed next to the *Fram* at the **Norsk Sjøfartsmuseum** (Norwegian Maritime Museum), 37 Bygdøynesveien,

t 24 11 41 50 (*open 15 May–Sept daily 10–6; Oct–14 May Fri–Wed 10.30–4, Thurs 10.30–6; adm, children free*). Amidst the usual maritime exhibits of figureheads and model ships are Norway's largest collection of maritime art, a display of dried cod, and some scenic footage of the Norwegian coastline and its underwater life. The large boat hall has a substantial collection of wooden boats from all over Norway, including Roald Amundsen's ship *Gjøa*, which was the first ship to cross the Northwest Passage (1903–1906).

In spring and summer there's a shuttle train from the maritime sector to one of Europe's largest open-air museums, the **Norsk Folkemuseum** (Norwegian Folk Museum), 10 Museumsveien, **t** 22 12 37 00 (*open 15 May–14 Sept daily 10–6; 15 Sept–14 May Mon–Fri 11–3, Sun 11–4; adm*), or it's a pleasant 10-minute walk inland. This reconstructed village is comprised of 150 buildings dating from the 13th to 19th centuries, arranged regionally, allowing visitors to experience traditional culture and history from all over Norway (including that of the indigenous Sami people from northern Lapland). During the summer, hosts in folk costume give pottery, silversmithing, weaving and candlemaking demonstrations. There's a 13th-century **stave church** – one of 30 or so simple churches built in Norway with wood timber placed vertically into the ground (in contrast to the stacked log cabin technique seen in other Norwegian buildings); they had elaborate interiors with symbolic designs including rose paintings and dragons' heads from the Viking era. The Folkemuseum hosts 'Norwegian Evenings' in English on Tues, Wed, Fri and Sat 5.30–7.30 in July and August; the programme features fairytales, folk music, dancing (the public can join in) and tastings of *lefse*, a traditional cake that you spread with butter and sugar.

Three of the best-preserved Viking ships ever to have been discovered can be seen a short walk away at the **Vikingskipshuset** (Viking Ship Museum), 35 Huk Aveny, **t** 22 13 52 80 (*open daily May–Sept 9–6, Oct–April 11–4, adm*). The ships had been placed in burial mounds on the western side of the Oslofjorden more than 1,100 years ago, in order to transport their owners to 'the other world'. The most well preserved is the elegant longboat *Oseberg* with its carved prow and 30 oarholes. Accompanying the ships are a number of other historical treasures, including smaller boats, richly carved sledges, and carriages, textiles and tools.

Outside the City

Oslo's array of green spaces are heartily embraced by its inhabitants: you'll see people of all ages and stages hiking (and cross-country skiing in winter) around the Holmenkollen (*see* pp.160–61) in the Nordmarka area north of the city, or jogging around the harbour and Frognerparken. In fact, Oslo is quite literally a 'green city', as you have to pay a toll fee to bring a car in, in an initiative to encourage people to use public transport. The islands within the **Oslofjorden** are also inviting oases, and boat trips in the fjord (*see* p.145) allow you to to enjoy the skyline from the water.

For a different perspective, take tram nos.18 or 19 from Jernbanetorget underground station and ride 10 minutes uphill to the **Ekeberg Heights** southeast of the city, to a castle-like building that once served as the merchant marine academy (Sjømannsskolen; it's now a business school), from where there are impressive views of downtown Oslo and the fjord, as well as the Holmenkollen ski jump. If you walk to the back of the academy and down towards a small field, you will come to a group of 6,000-year-old rock carvings depicting deer, elk and human figures – evidence of prehistoric inhabitants in the area.

Day Trips from Oslo

Like any capital, the 'City of Light' does not really reflect the country, and it is worth making a day trip or two to get a glimpse of Norway's fjord-scapes and mountains.

Henie Onstad Kunstsenter

t 67 80 48 80, www.hok.no. Høvikodden is a 35min bus ride from Oslo centre (nos.151, 161, 162, 252 or 261 from the Central Station and Nationaltheatret). The centre is a 5min walk from the stop (ask the driver to let you off here). Open Tues–Thurs 10–9, Fri–Mon 11–6; adm.

In beautiful surroundings by the Oslofjorden at Høvikodden just southwest of Oslo, this centre boasts Norway's largest collection of international modern art, which was acquired by figure-skater Sonia Henie and her shipowner husband Niels Onstad, aficionados of 20th-century painting and sculpture, especially work by Matisse, Picasso and Miró, postwar Abstract Expressionists and contemporary Norwegians. The collection is rotated to accommodate changing exhibitions of contemporary artists, and there is an impressive sculpture park, which includes some Henry Moores.

For skating fans, there is a room devoted to Henie's career, including her various medals (she won three in the Olympics), trophies and assorted memorabilia. Concerts and theatre performances are also held at the centre, and there's a first-class gourmet **Bolgen & Moi** restaurant and café (*expensive–moderate; closed Mon*) and nearby beaches if you want to have a swim at the end of the afternoon.

Holmenkollen

Way up in the hills to the north of Oslo, the **Nordmarka** is made up of forested hills and lakes, hiking trails and fine cross-country ski paths extending inland for a

Norway in a Nutshell

Considered one of the most interesting trips to make in Norway (as popular among Norwegians as foreign tourists), 'Norway in a Nutshell' combines an incredibly scenic journey on the Flåm Railway with a fjord cruise via express ferry from Oslo to Bergen and back. Taking 8 hours, it's available year-round and you can customize your route. It's a good way of experiencing the beautiful fjord region, including Aurlandsfjord, the narrow Naerøfjorden and the steep Stalheimskleiva road, and it is worth stretching the trip over a few days by making overnight stops in Gudvangen, Voss or Flåm and exploring the area on foot and by water. A colourful booklet is available from tourist offices, or see *www.visitbergen.com, www.visitoslo.com, www.visitflam. com, www.fjordpass.no, www.fjord-tours.com* or *www.nsb.no*.

Getting There

Take T-bane 1 from Frogner station in Oslo to the Holmenkollen stop (25mins). Or you can get off at the last stop, Frognerseteren/ Voksenkollen, and visit the **Tryvannstårnet** (*TV/observation tower; open daily May–Sept 10–5, Oct–April 10–4; adm*), situated 588m above sea level and affording, on a clear day, views of the Swedish border over to the east, Oslo to the south, and the forests of the Gudbrandsal valley to the north. You can take a walk in the atmospheric forest and follow the signposted trail back to Holmenkollen on foot, which takes 20mins. Oslo city itself is a pleasant half-hour downhill jaunt. In summer, there are small cafés around the forest.

Eating Out

Frognersetern Restaurant, 200 Holmenkollenveien (at final T-bane 1 stop), t 22 92 40 40 (*expensive–moderate*). A wooden lodge with a terrace with spectacular views of the Oslofjorden. Among the seasonal specialities you might encounter on the menu are salmon pâté, reindeer fillet, halibut and guinea hen. The famous apple tart with cream is served year-round, while the cloudberries with vanilla sauce are available only in late summer. There is also a cheaper self-service restaurant.

Holmenkollen Park Hotel Rica Restaurant, 26 Kongeveien, t 22 92 20 00 (*expensive–moderate*). Two restaurants set in an elegant hotel at the top of the Marka, both open for lunch and dinner. The main restaurant offers a sumptuous lunch buffet comprising a range of Norwegian specialities, herrings, cheeses and luscious desserts, while the gourmet dining room, which has several special menus to choose from, serves fresh seafood and game in season.

Holmenkollen Restaurant, near ski museum, t 22 14 62 26 (*moderate–inexpensive*). Delicious Norwegian food with a view. There's also a nearby cafeteria selling *smørbrød*.

distance of some 30km. Within this terrain is Holmenkollen, which as well as a ski resort is a good hiking spot in the spring, summer and early autumn, with several marked paths and lots of cafés along the way. In March Holmenkollen's annual **ski festival**, the world's oldest, attracts more than a million visitors over 11 days and is considered Norway's second national holiday. More than 50,000 people gather at the famous ski-jump (remember that this is the country where ski-jumping was invented), and there are other extreme sports competitions, as well as a festive parade and other traditional events.

The landmark **ski jump**, which is considered Norway's number one visitor attraction, offers breathtaking views from its 60m-high tower, but beware that, although there is an elevator, the last stairway before you reach the top makes for a pretty steep climb. Holmenkollen's **Skimuseet** (*ski museum; open daily 8.30–8.30; adm*), which charts 400 years of skiing history, also has a ski-jump simulator, while at the foot of the jump **Besserrudtjemet pond** is a fine place for a dip in warm weather. For information about skiing, contact the **Skiforeningen** (*see p.147*); for details of hiking, including route maps and hut locations, consult **Den Norske Turistforeningen** (*Norwegian Hiking Association, t 22 82 28 00, www.turistforeningen.no*).

Hadeland Glassverk

t 61 31 66 00; open daily 9–4; adm.

Located in Jevnaker, 75km north of Oslo, this is Norway's oldest company, dating back as far as 1762, and the purveyor of fine crystal to the royal Norwegian court. The

Getting There

From 23 June to 19 Aug an **express bus** runs to the Hadeland Glassverk from Oslo bus terminal (near the Central Station), leaving at 9.30 Mon–Fri, 10 Sat and Sun, then from in front of the university 8mins later. The trip takes about 1hr. Buses return to Oslo at 2.30 (Sat and Sun 4.30), though you should verify this with the driver on the outward journey.

The rest of the year a **regular bus service**, no.171, leaves from Oslo bus station (usually platform 14) and in front of the university every half-hour Mon–Fri and every hour on the hour Sat and Sun. You have to change buses in Hønefoss; the connection to Jevnaker leaves from platform 7.

Eating Out

The following are both located within the Hadeland complex.

Kokkestua Restaurant, t 61 31 66 00 (*moderate–inexpensive*). Norwegian fish and game dishes for lunch and dinner, plus soups, sandwiches and salads.

The Old Barn, t 61 31 66 00 (*moderate–inexpensive*). Traditional Christmas fare served in a festive, candlelit atmosphere. *Open Nov and Dec.*

fact that it is also Norway's fifth most-visited tourist attraction, attracting around 550,000 visitors in 2003, may seem like a good reason to avoid it, but this large cultural centre on the borders of the scenic Randsfjorden has plenty to do.

The Glassverk is set in a historic complex of some 25 red wooden buildings, many 200 years old. As well as the international glassworks, there are exhibitions on the history of glass, and demonstrations of glassblowing, candle-dipping and more, plus a good gift shop. From the start of November, especially at weekends, there are traditional Christmas activities, including horse and sleigh rides, and 50 Christmas trees decorated with candles, creating a fairytale atmosphere amidst the snowy landscape.

Blaafarveværket

t 32 78 49 00; open 22 May–18 June Tues–Sun 10–5; 19 June–22 Aug daily 10–6; 23 Aug–26 Sept Tues–Sun 10–5; adm.

'The Works', 75km west of Oslo in Åmot, was once the world's leading cobalt-blue pigment factory. Today it's a private foundation dedicated to conserving and presenting the cultural history of its heyday (1773–1893). Visitors can see the imposing 1770s **Glasshytten** (glasshouse) built after the discovery of cobalt ore in 1772; a **museum** with a permanent exhibition, 'From Cobalt Ore to Blue Pigment', and an annual exhibition featuring a prominent Norwegian artist; and the **wheelhouse**, with a display on the history of Blaafarveværket.

There are also concerts in spring and summer, a grassy park area with picnic tables along the banks of the Simoa, a children's farm, and two cafés serving simple fare. The

Getting There

The Blaafarveværket factory is 90mins from Oslo and you can take an excursion leaving 9.30–10am from the bus terminal (Nettbuss no.169, but check the number and times when you book on t 32 78 67 00; about NOK150). The return bus leaves for Oslo at about 4pm.

Eating Out

Bødtker Café, Blaafarveværket, no phone (*inexpensive*). Sandwiches and hot meals.
Thranestua Delicatessen, Haugfoss, no phone (*inexpensive*). Sandwiches, salads and tasty pancakes with ice cream and blueberries.

Getting There

Skien (*see* below) is about 2hrs from Oslo by regular train or by express coach; for timetables see *www.nsb.no*. Timekspressen (**t** 35 02 60 00, *www.timekspressen.no*) runs a day excursion package daily 23 May–17 Aug, with coaches leaving Oslo at 6.40 and 9.40am, arriving nearly 3hrs later to connect with the 3hr canal cruise. The bus heads back to Oslo at either 5 or 6pm. Other boat excursions can be booked thorough the tourist office.

Tourist Information

Telemark Reiser, 18 Nedre Hjellegate, Skien, **t** 35 90 00 30, *www.visittelemark.com* or *www.telemarkskanalen.no*.

Eating Out

Bring a picnic, or enjoy a hot meal or fresh waffles aboard one of the ships. Have dinner back in Oslo, or dine in **Skien** before returning:

Jegermesteren, 1 Nedre Hjellegate, **t** 35 52 41 73 (*expensive*). A fine dining spot offering Norwegian specialities according to season, from monkfish to reindeer.

China Twang, Nedre Hjellegate, **t** 35 52 80 70 (*moderate*). A quayside place for those craving something a little more exotic.

Kulcompagniet Bar & Grill, 5 Langbrygga, **t** 35 52 6170 (*moderate*). A lively spot on the quay from which excursions depart, with a popular terrace in spring and summer. The basic but tasty fare includes burgers, stir-fries, soups and salads.

Mølla gift shop sells striking cobalt-coloured glass and ceramics. You can haul yourself over the river on a timber raft and walk to Haugfoss bridge, or stroll on the path from the works to **Haugfoss** and enjoy the beautiful view of Haugfoss waterfall.

The excursion programme includes a visit by bus to the **former mines** 7km up the road. This part of the tour, during which visitors wear protective helmets and capes, is especially fascinating. Also on this site is the **Theodor Kittelsen Museum** (*same hours as Blaafarveværket*) with fanciful paintings and wooden sculptures of nature and mythical trolls by the well-known artist. There is also a lookout point at an altitude of 350m above sea level, usually with grazing sheep in residence.

Telemark

One of Norway's most popular holiday areas, Telemark is known for its waterways: the famous **Telemark Canal**, which celebrated its centenary in 1992, is Europe's only water course to have received a medal for restoration and preservation (in 1994). Stretching 105km from **Skien**, the birthplace of Ibsen, to **Dalen**, the canal was once considered the fastest route between eastern and western Norway, and even today it remains an important route for people, domestic animals, goods and timber.

Sign up for an excursion through its historic locks (*see* above) and enjoy nature at its best as you travel from Lunde to Akkerhaugen. The landscapes are diverse, ranging from sea to mountains and forests. Of the ships in the fleet, the MS *Victoria* is the *grande dame*, built in 1882 and still going strong; the MS *Telemarken* and MS *Henrik Ibsen* are slightly larger and more modern. All have open decks from which to enjoy the breathtaking journey, as well as plenty of room inside if shelter is required.

Other Day Trips from Oslo

If you are not planning on hiring a car and following the tour (*see* pp.167–72), you can still visit some of the most interesting places on it by public transport. You can make easy day trips from Oslo to **Drøbak**, a charming old sailing port at the narrowest

Getting There

Drøbak is less than 1hr from central Oslo by bus no.541 (from the corner of the Klingenberg cinema near the Nationaltheatret). In spring and summer (Wed–Sun) there are also ferry trips to Drøbak (90mins each way) from the harbour behind Oslo town hall (Rådhuset). Ask at the tourist office for bus and boat times.

Fredrikstad is 1hr from Oslo by rail; trains run throughout the day.

Tønsberg is 90mins–2hrs from Oslo by bus (*www.busslink.no*). Get off at Åsgårdstrand about 30mins from Oslo to see the former home of Munch (*see* p.156). You can then get another Busslink bus or local bus to Tønsberg.

Tourist Information

Drøbak: 4 Havnegaten, **t** 64 93 50 87.

Fredrikstad: 98 Voldgaten, Gamlebyen, **t** 69 30 46 00, *fredrikstad.turist@c2i.net*. Mid-June to mid-Aug there's an office at the harbour on Dampskipsbrygga, **t** 69 39 65 00.

Tønsberg: 36 Nedre Langgate, **t** 33 35 45 20.

part of the Oslofjorden (*see* p.167), **Fredrikstad**, the only intact Scandinavian fortress town (*see* p.168), and **Tønsberg**, Norway's oldest town (*see* p.171). *See* box above for details of how to get there and tourist information.

Overnighter from Oslo

Sandefjord

Airport confusion aside (Sandefjord Airport Torp is marketed by some airlines as an Oslo airport, though it's 120km south of Norway's capital), the coastal town of Sandefjord (*see also* p.172, 'Touring from Oslo') is beautifully located in Vestfold county in the heart of southwestern Norway. This pleasant area has a mild climate and 150km of coastline with plenty of beaches, watersports amenities and campsites.

A former whaling and fishing town with a a population of 40,000, Sandefjord makes a good base from which to enjoy Vestfold as a whole and surrounding towns such as **Tønsberg**, which boasts a 13th-century castle and Viking grave mounds (*see* p.171), the nearby island of **Nøtterøy** with its famed 'world's end point', and **Åsgårdstrand**, an unpretentious beauty spot that inspired Munch.

Viking-origin Sandefjord was later a spa town and the 'world capital' of whaling, shipping and fishing; in the city centre a massive rotating **bronze sculpture** by Knut Steen (1955) serves as a memorial to the whalers. This is still a wealthy town, though the whaling industry has been cut back considerably over recent decades (*see* p.135); today one of its primary moneyspinners is marine paint production. It is also an important gateway to Sweden, and has a daily ferry to Denmark, Finland and Latvia.

Sandefjord is a particularly pleasant place to spend time during the special summer market days (in June and on 1 and 15 July), when the quayside, or **Promenaden**, is animated with revellers crowding the waterfront terraces. Just above the harbour is a hilly park, **Preståsen**, which is a fine place to take a walk and enjoy panoramic views of the harbour and surrounding town.

A good place to look around is **Sandefjord Bad**, or Kurbadet (old spa building), in the centre of town at 7 Thor Dahls Gate (*open for guided tours and special events; ask at* *tourist office*). This distinctive complex of red wooden buildings, inspired by the Viking 'dragon' style, attracted royalty and members of the cultural élite for spa cures and assorted pamperings from 1837 until 1939. Recently restored, it's now a civic centre hosting cultural activities, with a museum wing containing a model of the facilities in 1900, a reconstruction of a treatment room and an exhibit of old postcards.

In the old town, along Bjerggata and Thaulowsgate, the architecture remains typically 'coastal Norwegian', with small, white wooden sailors' houses dating back to the early 1800s. The Bjerggata runs parallel to the Museumgata, where at No.39 you'll find the **Hvalfangstmuseet** (Whaling Museum), **t** 33 48 46 50 (*open May–Aug daily 11–5, Sept daily 11–4, Oct–April Mon–Sat 11–3, Sun 11–4; ask at tourist office for guided tours*), Europe's only museum on the natural history and cultural aspects of whaling. The zoological department has a life-size model of a blue whale.

Getting There

Direct **flights to Torp** are available from Amsterdam (KLM), London Stansted (Ryanair), Aberdeen (Coast Air, which also offers direct internal flights from Torp to Haugesund and Bergen), and Aberdeen and Newcastle (Widerøe, which also has direct flights from Torp to Bergen and Stavanger). For airline contact details, *see* p.3.

There is a **bus service** from Torp airport to Sandefjord train station (20mins), hourly Mon–Fri, less frequently Sat and Sun. A 10min taxi ride from the airport to the train station takes costs around NOK130.

From Oslo's Gardermoen airport, there's a **train** to Sandefjord (about 2hrs 15mins), with stops at Oslo's central train station and the Nationaltheatret. Trains run about every hour, no reservation is needed for 2nd-class carriages, and a round-trip costs NOK400. Times and prices are available at *www.nsb.no*. To get between Torp and Oslo, *see* p.145.

Tourist Information

Sandefjord: Reiselivsforening, 1 Thor Dahls Gate, **t** 33 46 05 90, *www.visitsandefjord.com* (*open 15 June–20 Aug Mon–Fri 9–6, Sat 10–4, Sun 12–4; rest of the year Mon–Fri 8.30–4*).

Festivals

Of Sandefjord's numerous festival and special events held throughout the year, it's worth watching out for the **Midsummer**

Festival concert at the Hjertnes Amfiteater (mid-June), featuring excerpts from musicals and operas, the **St Hans** celebration (23 June), including a midsummer night boat parade at the harbour and beach bonfires, and the **Vestfoldfestspillene** (festival of Norwegian and international art and culture, 27 June– 6 July), with music and dance events across the county, from rocky beaches to the wild rapids of the highlands.

Sports and Activities

Just outside town, the **Vesterøya** ('west peninsula') and **Østerøya** ('east peninsula'; a nature reserve with campsites) are scenic areas good for cycling, hiking and swimming. Other options include the hills of **Mølleråsen**, **Mokollen** and **Preståsen** a short walk from the town centre, offering lovely panoramic views. In **Bugårdsparken** there is a walking track around the lake.

For maps and information on **organized walking tours**, contact the tourist office. Vestfold county also has several marked **cycling** trails and roads (maps available at tourist office); for **bike hire** your best bet is the Spinn Sykkelshop at 2 Aagaardsplass, **t** 33 46 80 40.

Where to Stay

Rica Park Hotel, 9 Strandpromenaden, **t** 33 44 74 00, *www.rica.no* (*expensive*). A stylish, business-orientated chain hotel idyllically located by the marina, with its

Continuing the theme, the restored *hvalbåten* (whale-catching boat) **Southern Actor** at Pier 3 at the harbour (*t 33 46 05 90*) is representative of the modern whaling period. Its scale gives some idea of the vast size of the animals that were caught. In the same place is the **Gaia**, a scale replica of the *Gokstad* Viking ship excavated near Sandefjord in 1880 (*see* p.172). More than 5m wide and 24m long, it was rowed by 16 pairs of oars. You can go aboard both ships between 21 June and 15 Aug (*daily 9.30–5; adm*).

Located 1.5km outside the city centre at Pukkestad, the **Sandefjord Bymuseum** (*town museum, 21 Hystadveien; open only for guided tours via tourist office*) on the site of a 1790s farm offers a glimpse into 18th-century agricultural life. Aside the farmhouse, there's a barn with an agricultural exhibition, outbuildings with a town model, a shoemaker's workshop and historic interiors, and a lovely garden.

own health, fitness and spa centre complete with swimming pool. Rooms are well furnished and service is friendly.

Hotel Kong Carl, *see* p.172.

Comfort Hotel Atlantic, 33 Jerdbanealleen, **t** 33 42 80 00, *www.comfort.choicehotels.no* (*moderate*). A cosy hotel in the middle of town, with all mod cons. An evening buffet featuring a simple warm meal is included in the room price.

Sandefjord Herberge, *see* p.172.

Bjerggata Bed & Breakfast, 19 Bjerggata, **t** 95 04 46 67 (*inexpensive*). A B&B located within the historic Bjerggata quarter, with just one room with twin beds and a bath. Breakfast is served, and there is also a well-tended garden to relax in.

Lisbets Guesthouse, 33 Bjerggata, **t** 33 46 08 26, **mobile** (+47) 45 24 00 02 (*inexpensive*). A cosy guesthouse just a few minutes from the harbour in the Bjerggata quarter, with one room with twin beds, a shower and a toilet. There is a terrace with a brick fireplace and a barbecue. The owners, who live in the front house, speak English and are very hospitable.

Eating Out

Restaurant Fea (*expensive*), *see* p.172.

Mathuset Solvold, 9 Thor Dahls Gate, **t** 33 46 27 41 (*expensive*). A restaurant in an elegant building, which also houses the more casual Smak (see p.172), designed by Svein Lund, well known for his rendering of the royal family's summer house. The interior is cool and minimal, and the gourmet menu has a

global perspective (though French cuisine is the main influence) and uses the best local, seasonal products, such as fish or game. *Closed Sun.*

Kokeriet, Brygga (at wharf), **t** 33 46 62 62. (*expensive–moderate*). A restaurant/bar popular with local movers and shakers, specializing in fish. The interior harks back to the early days of Sandefjord's whale industry, and there is a popular terrace on the harbour front.

Da Vinci, 1 Aagaardsplass, **t** 33 46 86 80 (*moderate*). A restaurant with a pleasantly unexpected Italian ambience (its owner comes from a village near Naples) and a tapas/antipasti bar (*open daily from 3pm*). The delicious pasta dishes include tagliatelle with seafood, the fillet of beef makes for a superb main course, and the tiramisu is well worth saving room for.

Smak (*moderate*), *see* p.172.

Brødr (*moderate–inexpensive*), *see* p.172.

Fru Wolds Cafe og Spiseri (*inexpensive*), *see* p.172.

Halvorsens Bakeri og Konditori, 3 Christopher Hvidts Plass, **t** 33 47 19 20 (*inexpensive*). A granny-style tearoom and good place to buy goodies for a picnic. Accompany your cup of java with a *hvetestang*, a sweet roll with a bright yellow dollop of vanilla cream in the middle, topped with sprinkles of coconut, or a *skolebolle* ('school bun'), a variation on the same theme.

Milly's Kafé, 9 Thaulowsgate, no phone (*inexpensive*). Simple sandwiches and home-made pastries served in a little garden off the beaten path.

Touring from Oslo

Day 1: An Artists' Refuge, Santa Claus and Fish

Morning: Take the E6, direction Göteborg, then the 152 to the coastal village of **Drøbak**, an idyllic retreat of wooden houses with rose gardens and picket fences, which has become the Nordic residence of Santa Claus – there is a shop in the centre (*Julehuset; open daily*) with a permanent Christmas exhibition and Santa's own post office. But more important is Drøbak's role as a centre of art: wander the narrow streets with their galleries displaying works by contemporary Norwegian and international artists and ceramicists. The Drøbak Båtforenings Maritime Samlinger, 4 Kroketonna (*open May–Aug daily 11–7; Sept–April 11–4; adm*) is a small maritime museum.

Lunch: In Drøbak, *see* below.

Afternoon: The Follo Open-air Museum, Belsjøveien (*open May–early Oct Tues–Fri 11–4, Sat and Sun 12–5; adm*), in a series of old buildings from the area, has a permanent display on coastal cultural history as well as changing exhibitions. Book a ferry tour at the tourist office (*4 Havnegaten, t 64 93 50 87*) across the fjord to the fortress at Oscarsborg (*open June–Aug Mon–Fri 12.30 and 4.15, Sat and Sun 12 and 2.30*), a unique example of a Norwegian defence fortification. Another option is the Drøbak Akvarium, the only saltwater aquarium on the Oslofjorden, 4 Havnegaten (*open same hours as maritime museum; adm*).

Dinner and Sleeping: In Drøbak, *see* below.

Day 1

Lunch in Drøbak
Molle, 1 Torvet, **t** 64 93 00 36 (*moderate*). A well-rated restaurant with its own art gallery, serving a varied menu of simple sandwiches, salads and hot meals.

Det Gamle Bageri Ost og VInstue, market square, **t** 64 93 21 05 (*moderate–inexpensive*). A popular gathering place for those in the mood for a light meal and a glass of fine wine from the well-stocked cellar. Filled baguettes, quiche and fried Camembert are the house specialities. The building dates back to the 18th century, when it was used as a bakery and a brewery.

Dinner in Drøbak
Kumlegaarden Restaurant, 11 Niels Carlsensgate, **t** 64 93 15 04 (*moderate*) Traditional Norwegian recipes are the speciality of this dining room graced with fine art. Try the *komler* dumplings with whatever meat is being served that day.

Skipperstuen, 11 Havnebakken, **t** 64 93 07 03 (*expensive–moderate*). A traditional restaurant with a view of the harbour, popular among locals. The menu offers a wide choice of seasonal dishes with the emphasis on fish. Whale may also be on the menu, and is unashamedly enjoyed by customers for its similarity to beef steak.

Sleeping in Drøbak
Skiphelle Course & Conference Hotel, **t** 64 90 73 00, www.skiphelle.no (*moderate*). A hotel just a few minutes outside the centre at the beach, with 43 rooms, many with a view of the fjord, as well as some comfortable cabins. There is a restaurant, a bar and a lounge with a fireplace.

Reenskaug Hotell , Storgata 32, **t** 64 93 33 60, www.reenskaug.no (*moderate*). A family-run hotel dating back 100 years and located in the heart of town. There are 23 pleasantly furnished rooms, all of them equipped with minibar, cable TV and bath, plus an outdoor restaurant and a nightclub.

Day 2: Timber Town and the Gamlebyen Ramparts

Morning: Follow the E6 (direction Göteborg) to the 151 exit: **Son** is another charming village that has inspired artists past and present. Get back on the E6 and drive another half-hour, taking road 110 ('the prehistoric road', rich in rock carvings and burial mounds, including the world's largest cave painting, the *Oldtidsveien*) and the **Fredrikstad** exit. Park on the Vestsiden, the modern part of town, and rent a bike at the tourist office (*see* p.164), or take a passenger ferry to one of the skerries around nearby Hvaler. In summer, the harbourfront forms a popular promenade along the Vesterelva river. En route to the ferry point, you pass the cathedral, built in 1880, and many stately 1850 villas, residences of the 'Timber Barons' when this was a big timber port. It's a short ferry hop to the Old Town, Gamlebyen, heart of the city.

Lunch: In Fredrikstad, *see* below.

Afternoon: Scandinavia's only surviving fortress city has been gutted by fire again and again but has some interesting preserved buildings and cobbled streets. Completed in 1775 as a military warehouse and once Norway's largest bulding, the Tøihuset (*call for opening hrs, t 69 30 60 00; adm*) documents the city from 1567 to now. Nearby is the stone-walled food store (*grunnmurede provianthus*), built 1674–96 and the oldest preserved building in the fortress city, with walls up to 4m thick. Just east of Gamlebyen (also accessible by road 107) is Kongsten Fort, which comprises a part of the large Balaklava complex. Walk across a small footbridge to the neighbouring island of Isegran, a shipbuilding centre, for striking views of the fortress.

Dinner and Sleeping: In Fredrikstad, *see* below.

Day 2

Lunch in Fredrikstad

Gudesen Konditorier, 71 Voldportgaten, Gamlebyen, **t** 69 32 36 17, or Torvbyen, modern town, **t** 69 31 13 70 (*inexpensive*). Delicious pastries and open sandwiches.

Verdenspeilet Kaffebar, 27 Nygaardsgata, **t** 69 30 93 61 (*inexpensive*). A casually hip spot on the road leading from the car park towards the ferry point in the modern town, offering simple sandwiches and pastries and boasting an espresso machine.

Balaklava, corner of Kirkegaten and Voldportgaten, Gamlebyen, **t** 69 32 30 40 (*moderate–inexpensive*). A 1783 complex with several restaurants and a pension. The outdoor café, **Mulvadgården**, open spring and summer, serves sandwiches and salads and often hosts concerts.

Dinner in Fredrikstad

Restaurant Prestegården, 78 Færgeportgaten, **t** 69 32 30 40 (*expensive*). A 'gourmet' restaurant in the Balaklava complex (*see* above), specialising in elaborate seafood dishes and free range chicken with *foie gras*.

Mother India, 16 Nygaardsgaten, **t** 69 31 22 00. (*moderate*). An Indian outpost in the modern town, serving veggie courses and mean curries.

Sleeping in Fredrikstad

Hotell Fontenen, 9–11 Nygaardsgaten, **t** 69 30 05 00 (*moderate*). A pleasant family-run hostelry in the heart of the old town, with comfortable rooms and friendly staff.

Valhalla, 3 Valhallsgaten, **t** 69 30 09 70, *www.hotelvalhalla.no* (*moderate*). A striking white building on a hill above the modern town, with simple rooms. Breakfast is included in the price, which is lower after June 15, and parking is available.

Gamlebyen Pensjonat, 88 Smedjegaten, **t** 64 32 20 20, *www.gamlebyen-pensjonat.no* (*inexpensive*). An atmospheric spot in a former artillery building dating from 1733, with friendly owners, a TV in the living room, and bathrooms in the hall.

Day 3: Another Charming Hamlet and More Østfold Culture

Morning: Drive back to the E6, which takes you northwards to Moss (from where you can take the ferry to Horten tomorrow), then follow the local road through Moss to reach the small island of **Jeløy**. There, Galleri F15 (*t 69 27 10 33; open June–Aug Tues–Sun 11–7; adm*) is a contemporary art museum situated within a 19th-century manor house; two earlier mansions on the site burned down. The monthly exhibitions that are held here feature contemporary Norwegian artists and the occasional international guest. There is an excellent book/gift shop and a café, as well as a grassy terrain facing the fjord.

Lunch: In Jeløy, *see* below.

Afternoon: Wander amongst the grounds of the gallery, then go for a swim at the Refnesstranda waterfront, where there are changing rooms. There is an expensive hotel nearby (*see below*); if your budget won't quite stretch to this, returning to Moss from Galleri F5 you'll see a turn-off to the left a kilometre or so down the road – along this lies **Röd Gård**, an old farm that is now an arts, crafts and design centre where local artisans work and sell their wares: the ceramics, clothing and wall hangings are worthy of a museum. It's a short journey back to **Moss**, from where there are ferries that make a pleasant crossing from the Østfold to Horten in the Vestfold area of the Oslofjorden.

Dinner and Sleeping: In Jeløy or Moss, *see* below.

Day 3

Lunch in Jeløy

Restaurant Munch, Hotell Refsnes Gods, 5 Godset, **t** 69 27 83 00 (*expensive*). Traditional Norwegian fare served buffet-style in an elegant ambience. Reservations are essential.

Galleri F15 Café, *see* above, **t** 69 27 10 33 (*inexpensive*). Salads, sandwiches and delicious desserts served in the café of the modern art museum, or outside when the weather permits.

Dinner and Sleeping in Jeløy

Hotell Refsnes Gods, 5 Godset, **t** 69 27 83 00, *www.refsnesgods.no* (*expensive*). A former hunting lodge in an elegant 18th-century wooden mansion with stylish twin turrets. Its idyllic setting on the west side of the island with its spectacular views of the Oslofjorden has long attracted the *crème de la crème* of Norwegian society and culture, including King Oscar II in 1898. Painters Hans Gude and Edvard Munch were regular guests, and works by the latter (among others) decorate the walls of the hotel and its dining room.

Dinner and Sleeping in Moss

Moss Hotel, 21 Dronningens Gate, **t** 69 20 24 00, *www.moss-hotel.no* (*moderate–inexpensive*). A friendly, family-run, atmospheric hotel in the town centre, in a building that is more than 200 years old but is equipped with all modern amenities. The large rooms have recently been renovated; each one is different from the next. It's wise to book ahead, as there's a loyal clientele who return to soak up the homely ambience.

Lysthuset, Tollbodbrygga (harbour), **t** 69 20 83 20 (*moderate*). An excellent fish restaurant. *Closed autumn–late spring.*

Café Everts, 2 Værftsgaten, **t** 69 27 40 08 (*inexpensive*). A modest cafeteria offering simple Norwegian fare, including soups, salads, sandwiches and warm entrées. *Closed from 7pm.*

Day 4: The Idyllic Coast of Vestfold

Morning: If you didn't do it last night, make the short drive to Moss and take the ferry over to **Horten**. The harbour front is a good place to get acquainted with this former navy town by the sea, which provides a good example of an 1800s garrison town. Stroll along the lovely Horten canal until noon, when you can visit the old naval base on Karljohansvern, which has been converted into a cultural centre housing the Marinemuseet (*open May–Sept daily 12–4, Oct–April Sun 12–4*), the world's oldest navy museum, and the Norsk Museum for Fotograpfi/Preus Fotomuseum (*open daily June–Aug 12–6, Jan–May and Sept–Dec Thurs and Fri 12–4, Sat and Sun 12–6; adm*), which is known for its excellent exhibitions of work by both Norwegian and international photographers. There are some superb beaches nearby if you prefer to spend a morning sunbathing and swimming.

Lunch: In Horten, *see* below.

Afternoon: Borre, located about 5km inland from Horten and reached via road 19, is the oldest national park in Norway, boasting Scandinavia's largest collection of Viking graves – seven large ones and 30 smaller ones. Forest elves are said to have materialized here. Borre church in the community of Horten is considered to be one of the most beautiful examples dating from the Middle Ages. Follow the scenic coastal path south to **Åsgårdstrand**, which Edvard Munch immortalized in many of his paintings, and where you can visit the quaint yellow house in which he lived (*open June–Aug Tues–Sun 11–6*).

Dinner and Sleeping: In Horten, *see* below.

Day 4

Lunch in Horten

Lillescenen, 29 Storgaten, **t** 33 07 16 00 (*moderate–inexpensive*). Sandwiches, salads and soups served in a casual ambience.

Munchs Café/Frantzens Bakeri og Konditori, 5 Stansgaten, **t** 33 08 10 26 (*inexpensive*). A café-bakery offering home-made pastries and open sandwiches to eat in or take away for a picnic on the beach.

Dinner in Horten

Åsgårdstrand Hotell, 6 Havnegaten, **t** 33 08 10 40 (*expensive–moderate*). A hotel restaurant where you can indulge in a range of Norwegian specialities that form part of an extensive menu. Among house specialities is Åsgårdstrand soup, a delicious *mélange* of fish and shellfish served with crusty bread.

Fishland, guest harbour (Gjestehavn), **t** 33 04 88 10 (*moderate*). A popular restaurant in which you can choose from among a variety of fish according to season. The fish soup, which is a speciality of the house, is almost a meal in itself.

Sleeping in Horten

Hotel Horten Brygge, 2 Strandpromenaden, **t** 33 02 04 20, *www.hotel-horten-brygge.com* (*moderate*). Twenty-three comfy rooms at the guest harbour, with all amenities, a restaurant and an outdoor café.

Åsgårdstrand Hotell, 6 Havnegaten, **t** 33 08 10 40, *www.asgardstrand-hotell.no* (*expensive*). A historic conference hotel that has burnt down twice, with a beachfront location, stylish rooms and attentive staff.

Eiken Pensjonat, 36 Gamleveien, **t** 33 04 79 08/ 92 23 28 58, *www.eikenpensjonat.no* (*inexpensive*). A former girls' camp dating back to 1935, now a pleasant place to stay 2km from town along a beachfront walk. The cheaper rooms don't have a bath; if you want a bath and a balcony, splurge on room 203. A small rowing boat is available for guest use, and there is an *à la carte* restaurant on the premises in the summer.

Day 5: Viking Mounds and a Castle Keep

Morning: Take road 311 to **Tønsberg**, where, in 1904, archaeologists excavated Norway's richest find of cultural relics from the Viking Age. There are numerous Bronze Age graves and Viking mounds throughout the area, most notably on a hill above town, Slottsfjellet, Scandinavia's largest ruin park and the site of Norway's largest castle in the 13th century (it was destroyed in 1503). After your visit, stroll to the marketplace in the centre of town, which sells fruits, vegetables, flowers and leather goods hand-made by a Sardinian expatriate. There are also many parks and churches to explore. For those who enjoy art and architecture, the Haugar Vestfold art museum (*open June–Aug Mon–Fri 11–5, Sat and Sun 12–5; Sept–May Tues–Fri 11–4; adm*) is housed in a castle-like structure built in 1922 as a navigational school.

Lunch: In Tønsberg, *see* below.

Afternoon: A boat excursion out to the skerries is a wonderful way to experience Norway. The 3½hr cruise on the 1909 tramp steamer *Kysten I* sets sail at noon (*July only*) from the Honnørbryggen, the jetty just north of the tourist office. You can have lunch on board. The Vestfold Fylkesmuseum (*open mid-May–mid-Sept Mon–Sat 10–5, Sun 12–5; adm*) covers the history of Vestfold and has a reconstruction of a Viking ship and several equally impressive whale skeletons. Outside is a charming replica of an English garden. For the ultimate sunset, drive for half an hour along road 308, which links the islands of **Nøtterøy** and **Tjøme** and takes you to the southernmost tip of this peninsula, to a spot known as **Verdens Ende** ('world's end').

Dinner and Sleeping: In Tønsberg, *see* below.

Day 5

Lunch in Tønsberg

Grand Café, 65 Øvre Langgaten, t 33 35 35 00 (*moderate*). A stylish, historic hotel where local movers and shakers like to dine. The extensive buffet is popular, as is the *à la carte* menu. In warm weather the outdoor terrace is always full.

Garfo, 36 Storgaten, t 33 37 01 45 (*moderate–inexpensive*). A Portuguese restaurant on the main street in the town centre, offering sandwiches, coffee and pastries by day, and in the evening authentic cuisine served in a *cataplana* – a wok-style pan with a lid. The décor is modern, the staff friendly.

Dinner and Sleeping in Tønsberg

Esmeralda, 28 Nedre Langgaten, t 33 31 91 91 (*moderate*). One of several restaurants with outdoor terraces along the harbour front, specializing in fish.

Rainbow Hotel Brygga, 40 Nedre Langgaten, t 33 34 49 00, *www.rainbow-hotels.no*

(*moderate*). An efficient, comfortable hotel along the harbour front. Ask for a room with a view. Parking is available.

Tønsberg Vandrerhjem, 22 Dronnings Gate, t 33 31 21 75, *tonsvand@online.no* (*inexpensive*). A perfect youth hostel for families on a budget, ideally located next to the castle rock and Fylkesmuseum. Comfortably furnished, it has friendly staff.

Dinner and Sleeping in Tjøme

Engo Gard, 25 Gamle Engøvai, t 33 39 00 48, *www.relaischateaux.com/engogard* (*luxury–very expensive*). A stylish inn on an atmospheric island outside town, a member of the Relais et Chateaux group, with a gourmet restaurant serving excellent seasonal food and an impressive wine cellar.

Holme Gård Farm, 63 Holmeveien, t 33 39 01 23, *www.holmegard.no* (*moderate–inexpensive*). A small farm offering accommodation in the form of cabins of various sizes, located in an idyllic setting by the sea, on the small island of Brøtsøy in the village of Tjøme.

Day 6: Sandefjord's Historic Whaling Tradition

Morning: Drive to **Sandefjord** along road 303, which takes approximately 20 minutes. This former spa town (*see* pp.164–6) also has a rich history dating back as far as the Vikings. Make sure to visit the ***Gokstad* burial mound** on road 303, about 4km outside town, where a Viking ship dating from AD 800 was excavated. In Sandefjord itself, you can explore its life-size replica, the *Gaia* (*Pier 3, 21 June–15 Aug daily 9.30–5; adm*), situated in the harbour. At the same pier, you can also climb aboard the *Southern Actor* (*same hrs as* Gaia), a restored whale-catcher complete with its original steam engine, still fully operative. Walk from the harbour to the city centre past the whaling monument. The Hvalfangstmuseet (*see* p.165) is the only whaling museum in Europe.

Lunch: In Sandefjord, *see* below.

Afternoon: Cross from the Museumgata to the Bjerggata, which is the oldest and best-preserved area of Sandefjord, with its charming white artisans' and sailors' houses dating from the 1800s. Then take a short walk up the winding roads to the surrounding hills above the city (Mølleråsen, Mokollen and Preståsen), which afford panoramic views. You can rent a bicycle and spend a lovely afternoon exploring the scenic 'fingers' that separate the Mefjorden. There are beaches and hiking trails in each area, and you can venture as your bike can take you. Otherwise, drive and make sure to park off the road, as these are nature sanctuaries. The E18 takes you back to Oslo in the morning, unless of course you are flying out from Torp airport.

Dinner and Sleeping: In Sandefjord, *see* below.

Day 6

Lunch in Sandefjord
See also p.166.

Brødr Berggren, Brygga, **t** 33 48 30 40 (*Inexpensive–moderate*). A family-run fish shop at the harbourside, established in 1911 and Norway's oldest fishmonger. Queues of happy customers come for the fresh catch of the day. Potential picnic food includes shrimp, smoked salmon and herring, and be sure to try the *fiskekaker* (fishcakes) – minced fish with garlic and other spices, said to be the best in Norway.

Fru Wolds Cafe og Spiseri, Bytunet, **t** 33 46 42 71 (*inexpensive*). A charming spot in the small town park, offering simple fare such as soups, salads and sandwiches.

Dinner in Sandefjord
See also p.166.

Restaurant Fea, Hotel Kong Karl, 9 Torggata, **t** 33 46 31 17 (*expensive*). A stylish dining room specializing in fresh fish, including boiled cod or baked salmon in spring and summer, served with *Sandefjordsmør*, a parsley, cream and salt butter sauce.

Smak, 9 Thor Dahls Gate, **t** 33 46 27 41 (*moderate*). Mediterranean- and Asian-inspired dishes served in the same building as **Mathuset Solvold** (*see* p.174). *Closed Sun.*

Sleeping in Sandefjord
See also pp.165–6.

Hotel Kong Carl, 9 Torggata, **t** 33 46 31 17, *www.kongcarl.no* (*expensive*). One of Norway's prestigious De Historske Hotel group of beautifully preserved establishments offering fine lodging and dining. Once an inn for whalers and fishermen from 1721, it has traditional décor such as wood panelling and historical photographs and paintings.

Sandefjord Herberge, 24b Hystadveien, **t** 33 46 40 79, *sande-he@online.no* (*inexpensive*). A family-run pension within walking distance of the centre, with 13 cosy rooms with television, refrigerator and hotplate, and bathrooms in the corridor.

Norway: Southwest Norway

13

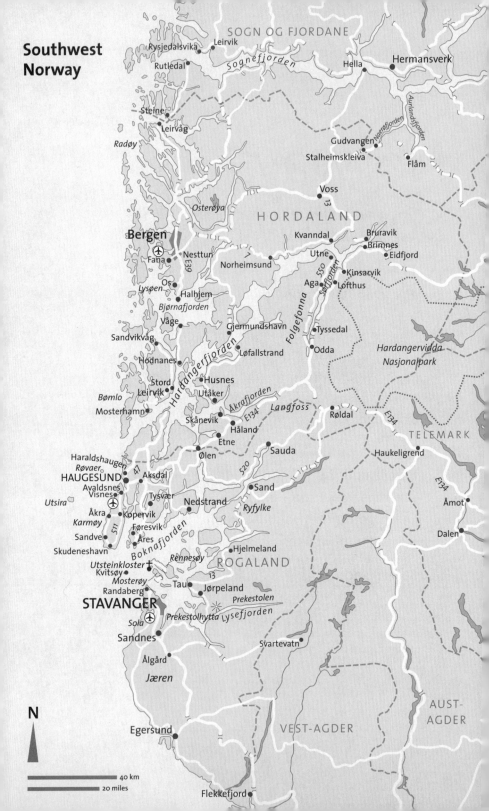

Stavanger

Stavanger, oil capital of Norway and its fourth largest city, is not what you might expect – there's no stench of oil in the air, no oil rigs despoiling the landscape. This is actually a pleasant part-medieval, part-modern city with the ambience of a smaller town, invigorating fresh air, miles of sandy beaches, forests, narrow fjords and dramatic mountains. Located in the Rogaland area of southwest Norway, it is famed for its unpredictable but mild weather, comprising 'at least three seasons in one day, because winter doesn't really count here,' as one local put it. July and August, the peak months embracing a number of festivals (*see* p.178), are the ideal time to enjoy the sea and the surrounding natural resources.

Stavanger's quaint harbour divides the historic part of town from the more modern environs. In Gamle Stavanger, the Old Town, the Stavanger Museum is comprised of five separate cultural institutions that include the unique canning museum, evidence of a once-important industry here. Stavanger's history has been well preserved along the alleys of Gamle Stavanger, which is lined with traditional 18th- and 19th-century timber houses ranging from the elegant to the functional. Around the guest harbour a variety of shops, cafés and restaurants lead up to the cobbled lanes of the centre. Among the many popular attractions are the ultra-modern Petroleum Museum and the Konserthus (concert hall), residence of the excellent symphony orchestra.

By boat you can reach the lovely Kvitsøy islands, where the fjord meets the open sea, or you can cycle to the picturesque countryside of Jæren just to the south or do some serious hiking in the magnificent scenery of the Lysefjorden to the east. Make sure to see Preikestolen ('Pulpit Rock') on the banks of the Lysefjorden, either by tour boat or by car and then on foot – experiencing the unique mount formation up close and personal is well worth the vigorous climb. Then there's the Utstein monastery north of the city, Norway's best preserved, and a true oasis for the spirit. Finally, the rich heritage of the Vikings can be traced during a visit to Jernaldergarden, a reconstructed Iron Age farm at Ullandhaug dating from the migration period AD 350–550.

History

Although it didn't gain city status until 1125, when construction of the modest medieval cathedral commenced, Stavanger is on a site that has been populated for more than 10,000 years. Indeed, the Rogaland region is rich in Viking history – many people from this area took part in Viking voyages, and, despite the fact that modern land development has obliterated many traces of the Viking age, there are still a few burial mounds and other related relics, many of which can be found in Stavanger's archaeological museum.

By 1900 Stavanger had become a dynamic fishing centre with more than 70 sardine canneries. Stock was depleted by the 1960s, but the discovery of oil in the North Sea led to a renaissance and, with the arrival of oil-related visitors, a more sophisticated image. The university is a world leader in information technology, and there are numerous cultural institutions and international schools as a result of the influx of foreign residents connected to the oil industry, as well as the Emigration Centre for

Stavanger

To Bjergsted, Norsk Grafisk
Museum and Konserthus

To Rennesøy,
Haugesund
and Bergen

Vågen

Østre Havn

Tou and Bergen

Norsk Oljemuseum

Fiskepiren

Hurtigbåt Domestic
Ferry Terminal

Norsk
Hermetikkmuseum

GAMLE
STAVANGER

ØVRE STRANDGATE

NEDRE STRANDGATE

LØKKEVEIEN

ØVRE STRANDGATE

NEDRE STRANDGATE

LARS HERTERVIGS GATE

WESSELS GATE

LØWOLDS GATE

KLINKENBERGGATA

OLAV KYRRES GATE

EIGANESVEIEN

JENS ZETLITZ GATE

ENGELSMINNEGATA

LØKKEVEIEN

ST OLAVS GATE

PRINSENS GATE

DRONNINGENS GATE

MADLAVEIEN

PEDER KLOWS GATE

To E39 (Sola, Sandnes
and Kristiansand)

To Ledaal, Breidablikk and
Rogaland Kunstmuseum

Norsk Telemuseum

Stavanger
Museum

Arkeologisk
Museum

To
Sandnes

SKANSEGATA

NEDRE HOLMGATE

ØVRE   HOLMGATE

VALBERGGATA

SKAGENKAIEN

KIRKEGATA

BREIGATA

SØLVBERGGATA

Valbergtårnet

Rodne Clipper
Sightseeing

Stavanger
Sjøfartsmuseum

ROSENKILDE-
TORGET

Sølvberget, Kulturhus and
Norsk Barnemuseum

VERKSGATA

VERKSGATA

PEDERSGATA

KLUBBGATA

KONGSGATA

BERGELANDSGATA

Marketplace

Domkirke

Breiavatnet

HAAKON VII'S GATE

OLAV V'S GATE

ST OLAV'S GATE

OLAV V'S GATE

KONGSGATA

STIFTELSESGATA

BREIBAKKEN

LANGGATA

LANGGATA

SAUDAGATA

Sentralstasjon and
Byterminalen

TEATERVEIEN

MUSEGATA

MUSEGATA

LAGÅRDSVEIEN

BIRKELANDS GATE

VIKEDALSGATA

N

200 metres
200 yards

Genealogical Studies and Contact between Norway and North America. So it's no
surprise that Stavanger has been designated Cultural Capital of Norway 2003–2005
and is a candidate for a European City of Culture 2008. Despite the Viking heritage,
the focus here is clearly on the future.

The City Centre

On central Haakon VII's Gate, the well-preserved and intimate 1125 **Domkirke** (*open
15 May–15 Sept Mon and Tues 11–6, Wed–Sat 10–6, Sun 1–6, Sun service 11am; 16 Sept–14
May Wed–Sat 10–3, Sun service 11am*) was originally constructed in the Anglo-Norman
style, probably with the help of English craftsmen (legend has it by Bishop Reinald of
Winchester, so he could preside over King Sigurd the Crusader's third wedding), but

now comprises an unusual mix of architectural styles. In 1272 it was badly damaged by fire, and around 1300 a completely new chancel was built in the Gothic style. Of all the Norwegian churches built in the Middle Ages, this is the only one that has retained its original style. In summer, public concerts, many of them connected with the chamber music festival held in late August (*see* p.178), are hosted here. The stately building beside the cathedral is **Kongsgård**, a former residence of kings, bishops and district governors, used as a high school for the last 150 years.

From the cathedral, take the stairs above the marketplace to get to the **harbour**, where you can buy sacks of shrimp from the indoor fishmarket just behind the fruit and veg sellers with their glossy plums, cherries, berries and apples. Along the harbourfront on Skansegata are pavement cafés where you can catch your breath and watch the parade of passers-by and the to-ing and fro-ing of fjord-cruisers.

You need to continue along Skansegata, past some warehouses, to get to the futuristic-looking **Norsk Oljemuseum** (Norwegian Petroleum Museum), **t** 51 93 93 11, *www.norskolje.museum.no* (*open June–Aug daily 10–7; Sept–May Mon–Fri 10–4, Sun 10–6; adm*). Its distinctive design of silver domes and features that recall the Norwegian bedrock, the coastal landscape and oil installations out at sea, carried out by Lunde & Løvseth architects, has been nominated for several European awards. The interesting exhibitions trace the history of the oil industry in the North Sea from the discovery of oil in 1969 to the present, through hi-tech interactive displays, huge models and excellent reconstructions. Its Bolgen & Moi café with waterfront view is better by day, when the food is slightly less expensive and the service less formal. Near by is the Magasin Blaa shopping complex (*see* p.179).

As you head back to the centre up Valberggata, the imposing structure on your right is the **Valbergtårnet**, an 1850 watch- and firetower housing the **Vektermuseet** (Watchmen's Museum), **t** 51 89 55 01 (*open Mon–Fri 10–4, Thurs 10–6, Sat 10–2; adm*) and a candlelit cocktail bar with a view of the city and fjords.

West of the harbour is **Gamle Stavanger**, the historical quarter, with 173 mainly small and white-painted wooden houses built at the end of the 18th century and beginning of the 19th. Stavanger has received many awards for its fine preservation of this area, which now has several galleries and crafts workshops, as well as some pleasant museum cafés. South past the Breiavatnet pond at 16 Muségata, the **Stavanger Museum**, **t** 51 84 27 00 (*open daily 15 June–15 Aug 11–4, 16 Aug–Nov and Jan–14 June Sun 11–4 or by appt; adm*), founded in 1877 and housed in a stately edifice, demands a full afternoon, with its 26 exhibitions focusing on Stavanger's natural and cultural history in the 19th century. The Stavanger Museum actually comprises five separate buildings, including the Norsk Hermetikkmuseum, the Stavanger Sjøfartsmuseum, and the Ledaal and Breidablikk patrician residences.

Off Muségata, the **Arkeologisk Museum i Stavanger** (Museum of Archaeology), 30 Peder Klows Gate, **t** 51 84 60 00 (*open June–Aug daily 11–5, Sept–May Tues 11–8, Wed–Sat 11–3, Sun 11–4; adm*) traces the relationship between culture and nature in Norway's rich 15,000-year history and puts a human face on the much-mythologized Vikings. There are permanent and changing exhibitions, including interactive areas, instructive models and unique objects of antiquity.

Getting to Stavanger

SAS has daily **flights** to Stavanger from London Heathrow, Newcastle, Aberdeen, Oslo, and Copenhagen; Braathens has daily flights from Aberdeen, Oslo, Bergen, Kristiansand and Trondheim; Widerøe's Flyveselskap ASA has a daily flight from Newcastle. For airline contact details, *see* p.3.

Fjord Line/Flaggruten (*www.fjordline.com*), see p.6, operates Bergen–Haugesund–Stavanger–Newcastle car **ferries**. Stavangerske Boknafjorden (Fiskepir terminal, **t** 51 86 87 80, Mortavika terminal, **t** 51 72 42 50, timetable info **t** 51 53 96 00, *www.stavangerske.no*) runs express ferries to Haugesund and Bergen and other locations in the Rogaland region.

Getting from the Airport

Stavanger's Sola airport is 17km from the centre. **Airport buses** leave every 20mins, making the 20min journey to such city-centre locations as the bus and train station and the harbour front for NOK100.

Getting Around

Most of Stavanger's sights are within easy walking distance of the harbour separating the historic quarter, Gamle Stavanger, from the centre with its labyrinthine backstreets filled with shops and restaurants.

Just behind the cathedral and Breiavatnet pond are the Byterminalen (**bus station**) and Stavanger Sentralstasjon (**rail station, t** 51 56 96 10, 24hr booking/info line **t** 81 50 08 88, *www.nsb.no*). Boats, buses and trains come under the auspices of Kolumbus, Rogaland Kollektivtrafikk (timetable info, **t** 177 or **t** 51 53 96 00, *www.kolumbus.no; Mon–Fri 7am–9pm, Sat 8–3.30, Sun 11–6*), which has a ticket office at Byterminalen (*open Mon–Fri 7–6, Sat 8–3*).

Taxis can be found around at stands at the train/bus station and at other central locations, or call Norges Taxi Stavanger, **t** 08 000, or Stavanger Taxi, **t** 51 90 90 90.

Car Hire

A compact car costs around NOK1,200–1,400 a week.
Avis, 15 Skansegata, **t** 51 93 93 60.
Budget, 125 Lagårdsveien, **t** 51 52 21 33.

Hertz, 13 Olav V's Gate, **t** 51 52 00 00, airport **t** 51 65 10 96.
Rent-a-Wreck, 2 Våenesveien, Røyneberg, **t** 51 64 70 50.

Tourist Information

Stavanger: Destinasjon Stavanger, 1 Rosenkildetorget, **t** 51 85 92 00, *www.visit stavanger.com* (*open June–Aug daily 9–8; Sept–May Mon–Fri 9–4, Sat 9–2*).

For NOK40 you can buy a **day ticket** valid for the Stavanger Museum, maritime museum, canning museum, and Ledaal and Breidablikk.

Guided Sightseeing

The informative 2hr City Sightseeing **coach tour** (June–Aug) is a good way to get quickly acquainted with Stavanger's history and attractions. Starting from the tourist office at 2pm (book by 1pm; **t** 51 85 92 00), it begins with a visit to Gamle Stavanger, then goes by the Ledaal and Breidablikk villas and the Three Swords monument. There is a stop to enjoy views of the city and the Ryfylke islands in the Boknafjorden from the **Ullandhaugtårnet** telecommunications tower, built in 1964 and 64m tall. The tour concludes at the cathedral.

For **fjord boat tours**, contact Rodne Clipper Fjordsightseeing (18 Skagenkaien, **t** 51 89 52 70). Scenic **helicopter flights** over the city, Lysefjorden and Ryfylke islands include a 30min trip to Pulpit Rock for around NOK1,000; book at the tourist office or by calling **t** 88 00 1414, *www.norcopter.com*.

For **cycling trips** in Rogaland, try Naboen Utlei (**t** 51 81 03 00, *www.naboen.no*) or Scanone Tours (**t** 51 85 09 10, *www.scanonetours.no*), which offers one-way bike hire along the North Sea route. Brochures for package tours along the North Sea route combined with island-hopping on Ryfylke are available at *www.visitsandnes.com*, or call **t** 51 66 20 96.

Festivals

Music events in the city include the **Tradjazz International Festival** (16–19 Jan), **May Jazz** (6–10 May; *www.maijazz.no*), **Sandnes Bicycle Blues Festival** (mid-June) and **International Chamber Music Festival** (16–23 Aug; *www.*

icmf.no). Other cultural highlights include the **Chapter 03 International Literary Festival** (19–23 Sept; *www.kapittel.com*) and the **Family & Youth Film Festival** (mid-Nov), while for gastronomes there's the **VinFest Wine Festival** (mid-Mar) and the **Gladmat Food Festival** (23–26 July; *www.gl indooradmat.no*).

Shopping

The small streets above the marketplace are where most of the unique souvenir and crafts shops are located, mainly on **Kirkegata**, **Sølvberggata** and surrounding streets, selling traditional silver, pewter, knitwear, rose paintings, animal skins and more.

Magasin Blaa at 2 Verksgate near the Petroleum Museum is a modern complex with 20 excellent shops, including Marimekko and other Scandinavian design addresses. **Stavanger Storsenter**, which includes the Steen & Strøm department store and H&M, extends from the marketplace to 5 Klubbgata. The **Straen Senter**, up the steps behind the tourist office, is smaller; the Meny grocery store has good fresh foods.

Kvadrat, Norway's largest shopping centre, is along the E39 between Stavanger and Sandnes. It has 160 shops, a department store, a pharmacy, a state off-licence, a post office, a bank and a tourist office.

Shop opening hours are Mon–Wed and Fri 9–5, Thurs 9–7 and Sat 9–3. Shopping malls are open Mon–Fri 10–8 and Sat 10–6.

Markets

The flower, fruit and veg stalls and indoor fishmarket along Rosenkildetorget by the harbour (Mon–Sat 8–3) are always crowded with locals and tourists. It's easy to make a movable feast with a box of berries, a bag of shrimps and a loaf of bread from Skagen Bageri (18 Skagen) or Baker Brun at the nearby Arkaden shopping centre.

Where to Stay

The **B&B Circle** consists of several charming, well-established family homes in the heart of Stavanger, including Ye Olde Stable. A brochure is available from the tourist office.

Rica Forum Hotel, 17 Gunnar Warebergsgaten, **t** 51 93 00 00, *www.rica.no* (*expensive–moderate*). A large luxury hotel next to the Stavanger Forum congress hall in a modern, circular glass structure 2.5km from the train station. The rooms have magnificent views, as does the restaurant and 'sky bar'.

Victoria Hotel, 1 Skansegata, **t** 51 86 70 00, *www.victoria-hotel.no* (*expensive–moderate*) Stavanger's 'first luxury hotel', as stylish as when it opened in 1900. Rooms are elegantly decorated in subdued colours, and some have harbour views. The excellent restaurant, bar and outdoor terrace attract a local crowd, and the staff are friendly.

Best Western Havly, 1 Valberggata, **t** 51 89 67 00, *www.havly-hotell.no* (*moderate*). A hotel in a narrow street off Skagenkaien, convenient for nearby restaurants and cafés and with comfortable, quiet rooms.

Charlottenlund, 45 Kongsgata, **t** 51 91 76 00, *www.charlottenlund.no* (*moderate*). An 1820s summer house with just 5 rooms, family-run, friendly and homely. Room 1, with its light and airy ambience and charming yellow décor, is popular with honeymooners. *See* also 'Eating Out'.

Golden Tulip Rainbow Hotel Maritim, 32 Kongsgata, **t** 51 85 05 00, *www.rainbow-hotels.no/maritim* (*moderate*). A quiet hostelry opposite a park, providing a home from home for tourists and business travellers. It's convenient for the city centre and the airport bus stop by the train station.

Skagen Brygge Hotel, 30 Skagen, **t** 51 85 00 00, *www.skagenbryggehotell.no* (*moderate*) A modern hotel with all conveniences, including a popular bar attracting a local crowd. Ask for a room with a view of the scenic harbour and old town.

Ye Olde Stable (Den Gamle Stallen), Villa Blidensol, 112 Øvre Strandgate, **t** 51 52 53 46, *www.gamlestallen.com* (*moderate*). Original (if slightly dark) B&B accommodation for up to 4 people in a 300-year-old stable, with modern furnishings, a small kitchen and a sleeping area reached by a ladder. The surrounding Old Stavanger area is charming and there is parking.

Commander Hotel, 9 Valberggata, **t** 51 89 53 00, *www.commandor.no* (*moderate–inexpensive*). A family-run hotel located on a quiet street parallel to the harbour front, with clean, simply furnished rooms.

Skagen Hotell & Gjestehus, 7 Skansegata, **t** 51 93 85 00, *www.shg.no* (*inexpensive*). A tranquil budget establishment not far from the harbourfront, with simple, mainly white rooms equipped with telephone and TV. Its **Broremann Bar** attracts a hip local crowd.

Stavanger Bed & Breakfast, 1a Vikedalsgata, **t** 51 56 25 00, *www.stavangerbedandbreakfast. no* (*inexpensive*). A clean and basic place near the bus and train stations, with toilets in the hall. The friendly staff are a fount of information, and breakfasts are hearty.

Eating Out

Craig's Kjøkken & Bar, Breitorget (behind Kulturhus), **t** 51 93 95 90 (*expensive*). A stylish but relaxed restaurant serving serious bistro cuisine and even more serious wine. Genial Oklahoma-born Craig Whitsun presides over a hand-picked staff. *Closed lunch and Sun*.

Charlottenlund Restaurant, 41 Kongsgata, **t** 51 53 33 00 (*moderate*). An elegant, old-fashioned eatery along the Breiavatnet lake (*see* 'Where to Stay'), serving tea and cake, and more elaborate meals. The terrace is lovely in summer, and Sunday dinner is popular among locals. *Closed lunchtimes outside summer*.

Gaffel & Karaffel, 20 Øvre Holmgate, **t** 51 86 41 58 (*moderate*). An excellent, unpretentious restaurant with a seasonal menu featuring Norwegian ingredients interpreted in a pure and delicious manner, including wild salmon and reindeer. *Closed lunch and Sun*.

N.B. Sorensens Dampskibsexpedition, 26 Skagen, **t** 51 60 20 80 (*moderate*); dining room, **t** 51 84 38 20 (*expensive*). An old wooden warehouse and former chandlery with a pub/restaurant on the ground floor and a gourmet dining room upstairs. Downstairs you can feast on all-day English breakfasts, classic burgers and more; upstairs enjoy the 4-course menu. *Dining room closed lunch and Sun*.

Vertshuset Mat & Vin, 10 Skagen, **t** 51 89 51 12 (*moderate*). A cosy environment in which to enjoy good grub, from reindeer steak and wild salmon to *komler*. *Closed Sun eves*.

Bolgen & Moi Ostehuset, 3 Klubbgata, **t** 51 86 40 10 (*moderate–inexpensive*). An upmarket lunch room/gourmet food shop serving up delicious salads, sandwiches and mini pizzas, plus great coffees and fine wines by the glass. *Closed from 6pm Sat and all day Sun*.

Café Sting, 3 Valberggata, **t** 51 89 38 78 (*moderate–inexpensive*). A hip restaurant and café opposite the Valbergtårnet, with Norwegian 'fusion' cooking – Asian dishes, salads, sandwiches and whatever has inspired the chef. It's also a gallery and music venue. *Closed Sun lunch (open from 2pm)*.

India Tandoori Restaurant, 14 Valberggata, **t** 51 89 39 35 (*moderate–inexpensive*). A good, family-run place to indulge in onion bhaji, mango lassi and a well-spiced vindaloo, on a back street near the harbour. *Closed lunch*.

Ekofisk, 13 Nedre Strandgate, **t** 51 52 54 09 (*inexpensive*). A fish shop popular among locals for quick, cheap lunches or snacks. In summer there are a few outside tables with harbour views. Try smoked salmon on crusty bread or *bacalao*. *Closed eves and Sun*.

Food Story, 3 Klubbgata, **t** 51 56 37 70 (*inexpensive*). A modern café/food shop with a simple, healthy menu of fresh juice, fruit and yoghurt, lentil soup, pasta of the day, salads and sandwiches. *Closed eves and Sun (open until 8pm Thurs and Fri)*.

Newsman, 14 Skagen, **t** 51 84 38 80 (*inexpensive*). A place with broadsheets hanging on the walls and daily papers (mainly Norwegian) to peruse over a coffee or tankard of ale. In the evenings there's a pub-style menu.

Entertainment and Nightlife

The **Stavanger Konserthus** at Bjergsted (**t** 51 53 70 00) is home to the city's internationally acclaimed symphony orchestra, as well as a venue for opera, pop music, theatre and dance.

For rowdier pleasures, try **Hansen Hjørnet** (18 Skagenkaien, **t** 51 89 52 80), one of the liveliest spots on the harbour, and **Taket** (15 Nedre Strandgate, **t** 51 84 37 20), an upmarket club opposite the harbour and above the trendy Timbuktu bar, kicking off at around midnight.

Just north, the **Norsk Telemuseum** (Norwegian Telecom Museum), 12 Dronningens Gate, t 51 76 32 49 (*open mid-June–mid-Aug Wed–Sun 12–4; mid-Aug–mid-June Sun 11–4; adm*), in a restored wooden house, covers the history of wireless communication and telecommunications, as well as modern developments and events.

Further north, just past the tourist office, the **Stavanger Sjøfartsmuseum** (Maritime Museum), 17–19 Nedre Strandgate, t 51 84 27 00 (*same hours as Stavanger Museum; adm*), in some restored harbour-front warehouses dating from 1770–1840, has an exhibition on local maritime history over the last 200 years, from the era of herrings and sailing ships to the present-day oil industry. There are interesting reconstructions of a shipowner's office, a general store, a sailmaker's loft and an early-1900s merchant's apartment. The museum also owns and operates two sailing boats: the 1897 yacht *Wyvern*, commissioned by English timber merchant Frederick Croft, which has crossed the Atlantic more than a dozen times and sailed around the world in the 1940s and '50s; and the 1848 sloop *Anna*, originally used to transport goods up the fjords and along the coastline and believed to be one of Europe's oldest surviving vessels.

The nearby **Norsk Hermetikkmuseum** (Canning Museum), 88a Øvre Strandgate, t 51 84 27 00 (*same hours as Maritime Museum; adm*), set in an old canning factory where fishballs and canned brisling were once produced, has displays on the factory and its working conditions. Smoking still takes place on the first Sunday of the month and on Tuesdays and Thursdays from 15 June to 15 August, when you can sample brisling straight from the ovens.

On the seafront at the tip of the western harbour at Bjergsted, further north near the Konserthus, a restored 1913 canning warehouse houses the **Norsk Grafisk Museum** (Printing Museum), 24 Sandvigå, t 51 52 88 86 (*open 15 May–15 Aug Mon, Wed and Fri 11–3; 16 Aug–14 May Sun 11–4; adm*) with printing presses and related equipment for newspapers, lithography and bookbinding from 1850–1950, much of it still operational. There are guided tours and demonstrations of old printing techniques.

At the **Sølvberget** (Stavanger Culture House) at 2 Sølvberggata there is a library and a cinema, as well as the new **Norsk Barnemuseum** (Norwegian Children's Museum), t 51 91 23 93 (*open Tues–Sat 11–3.30, Sun 12.30–4.30; adm*), with its exhibition of old toys, its labyrinth and its collection of other childhood-related items popular with both kids and nostalgic adults.

You might like to see some of the Stavanger Museum departments in the morning, then in the afternoon visit the Museum of Archaeology (*see* p.177) and the Rogaland Art Museum (*see* p.182) and walk along **Eiganesveien**, a tree-lined street with some grand mansions, east of the cathedral. At No.45, **Ledaal** (*open 15 June–15 Aug daily 11–4; 16 Aug–Nov and Feb–14 June Sun 11–4 or by appt; adm*) is a royal residence and summer home that was originally built for shipowner and merchant Gabriel Schanche Kielland in 1799–1803 and is considered one of western Norway's most important neoclassical buildings. The furnishings, mainly rococo, Empire and Biedermeier, include the king's 250-year-old four-poster bed and a 1680 pendulum clock. At No.40a, **Breidablikk** (*same hrs as Ledaal; adm*) is a stately villa built by merchant and shipowner Lars Berentsen in 1881–2. The original exterior and interior have been preserved, and you can see books, bric-a-brac, old farm tools and more.

The **Rogaland Kunstmuseum** (Art Museum), 55 Henrik Ibsen's Gate, **t** 51 53 05 20 (*open Tues–Sun 11–4; adm*), a pleasant 20min walk from the centre along Eiganesveien, includes a unique collection of 18th- and 19th-century art, focusing on Norwegian romanticist painter Lars Hertervig (1830–1902), born in Tysvær (*see* p.194). There is an overview of Norwegian art from the 19th century to the present, work by eight Norwegian artists of the inter-war generation (in a separate pavilion), and a permanent exhibition of sculpture by British artist Anthony Gormley that opened in 2003.

As you walk back towards town, make sure to see the elegant mansion at No.28 Eiganesveien, where 'cat lady' Kari Mills has given numerous stray felines shelter; you are bound to spy several peeking out of each window, or happily sleeping on sills. Her antiques shop and art gallery are worth visiting whether you are a cat-lover or not.

Sculpture enthusiasts not sated at the Rogaland Museum will also be interested in Gormley's **Broken Column** project of 23 sculptures of figures in site-specific and altitude-specific locations throughout Stavanger. Ask at the Kunstmuseum for details.

Outside the Centre

A pleasant 3km walk south of the centre in the direction of Sandnes, or a 10-minute ride on bus no.130 from the main bus station, **Mosvagen Forest Park and Wildlife Refuge** has footpaths, a lagoon and a large bird and wildlife population. Just south of it on road 510 from Stavanger to Sandnes is **Jernadergarden**, also known as the **Ullandhaug Farm Reconstruction**, **t** 51 84 60 71 (*open 15 June–Aug Mon–Sat 11–4, Sun 12–4; rest of year Sun 12–4, adm*), a replica of an Iron Age farm dating from the migration period AD 350–550. The best day to visit is Sunday, when there are numerous activities, including people in period dress, demonstrations and cookery.

Three Swords in the Rock (*Sverd i fjell*) at Hafrsfjord beach towards Sola (10 minutes by the twice-hourly bus no.7 from the main bus station) is a memorial to Harald the Fairhaired, who united Norway in a battle here in AD 872. You can combine a bike trip to this popular recreation area with a dip in the sea; from the city centre, cycle along Mosvannet lake, then continue along road 510 towards Sola (30mins each way).

On the banks of the **Lysefjorden** 15km east of the city is magnificent **Preikestolen** ('Pulpit Rock'), a dramatic rock fissure reached by a 2hr trail from the Preikestolhytta (Pulpit Rock Hut) along a steep but well-paved path that gives way to steeper, rather soggy terrain, then to thrilling granite slabs and windswept cliffs. For die-hard hikers there are other options from the same starting point: the Vatnerindane ridge circuit (2hrs); and Ulvaskog, the Refsvatnet circuit and the summit of Moslifjellet (all 3hrs). You need to buy a ticket (NOK5) at the hut. Buses run from Tau to the hut from 17 June to 1 September, linking up with ferries from Fiskepiren in Stavanger at 8.20 and 9.05am (buses return at 2.20 and 4.15). Out of season, take a taxi to the hut from Jørpeland. Make sure you wear a windbreaker and proper shoes, and bring food and water. The hut has a youth hostel and a café serving meals from 28 May to 14 September. For more details, enquire at Stavanger tourist office. The 3½–4hr **Lysefjord–Pulpit Rock Boat Tour** leaving Skagenkaien quay near the Victoria Hotel at noon daily (*call for details of monthly schedule*, **t** 51 53 73 40; *tickets sold on quay 20mins before departure or at tourist office*) is another way of viewing Preikestolen.

Day Trips from Stavanger

Sandnes

Just south of Stavanger by car, bus or train, the country's fastest-growing city has also been also dubbed Norway's 'bicycle town' – it has 200 cycles that can be borrowed free, and mountain bike hire for trips into the surrounding countryside, and is where DBS bicycles are made. There's a good trip from Sandvedparken along Bråsteinsvatnet to the Melsheia area, where you can walk through the lush **Rogaland Arboretum** parkland. It takes about an hour each way. **Kongeparken**, Scandinavia's largest leisure park, is nearby in a lovely lakeside setting, Edlandsvatnet, in the small town of Ålgård.

Utstein Kloster

t 51 72 47 05; open May, June and Aug–15 Sept Tues–Fri 10–4; July Tues–Fri 10–4, Sun 12–5; adm.

On the island of Mosterøy just north of Stavanger, this monastery was as a royal residence of Harald the Fairhaired at the end of the 9th century. In 1250 it was acquired by Magnus Lagabøter (the 'law mender' who, as king, would draft Norway's constitution). Magnus gave Utstein to Augustinian canons, who built their abbey around his fortress at the end of the 13th century. After the Reformation, it became one of the largest private estates in western Norway, and today it is open for guided tours, seminars and summer concerts in the chapel. The peaceful monastery and surrounding green areas make for a tranquil excursion to the country.

Getting There

Sandnes
Sandnes is a 15min drive south of Stavanger on route 13. Frequent **buses** include no.2 from Stavanger's main bus station, taking about 30mins. **Trains** take only 10mins but are a bit more expensive.

Utstein Kloster
It's 22km to Utstein Kloster from Stavanger, via the tunnel to Sokn on Rennesøy. **Bus** no.10 from the main bus station (7, 9, 2.40, 3.10, 4.10, 5.10) goes to Sokn, where you change to no.33. Return buses leave the monastery at 3.28, 4.08, 5pm and 6pm.

Tourist Information

Utstein Kloster: contact Stavanger office.
Sandnes: 22 Vågsgaten, **t** 51 97 55 55, *www. visitsandnes.com (open June–Aug, Mon–Fri 8–7, Sat 10–5, rest of year Mon–Wed and Fri 10–4, Thurs 10–6).*

Eating Out

Sandnes
N.B. Sorensens Dampskibsexpedition, Sandnes Kulturhus, **t** 51 60 20 80 *(moderate)*. Good steaks, seafood, pasta and salads served in an historic old ship's chandlery.
Gamla Værket Gjæstgiveri & Tracteringssted, 38 St Olavs Gate, Sandnes, **t** 51 68 51 70 *(moderate–inexpensive)*. Breakfasts, lunches and dinners in a restored brick factory. One menu has Norwegian and local dishes, the other Mediterranean dishes. The hotel also has a traditional pottery workshop.

Utstein Kloster
Utstein Kloster Hotell Restaurant, Mosterøy (2km from monastery), **t** 51 72 01 00 *(moderate)*. Hotel restaurant open all day. Norwegian cuisine includes fish soup with home-made bread, and summer desserts with local fruit. Located at the water's edge, the hotel has minimally furnished, peaceful, airy rooms. *Closed Sun eve.*

Haugesund

Although it is not a stately capital like Stockholm or Helsinki, Haugesund, like them, is a town that it is best approached by boat, with its charming inner harbour lined with 19th-century wooden buildings and lively cafés, restaurants and hotels. At the heart of Norway's west coast, synonymous since Viking times with seafaring and trade, it has plentiful herring resources and remains an important site for fish export, as well as being Norway's leading shipbuilding centre.

While it may at first seem a sleepy little burg reminiscent of American small towns in the 1950s, it boasts the longest shopping street in Norway (most of the shops are nondescript, alas) and is a well-known congress destination. After its mild winters (thanks to the Gulf Stream), it erupts with energy in summer, hosting one festival after another, including jazz and film festivals in August (*see* p.187), and the harbour takes on a festive atmosphere, with a rainbow of sailing flags.

Haugesund is also the gateway to the wet, wild and rugged land- and seascapes of Haugelandet ('hill country'), which embraces nearby Stavanger and Bergen and numerous charming, laidback towns and villages with friendly – and often eccentric – citizens, most of them fishermen, farmers or craftspeople. The fjords here, which locals call the 'highway to the world', are graced by breathtaking waterfalls, including Langefoss, Vøringfoss and Skykkjedalsfoss, the highest in the region at 1,000ft. The scenic drive to Bergen via the Hardangerfjorden is one of Norway's most magnificent, especially in early spring when the famous fruit trees (half a million of them) are in glorious bloom, or in late summer, when the crunchy apples, luscious plums and morello cherries can be sampled at roadside stands. Locals attribute their unique flavour to the hearty air, rich soil and pure water of the fjords.

History

The Haugelandet region is known as 'Norway's birthplace', and for good reason. For more than 3,000 years, chieftains or kings levied tolls on passing ships at Avaldsnes, on the Nordvegen strait between Karmøy and Haugesund. These chieftains ruled the Vikings, who when not fighting amongst themselves were busy plundering neighbouring countries. The first church built at Avaldsnes by King Håkon Håkonson in 1205, St Olav's (*see* p.191), still stands as evidence of the area's rich history, and there are many monumental burial sites, carved stones and other treasures, discovered both on the seabed and on land.

It was in this region, following the Battle of Hafrsfjord in AD 870, that Norway's first throne was established by Viking king Harald the Fairhaired and Norway acquired its name from the strait of Nordvegen. Haraldshaugen, the national monument erected as a tribute to Harald, who united Norway as a kingdom, is situated just north of Haugesund (*see* p.186).

While archaeologists continue to mine the area for historical documentation, technological development is continuing apace. The Norwegian oil industry is firmly entrenched in the region, with the gas pipeline from the North Sea to Kårstø east of Karmøy following the route of the Vikings, as well as others before and after them.

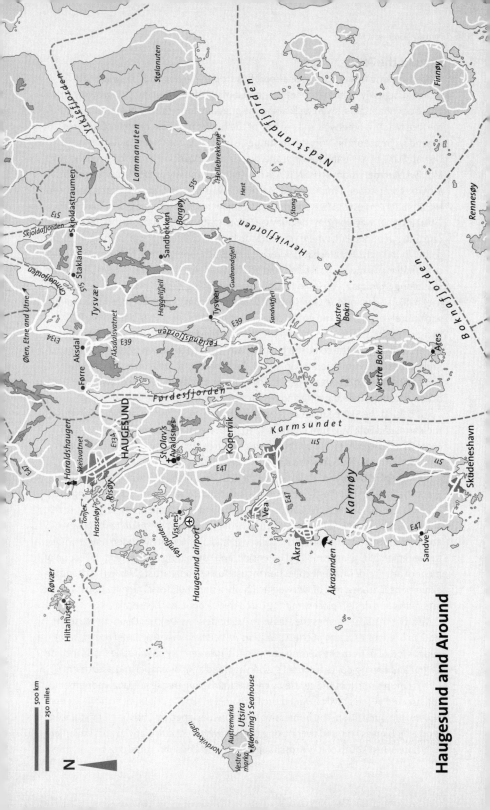

Haugesund and Around

N

500 km
250 miles

Røvær
Hiltahuset

Austremarka
Vestre-marka
Utsira
Klovning's Seahouse
Nordhvitdgen

Åkra
Åkrasanden
Karmøy
Sandve
E47
Vea
Visnes
Føynafjorden
Haugesund airport
St Olav's
Avaldsnes
Kopervik
Karmsundet
Skudeneshavn
517
515
E47

HAUGESUND
Haraldshauget
Skeisvatnet
Tonjer
Hasseløy
Risøy
E134
E47

Forre
Aksdal
Aksdalsvatnet
E39
Ølen, Etne and Utne
E134

Tysvær
Stakland
515
Skjoldastraumen
Skjoldafjorden
513
Ølsfjorden
Yklsfjorden

Stølanuten
Lammanuten

Sandbekken
Heggelifjell
Borgøy
515
Hellebrekkene
Hest

Tysvær
Gudbrandsfjell
E39
Sandvikfjell
Forlandsfjorden
Førdesfjorden

Herwikfjorden
Stong
Austre Bokn
Vestre Bokn
Åres
Boknafjorden
Nedstrandsfjorden
Finnøy
Rennesøy

Around the Town

Disembarking from the boat or airport bus stop, or parking your car, you'll find yourelf practically right in front of the tourist office of this friendly, still-growing town of 31,000 inhabitants. If you walk along the quayside from the Hotel Amanda towards the Rica Maritim hotel, you will see two of the town's most memorable sculptures: **Amanda**, symbol of the Norwegian statuette (similar to the Oscars or Baftas in the USA and UK), by Kristian Kvakland; and, just past the Maritim, an almost recognizable **Marilyn Monroe**, whom artist Nils Aas has seated demurely on her famous bottom. Monroe's stepfather, a man named Mortensen, was born outside town, and visitors to the annual Film Festival (*see* p.187) seem to enjoy this incongruous work of art.

Making your way up from the quay via Skippergata, you pass the Lothes restaurant, café and bar on the left, where you can stop by for a coffee, snack or evening meal (*see* p.189). To the right, **Haraldsgata**, Norway's longest shopping street, has the atmosphere of a small 1950s town – you won't find the familiar high-street shops here. Just to the east along Skåregata, you'll see the Markedet shopping centre; behind is the **Rådhus** (city hall) (*guided tours in English Mon–Wed and Fri 1pm*), a striking rose-hued building with stately pillars, a grand entrance, a charming fountain, and, inside, colourful murals depicting town history and some distinctive light wood furniture from the region. Built in 1931, the colourful building was a gift to the town from shipowner Knut Knudsen, commemorated in one of the many sculptures surrounding the **Rådhus Plassen**. This square hosts many outdoor events, including fireworks displays, cobblestone dancing and parades commemorating various festivals.

Just behind the **Skåre Kirche**, or town church, also on Skåregata, an old dairy houses the **Karmsund Folk Museum Centre, t** 52 70 93 60, *www.museumsnett.no* (*open Mon–Fri 10.30–2, Sun by appointment; adm*), with exhibitions about daily life in the town and rural areas in the 19th and 20th centuries.

The **Kirkegård Byparken** (town square park) to the north of here on Havnaberggata is another site for civic festivities and has a distinctive bandstand. Overlooking it from No.4 Erling Skjalgssons Gate is the **Haugesund Billedgalleri, t** 52 72 34 71, *www.haugesund-billedgalleri.net* (*open Tues–Sat 12–4, Thurs 12–7, Sun 12–5; longer hours in summer*), an acclaimed art gallery spread over a white wooden house unique to the region plus a large modern extension, and containing an excellent collection of modern art. The permanent collection focuses on regional artists, while the changing exhibitions feature a mix of Norwegian painters and sculptors. The gift shop has good arts, crafts and design pieces, and the café serves a popular cheesecake.

West of the gallery, across the Hasseløy Bru bridge, the **Dokken Open-air Museum**, 11d–13b Brugata, **t** 52 70 93 60 (*guided tours mid-June to mid-Aug Sun–Fri 12–5, adm*) depicts local life from the herring boom in the 19th century onwards. Exhibits include sailing and rowing boats, a cooper's workshop, and a 1950s chapel and apartment.

Ten minutes north of the centre by car is **Haraldshaugen**, the national monument, constructed at the grave of Harald the Fairhaired in 1872 to celebrate 1,000 years of Norwegian unification. The impressive structure, designed by Christian Christiansen, is on a high grassy mound overlooking the sea. with a spectacular view of the Tonjer lighthouse. Just south of it is **Krosshaugen**, an early-Christian stone cross.

Getting There

Haugesund airport on the island of Karmøy serves the Haugelandet area, which includes Stavanger and Bergen, each of which also has its own airport. Ryanair has one daily flight to Haugesund from London Stansted. Coast Air has flights to Haugesund from Aberdeen, Bergen and Sandefjord. SAS has flights from Oslo (45mins) and other destinations within Norway. For airline contact details, *see* p.3.

Fjord Line/Flaggruten runs a **ferry** between Newcastle and Haugesund (*see* p.6).

Haugesund is 110km from Bergen, which can be reached by **hydrofoil** in 2hrs 50mins, or 3hrs 30mins by car/bus (via 2 ferries). Stavanger, 77km away, can be reached by hydrofoil in 1hr 20mins, by car or bus in 2hrs. The 460km drive from Oslo takes about 8hrs direct on the E134.

Getting from the Airport

Buses to Haugesund bus station (**t** 177 or **t** 52 70 35 00, *www.kystbussen.no*; NOK40) leave 25mins after the Ryanair flight arrives and take 20mins. They leave the bus station for the airport 2hrs before outgoing flights.

Getting Around

Haugesund is a small town that is easily explored on foot, with a simple grid plan.

Taxis can be found at stands around town, or call **t** 52 80 80 80.

The free map 'On Green Wheels', available in English at tourist information centres, has tour suggestions and other useful information for **cyclists**. See also *www.bike-norway.com* and *www. northsea-cycle.com*. For **bike hire**, contact the Karmøy Tourist Information Centres at Skudeneshavn or Avaldsnes (*see* p.192), or see *www.karmoy.org*.

Car Hire

Driving is the easiest way of seeing the Haugelandet area, and you can take cars on the ferries.

Avis, 64 Haraldsgata, **t** 52 84 02 23, and airport.

Europcar, 178 Karmsundgata, **t** 52 84 04 50, and airport.

Hertz, 189 Karmsundgata, **t** 52 84 20 00, and airport.

National Rental Car, Haugesund Travel, 215 Karmsundgata, **t** 52 70 35 50.

Tourist Information

Haugesund: 1 Kaigata, **t** 52 73 45 26, *www. haugesund.net*.

Festivals

Among local cultural highlights are the **Fartein Valen** chamber music festival, a tribute to the composer (24–7 April); **Skånevik Blues Festival** (3–6 July, *www.skanevik-blues.com*) on the Hardangerfjorden; the **Silda international jazz festival** (6–10 Aug; **t** 52 74 33 70, *www. sildajazz.no*), with a swinging parade featuring hundreds of musicians and tap dancers, concerts at numerous venues, including small surrounding islands reached by little ferries, and exhibitions; and the **Norske Filmfestivalen** (Norwegian Film Festival; 16–24 Aug; **t** 52 73 44 30, *www.filmfestivalen.no*).

Those lucky enough to be here around the longest day of the year can take part in the **Midsummer Festival Tysvær** (19–23 June), which includes a large bonfire on a headland, Slusedagen, with marked boats making their way through the sluices, and a dance at the beach at Skjoldastraumen.

Around the same time, **Borgøydagen**, a celebration on the idyllic island of Borgøy in the Skjoldafjorden, where artist Lars Hertervig was born, includes a small market and guided tour, including Hertervig's favourite path across the island. There's a café (*open Sun*).

Shopping

Haugesund's inordinately long shopping street, **Haraldsgata**, parallel to the quayside, has about 100 shops and many restaurants. Also in the heart of town, the **Markedet** shopping centre in the heart of town (92 Skåregata) has a wide variety of shops, including a branch of the **Steen & Strøm** department store.

Market Days

There is a fruit, vegetable and flower market in front of the town hall (Rådhus) Mon–Fri 9–3.

Where to Stay

Radisson SAS Park Hotel, 1 Ystadveien, **t** 52 86 10 00, *www.radissonsas.com* (*expensive*). A modern conference hotel 3km south of the centre, with views over the Karmsundet, a restaurant, an indoor pool and a mini golf course.

Rica Maritim, 3 Åsbygata. **t** 52 86 30 00, *www.rica.no* (*expensive*). Rated as one of Haugesund's 'luxury' hotels for its quayside location, elegantly decorated rooms and gourmet restaurant, **Brovingen** (*see* below), this is the hub of the busy jazz and film festivals (*see* p.187). It has a theatre in its conference centre, where you can watch a 5-screen video of the Haugelandet area to inspire you before you start your travels, as well as *Kystfolk*, a documentary about coastal folk (in Norwegian).

Comfort Hotel Amanda, 93 Smedasundet, **t** 52 80 82 00, *www.choice.no* (*expensive–moderate*), An American-inspired building opposite the harbour, near the boat landing to Stavanger, built at the beginning of the 20th century and catering to movie buffs year-round, with its Citizen Kane Suite and rooms paying tribute to screen sirens such as Marilyn Monroe.

Best Western Hotel Neptun, 207 Haraldsgata, **t** 52 86 59 00, *www.bestwestern.com/no/ neptun* (*moderate*). A low-key hotel that was built on the city's main shopping street in 1920, with the feel of an old-fashioned boarding house, a comfortable lounge and a well-tended breakfast room where you can select from an excellent buffet that includes smoked salmon.

Hendersons Airport Hotel, 24 Helganesveien, Karmøy, **t** 52 84 25 00, *www.hendersons.no* (*moderate*). A conference hotel 2km from the airport and 20mins by car or airport bus from Haugesund, with well-appointed, modern, reasonably stylish rooms. The staff are friendly and there are 2 restaurants, a fitness and recreation centre, and a congress hall in a 1915 Jugendstil villa. Ask about the special offer combining a night's stay with 24hr Hertz car rental.

Skeisvang Gjestgiveri, 20 Skeisvannsvegen, Skeisvatnet (10min drive northeast of centre), **t** 52 71 21 46, *www.skeisvang-gjestgiveri.no*

(*inexpensive*). A homely family-run guesthouse with a living room with a fireplace, a piano, a large-screen TV and a CD/DVD player. It's a 5min walk from a fitness centre with an indoor pool and a wooded area with hiking and swimming in a small lake. Rooms are light, airy and pleasantly spartan; some have TV but none has a phone (though you can check your emails in the office). Family apartments are also available.

For information on **camping** by the sea and **winter chalet rentals**, contact Haraldshaugen Camping, **t** 52 72 80 77, *www.nafcamp.com/ haraldshaugen-camping*. To lodge in an atmospheric **sea house**, call **t** 52 72 55 57 or see *www.hagland.no* or *www.rovar.no*.

For low-priced **family and youth hostels** in the region, see *www.hostelbooking.com* or *www.vandrerhjem.no*.

The **Haugesund Tourist Brochure** also lists alternative types of accommodation.

Eating Out

Brovingen Mat & Vin, Rica Maritim Hotel, 3 Åsbygata, **t** 52 86 30 00 (*very expensive*) Serious and sophisticated French-inspired dining, sometimes cooked by visiting chefs 'in residence', accompanied by attentive service and quayside views. There are 3-, 5- and 7-course menus to choose from, with special wines for each course. Traditional Christmas food is served from the end of Oct to the end of Dec, including half-fermented trout (*rakørret*), cod prepared in a potash lye (*lutefisk*), and lightly smoked ribs of lamb (*pinnekjøtt*). Save room for the cloudberry cream (*multekrem*). *Booking essential.*

Bestastua, 132 Strandgata, **t** 52 86 55 88 (*expensive*). A classically decorated restaurant hung with distinctive Norwegian paintings and serving native specialities such as fish soup and fish and game (according to season) to families and romantically inclined couples. Downstairs it has a modern leather and dark-wood bar and nightclub.

Escalon Tapas, 169 Strandgata, **t** 52 86 62 10 (*moderate*). A restaurant providing a little bit of Spain in the centre of town, plus outdoor dining in summer. The casual *cantina* offers a delicious tapas buffet, paella and *bacalhao* as main courses, and simpler fare such as steak with jacket potato, and lightly spiced monkfish. There's a bargain 2-course menu between 3 and 7pm and a wine bar in the cellar. *Closed Sun.*

Naustet Spiseri, 3 Åsbygata, t 52 86 30 00 (*moderate*). A cosy, historic 4-storey sea house attached to the Rica Maritim hotel (*see* p.188) but without the pretentious feel of many hotel restaurants. The Mediterranean-inspired menu with fresh seafood makes this a favourite spot among local chefs on their night off.

Willy Knickersen, 169 Haraldsgata, t 52 80 46 60 (*moderate*). A restaurant affiliated with other popular quayside spots MM Café and Nitti; all serve 'good time' food such as burgers, ciabattas, stir-fries, pasta and the catch of the day. *Closed lunchtimes Mon–Fri (open from 3pm).*

Lothes Mat & Vinhus, 4 Skippergata, t 52 71 22 01 (*expensive–inexpensive*). A gourmet restaurant in a former tugboat captain's office in a complex of historic buildings dating back to the 1850s, with a stylish bar that was once a pigsty. The café with its high ceilings, many windows and modern ambience serves simple salads and soups, while the restaurant – for which reservations are essential – offers seasonal fish and game, as well as beef and lamb, and also has an excellent wine list. *Closed Sun.*

Egon, 93 Smedasundet, t 52 72 56 02 (*moderate–inexpensive*). A popular chain offering reliable family fare, including nachos, pizza, bacon and eggs, and steak, chicken or salmon with salad, bread, jacket potato and vegetables.

Haraldsvang Kafe & Restaurant, entrance to Haraldsvang Nature Park, Skeisvatnet, about 5km northeast of centre, t 52 71 63 31 (*moderate–inexpensive*). An ideal place to stop after a day's hike or bike ride, in a scenic area rich with birdlife. It's great spot for Sunday lunch and to try out family recipes such as *komler* or *fårikål* (a national dish featuring lamb with cabbage and peppercorns). Save room for chocolate cake or Maud's Pudding (similar to *crème caramel*). Call ahead to check there's not a private function on.

Fiskakommen, 1 Kaigata, t 52 71 50 48 (*inexpensive*). A quayside fish shop selling shrimp, smoked salmon and fishcakes for those wanting a snack on the run. *Closed eves and Sun.*

Haugli Konditori, 111 Haraldsgata, t 52 70 32 20, and branches around town (*inexpensive*). A reliable bakery-café offering reasonably priced *smørbrød*, sweet rolls and the like either to eat in or take on a picnic. *Closed eves and Sun.*

Entertainment and Nightlife

Festiviteten Konserthus, 4 Knut Knutsen OAS Gate, t 52 73 44 30, *www.festiviteten.no*. The city's theatre and concert hall, is centrally located and hosts a variety of high-quality musical and theatrical productions.

Byscenen, 170 Haraldsgata, t 52 80 46 50. A lively concert and entertainment venue with a variety of music, from pop to jazz.

Edda Kino, 183 Sørhauggata, entrance on Skåregata, t 52 71 90 07. A new 5-screen cinema that shows many English-language films with Norwegian subtitles and has comfortable seats and a café.

Bars and Clubs

There are a large number of bars dotted along the quayside, as well as plentiful bars and clubs along Haraldsgata, to suit a wide variety of tastes.

Dikselen, 170 Haraldsgata, t 52 80 46 65. A popular outdoor and indoor meeting place in the heart of town, liveliest on weekend evenings and offering a wide selection of coffees and food.

Kompasset Bar, 3 Åsbygata, t 52 86 30 00. A lively piano bar in the Rica Maritim hotel (*see* p.188), a popular pre- and post-dinner meeting spot with a great range of cocktails. The **Seaside Nattklub & Disco** is in the same hotel. *Closed Sun.*

Willy's Vinkjeller, 169 Haraldsgata, t 52 80 46 60. An atmospheric wine cellar attached to Willy Knickersen restaurant (*see* above). Other nearby 'hot spots' owned by this chain include **Metz**, **Flytten Pub** and **Mack Kjelleren**.

Day Trips from Haugesund

Røvær

These idyllic islands about 10km northwest of Haugesund and served by a regular boat service have around 100 inhabitants and make for a pleasant day's outing of bird-watching, flora- and fauna-spotting, shore-fishing or hiking to scenic **Bråvarden** hill on the main island, Røvær. There is an old herring-packing building with 32 inexpensive beds (**Røvær Sjøhuset**, t 52 71 80 35, *www.visitrovar.no; open Sat and Sun*) if you fancy staying. Its owners can arrange guided tours of the island and **Hiltahuset Museum**, with its exhibitions on local life on Røvær 100 years ago and the tragic drowning of 30 islanders in 1899. For excursions and fishing trips (*Mar–Oct*), call t 94 54 07 56.

Utsira

The island of Utsira, 75 minutes from the mainland by boat, makes for an exhilarating day out, not only because of the delightful ride from Haugesund, but for the variety of things to experience, including at least 310 bird species and assorted fauna. Norway's smallest commune at 6 square km and with a population of just 250, Utsira has been inhabited since Neolithic times. Between 1300 and 1500 it was owned by a monastery, and after the Reformation it became the property of the Crown. By the 1800s tenant farmers had taken over the land, and in 1924 it became a municipality, later inaugurating Norway's first female lord mayor, Aasa Helgesen.

Sights of historical interest include a **maritime museum** (Mikal L. Klovning's Seahouse), t 52 70 93 60 (*open by appointment*), which includes boats and fishing equipment

Getting There

Røvær

Daily boats for Røvær leave the quay 200m from Hotel Amanda in Haugesund, taking about 30mins. For times, contact Haugesund tourist office.

Utsira

Boats depart daily from the Utsira ferry quay on Risøy, which is best reached by taxi, or cross Risøy Bru bridge in front of the Rica Maritim hotel, then follow the signs for Utsira and Great Britain ferries (15mins away). For sailing times, contact Haugesund tourist office (*see* p.187) or see *www.utsira.kommune.no*.

Tourist Information

Røvær: contact Haugesund tourist office.
Utsira: at Dalanaustet restaurant (*see below*), t 52 75 01 00, *www.utsira.kommune.no* (*open Mon–Fri 8.30–4*). For information about

staying in one of the unique sea houses, contact **Utsira Overnatting**, t 52 74 92 52, **gsm** 45 47 02 37.

Eating Out

Røvær
Hiltahuset Museum Café, Hiltahuset, Røvær, no phone (*inexpensive*). A pleasant museum café offering good views and serving up a selection of simple but delicious Norwegian fare, including fish soup, *komler* and some excellent home-made desserts. *Closed winter.*

Utsira
Dalanaustet, Nordvikvågen inner harbour, t 52 74 91 50 (*moderate*). A charming restored maritime warehouse from the 1870s, serving salads, *smørbrød*, soup and other hot dishes, and desserts. Call in advance to make sure it's open out of season.

from the herring fisheries period. The nearby **Måkehus** ('Seagull House'), a sort of monument, serves as a reminder that until 1945 seagulls were hunted and captured so their feathers could be used in eiderdowns, and that they were a substitute for chicken in hard times. Also worth a look are the 68m **Utsira Fyr** or lighthouse (*t 52 75 19 75; guided tours in summer*), built in 1844, and the modest wooden church nearby, completed in 1785 (*guided tours arranged through church warden, t 52 75 01 00*). The inner harbour of **Nordvikvågen** has a number of unique and lovingly preserved buildings from the fishing era.

Serious hiking can also be enjoyed on the **Vestremarka** and the **Austremarka** with their old paths, some with stone walls.

Overnighters from Haugesund

Karmøy

This island – the name of which comes from the old Norse word *kormt* or 'shelter' – is the gateway to Viking history in the Haugelandet region. Its local centre **Avaldsnes**, now an industrial area with Norway's largest fishing harbour and Europe's biggest aluminium factory, was a royal residence for 500 years. Its main sight is **St Olav's** on the way out of town (*open June–Aug Mon–Sat 11–5, Sun 12–5; ask at nearby tourist office about guided tours*), built by King Håkon Håkonson in 1250 as part of the royal manor and once a stopping place for pilgrims en route to Nidaros (now Trondheim); it is still considered a holy area. Reconstructed in the 1920s, the modestly elegant grey-stone church still holds services. According to legend, when the top of the huge 'Virgin Mary's Sewing Needle' stone touches the church wall, Doomsday will be upon us; it is dangerously close, and some say that former priests have come in the night to saw pieces of the top away. St Olav's Days (27–29 July) are celebrated with concerts, guided pilgrims' walks and services.

The area around St Olav's is the site of several digs. In 1986 archaeologists discovered 35m of secret underground passage that led down to the sea, beneath which were the remains of a building that may have belonged to the royal manor from the Viking era or Middle Ages. In fact, the **harbour**, which dates from the Middle Ages, contains many archaeological treasures, including a ship from 1250. The **storehouse** around St Olav's is the only remaining building from a large priest's farm complex, parts of which date back to the 1600s, and the **longhouse** is a 1997 reconstruction of an AD 950 house found in Oma, a farm site south of Stavanger. Its roof is covered in layers of small wooden shingles (more than 100,000), pieces of muscovite in the small window frames allow in some daylight, and there is furniture copied from archaeological finds or saga records. The house would have been home to an extended family of children, parents and grandparents. In May 2005 the **Avaldsnes Nordvegen Historiesenter** will open as a museum here, set in a wood and glass complex inspired by Viking architecture and hosting exhibitions about the rich history of the area.

It's a 10-minute stroll along a path just down from the church and across two small bridges to the island of **Bukkøy**, site of the **Viking Farm** (*call t 52 83 84 00 for hrs; adm*),

Getting There

From Haugesund it's a 10min **drive** to Karmøy: follow road 47 in the direction of Karmøy/Skudeneshavn, crossing the Karmsund bridge. After about 3km there's a turnoff to Avaldsnes. Skudeneshavn is another 27km on road 47, or take the rural road 511 via Kopervik, down the east coast of the island.

There are **buses** to Avaldsnes from Haugesund bus station, making the 30min ride about every hour, and buses to Skudeneshavn.

Tourist Information

Avaldsnes: Nordvegen Historiesenter (officially open from May 2005), **t** 52 83 84 00, *www.karmoy.org (open Mon–Fri 9–5, Sat 10–4).*
Skudeneshavn: town centre, **t** 52 82 72 22, *www.karmoy.org (open June–22 Aug Mon–Sat 11–4).*

Where to Stay

The tourist office has a list of **farms** and **fishermen's** sea huts in Skudeneshavn and other local spots.
Henderson's Airport Hotel, *see* p.188.
Norneshuset Overnatting, 7 Nordnes, Skudeneshavn, **t** 52 82 72 62, **gsm/mobile t** 90 05 90 07, *www.norneshuset.no (inexpensive).* A wharfside pension with 5 rooms individually furnished with antiques, all with shower and toilet, plus a living room with TV and game table, and a fully equipped communal kitchen where guests can prepare their own breakfast at any time they fancy. It's set in a unique former warehouse shipped from Riga in the 1830s. They also let 2 flats by the week.
Skudenes Camping, 129 Posteveien, Skudeneshavn, **t** 52 82 81 96, **gsm** 92 09 85 65, *www.skudenescamping.com (inexpensive).* Seven huts and 1- to 4-person rooms where one can stay all year round.

Vikholmen Fyr, entrance to Skudeneshavn harbour, **t** 52 82 85 97 or **t** 97 07 29 48, *www.skudenes-sjomannforeneing.com (inexpensive).* An 1875 lighthouse 5mins from the town centre, accessible only by boat (included in the weekly rate). Duvets, pillows and mattresses are supplied but not bed linen. *Closed autumn and winter.*

Eating Out

From May 2005 there will be a restaurant serving Norwegian fish and meat specialities (*open daily 12–6*) at the new Nordvegen Historiesenter in old Avaldsnes.
Lanternen Kro & Restaurant, between marketplace and harbour, Skudeneshavn, **t** 52 82 86 74 (*moderate*). A popular seaside meeting place in an historic sea house with an outdoor terrace. The delicious fish specialities include monkfish, shrimp and crab. *Closed Mon–Fri outside summer.*
Vertshuset Smiå, 4 Søragada, Skudeneshavn, **t** 52 83 69 90 (*moderate*). A cosy spot set in a mid-1800s building on the edge of Gamlebyen, with outdoor dining in warm weather and an open hearth where locals gather on chilly evenings. Highlights of the upstairs dining room include creamy fish soup, catch of the day, monkfish and roast lamb. Save room for the classic caramel pudding, or fresh berries with ice-cream. There's live music Thurs–Sat. *Closed Mon–Fri lunch, and Sun.*
Verdens Minste Kafé, 23 Søragadå, Skudeneshavn, **t** 52 85 27 50 (*inexpensive*). The 'world's smallest café', offering tea, coffee and yummy pastries on the main street of Gamlebyen. *Closed eves and Sept–May.*
Gruvemuseum Café, Visnes, **t** 52 83 84 00 (*inexpensive*) A good place for lunch, with delicious Norwegian specialities. *Closed eves, Sat, Sun and 19 Aug–19 May.*

with its farmyard fenced in accordance with traditional methods, its reproduction of a round, wattled henhouse thatched with heather, and its farm animals. Just outside is a reconstruction of a small burial mound where important people were buried with many of their possessions. There is a Viking boat by the shore, and you can walk through the forest. In summer there are guided tours of the farm by a 'Viking host' and his wife, who recount ancient sagas, and in the first week of June there's a Viking festival.

Visnes, across from Avaldsnes on the west of the island, has several interesting sites, including the **Gruvemusem** (Museum of Mining), **t** 52 83 84 00 (*open mid-June–Aug Mon–Fri 10–5, Sun 11–5; adm*), a copper mill that was in operation until 1972 and where the copper for the Statue of Liberty was mined. Just nearby is the **Lyngsenter** (Heather Centre), **t** 52 83 16 63 (*open 21 May–Aug Mon–Fri 10–5, Sun 11–5*), with an exhibition on the relationship between the coastal community and the heather which covers the surrounding hills in spring, and a shop selling gems and heather-related souvenirs. For a map of **hiking trails** around this picturesque area, ask at the mining museum.

Sightseeing boat trips (*ask at tourist office*) run from Visnes to **Skudeneshavn**, a charming, well-preserved fishing community at the southernmost tip of Karmøy that is both Norway's smallest town and Haugelandet's most-visited attraction. Guided tours begin at **Mælandsgården**, the local museum (*t 52 84 54 60; open 20 May–mid-Aug Mon–Fri 11–5, Sun 12–4; mid-Aug–Sept Sun 12–7 and by appt; adm*), at the entrance to the Gamlebyen quarter with its labyrinth of small streets, white wooden cottages and wharf warehouses in the attractive Empire style of the day. The museum is housed in an old merchant's residence with a store, a maritime warehouse and old workshops.

On the first weekend in July, the town hosts the largest gathering of coastal culture in western Norway, the **Skudenesdagen** ('Skudenes Days'), with boats in and around the harbour, an outdoor market, art exhibitions, crafts demonstrations and more. On 3–7 July the **Skip Festival** is another, more tourist-orientated festival of coastal culture, with boats of all kinds, from vintage wooden vessels to sailing ships, plus art exhibitions, concerts, outdoor markets and entertainment.

There are many lovely **beaches** with white sands and crystal-clear water on the island's west coast, stretching from Sandve north as far as Åkra. Here you'll find diving and windsurfing facilities, and you might even spot the occasional dolphin.

Other Overnighters from Haugesund

Northeast of Haugesund on the E134 (to Oslo) are beautiful landscapes, especially after Ølen and Etne, when you approach the stunning Hardangerfjorden on road 550, where you'll find Odda, Aga and Utne. From Utne you can take a ferry to Bergen. Even if you are not following our tour (*see* pp.194–9) you can make separate trips by public transport to Tysvaer, Ølen, Etne, Skånevik, Odda, Tyssedal, Utne and Lofthus.

Getting There

There are **buses** to many of the best destinations from Haugesund's main station (215 Karmsundsgata) or Sørhauggata by the post office. Look for the destinations on the bus rather than a number, such as Aksdal (in Tysvær), Ølen, and Skånevik (for Etne). There are several daily buses to Aksdal (the main community of Tysvær), but owing to complicated timetables and limited schedules, it is wise to either stay overnight or rent a car when going beyond the Tysvær area.

Tourist Information

Tysvær: Aksdal Senter, **t** 52 77 52 00, *www.tysver.kommune.no/turistinfo*.
Ølen: Kommunehuset, **t** 53 76 67 00, *www.olen.kommune.no*.
Etne: **t** 53 75 63 63, *www.etne.kommune.no* (*open Mon–Fri 9–4.30, Sat 10–2*).
Skånevik: t 53 75 55 00 (*open mid-June–mid-Aug*).
Hardanger: Hardanger Brygge, Norheimsund, **t** 56 55 38 70, *www.hardangerfjord.com*.

Touring from Haugesund

Day 1: A Second World War II Museum, Quakers and Emigration to America

Morning: Leave Haugesund via road E134 in the direction of Oslo; after 7km (just before the tunnel) there is a turn-off for the **Arquebus War History Museum** in Førre (*open May–Aug Sun–Fri 11–5; adm*), a major Second World War museum focusing on the German occupation. With costumes, weapons and memorabilia, it documents Norway's shame as well as glory. Continue east along the E134, then turn right down the E39 and head for the sleepy town of **Tysvær**, east of the Førlandsfjorden.

Lunch: In Tysvær, *see below*.

Afternoon: Tysvær's Tysværtunet community centre has a library with an exhibition on emigration to America (*open Mon–Fri 10–7, Sat 10–2, Sun 1–5; adm, children free*). Just northeast, **Sandbekken** contains the beautifully restored Cleng Peerson House (*open Sun 15 June–15 Aug 1.30–3.30*), moved here from Hesthammer in 1983 to celebrate the bicentenary of the birth of Peerson, who in 1821 set out for America to help Quakers, who were persecuted in Norway, find a better life. At **Stakland** just to the north, Norway's only Quaker meeting house can also be visited by request (*ask at Cleng Peerson House*). Spend the night back in Tysvær, or continue to scenic Ølen, about an hour (50km) along the winding E134.

Dinner and Sleeping: In Tysvær or Ølen, *see below*.

Day 1

Lunch in Tysvær

The grocery store inside the Aksdal Senter shopping centre is also a good place to stop if you are putting together a picnic.

Tysværtunet Café, just behind Aksdal Senter, no phone (*inexpensive*). A café serving warm Norwegian speciality dishes, as well as sandwiches and pastries. There is a large public swimming pool in the same complex if you need to work up an appetite. *Closed eves and Sun*

Tysvær Konditori, Aksdal Senter, no phone (*inexpensive*). A bakery selling pastries and open sandwiches. *Closed eves and Sun.*

Dinner in Tysvær

Tysvær Kro & Motell, t 52 77 59 00 (*moderate*). A simple but pleasant restaurant offering delicious Norwegian cooking, including *komier* and cod steamed in white wine, all prepared by the proprietor's wife. *Closed for lunch except for groups by appointment.*

Sleeping in Tysvær

Tysvær Kro & Motell, t 52 77 59 00, *t-motel@online.no* (*moderate*). A modest family-run hostelry with an idyllic location by Aksdal lake. There is an outdoor terrace and a pleasant area where you can take a vigorous walk around the lake and a dip. On summer evenings, when darkness falls late, the Norwegian light and the sounds of the birds are quite special.

Sleeping in Ølen

Eide Gard, t 53 76 82 23, **gsm** 90 19 53 10, *www.eidegard.no* (*moderate*). A lovingly restored traditional cabin dating from 1880, in the pastoral Ølen valley. Six to 16 people can lodge family-style in the charmingly furnished rooms with their antiques and embroidered linens. The bathroom, complete with clawfoot bath, is white on white with a glass-tiled shower and a loo with a view. Meals can be arranged for groups in advance, and baking and painting courses are available for small groups.

Day 2: Traditional Farm Towns, Fjords and Islands

Morning: If you stayed overnight in Tysvær, follow the twists and turns of the E134 to reach the traditional farming town of **Ølen**, where you can enjoy all sorts of coastal fun, including bathing and fishing, and which could make an interesting base for a day or two if you have longer to spend. The same could be said for **Etne** a further 2km up the E134. Both of these scenic locations, where many Norwegians have summer cottages and which are infinitely preferable to dreary Odda (closer to the Hardangerfjorden), are handy for day trips to **Langfoss**, about 50 minutes' drive further up the E134 at the Åkrafjorden – at 6.5m, this is the fifth highest waterfall in Norway. There is a picnic area, a snack kiosk, toilets and an information centre (*open May–Sept*). Then follow one of the country roads at random – there are all sorts of unexpected beauty spots to discover in the environs.

Lunch: In Etne, *see* below.

Afternoon: Surrounded by mountains, fjords, farms and unique little islands, the charming hamlet of **Etne**, which has only 4,000 inhabitants, was once the home of King or Viking chief Erling Skakke and poet Olav Vik, whose poems are carved on trees in the **Osnes recreation area**, where you can hike, bathe and fish. For spectacular views of the Etnefjord, start at the bathing spot of Honsvikjo and make the steep climb to the **Borgarårsen fortress**, taking a breather at a resting place halfway up, by a large rock known as Gåstein.

Dinner and Sleeping: In Etne, *see* below.

Day 2

Lunch in Etne

Fugl Fønix, Etnessjøen, t 53 77 14 40 (*moderate–inexpensive*). The only really reliable place to eat in the area, offering ciabatta sandwiches, a variety of soups, spicy noodles with beef and the like. Make sure to leave enough room for one of the luscious desserts, which are created on the chef's whim, accompanied by an espresso or a fruit shake. On Fri an all-you-can-eat buffet is available, and as we went to press plans were underway to open a summer café on the beach.

Dinner and Sleeping in Etne

Fugl Fønix, Etnessjøen, t 53 77 14 40, *www.fuglfonix.no* (*moderate*). A group of young men operate this unique 'artists' hotel' providing an urban oasis in the middle of nature. The guest rooms are modern and minimal, with unique, colourful touches and original art that is refreshingly good as well as easy on the eye. There is also an apartment for long stays. The inviting and filling breakfast buffet goes beyond the routine, and the friendly young staff are happy to advise you on some great outings in the area. As far as dinner is concerned, you need go no further either. In the evenings, the lunch spot turns into a hip, modern restaurant with an imaginative crossover menu that changes with the seasons, featuring fresh local products. It's so good that many people drive here from Haugesund for a night out. Whether you choose fish, fowl or meat, make sure to accompany them with a side order of the *Fugl pommes* – chips with attitude! The wine list is reasonably priced for Norway and covers a range of regions. After dinner, you can have a nightcap in the bar, where concerts are sometimes held, visit the on-site art gallery with its changing exhibitions, or take a look at the upstairs studio of co-proprietor and artist-in-residence Jan Terje Rafdal.

Day 3: Historic Etne and a Pastoral Landscape

Morning: Enjoy **Etne**'s many historic sites, including **St**ø**dle** church, built as a private chapel in 1176, extended in wood in 1650 and boasting, just to the west, a burial mound and stone monument; the timbered medieval Grindheim church, with more than 200 burial mounds, a 4m-tall rune stone and a stone cross; and Gjerde church (1676), which also has a rune stone, plus unusual wall decorations. A bronze statue of Magnus Erlingsson, King of Norway 1161–84, by Per Ung can be found just outside the town hall, while just outside the Fugl Fønix hotel is a 1999 sculpture of a woman's torso in Carrara marble by Marton Varo. Nearby Sæbøtunet (rural museum; *open 21 June–17 Aug Mon–Fri 11–4, Sat 10–1; adm*) has displays on town history.

Lunch: Buy a picnic from Etne before you leave, *see* below. and eat it on the hike.

Afternoon: Hike up the old Stavanger post road (1785) to **Skånevik** (3hrs each way), to see fine views of Sunnhordland valley and the Folgefonna glacier. At the park close to the ferry quay is a memorial to the *Folgefonde*, which sank in 1908 with the loss of 26 lives. Alternatively, make the scenic round-trip to Skånevik by car, taking the old road along the fjord and returning on the mountain route through the valley from Håland back to the E134. Skånevik's Norwegian Motor Museum (*open 23 June–16 Aug Tues–Sun 11–4; adm*) displays cars dating from 1898, while there's a replica of the 8m-long *King Magnus* Viking ship that can be hired for short trips for up to eight people (*t 53 75 56 59, or ask at tourist office*). The tourist brochure lists activities in the area, plus burial grounds and preserved wooden buildings to visit.

Dinner and Sleeping: In Etne or Skånevik, *see* below.

Day 3

Lunch from Etne
Saltnes and **Larsen**, Etnessjøen, no phone (*inexpensive*). Two good bakeries on the main street where you can buy sweet rolls and breads to combine in a picnic with cheese, smoked salmon, grilled chicken and fruit from the nearby Spar grocery.

Dinner in Etne
See also p.195 (Day 2).
Old River Saloon, Etne Hestegard, **t** 97 18 05 47 (*moderate*). An American-inspired saloon 5mins from the centre of Etne at a farm with some 20 breeds of horses. Some locals say it is a place where people come to drink too much beer and act crazy, others find it a cool place to let their hair down. It's normally open Sat night only, and sometimes Fri, but if you call proprietress Auslaug Male in the afternoon she will be glad to prepare a beef steak or similar fare for you that evening. You can also book horse and carriage rides or riding excursions. *Closed lunch and Sun–Fri except by appointment.*

Dinner in Skånevik
Skånevik Fjordhotell, quay, **t** 53 75 55 00 (*moderate*). A hotel bar and restaurant with fjord views and a seasonal menu of delicious, hearty fare, including good fish soup.

Sleeping in Skånevik
Skånevik Fjordhotell, quay, **t** 53 75 55 00, *www.skaanevik-fjordhotel.no* (*moderate*). A family hotel right by the ferry dock to Utåker and the fast boat dock to Bergen, Haugesund and Stavanger. Rooms are comfortable and equipped with telephone and TV, and there is a gym with a sauna.
Skånevikstranda Fjordstover, Børkjenes, **t** 41 62 32 40, *www.fjordstover.no* (*moderate*). Two houses on a hill between Etne and Skånevik, with views of the Skånevikfjorden. Each has a cosy living room with a fireplace, plus a well-equipped kitchen. There is rowing boat and motorboat hire.

Day 4: Hydropower, Fruit and a 13th-century Village

Morning: Leaving Skånevik, return to the E134 and turn off to route 550 along the Sørfjorden. An hour north brings you to **Odda**, the bleak gateway to the magnificent Hardangerfjorden. The hamlet of **Aga**, signposted off the road to Odda, is home to Agatunet (*open for guided tours mid-May–Aug daily 11–6*), a 13th-century sheriff's farm that was gradually transformed into a nine-family village with some 30 buildings, now listed summer homes. In spring and summer there are crafts shops, galleries, a café serving local specialities, and a bakery. This area is known as 'the orchard of Hardanger', and May is the most popular month to enjoy its bursts of colour. It was here that Cistercian monks, who lived in a monastery in Lofthus until the Reformation in 1537, planted the first fruit trees between 1200 and 1210. Today, with more than 500,000 trees around Sørfjorden, fruit production is the main local industry. Roadside stands sell morello cherries, plums and apples.

Lunch: In Odda or Aga, *see* below.

Afternoon: Across the Sørfjorden via road 13, at **Tyssedal**, an impressive 1908 hydroelectric power plant houses the Norsk Wasskraft og Industristad Museum (Norwegian Museum of Hydropower and Industry; *open mid-May–Aug daily 10–5; Sept–mid-May Tues–Fri 10-3; adm, children free*). The art gallery at the nearby Tyssedal Hotell (*see* below) shows landscapes by local painter Nils Bergslien (1853–1928) and his contemporaries, plus some fascinating fairytale paintings. Retrace your route back to Odda on the other side of the fjord (direction Bergen).

Dinner and Sleeping: In Odda or Tyssedal, *see* below.

Day 4

Lunch in Odda

Hardanger Hotell & Restaurant, Odda, t 53 64 64 64 (*moderate–inexpensive*). A rather nondescript but central dining room with a real espresso machine, offering sandwiches, salads and soups. *Restaurant closed Sun*.

Lunch in Aga

Aga Tunkafe, Agatunet, Aga, no phone (*inexpensive*). A café dating back to the 13th century, situated within the old sheriff's farm complex and serving traditional open sandwiches on home-baked breads, a soup of the day, and usually a dessert made with freshly picked plums, apples or cherries (make sure to stock up on a bag of fruit from the road stands en route – there is definitely a difference in taste, colour, fragrance and texture, and prices are better than in the supermarkets). If no one is around, an honour system is used for sales.

Dinner and Sleeping in Tyssedal

Tyssedal Hotell & Restaurant, 3 Gamleveien, t 53 64 69 07, *www.tyssedal-hotel.no* (*moderate–inexpensive*). A unique brick-red, gabled building in a seriously scenic location, dating back to 1913 and operated by a power company. The 26 guest rooms are comfortably furnished and have all the requisite modern amenities. The hotel restaurant offers a daily seasonal 2-course menu featuring either Norwegian specialities or something a little more 'international' in scope. The wine list includes a number of bottles that you can sample by the glass. The staff are friendly and attentive.

Sleeping in Odda

Hardanger Hotell & Restaurant, t 53 64 64 64, *www.hardangerhotel.no* (*inexpensive–moderate*). A hotel that's rather short on ambience but that offers a number of clean, comfortable rooms. There is also a restaurant, serving lunch and dinner.

Day 5: A Stone Church, a National Park and Waterfalls

Morning: Drive for an hour along road 13 (on the same side of the fjord as Tyssedal) to reach **Kinsarvik** and one of Norway's earliest stone churches, containing fragile chalk paintings and a 17th-century pulpit. According to legend, the church, which was restored in 1880 and again in 1961, was built in the Roman style by Scots in 1160. The nearby **Hardangervidda National Park** has many hiking trails, one of which leads past the Husedalen waterfalls; you can stay overnight in nearby Lofthus (*see below*). Alternatively, make the short ferry ride from Kinsarvik to Utne, a charming village in the heart of the fruit-growing region and a popular beauty spot, as well as a place to pick up the ferry to Kvanndal, where you connect with route 7 to Bergen.

Lunch: In Utne, *see* below.

Afternoon: **Utne**'s economy once centred on the orchards that still adorn the slopes of the Sørfjorden, but it was also kept afloat by fishing and its charming painted furniture, which you can still enjoy at the Hotel Utne (*see* below). The open-air Hardanger Folk Museum in the centre of town (*open May and June Mon–Fri 10–3, Sat 10–4, Sun 12–4; July and Aug Mon–Sat 10–6, Sun 12–4; adm*) includes historic houses, boats, shops and a school, along with exhibitions on local weddings, fiddle-making, fishing, music, orchard crops and the wood carvings of local artist Lars Kinsarvik. Also represented are 19th-century romantic painters Adolph Tidemand and Hans Frederik Gude, who were considered to be in the vanguard of Norwegian artists and whose works depicted the bourgeois nationalism of the period.

Dinner and Sleeping: In Utne or back in Lofthus, *see* below.

Day 5

Lunch in Utne

Hotel Utne, across from the ferry point, **t** 53 66 64 00 (*moderate*). A charmingly decorated hotel restaurant serving traditional, seasonal Norwegian dishes.

Dinner and Sleeping in Utne

Hardanger Gjestegard, Alsåker, **t** 53 66 67 10, *www.hardanger-gjestegard.no* (*expensive–moderate*). A 19th-century ciderhouse alongside the picturesque Hardangerfjorden, extensively renovated in 1989 and now a complex with a self-catering guesthouse, two refurbished millhouses and a boathouse, plus a restaurant and wine cellar. The restaurant is a good place to try delicacies and traditional home-style Norwegian cooking, including potato griddle cakes and salt meat and barley. If you'e lucky, you may get to sample a glass of the fine wine that used to be produced here.

Hotel Utne, across from ferry point, **t** 53 66 64 00, *utnehot@online.no* (*moderate*). A guest house built in 1722 and run by the same family for five generations. It has always been a favourite among artists, who have donated paintings depicting the area to adorn the hotel.

Dinner and Sleeping in Lofthus

Hotel Ullensvang, Lofthus, **t** 53 67 00 00, *www.hotel-ullensvang.no* (*expensive–moderate*). A large, historic hotel run by four generations of the same family, who continue to expand and improve the now-modern hostelry, complete with dining room, disco and conference facilities. The hotel restaurant serves a discerning menu using fresh regional ingredients according to season. If you get the chance, make sure to try the cider-marinated salmon with sour cream and brine, or the traditional *komler*.

Day 6: A Scenic Approach to Bergen

Morning: Take the ferry from in front of the Hotel Utne to Kvanndal, a scenic trip along the famous **fruit orchard route** beyond Hardanger. From Kvanndal you can make a detour a short distance east along route 7 and then road RV550 to **Ulvik**, a tiny village nestled on the Hardangerfjorden shoreline; in spring, bright red orchards punctuate the verdant hills above. Ulvik's historical claim to fame is to have produced the first Norwegian potatoes, back in 1765. Further east still (about 9km), **Osa** is a farm-dotted landscape along the Osafjorden. About a kilometre above the fjord, the abstract **Steam Nest sculpture** (*open daily mid-May–mid Aug 10–4; adm*), resembling an enormous bird's nest, was created by Takamasa Kuniyasu for the 1994 Lillehammer Winter Olympics, and relocated here. On the way to the sculpture, the **Hjadlane Gallery for Samtidskunst** (*open daily May–Sept 11–6; adm*) hosts changing exhibitions of contemporary art. Go back along route 7 via **Norheimsund**; this is the most scenic route to Bergen, taking about an hour and a quarter. Norheimsund is a little port town also known for its furniture-making.

Lunch: In Norheimsund, *see* below.

Afternoon: Continue along route 7 until you arrive in Bergen. En route from Hardanger to Bergen, beware of narrow roads and unpredictable weather conditions, which may affect your schedule. For Bergen sightseeing, *see* pp.200–208.

Dinner and Sleeping: In Bergen, *see* below. In the morning, take the E39 south from Bergen to Halhjem, then a ferry to Sandvikvåg on the island of Stord. The E39 continues south from here via Leirvik, through a tunnel and on to Haugesund.

Day 6

Lunch in Norheimsund

Privaten Restaurant, Sandven Hotel, 4 Sandvenvegen, t 56 55 20 88 (*expensive–moderate*). A family-run hotel dating back more than 100 years, renovated by former glacier guide Tron Bach, who transformed 4 rooms into an intimate restaurant serving fine cuisine. Try the Sandven soup with smoked lamb and root vegetables.

Dinner in Bergen

See also pp.205–206.
Boha, 6 Vaskerelven, t 55 31 31 60 (*expensive*). A recent addition to Bergen's culinary scene, with Med-inspired dishes using the best local ingredients. *Closed lunch and Sun.*
Dickens, 4 Kong Olav V's Plass, off Ole Bulls Plass, t 55 36 31 30 (*moderate–inexpensive*). An established address for Bergeners who like to see and be seen while having a simple meal, coffee and dessert, or enjoying a cold beers on the outdoor terrace.

Sleeping in Bergen

See also pp.204–205.
Augustin Hotel, 22–4 Carl Sundts Gate, t 55 55 30 40 00, *www.augustin.no* (*moderate*). Norway's oldest family-run hotel, in a 1909 Jugendstil building with modern additions across the waterfront from Bryggen and near the central shopping streets. Rooms are modern and stylish, and the restaurant, **Kjøbmandsstuen**, serves good local specialities in season. In the cellar is the atmospheric 400-year-old **Altonakjellern** bar (*see* p.206).
Crowded House Travel Lodge, 27 Håkons Gaten, t 55 23 10 10, *www.crowded-house.com* (*inexpensive*). A pleasant 'youth hostel' for grown-ups, offering clean, simply decorated single, double and family rooms with wash basin and telephone at budget prices. Showers and loos are in the corridor, and there is a lounge, a laundry room and a communal kitchen. The stylish café on the ground floor serves good breakfasts, great espressos, and sandwiches and snacks.

Bergen

The capital of west Norway, Bergen is renowned for its beauty. Built on seven hills that look down over a peninsula and a harbour where pleasureboats and large transport ships glide peacefully by, against a backdrop of colourful restored wooden 18th-century houses gracing the hillside, the city feels like a page from a book of fairytales. Today it has a population of more than 200,000, making it about half the size of Oslo, and although it has the sophistication of a large city, it retains the charm of a village. As for the lousy weather, Bergeners, who consider themselves almost like ducks, are near-oblivious to the 260 or so days of rain each year. The old saying 'If you don't like the weather, wait a minute' is worth remembering – but carry a good umbrella and a macintosh.

Bergen was a European Cultural Capital in 2000, and has many cultural attractions in addition to its museums and concert hall, including the villa of virtuoso violinist

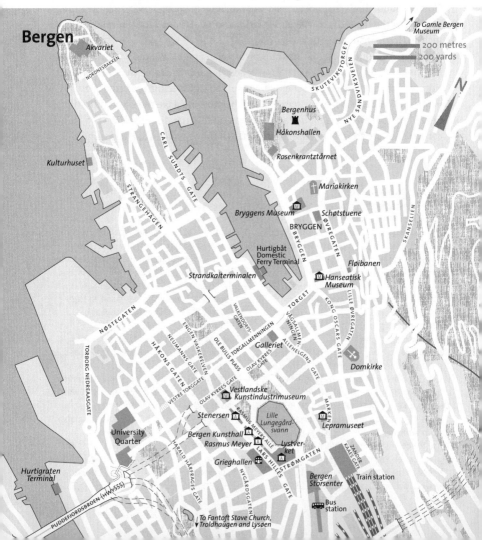

Ole Bull, a native of the city who contributed greatly to Norwegian culture by collecting old folk tunes during his travels along the fjords, and Edvard Grieg's summer home at nearby Troldhaugen, which allows a view of the human side of the composer who enjoyed nothing better than a spot of fishing after a day at the piano.

Bergen is also the starting point for the popular Hurtigruten, or Norwegian Coastal Voyages, said to be one of the most beautiful cruises in the world (*see* pp.208–9); you can also take the 'Norway in a Nutshell' tour from here instead of from Oslo, *see* p.160.

History

Founded by King Olav Kyrre ('the peaceful') around 1070, Bergen over the next two centuries not only evolved into an international trading centre but also became Norway's first capital and a seat of royalty. Oslo took over as capital in 1299, but Bergen remained a clerical and commercial centre, and, with its strategic position, maintained good business relations with the rest of Europe.

The city grew up around its lively harbour, the hub of commerce, seafaring and craftsmanship. The German Hanseatic League, a medieval guild of merchants, had one of its main offices on the wharf of Bryggen. The Hansas controlled most of the trade from the Middle Ages until the beginning of the 16th century, when its power and influence started to decline due to competition from Dutch and English shipping companies, internal conflicts and the Black Death, which killed off one third of Europe's population.

This is a city that has survived fires, wartime occupation and explosions – including the great fire of 1702, after which the distinctively painted Hansa houses and warehouses of Bryggen were built – and still stands proud. It has long been a crossroads for people from all over the world, many of whom have stayed, making it Norway's most international and multicultural city.

Torget and Around

At the eastern end of the busy harbour, **Torget**, Bergen's main square, is a lively meeting place with inviting restaurants and cafés; its daily open-air fishmarket is a good spot in which to sample smoked salmon, herring, crab and shrimp, sold in small portions or in sandwiches by the fish merchants. Across from the market at 1 Vågsallmenningen, the tourist information centre/**Fresco Hall**, the old stock exchange, built in 1862 and extended in 1893, is decorated with murals painted by Axel Revold in 1921–3 and divided into three themes. The North County Wall features three panels representing the fishing industry in the region; the Bergen Wall has four panels showing heavily loaded vessels arriving at Bergen harbour; and the World Wall illustrates humankind's importance in the busy machine age, the cultivation and processing of the products of nature, and the abundance of nature.

Bergenhus and Bryggen

At the western end of the quay, the crescent-shaped **Bergenhus fortress** dominates the entrance to the harbour. In its surrounding park, the **Rosenkrantztårnet** (Rosenkrantz tower), the residence of governor Erik Rosenkrantz in 1560–8, contains an exhibition

Getting to Bergen

Owing to increased demand, **airlines** serving Bergen are expanding their schedules; check their websites for up-to-date information. To accommodate travellers taking the Hurtigrute coastal trips (*see* pp.208–209), there are also new summer charter flights from Exeter, Bournemouth, Norwich and Edinburgh.

Braathens has a weekly flight from London, arriving Fri evening and leaving Sun afternoon, and flights from Manchester. Norwegian Airlines has a weekly flight from London Stansted, arriving Fri afternoon and leaving Sun afternoon, a non-stop service from Manchester, and 2 daily direct flights from Aberdeen. Scandinavian Airlines System (SAS) has flights from London Heathrow and a weekly flight from Manchester, arriving Fri afternoon and returning Sun afternoon. SAS/Widerøe has a direct flight from Aberdeen on Fri mornings, returning Sun morning.

For airline contact details, *see* p.3. *www.visitBergen.com/transport* has further details.

For Bergen–Haugesund–Stavanger–Newcastle car **ferries**, *see* p.6. Haugesund is 1hr 30mins from Bergen, Stavanger 2hrs 30mins.

There are comfortable daily Kystbussen ('**coast buses**') from Stavanger and Haugesund (**t** 177 or **t** 52 70 35 00, *www.kystbussen.no*).

For the scenic **Norway in a Nutshell** trains between Oslo and Bergen, *see* p.160.

To reach Bergen from Stavanger by car, take the ferry to Tau, then follow route 13, the main road through Ryfylke to Sand. From there, route 520 (the Røidal Road; closed in winter) takes you past some impressive sights via Sauda, or just continue on route 13 to Røldal and then on to Odda, a former industrial town. From there follow the route laid out on pp.194–9 ('Touring from Haugesund'). Note that pre-booking is not possible for car ferry crossings, so make sure you take a possible wait into account.

Getting from the Airport

There is a frequent **airport bus** from the Radisson SAS Royal Hotel Bryggen, via the Radisson SAS Hotel Norge (near the Kunstindustrimuseum) and the bus station at 8 Strømgaten. For times, call **t** 177, the airlines, the SAS hotels or the tourist office.

Getting Around

There are free **city buses** to the bus and railway stations from Olav Kyrres Gate in the centre (near the post office), and from outside the bus station to the centre.

To hire a **city bike** (available at 10 locations around the city), buy a 'lender's card' at the tourist office or town hall (around NOK100, plus a deposit). Bikes can be used for 3hrs before needing to be checked out again.

For **taxis**, call Bergen Taxi, **t** 070 00 or **t** 55 99 70 10 (advance booking).

Car Hire

Avis, 20a Lars Hilles Gate, **t** 55 55 39 55.
Budget, 58 Storetveit, Minde, 5mins south of centre (rentals also possible at tourist office or Bergen airport), **t** 55 27 39 90..
Centrum Bilutleie (cars and vans), 20 Lars Hilles Gate, **t** 55 21 29 50.
Hertz, 89 Nygårdsgaten, **t** 55 96 40 70.

Tourist Information

Bergen: 1 Vågsallmenningen (in Fresco Hall opposite fishmarket), **t** 55 32 14 80, *www.bergen-travel.com*.

of medieval life, and the **Håkonshallen**, **t** 55 31 60 67 (*both open 15 May–Aug daily 10–4, guided tours of hall and tower every hr; Sept–14 May Fri–Wed 12–3, Thurs 12–6; closed during Bergen International Festival and on special occasions; adm*), built during the reign of Håkon Håkonsson (1247–61), was the largest and most imposing building of the royal residency when Bergen was at the height of its political prominence.

Between the Bergenhus and Torget, the historic harbourside quarter of **Bryggen** was formerly known as Tyskebryggen after the merchants of the German Hanseatic League. Bergen's very first buildings were built along the harbour here, for centuries the heart of town, bearing witness to its unique history. The 1702 fire means there is

The **Bergen Card** (24hrs NOK150/children 3–16 NOK65; 48hrs NOK230/100) allows free bus travel within the city, free parking, free admission to most museums and attractions, and discounts on other sights. It is sold at the tourist office, train station, Hurtigbåt ferry terminal, campsites and some hotels, and the Montana Youth Hostel (30 Johan Blyttsvei, outside Bergen in Landås).

Guided Sightseeing

There are interesting English-language historical **walking tours** of Bryggen that include admission to the Bryggen museums, starting from the Bryggens Museum daily at 11 and 1 (*June–Aug*) and lasting 90mins. Tickets (NOK70, children under 10 free) can be bought at the museum and re-used the same day for return visits to all Bryggen museums. Contact **Bryggen Guiding**, **t** 55 58 80 10.

The 1hr Bergen Expressen **sightseeing train** (every 30mins in summer, every hour the rest of the year, from 11 to 3, 5 or 7 depending on time of year) through the central streets goes past the fishmarket, along colourful old Bryggen, then up to Mount Fløyen for a panoramic city view between the seven hills. Tickets can be bought on board or at the tourist office.

'Bergen In a Nutshell' guided bus tours combine trips (**t** 55 20 20 20; 8 languages; May–Sept every 30–60mins 9.45–8.45; adults NOK120, children NOK60) around the harbour and Bryggen areas in glass-roofed red double deckers with a cable car ride (every 7mins 9am–10pm) to Ulriken, the highest of the 7 hills, with a panoramic view of the others and of 7 fjords, and a light show.

Bergen Guided Bus Tours have a choice of 3hr excursions: Tour 1 (10am) goes to Gamle

Bergen open-air museum (*see* p.209) and Troldhaugen (*see* p.210); Tour 2 (2pm) consists of extensive city sightseeing, then carries on to Fantoft (*see* p.210) and Troldhaugen.

The **Attractions Bus** (**t** 55 55 44 64; 15 June–17 Aug daily 10–5 from tourist office) runs 1hr hop-on hop-off trips with a taped commentary in English and other languages; it visits most Bergen attractions. Tickets are valid 24hrs.

White Lady Fjord Sightseeing (**t** 55 25 90 00) offers a 1hr **boat tour** of the historic harbour (with wonderful views of the Gamle Bergen open-air museum and aquarium) and a 4hr half-day excursion giving you the chance to experience west Norwegian coastal scenery at its best. Tours depart from fishmarket pier at Torget; tickets can be bought at the pier or at the tourist office across the street.

Festivals

Events worth seeking out include the **Bergen Music Fest (Ole Blues;** *23 April–2 May*), the **Bergen International Festival** of dance, theatre and music (*19–30 May; www.fests pillene.no*) and its companion event, the **Music Factory and Night Jazz** (*19–30 May; www. nattjazz.no*); the **Dragon Boat Festival and Harbour Regatta** (*4–5 June*), the **Bergen International Festival of Chamber Music** (*18–26 Sept*); the opening of **Christmas Street** (*25 Nov*) and the **Festival of Lights** (*27 Nov*). Dates can vary slightly from year to year; check with the tourist office.

Shopping

Bergen has several large shopping centres, including **Galleriet** and **Bergen Storsenter**,

very little of medieval Bergen to be found, though there are some excavated remains from the period in the **Bryggens Museum**, 3 Dreggsalm, **t** 55 58 80 10 (*open May–Aug daily 10–5; Sept–April Mon–Fri 11–3, Sat 12–3, Sun 12–4; adm*), including the foundations of 12th-century buildings and some ceramics, and the surviving 18th-century timber buildings have led to Bergen being listed a UNESCO World Heritage City.

Wandering through Bryggen's narrow alleyways with their overhanging balconies is like stepping back in time. About 60 of its spectacular, colourfully painted preserved wooden buildings are taken up by offices, shops, artists' ateliers and workshops, and cafés and restaurants. One of the oldest and best preserved, a rough timber building and many pedestrian shopping streets, such as **Torgallmenningen**, **Hollendergate** (behind Torget) and **Marken**. The many speciality and museum shops where you can buy handicrafts and assorted souvenirs include **Husfliden** (3 Vågsallmenningen, t 55 54 47 40) and **Juhls' Silver Gallery** (Bryggen, t 55 32 47 40), selling a line of 'Tundra' jewellery inspired by northern Lapland.

Shops are **open** Mon–Wed and Fri 9–4.30, Thurs 9–7, Sat 9–3.

Markets

The central **fishmarket** (*open June–Aug Mon–Fri 7–5pm, Sat 7–4; Sept–May Mon–Sat 7–4*) is at Torget, where you'll also find fruit from the Hardangerfjorden orchards, veg, flowers, handicrafts and souvenirs. Just opposite is the **Kjøttbasaren**, a restored 1887 meat market with a food hall containing several eateries, a deli and a fishmonger with great fishcakes. You'll also find handicrafts and gifts such as knitwear and wooden Viking memorabilia.

Arts and crafts market days take place in mid-June around the Lille Lungegårdsvann, next to Rasmus Meyers Allé.

Where to Stay

The **Bergen Package** offers cut-rate hotel accommodation with full breakfast and a Bergen Card; it is sold at the same places as the Bergen Card (*see* 'Tourist Information').

Solstrand Fjord Hotel & Bad, Os, t 56 57 11 00, *www.solstrand.com* (*expensive*). A spa hotel 30km outside the centre and 10km from Lysøen, on the picturesque Bjørnafjorden, operated by the Schau-Larsen family since 1929. The historic building dates back to

1896 but the 135 rooms have all mod cons. The restaurant offers refined cuisine using fresh local ingredients. Besides the spa programme, guests can swim, play tennis, row, fish or hike, and there is also a golf course 5mins away.

Neptun Hotell Rica Partner, 8 Valkendorfsgaten, t 55 30 68 00, *www.rica.no* (*expensive*) A unique hotel just south of the harbour, with stylish rooms and 700 works of art, both contemporary and by old Norse masters. The **Ludwig Bar** is a popular meeting place among cultured locals, **Pascal Mat & Vin** is an in-house bistro, and **Lucullus**, its gourmet restaurant (*see below*), is said to have Norway's largest wine cellar.

Grand Hotel Terminus, 6 Zander Kaaes Gate, t 55 21 25 00, *www.grand-hotel-terminus.no* (*expensive–moderate*). An elegant hotel popular with discerning visitors since 1928, just across from the train station and a five-minute walk from the centre. Rooms are quiet and beautifully decorated, and the restaurant serves exquisite Norwegian cuisine, including dishes unique to Bergen.

Augustin Hotel (*moderate*); *see* p.199.

Best Western Hotel Hordaheimen, 18 Carl Sundts Gate, t 55 33 50 00, *www.hordaheimen.no* (*moderate*). A traditional hotel run by the Norwegian Agriculture Association, originally established as a 'home from home' for Norwegian travellers from the countryside. The rooms are simply decorated but comfortable and the staff are welcoming. The restaurant, **Hordastova** (*see* opposite), offers simple and hearty Norwegian cooking.

Hotel Park Pension, 35 Harald Hårfagres Gate, t 55 54 44 00, *www.parkhotel.no* (*moderate*). A charming family-operated hotel in the

dating back to 1704, now houses the **Hanseatisk Museum**, 1a Finnegårdsgate, t 55 31 41 89 (*open June–Aug daily 9–5, May and Sept daily 11–2, Oct–April Tues–Sat 11–2, Sun 12–5; adm*), which has been furnished in the style of that period to give a flavour of the austere living and working conditions of Hanseatic merchants and apprentices.

Back up next to the Bryggens Museum, the **Mariakirken** (St Mary's church), t 55 31 59 60 (*open 22 May–Aug Mon–Fri 11–4; rest of year Tues–Fri 12–1.30; adm in summer*), the oldest building in Bergen to be still in use, was built more than 850 years ago and served as a church for the Hanseatic merchants from 1407 to 1766. With its distinctive twin towers, it is one of the most outstanding Romanesque churches in Norway.

university quarter just to the south of the city centre, with 40 cosy and individually decorated rooms.

Best Western Victoria Hotel, 29 Kong Oscars Gate, **t** 55 21 23 00, *www.victoriahotel.no* (*moderate*). A historic, family-run B&B hotel with old photos and paintings of Bergen in its corridors. Located in the antiques quarter, it has views of the hilltop houses above.

Bergen Gjestehus, 20a Vestre Torggate, **t** 55 59 90 90, *www.hotelbergen.com* (*moderate–inexpensive*). A friendly guesthouse near the main shopping streets, with large rooms, an apartment for longer stays, a welcoming pub and and parking outside.

Crowded House Travel Lodge (*inexpensive*); *see* p.199.

Eating Out

Good bakeries are **Baker Brun**, **Godt Brod**, **Lie Nielsen** and **Helgesen**, with outlets all around town. They sell open sandwiches and the local speciality, *stillingsboller* (cinnamon buns).

Lucullus, 8 Valkendorfsgaten, **t** 55 30 68 00 (*very expensive*). An elegant restaurant within the Neptun Hotell (*see* p.204), with attentive service and an imaginative menu by chef Frederik Hald that changes seasonally and features regional ingredients. *Closed lunch and Sun.*

Boha (*expensive*); *see* p.199.

Enhjørningen/To Kokker, 1 Enhjørningsgarden, **t** 55 32 79 19/**t** 55 32 28 16 (*moderate–expensive*). Two restaurants in adjacent old Hanseatic wharfhouses in Bryggen, with the same owner. Enhjørningen specializes in seafood, To Kokker in meat and local produce. *Closed lunch outside summer, and Sun.*

Fiskekrogen, Zachariasbryggen, at fishmarket, **t** 55 55 96 55 (*expensive–moderate*). Excellent seafood served in an intimate setting with views of the water. In summer there is a popular terrace. *Closed lunch.*

Kafe Krystall, 16 Kong Oscars Gate, **t** 55 32 10 84 (*moderate*). An elegant, unpretentious restaurant serenely situated behind the medieval Korskirken quarter, minutes from Torget. With only 4 tables in a candlelit 1920s ambience, it feels like the private dining room of a Bergen *grande dame*. The seasonal menu changes every three weeks and is seasonal. *Closed lunch, and Sat and Sun (open Sat in summer by arrangement for small groups).*

Potetkjellern, 1a Kong Oscars Gate, **t** 55 32 00 70 (*moderate*). An unusual 'concept' restaurant serving potatoes in all shapes and styles, as a starter, main course or even dessert, with more conventional fish and meat dishes served 'on the side'. *Closed lunch, Sun, Easter and Christmas.*

Lido, 1 Torgallmenningen, **t** 55 32 59 12 (*moderate–inexpensive*). A cafeteria-style, fairly priced place where ladies who lunch come either before or after a shopping trip in the neighbourhood.

Dickens (*moderate–inexpensive*); *see* p.199.

Dr Livingstone Traveller's Cafe, 12 Kong Oscars Gate, **t** 55 56 03 12 (*moderate–inexpensive*). A lively place serving 'world food', burgers, pasta, sandwiches and salads. In summer there's a terrace facing the historic hillside houses. *Closed lunch Mon–Thurs.*

Mago, 5 Neumanns Gate (next to large cinemaplex), **t** 55 96 29 80 (*inexpensive–moderate*). An ecologically conscious place serving organic produce, free-range meat, non-farmed fish and fresh juices.

Between June and August it hosts concerts every Tuesday night; tickets can be bought at the door. Across from the church, the **Schøtstuene**, 50 Øvregaten (*open June–Aug daily 10–5, May and Sept daily 11–2, Oct–April Sun 11–2; adm*) is the site of the former Hanseatic assembly rooms, where merchants gathered for meetings and meals and taught the apprentices.

Continue along **Øvregaten**, a charming 800-year-old cobblestoned street, back east into town. At the far end on your left is the **Fløibanen** funicular railway terminal, from where you can take a seven-minute ride (*every 30mins Mon–Fri 7.30am–11pm, Sat 8am–11pm, Sun 9am–11pm; until midnight May–Aug*) to the top of **Mount Fløyen**

Hordastova, 18 Carl Sundts Gate, **t** 55 33 50 00 (*inexpensive*). A 'cafeteria' restaurant in the Hotel Hordaheimen (*see* opposite), serving authentic Norwegian cooking at reasonable prices but no alcohol.

Kafé Kippers, Kulturhuset, 12 Georgenes Verft, **t** 55 31 50 70 (*inexpensive*) A café/cultural complex located just outside the centre near the aquarium but worth the trip for its terrace overlooking the sea. You can combine a light lunch or snack with an exhibition or a concert.

Vågen Fetevare, 10 Kong Oscars Gate, no phone (*inexpensive*). A laidback café with eclectic furnishings, a hip clientele and strong coffees. The speciality is *blingser*, an open sandwich on freshly baked bread, with ham, cheese or other tasty toppings, but save room for the chocolate cake. *Closed eves*.

Zupperia, 9 Nordahl Bruns Gate, **t** 55 55 81 14 (*inexpensive*). A cosy soup bar popular among both students and visitors to the museum of decorative arts upstairs (*see* p.207) . As well as soups, there are stews, salads and sandwiches.

Entertainment and Nightlife

The Bryggens Museum hosts **Bergen Folklore** evening, traditional Norwegian folk dances and music, Wed at 9pm (*18 June–20 Aug; 3–17 Aug it's held in the Schøtstuene, Sun 9pm*). Tickets are sold at the tourist office and on the door.

From 5 June to 29 Aug (Thurs and Fri 7pm), you can experience festive traditions at **Fana Folklore Folk Dancing**, an evening of national costumes, song and dance in a country setting (**t** 55 91 52 40, or ask at tourist office or your

hotel; NOK270). This includes a concert in the 800-year-old Fana church, a traditional meal, folk music, dancing and singing, and transport.

Folk music and songs are also performed Mon Sept–April at **Café Columba**, 14 Øvregaten; call **t** 55 31 23 18 for times.

Bars and Clubs

Bergen Jazz Forum is a series of Fri-night concerts at Kulturhuset outside the centre at 12 Georgenes Verft, **t** 55 30 72 50, Sept–May. On Sat (2–5.30) **Den Stundesløse**, 3 Øvre Ole Bulls Plass, **t** 55 31 55 70, hosts jazz concerts.

Altonakjellern, Augustin Hotel, 24 Carl Sundts Gate, **t** 55 30 40 72. An old wine cellar decorated in a modern, minimal style, offering privacy and the chance to enjoy good wines by the glass.

Baklommen, 1 Enhjørningsgarden, **t** 55 32 28 16. A cosy bar in an old Bryggen wharfhouse.

Banco Rotto, 16 Vågsallmenningen, **t** 55 55 49 60. A veteran spot on the nightclub scene, in a former bank with a restaurant and bar.

Dyveke and Frille, 7 Hollendergate, **t** 55 32 30 60. Two charming wine cellars on a quiet medieval street; fine wines by the glass.

Fincken, 2A Nygårdsgaten, **t** 55 32 13 16. A stylish lounge-style restaurant/bar, one of the city's first to cater to gay clientele.

Madam Felle, Radisson SAS Royal Hotel Bryggen, **t** 55 54 30 00. A nightclub and jazz bar attracting a lively crowd of 40-plussers.

Rick's Cafe og Salonger, 3 Veiten, off Ole Bulls Plass, **t** 55 55 31 31. A nightclub complex for 20- and 30-somethings.

Zachen Piano Club, Zachariasbryggen, by fishmarket **t** 55 55 96 40. A piano bar that's run as a popular karaoke venue Sun, Mon and Wed.

for magnificent views of Bergen and its surroundings, weather permitting. In summer the restaurant and café are open daily and concerts are held every evening. This is also a great spot for a mountain walk.

From the Fløibanen terminal, continue east along **Lille** ('little') **Øvregaten**, with a delightful mix of old timber houses in many colours and stately 19th-century villas lining the steep cobbled streets off to the sides, which lead back down into town past quaint shops and cafés. At the end of it is the prominent **Domkirke** (*open 19 May–Aug Mon–Sat 11–5, Sun 9–1, rest of year Tues–Fri 11–2, Sat 11–3, Sun 10–1; English* *services June–Aug Sun 9.30am, organ concerts Sun 7.30pm*), a 13th-century cathedral rebuilt many times over the years and hence combining a variety of architectural styles, including a Gothic choir and lower tower.

Continue along Kong Oscars Gate to the unusual **Lepramuseet** (Leprosy Museum), **t** 55 96 11 55 (*open 15 June–Aug daily 11–3; adm*), on the site of what was a hospital for lepers for 500 years (the present-day buildings around the cobbled courtyard are 18th century). The unique wards both portray the grim conditions in which the lepers lived and house an exhibition about Norway's' contribution to leprosy research. Part of the complex includes the hospital chapel, St George's (*same hours as museum*), which was built in the Middle Ages, then rebuilt after the great fire of 1702. It is now used for special services for students and various groups.

As you head back to town, the body of water that you see just down the road is Bergen's central lake, **Lille Lungegårdsvann**, which plays host to many of the city's festivals and summer events. On the southern side of it, on Lars Hilles Gate, is Bergen's 'museum row' and the **Grieghallen**, an impersonal concrete concert hall with excellent acoustics.

The **Bergen Billedgalleri** (Art Museum), **t** 55 56 80 00 (*open 16 May–14 Sept daily 11–5, rest of year Tues–Sun 11–5; adm*) houses the city's art collection in three buildings alongside Lille Lungegårdsvann lake, including the **Lystverket** ('Light Works', *10 Lars Hilles Gate*), the former power company offices (1928), newly renovated and displaying Norwegian and international art from the 13th century to the present, as well as some 14th-century Russian and Greek icons. It also has temporary exhibitions of contemporary art, an excellent bookshop, and a branch of the upmarket Bolgen & Moi restaurant. The **Rasmus Meyer**, 7 Rasmus Meyers Allé, has an excellent collection of Norwegian masterpieces from the 18th century to 1915, including a rare selection of Edvard Munch works, and paintings by J.C. Dahl, Christian Krohg and Harriet Backer, plus some interiors from 18th-century Bergen homes. The **Stenersen**, 3 Rasmus Meyers Allé, shows 20th-century art by Picasso, Miró, Munch and others, and boasts northern Europe's largest collection of works by Paul Klee. It also hosts temporary exhibitions throughout the year.

On the same street is a green building housing the **Bergen Kunsthall** (Contemporary Art Centre), 5 Rasmus Meyers Allé, **t** 55 32 14 60 (*open Tues–Sun 12–5; adm*), which has changing exhibitions of contemporary art, including video installations, and contains the ultra-modern Landmark café/bar, open after museum hours and often hosting free concerts and video installations.

Just up the road is the **'Permanenten'/Vestlandske Kunstindustrimuseum** (West Norway Museum of Decorative Art), 9 Nordahl Bruns Gate, **t** 55 33 66 33 (*adm*), including a 'People and Possessions' collection that features art and design (Bergen silverware, porcelain, furniture, clothing, textiles and jewellery) dating back 500 years. The 'Art of China' exhibition includes northern Europe's largest collection of Buddhist marble sculptures, plus porcelain, jade, bronzes, textiles and paintings. You can also see the world's oldest violin, which dates back to 1562 and once belonged to revered local composer Ole Bull. There's a soup bar in the basement (*see* p.206).

Outside the Centre

A pleasant 20-minute walk from the city centre, following Carl Sundts Gate along the harbour to the end, or alternatively a ride on bus no.11 from outside the Strandkaiterminalen (fast ferry terminal) or opposite the old city hall on Allehelgens Gate, or on the old ferry MF *Vågen* from the fishmarket (*May–Aug daily 10–6*) is the **Akvariet** (aquarium), 4 Nordnesbakken, **t** 55 55 71 71 (*open daily May–Sept 9–8, penguin feeding times 12, 3 and 6; Oct–April 10–6, penguin feeding times 12 and 3; adm*), with one of Europe's largest collections of fish and invertebrates from the North Sea, tropical saltwater and freshwater sections, and three species of penguins (Humbold,

Hurtigruten

Trips on the Norwegian Coastal Express ships or Hurtigruten ('quick routes'; **t** 81 03 00 00, *www.hurtigruten.com*) are promoted as one of the world's most beautiful voyages. It's a form of transport that began out of necessity in 1891, as an express shipping service along the not-so-accessible Norwegian coast, beginning at Bergen and heading far north beyond the Arctic Circle to the Nordkapp (North Cape) and Kirkenes, near the Russian border. It has since evolved into a unique excursion for tourists, which was one of its ambitions from the beginning.

Although it offers comfortable cabins, an extensive breakfast and lunch buffet and a sit-down dinner, it must be stressed that this is not a luxury cruise. And there's another caveat for those expecting a lively *Love Boat* atmosphere – the majority of passengers tend to be pensioners, who stick together and dominate the early dinner hour, interspersed with the occasional honeymooning couple or family. There are no films, aerobics classes or lectures. This no-frills journey is about non-stop fabulous scenery and pure relaxation: finding a good spot on one of the decks to read a book, listening to your CD player, or taking a nap between craning your neck at the panoramic views. Cameras are essential and binoculars are a good idea. There are some rather pricy excursions at many of the ports during daylight hours, for those who want to visit the impressive Ishavskatedralen (Arctic Cathedral) at Tromsø or see some puffins or reindeer at the Nordkapp.

The food in the dining room (*included in one-way and round-trip voyages; port-to-port passengers pay on board*) is pleasant comfort food for the masses; the daily lunch buffet tends to be heavy on salads, herring, smoked salmon and basic cheeses. The cafeteria, which has longer hours, serves reasonably priced hot dishes as well as a variety of sandwiches and snacks. After a few days aboard, you'll probably want to make a quick run into town at one of the ports of call to stretch your legs, make a supermarket run for something different, grab a cappuccino or enjoy a takeaway pizza or Chinese meal.

For resident Norwegians who travel both in and out of season, the ships serve the west coast like a sophisticated water taxi. For tourists, in addition to the magnificent views along the way, the journey provides a way of observing a working ship in operation. Spring and autumn are the ideal months in which to see the valleys along the fjord, seemingly sprayed with flowers, the mystical snow-covered mountains, the storybook houses on the water's edge in quaint villages, the thousands of islands

Genthoop and Rockhopper), which are the most popular attraction. There's also a café and a souvenir shop.

Short Excursions from Bergen

Five kilometres north of the centre via the E39 and then the E16 (or by bus, see below), the **Gamle Bergen Museum**, **t** 55 39 43 00 (*open daily 12–16 May and 18 May–11 Sept 9.30–5.30; guided tours every hour 10–5; adm*) is a reconstructed small town of more than 40 Bergen houses from the 19th and early 20th centuries, with various

and skerries, the elegantly designed bridges, and the mysterious, solitary lighthouses in the middle of the open sea. Those who want to witness the cosmic miracle of the Northern Lights, or Aurora Borealis, when the sky is streaked with purple and electric green against a halo of white light, should go in January or February, when the sky around the Arctic Circle tends to be dark and clear. In June and July, the midnight sun is in full glory above the Arctic Circle south of Bodø, and the magnificent sunsets take on an unexpected range of colours.

Over the years there have been 70 different kinds of ship in the fleet, dropping their anchor at nine ports of call. In recent years, with the extension of the road system, the vessels are less vital to the once-remote towns of the north. Today there are 11 ships in a fleet operated by two companies, providing one daily service to 34 ports of call on the coastal route, including the Art Nouveau town of Ålesund and the university town of Trondheim, and across the Arctic Circle to Tromsø, Hammerfest, the Nordkapp and Kirkenes, on the Norwegian-Finnish border.

Traditionally, the trip begins in Bergen and arrives back 12 days later, though you can make shorter, cheaper voyages – six days to Tromsø, from where you can fly back to Bergen or Oslo, or four days to Trondheim, from where you can return to Bergen or Oslo by train. Discounts are available on some cabins and certain sailings for over-67s, students, and families with children, with advance booking. Prices hinge on both the class of cabin you choose and when you sail – June, July and August are about 30 per cent more expensive than April, May, September and October. There are also last-minute bargain rates; tourist offices in the various ports have the latest information. Cars are allowed on board and bicycles can also be provided.

For all-inclusive packages with flights and up to three nights in Bergen, costing about £2,500, contact Norwegian Coastal Voyage at 3 Shortlands London W6 8NE, **t** 0208 846 2666, *www.norwegiancoastalvoyage.com*.

US packages differ slightly from UK packages: for two nights in Oslo, one night in Bergen and the complete 11–12 day voyage, you should reckon to pay between $2,370 and $5,600, depending on your choice of cabin. Contact Norwegian Coastal Voyage at 405 Park Avenue, Suite 904, New York, NY 10022, **t** (212) 319 1300 or **t** 800 323 7436, *www.norwegiancoastalvoyage.us*.

If you decide to make a trip on the spur of the moment once you are already in Bergen, tickets may be bought at Kystopplevelser AS, 4 Strandveien (in Strand Hotel), **t** 55 31 59 10, *www.kystopplevelser.no*; or at any travel agent in the city.

Getting There

Gamle Bergen: most buses from Bryggen, including nos.9, 20, 21, 22, and 50, go to the museum.

Fantoft stave church and **Troldhaugen**: take any bus from platform 20 (every 15–20mins; 10mins to stave church) at the main bus station. The church is about 10mins' walk from the stop (cross the road, turn right and walk up the hill behind the car park). For Troldhaugen, walk back to the bus stop and take any bus, alighting at Hopsbroen. Turn right, then left at Troldhaugsveien, following the signs to Troldhaugen (about 10mins). By car follow the E39 south out of town (towards Nesttun) for about 1.5km. At the 2nd pedestrian bridge crossing the main road, turn left, signposted Fantoft Studentby.

Lysøen and **Old Bull's Villa**: take the Lysefjordata bus to Buena Kai (50mins from Bergen bus station, gate 19 or 20), then take the Ole Bull ferry across the fjord to the island. Call **t** 177 for a bus timetable. By car, take the E39 south out of the city, then right on to road 553, signposted Fana. At Fana church, continue straight on, over the Fanafjell mountain to Sørestraumen. Follow signs to Buena Kai for the ferry.

shops and workshops, an exhibition of toys and a restaurant set in a 'great-grand-mother's living room'. The interiors can only be seen by guided tour.

A similar distance from the city in the opposite direction, just off the E39, the **Fantoft stave church**, t 55 55 44 54 (*open daily 15 May–15 Sept 10.30–2 and 2.30–6; adm*) was built in Sogn in 1150 and moved here in 1883. It burnt down in 1992 but has been rebuilt just as it was. Guided bus tours (35% discount for Bergen Card holders; *see* p.203) leave from the Bergen tourist office. Tickets are sold at the office, on the bus and at most hotels.

Also south of Bergen (8km), the **Edvard Grieg Museum, Troldhaugen**, Hopsbroen, t 55 92 29 92 (*open May–Sept daily 9–6; Oct and Nov Mon–Fri 10–2, Sat and Sun 12–4.15; Jan–April Mon–Fri 10–2, plus Sat and Sun 12–4 in April; adm*), which consists of the museum and Grieg's villa, hut and tomb, provides a human glimpse of the sensitive composer of *Peer Gynt*, including his favourite fishing spot along the lake. The on-site Troldsalen concert hall hosts concerts in summer and autumn, with musicians from Norway and abroad performing works by Grieg and other composers (tickets can usually be bought at the hall on the same day, or at the tourist office).

Twenty-five km south of Bergen at picturesque **Lysøen** (the 'Island of Light') is **Ole Bull's Villa**, t 56 30 90 77 (*open 18 May–Aug Mon–Sat 12–4, Sun 11–5; Sept Sun 12–4; adm, includes guided tour*), an extraordinary structure complete with onion dome and fairytale trellis décor, built as a summer home for the charismatic violin virtuoso in 1873. These days, like the former Grieg residence, it operates as a museum containing numerous personal artefacts. It has breathtaking views from the 13km of scenic walkways that Bull laid out for the pleasure of his visitors, secluded swimming and picnic spots, and a café.

Language

Norway has 2 official languages, Bokmål and Nynorsk, which are similar to each other and understood by nearly all Norwegians. Considered the national language, **Bokmål** ('language of books', also known as **Riksmål**) is a modern variation of the language used by the former Danish rulers, and is the first language of more than 80% of the population, employed both by the media and in schools. **Nynorsk** ('New Norwegian'), the language used prior to Danish rule, still predominates in the western fjords and in parts of central Norway, which may have one or more dialects.

Pronunciation

Vowels

Pronunciation is easier if you memorize the various vowel sounds:

å pronounced as in 'ha'.

ø pronounced as in 'fur', but keeping the 'r' silent.

æ pronounced as in 'ca't (t silent) when before an 'r', otherwise like 'ay'.

ei pronounced like 'ay'.

øy a soft sound between the 'ø' sound and 'toy'.

Consonants

Consonants are pronounced as in English, with the following exceptions:

c, q, w and **z** found only in foreign words and pronounced as in the original language.

g before 'i', 'y' or 'ei' pronounced as in 'yes'.

rs nearly always pronounced 'sh' as in 'shove'.

j in 'gj', 'hj' and 'lj' pronounced as a 'y' (and the **h** in 'hj' is silent and thus pronounced as a 'y').

hv pronounced as 'v'.

k before 'i', 'y' or 'j' pronounced as in Scottish loch or with a hard 'k'.

sj, sk before 'i', 'y', 'ø' or 'øy' pronounced 'sh' as in show.

Useful Words and Phrases

do you speak English?	*snakker du engelsk?*
yes	*ja*
no	*nei*
do you understand?	*forstår du?*
I don't understand	*jeg forstår ikke*
my name is...	*mitt navn er...*
please/	*vær så god*
you're welcome	
thank you (very much)	*takk (tusen takk)*
excuse me	*unnskyld*
good morning	*god morgen*
good afternoon	*god dag*
goodnight	*god natt*
goodbye	*adjø* (pronounced *hay-do*)
today	*i dag*
tomorrow	*morgen*
in the morning	*om morgenen*
in the afternoon	*om ettermiddagen*
in the evening	*om kveiden*
where is/are?	*hvor/hvor er?*
when?	*når?*
what?	*hva?*
how much/many?	*hvor mye/hvor mange?*
why?	*hvorfor?*
which?	*hvilket?*
can you show me how to get to?	*kan de vise meg veien til?*
what time is it?	*hvor mange er klokken?*
big/small	*stor/liten*
cheap/expensive	*billig/dyrt*
early/late	*tidlig/sent*
hot/cold	*varm/kald*
good/bad	*god/dårlig*
near/far	*i nærheten/langt borte*
left/right	*venstre/høyre*
vacant/occupied	*ledig/opptatt*
a little/a lot	*litt/mye*
more/less	*mer/mindre*
and	*og*
or	*eller*
not	*ikke*
nothing	*ingenting*

very	*veldig*	June	*juni*
inside	*innenfor*	July	*juli*
outside	*utenfor*	August	*august*
up/down	*opp/ned*	September	*september*
with	*med*	October	*oktober*
without	*uten*	November	*november*
		December	*december*

Notices, Signs and Sights

Numbers

open	*åpen*		
departure	*avgang*		
bridge	*bro/bru*		
entrance	*inngang*		
vacant	*ledig*		
occupied	*opptatt*		
police	*politi*		
no smoking	*røyking forbudt*		
closed	*stengt*		
hospital	*sykehus*		
cycle path	*sykkelsti*		
special offer	*tilbud*		
toilet	*toalett*		
ladies	*damer/kvinner*		
gentlemen	*herrer/menn*		
pull/push	*trekk/trykk* (lift button, or *skyv* (on doors)		

0	*null*	1	*en*
2	*to*	3	*tre*
4	*fire*	5	*fem*
6	*seks*	7	*sju*
8	*åtte*	9	*ni*
10	*ti*	11	*elleve*
12	*tolv*	13	*tretten*
14	*fjorten*	15	*femten*
16	*seksten*	17	*sytten*
18	*åtten*	19	*nitten*
20	*tjue*	21	*tjueen*
22	*tjueto*	30	*tretti*
40	*forti*	50	*femti*
60	*seksti*	70	*sytti*
80	*åtti*	90	*nitti*
100	*hundre*	200	*to hundre*
1,000	*tusen*		

exit	*utgang*
no trespassing	*uvedkommende forbudt*
wharf/quay	*brygge*
church	*kirke*
cathedral	*domkirke*
old quarter	*gamlebyen*
museum	*museet*
town hall	*rådhus*
castle	*slott*

Getting Around

car	*bil*
bus/coach	*buss*
one-way ticket	*énveisbillet*
aeroplane	*fly*
train	*tog*
tram	*trikk*
return	*tur-retur-billett*
adult	*voksen*
child	*barn*
airport bus	*fly bussen*
ferry	*ferry/ferge*
train station	*jernbanestastjon*

Days and Months

Monday	*mandag*
Tuesday	*tirsdag*
Wednesday	*onsdag*
Thursday	*torsdag*
Friday	*fredag*
Saturday	*lørdag*
Sunday	*søndag*
January	*januar*
February	*februar*
March	*mars*
April	*april*
May	*mai*

Shopping

pharmacy/chemist	*apotek*
bookshop	*bøkhandel*
shop	*butikk*
money	*penger*
department	*storehus/atormagasin*
grocery	*storelandhandel*

Denmark: Introduction

15

When you think of Denmark, the picture that comes to mind may be of tall blond Vikings munching bacon sarnies and Danish pastries and swilling them all down with beer while playing with Lego bricks. A cliché – and although some elements may have a certain ring of truth about them, Denmark amounts to much more than that.

A small country on the perimeter of Europe, covering mainland Jutland and 406 islands, Denmark has had some very warlike and expansionist periods – notably lots of raping and pillaging in western Europe between the 8th and 11th centuries, much disagreement with Sweden in the 16th and 17th centuries and, for several centuries, sovereignty over Sweden, Norway and parts of northern Germany (Schleswig Holstein). With its own fair share of internal strife in the Middle Ages, it has gone from being an absolute (though reasonably benevolent) monarchy (1660–1849) to being politically one of the most democratic countries in the world. The Danes seem to excel in foresight and rational consideration; there is something uncannily reasonable about everything that they do – from bike lanes and property laws to paying exorbitant tax (50–100 per cent in many cases) in order to reap the benefits of a fantastic welfare system. Foresight in public policy has meant, for example, that childcare issues in relation to working women and a falling birth rate were on the agenda as early as the 1960s, with the result now that every parent in Denmark is entitled to subsidized childcare until their children are in their early teens. This now means that this predominantly Lutheran country has one of the highest birth rates in the EU, only exceeded by Catholic France and Ireland.

The one fly in the ointment of this laudable policy of looking after its population so well is Denmark's very recent draconian asylum laws, which are so tough that the UN High Commissioner for Refugees wrote to the government questioning the legality of the plans under international law, and Sweden, Belgium and France expressed their 'profound concern'. The change has come about since a Liberal-led coalition backed by the far-right Danish People's party came to power in 2002. These policies sit uncomfortably with Denmark's generosity to the Third World and also its history of refugee support. About 8 per cent of its 5.3 million population are non-Danes, including EU citizens; the figure for non-white refugees and immigrants is nearer 5 per cent.

For the tourist, however, Denmark is a very friendly place. The Danes also like the English – football, a love (oh, what a love!) of monarchy ('probably the oldest monarchy in the world' – dating back to Gorm the Old in the early 10th century), a history of royal intermarriage, beer and a reluctance to change their currency may have something to do with it. Fortunately, they seem to have forgiven us for destroying large areas of Copenhagen in an unprovoked attack in 1807 during the Napoleonic Wars, when they were neutral. Culturally, the Danes have as much to offer as anybody else (*see* p.241). And if you are more interested in chilling out – again, Denmark is good at it. Copenhagen is now home to ten restaurants with Michelin stars, not to mention a vast quantity of cafés, bars and restaurants where you can *hygghe* down (an untranslatable, sociable, national Danish pastime, which roughly translates as 'cosy') at less expense; or you can relax and enjoy one of the many international and national festivals that the Danes host so well.

Denmark: Travel and Practical A–Z

Travel

Entry Formalities

Visas and Passports

For tourist visits of up to three months, EU citizens must present either a passport or an ID card that is valid for the duration of their stay in order to enter Denmark.

Citizens of other countries must have a valid passport. Some non-EU citizens are required to produce a visa. The web address for the Danish Ministry of Foreign Affairs is *www.um.dk* or, for detailed information on visa requirements, visit *www.udlst.dk* (Danish Immigration).

Customs

Duty-free customs allowances depend on whether you arrive from an EU country or a non-EU country. While EU nationals can now import a limitless amount of goods, the proviso that they are for personal use ensures a cap: limits are 800 cigarettes/400 cigarillos/200 cigars/1kg of tobacco; 10 litres of spirits, 90 litres of wine (60 litres maximum sparkling wine) and 110 litres of beer.

For non-EU travellers, tobacco and alcohol allowances are: 200 cigarettes/100 cigarillos/50 cigars/250g of tobacco; 1 litre of liquor over 22% alcohol, 2 litres under 22% alcohol, 2 litres of sparkling wine, 2 litres of wine, 50g perfume or 0.25 litres *eau de toilette*. US citizens should contact US Customs (**t** (202) 354 1000, *www.customs. gov*) or read its pamphlet *Know Before You Go*.

Citizens from countries outside the EU and Scandinavia may be able to claim a VAT refund when goods purchased in Denmark are shipped to another country. VAT can also be refunded at the airport upon presenting a completed VAT refund form (if you are eligible, ask for this when you buy the goods). To achieve the VAT refund, the minimum purchase per shop must be 300kr. *See* p.221.

Getting Around

By Train

DSB national trains: for information and to reserve seats, **t** *70 13 14 15, www.dsb.dk.*

Denmark has a very efficient and comfortable train system – rubbish bags provided! Nor is it overly expensive. Up to two children under 12 can travel free with any adult on any train and, if the children are between the ages of 12 and 15, they can have half-price tickets (as long as you accompany them). Seniors (age 65 or older) receive a discount of up to 25% for travel on Fridays, Sundays and holidays, and discounts of 50% every other day of the week. No identification is needed when you buy your ticket, but the conductor who checks your ticket might ask for proof of age.

There are also government discounts – depending on the type of traveller, days or hours travelled, and destination. These often change so it's always best to ask for a discount based on your age and the number of days (or hours) you intend to travel.

Trains are either regional, intercity or international. You can get timetables and make reservations at the station. If you are travelling regionally or internationally, it is a good idea to book, as you are not guaranteed a seat. The most crowded times on Danish trains are Fridays, Sundays and national holidays, although it is still advisable to book outside these times.

Trains from Copenhagen take you to all major cities, going as far north as Frederikshavn (6½hrs) on the northeast coast of Jutland, stopping at Odense on Funen (2hrs), Århus (3hrs), Randers (4¼hrs) and Aalborg (5¼hrs) among other places; trains also go to Esbjerg (3hrs) in southwest Jutland (also stopping at Odense) and further south to Padborg (3hrs 40mins), Sønderborg (3¼hrs); and northwest to Struer (4hrs 40mins) (via Viborg 4hrs) and Thisted (6hrs). Timings are approximate, as some trains are faster than others; check the timetable. *Lyntog* are 'Express Trains'. Some journeys may require a change. You do not usually need to book for regional trains, though you may need to pay a supplement on some of them. A **Copenhagen Card** (*see* p.235) will enable you to travel free on regional trains in the Copenhagen area.

By Bus

If you are planning to travel in rural Denmark, a car is much the best option. However, trains followed by bus connections are do-able, although you will need to plan and timetable your trip quite closely to make sure that you can get the connection and are not left stranded anywhere. Buses are efficient and punctual, but not as frequent as you might wish. If you do need or decide to travel by bus, head for the railway station, as the bus station or terminal is usually close by; in much of Scandinavia, buses take passengers to destinations not served by the train, so the bus route often starts at the railway station. The arrival of trains and departure of buses are usually closely timed.

If you are not sure of anything, just ask. Your bus driver will doubtless speak flawless English.

City buses are much more regular than their more rural counterparts. Bus stops usually have maps, or you can get a timetable from the bus station or the tourist office.

Bus tickets can be bought on the bus, but discount clip cards (*see* p.234) are only available in advance from sales outlets such as tobacconists, newspaper kiosks, bars, supermarkets or from ticket machines near the main stops. Once you get on, punch your ticket in the machines at the front or back of the bus; inspectors do stage random checks to make sure you've punched your ticket. Fines for fare-dodgers are about €25.

By Car

You really don't need a car if you are planning to visit Copenhagen and go on day trips. In Esbjerg and Århus, however, while you don't need one in town, a car is the most convenient option for day trips and travelling further afield (although all day trips *can* be done by bus if necessary).

Hiring a Car

Hiring a car in Denmark is not especially cheap, not least because there is a government tax of 25% on all car rentals. This is usually charged separately from the original quote when you pick up the car, so check in advance. Also, while it may be worth every penny if you don't want the bother of public transport into town, be aware that cars picked up at a Danish airport are subject to a one-time supplemental tax of 190kr, so you might prefer to book your car from a different location. You should still be able to deliver it back to the airport but do check! If you belong to

Hiring a Car

Hertz, Avis and Europcar have downtown outlets in Århus, Copenhagen and Esbjerg, as well as desks at the three airports. Budget has offices in central Copenhagen, the airport, and in Århus. National also has offices in central Copenhagen and the airport, plus downtown offices in Esbjerg and Århus. Local numbers and addresses are given under each city.

In the UK

Avis, t 0870 606 0100, *www.avis.co.uk*, *www.avisworld.com*.
Budget, t (01442) 280181 or **t** 0800 181181, *www.budget.co.uk*.
Europcar, t 0870 607 5000, *www.europcar.com*.
Hertz, t 0870 599 6699, *www.hertz.co.uk*.
National, t 0870 536 5365, *www.nationalcar.com*.

In the USA

AutoEurope, t 888 223 5555, *www.autoeurope.com*.
Avis, t 800 331 1084, *www.avis.com*.
Europcar, t 877 940 6900, *www.europcar.com*.
Hertz, t 800 654 3001, *www.hertz.com*.
National, t 800 227 7368, *www.nationalcar.com*.

certain travel clubs or organizations (such as AAA or AARP) you may be entitled to a small discount.

Car deals will also be cheaper if you reserve and pay in advance (usually two weeks, but occasionally as little as 48hrs). If you arrange your rental on arrival at the airport, you can be charged as much as double.

Driving in Denmark

Unsurprisingly, driving in Denmark is very straightforward. Roads are usually well marked, though you need to know which towns you are planning to pass through as, in many instances, your destination will only be marked when you are quite near.

Fuel has been unleaded since 2000 and it is compulsory to wear a seatbelt in the front and also in the back if they are fitted. Children under 3 are not allowed in front except in a child safety seat. In the rear and between the ages of 3 and 7 children must use a child safety seat or booster cushion.

Speed Limits

Speed limit without a trailer
Built-up areas: 50kph (31mph)
Major roads outside towns: 80kph (50mph)
Motorways: 110kph (68mph)

Speed limit with a trailer
Built-up areas: 50kph (31mph)
Major roads outside towns: 70kph (43mph)
Motorways: 70kph (43mph)

You must also drive with (dipped) headlights at all times regardless of time or weather.

The Danes drive on the right and generally more or less keep to the speed limit, though you may find people driving faster on the motorways. Motorways, or *Motorvej*, are mainly two lanes in either direction. There are no toll roads.

In and near towns, there are cycle lanes on both sides of the road – and there are a lot of cyclists of all ages, shapes and sizes, some with children or small animals in a kind of trailer, usually on the front of the bike.

Parking meters operate in some towns and street parking is usually restricted to one hour. Illegally parked cars are often impounded. A parking disc system operates in major towns – you can get discs from petrol stations, tourist offices and tobacconists.

Motoring offences attract an on-the-spot fine. An official receipt should be issued. Non-payment may result in the vehicle's being impounded. See 'Liquor Laws', p.219.

Practical A–Z

Climate and When to Go

Because Denmark is almost entirely surrounded by sea, it has a moderate, maritime climate. The average temperatures range from 0°C/32°F in February to 17°C/62°F in July. Temperatures vary slightly from day to night. Average annual rainfall is 24 inches. Days are short in winter, with about 5 hours of daylight in December and January. Daylight in summer lasts 16–18 hours on clear days. You can check the Danish meteorological website for 5-day forecasts: *www.dmi.dk*.

Disabled Travellers

The Danish tourist authorities are very aware that disabled people have a right to expect decent access to museums, attractions, hotels and restaurants, etc., and in 2004 they launched a labelling scheme for accessibility with criteria that must be met in order to be part of the scheme.

The accessibility scheme has requirements and regulations in regard to the following seven disability groups: wheelchair users, people with mobility impairments, the visually impaired and hearing-impaired, people with asthma and allergies, people with mental disabilities, and people with reading difficulties. If a business is approved for wheelchair users, for example, a fact sheet is made that makes it easy and accessible for the consumer to obtain information about parking, accessibility to and within the business, and access to borrowing or renting technical aids.

Visit *www.visithandicapguide.com* for useful information about accessibility – and lack of it – on a long list of accommodation and attractions in Denmark. At the time of writing, the site primarily deals with businesses in west Jutland, but in the span of a couple of years it will also have information about businesses in the rest of the country. The information on the database, which is in Danish, English and German, is made as a kind of 'condition report', where information on accessibility – or lack of accessibility – is registered.

The registration of accessibility to the individual businesses is made by user groups consisting of people with disabilities, who have received special training to register accessibility.

You can also find information on *www.visitdenmark.com* and from individual tourist offices. Staff are usually very helpful and are able to suggest and book hotels with proper access as well as provide local information on access.

Drugs

Penalties for the possession, use, purchase, sale, or manufacturing of drugs are severe. The quantity of the controlled substance is more important than the type of substance. Danish police are particularly strict with cases involving the sale of drugs to children.

Electricity

Denmark, like most other European countries, has 220-volt AC, 50Hz current and uses two-pin continental plugs. Visitors from the UK will need an adaptor for electric appliances, whereas North Americans need a transformer in order to use their 110/125V appliances.

Embassies and Consulates

Danish Embassies Abroad

UK: 55 Sloane Street, London SW1X 9SR, t (020) 7333 0200, f (020) 7333 0270, *lonamb@um.dk*.

USA: 3200 Whitehaven St, N.W., Washington D.C. 20008, t (202) 234 4300, f (202) 328 1470, *wasamb@um.dk*.

Canada: 47 Clarence Street, Suite 450, Ottawa, Ontario, KIN 9K1, t (613) 562 1811, f (613) 562 1812, *ottamb@um.dk*.

In Copenhagen

UK: Kastelsvej 40, 2100 Copenhagen, t 35 44 52 00.

USA: Dag Hammerskjølds Allé 24, 2100 Copenhagen, t 35 55 31 44.

Canada: Kr. Bernikowsgade 1, 1105 Copenhagen, t 33 48 32 00, f 33 48 32 20.

Germany: Stockholmsgade 57, 2100 Copenhagen, t 35 45 99 00.

Ireland: Østbanegade 21, 2100 Copenhagen, t 35 42 32 33.

Norway: Amaliegade 39, 1256 Copenhagen, t 33 14 01 24.

Sweden: Sankt Annæ Plads 15A, 1250 Copenhagen, t 33 36 03 70.

For a complete list of embassies visit the home page of the **Danish Ministry of Foreign Affairs**, *www.um.dk*.

Health and Emergencies

Most areas have doctors on duty 24 hours a day on Saturdays, Sundays and holidays; weekday emergency hours are 4pm to 7.30am. Every doctor speaks English.

In an emergency dial t 112 to contact the police, ambulance or fire service. Speak slowly and distinctly. State your phone number and address. Emergency calls from public pay phones are free.

Health Insurance

Citizens of EU countries are covered, while visiting Denmark, by public health insurance within the limits agreed upon between your own country and the Danish authorities. Take a stamped E111 form with you (available from post offices). Also, as a temporary foreign visitor, you are entitled to free medical treatment in hospitals and emergency wards if you are taken ill or have an accident, provided that you have not travelled to Denmark with the intention of obtaining treatment and are physically unable to return to your own country. However, you will need insurance if you wish to be covered for the cost of being flown home.

If you are a citizen of a non-EU country, you should ensure that you have adequate health insurance. Check with your travel agency or your insurance company.

The Internet

All big towns have internet cafés and even some of the smaller ones as well. Most hotels, especially the more commercial ones, offer internet access, although this can vary from plugging in your laptop in your room to picking up your emails on the one computer in reception.

Liquor Laws

To consume alcohol in Danish bars, restaurants or cafés, customers must be 18 or older. There are no restrictions on children under 18 who drink at home or, for example, from a bottle in a public park. Danish police tend to be lenient unless drinkers become raucous or uncontrollable. There is no leniency, however, in the matter of driving while intoxicated. It's illegal to drive with a blood-alcohol level of 0.8 or more, which could be produced by two drinks. If the level is 1.5, motorists pay a serious fine. If it's more than 1.5, drivers can lose their licence. If the level is 2.0 or more (usually produced by six or seven drinks), a prison term of at least 14 days might follow.

Maps

Most tourist offices will provide free town plans and also sell various maps of the country.

Media

No English-language radio or TV stations broadcast from Denmark. Only radios and TVs with satellite reception can receive signals from countries such as Britain. News programmes in English are broadcast from Monday to Saturday at 8.30am on Radio Denmark, 93.85 MHz. Radio 1 (90.8 MHz VHF) features news and classical music. Channels 2 and 3 (96.5/93.9 MHz) include some entertainment, broadcast light news items, and offer light music. Most TV stations transmit from 7.30am to 11.30pm. Most films (many of which are American) are shown in their original languages, with Danish subtitles.

Money and Banks

The Danish currency is the krone (kr or DKK) which is divided into 100 øre.

Coins are circulated in the following denominations: 25 øre, 50 øre (both copper) 1 krone, 2 kroner, 5 kroner (silver, each with a hole in the centre), 10 and 20 kroner (both brass). Bank notes are issued in denominations of 50kr, 100kr, 200kr, 500kr and 1,000kr. There is no limit on the amount of foreign or Danish currency you can bring into Denmark.

Many restaurants and hotels allow you to pay with euros. Personal cheques from outside Denmark and traveller's cheques are usually not accepted in shops, but the banks will exchange euro cheques and official traveller's cheques. Nevertheless, most shops will accept euro and traveller's cheques issued in Danish kroner, as well as credit cards like Visa (although not all shops and restaurants,

Public Holidays

Most museums, as well as banks and shops, are closed on the following national holidays:

Dec 24–26: Christmas – called *Jul*.
Jan 1: New Year's Day – called *Nytårsdag*.
June 5: Constitution Day – called *Grundlovsdag*.
Maundy Thursday – called *Skærtorsdag*.
Good Friday – called *Langfredag*.
Easter Sunday – called *Påske søndag*.
Easter Monday – called *2 Påskedag*.
Day of Prayer – called *Store Bededag*.
Ascension Day – called *Kristi Himmelfartsdag*.
Whit Sunday – called *Pinse søndag*.
Whit Monday – called *2 Pinsedag*.

especially small ones, will accept international credit cards as the costs are prohibitive).

For help with stolen credit cards call the 24-hour Danish **PBS Hotline, t** 44 89 29 29.

Opening Hours and National Holidays

Banks: Open Monday to Friday 9.30–4, with late hours until 5.30 on Thursdays (closed Saturdays and Sundays). ATMs outside the banks are open 24 hours a day.

Churches: Usually open until 3pm, sometimes until 4 or 5pm. However, they are not generally open before 12pm on Sundays because of services and often close mid-afternoon.

Museums, attractions and restaurants: Often close on Monday. Some museums stay open late on Wednesdays, often as late as 8–10pm. Most museums and attractions have admission charges and it is usually worthwhile getting a 'city' tourist card if you are planning on seeing as much as you can. These usually come in 24hr, 48hr and sometimes 72hr or week-long periods and include travel on public transport during the allotted period. Many museums are free on Wednesdays.

Shops: Usually open during regular working hours during the week (9.30–5.30, although independent boutiques might open as late as 11am), but close at lunchtime (1 or 2pm) on Saturdays. Shops are not open on Sundays.

Pharmacies: Known as *apoteker*, these are open Monday–Thursday 9–5.30, Friday 9–7, and Saturday 9–1.

Packing

Temperatures are slightly colder than the UK (and obviously vary slightly). The average high in Copenhagen in June, for example, is about 19°C/66°F, but has hit up to 29°C/84°, so pack for all eventualities. However, in the spring you can probably get away with bringing just a sweater and a light coat or mac (though if you bring layers, you won't find yourself with sartorial problems).

You can get a 5-day weather report at *www.dmi.dk*.

Danish dress sense is usually pretty casual even in sophisticated settings, but you don't see many people looking grubby or crumpled. Unless you want to dress up, you can get away with smart casual on virtually any occasion.

Post Offices

The general opening hours for post offices in Denmark are on weekdays from 9/10am to 5pm/5.30–6pm and on Saturdays from 9am to 1pm. They are closed on Sundays. All mail to North America is sent airmail without extra charge. The cost for mail weighing 20 grams (0.175 oz.) is 5.50kr (70¢). Mailboxes are painted red and display the embossed crown and trumpet of the Danish Postal Society.

Price Categories

Hotels usually have a 'rack' rate, which is their official hotel rate, but these vary according to the season (high May–Sept, low Oct–April). Always check for deals, as many hotels have weekend or one-off deals during the year. Many hotels also offer a lower rate if you book on the web. Room rates do not automatically include breakfast – always check. Many hotels offer free internet access, especially in town.

Eating out is generally more expensive than in the UK, but the quality of food is often higher and you get more for your money. Many restaurants offer fixed rates for 2+ courses, which often makes moderate or expensive meals less expensive for what you get than you might think.

Shopping

Danish shopping is pretty much like elsewhere in Europe, except it is more expensive, and in this day and age you can get virtually anything anywhere.

However, for presents, amber is not unreasonable and there is some very pretty jewellery available. Anything to do with Danish design is always good – Georg Jensen and Royal Copenhagen spring to mind – or even better, perhaps, keep an eye out, especially in Jutland or in any of the more rural areas, for hand-blown glass and other crafts that are individual.

If you are interested in clothes, look out for Danish designers such as munthe plus simonsen.

Taxes

The current VAT rate is 25%. VAT is included in hotel and restaurant bills, entrance fees, etc. and cannot be refunded on these services.

Tax-free shopping is possible in many major shops and department stores for visitors from non-EU and non-Scandinavian countries. To achieve the VAT refund (when you leave the country), the minimum purchase per shop must be 300kr.

A useful home page is *www.globalrefund. com*. Global Refund is the world leader in tax refunding, with more than 210,000 affiliated retailers in 34 countries and on three continents. In Denmark you can buy tax-free in more than 4,000 shops and get your tax refund when leaving Denmark or the EU.

Hotel Price Categories
Prices are for a double room per night, with bath/shower and WC in high season.
expensive over 1,000kr
moderate 500–1,000kr
inexpensive below 500kr

Restaurant Price Categories
Prices are for a three-course meal without wine.
very expensive over 600kr
expensive 400–600kr
moderate 200–400kr
inexpensive below 200kr

The refund is 13–19% of your purchase, and the procedure is as follows:

1 When shopping in TaxFree stores, collect a Global Refund TaxFree Cheque.
2 Get your Tax Refund when leaving Copenhagen or the EU. Just show your purchases, receipts and passport to customs officials and have your TaxFree Cheques stamped.
3 Global Refund refunds your money.

Smoking

The attitude of the Danes to smoking is generally quite liberal, and 34% of the population are smokers. Smoking is permitted in most cafés and restaurants, specially designated compartments in trains and the S-tog, but not in the metro and on buses.

Wherever you are, it is always a good idea to check for no-smoking signs before you light up and to show consideration for non-smokers in general.

Telephones

Local Danish phone numbers have eight digits. The international dialling code from abroad is +45, and there are no area codes. Do not use the +45 prefix when calling within Denmark.

For international calls from Denmark, dial 00 + national code + area code minus the first zero + personal number.

International dialling codes: Britain +44, France +33, Germany +49, Ireland +353, Italy +39, Japan +81, Norway +47, Sweden +46, USA +1.

For domestic **directory enquiries** dial **t** 118; for international dial **t** 113.

If you have problems getting a connection, contact the International Telephone Service Department at **t** 141 or **t** 80 60 40 55; all calls are free (although you will be charged if the operator connects you).

Public **pay phones** accept coins (not the little copper coins) or prepaid **Telecards**. For international calls use 5–20kr coins, but beware – the telephones do not give back change, no matter if you are connected or not. Telephone cards come in denominations of 30, 50 and 100kr and are available from kiosks and post offices.

Mobile phones should work without any problems as Denmark is part of the worldwide GSM network .

Time

Denmark follows Central European Time (CET), which is one hour ahead of Greenwich Mean Time (GMT) and six hours ahead of Eastern Standard Time (EST). The clocks go forward on the last Sunday in March, and back again on the last Sunday in October. The 24-hour clock is commonly used.

Tipping

Tips are usually included in all services, meaning that the service at restaurants and hotels is normally included in the price. However, if you liked the meal and the service, you are very welcome to add a little something to the bill.

Tourist Information

UK

Danish Tourist Board, 55 Sloane Street, London SW1X 9SY, **t** (020) 7259 59 59 (*open Mon, Wed and Fri 10–1*); 24hr brochure line, **t** 09001 600 109, **f** (020) 7259 5955, *dtb.london@dt.dk*.

USA

Danish Tourist Board, 655 Third Avenue, 18th floor, New York, NY 10017, **t** (212) 885 9700, **f** (212) 885 9726, *info@goscandinavia.com*.

Denmark: Food and Drink

17

Traditionally, Danish food has been based around sturdy home-made victuals, meat and particularly fish – just what you would expect from a seafaring nation totally surrounded by water and whose success in trade was (and still is to an extent, with North Sea oil) dependent upon the sea.

However, whereas once you would have been offered gruel, fruit soup or porridge as a sturdy main course, Danish cuisine has moved on, using fresh traditional ingredients but increasingly infused with continental inspiration, particularly French and Italian. Go to any of the big towns – in relation to this book, particularly Copenhagen and Århus – and you will find international cuisine in which the Danes don't just replicate well-known foreign dishes, but create simple foods using a combination of ingredients from all over the world. There seems to be a particular penchant for French flavours and combinations and there are lots of French/Danish restaurants. Perhaps if Britain hadn't used bullying tactics in the Napoleonic Wars and attacked Copenhagen, ruining vast tracts of it, there would be an interesting Danish/English cuisine based around Yorkshire pudding, gravy and marinated herring...or perhaps not.

Restaurant Generalities

Breakfast is very often served buffet-style and is usually copious; you can easily fill up for the day if you want to. There will often be a selection of breads, including the heavy and delicious bitty rye bread, which you can combine, English-style, with butter and jam, or Scandinavian or Dutch style with cheese and salamis and other cold meats. Fruit juice, milk, tea and coffee are usually on offer as well as breakfast cereals and several types of yoghurt (good combined with the cereal as well as eaten on its own).

If you are in a superior establishment, you will probably also be offered Danish pastries – very dangerous not just for the waistline but also to one's ability to move at speed, so be warned. The Danish make no claims on Danish pastries and actually call them *wienerbrød* (Viennese bread). They can come in a bewildering number of delicious varieties.

Lunch usually takes place around midday–2pm and more often than not is *smørrebrød* – a Danish sandwich. Unlike English sandwiches, which you can eat on the move, these definitely need a sit-down and a knife and fork, as they are open-topped. *Smørrebrød* actually means 'buttered bread', but is far more than bread and butter. Usually on rye bread (although increasingly continental influences are being felt and Italian breads are now often offered as well), these sandwiches are piled high with any number of ingredients – spiced, smoked and marinated herring, boiled eggs, shrimps, salad, cold meat, cheese, smoked salmon... *Smørrebrød* is an art and you can experiment with topping combinations to your heart's content. Hans Christian Andersen, it is said, favoured his with bacon, tomato, liver paté with truffles, and meat jelly.

Traditionally, *smørrebrød* is washed down with beer and schnapps (take care!) and served from *det store kolde bord*, a big buffet of traditional cold and warm ingredients. Traditionally, the *smørrebrød* course is then followed by fish dishes, usually mackerel, salmon or pickled herring, then meat such as liver paté, meatballs and *æbleflæsk* (bacon with roast apple), and finally cheese, biscuits and fruit. Danes often follow this traditional pattern for festivities and long lunches.

Supper is usually served between 6 and 9pm, although many restaurants, especially in the bigger cities, will close the kitchen a bit later.

Although, in general, eating out in Denmark seems to be more expensive than elsewhere (unless you snack or eat in a café or bar, a meal for under 200kr is quite hard to come by), you usually get good food and, if you decide to eat several courses, you will find that many restaurants offer set prices for two, three or more courses so, proportionately, your meal is cheaper the more courses you have. You can usually choose *à la carte* in these circumstances as well.

Food Specialities

If you get the opportunity, you should try out national dishes such as boiled or sugar-browned potatoes, boiled red cabbage, brown sauce, roast pork or roast duck, and almond rice with cherry sauce for dessert (a Christmas speciality). Other original contributions to the gastronomic pantheon include smoked eel with scrambled eggs, pork with red cabbage, apples and prunes, and liver paste with pickled cucumbers or gherkins, *kranskage* (almond cake rings), *æblekage* (apple charlotte) with fried breadcrumbs and fruit preserves. Hot dishes include boiled cod with mustard, butter and chopped hard-boiled eggs, horseradish and boiled potatoes, and roast duck, pork or goose with apples, prunes, caramelized potatoes, red cabbage and gravy.

Drinks

The Danes enjoy a drink, it has to be said – and why not, as they produce 'probably the best lager in the world' (and lots of fab museums associated with the name as well). *Skål* (cheers) is undoubtedly a word you should learn if you wish to endear yourselves with the locals. Beer is the national drink, and Carlsberg and Tuborg are the big names. Don't be surprised if a beer costs you considerably more in a bar than in a supermarket – somewhere in the region of 25–45kr. Look out for Happy Hours, usually before about 8pm, although many last until 10pm.

The other traditional drink is *acquavit*, a vodka that comes in a huge number of flavours (the most popular is flavoured with caraway seeds), which is made in Aalborg (*see* p.304). It is usually drunk as a chaser after a beer. If you sip it, you will get much more inebriated and have a worse hangover than if you just knock it back. Eating something before each shot (even just a bite of of bread) also helps. From personal experience, if you are knocking it back with seafood (especially crayfish or

Danish Menu Reader

Kød (Meat)
and/andesteg duck/roast duck
bøf beef
dyresteg roast venison
hakkebøf ground beef burger
flæskesteg roast pork
lammesteg roast lamb
kylling chicken
lamme koteletter rack of lamb
lever liver
lever postej liver paté
oksekød beef
pølse hot dog
skinke ham
svinekød pork

Fisk (Fish)
ål eel
fiskefilet fish fillet
fiskefrikadelle fried fishball
fiskesuppe fish soup
flynder flounder
forel trout
helleflynder halibut
hummer lobster
krabbe crab
kuller haddock
laks salmon
makrel mackerel
musling mussel
ørred trout
øsers oyster
rejer prawn
røget laks smoked salmon
røget sild smoked herring
rødspætte plaice
sild herring
skaldyr shellfish
søtunge sole
torsk cod
torskerogn cod roe
tun tuna

Frugt og Grøntsager (Fruit and Vegetables)
abrikos apricot
æble apple
ærter pea
agurk cucumber
appelsin orange
banan banana
blåbær blueberry
blomkål cauliflower
brombær blackberry
bønner beans
champignon mushroom
citron lemon
dild dil
fersken peach
grøn bønne green bean
gulerødder carrots
hvidløg garlic
hindbær raspberry
jordbær strawberry
kål cabbage
kartoffel potato
løg onion
rødkål red cabbage

Desserts
chokolade chocolate, also hot chocolate
is ice cream/ice
fløde cream
fromage a pudding
kage cake
kringle type of Danish pastry
pandekage pancake
tærte tart
vaffel waffle
vanilleis vanilla ice cream
wienerbrød Danish pastry

Other Terms
æg egg
appelsinjuice orange juice
bolle soft bread roll
brød bread
citronvand lemonade
eddike vinegar
kaffe coffee

mælk milk
mineralvand mineral water
nødder nuts
olie oil
ost cheese
peber pepper
peberrod horseradish
purløg chives
ris rice
rundstykker crusty rolls
salat salad
senap mustard
smør butter
sodavand mineral water
suker sugar
suppe soup
te tea
vand water

Cooking Terms
bakt baked
benfri boneless
dampet stewed
frisk fresh
friturestegt deep-fried
hakket chopped, minced
gennemstegt well done
grilleret grilled
gryderet stew
hvide white (as in white potatoes, rice, etc.)
kogt boiled
kold cold
marineret marinated
mellemstegt medium cooked
ovnstegt roasted
pocheret poached
røget smoked
rår raw
stegt fried
varm warm, hot

Some Traditional Dishes
Æggekage rich Funen omelette served with
   dark bread
Medisterpolse Danish sausage, usually served
   with sautéed mushrooms
Fiskfrikadelle fried fishball

Flæskeæggekage scrambled eggs with bacon
Flæskesteg med rødkål roast pork with red
   cabbage
Frikadelle fried ground pork, home-made
   meatballs commonly served with boiled
   potatoes and red cabbage
Gravadlax cured or salted salmon marinated
   in dill and served with a sweet mustard sauce
Gule ærter split pea soup, boiled with pork,
   cured gammon or possibly *medisterpolse*
Hakkebøf ground beef burger, usually covered
   with fried onions and served with boiled
   potatoes, brown sauce and beets
Husets platte Traditional Danish platter
   (served on two plates)
Kryddersild herring pickled in various types
   of marinade
Løskesteg roast pork, usually with crackling
   served with potatoes and cabbage
Karbonader burgers, often made with
   minced pork
Marineret sild marinated herring
Mørbradbøffer small steaks of pork
   tenderloin, commonly in a mushroom sauce
Pølsevogn fish and chips

Alcohol
hvidvin white wine
rødvin red wine
mousserende vin sparkling wine
husets vin house wine
gløgg mulled wine
fadøl draught beer
øl beer

Menu Terms
børnemenu children's menu
daggens middag set menu
daggens ret daily special
forretter starters
frokost lunch
hovedretter main dishes
middag dinner
morgenmad breakfast
retter dishes, courses
spisekort menu
tagselvbord self-service buffet

langoustines), eat heartily beforehand if you can – after all, they are not much more than oversized prawns, and they really don't soak up much!

Peter Heering is a popular Danish liqueur made from cherries. it is sipped straight or tastes good poured over vanilla ice-cream.

Wine is generally expensive in restaurants and will bump up your bill. You may find a house wine at around 130kr, but it is not unusual for a bottle to be around the 150–200kr mark.

Denmark: Copenhagen and Around

18

Around Copenhagen

20 km
10 miles

N

Höganäs

SWEDEN

Gilleleje

Hornbæk

Helsing-
borg

Græsted

Helsingør

Frederiksværk

Helsinge

Esrum
Sø

Humlebæk

Hundested

Arresø

Fredensborg

Rørvig

Roskilde Fjord

Hillerød

E47/E55

Nykøbing

Rungsted

Isefjord

Horsholm

Slangerup

Frederikssund

Farum

Nærum

Øre

Skibby

Stenløse

Lyngby

Klampenborg

Holbæk

Sund

Zealand

COPENHAGEN

Roskilde

21

Hedehusene

Ishøj

E20

Tarnby

To
Odense

E20

Ejby

Køge Bugt

Ringsted

Køge

E47

Falsterbo

Copenhagen lies on the eastern side of Zealand, the largest of Denmark's 406
islands. After visiting the capital, there are plenty of day trips to do, and it's easy to
travel by train from Central Station. Most of the excursions are to destinations in
northern Zealand, a surprisingly rural area given its proximity to the city.

Copenhagen

Wonderful Copenhagen! trumpets the Tourist Board, quoting the rather kitsch Danny Kaye song – surely a PR exercise that sets you up for disappointment. But, actually, no. Copenhagen is lovely and you could easily spend a couple of weeks here without running out of things to do. It is full of world-class museums, attractive parks, several castles, fabulous eating places, a good nightlife and the certain knowledge that, however hard you try, you will never get run over – there are far fewer cars on the road than you are probably used to, lots of pedestrianized areas, and people just don't jay-walk. If you are not convinced, the UK's trendiest style magazine, *Wallpaper**, ranks Copenhagen as one of the world's coolest cities.

It is also a very pretty city, with green spaces, city squares and lots of water, and is small enough to make for easy walking, though jumping on and off buses is very straightforward. Alternatively, ride a bike. The Danes respect and encourage their cyclists and provide wide lanes on both sides of the roads for them. Many people seem to be especially fond of bikes with a kind of front trailer, which they use for shopping or, just as often, for transporting their animals and small children. There is a certain Danish attitude that is reflected in the fact that every summer 2,000 civic bikes are provided for Copenhagen's populace – a bit like with a supermarket trolley, you pay 20kr, take a bike and when you take it back to an official rack you get your money back. This was tried in Cambridge, UK, a few years back and all the bikes disappeared within a nano-second, never to return. In Copenhagen it works remarkably well and, although about half the bikes disappear over the summer, most of them are returned over the winter.

The Danes, of course, also know a thing or two about stylish design. Whether you are in a café, walking in the streets, shopping or doing your cultural thing, you can't fail to see how they understand the concepts and interaction of space, shape and colour.

The Danes themselves are generally charming and very helpful. This is not a place to be worried about asking for directions in the street. Everyone, from the bus driver to the hotel receptionist, speaks some (usually very good) English. The people seem relaxed – even here, in the home of Denmark's political, financial and artistic institutions, you don't get the rushed, no-time mentality of some European and US cities.

If you want to travel outside Copenhagen, there are plenty of easy day trips, from Viking remains to Baroque-inspired castles and gorgeous modern museums in lovely gardens. These trips all start at Central Station. You will discover the Danes' fabulous trains (there are a number of different sorts) right from the start if you make the easy trip in from the airport by train. Graffiti-free, comfortable and complete with plastic bags provided for your rubbish, they always run on time; however, do check train times as they can be infrequent, depending on where you are going.

And at the end of the day, there are plenty of places to *hygghe* down – the all-important, convivial but essentially untranslatable Danish word that is generally taken to mean 'cosy' but is actually a verb as well as an adjective, that usually involves alcohol and can mean everything from cosying up all warm and intimate *à deux* to family get-togethers or partying loudly into the early hours with your mates.

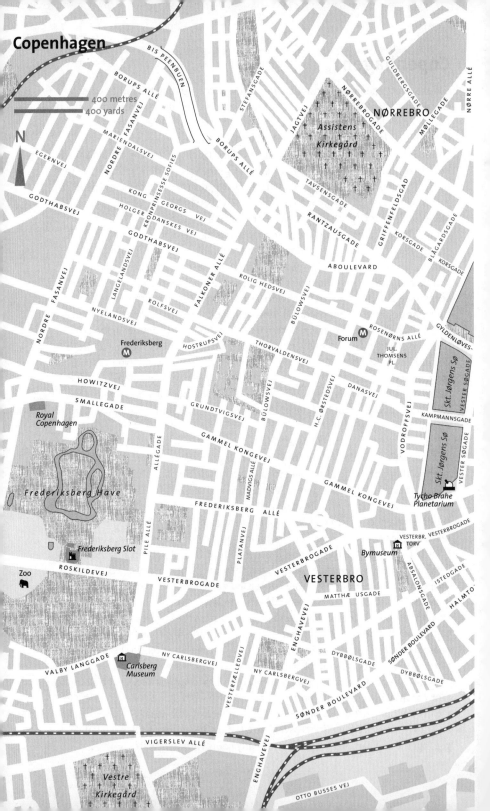

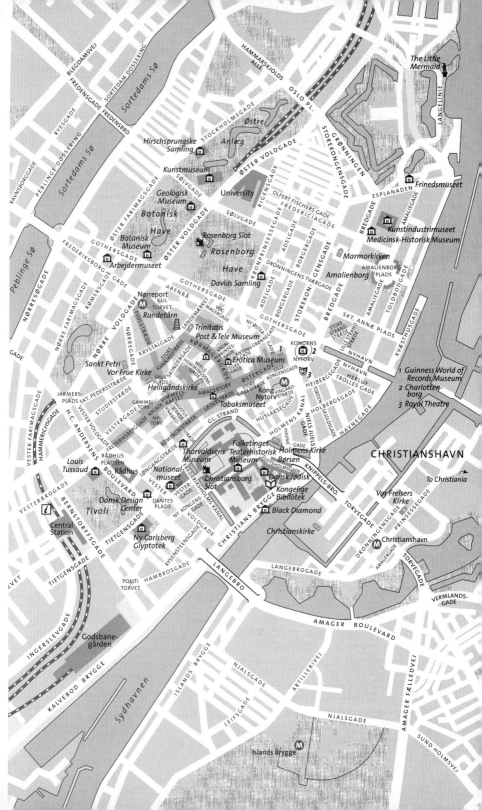

The Little Mermaid

HAMMARSKJOLDS ALLE
OSLO PL.
LANGELINIE

STOCKHOLMSGADE
Østre Anlæg
Hirschsprungske Samling
Kunstmuseum
SØLVGADE
University
Geologisk Museum
Botanisk Have
Botanisk Museum
ØSTER VOLDGADE
Rosenborg Slot
Rosenborg Have
Arbejdermuseet
Davids Samling
GOTHERSGADE
Nørreport
TORVET
Rundetårn
Trinitatis
Post & Tele Museum
Sankt Petri
Vor Frue Kirke
Helligåndskirke
Erotica Museum
Kong Nytorv
Tobaksmuseet
Thorvaldsens Museum
National-museet
Louis Tussaud
Rådhus
Dansk Design Center
Tivoli
Ny Carlsberg Glyptotek
Central Station
Godsbane-gården

ESPLANADEN
Frinedsmuseet
BREDGADE
Kunstindustrimuseet
Medicinsk-Historisk Museum
Marmorkirken
Amalienborg
AMALIENBORG PLADS
TOLDBODGADE
SKT. ANNÆ PLADS
NYHAVN
KONGENS NYTORV

1 Guinness World of Records Museum
2 Charlotten-borg
3 Royal Theatre

CHRISTIANSHAVN
To Christiania
Vor Frelsers Kirke
Christianshavn

Folketinget
Teaterhistorisk Museum
Holmens Kirke
Børsen
Dansk Jødisk
Christiansborg Slot
Kongelige Bibliotek
Black Diamond
Christianskirke

LANGEBRO
LANGEBROGADE
AMAGER BOULEVARD
VERMLANDS-GADE

Sydhavnen
ISLANDS BRYGGE
NJALSGADE
LEIFSGADE
ARTILLERIVEJ
AMAGER FÆLLEDVEJ
SUND HOLMSVEJ

Islands Brygge

Getting There

Over 75 airlines fly to Copenhagen. Easyjet flies from Stansted once a day; British Airways also have several flights a day from London Heathrow. SAS, Maersk and Finnair also fly.

Getting from the Airport

The airport is 8km from the centre and a **train** runs six times an hour and take 13 minutes to Copenhagen Central (Hovedbane-gården) (about 21kr). One train an hour runs between midnight and 1am at 26 minutes past. You can easily pick up a cab if you need one at the station. A **taxi** from the airport will cost about 180kr.

Getting Around

By Bus, Train and Metro

Tickets are timed and cover 95 zones within the greater Copenhagen area. One ticket covers all transport as long as you are within your time and in the zone you have paid for. (You may have to pay a surcharge on some international and InterCity trains.) The price relates to the number of zones you pass through – the most expensive zone determines your fare, regardless of whether you get off or not. Zone maps are on display at stations and bus stops. The zone you are in is marked in red.

Ordinary basic tickets can be bought at vending machines at stations, ticket offices and on buses from the driver. However, it is cheaper to buy discount **clip cards**, which will cover 10 journeys. Buy these at stations, HUR ticket offices and many newsagents and supermarkets. Before your journey, punch your card in a yellow card-clipping machine. The text on the discount clip explains exactly how it works. Children under 12 travel free when accompanied by an adult. A 24hr ticket is also available for all zones at HUR ticket offices and manned stations. Two children under 10 can travel free with an adult on this ticket.

If you are planning to do a lot of sightseeing and buy a **Copenhagen Card** (*see* below), this will entitle you to free transport across the zones and will cover any day trips suggested in this book. For more information contact:

HUR service centre: *www.hur.dk*, t 36 13 14 15.
DSB S-trains: *www.s-tog.dk*, t 33 14 17 01.
DSB domestic trains: *www.dsb.dk*, t 70 13 14 15.

By Taxi

Vacant cabs have FRI (free) on display and can be hailed in the street or phoned. Taxis usually take credit cards and can provide you with a receipt. Most drivers speak English and German. The start-up fare is 23kr with an additional 10kr per km between 6am and 4pm, and 11kr per km from 4pm to 6am. Fares are slightly more expensive per km on Fri and Sat nights, Sun and national holidays.

By Boat

A new harbour bus service links the Black Diamond on Christians Brygge with Nordre Toldbord, with stops along the waterfront at Knippelsbro, Nyhavn, and Holmen North. Shuttle boats (nos. 901/902) run six times an hour between 6am and 6/7pm throughout the year. The whole journey takes about 20 minutes. Otherwise DFDS canal tours offers an unguided hop-on hop-off waterbus service between Copenhagen and Fisketorvet shopping centre or a guided tour (1½hrs) along the canals every 30mins, leaving from Nyhavn. See *www.canaltours.com*.

Bike Hire

Hire a bike or, in summer, free city bikes are available from special stands around town. Like a supermarket trolley, you pay 20kr into the slot, which you get back when you return it to a designated stand. They are only for use in the city centre.
Kobenhavns Cykelbørs, Gothersgade 157, t 33 14 07 17 (*open daily 8.30–5.30, Sat 10–1.30*).
Kobenhavns Cykler, Central Station, t 33 33 86 13 (*open daily 8–5.30, Sat 9–1*).

Car Hire

Unless you are planning trips (and most of them are easily done by train), a car is a bit more trouble than it is worth. No one under 20 can hire a car. All these are at the airport:
Avis, t 32 51 22 99.
Budget Rent-a-car, t 32 52 39 00.
Europcar/InterRent, t 32 50 30 90.
Hertz, t 32 50 93 00.

Tourist Information

At Vesterbrogade 4A (opposite the Tivoli main entrance, close to Central Station), **t** 70 22 242 (open Jan–April Mon–Fri 9–4, Sat 9–2, closed Sun; May–June Mon–Sat 9–6, closed Sun; July–Aug Mon–Sat 9–8, Sun 10–6; Sept–Dec Mon–Fri 9–4, Sat 9–2, closed Sun).

Copenhagen Card

This can be bought for periods of 24, 48 or 72 hours at a stretch and covers entry to over 60 attractions (199–399kr). For others it offers a discount. It also covers public transport on public buses, boats and trains within the Greater Copenhagen area. If you are planning to see a lot of attractions, it is very good value, as museums tend to cost between 500 and 750kr admission. An adult card will also cover two children up to the age of 9. Cards can be bought at the tourist office.

Festivals

Copenhagen is renowned for its festivals, with themes ranging from rock and jazz to film, ballet, design and the visual arts. They tend to take place in the spring/summer and have high cultural status. For a full list of festivals, visit www.woco.dk.
Night film festival: www.natfilm.dk.
International film festival: www.copenhagenfilmfestival.com.
International jazz festival: www.festival.jazz.dk.

Shopping

Copenhagen offers lots of great shopping opportunities. Everyone talks about Strøget as a major shopping area; there are lots of shops but nothing terribly individual. Like London's Oxford Street, it covers a multitude of price brackets, but its side streets are more interesting. Branching off from Amagertorv:
Købmagergade is good for mid-price stores such as Benetton and Diesel and also has plenty of independent shops; the **Grønnegade** quarter towards the eastern end of Strøget is an atmospheric, half-timbered, twisty-windy area with lots of trad and contemporary design products as well as plenty of good

fashion – from classic chic to hip street gear; **Kompagnistræde** and **Læderstræde**, running into each other, offer an absorbing afternoon's browsing, while the **Latin Quarter** offers a lot of record shops and trendy clothes – new and secondhand. The designer Bond Street of Copenhagen is **Kronprinsensgade** with stores such as munthe plus simonsen, Stig P and Bruuns Bazaar. **Vesterbrogade** offers not especially classy shopping but has a number of factory outlets, several with an emphasis on leather – the usual (downmarket) high street type thing. **Nørrebro** is a good place for bric-a-brac, antiques or clothes for 20–30- somethings, especially along **Elmegade**, **Blågårdsgade** and **Ravnsborggade**. Up near the Amalienborg, streets such as **Bredgade** and **Store Longensgade**, as well as little streets off Nyhavn, such as **Store** and **Lille Strandstræde**, are fabulous for window-shopping if your pockets are not sufficiently deep (and not many people's are).
Rosenthal, Frederiksberggade 21, is an interesting gallery, with price tags ranging from 200kr for a designer Bjørn Wiinblad memento Copenhagen mug to 3,800kr for lovely hand-blown bowls and candlesticks.
Illum department stores, Østergade 52. Stylish department store. There is a very nice 'shiplike' café on the 4th floor. Open Mon–Sat 10–7.
Georg Jensen, Amagertorv 4. This is the flagship store where you can buy (or simply admire) classic silver designs in jewellery and homeware (antiques and the Georg Jensen museum are in the basement).
Magasin du Nord, Kongens Nytorv. Lovely department store, with delicious, upmarket supermarket downstairs – also, lots of cafés with a 2Go café and pizza place in the basement and a stylish bar-eatery serving smørrebrød on each floor, many with leather sofa views over the square. There is also a huge and very reasonable café at the top.
Rådhusarken, Jerbandgade. Shopping mall just off Rådhus Pladsen, the other side from Strøget.
Klaedebo, Blågårdsgade 3, Nørrebro. The place for loose, designer, hippy-pretty gear. It's run by four local designers in a former basement

cheese shop, and they are happy to do alterations. There is also a children's range.

Frogeye, Blågårdsgade 2A, Nørrebro. For trendy footwear from New York, Paris, Barcelona and Berlin. If you plan on spending, be warned, they only take Danish credit cards.

Juice, Elmegade 14–17. Trendy gear for girls and guys.

Where to Stay

In most hotels in Copenhagen, rates can vary dramatically depending on whether it is the winter or summer season. From time to time, they also offer special deals. Always ring and/or check their websites. In high season, you will be hard pushed to find a double for much under 700kr. Reception staff are usually very helpful and speak excellent English.

Hotel Sankt Petri, Krystalgade 22, t 33 45 91 00, f 33 45 91 10, *www.hotelsktpetri.com* (*expensive*). This gorgeous, newly converted five-star hotel in the old quarter right by the cathedral was originally a much-loved department store. Very Danish, very stylish, orchids in all the rooms, bespoke artwork, and an elegant and lively atrium on the ground floor.

Admiral Hotel, Toldbodgade 24–28, t 33 74 14 14, *www.admiralhotel.dk* (*expensive*). Situated in a 200-year-old granary, Admiral Hotel is now a lovely wood-beamed hotel with individual rooms, each decorated in cosy but modern Danish design.

No. 71, Nyhavn 71, t 33 43 62 00, f 33 43 62 01, *www.71nyhavnhotelcopenhagen.dk* (*expensive*). A lovely converted warehouse at the end of Nyhavn, No.71 is close to the action but you won't be troubled by sound pollution. Following the Danish chic/French colonial style, many of the rooms (a few on two levels with an interconnecting spiral staircase) have a view over the Sound. The downstairs basement bar and restaurant are a gourmet haven of candlelit *hygge*.

Radisson Royal SAS, Hammerichsgade 1, t 33 42 60 00, f 33 42 61 0, *www.radissonsas.com* (*expensive*). Considered a 'landmark of the jet age' when it was first built and designed by Arne Jacobsen in 1956, though modern tastes might now consider it more of a vile tower block. However, it retains its iconic status inside. Although all rooms, except room 606, have been updated, they are all furnished with Arne Jacobsen designs – keep an eye out for the chairs. Breakfast on the 20th floor is great.

Hôtel d'Angleterre, Kongens Nytorv 34, t 33 12 00 95, f 33 12 11 18, *www.dangleterre.dk*. This is Copenhagen's oldest and most dignified hotel with typically gracious décor.

There are plenty of nice three- and four-star hotels around Central Station. Although not quite as central or as picturesque as the old town or Nyhavn, rooms are cheaper (check for deals). You will be well placed for day trips , and there is still plenty to do close by.

Ibis Copenhagen Star, Colbjørnsensgade 13, t 33 22 11 00, f 33 21 21 86, *www.ibishotel.com* (*moderate–inexpensive*). Just behind Central Station, this is part of the Accor hotel group. Comfortable with standard décor, it does some good deals. Breakfast extra.

Ibis Copenhagen Triton, Helgolandsgade 7–11, t 33 31 32 66 (*moderate–inexpensive*). Another in the Accor chain – uninspired decoration but value for money in a cosmopolitan city.

Hotel Centrum, Helgolandsgade 14, t 33 31 31 11, *www.hotelcentrum.dk* (*moderate*). A bright modern hotel in the area behind the station – standard stuff, though you also get free access to the posh swim centre near by.

Cab Inn hotels, *www.cabinn.com* (*moderate–inexpensive*): **Scandinavia**, Vodroffsvej 55, t 35 36 11 11; **Express**, Danesvej 32, t 33 21 04 00; and **City**, Mitchellsgade 14, t 33 46 16 16. The Cab Inn chain offers very good value for money. It is based on the concept of rooms being like a ship's cabin – functional and attractive but not exactly palatial. In the smaller rooms, or rooms with extra beds, be prepared for bunks to maximize space. However, excellent value with good service, a nice ambience and good breakfasts (extra).

Saga Hotel, Colbjørnsensgade 18–20, t 33 24 49 44, *www.sagahotel.dk* (*moderate–inexpensive*). Friendly and family-run, its 79 rooms vary in size from single to family rooms for 3 or 4, with and without bath. Very good value and close to the centre.

Euroglobe, Niels Ebbesens Vej 22, Frederiksberg, **t** 33 79 79 54, *www.hoteleuroglobe.dk*
(*inexpensive*). A bit further out (take bus 29
from Rådhus Pladsen) towards Nørrebro,
this hotel in an old villa offers simple rooms
sharing bath and kitchen facilities.

Løven, Vesterbrogade 30, **t** 33 79 67 20, *www.*
loeven.dk (*inexpensive*). Although this can be
a bit on the noisy side, its plain, basic rooms
(with and without bath) are very good value
for the area.

Eating Out

A cheap meal in Copenhagen is hard to
find, unless you eat in one of the many cafés,
which usually serve up a good plate of food
and a beer for 100–150kr. Alcohol never
comes cheap. Copenhageners like their food
and, as in most capital cities, the choice of
styles is bewildering, although there is a
preponderance of very good French, Italian
and Danish fare.

Kommandanten (Michelin**), Ny Adelgade 7,
t 33 12 09 90, *www.kommandanten.dk* (*very*
expensive). The only restaurant with two
stars, serving delicious seasonal Danish-
French cuisine with tempting dishes such as
fried Norwegian lobster *à la nage*, with
aniseed and spring onions.

Restaurationen (Michelin*), Møntergade 19,
t 33 14 94 95, *www.restaurationen.dk* (*very*
expensive). This charming, pretty restaurant
offers one fixed menu of five courses: three
starters, one main course and a dessert,
which is always composed of three
individual dishes. Inspiration is French,
Danish and Italian. Finish off with a choice
of cheese, one of 100 *digestifs* or a Cuban
cigar. Reviewers extol its virtues.

Kong Hans Kælder (Michelin*), Vingårds-
stræde 6, **t** 33 11 68 68, *www.konghans.dk*
(*very expensive*). Originally part of a 16th-
century royal vineyard, this restaurant is
located in the oldest building in Copenhagen, complete with Gothic arches. Years
later, Hans Christian Andersen lived in its
garret. Now, it offers fabulous food based
predominantly on French cuisine but with
an interesting twist.

Era Ora (Michelin*), Overgaden Neden Vandet
33B, **t** 32 54 06 93, *www.era-ora.dk* (*very*

expensive). A succession of fresh, light, very
simple Umbrian dishes make this one of the
best restaurants in town.

Le Sommelier, Bredgade 63–65, **t** 33 11 45 15
(*very expensive–expensive*). Understated,
stylish French décor with 1930s posters on
the walls. Delicious food if you're into
halibut with oysters, beef with cherries,
sublime *terrine de foie gras*, or, for pudding,
a 'chocolate plate with five different choco-
late-inspired confections' – though by this
stage, it is probably best shared.

Sankt Gertruds Kloster, Hauser Plads 32, **t** 33 14
66 30 (*very expensive–expensive*). This
unique restaurant has an extraordinary
interior located in the cellars of what
remains of a 14th-century chapel/convent.
Start with a drink in the candlelit library and
move on, through stone-flagged corridors, to
the restaurant under the arches. The food is
delicious, service helpful and the impressive
wine cellar boasts 35,000 bottles. *Open daily*
5pm–11pm.

Café a Porta, Kongens Nytorv, **t** 33 11 05 00
(*expensive–moderate*). Next door to Magasin
du Nord, this is a French-inspired, dark wood
bistro with dark, tooled-leather effect walls,
a coffered ceiling, '*boule*' lights and lots of
plants – the opposite of Danish airy and
bright, but cosy and attractive all the same.

Restaurant Alsace, Ny Østergade 9/Pistol-
stræde, **t** 33 14 57 43, *www.restaurantalsace.*
dk (*expensive–moderate*). A nice little restaurant off Strøget in a quiet, cosy, cobbled little
courtyard with a fountain, surrounded by
higgledy-piggledy 17th-century houses.
Dishes vary from traditional Alsace cuisine
to ravioli, Danish sole and a good beef steak.

Cafe Truffle, Vestergade 29, **t** 33 13 15 00
(*expensive*). Taking inspiration from every
continental culinary tradition, this stylish
restaurant with its charming courtyard is
well worth the price. *Open Mon–Sat 11am–*
12am; closed Sun.

Salt Bar & Restaurant, Admiral Hotel, Toldbodgade 24–28, **t** 33 74 14 44 (*expensive–*
moderate). The ground-floor restaurant of
the Admiral Hotel – good food, excellent
service and lovely surroundings. *Open 12–5*
and 7–10pm.

Fyrskibet, Nyhavn, **t** 33 11 19 33 (*expensive–*
moderate). The food is nice but you're here

for the location – on a lovely old red boat with wonky floors, near Nyhavn Bridge. *Open Mon–Sat 11.30–10.15.*

Cap Horn, Nyhavn 21, **t** 33 12 85 04 (*moderate*). One of the famous old-fashioned rustic restaurants in Nyhavn and one of the city's first eco restaurants. It's always busy – if you want to eat out, they provide heaters and blankets if necessary. *Open 11.30am–1am.*

Kamelspicehus, Sundevedsgade 4, **t** 33 25 32 41 (*moderate*). Offering eclectic Mediterranean cuisine, with leather chairs, wood-burning stoves, candlelight, live music and abstract paintings, this is a world away from the streets of Vesterbro outside. It has the reputation of being a place for price-conscious foodies. *Open Mon–Sat 5.30–midnight.*

Bacchus Vinbar & Bistro, Viktoriagade 8, **t** 33 22 67 97 (*moderate*). Down in a cellar, Bacchus has a unpretentious authentic bistro atmosphere. It offers 400 different wines, of which about 40 are available by the glass. Very good value for money. *Open Mon–Thurs 4pm–1am, Fri–Sat 4pm–2am.*

Bastionen & Løven, Voldgade 50, Christianshavn, **t** 32 95 09 40 (*moderate*). An old mill with a lovely garden – so romantic you might not feel you care about the food, which is good, so you get the best of both worlds. *Open daily 10–12am.*

Brasserie Degas, Jernbanegade 7, **t** 33 11 08 91 (*moderate*). Good traditional French food. *Open Fri–Sat 10am–3am, Sun–Thurs 10am–1am.*

Barcelona, Fælledvej 21, Nørrebro, **t** 35 35 76 11 (*moderate–inexpensive*). Spanish café with a tiny outdoor area and a good traditional French/Spanish restaurant on the first floor. There is also a small disco. *Open Sun–Wed 11am–2am, Thurs–Sat 11am–5am, Sun 11–10.*

Circus, Rosenvængets Allé 7, Østerbro, **t** 35 55 77 72 (*moderate–inexpensive*). This tiny restaurant has original 19th-century frescoes and offers excellent lunch food and a good-value dinner, with the intriguing Italian 'sushi' – fresh Italian ingredients made up Japanese style. *Open Mon–Thurs 10am–12am, Fri–Sat 10am–1am, closed Sun.*

Lo Stivale, Godthåbsvej 8, Frederiksberg, **t** 38 10 37 64 (*moderate–inexpensive*). An unpretentious place, and simply one of the best Italian restaurants in town. *Open Tues–Sat 5pm–12am.*

Restaurant Biblioteket, Toldbodgade 5, **t** 33 32 32 14 (*moderate–inexpensive*). Slightly off the beaten track, Restaurant Biblioteket (Library) is in a side street off Nyhavn and is less touristy and cheaper than most other places in the area. Good lunchtime sandwiches include tartar and smoked eel. *Open Mon–Sat 11.30–4, Thurs–Sat 6pm–10pm.*

Riz Raz, Kompagnistræde 20, **t** 33 15 05 75 (*inexpensive*). In the heart of the city, this lively restaurant specializes in Eastern Mediterranean cuisine. It is mainly known for its extensive cold and hot buffet. There is an impressive selection of beetroots, beans, lentils, rice, feta cheese, aubergines, olives, humous and falafel. Lots of people start here before a night out on the town. *Open daily 11.30am–12am.*

Kaffesalonen, Peblinge Dosseringen 6, **t** 35 35 12 19 (*inexpensive*). Stylish, with a great location near the water. Sip cocktails on the landing stage and look at the swans. *Open Mon–Fri 8am–12am, Sat–Sun 10am–midnight.*

Atlas Bar, Larsbjørnstræde 18, **t** 33 15 03 52 (*inexpensive*). This colourful basement bar-café-restaurant serves excellent 'world food' and is a favourite of the local trendies. It also offers several vegetarian meals and generous portions. *Open Mon–Sat 12–10.*

Bombay, Lavendelsstræde 11–13, **t** 33 93 92 98 (*inexpensive*). Good-value, mildly spicy food from northern India in a stylish but low-key setting. *Open daily 4–11pm, closed Mon.*

Kate's Joint, Blågårdsgade 12, Nørrebro, **t** 35 37 44 96 (*inexpensive*). A lovely, friendly, relaxed restaurant serving excellent world food (Indian-influenced) for a pittance. Music ranges from salsa to oriental ambient. *Open 5.30–11pm.*

Restaurant Tibet, Blågårdsplads 10, Nørrebro, **t** 35 36 85 05 (*inexpensive*). The only Tibetan restaurant in Denmark, serving traditional simple dishes at real value prices. *Open Tues–Sun 11–11.*

Entertainment and Nightlife

Nightlife in Copenhagen changes fast and starts late – things rarely get going until after midnight on Friday and Saturday night. The city has an ever-changing range of clubs, restaurants and bars catering to all tastes – cutting-edge dance music, world-class jazz, or pop. It also has several popular DJ/bar/restaurant 'hybrids' that change mood and function over the evening. There is no one defined nightlife area, although both Nyhavn and Boltens Gård are popular. Dress codes and admission prices are not strict.

There are late licensing hours in Copenhagen, with cafés typically open until 1 or 2am, bars until 2–5am and clubs until 5am. The minimum age for drinking is 18 and a beer will set you back 20–30kr, while a gin and tonic, on average, will cost 45–50kr.

Hotel Sankt Petri (*see* 'Where to Stay'). This stylish five-star hotel is a find – and not just for the super-rich. It positively welcomes punters from outside and you won't find a hushed, five-star-hotel palm-decked atmosphere here. If you are feeling broke, have one drink anyway and watch the world go by.

Copenhagen Jazzhouse, Niels Hemmingsensgade 10, t 33 15 26 00. A safe bet for a good night out, with live music and DJs. There is a well set-up bar upstairs and one of the city's largest dance floors downstairs – an institution in the city's nightlife. *Open Sun–Wed 6pm–12am, Thurs–Sat 6pm–5am.*

Møjo, Løngangstraede 21, t 33 11 64 65, booking t 23 44 97 77, *www.mojo.dk*. Tiny, cosy place known for its laid-back live jazz and blues every night. Book if you want to be certain of getting in.

Nasa, Boltens Gård, Gothersgade 8F, t 40 56 91 01. If you want to experience a celebrity hang-out, this is your place. It's seriously rich and posh; don't expect to get in without wearing your glad rags. Even then, you might not manage it – though girls will probably have an easier time of it than guys. *Open Fri–Sat 11pm–5am.* If you fail on the social/sartorial front, fear not – patronize one of the other clubs on the street, such as the **Zero Nightclub**, **Lounge**, or the **Blue**

Buddha. Otherwise one of the many lively Nyhavn bars will give you a good night out.

Rust, 8 Guldbergsgade, Nørrebro, t 35 24 52 00. Formerly a political café and rock club, Rust is one of Copenhagen's leading nightclubs and is usually in the forefront of musical trends. It features both live music (Thurs) and club nights. It has three main areas, a laid-back cocktail bar, a main bar (and concert venue) and a dance floor. More intimate than other rival clubs, it is popular with students and super-cool locals alike.

Ideal Bar, Vega, Enghavevej 40, Vesterbro, t 33 25 70 16. Housed in the same venue, Ideal Bar and Lille Vega are Copenhagen hot-spots with the hip and trendy. Typically, the spacious two-storey venue hosts house, Latin, rare-soul Djs and, once a month, the Vegatronic event: said to be the biggest and best electronic club in Scandinavia. *Open Wed–Thurs 6pm–2am, Fri–Sat 11pm–5am.*

Columbus, Nørrebrogade 22, t 35 37 00 51. Very good, lively French-Danish restaurant with a salsa disco on the first floor; popular with the Hispanic community of Copenhagen. *Open Thurs–Sat 5–11pm, disco until 5am.*

Pappa Hotel, Kalvebodspladsvej 19, Vesterbro, t 33 11 29 08. Pappa Hotel offers fast, simple food straight from the barbeque. It holds parties every weekend, and there are volleyball nets, a dance floor and other activities in the 6,000m² area. *Open 10pm–late.*

Sofiekælderen Overgaden Oven Vandet 32, Christianshavn, t 32 57 27 87. In a cellar by the romantic canals of Christianshavn, this is small, cosy bar-café-restaurant. Known for jazz in the '70s, it now favours hip-hop and urban beats. There is excellent live music on Thursdays. It won an award in 2003 as 'best concert venue' in Copenhagen. *Open Mon–Wed 4pm–12am, Thurs–Sat 4–3am, Sun 2pm–midnight.*

Latin Quarter, Nørrebrogade 22, t 35 37 00 51. All things to all people: a café by day, tasteful candlelit restaurant by night, and after 10pm you can dance the night away, Latin-style – including free salsa lessons – on the dance floor upstairs. *Open Mon–Wed 12–12, Thurs 12pm–3am, Fri–Sat 11am–5am, Sun 11–6pm.*

History

Copenhagen, on the far eastern side of Zealand, might seem a bit out on a limb, on the edge of Denmark, a mere 4.2km away from Sweden at its nearest point. However, in the period between 1380 and 1523 it was pretty central, as nearby Sweden and Norway were ruled by the Danish monarchy. Sweden ruled itself again from 1523, but Norway did not gain independence until the 19th century.

The earliest evidence of a town on this site dates from 1025, when there was a village called Havn on the island now known as Slotsholmen. In the 1160s, the king, Valdmar I, gave the village to Bishop Absalon of Roskilde, his adviser, as a thank-you for his political support and in 1167 the bishop began to build a castle to protect it from sea maurauders (remnants can be seen under Christiansborg Slot, *see* pp.246–7). At this time, Roskilde (*see* pp.259–63) was the most important town in Denmark, with a cathedral being built in which Danish monarchs have been buried ever since. Gradually, Havn (eventually Kømandshavn, meaning 'merchants' harbour') began to flourish as a trade centre. Although during the medieval period the town changed hands several times, it was crown property by 1417 and remained so. By this time, Absalon's castle (destroyed by the Hanseatic States in 1369) had been replaced, and in 1416 King Erik of Pomerania settled there. It became the official capital in 1443.

Much of Copenhagen today reflects the building enthusiasm of one of Denmark's much-loved kings, Christian IV (1588–1648). In power for 60 years, he showed a lack of talent in the area of foreign policy but was responsible for many of Copenhagen's Renaissance architectural gems, including Rosenborg Slot (*see* p.250), the Rundetårn Observatory (Round Tower, *see* pp.244–5) and the Børsen by the river, Europe's first stock exchange, as well as the canals. The Amalienborg (*see* p.252) was built in the 1760s by Frederik III (1648–70) and became the official royal residence in 1794.

Relatively little of Copenhagen's medieval past has survived as, inevitably, it suffered a couple of 'great fires', which destroyed one period of its architectural history, only to usher in a new one. The fires of 1728 and 1795 were responsible for razing large tracts of the town (the population already depleted by the plague in 1711, when 20,000 of its 60,000 inhabitants died), and thereafter, Britain must take responsibility for destroying much of the centre. This occurred in 1807 when, under the command of Horatio Nelson (who reputedly went shopping afterwards for a few knick-knacks for Lady Hamilton), the Navy bombarded the city to prevent it from falling into French hands during the Napoleonic Wars.

For a while, Denmark was financially up a gum tree. Going bankrupt in 1813, the Danes had to cede Norway to Sweden after more than 450 years, but gradually Copenhagen recovered and from 1830 to 1850 it slowly grew beyond the ramparts into the new working-class quarters such as Vesterbro, Nørrebro and Østerbro. Today the city is a vibrant mix of old and new, its past co-existing with the very latest trends in architecture, design and fashion.

Vesterbro and Tivoli

Vesterbro and Tivoli are the areas to the east and west of Central Station southwest of the centre. They both grew up during the 19th century, and in the 1970s Vesterbro

Danish Art and Design

Culturally, the Danes have much to offer. The architect and designer Arne Jacobsen has so influenced design that his new idiom of the 1960s seems almost unremarkable these days, and most children in the West have grown up with the fairytales of Hans Christian Andersen. Composer Carl Nielsen, writers Peter Høeg (*Miss Smilla's Feeling For Snow*) and Karen Blixen (*Out of Africa, Babette's Feast*), and the film-maker Lars von Trier (*Breaking the Waves, Dancer in the Dark*) and Dogme 95 (*Festen* – also staged as a play at the progressive Almeida theatre in London in 2004) are all relatively familiar names. Less well known, perhaps, but just as important are nuclear physicist Nils Bohr and the 16th-century astronomer Tycho Brahe, not to mention a great many artists, such as P.S. Krøyer, Michael and Anna Ancher and Asger Jorn, who deserve to be better known in popular culture outside their native Denmark.

was Copenhagen's red light district. Remnants of this past are still visible, with the odd stripper bar, but on the whole Vesterbro is on the up, and increasingly popular.

The **Bymuseum** (City Museum), Vesterbrogade 59, t 33 21 07 72, *www.bymuseum.dk* (*open May–Sept Wed–Mon 10–4; Oct–April Wed–Mon 1–4; closed Tues; film 11.15, 12.45, 2.45; adm*) is a good place to start your sightseeing. Apart from its strange concept of telling the city's story backwards, like peeling off the skins of an onion – which, frankly, is confusing – it is in interesting trawl through the history of Copenhagen, including a whole room (and 25min film) devoted to the writer and philosopher Søren Kierkegaard, who some people claim laid the foundations of existentialism. There is a nice café, too.

At the end of Vesterbrogade, you come to **Frederiksberg Have**, t 38 87 24 81, which contains the Frederiksberg palace. Although closed to the public (it is a military academy), it is a pretty building set in a nice park, with an unusual number of cranes walking the paths and a few fountains (a good place for a picnic). It is also next door to the **Zoo** at Roskildevej 32, t 72 200 280, *www.zoo.dk* (*open Mon–Fri 9–5, Sat, Sun and hols 9–6; adm*), a centre for the breeding of endangered animals, including tiny Golden Tamarinds. There is also a children's zoo, a zoo stage and thematic adventure trails, each of which presents animals from different parts of the world. To go back in the direction of Central Station up Vesterbrogade, hop on bus 6A, 14 or 15 on the opposite side of the road, just outside the zoo.

Just up from the zoo is the **Royal Copenhagen Porcelain Factory** at Smallegade 47, t 38 14 92 97 (*open for guided tours only, Mon–Fri, at 9, 10, 11, 1, and 2; adm*), where you can see potters and artists at work. In the opposite direction, the **Carlsberg Museum** at Valby Langgade 1, t 33 27 13 14 (*open Mon–Fri 10–4; adm free*), is one for beer buffs; the **visitor's centre**, Gamle Carlsbergvej 11, t 33 27 113 14, *www.carlsberg.com* (*open Tues–Sun 10–4*), is just around the corner and includes a complimentary drink.

At Gammel Kongevej 10, on the banks of the Skt. Jørgens Sø, a pretty stretch of water with swans, you will find the **Tycho Brahe Planetarium**, *www.tycho.dk* (*open Fri–Tues 10.30–8.30; Wed and Thurs 9.45–8.30pm; holidays 9.30–8.30; adm*), named after the astronomer who invented instruments that could accurately plot the sun's course. There is a permanent exhibition, the Active Universe, about natural science, astronomy and space travel, as well as a marvellous opportunity to sit back and watch the universe unfold across the 1000m² domed screen, which is also used to show 3-D IMAX movies on the natural world, screened every hour.

The **Tivoli Gardens**, Vesterbrogade 3, **t** 33 15 10 01, *www.tivoligardens.com* (*open May–Sept 11am–11/12pm/1am, depending on the day; adm*), inaugurated in 1843, have become a symbol of Copenhagen. If you are walking past, day or night, you would be forgiven for thinking mass murder was taking place – but the shrieks are simply those of punters having a jolly good scream as they whizz up and down and side to side on the rides, some of which take you to speeds of up to 70kph. Although criticised by some for its commercialism, Tivoli really is great fun and definitely worth a visit at night, when the fairy lights and the Chinese lanterns come on and everything looks magical (and on Wed and Sat there are firework displays at 11.45pm). It also offers theatre performances and concerts (book in advance), and side by side with the popcorn there are also a number of very good restaurants. The Danes love Tivoli and make up 73 per cent of its guests, and it has hosted a number of royal birthdays including the Queen's 60th in 2000. If you have a Copenhagen Card, you can enter free, even if you are not planning to take any of the rides. You can buy ride tickets individually, or as multi-ride tickets. From mid-November the gardens are open for the Christmas period, complete with 450, 000 fairy lights (all recycled; Tivoli is keen to be as eco-friendly as possible), 1,100 Christmas trees, 4½ tons of wood chips, 60 stalls, 136 Christmas elves, some rides, Santa (of course) and an outdoor skating rink.

On the northwest corner of Tivoli towards Central Station, you will see the tall tower-block **SAS Radisson Royal Hotel**, Hammerichsgade 1, **t** 33 42 60 00, **f** 33 42 61 00, originally designed by style guru Arne Jacobsen; if it's unoccupied, they will allow you to see Room 606, which retains its legendary 1960s design.

The **Dansk Design Center**, H.C. Andersens Boulevard 27–9, **t** 33 69 33 69, *www. ddc.dk* (*open Mon–Fri 10–5, Wed 10–9, Sat and Sun 11–4; adm*) is worth visiting for its permanent and temporary exhibitions on design, for which the Danes are famous. The five-storey, 80-million-kroner building was designed by the world-famous Danish architect Henning Larsen. Inside, the permanent exhibition encompasses both classic and contemporary design, mainly from Denmark, and there are constantly new temporary exhibitions; 'Seventy-five Years of Bang and Olufsen' and 'The Fascination of the Mercedes Design' are two recent examples. Guided tours of the exhibitions are offered every day of the week but should be booked in advance.

Also at this end of H.C Andersens Boulevard is the fabulous **Ny Carlsberg Glyptotek**, Dantes Plads 7, **t** 33 41 81 41, *www.glyptoteket* (*open Tues–Sun 10–4; adm, free Wed and Sun*), which no one should miss. The art collections are housed in four connected buildings, ranging from a grand 19th-century building with marble floors, coffered gilt ceilings and a lovely palm-filled Wintergarden to a modern French Wing, also designed by Henning Larsen, all of which are as much part of the aesthetic experience as the art itself. The collection concentrates on ancient art of the Mediterranean area and French and Danish art of the 19th and early 20th centuries. There are lovely sculpture galleries on the ground floor, including classicist art by pupils of Denmark's great sculptor Bertel Thorvaldsen (*see p.248*) alongside 35 works, including *The Kiss*, by the French sculptor Auguste Rodin. The French galleries take you from outdoor painted scenes by precursors of the Impressionists such as Courbet and Corot, through works by masters such as Monet, Sisley, Cézanne, Manet, Degas and Berthe Morisot, to the Post-Impressionists, including Van Gogh, Gauguin and Bonnard. Then there are the galleries of ancient art – don't miss the wonderful, atmospheric, state-of the-art Egyptian gallery, which has a good collection of mummies and sarcophagi. At the time of writing, Project 2006, a refurbishment programme, is under way, but you can still see a fine selection of the museum's collections housed in the modern French Wing. The whole museum will reopen on 28 June 2006.

Also in the Tivoli area, on the Rådhus Pladsen side, is the waxwork museum **Louis Tussaud**, H.C. Andersens Boulevard 22, **t** 45 33 11 89 00, *www.louistussauds.dk (open summer 10am–11pm; winter 10–6; adm)*. Louis was a nephew of dear Madame, and this museum is much like the museum in London, only smaller. Understandably given its location, it has a whole section on fairytales with tableaux from stories such as *The Sleeping Beauty* and *The Emperor's New Clothes*. It also has a Chamber of Horrors.

Opposite on the same road, just off the Rådhus Pladsen, you will see a large bronze statue of Hans Christian Andersen, pointing towards the Tivoli.

The **Rådhus**, or City Hall, is an early 20th-century building adorned with fantastical animals *(open Mon–Sat 9.30–3; free; guided tours Mon–Fri at 3, Sat at 10 and 11; adm)*. Inside, there is an elegant hall and you can climb the tower. Not included in the price of your guided tour is **Jens Olsen's World Clock, t** 33 66 25 82 *(open Mon–Fri 10–4, Sat 10–1; adm)*, which is probably the most interesting bit. The clock, which has 15,448 individual parts, was designed by Olsen, a watch- and instrument-maker born in Ribe in 1872. He planned the clock for 50 years and was finally given the money to construct it in 1943 (sadly, he died in 1945). It was set in motion in 1955. The clock is famous for its accuracy, losing just milliseconds each century. It shows local time, sidereal time (a time system linking the earth's motion to faraway stars), solar time, sunrise and sunset times, celestial pole movement and the movement of the planets.

Strøget and the Latin Quarter

Just west of Rådhus Pladsen is **Strøget** – five streets (Frederiksberggade, Nygade, Vimmelskaftet, Amagertorv and Østergade) that link the Rådhus square with Kongens Nytorv near the harbour. It was pedestrianized in 1962. West to east, it becomes progressively posher, starting with high-street chains such as H&M and Benetton, and ending with designer-label shops, such as Georg Jensen.

Along Strøget, the area just after Gammeltorv/Nytorv (Old and New Squares; the fountain shows *Caritas – Charity* – and dates from 1608) is the oldest in Copenhagen. The first two streets on the south side, Knabroestræde and Badstuestræde, were where butchers set up shop in 1377 until they moved their booths to Købmagergade in 1400; and Hyskenstræde (which means 'little house'), referred to as 'old' even in the 15th century, is thought to have been the site of a public lavatory in the 14th century.

A little further down Amagertorv on the north side is the **Helligånds Kirke** (Holy Ghost Church), Niels Hemmingsensgade 5, **t** 33 37 65 40 *www.helligaandskirken.dk (open Mon–Fri 12–4)*. A hospice stood on this site as early as 1296 and in 1474 was incorporated into an Augustinian monastery, which became a hospital after the Reformation in 1536. The present church is part of the old monastery building, which was extended, and the tower added in 1582. The spire dates from 1594. An international organ festival is held here on Fridays at 4.30 in summer. If you're lucky, they might have lit the whole place up with candles.

Almost opposite is the **Tobaksmuseet** (Tobacco Museum), Amagertorv 9, t 33 12 20 50 (*open Mon–Thurs 10–4, Fri 10–7, Sat 10–4; free*). Here, you will find pipes from all over the world, from primitive African ones to delicately carved meerschaums, including one the size of a needle.

Further down on the right, you will come to a family crowd-puller, the **Guinness World of Records Museum**, Østergade 16, t 33 32 31 31 (*open Jan– April Mon–Thurs 10–6, Fri–Sat 10–2; May daily 10–8; June–Aug daily 9.30am–10.30pm; Sept–Dec daily 10–6; adm*). This covers 13 galleries of the tallest, fastest, biggest, smallest, etc., and an activity room where you can pit yourself against Guinness world record holders.

The old university area, now often called the **Latin Quarter**, is north of Strøget and best reached either off Nytorv or heading down Købmagergade, past the department store Illum (with a lovely café at the top if you are in need of sustenance). The Latin Quarter is an individual, atmostpheric area with shops, museums and historic buildings which are much more interesting than most of those along Strøget.

You would have to be blind to miss the **Erotica Museum** at Købmagergade 24, t 33 12 03 46, f 33 12 03 18, *www.museumerotica.dk* (*open May–Sept 10am–11pm; Oct–April 10am–8pm; adm*). This pricey museum (and you can't use a Copenhagen Card) is not for the bashful. If you are curious, you will be faced with a world view of male anatomy on the first floor, including Indian lingums, miniature paintings and reproductions of fruity goings-on on Greek urns, followed by a quite interesting social history section on the story of prostitution in Copenhagen, and the love lives of Hollywood actors and actresses (someone here has a big interest in Marilyn Monroe). The third floor is devoted to the porn industry and some unedifying stuff that you will probably wish you hadn't seen – particularly in the 'Shock' video department.

The **Post and Tele Museum** further down at Købmagergade 37, t 33 41 09 00, *www.pt-museum.dk* (*open Tues–Sat 10–5, Wed 10–8, Sun 12–4*), is probably not of enormous interest, as everything is in Danish, but it has a nice rooftop café that is a bit of well-kept secret. A good place for lunch or a coffee, especially on a fine day.

On the same road, down on the right, is the **Rundetårn** or Round Tower, Købmagergade 52a, t 33 73 03 73, f 33 73 03 7 (*open Sept–May Mon–Sat 10–5, Sun 12–5; June–Aug Mon–Sat 10–8, Sun 12–8; adm; observatory open mid-Oct–Mar Tues–Wed 7pm–10pm; mid June–early Aug Sun 1–4; adm*). The Rundetårn is 34.8m high; it was built by Christian IV as an observatory in 1642 and used by the University of Copenhagen until 1861. The current observatory dates from 1928. You walk to the top up a 200m-long and 4.25m-wide cobbled spiral ramp (with steps for the last bit). In 1715, Tsar Peter of Russia rode his horse to the top, followed by his wife in her coach and six. In 1902 a car drove up and down for the first time. These days there is an annual, comic unicycle race, open to all ages – the winner must get to the top without touching the ground with his or her feet. (Incidentally, the reference to the biggest dog 'with eyes like towers' in Hans Christian Andersen's first fairytale, *The Tinderbox*, actually referred specifically to the circular Rundetårn, not just any tower.)

At the top, there are wonderful views of the city, which make the walk worthwhile. Halfway up (or down), pop into the 900m² 'Library'. This is above the vaults of the Trinitatis Kirke next door and was used as a university library between 1657 and 1861. It was reopened in 1987 and now hosts some lovely changing exhibitions of art, culture, history and science. It is also used as a concert hall and there are about 100 public concerts here every year.

The **Trinitatis Kirke** (1637–57) was started by Christian IV but finished by Frederik III. Although the roof and parts of the library were damaged in the fire of 1728, it remained undamaged in the 1795 fire and 1807 bombardment. The white interior is predominantly 18th-century with a richly Baroque altarpiece, pulpit and organ (all 1731, though only the front of the organ remains – the instrument was replaced in 1956) and a massive rococo clock dating from 1757 on the wall opposite the pulpit. The pew ends are decorated with carved sea shells and the ceiling is gilded.

Opposite the church is the **Regensen**, a student residence built, once again, by Christian IV, between 1618 and 1628. It is arranged around a courtyard (*open to the public*) and has a lime tree in the middle, planted by the warden on 12 May 1785. A yearly feast is held in honour of the tree and it has become a tradition that the students from Regensen manifest their 'ownership' of the Rundetårn by 'storming' it.

Slightly further west is the **Vor Frue Kirke** (formerly known as St Mary's Church), Copenhagen's light and airy cathedral where Crown Prince Frederick married Australian commoner Mary Donaldson on 14 May 2004. In this he followed in the footsteps of his forebears: Margrethe I, who was married in the original church in 1363 at the age of nine to the Norwegian King Haakon, and King Christian I and Queen Dorothea, who were crowned and married here in 1449. These days, with its 60m-high nave and galleries, it can seat over 1,100 people.

St Mary's Church was founded between 1190 and 1200 by Bishop Absalon of Roskilde and would thus have been a Gothic building (visit Roskilde cathedral to see what it might have been like, *see* pp.260–62). However, like much else in Copenhagen, it suffered badly in the 1728 fire and, although the chancel survived, it didn't last long when the British, who used the church's very tall spire as their sighting point, fired on the town on 5 September 1807 and set the entire building on fire.

The current, neoclassical building, completed in 1829, retains only the walls of the side aisles and the tower of the medieval building. It is 83m long and 33m wide, painted in beige and white, with modern 'downlighter' chandeliers and a large, modern chrome organ. The tower is 60m high and houses the four church bells (Stormklokken weighs 4 tons and is the largest bell in Denmark; the smallest bell in the tower, used at morning service, is the oldest bell in the country, dating from 1490 and taken from Antvorskov Klosterkirke). The 12 apostles (Judas replaced by St Paul) along the walls, the huge figure of Christ on the altar and the font, *John Preaches in the Desert* above the porch and *Christ's Entry into Jerusalem* above the doors, were all created by the sculptor Bertel Thorvaldsen (*see* p.248).

Famous Danes to have had their funeral services here include Hans Christian Andersen, Thorvaldsen and Søren Kirkegaard.

There is a small museum if you climb a spiral staircase behind the altar (you will have to go on to the altar to reach it), which is free but everything is in Danish.

Very near to the cathedral is **Sankt Petri Kirke**, Skt. Peders Stræde 2, **t** 33 13 38 33 (*open Tues–Sat 11–3*). This is a pretty, now mostly 19th-century church, although part of the 15th-century building can be seen facing Nørregade. A church has been on this site since the 12th century although the actual building has suffered through various fires and the 1807 bombardment. It has a vaulted sepulchral chapel (built 1681–83) containing ornate tombs and memorials.

Christiansborg and Around

The area around Christiansborg has a lot to offer, not least the fabulous **National Museet**, Ny Vestergade 10, **t** 33 13 44 11, *www.natmus.dk* (*open Tues–Sun 10–5*). As usual, the building is light and bright – no dusty nooks and crannies here – and the objects are displayed to great effect, with plenty of space around them, amazingly some not even under glass. The descriptions are good and also in English. On three floors, the main collections cover Danish history from prehistory to modern times (including period rooms laid out on the first floor; don't miss Room 117, the Renaissance bourgeois interior from Aalborg); a coin and medal collection; beautiful collections of ethnographic material; and Classical and Near Eastern antiquities (including the best collection of Roman swords in the world), as well as an interactive children's museum. Rooms 10 and 11 display seven oak-coffin burials from the Bronze Age, dating from c. 1400 BC, which were found in the same area of Jutland as Tollund and Grauballe Man (*see* pp.298 and 297). Of these, the most extraordinary are perhaps the Egtved grave, in which a young woman was buried with her clothes – very *Hiawatha* – made up of a string skirt, bodice, belt, dagger and hairnet (we know she was blonde), which have all survived, and another of a young man, complete with a full head of hair and earrings in his ears. The Iron-Age, silver *Gundestrup Cauldron* in Room 13, found in a peat bog and decorated with animals and mysterious figures (including the god Cernunnos), is another highlight. Note, too, what looks like a human sacrifice – a god holding a man over a cauldron (*see* p.297). As you wander through, you really feel the collection has been laid out for your own private enjoyment. There is also a nice gallery café and a small garden.

Down the road from the National Museet is **Christiansborg Slot**, on the island of Slotsholmen (across the Frederiksholms Kanal), where the first village of Havn was sited by the 11th century. Here, too, Copenhagen's first castle was built by its official founder Bishop Absalon. The current palace is the fourth one on the site, the last three all called Christiansborg. The first was destroyed in 1367 and the second demolished in 1731 by Christian IV, who built a Baroque palace in its stead. However, a fire destroyed everything but the stables in 1794 and a third building was built in neoclassical style between 1803 and 1828. Most of this was also destroyed by fire and the current palace, in neo-Baroque style, was built between 1907 and 1928. Parts of the neoclassical palace remain in the northern façade. The current palace houses the

Folketinget or state parliament, **t** 33 37 55 00, *www.folketing.dk* (*open June–Sept daily at 2pm; rest of year Sun 2pm; adm free*), the state rooms, *see* below (*open daily May–Sept; guided tours only, in English, at 11, 1 and 3; adm*), the Royal Stables and the Royal Library or **Kongelige Bibliotek** (*open Mon–Sat 8am–11pm*), *see* below. The Prime Minister's department and the High Court are housed here as well. The **Royal Stables** are the longest-surviving part of the castle, and the Queen's horses are still kept here in Classical splendour (*open Sat–Sun 2–4; adm*). A small **Teaterhistorisk Museum**, Christiansborg Ridebane 18, **t** 33 11 51 76 (*open Wed 2–4, Sat and Sun 12–4; adm*) is housed, appropriately, in the palace theatre dating from 1767. Costumes, scenography, set models, paintings, drawings and photos illustrate the history of the Danish theatre from the 18th century to the present. The public are admitted to the boxes, the stage and the old dressing rooms. You can also visit the **ruins** of the first two castles in the cellars of the current palace (*open May–Sept daily 9.30–3.30; Oct–April, Tues, Thurs, Sun 9.30–3.30*), which are atmospheric and well worth a look.

The guided tour of the **state apartments** lasts about an hour, when you will follow the 'dinner party route' followed by visiting dignitaries and learn, amongst other things, that Queen Margrethe has a flair for interior design and designed the red stair carpet herself. There are lots of portraits, lots of gilt, lots of stories, the throne room (the thrones haven't been used for a coronation since 1840 when the last king of Denmark was 'crowned'; Denmark has been a democracy since 1849 and all subsequent 'powerless' monarchs have been inaugurated by a proclamation given by the prime minister 24 hours after the death of the previous monarch), and some excellent modern tapestries depicting the history of Denmark by one Bjørn Nørgaard (given to the Queen for her 50th birthday), which include motifs such as Bob Dylan, Donald Duck and the Beatles. You will certainly be up on your Royal Danish genealogy by the time you emerge, and in no doubt of the fondness with which the Danes regard their Queen and her family (though by other accounts they are not too fond of her French husband, who hasn't learnt to speak Danish well, despite being fluent in several other languages).

Also on Slotsholmen are the **Royal Defence Museum**, Frederiksholms Kanal 29, **t** 33 11 60 37 (*open Tues–Sun 12–4; adm, under-15s free*), and the **Dansk Jødisk Museum** (Danish Jewish Museum), **t** 33 11 22 18 (*main entrance from the garden of the Royal Library, via Christians Brygge or Proviantpassagen by Christiansborg; open Tues–Fri 1–4, Sat and Sun 10–5, closed Mon*). The Dansk Jødisk Museum was inaugurated in June 2004 and is located in the oldest part of the Kongelige Bibliotek (Royal Library; originally it was the boathouse for Christian IV). The museum is spectacular and is the first one dedicated to minorities in Denmark. It presents Danish-Jewish culture, art and history extending back to the first Jewish immigration around 400 years ago. Its designer Daniel Libeskind (who also designed the Jewish Museum in Berlin) calls the Museum 'Mitzvah', the Hebrew word meaning good deeds, compassion and brotherly love. He regards this 'Mitzvah' partly as an expression of gratitude to the Danes for the rescue of Danish Jews in October 1943 and also as 'a forward-looking ethical reminder of brotherly love and peaceful co-existence'. All information is written in both Danish and English.

If you like 19th-century Danish sculpture, round the corner you will find the **Thorvaldsens Museum**, Bertel Thorvaldsens Plads 2, **t** 33 32 15 32, *www.thorvaldsens museum.dk* (*open Tues–Sun 10–5, closed Mon; adm, Wed free*). The museum contains almost all of Thorvaldsen's works (he created over 90 free-standing sculptures, just under 300 reliefs and more than 150 portrait busts), as well as his collection of art, his large collection of books, and some of his private possessions such as clothing, decorations, spectacles, snuff boxes, a flute and some of his tools. You can also see his tomb – he died in 1844 and his body was transferred from the cathedral to the courtyard of the museum when it opened in 1848.

Just on the waterfront, down from the palace, is the **Black Diamond**, Christians Brygge 1, **t** 33 47 47 47 (*open Mon–Sat 10–9*), the new, shiny black extension to the Kongelige Bibliotek opened in 1999, designed by the architects Schmidt, Hammer & Lassen. The downstairs exhibition area houses a variety of cultural historical exhibitions, the **National Museum of Photography** with about 25,000 photographic works of art from 1839 to the present, and the **Queen's Hall** where concerts and live music based on printed music from the library's own collections are performed. The Kongelige Bibliotek contains more than 4.5 million books, and is the largest book collection in Northern Europe – nip in if you are curious to see original manuscripts by Hans Christian Andersen, Karen Blixen and Søren Kirkegaard, among others. Just up from here, you will see a tall barley-sugar twist spire – actually three dragons entwined. This belongs to the **Børsen** or Royal Exchange, built by Christian IV between 1619 and 1640, and is 54m high. It is not open to the public.

If it's a hot summer's day and you need a dip, there is an open-air pool, the **Havnebadet,** close by in the harbour at Islands Brygge, opposite the Marriott Hotel (*open 1 June–31 Aug*), which opened in 2002 and is proving very popular.

On the other side of the Frederiksholms Kanal from the Børsen, you will see **Holmens Kirke**, which is the church of the Royal Navy and is another of Christian IV's building projects. Queen Margrethe got married here in 1967. Pop in and have a look at the carved 17th-century altarpiece, the baptismal font, made by Holmen's blacksmith in 1646, and Denmark's tallest pulpit (which reaches right to the roof). The external east portal was originally from Roskilde cathedral (*see* pp.260–62). Several famous Danes, such as the composer N.W. Gade, are buried in the chapel, built in 1705–8. If you continue northeast, you are going in the right direction for Nyhavn and the Amalienborg (*see* p.251).

The Botanical Gardens and Around

The area immediately north and northeast of the Latin Quarter is dominated by four really good museums, the botanical gardens and, parallel, Rosenborg Slot and its gardens. Altogether, it is a lovely green, cultured area and excellent for picnics.

The **Arbejdermuseet** (Workers Museum), Rømersgade 22, **t** 33 93 25 75, **f** 33 14 52 58 (*closed for refurbishment until August 2004; adm*), is housed in the original Workers' Building of the Danish workers' movement. Using very little text, the museum concentrates on setting up reconstructions of what life was like for the working classes between the end of the 19th century and the 1950s. There are four core exhibitions (as well as temporary exhibitions throughout the year); the People's Century is a traditional exhibit about the workers' movement and its fight for better living conditions. The others – 'The 1950s', 'Sørensen's flat' and 'Hard Times' – are reconstructions, allowing you to walk through a 1950s shopping street (when times weren't hard), visiting its shops and tasting some of their goods, and experiencing the harshness and lack of space in two working-class flats in 1915 and 1930 – two-room affairs lived in by families of eight or more.

On Gothersgade you will find the **Botanisk Have** (Botanical Gardens), Gothersgade 128, **t** 35 32 22 40 (*open summer 8.30–6, winter 8.30–4pm; adm free*), which are a green haven of peace and quiet with water features, bridges and lots of birds. The elegant glass palm house is modelled on the greenhouse at Kew and you can climb up the spiral staircase to look down on the hot, tropical foliage below. The **Geologisk Museum**, Øster Voldgade 5, **t** 35 32 23 45, *www.geological-museum.dk* (*open Tues–Sun 1–4; adm, free Wed*), can also be found in the grounds. At the palm house end of the gardens, across the road, is the wonderful **Kunstmuseum**, Denmark's national gallery, Sølvgade 48–50, **t** 33 74 84 84, **f** 33 74 84 04, *www.smk.dk* (*open Tues and Thurs–Sun 10–5; Wed 10–8; adm, free Wed*). This should be a must on everybody's schedule. The audio guide is good (and not expensive) and worth taking if you want to do more than just wander through. Alternatively there are free guided tours in English at weekends at 2pm (or you can book a private guide in advance, **t** 33 74 84 84).

Housed in two buildings linked by footbridges – one 19th-century, the other another lovely light, bright Danish glass affair – the museum collection spans international art from about 1400 to the present. Italian art is particularly well represented and features paintings by artists such as Lorenzo Monaco, Andrea Mantegna (one of the first artists to adopt elements and style from Classical Roman works; look at his famous *Christ as the Suffering Redeemer*), Filippino Lippi (*Joachim Meeting Anne outside the Golden Gate in Jerusalem*, the moment that the miracle of the Virgin's conception takes place; Lippi himself was the product of a 'holy union', his parents both being in holy orders at the time), and Lucca della Robbia, famous for his poly-chrome clay sculptures, particularly of the *Virgin and Child*. Other famous artists represented include the Dutch painters Rubens, Rembrandt and van Dyck.

The post-1900 collection is reached by a bridge over the glass-sided sculpture gallery and is also full of amazing stuff, including works by Munch, Picasso, Braque, Modigliani, Emil Nolde, Léger and Matisse – including the portrait of his wife from 1905 (also called the *The Green Line*), which shocked everyone who saw it and was considered an appalling *'fauve'* ('wild beast') of a painting, and which had great impli-cations for the development of artistic style, colour and intent. Overwhelmed though you might be by some of the 'greats' in the history of art, do not cut your time short and miss out on the Danish school and modern works such as Kurt Trampedech's extraordinary sculpture, *Morning* (1943), the sad bodies of Ejner Nielson, Svend Wiig Hansen's *The Earth Weeps* (1981) or Per Kirkeby's *Untitled* (*Winter Picture*, 1995). For those with children, there is also a **children's museum** (with a workshop). Groups must be booked in advance (**t** 33 74 84 84, Mon–Fri 10–2) but on Saturdays and Sundays there is a free guided tour for families, which can be followed by a session in an open workshop. If you need a rest, the museum café is a good place for lunch or coffee, decorated with the humorous designs of Lars Nørgård.

Around the corner, at Stockholmsgade 20, is the **Hirschsprungske Samling, t** 35 42 03 36, **f** 35 43 35 10, *www.hirschsprung.dk* (*open Wed–Mon 11–4; adm, free Wed and children free*), a nice little collection that is definitely worth a visit, especially if you have a Copenhagen Card. Housed in an charming 19th-century house, it displays 19th-century Danish portraits and landscapes, including paintings by the Skagen school (Danish Impressionists for want of a better description), with some lovely paintings by Anna and Michael Ancher and P.S. Krøyer in particular. If you are not planning a trip to Skagen (*see* pp.304–305), where there are many collections, this is a good place to introduce yourself to the works of these painters. If you have visited (or are going to visit) the Kunstmuseum, look out for the deathbed scene of Queen Sofie Amalies with her son by Kristian Zahrtmann (1843–1917), as there is another (equally disapproving) painting of the scene in this collection with which you can compare it.

Rosenborg Slot and the **King's Gardens** are a stone's throw from the museums at Øster Voldgade 4A, **t** 33 15 32 86, *www.rosenborg-slot.dk* (*open Nov–April Tues–Sat 11–2; May daily 10–4; June–Aug 10–5; Sept 10–4; Oct 11–3; adm*). This Dutch Renaissance *slot* (castle) was designed and built by Christian IV between 1606 and 1634 as a 'summerhouse' (it was in the countryside outside the town at the time), although he and subsequent monarchs used it as their main abode. He died here in 1648. From 1658, it was used as treasure of the realm, and since 1838 has been a museum of the history of the Danish royal family from Christian IV to Frederick III.

The castle, guarded by soldiers with guns (held upright in the crooks of their elbows, which makes them look somewhat nonchalant), has 24 rooms over three floors reached by spiral staircases, plus the treasury under the castle, where the crown jewels are kept. About half the rooms retain the decoration from Christian IV's time, with sumptuous wainscoting, painted ceilings and carved wood, and include his 'winter room', writing closet, bedroom and even a fully tiled blue-and-white Delft lavatory with an embossed ceiling. Buy an English guidebook, as there are no explanations in English.

The crown jewels are in the basement. Turn right out of the castle and right again by the first soldier; don't dawdle, as you will present a security hazard and be told to move along. The crown jewels are what crown jewels should be – big and sparkly – and you can get up very close to the cabinets to have a good look. Here you will be able to see the gold- and jewel-encrusted sword of state from 1551, Christian IV's crown (1596) smothered in diamonds, pearls and very delicate enamelled figures, the Crown of Absolutism from 1671, which has an 'I mean business' orb on top, and the Queen's crown, also dating from 1671. The rest of the collection – royal accessories including some very serious diamond necklaces, ceremonial saddles, swords, miniatures, etc. – is also impressive.

Across the park is the **Davids Samling**, Kronprinsessegade 30–32, **t** 33 73 49 49, *www.davidsmus.dk* (*open Tues and Thurs–Sun 1–4, Wed 10–4; free*), a small and charming decorative arts museum set up over four floors in an early 19th-century neoclassical house. The first floor displays Danish and English art and design from the

17th and 18th centuries; floor two has French furniture and china; the third floor is given over to English and German furniture, Meissen porcelain, lacquerwork and chinoiserie. It's like wandering through a very finely stocked stately home. The fourth floor is home to a very impressive Islamic collection – much of it on a par with the collection in the British Museum. Unfortunately not much is labelled in English; however, the bookshop has plenty of material at unbelievably reasonable prices.

Kongens Nytorv, Nyhavn, the Amalienborg and Beyond

Kongens Nytorv (King's New Square) is a large, elegant square at the bottom of Strøget. Originally just outside the medieval east gate of the city and the site of the town gallows, it was linked to Nyhavn (*see* below) by Frederick III, but not converted into the open neoclassical square that we see today until 1670 by Christian V (1646–99). He is commemorated in the centre by a **statue** (the original dated from 1688 but this is a copy). The square is illuminated during December and features a skating ring throughout the winter.

The **Royal Theatre** on the west side has stood on the same spot since 1749, although it has been rebuilt twice in 1773–4 and 1872–4. It stands next door to the **Charlottenborg**, Nyhavn 2 (*open Thurs–Tues 10–5, Wed 10–7*), built in 1672–83 by Frederick III's son Ulrik Frederik Gyldenløve, a very early example of Danish Baroque architecture. It has belonged to the Royal Academy since 1734 and has frequent temporary art exhibitions. One of Copenhagen's major department stores, **Magasin du Nord**, is also on the square as is the **Hotel d'Angleterre**, one of Copenhagen's oldest and most dignified hotels.

Kongens Nytorv issues on to **Nyhavn**, Copenhagen's now-popular, trendy canal area, which has plenty of places to eat and drink as you while away many a pleasant after-noon and evening. Now highly desirable, in days of yore this was a very dubious area, generally only catering to drunken and sex-starved sailors with a more limited budget.

The road itself, with 18th-century pastel-coloured houses on each side, and origi-nally with warehouses at the end, is divided in two by the canal where various yachts are moored. The canal was planned by Frederick III to allow ships to sail all the way up to Kongens Nytorv and enabled the merchants to build their homes directly by the water. It was completed in 1673.

The cafés, restaurants and bars are concentrated on the east side and bear names that relate to the canal's less gentrified past – Hong Kong, Cap Horn Skipperkroen (The Skipper's Inn), Havfruen (The Mermaid) and Hyttefadet (The Tank). Many stay open beyond midnight and provide blankets if you want to sit outside but are feeling a tad chilly.

Nyhavn also has strong links with Danish folk-hero Hans Christian Andersen (1805–75), who lived here on and off throughout his life and wrote his first fairytale, *The Tinder Box* (1835) at No.20 where he had moved a year earlier. In 1848, he moved into No.67, where he lived for 17 years before his landlords gave him notice, and then in 1871 he returned to live at No.18, where he lived until shortly before he died on 4 August 1875.

East of Nyhavn, you come to the **Amalienborg** (*open Jan–April Tues–Sun 11–4; May–Oct daily 10–4; Nov–17 Dec Tues–Sun 11–4*), Copenhagen's answer to Buckingham Palace. Unlike Buckingham Palace, the public are not kept away behind a gate and can walk straight into the central octagonal courtyard round which the four rococo Amalienborg palaces stand. The courtyard is cut by two perpendicular streets, of which the grandest leads from the harbour, at the time the main artery of Copenhagen, to the Marmorkirken (Marble Church).

The Amalienborg is the Queen's winter residence (she heads off to Fredensborg in summer, *see* p.264) and when she is in residence you can see the **changing of the guard** daily at noon. The guard leave the Rosenborg at 11.30 and walk through the streets. The **equestrian statue** in the middle depicts Frederik V, the founder of the Amalienborg Palace complex and the Frederiksstad area around it.

Although they look very similar from the outside, inside the palaces are very different. Amalienborg was originally conceived as town mansions for families of the nobility at the beginning of the 1750s. The royal family moved in (and the previous noble family residents moved out) in 1794, after the fire at Christiansborg Slot. Today, you can visit two of Amalienborg's palaces: Christian VIII's Palace, which has been partly turned into a museum of the Glücksburg dynasty; and Christian VII's Palace, which is used by the Queen to receive and entertain guests, but which is occasionally open for guided tours or special exhibitions.

The museum in Christian VIII's Palace is a continuation of the royal collections at Rosenborg Slot (*see* p.250) and houses exhibitions covering the period 1863–1972 spanning four generations of the Glücksburg line: Christian IX, Frederik VIII, Christian X and Frederik IX.

The central road axis running through the Amalienborg courtyard has the Marmorkirken at one end and the sea at the other (the new opera house can be seen on the opposite shore of Christianshavn). The **Marmorkirken** (Marble Church), Frederiksgade 4, **t** 33 15 01 44 (*open Mon, Tues and Thurs 10–5, Wed 10.30–6, Fri–Sun 12–5*), was planned as part of the 18th-century Amalienborg complex, although it was costing so much that plans were shelved for a while and the neo-Baroque church was not completed until 1849. Its copper-covered dome is one of the largest in Europe and has an internal diameter of 30m. The church interior is circular. For a view of the city, join a guided tour at 1pm or 3pm between 15 June and 31 Aug (*adm*) and climb to the top of the cupola (*closed apart from these times*).

From here head up to the Kunstindustrimuseet (Industry Museum), the Frinedsmuseet (Danish Resistance Museum) and, further up on Langelinie, *Den Lille Havfrue*, Copenhagen's *Little Mermaid*.

Housed in the 18th-century Frederiks Hospital, the **Kunstindustrimuseet**, Bredgade 68, **t** 33 18 56 56, **f** 33 18 56 66, *www.kunstindustrimuseet.dk* (*open Tues–Fri 10–4, Sat and Sun 12–4*), is Copenhagen's decorative art and design museum, which has a traditional permanent collection including Japanese, Chinese and European medieval and rococo arts and crafts as well as a major section on 20th- and 21st-century design. English labelling is limited. The modern section takes you chronologically through the history of Danish design, from the functionalism and Bauhaus concerns of the

1920s–40s and the sober simplicity and natural materials of the 1950s, to the brash, bright 'pop' colours of mass-designed plastics in the 1960s, and the wood, elegance and ecological concerns of the 1980s onwards. The emphasis is on the 'slowness of Danish design' – the quality and finish of the materials, the craftsmanship that gives it a meditative quality. Simple colanders, saucepans, toilet designs and some nasty-looking forceps sit side by side with Arne Jacobsen icons, Lego, eco-friendly furniture made out of recycled newspapers and corrugated cardboard, a transparent perspex baby grand piano and a 2001, chromium-plated steel and aluminium Harley Davidson – with not one fingerprint on it. At times, it is like wandering through an exceptionally cool and surprising designer furniture and lifestyle store.

In the same building, at Bredgade 62, is the medical history museum, **Medicinsk-Historisk Museum**, t 35 32 38 00, f 35 32 38 16, *www.mhm.ku.dk* (*open Wed–Fri and Sun, only with guided tours at 11 and 1, available in English in Aug*). This museum is worth visiting if you are a student of medical history, with over 80,000 artefacts dating from the 18th century to the present, as well as books and pictures, or – if you are into the grisly details of past medical practices – amputation tools, dental equipment, enema syringes, syphilis chairs and the faeces of a cholera patient (though, given the symptoms, anything solid would be unusual). Not for the squeamish.

The **Frinedsmuseet** (Danish Resistance Museum) is at Churchillparken 7, t 33 13 77 14, f 33 14 03 14, *www.natmus.dk* (*open May–mid-Sept; adm; free guided tours in English on Tues, Thurs and Sun at 2pm*). It's a fascinating and well laid-out museum illustrating the activities of the Danish resistance movement between 1940 and 1945, including sabotage, the underground press and the rescue of Danish Jews in 1943, as well as daily civilian life under German occupation. Full descriptions and interviews on film and audio make the period come alive and the risks people ran seem very real. There is some very affecting memorabilia from the concentration camps, sad goodbye letters written by soldiers who knew they were going into battle, and a chilling execution post. An outdoor café is open during the summer season.

North, along Langelinie, you come to the ***Little Mermaid***, created in 1913 by Edvard Erikson and paid for by the beer magnate Carlsberg. She is small and, unfortunately, a bit of a disappointment, even though she has become a PR symbol for Copenhagen. Further down, there is another statue, ***Gefion Springvandet*** (Gefion fountain) next door to the English church, St Alban's. Also financed in 1909 by Carlsberg, and created by Anders Bundgaard, *Gefion* is more arresting than the mermaid and depicts the goddess ploughing the land with four great bulls, having been told by the king of Sweden that she could keep any land that she managed to plough in a single night. Being a canny lass, she transformed her four strapping sons and ploughed up a great tract of Sweden. At dawn she picked it up (creating Lake Vänern) and flung it into the sea, where it became Zealand.

Christianshavn

Christianshavn lies south of the city on the island of Amager, which shows signs of being settled since the early Stone Age. It is also highly fertile, and in 1521 Christian II brought several Dutch market gardeners (who he thought were better than the

Danes) and their families to work there. In 1618, Christian IV decided to build a town at the north end of the island, so the engineer Johan Semb constructed a new part of town, Christianshavn, including a dam, on top of which the first 'Amagerbro' (the bridge, known today as Knippelsbro) was built to connect the two islands.

Christianshavn is a pretty area on the whole, especially around the canal and on Overgaden Neden Vandet ('upper street below the water') and Overgaden Oven Vandet ('upper street above the water'), where charming, multicoloured 17th-century houses jostle with a canal filled with barges and wooden sailboats.

Off the main road, Torvegade, on Amagergade, you will find one of the prettiest half-timbered houses at No.11, complete with a gallery. Not far away, just off Dronningensgade, you come to the landmark **Vor Frelsers Kirke**, Sankt Annaegade 29, **t** 32 57 27 98, *www.vorfrelserskirke.dk* (*open April–Aug 11–4.30; Sept–Mar 11–3.30, Sun 12–4.30; free; spire closed Nov–Mar; adm*), the Church of Our Saviour, built in 1682–96 by Lambert van Haven. The tower was not completed until 1752, when the king, Frederik V, climbed to the top (there are 400 steps, and it is 90m high), something his descendant Prince Joachim repeated in 1996 when the newly restored spire was rededicated. Inside there is a Baroque altar piece and an organ dating from 1700, with more than 4,000 pipes. The church's history has not been without upset: in 1721, its pastor, Pastor Trojel, was thrown in prison for life for criticising once too often the 'impious way of living' of King Frederik IV, who over the years had had a series of morganatic wives. The final taking of Anna Sophie Reventlow as his legal queen and wife only days after the death of his first queen, Louise of Mecklenburg-Güstrow, in 1721 was too much for the pastor, and proved his undoing. The church was also badly damaged in 1807 by the British who aimed (successfully) at its spire. N.F.S. Grundtvig, composor of many of Denmark's best-loved hymns, was pastor here from 1822 to 1826 until he fell out with the authorities who criticized his work for being too secular.

The other church definitely worth having a look at is the **Christianskirke** at Strandgade 1, **t** 32 96 83 01 (*open Mar–Oct 8–6; Nov–Feb 8–5*), built between 1755 and 1759 by the court architect, Niels 'Nicolai' Eigtved, for Frederik V, who was responsible for so many of Copenhagen's 18th-century buildings – including the Marmorkirken, the Amalienborg and the Frederiks Hospital (home to the design and medical museums, *see* pp. 252–3). Built in the rococo style, it puts you in mind of a theatre with the altar on the far wall and seating galleries on the remaining three sides. Royalty sit directly opposite the altar. The altar is surmounted by the pulpit, which is surmounted by the organ – a traditional arrangement in the Reformed Church. It has wonderful acoustics and hosts plenty of concerts. Downstairs in the crypt are 48 chapels where the great and the good were interred. This was Eigtved's last project; he died a year later. N.F.S. Grundtvig (*see* above) preached here between 1832 and 1839.

Christiania is another – far more modern – interesting place to visit in Christianshavn, although it may not be everyone's cup of tea. Thirty-plus years ago, in 1970, in the aftermath of the 1968 riots, a group of people got together to create an area where they could live an alternative lifestyle. The police tried to move them on but there were so many people that it became a political issue which ended up in

Parliament. Eventually Christiania agreed to pay for the use of water and electricity, and in return receive political acceptance as a 'social experiment'. The experiment was to continue until a competition of suggestions for the use of the area could be arranged. In 1973, the government changed and wanted to clear the area and close it down. Since then, the government and the inhabitants of Christiania have had a love-hate relationship and the community is still under threat. There is nothing much to see here but people come to look for evidence of its 'free' status and to hang out and/or buy soft drugs. Despite soft drugs being illegal in Denmark, you can buy them openly at stalls along Pusher Street. Hard drugs are strictly *verboteno*. However, be warned that, even if they turn a blind eye in Christiania, the police have every right to arrest users, regardless of where they have bought their gear.

Day Trips from Copenhagen

Arken

Skovej 100, Ishøj, t 43 54 02 22, f 43 54 05 02, www.arken.dk; take the train to Ishoj and then the 28 bus – the walk is signposted and takes 30–40mins; open Thurs–Tues 10–5, Wed 10–9; adm.

Arken, 17km south of Copenhagen, is a marvellous ship-like modern art museum on sand dunes overlooking the sea that you should visit as much for its innovative architecture, designed by Danish architect Søren Robert Lund, as for its exhibitions. It is a fairly small space and has a permanent, rotating collection of pictures, sculptures and installations, and it also presents excellent temporary exhibitions, most recently one on Picasso.

Take a break in the delicious café (*moderate–inexpensive*), but go upstairs from the shop area so that you can take advantage of the sea view.

Helsingør

Helsingør, a harbour town about 60km away Copenhagen, chiefly lays hold on the imagination because of **Kronborg Slot**, more widely known as Elsinore, home to Shakespeare's *Hamlet*.

A mere 4.2km across the Sound from Sweden, the town has medieval roots and has played a major role in Danish trading history. Until about 1230, the Sound was a major source of herring (which then suddenly disappeared into the Baltic) and then, from 1429, became a source of serious cash when King Erik of Pomerania introduced the 'Sound Dues' – a fee for all boats passing to and from the Baltic. If you didn't pay in money, you could pay in cattle – a regular 'cash cow', so to speak. The Sound Dues were a major (and much resented) source of revenue until 1857, when they were abolished. King Erik also established the town as an important ecclesiastical centre, helping to found three monasteries here.

Getting There

Take the train to Helsingør from Copenhagen Central Station. They run every 20mins and the journey takes about 50mins.
From Helsingør train station, it is approximately 15 minutes on foot to Kronborg. Follow the harbour front until you see the castle.

Tourist Information

Helsingør: The tourist office is opposite the train station, t 49 21 13 33, *www. helsingorturist.dk (open June–Aug Mon–Sat 9–7, Sun 9–noon; Sept–May Mon–Fri 9–5, Sat 9–1).*

Markets
Wed, Fri and Sat am, on Axeltorv.

Eating Out

There are plenty of options for a bite to eat, not least an open sandwich and a beer in one of the pubs on the town square (*inexpensive*). Other options include:

Kronborg Havbad, Strandpromenaden 6, t 49 20 13 30 (*moderate*). This restaurant serves traditional Danish dishes and has a large, attractive terrace overlooking the marina.

Restaurant Brohuset, t 49 21 64 81 (*moderate–inexpensive*). Situated in the grounds of the castle on the bridge as you approach, this provides a very easy and pretty option.

Anno 1880, Kongensgade 6, t 49 21 54 80 (*moderate–inexpensive*). A charming rustic building with a pretty garden where you can eat traditional Danish fare outside.

Amici Miei, Stengade 15, t 49 26 26 71 (*moderate–inexpensive*). A pleasant Italian restaurant with outdoor tables.

Kronborg Slot

t 49 21 30 78, www.kronborgcastle.com; open May–Sept daily 10.30–5; Oct Tues–Sun 11–4; Nov–Mar Tues–Sun 11–3; April Tues–Sun 11–4. Coastal batteries open all year dawn to dusk.

This Dutch Renaissance castle with its copper-roofed spires and cannons overlooking the Sound is reached along the coastal road. You enter across a deep moat.

On your way in, you may come across an embarrassed-looking Hamlet, book in hand, and his Ophelia – a tourist gimmick probably best forgotten, although the *Hamlet* exhibition inside is quite interesting. Shakespeare's unhappy and confused prince did not actually exist (although there is a Prince Amleth lurking in Danish history around the year 800), but Shakespeare really did know a thing or two about the castle and the people who lived here; the short-lived emissaries, Rosencrantz and Guildenstern, for example, are local family names, and there was a gravedigger at the castle called Johann ('Go, get thee to Yaughan: fetch me a stoup of liquor.' Act V, Sc. 1). It is known that several English and Scottish actors from Shakespeare's circle performed as guest actors, both at Kronborg and in the town, and they may have provided the inspiration for his setting. The town was also a major trading post, so he may also have received information from sailors.

Erik of Pomerania built the first castle, which was called Krogen, on the site in 1420 as a strategic fortress, at the seaward approach to the Sound, where Kronborg is now located. It consisted of a number of buildings inside a surrounding wall. This first castle was transformed by Frederik II into a Renaissance palace between 1574 and 1585. It was renamed Kronborg but it was destroyed by fire in 1629, leaving only the chapel intact. Christian IV had rebuilt it by 1639. However, in 1658 it was commandeered by the Swedes, who pillaged the castle and the town. They left in 1660 and thereafter Kronborg was refortified and the Crownwork, an advanced line of defence, and a new series of ramparts around it were added. After its completion, Kronborg was the strongest fortress in Europe.

Kronborg ceased to be a royal residence in the 17th century and became a prison and then, from 1785 until 1922, an army barracks. Since then it has undergone extensive work and has been restored to look as it did during the reigns of Frederik II and Christian IV. In 2000, it joined ranks with the Egyptian pyramids and the Acropolis in being awarded UNESCO World Heritage status.

The apartments are not very well labelled; you will get more information from one of the guided tours available during the day. At 62m by 11m, Christian IV's massive ballroom is one of the largest in Europe – and it was here that theatre performances, including some by the English actors from the Globe theatre, took place. Look out, too, for the 'Queen's door' on one side – the keyholes on both sides don't match up so that no one could peek through at her. The tapestries originally represented 100 fictional and historical monarchs of Denmark. All but 15 have been destroyed – the remaining eight can be seen in the National Museet (*see* p.246). The courtyard is where international dance and theatre performances of *Hamlet* are staged. The first took place in 1937 and starred Laurence Olivier and Vivien Leigh. They fell in love here and subsequently got married. Richard Burton, John Gielgud and Kenneth Branagh have also all performed the role here.

In the courtyard, the hooks are where hunters hung up deer and other game for the kitchens. Across the courtyard, don't miss the dank and gloomy underground Casemates where, at one time, hundreds of soldiers were stationed, complete with kitchens, stables, brewery, etc., but in an area at one time used for prisoners. Here, you will also see the statue of the legendary hero Holger Danske who, like King Arthur, sleeps until his country needs him when he will awake to save it from peril. Interestingly, one of the resistance groups against the Germans during the Second World War took his name.

Helsingør Town

Other attractions in Helsingør include the Bymuseum, the Vinmusem and the Tekniksmuseum. The **Bymuseum**, Karmelitehuset, Sankt Anna Gade 36, **t** 49 28 18 00 (*open daily 12–4*), the city museum, is in a lovely old Carmelite convent dating back to 1516, and displays the history of the Sound Dues and the city's trading life. The **Vinmuseum**, Strandgade 93, **t** 49, 21 09 29, is situated in a wine vault founded in 1760. The **Tekniskmuseum**, Fabriksvej 25, **t** 49 22 26 11, *www.tekniskmuseum.dk* (*open all year Tues–Sun 10–5; June 21 –2 Aug also open Mon*) has an impressive collection of steam engines, inventions, electrical appliances, bicycles, cars and over 30 aeroplanes ranging from gyroplanes to helicopters and DC-7s and 8s. It also has the 1906 flying machine belonging to the pioneer J.C. Ellehammer, who the Danes claim was the first man to fly in 1906, although it was never internationally recorded.

Take your time wandering around the old quarter, especially along Strandgade and the streets off to the right – on Odernesgade, No.66 dates from 1459, and Nos.70, 72, and 74 are all 16th-century late Gothic. No.76 is in the Renaissance style and dates from 1579, while No.64, dating from 1739, is in the ornate Baroque style.

The newly restored **cathedral**, Sankt Olai Domkirke in Sankt Anna Gade 12, *www. helsingordomkirke.dk (open May–Aug 10–5; Sept–April 10–2)*, was founded in 1200 but completed in the 16th century. It is home to some lovely church furniture, including a huge altar (1664), which is over 11m high. Don't leave without having a look at the baptismal chapel where there is a 'black board' on which parishioners were named and shamed if they committed *faux-pas* in church.

Louisiana, the Karen Blixen Museum and Bakken

Louisiana

Gammel Strandvej 13, Humlebæk, t 49 19 07 19, www.louisiana.dk; open Thurs–Tues 10–5, Wed 10–10; adm.

This impressive modern art museum is set in romantic green, sculpture-scattered gardens overlooking the sea. The collection ranges from early Danish modernism, the works of the CoBrA group, through to European and American art of today. Artists include giants such as Francis Bacon, Jean Dubuffet, Pablo Picasso, Henry Moore, Alberto Giacommetti (amazing rooms of startling elongated figures), Asger Jorn, Carl

---

Getting There

These three are all stops on the **train** line to Helsingør, so can be mixed and matched on a day trip if you prefer. In order of train stops, Klampenborg is home to Bakken Amusement Park, the Karen Blixen Museum is at Rungsted Kyst and, three stops on, Humlebæk gives you Louisiana. For a day trip, visit Louisiana first and work backwards.

Louisiana

Take the S-train, direction Helsingør, from Copenhagen Central and alight at Humlebæk. The journey takes 40mins and trains run at 20min intervals. The museum is a 20min walk from the station.

Karen Blixen Museum

As above, but get off at Rungsted Kyst. The journey takes about 30mins. Or, if coming from Louisiana, it's a 10min ride on the Copenhagen train. From the station, it's a 15–20min walk (signposted), or take bus 388.

Bakken

From Copenhagen, as above. Get off, 20 minutes later, at Klampenborg. If you are coming from the Karen Blixen Museum, pick up the Copenhagen train – it is a 12min journey – or take the 388 bus from Rungsted station. From the station, it is a 7min walk through the deer park to Bakken. The final train leaves at 12.20am to allow people to return to Copenhagen after the park shuts.

Eating Out

Your best bet at Louisiana and the Karen Blixen Museum is either to take a picnic and have it in the grounds, which are lovely on a sunny day, or eat at either of the museum cafés, which are both very nice and serve up sandwiches, tea, cakes, etc.

At Bakken, there is a wealth of very unhealthy and totally appropriate fairground fare, as well as sit-down restaurants and bars.

Henning Pederson, Per Kirkeby, Roy Lichtenstein, Ellsworth Kelly and Josef Albers, to name a few. There is also a children's wing where activities are arranged for 4–16-year-olds, although all are welcome. There are workshops (2–4pm) at weekends and family guided tours every Sunday at 11am. Ring for information.

Karen Blixen Museum

Rungstedlund, Rungsted Strandvej 111, Rungsted Kyst, t 45 57 10 57,
f 45 57 10 58, www.karen-blixen.dk adm; open May–Sept Tues–Sat 10–5;
Oct–April Wed–Fri 1–4, Sat–Sun 11–4.

Out of Africa author Karen Blixen (Isak Dinesen) grew up here from her birth in 1885 and lived here again on her return from Africa (1914–31), until she died in 1962. Her rooms are almost exactly as they were when she lived here – some of the furniture came from her farm outside Nairobi, including Denys Finch Hatton's favourite chair and the chest that her steward, Farah, gave her. There is an exhibition of her paintings and another on her life, including essays, poems, letters and drawings from her child-hood and an interesting slideshow of her life in Africa. There are also recordings of Blixen reading her own stories. Outside, there are 14 acres of land, comprising a garden and grove, which is maintained as a bird sanctuary and is open all day. Karen Blixen is buried in the grove under the large beech tree at the foot of 'Ewald's Hill'.

Bakken Amusement Park

Dyrehavevej 62, Klampenborg, t 39 63 73 00, www.bakken.dk;
open April–Aug daily 1pm–12am; free.

Bakken is the world's oldest amusement park; a fun-park of one sort or another has been on this site since the 16th century. Rollercoasters (prepare to scream – if people scream loud enough, they often extend the ride), merry-go-rounds, waltzers, ghost-trains, hot dogs – the usual thing but great fun and very popular with the locals. The park is on the edge of Dyrehaven (deer park), which is a nice picnic spot. Bakken is closely involved with the park and closes in late August to avoid disrupting the mating season; it gives all proceeds to its upkeep and prohibits cars – you can only use bikes and horse-drawn carriages (*180kr for half an hour – make a fuss if you get a 'little half-hour'*).

Roskilde

Founded by Harald Bluetooth in the 990s, Roskilde is an older town than Copenhagen and was much more important for centuries. The many barrows in the area indicate that it was densely populated. It grew rapidly and by the Middle Ages was considered one of the biggest and most important cities in northern Europe, with a population of 5,000 to 10,000 people. It has been called Denmark's first capital city and was an important centre for both the Crown and the Catholic Church, which

Getting There

Take the train to Roskilde from Copenhagen Central Station. They run regularly, and the journey takes about 25mins.

Tourist Information

Roskilde: Gullandsstraede 15, t 46 31 65 65, f 46 31 65 69, www.visitroskilde.com (open 23 Aug–Mar Mon–Thurs 9–5, Fri 9–4; April–27 June Mon–Fri 9–5, Sat 10–1; 28 June–22 Aug Mon–Fri 9–6, Sat 10–2).

Festivals

In the first week of July, Roskilde holds a massive rock festival – the largest in northern Europe. Artists have included Blur, Suede, the Beastie Boys, Björk, Oasis, David Bowie, Bob Dylan, Paul Simon and Eric Clapton. Camping is free if you have a ticket for the festival; information from www.roskilde-festival.dk.

Eating Out

Rådhuspladsenkeldern (*moderate*). Just by the Domkirke, this underground cellar is lovely, serves traditional Danish food from marinated herrings to smoked haunch of venison, and has a nice courtyard for eating out in summer.

Snekker Café (*moderate*). This café/restaurant is part of the Viking Ship Museum complex and is housed in the big black cube building as you come in. It has an attractive modern interior with an open kitchen and the restaurant area looks over the harbour. The food is good; the café serves Mediterranean-style food, and you can get Danish cuisine in the restaurant.

established it as a bishopric in 1020 – soon afterwards the town was also home to 14 parish churches and five convents and monasteries alongside the cathedral.

Roskilde retains a charming market town atmosphere (although it is home to several major companies and over 52,000 inhabitants) and is pleasant to wander through. Its main claims to fame are its cathedral and the Viking Ship Museum, both of which should be musts on anyone's intinerary. Get a town map at the station, as this shows you a pretty route down narrow streets and across grassy meadows from the Domkirke (cathedral) to the museum near the harbour.

The Domkirke

Domkirkepladsen, t 46 31 65 65, www.roskildedomkirke.dk; open April–Sept Mon–Fri 9–4.45, Sat 9–12, Sun 12.30–4.45; Oct–Mar Tues–Sat 10–3.45, Sun 12.30–3.45; adm; English tours (fee), summer Mon–Fr 11am and 2pm, Sat 11am, Sun 2pm.

The Domkirke was begun in the 1170s by Bishop Absalon (founder of Copenhagen). Since then additions have been made, but it has generally survived the curse of fire and represents 800 years of architectural history; if you walk around the cathedral, you can see the changing styles. Since the 15th century it has been the preferred burial place for the monarchy – there are 39 royal sepulchral tombs dating from Margrethe I to the present.

The first church was built here by the wonderfully named Harald Bluetooth in the 900s. This was then replaced by a stone church in the 11th century by King Canute's sister Estrid. Another stone church may have existed before the brick cathedral was begun in the 12th century, commissioned by Bishop Absalon. The art of brick-burning was new in Denmark at that time and the cathedral is one of the earliest examples of a brick construction. It was completed in the 13th century, but along the way Absalon's design was altered by his successor Peder Sunesøn, who was familiar with Paris and the new, exciting French Gothic style. Roskilde was one of the first places to adopt the new style outside Paris.

When you come into the church through the southwest porch, you walk directly into the nave into a white, light space with bare-brick columns, medieval frescoes and Renaissance elements, such as the ornate pulpit, organ, altar and royal pews, all dating from the time of Christian IV. The latter were added to suit the Protestant service in which the sermon had become crucial – before this, the nave had no pulpit or pews, just side altars where priests said masses for the dead. As you come in, don't miss the 24-hour mechanical clock around the corner from the chapel on your right. It dates from the late 15th century and, when it strikes the hour, St George kills the dragon, which then lets out a terrible wail. Further down the nave are lovely medieval frescoes that were originally part of Catholic chapels (of which, in the early 16th century, there were some 75); none of these exists now. More frescoes can be found, notably in the **Chapel of the Magi** (also called Christian I's chapel) on the south side of the nave and the **Chapels of St Birgitte and St Andrew**, next door to each other on the north side. The Chapel of the Magi dates from 1462 and the frescoes illustrate the life of Christ, saints and Judgement Day. The frescoes in the chapels opposite date from 1511. St Andrew's chapel contains a large image of the death of John the Baptist, while St Birgitte's shows the fathers of the church – Augustine, Hieronymous, Gregory and Ambrosius – as well as several more saints, including Birgitte sitting on a dragon with Pope Lucius, the cathedral's patron saint. Don't miss the small green devil in St Birgitte's chapel, who sits in a corner with his ink well and large pen to write down the names of those who come in late or are gossiping. The oldest frescoes are at the east (altar) end, which is the oldest part of the cathedral.

The cathedral is famous for the many tombs, sarcophagi and memorial tablets that can be found on its walls and floors – the oldest are in St Birgitte's chapel, dating from about 1250 (and brought in at some point from the cemetery outside). Behind the chancel, the narrow black tombstone is said to be that of a three-legged 'ghost horse' with coal-red eyes. Seeing it does not apparently bode well for your future health; in the past, people used to spit on it as they passed.

Royal burials took place here after the Reformation in 1536, but there are nonetheless some important medieval royal graves. These are in the walls of the chancel and are marked by Renaissance frescoes. They belong to Estrid (founder of the first stone church), her son Svend Estridson (d. 1074) and his close friend Bishop Vilhelm. Harald Bluetooth is thought to have been buried in the original wooden church in 986 and is also represented, although his tomb is not here.

In the west corner, you can see the sarcophagus of Denmark's only other reigning queen, Margrethe I (d. 1412), whose body was transferred here from Søro Abbey in 1423. Her tomb has been damaged and many of the figures are restored; some of the original figures can be seen in the cathedral museum. Just behind her is her brother

Duke Christopher (d. 1368). Chronologically the next tomb after that is Christian I's Chapel (d. 1481) (*see above*), which was designed as a sepulchral monument so you cannot see his tomb below the floor. The enormous Renaissance sepulchres you see here belong to Christian III (d. 1559) and Frederick II (d. 1588). The chapel's middle column is called the kings' column because the heights of royal visitors have been marked on it through the years. The tallest to date is Christian I himself, who apparently stood at 2.195m; the smallest is Christian VII (1.641m), smaller even than Chulalongkorn of Thailand who was 1.654m tall. Its base dates from the 12th century and has a Romanesque hand-carved frieze of palmettes.

Christian IV's chapel (d. 1648) is the first post-Reformation royal sepulchre and can be found on the north side just before the altar. Alongside Christian IV are several more members of his family. The tombs of absolute monarchy – those of Christian V (d. 1699) and Frederik IV (d. 1730) and their queens – are to be found in the chancel behind the altar. Styles change as you reach Frederik V's chapel (d. 1766), opposite that of Christian IV. Neoclassicism is the order of the day and the king is buried in a classically inspired sarcophagus with the female figures of Norway and Denmark weeping on either side. Twelve other sepulchres in varying styles are also in this chapel. The most recent sepulchre, the Glücksberger Chapel, dates from 1924 and is on the north side of the cathedral. It holds three royal couples. However, the most recent, Frederik IX (d. 1972) and his wife Ingrid are buried outside at the request of the royal family.

The Viking Ship Museum

Vinderbode 12, t 46 0 02 00 www.vvikingesskibsmuseet.dk; open daily 10–5; adm; boat trips 30kr/50kr.

This fabulous museum brings the Vikings vividly to life and could easily take up your whole day, especially if you watch or take part in various Viking craft demonstrations and workshops, or talk with the artisans and wainwrights working in the museum. You can also sail in a Viking ship replica (*May–June, weekends and hols only; 19 June–3 Sept daily; duration 50mins*), taking a turn with the oars and helping with the sail. Ask about activities at the information desk.

Housed in a gorgeous glass-fronted building right on the water (opened in 1969 and in 1997 designated a listed building), the core of the collection is the five Viking boats that were dredged up from Roskilde Fjord in 1962. These five boats are all of different types (what a haul for the archaeologists!) and appear to have been deliberately scuttled in the late 11th century, near Skuldevej, 20km north of Roskilde, to act as a barrier to protect the harbour from invasion.

They have been lovingly restored and several of them have been recreated with authentic tools and materials in the boatyard next door to the museum. The most recent is the largest, *Skunkdelev 2*, a great 10m-long longship, designed for a crew of 70 to 80 men. It will be launched in September 2004 and plans are afoot for a maiden voyage to Dublin where the original was made in 1042–3.

The museum exhibits are very well explained and laid out (don't miss the video explaining how the boats were put together). There are five special exhibitions telling amazing stories of the Vikings and their ships, including a thrilling, hour-by-hour reconstruction of a Viking attack and an exhibition on the Vikings in Ireland. For children (aged 9–90) there is also the opportunity to dress up in Viking clothes, write in runes and stand on board a Viking ship model in the museum, taking a closer look and handling rope, trading goods and weaponry. And if you have the habit of falling in love with difficult people, take heed of some heartfelt Viking advice (I think we can now assume it to be for either sex):

To love a woman whose ways are false
Is like sledding over slippery ice
With unshod horses out of control,
Badly trained two-year-olds,
Or drifting rudderless on a rough sea
Or catching a reindeer with a crippled hand
On a thawing hillside: think not to do it!

The museum shop has the usual nice stuff – jewellery, clothing, books, ceramics – and, taking its theme very seriously, rabbit skins (a mere 45kr) and cows' horns (120kr).

Frederiksborg and Fredensborg

Frederiksborg Slot

Hillerød, t 48 26 04 39, www.frederiksborgmuseet.dk; open April–Oct 10–5, Nov–Mar 11–3; adm.

Your imagination will be caught the moment you walk over the cobbles, past the fountain and inside this lovely, fairytale Renaissance castle with its copper spires and

Getting There

For **Frederiksborg**, take the train to Hillerød from Copenhagen Central Station. They run at 20min intervals; the journey takes about 40mins. For **Fredensborg** from Hillerød, take the local Helsingør train, which runs every 30mins and takes about 10mins, or take a taxi. From Copenhagen, either take the S-train to Hillerød and go from there as above, or take the regional train to Helsingør and then the same local line towards Hundested, which will take about 20mins.

Tourist Information

Hillerød: *Møllestraede 9, t 48 24 02 00, f 48 24 02 62, www.hillerodturist.dk (open Mon–Fri 10–5, Sat 10–1)*

Fredensborg: *Slotsgade 2, t 48 48 21 00 (open April Mon–Fr 12–5; May–mid-Aug daily, Sat–Sun 12–4; closed Nov–Mar).*

Eating Out

Frederiksborg

There are plenty of places to eat. Try **Brasserie Kong Christian**, Slotsgade 59, t 48 24 53 50, for a hearty lunch.

Fredensborg

There are three nice café restaurants on Jernbanegade. Otherwise there are lots of places to choose from.
Restaurant Skipperhuset, Skipperallé 6, t 48 48 17 17. Home-made lunches and supper at a pretty location on the lake near the castle.

formal garden overlooking the lake. Buy the guide, as labelling is spartan and you will want to know a bit more about the 60 or so rooms open to the public. Built by Christian IV (1588–1648), Frederiksborg has, inevitably, had its fair share of fires and some of the rooms have been reconstructed but this does not detract from its appeal.

Highlights are the 'Rose' or Knights' Room, an ornate low-ceilinged dining room decorated with gilt-leather, a stuccoed ceiling and five marble columns; the exuberant Baroque chapel with its galleries, royal loggias and festoons of cherubs and fruit; and the Great Hall with its minstrels' gallery and amazingly ornate walls and ceiling. If you like Renaissance furniture and portraits, this is the place for you (look out for the curious 'his-and-hers' changing portrait of Frederick I and his wife just past Room 49).

The castle houses the **Museum of National History**, Denmark's national portrait gallery. On the third floor is the modern collection concentrating on the 20th and 21st centuries, including some Andy Warhol prints of Margrethe II.

Fredensborg Slot

Open July daily 1–5; adm; guided tours only (last tour 4.30);
no advance booking; gardens open all year, daily from sunrise to sunset.

Five miles north is the 18th-century palace of Fredensborg, summer home to the Queen and the permanent pad (in the 'annexe') for Crown Prince Frederik and Princess Mary Donaldson. It was not until the 19th century that the palace became the setting for the life of the royal family for lengthy periods. 'Europe's parents-in-law', Christian IX (1863–1906) and Queen Louise, gathered their daughters and sons-in-law, all of whom represented many of Europe's royal and princely houses, at Fredensborg Palace every summer. Now the present royal family uses the palace for three months in the spring and three in the autumn. If you are desperate to see the chapel, public church services take place every Sunday except in July.

Overnighter from Copenhagen

Odense

Odense is on the train line from Copenhagen to Esbjerg. Trains leave
every 2 hours or so from Copenhagen and take 90mins.

Odense, an agreeable olde-worlde town close to the sea, is situated midway between Copenhagen and Esbjerg, on the island of Funen. It's well known as the birthplace of Hans Christian Andersen and of the composer Carl Nielsen, and both have houses you can visit. For further attractions in the town and for practical information on where to stay, etc., *see* 'Day Trips and Overnighters from Esbjerg', pp.284–5.

Denmark: Jutland

Jutland

40 km
20 miles

N

Hanstholm
Thy
Thisted
Nykøbing M.
Nissum Bredning
Struer
Holstebro
16
Ringkøbing
Ringkøbing Fjord
Herning
Ikast
Skjern
Tarm
Brande
JUTLAND
Ansager
Grindsted
Varde
28
Billund
Legoland
28
Oksby
ESBJERG
E20
176
Egtved
Nordby
Fanø
Tjæreborg
Bramming
Brørup
Vejen
Sønderho
Ribe
Rødding
E45
Haderslev

Hirtshals
Råbjerg Mile
Grenen
Skagen
597
40
Hjørring
Strandby
Sindal
Frederikshavn
Brønderslev
E39
Sæby
Aabybro
Læsø
Nørresundby
Dronninglund
Nibe Bredning
Aalborg
Langerak
Hals
E45
Støvring
Nørager
Hadsund
Hobro
E45
Skive
Viborg
Randers
16
Auning
Grenaa
Djursland
Hadsten
Hornslet
Tirstrup
Bønde
Tastrup
Silkeborg
Mols
Låsby
Nr Vissing
Himmelbjerget ▲
Ry
ÅRHUS
Ebeltoft
Møssø
Skanderborg
Moesgård
Horsens
Samsø
Bredsten
Vejle
Fredericia
Bramdrupdam
Middelfart
Kolding
E20
Odense
To Copenhagen
FUNEN
Nyborg

Originally settled by the Jutes, the marshy, fertile agricultural Jutland peninsula is
the only part of Denmark that is attached to the rest of continental Europe; the rest,
including the capital Copenhagen, is on a series of islands in the Baltic Sea between
Jutland and southern Sweden. Jutland's east coast is inset by fjords, the west and north
have dunes and marshes, and there are some well-preserved old towns and cities.

Esbjerg

Esbjerg, on the west coast of Jutland, is Denmark's youngest city; it dates from just 1868. Originally a landscape of moors and farmland, it became important after Denmark lost its possession of Schleswig-Holstein in 1864 to Germany (which is still hanging on to it), only 85km to the south. Schleswig-Holstein had been the centre for exporting grain to the UK and, in response to the new need, this tiny seaside village began to spread and a port was built to export to markets in the south.

The port, the largest in Denmark, was opened in 1874 and within ten years Esbjerg had a population of 20,000 inhabitants. It has thrived ever since, expanding its exports and its position as a fishing centre and a gateway to Europe and the rest of Jutland. It now counts itself Denmark's fifth largest town, with a population of approximately 83,000. Oil and natural gas deposits in the North Sea have also made it the centre of Denmark's oil industry since the 1980s. As in the past, virtually everyone who lives in Esbjerg has family who works at sea – in the fish, oil or gas industries – and even if you never saw the harbour, on days when the fish comes in you would get a whiff of it on the air. Although the 19th-century origins of the city can be seen in many of its buildings, Esbjerg lacks the romance of some Danish cities. However, it is an airy and pleasing town, though on the small side, built on the US grid-system, with straight, wide streets and square town sections. It has enough to keep you occupied for a day or so (but check opening times as not everything is open all the time) and is very well placed as a base for exploring one of the country's best holiday areas – which offer beaches, medieval towns and amusement parks.

From Torvet South to Havnegade

As with all Danish cities, the best place to begin a tour of the city is from the main square or **Torvet**, which is home to two or three cafés, the bank, post office and the tourist office (housed in what was formerly the county jail). If you arrive by train or bus, you will get off about 300m east of the square. The ferry docks 1km to the south. In the centre of Torvet you will see the **statue of Christian IX**, who was on the throne in 1868 when Esbjerg was founded. From here, walk along Torvegade, one of the city's main shopping streets. Carry on until you reach Havnegade where you will see the **Esbjerg Kunstmuseum**, Havnegade 20 (*open daily 10–4; adm*), in front of you, on the edge of the town park with a fine view of the harbour. This gallery, opened in 1962, is one of the best galleries of Danish art in the country. It contains some 800 paintings and lithographs, dating from about 1920 to the present day, including works by important 20th-century Danish artists, including the internationally renowned CoBrA group (**C**openhagen, **Br**ussels, **A**msterdam), such as Richard Mortensen, Robert Jacobsen, Svend Wiig Hansen and Per Kirkeby, and more recent artists such as Christian Lemmerz, Michael Kvium and Peter Bonde. *Esbjerg*, a 3m-high sculpture by Robert Jacobsen, stands in the museum gardens and represents the vital energy of the bustling port town. The Kunstmuseum is one of Denmark's more experimental centres of culture and some of its temporary exhibits, including an inauguration exhibition of a collection of dead pigs collected by the infamous Christian Lemmerz, a

Getting There

From the UK

Ryanair **flies** direct from Stansted; alternatively, British Midland (BMI) flies direct from Aberdeen to Esbjerg. The airport is 12km outside Esbjerg. **Buses** leave hourly from outside the terminal building and cost 17kr; a **taxi** will cost about 120kr to the city centre.

Alternatively, you can reach Esbjerg from the UK on the **ferry** from Harwich in Essex. DFDS Seaways ferries run once a day, usually around 6pm, on Mon, Wed and Fri; the journey takes about 22hrs. Check *www.ferrybestprice* for details.

From Copenhagen

Trains run hourly throughout the day between Copenhagen and Esbjerg, take 3¼ hrs and cost 241kr; the last train in either direction leaves at 10pm. Trains arrive at the harbour train station.

Getting Around

On Foot

Esbjerg is an easy place to walk around because the grid-system of streets makes it difficult to get lost for very long. The centre is also small enough not to be taxing on shoe leather.

By Bus

There are lots of buses in Esbjerg and you can pick up a bus map from the tourist office on Torvet. They are particularly useful for travel outside the immediate centre. Buses run on time but are often only timetabled once an hour, so check before you set off. Most buses can be boarded at the bus station outside the railway station.

By Taxi

Much of the centre of Esbjerg is pedestrianized so you won't have much luck hailing a taxi and, frankly, you won't need to unless you are going further afield. To hail a cab, you will need to be on one of the busy perimeter roads. However, much the best thing is to ask your hotel to call one. If you are out and about, many of the museums will also oblige.

By Bike

Biking is a safe and fun option for getting around Esbjerg if you don't want to walk. As elsewhere, there are well-marked cycle lanes which are easy to follow and keep you out of the way of the traffic. Hire bikes at **Skræntens Cykeludejning**, Skrænten 2, **t** 75 45 75 05, where you can find normal bikes, children's bikes and even tandems for hire.

Car Hire

Hiring a car will only be of use if you are planning to tour outside Esbjerg. These have offices at the airport and in the centre:
Hertz, t 75 16 04 07.
Avis, t 75 13 44 77.
Europcar, t 75 12 38 93.
National, t 70 22 22 01.

Tourist Information

Esbjerg: Skølegarde 33, **t** 75 12 55 99 (*open summer Mon–Fri 9–5, Sat 9.30–3.30; rest of year Mon–Fri 10–5, Sat 10–1*). The very helpful tourist board can and will help you plan your stay and will book holidays, such as cycle or golfing trips, tickets and hotels, as well as provide you with information and guided tours in and around Esbjerg.

If you are planning to stay a few days and explore more widely, the **Esbjerg Passport** (adults 135/160kr, children 80/90kr; the latter is the high season price) will buy you unlimited travel on the bus for two days, as well as free boarding on the ferry across to Fanø (*see* pp.276–8), free entry into the Fisheries Museum, the swimming stadium (Svømmestadion Danmark) and the harbour sightseeing tours. You can buy the pass at the tourist office at Esbjerg and Fanø. It will also grant you a discount to other city museums.

Festivals

Esbjerg hosts a number of annual festivals, including a **rock festival** in June and the weeklong party, the **Esbjerg Festival**, in early August, which features performances, exhibitions, jazz, opera. pop, with top Danish and international names and open-air concerts. There is also a **chamber music festival** later in the month. Check for final programmes and dates in July at *www.esbjerg-festuge.dk*.

Shopping

Esbjerg is the major town for shopping in south Jutland and sells most things. The main shopping streets are Torvegade and Kongensgade. A wide selection from fresh food and delicacies to fashion and decorative art is found along **Torvegade** while **Kongensgade** has some 156 speciality shops. Most shops are open Mon–Fri 9.30–5.30, but don't expect to do much shopping at the weekend; nothing will be open after 2pm on Sat and shops are shut on Sun.

If you are looking for presents, check out the shops at the **Esbjerg Museum**, which has a nice choice (including amber jewellery), and the smaller shop at the Kunstmuseum.

Near the centre, antiques can be found at Klintes-gade Antik, Strandbygade 48, **t** 75 25 90 90, and commercial art at Galleri Dykra, Havne-gade 13, **t** 75 15 46 57, Sand's Galleri, Skolegade 60, **t** 75 12 02 07, Vestjysk Kunstgalleri, Strandy-gade 92, **t** 75 13 55 90, *www.voigtfineart.dk*, ceramics at Keramic-voerkstedet Broendingen, Jyllandsgade 44, **t** 75 12 99 15, and amber at Ravhuset Kongensgade 17, **t** 75 13 89 70.

Sports and Activities

Svømmestadion Danmark, G. Vardevej 60, **t** 76 11 42 40, *www.svvdk.dk* (*open daily 8am–9pm, weekends and public hols 8am–7pm; adm*). Denmark's largest swimming stadium with 10 different baths and pools, including a competition pool and one for water polo as well as pools for small children and a tropical swimscape.

Breinholtgård Golfklub, Kokspangvej 17–19, **t** 75 11 57 00. International 27- and 9-hole golf courses, 11km from the centre of town.

Esbjerg Golfklub, Sønderhedevej 11, Marboek, **t** 75 26 92 19/75 26 92 72. International 18- and 9-hole golf courses, 15km from the centre of town.

Fun World, Glamerstervej 6–12, **t** 75 46 84 00. Lots of activities, including bowling and go-karting.

Where to Stay

Hotel Britannia, Torvegade 24, **t** 75 13 01 11, *www.britannia.dk* (*expensive*). Very central, this 4-star hotel is stylish and modern, filled with functional, contemporary light design and furnished with Danish designer furniture. It has a good restaurant and bar-café (**Green Garden**, *see* over).

Hotel Hjerting, Strandpromenaden 1, **t** 75 11 70 00 (*expensive–moderate*). 9km out of town in Hjerting, this is a prettier hotel than you will find in town, overlooking Ho Bay and next to the beach. It has pretty rooms with a choice from standard to a 2-room suite and a good restaurant (**Restaurant Strandpavillion**, *see* over). There's an on-site 'cosy' English pub, popular with locals.

Hotel Ansgar, Skolegade 36, **t** 75 12 82 44, *www.hotelansgar.dk* (*moderate*). This attractive 3-star, white building in the centre has been a hotel since 1948 and prides itself on its peace and tradition. Rooms are white and generally attractive, with a splash of bright colour. Only breakfast is served.

Palads Hotel Cab Inn, Skolegade 14, **t** 75 18 16 00, **f** 75 18 16 24, *www.cabinn.dk* (*moderate–inexpensive*). Part of the Cab Inn hotel chain based on a ship-like 'cabin' approach (including, in some rooms, bunkbeds), this is a comfortable 3-star hotel with nice staff, free internet access and good rates. Particularly good if you want to sleep more than two in a room, although its green and purple décor might not be everyone's first choice.

Park Hotel, Torvegade 31, **t** 75 12 08 68 (*moderate–inexpensive*). Small hotel in the centre of Esbjerg.

Hotel Bell-Inn, Skolegade 45, **t** 75 12 01 22 (*inexpensive*). A nice hotel, situated in the city centre. Bargain rooms. Also a restaurant.

Guldager Kro, Stationsvej 104, **t/f** 75 16 70 08 (*inexpensive*). This romantic inn 8km northwest of Esbjerg in Hjerting is over a century old.

Eating Out

Den Røde Okse, Tarphagevej 9, **t** 75 15 15 00 (*expensive*). Lovely, bright, airy and stylish interior with dark-wood wicker chairs;

unfussy, classy décor. Interesting gourmet food, principally French and Danish.

Green Garden, Hotel Britannia, Torvegade 24, t 75 13 01 11 (*expensive–moderate*). Gourmet food amid modern, art-clad décor with an emphasis on fish. Prices can add up but a 2-course gourmet menu for under 180kr can't be bad. *Open 6pm–12am (kitchen closes 10pm), closed Sun.*

Kunstpavillionen Restaurant, Havnegade 2, t 75 12 64 95 (*moderate*). Part of the art museum complex, this has views of the harbour but it is often booked for functions so ring ahead if you want to eat here, especially at weekends; open evenings too. There is also a nice café (*open Mon–Fri 8.30–3*), open as well when there are concerts at weekends and in the evenings, serving wholesome food and home-made cakes.

Dronning Louise, Torvet 19, t 75 13 13 44, *www.dr-louise.dk* (*moderate–inexpensive*). A pub-cum-restaurant-cum-nightclub (*downstairs, Fri and Sat*), clearly divided down the middle, offering hearty portions of Danish and some international cuisine. *Open daily 10am–late.*

Bone's Skolegade 17, t 75 13 61 18, *www. bones.dk* (*inexpensive*). Another popular chain, this time themed with fun pirate-ship-related décor. An early-bird menu is especially good if you have hungry children in tow. *Open Sun–Fri 4.30–10.30, Sat 12–10.30.*

Jensen's Bøfhus, Kongensgade 9, t 75 18 18 70 (*inexpensive*). Danish chain offering steak-related fare. This one is off the street and has a nice courtyard at the front for eating out in summer. *Open daily 11–11.*

Entertainment and Nightlife

Although Esbjerg is small in comparison with Copenhagen or Århus, it offers quite a lot of choice for a night out, especially at weekends

Ballet, opera, etc. takes place at the **Musikhuset Esbjerg**, Havnegade 18, t 76 10 90 00. Also check out the **Musikkonservatorium**, Kirkegade 60, opposite Sankt Nikolaj Church.

Look out for rock, jazz and theatre at the **Multihus Tobaksfabrikken**, Gasværksgade 2, t 75 18 02 22, *www.tobbakken.dk*. For smaller

venues, there's **De Studerendes Hus**, Finsensgade 1, t 75 45 09 22, parallel with the northern stretch of Torvegade and, further out of town, **Jazz Esbjerg**, Cederlunden 10, Esbjerg East, t 75 14 14 12.

The city also boasts several symphony orchestras, and the Esbjerg Ensemble presents numerous concerts throughout the year. On a number of Wednesdays in summer, city officials offer free entertainment under an open sky (the tourist office will have details).

For dancing the night away, there are a number of **nightclubs**. These tend to open around 11 or 12 midnight on Fri and Sat and in some instances are free up to midnight; they shut at 5am. You can also strut your stuff at some of the pubs, such as the 007 James Bond Bar on Skolegade (a good pick-up joint by all accounts), which often turn into clubs around midnight as well.

Twist and Shout, Kirkegade 21, t 76 12 10 22, *www.twistandshout.dk*. There are usually other gigs going on the rest of the week. *Open Fri and Sat 11–5, free entry before 12am.*

Papa's Cantina, under Dronning Louise, Torvet 19, t 75 13 13 44, *www.dr-louise.dk*.

For drinking, Torvet and Skolegade are the main drags for bars and pubs. These open around 10–11am. The coolest is **Industrien**, Skolegade 27, t 75 13 61 66, a stylish bar in Danish style, with candles and mirrors, which has a very reasonably priced menu and is popular with students from the music school. It also has live music on and off each month so is worth checking out for that as well (*closed from 4.30 on Sun*). If beery English and Irish pubs are your thing, there are plenty to choose from. Check out **You'll Never Walk Alone**, Kongensgade 10, t 75 45 40 60, a popular venue where English and Celtic folk musicians sometimes play. On Torvet, there are two large cafés, the **Dronning Louise** (Queen Louise) and the **Christian IX**, historically married to each other and once again a couple side by side in the town square.

And if you just want a wander after dark, make your way down Torvegade, which has a 'Light Avenue' and a 'Scattering of Stars' sunk into the cobbles. These 288 lights are an artistic representation of a part of the night sky that was visible over Torvegade at midnight on 1 January 2000.

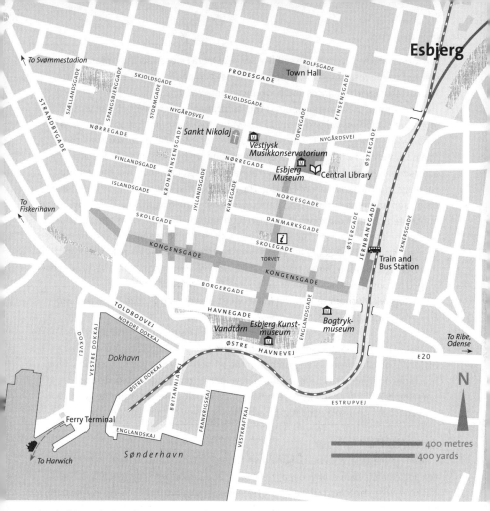

kind of Danish cross between Damien Hirst and Marc Quinn, have given rise to a great deal of controversy.

Inside, the hung collection is on the first floor – consisting of five rooms – and the stores are in the basement. Don't miss these, as this is where you can pull out whole walls of paintings from a kind of long filing cabinet and see parts of the collection that are not currently being exhibited upstairs. The museum is very keen on interaction between the public and the art; there is also the opportunity to blindly handle small sculptures in enclosed cabinets, which have room for you to put your hand in to feel the sculpture before you open it up to see what it is. If you are not in a rush (and Denmark isn't a place to rush), it is worth spending some time down here – it's not often that you are given *carte blanche* to get this close to a national collection of art.

Once you are in the museum, you are actually in the same building as the fabulous **Musikhuset Esbjerg**, the Esbjerg Performing Arts Centre. Looking at this clean-cut, modern, almost abstract white building, it will come as little surprise that it was designed by the Danish architects Jørn and Jan Utson, a father and son combination, the former the architect of the sail-like Sydney Opera House. It is the cultural meeting place of southwest Jutland, and lots of concerts and performances take place here. You can check performances and book ahead on *www.mhe.dk*.

To the right of the Kunstmuseum is the **Vandtårn** or water tower, at Havnegade 22 (*open June–mid-Sept daily 10–4; mid-Sept–May Sat and Sun, plus school holidays in autumn and winter; adm*). It was built in 1896–7 for a population which, until then, had no waterworks, the water supply being managed by wells and water posts spread across the town. Built on a Bronze Age burial mound, it looks out over the sea and soon became the landmark of Esbjerg. The architect, C.H. Clausen (1866–1941), based his design on a medieval German pattern, Haus Nassau in Nürnburg, Germany. It now houses temporary exhibitions. It is 35.5m high and, for a good view of the city and the port, climb the six floors to the top. You will also be able to see Fanø to the south and, on a good day, the tower of Ribe's Domkirke, 30-odd kilometres away. In a thoughtful manner typical of the Danes, there are boxes for children and the more vertically challenged amongst us to stand on to look out of the windows.

The **Bogtryk Museum**, or Printing Museum, at Borgergade 6 (*open June– mid-Sept Fri–Wed 12–4, closed Thurs; mid-Sept–May Tues–Fri 1–4; adm*), is a short walk from Havnegade down Englandsgade on to Borgergade. This printing museum is the largest in Denmark and is set out like a medium-size printing office. It charts the history of printing from its beginnings in the 15th century and you can see how type, machines and processes have gradually developed from hand-set type to the amazing printing technology we employ today. Working presses from the last 100 years or so are on display, and it is possible to see many of them in operation.

Down to the Harbour

From Havnegade, it's a quick hop down to the harbour, the working hub of this seaside city. It is here that you realize how big and important Esbjerg really is. The harbour front stretches out over 5km, from Fiskerihavn (up by the fisheries museum, *see* below) to Sønderhavn down by the Vandtårn and the Kunstmuseum, and has a quay area of 10km². Plans are afoot at Sønderhavn for the construction of Denmark's tallest building, intended to house a hotel, with additional shops, cafés and cruise line terminals in the surrounding area.

Measured by turnover, this harbour is amongst Denmark's biggest in terms of fishing and shipping, and is also a base for the offshore oil and gas activities in the Danish North Sea. In recent years, about 17,000 vessels have called in annually, with almost two million passengers. Before the harbour was constructed, the coastline ran along the base of the cliffs. Most of the harbour area as it is today is man-made, created from sand pumped from the harbour entrance. After being established, the areas are sown with a mixture of grass and corn to prevent the sand from drifting. Each year, 1.2 million cubic metres are removed to maintain the depth of the water.

The first ship entered on 24 April 1868. In recent times, the harbour has flooded three times, in 1981, 1990 and 1999 (when Denmark experienced its first hurricane), and the quays (3m high) were a metre under water. New areas are being constructed at 5m and a flood alert service has been set up to warn all the businesses in the harbour so they can take necessary precautions.

If you see a trawler in port called *Peter Marlene*, this is the largest trawler in Denmark. Built in Scotland in 1995, it weighs 1,460 gross tons and is 57.44m long and 12m wide.

If you head away further west from Sønderhavn, you can visit *Horns Rev*, the **Lightship Museum** in the old fishing harbour (*open April–May Mon–Fri 10–2.40; June–Aug Mon–Fri 10–3.30; Sept Mon–Fri 10–2.30; closed Oct–Mar; adm*), the last of the Esbjerg lightships. It was in service between 1913–14 and 1984. The museum exhibits explain what life was like on board, protecting shipping off the west coast of Jutland. You can also take guided harbour tours from here (*1½hrs, June–Sept*).

From Torvet North to Nørregade

Head north from Torvet, past the tourist office, and past a rather nice bakery on your right, and you come to the **Esbjerg Museum**, Torvegade 45, **t** 75 12 78 11, *www. esbjergmuseum.dk* (*open daily 10–4; closed Mon Sept–May, except school holidays in autumn and winter; adm, Wed free*), which specializes in local history and archaeology and has a number of interesting permanent exhibits based on the town and its surrounding area, including a display that shows reconstructions of early 20th-century façades of shops and home interiors within the city. Visit the grocers, look in the windows of the dress shop and the barber's and see what was happening on the dockside down at the port, where they loaded eggs, bacon and butter bound for England, by hand, as late as 1972. The home interiors show a 'working-class' apartment and rooms from a 'director's' home, complete with a maid's room, a wainscoted drawing room and office, and a blue-and-white china faïence loo.

On the same floor, there is an exhibition showing artefacts from Stone Age, Iron Age and Viking settlements around Esbjerg, with the usual pots, tools and explanations of how life was lived. The star turn here, especially for kids, is the reconstruction of an Iron Age farmhouse with a stable at one end of the building and living quarters at the other, complete with a stuffed cow, pig, sheep and chicken, which unlike in English museums are not remotely mangy and are eminently strokable.

The third floor has an excellent amber exhibition, explaining the geology, geography and uses made of this 'Danish gold' – for which the west coast of Jutland is famous – with exhibits dating back to 8,000 BC. Here you will discover some interesting facts: that amber, with a density of just over 1, will float in salt water but sink in fresh, that as a varnish it improves the sound of stringed instruments, that it is traditionally a remedy against rheumatism, and that Martin Luther wore it to prevent kidney stones.

If, having seen the water tower on Havnegade, you want to see more of C.L. Clausen's work, walk a block along Nørregade until you reach Kirkegade. Turn right and you will come to the former electricity works, or **Vestjysk Musikkonservatorium**, now the Academy of Music, Kirkegade 61, **t** 76104300, *www.vmk.dk*. Built in 1907, it is an impressive example of how you can transform an old industrial building into a cool, modern space. A lot is made of the constrast between rough and smooth surfaces, modern glass and steel structures alongside railways sleepers and massive cranes from the early part of the last century. As well as the teaching facilities, there is a large concert hall – formerly the old machine hall. It still has its old lacunar ceiling and along the walls are 22 *Nocturne* paintings by Danish artist Hans Tyrrestrup. It is regarded as one of the best concert halls in Denmark and houses a rare concert organ with 44 stops – there are only two others like it in Denmark.

Outside there is a huge sculpture (1998) by Thorbjørn Lausten. Called *The Clock*, it consists of a modern sundial in steel and neon, which is controlled by satellite, and a sandstone block from which water gushes – the 'performance' is eerily accompanied by the sculpture's own ever-changing music from speakers sunk below ground level, from which you can also hear performances directly from the concert hall.

Opposite at Kirkegade 58 is **Sankt Nikolaj Kirke**, **t** 75 12 10 27 (*open Tues–Fri 9.30–12; free*), a Catholic church designed in the mid 1960s by the architect Johan Otto von Spreckelsen (1929–87), a Danish architect who designed many Danish churches and became world-famous for his Grande Arche, or Triumphal Arch of Humanity, at La Défense in Paris, which was unveiled in 1989 after he died. This church was consecrated in 1969 and has a modern, white octagonal interior. The crucifix above the altar was made by a German artist in Münster, Jacob Werner Korsmeier. The body is cast in bronze and depicts the living, resurrected victorious Christ, with a crown on the cross.

Continue to walk down Kirkegade, past the cemetery and towards the sea, and take a left on to Kongensgade. Depending on who you listen to, this is either the longest pedestrian street in Denmark, or second only to Copenhagen's Strøget (*see* p.243). It has a good selection of high street-type shops. Look up to see how the buildings come in a variety of architectural styles. If the spirit moves you, make a quick detour and have a look at the **old courthouse** at Skolegade 33, and a collection of sculptures by the Danish sculptor Henry Heerup (a member of the CoBrA group) in the little garden nearby, Skolegade 35; there is also a café here.

Outside the Centre

Don't leave Esbjerg without hopping on the nos.1 or 3 bus, which both leave about once an hour from outside the train station on Jernbanagade, to go 4km northwest of the centre to the **Fiskeri-og Søfartsmuseet** (Fisheries Museum), Tarphagevej 2, **t** 76 12 20 00 (*open daily Sept–June 10–5; July–Aug 10–6; adm*). If you fancy a brisk walk, it will take you about 45 minutes from the centre of town.

This may not sound like the most exciting trip, but this museum, dedicated to fishery and seamanship, is great fun, not least because the first two things you see are the skeleton of a large male sperm whale, 13.2m long and, in life, weighing in at 25 tons, found beached on the island of Rømo in 1996 with 15 others; and a stuffed walrus, humanely put down after it was found, badly malnourished – 660kg instead of over 1,000kg – stranded on a beach in 1999. It's probably the closest you will ever get to one of these extraordinary animals – so close you can even see the 'toenails' on its five-toed flippers.

The museum has two large permanent displays, both on the ground floor: the fisheries section, which displays tools, vessels, paintings and models of the breakthrough made by Danish saltwater fishing in the years 1880–1940, and the shipping section, which shows ships, people and seafaring from the sailing ships of the Viking era to present-day container traffic and offshore activities. Here, you will learn what life was really like for the fishermen and their families, and the jobs they did.

The museum contains a sealarium, a mink enclosure and a fabulous aquarium. The sealarium is home to several extremely cute common and grey seals, both natural species to the North Sea (in the spring there are usually babies). You can watch them from above or below, as their tank is glass on one side. Feeding times are at 11am and 2.30pm. Also outside, and adjacent to the sealarium, is the mink enclosure, complete with its own lake and brook. Mink, like seals, are indigenous to Denmark and can be found in the wild, where they live on small rodents and the eggs and young of ground-breeding birds such as gulls, terns, lapwings and wading birds in general. The minks are fed after the seals in the morning with live fish that they catch themselves in the lake.

Back inside the museum, there is a fascinating 25-tank saltwater aquarium with most fish species from the North Sea. Beginning at the water's edge, the aquarium is arranged so that you gradually plough the depths of the ocean, learning about the different habitats at different depths and the physical characteristics of the fish that live there. The tanks are designed for the best effect, including sloped, triangular tanks as if you are looking at a cross-section of shoreline, circular tanks, and mirrors, which really help you to understand the meaning of the word 'shoal'.

There is also an outdoor area with a harbour reconstruction, a stretch of sand dunes, a Second World War shelter, a ropewalk and a lifeboat station, all of which can be climbed on and investigated.

Check with the museum or the tourist board for special exhibitions and activities inside and outside the museum. These occur all year, but especially in summer, and include functioning workshops – such as blacksmithery, emptying fish traps on the seashore, and taking tours in the fishing cutter *Claus Sørensen*.

Just over the road from the museum is Esbjerg's new waterfront landmark, **Mennesjet ved Havet** ('Man Meets the Sea'), a massive, white, 9m-high concrete sculpture of four seated figures created by the Danish sculptor Svend Wiig Hansen to commemorate the city's centennial as an independent municipality in 1994. Rigid and enormous, they put you in mind of ancient Egyptian monolithic statues or the strange, inexplicable figures on Easter Island, and are intended to represent 'pure' humanity before 'man got his hands dirty'. They can be seen from a distance of 10km.

If you feel like a walk or a picnic, or the kids are desperate for a big playground, visit **Vognsbøl Park**, Gl. Vardevej 83, **t** 75 45 22 00, a few kilometres west of the centre (catch the no.4 bus heading north from Havnegade). This will take you through 178 hectares of forested parkland complete with a good network of paths, playgrounds, picnic tables (including facilities for the disabled), a café and activities for kids. If you stay on the bus, you will reach the **deer park** a little further on.

Day Trips and Overnighters from Esbjerg

Fanø

Fanø, a pretty, low-lying island with 18km of lovely wide beaches along its western coast, lies in the Wadden Sea ten minutes by ferry from Esbjerg. The sea is Denmark's largest nature reserve and one of the world's most important wetlands for migratory waterbirds; between 10 and 12 million waterbirds pass through it each year. It is also home to a third of Denmark's seal population.

Fanø is a popular tourist island; its population of 3,200 rises to 20–30,000 over the summer months. It was originally the king's hunting ground; the inhabitants bought its charter in 1741 and thereafter became heavily involved in coastal traffic, including smuggling. They established working harbours long before Esbjerg's opened in 1874. By 1897, Fanø owned one of the largest merchant fleets after Copenhagen. It only began to decline with the arrival of the steamship and the new port in Esbjerg.

Fanø rewards a visit, especially if the weather is good. With its charming cottages and sandy, grass-strewn dunes, it is a stark contrast to 19th-century urban Esbjerg. If you have the time and the inclination, this is a gentle place to spend a weekend, enjoying the sea and the outdoors. You are bound to see lots of bird life and you may also come across some seals. If you want something a bit more energetic, there are plenty of sports and outdoor activities, including biking, nature walks, cycling, wind-surfing, kite-flying, golf or horse-riding.

Nordby

The ferry comes into Nordby, Fanø's main town in the north of the island. On the way across, you will see offshore windmills in the sea. The tourist board is on the harbour; although Fanø is small, pick up a map. The charm of Nordby is wandering round its pretty streets with old maritime houses, most of which still have thatched, mossy roofs and picket fences. Along the harbour, look out for **The Trappen** (The Steps), which is a typical alley with houses dating back 200 years. The gardens along here are behind high cement walls to protect them from sea storms and salt water. If you are interested in Fanø's past, visit the **Fanø Shipping and Costume Collection** on Hovedgaden 28, **t** 75 16 22 72 (*open May–Sept daily 11–4; Oct–April weekdays 11–1, closed Sun*), and the **Fanø Museum** on Skolevej 2 (*weekdays 11–2; July–Aug 11–4*). The former is especially good at describing the hard lives of the sailors' wives, who were often alone for years if their men were sailing the seven seas. The costume collection is also fasci-nating – women wore lots of skirts (dampened, pleated, bound with braid and sent to the baker who steamed them in a warm oven!) and had a specific costume for each stage of their lives – including a party dress, the hem of which trumpeted their marital or single status. The Fanø Museum houses reconstructions of cottage rooms and displays of domestic items as well as an interesting collection of sailors' memen-toes. Also of interest is **Nordby church**, which can hold up to 700 people, and has been

Getting There and Around

Scandline runs regular **ferry** services to Nordby from Esbjerg harbour. Services run every half-hour or so from Oct to May and every 20mins from June to Sept (30kr return). You can take a car over, but this is expensive (325kr in high season for a car with up to 9 passengers).

There are three **taxis** on the island, t 75 16 62 00, and buses run between Nordby and Fanø Bad, Rindy Strand and Sønderho; get a timetable at the tourist office.

Otherwise, your feet or a bike are your best options.
Fanø Cykler, Hovedgaden 96, t 75 16 25 13
Unika Cykler, Mellemgaden 12, t 75 16 24 60
Havnekiosken, Langelinie 9, t 75 16 21 20

Tourist Information

Fanø: the tourist office is at the harbour, t 75 16 26 00, *www.fanoeturistbureau.dk (open June–Aug Mon–Fri 8.30–6, Sat 8–7, Sun 10–5; Sept–May Mon–Fri 8.30–5.30, Sat 9–1)*. As well as general information, they can also help with accommodation.

Festivals

Kite-flying festivals are held all along the coast of Fanø, usually towards the end of June. **Midsummer's Day** is celebrated on the beach at Fanø Bad, including a bonfire in the evening.

Activities

Horseriding: Rindby Rundridning/Baun, Rindbyvej 8, Rindby, t 75 16 37 43; **Farmen**, Gl Toftvej 10, Sønderho, t 75 16 41 61.
Buggy-riding without kites: Drageland, Hovedgaden 34, t 75 16 20 87.
Golf: Fanø Bad, t 40 43 38 50/76 66 00 77.
Tennis: Fanø Bad, t 76 66 00 77.

Where to Stay

There are four bed-and-breakfasts on Fanø, from 400kr for a double room. There are also campsites and holiday homes. Contact the tourist board for information and booking.
Sønderho Kro, Kropladsen 11, Sønderho, t 75 16 40 09, *www.sonderhokro.dk (expensive)*. If you are staying the night, this is perhaps the place to stay if you want to treat yourself. Built in 1722, it is the town's oldest building and one of Denmark's oldest inns. It is cosy and intimate and only a few metres from the dyke, with views over marshland and sea. There is also a lovely garden where you can dine in the shade of tall trees. Only 13 rooms, and recommended by *Relais & Chateaux*; book well in advance.
Nørby Kro, Strandvejen 12, Nordby, t 75 16 35 89, f 75 16 62 98, *www.noerbykro.dk (expensive–moderate)*. Towards the beach at Fanø Bad, this pretty though slightly more chintzy hotel is set in a 300-year-old parish bailiff's thatched farm buildings, which have been thoroughly restored. It also has a nice restaurant.
Fanø Krogaard, Langelinie 11, Nordby, t 75 16 20 52, f 75 16 23 00, *www.fanokrogaard.dk (moderate)*. This old royal privileged inn from 1664 is very close to the harbour and has views out over the sea. It boasts charming, light, bright rooms (including very reasonable 4-person family rooms) from which you can see seals sunning themselves if you are lucky. It also has a nightclub.

Eating Out

There are plenty of bakeries, cafés and restaurants in Nordby, Fanø Bad and Sønderho.
Sønderho Kro, Kropladsen 11, Sønderho, t 75 16 40 09, *www.sonderhokro.dk (expensive–moderate)*. Atmospheric, tiled and low-beamed restaurant serving gourmet Danish cuisine.
Café Nanas Stue, Sønder Land 1, Sønderho t 75 16 40 25 *(moderate–inexpensive)*. Tile-decorated café/restaurant offering traditional food and music in the evenings.
Fru Pille Ville, Hovedgaden 57, Nordby, t 75 16 22 11 *(inexpensive)*. Standard family restaurant offering standard fare.

restored to the way it was in 1786; look out for the bronze, late 15th-century font, an altar and pulpit from 1622 and several 'votive ships'. According to modern research, although they are called 'votive', there is no evidence of any religious rite or tradition – they are merely a representation of the profession of the men of the parish.

There are plenty of small gift shops in Nordby, and also a **glass-blowing studio** at Hovedgaden 47. If you are there at the right time, you will see the glass-blowers at work, making gorgeous, multicoloured bowls, candlesticks, plates and even fridge magnets, which sell for between 30 and 3,300kr.

Fanø Bad and Sønderho

To reach **Sønderho**, a pretty village 12km away at the south end of the island, hop on a bike, or catch a bus or taxi. The nicest route is slightly longer (about 15km) via **Fanø Bad**, on the west side, where there is a lovely long, wide beach along which you can ride your bike or drive your car – as Sir Malcolm Campbell did in 1924 when he raced *Bluebird* here to set a world speed record of 220kph. If you cycle along here and then through the plantations, it takes about 1½–2 hours. As you come into Sønderho, there is a **windmill** (1895) on your right (a museum; *open summer and school hols 3–5pm*) and, if you carry on and take a left, you come to the **village church** which has 15 votive ships hanging from its ceiling – more than any other church in Denmark.

Other places to visit are: the **Hannes Hus**, Øster Land 7 (*open intermittently 3–5*), a 17th-century sea captain's home; the **Fanø Art Museum**, Nord Land 5, **t** 75 16 40 44 (*open April–Nov Tues–Sun 2–5*), which has several rooms filled with paintings from the last hundred years, mainly showing local life; the **Fanø Tile Collection,** housed in Denmark's smallest dairy (now a café, Café Nannas Stuew) and showing the Dutch/Friesian tiles that sailors brought home between 1650 and 1910, typical of Fanø interiors; the **old fire station** with a fire engine dating from 1895; and, again if it is open, the **old lifeboat station** along the beach, which is under restoration.

Legoland

Nordmarksvej 9, Billund, t 75 33 13 33, www.lego.com; open April–June and Sept–Oct 10–6 (rides close 5pm), weekends 10–8 (rides close 6pm); July and Aug 10–9 (rides close 8pm); some height restrictions apply to anyone between 90cm and 1m 20cm; adm, children (3–12) 160kr, adults 180kr, senior citizens 160kr, 2-day ticket 260kr.

This amusement park is huge fun for everyone. It is now much more than the original model-park, although this is what is still truly extraordinary about the place. Depending on how keen you are to do all the rides, it is advisable to start at the far end of the park and work your way back to the models, which are open for another hour or so after the rides finish.

There are plenty of fun rides in the **Legoredo**, **Borgland** and **Adventureland** areas. Don't miss the X-treme Racers rollercoaster or Power Builder – a powerful robotic arm

Getting There

Follow the E20 until exit 63 (Bramdrupdam). Take route 441 towards Bredsten and then route 28 to Billund, or route 176 via Egtved.

By bus from Esbjerg, take the no. 44 or 913X from the bus station next to the railway station, and change at Grindsted on to the 907X or 244 (timetable: *www.rejseplanen.dk*).

Where to Stay

Hotel LEGOLAND, Aastvej 10, 7190 Billund, t 75 33 12 44, *www.hotellegoland.dk* (*expensive*). Lego-run, modern, family-orientated hotel bang in the middle of Legoland with restaurant serving gourmet and kids' food, so you are not doomed to a youthful diet throughout your stay.

that you programme from a choice of movements according to your height, for a bespoke 15–30-second acrobatic ride (*minimum height 1m 20cm*). Elsewhere there is lots of stuff for small kids in **Duploland**, including a brilliant Lego 'orchestra' fountain that 'plays' both water and jolly tunes such as 'Yes, We Have No Bananas' and 'Pollywollydoodle' when you jump on ground-level sensors.

Miniland (which is obviously what makes Legoland Legoland and not just any old amusement park) is fascinating, not only because of the thousands of bricks that go into each model (this is a *job* for some people!), but because of the detail involved. Every model looks just as good from the back as from the front and, when you look closely, you can tell that a lot of imagination and humour has gone into the designs. Note the fat red swimsuited lady with the conical, Madonna-like frontage having her picture taken by the man with the fat bottom on the beach of the model of 'Oil Production in the North Sea'; also the frogmen, the people running into the waves... Many of the models have working parts – lots of boats and trains whizzing about, a working oil rig, helicopter blades whirring, and planes taxiing along the runway in Billund Airport (the real version of which is actually visible beyond the park from the viewing platform). Miniland is also where you can get a preview of the picturesque medieval town of Ribe or Copenhagen's Amalienborg Palace and harbour area, not to mention downtown Los Angeles, complete with film crew, a working funicular and three skyscrapers, made with a total of 740,000 Lego bricks. For sheer wow-factor, float in a boat past some of the great buildings of the world, including Abu Simbal (264,000 bricks), the Acropolis (265,000 bricks), Kronborg Castle (Elsinore, *see* p.256 – 105,000 bricks), and, to cap it all, the 9m-high Statue of Liberty (1.4 million bricks). There is also an adorable safari ride in self-drive buggies where it is as funny to watch three-year-olds in big nappies bombing about, very pleased with themselves, as it is to look at the huge models of safari wildlife – many with sound effects.

Before you leave, don't miss out on Titania's Palace, an amazing 19th-century fairy doll's house built by the English painter Sir Neville Wilkinson, 14th Earl of Pembroke, complete with Old Master paintings, monogrammed linen, Staffordshire china, gold dishes, stained-glass windows and suits of armour on the stairs. The motto over the doorway of the Hall of the Fairy Kiss, *Nihil Sine Labore* (Nothing Without Work), must have had resonance for its maker, who took 15 years to complete it. There is also a collection of mechanical toys dating from between 1850 and 1950 that is well worth a visit, and a computer interactive zone.

Ribe

Ribe, twinned with Ely near Cambridge, is a lovely, atmospheric town and one of the oldest in Denmark. Established by 700, it was first mentioned in written sources in 860 when St Ansgar, the German missionary who brought Christianity to Denmark, chose it as the site for his second church. By 948 it was a bishopric, had a cathedral and was a major trading town on the routes south to England and mainland Europe.

As a predominantly 16th- and 17th-century town, Ribe has survived more or less in its entirety owing to a 200-year run of bad luck. The Reformation put paid to the church; a 'great fire' in 1580 that demolished the town was followed by a flood in 1634; war in the 1650s with Sweden didn't help; and the plague in 1659 killed off 70 per cent of the population (which fell from 6,000 in 1640 to 1,600 in 1660). Most importantly, the introduction of absolute monarchy in 1660 meant that the king no longer travelled around the country but stayed put in his new capital in Copenhagen, and Ribe lost its royal privileges. On top of that, competition with Copenhagen and the gradual silting up of the river that linked its harbour to the sea affected its position as an important coastal trading town. The result was that Ribe's inhabitants patched up their old houses rather than build modern new ones, as more prosperous town dwellers did elsewhere.

The Domkirke (Church of Our Lady)

Opening times vary according to the season, but usually open summer Mon–Fri 10/11–4/5.30, Sun and public holidays 12–4/5.30; winter Mon–Fri usually 11–3/4, Sun and public holidays 12–3/4pm; adm.

The cathedral stands in the centre of Ribe. Now 1.5m below street level, it followed tradition and was originally built at the town's highest point, 2–3m above everything else. It was begun between 1150 and 1175 and is in the Romanesque style. Before you go in, walk around it. On the south side you will see the 'Cat's head' door, which has a large head surrounded by mice with five more cat heads below it. The story goes that there were two brothers, one wealthy, the other poor. To help his poor brother, the rich merchant brother asked for something that he could sell while abroad. All the poor brother had was his cat so the merchant took that. Shipwrecked on an island overrun with mice, the rich brother sold the cat for a huge sum. On his return, he advised his now less-poor brother to buy and sell five more cats (but not to flood the market). Grateful for his good fortune, the newly wealthy brother is said to have given the door to the church (although the door is 19th-century, the decoration is 14th-century) .

The relief above the door, which dates from 1130, shows the deposition from the cross and the sandstone epitaph of King Christopher I, made in 1259; it is formed from one piece of granite and is the largest medieval sculpture in Denmark. The decoration on the west door was designed by artist AnneMarie Carl-Nielsen, wife of composer Carl Nielsen (*see* p.285) in 1904. The 'angry angel' is a portrait of her daughter.

The cathedral is made from yellow tufa, originally cut in Cologne and transported by boat to Ribe – the quarry still exists and the same stone has been used for renovation. The square, red-brick north tower replaced the original matching tower, which

Getting There

Ribe is good alternative to staying in Esbjerg as it is only 25km from the airport. There is no direct bus but you can take a **bus** to Esbjerg and, from there take a **train** to Ribe. Alternatively, a **taxi** will cost you approximately 350kr and take about 25mins (contact *www.ribetaxa.dk*).

If you're planning to drive about a bit, it really is worth hiring a car. There are signs to Ribe from the airport. To visit from Esbjerg (30km), leave the city from the harbour area and take the A24 going south.

Tourist Information

Ribe: Torvet 3, **t** 75 42 15 00, *www.ribe.dk* (*open high season Mon–Fri 9–6, Sat 10–5, Sun 10–2; off season Mon–Fri 9.30–4.30, Sat 10–1*). The tourist office is incredibly helpful and will help you to arrange accommodation as well as tours (guided or not) around the town and the local area. Their town guides (50kr for 1½hrs per person) cannot come too highly recommended. They also provide some very good weekend deals for two people and families.

The **Ribe Pass** gives you 20% off most entry fees in and around Ribe; get full details from the tourist office.

Where to Stay

Hotel Dagmar, Torvet, **t** 75 42 00 33, *www. hoteldagmar.dk* (*expensive*). This is the most historic inn in the whole of Denmark with lovely rooms and breakfast – stay here if you can!

Ribe Byferie, Damvej 34, **t** 79 88 79 88, *www. ribe-byferie.dk* (*moderate–inexpensive*). Five mins from the town centre, these are comfortable self-catering appartments for 4–7 people; good for families and groups.

Danhostel (youth hostel), Skt. Peders Gade 16, **t** 75 42 06 20, *www.danhostel.dk/ribe* (*inexpensive*). All rooms with bath. Lovely view over the river, cathedral, old town and tidal flats.

Backhaus, Grydergade 12, **t** 75 42 11 01 (*inexpensive*). A stone's throw from the cathedral, this pretty restaurant also offers rooms (no private bath).

Fru Mathies, Saltgade 15, **t** 75 42 34 20 (*inexpensive*). Pleasant rooms in a hotel/pub; also family rooms.

Den Gamle Arrest, Torvet 11, **t** 75 42 37 00, *www.dengamlearrest.dk* (*inexpensive*). Old jailhouse just opposite the cathedral with charming, simple double rooms and shared bathrooms. Also a café, restaurant and pretty courtyard.

Eating Out

There are lots of nice restaurants and cafés in Ribe. This list represents a few of them.

Hotel Dagmar, Torvet, **t** 75 42 00 33 (*expensive–moderate*). Delicious gourmet food in an attractive dining room or, in summer, lunch on the square.

Voegterkoelderen (Watchman's Cellar), Torvet 1, **t** 75 42 00 33 (*moderate–inexpensive*). Below (and belonging to) the Hotel Dagmar, this informal basement restaurant serves tender steak, fresh fish, spare ribs and lots of beer. It is popular with the locals and there is a very reasonable 4-course lunch menu.

Sælhunden (the Seal), Skibbroen 13, **t** 75 42 09 46 (*inexpensive*). Down on the harbour, this old pub is probably best for a lunch but still nice in the evening (lots of hearty steaks). *Smørrebrød* and all things Danish (including the menu). *Open 11–11.*

collapsed during Christmas mass in 1283 and killed 100 people. It is known as the civic tower and has been the offices of the mayor and the town archive for 150 years.

The cathedral has a nave flanked by two aisles on either side – the only church of this kind in Denmark. The outer aisles were added after a fire in 1402 to what were then the outside walls. As you enter, on the right-hand side of the inner door into the church there are deep grooves in the stone work; these were made (before 1350) by men sharpening their weapons on the stone as a way of blessing them. Other downward strokes are where locals (up until the 1950s!) came to 'drink the church' – scraping stone dust off the walls and taking it home to make a 'holy tea'.

Inside, the cathedral is light and bright with some lovely medieval, typically Danish linear frescoes on the walls – a red-headed, 15th-century *Madonna and Child*, the apostles Andrew and Bartholomew dressed as merchants and, on the second pillar on the left, a young man standing on an old man's back – good overcoming evil, or the building of one generation on the back and shoulders of previous generations?

As you wander down the aisle, look out for fossils in the marble floor. In front of the altar, there is a worn-down grey slab – the tomb of King Eric Emmune, murdered in 1136 by a farmer who resented paying tax. In the aisle to the left is an open stone sarcophagus – also that of a murdered king, Christopher I, who suffered at the hands of his abbot who felt sufficiently peeved to pop poison into the communion wine.

The altar is decorated with glittering glass mosaics, ceiling frescoes and stained-glass windows. Created between 1982 and 1987 by the famous Danish artist Carl-Henning Pederson, they are wonderfully integrated and put you in mind of artists such as Joan Miró and Picasso. Although he has never given an explanation of them, from right to left they are called *The Light of Heaven*, *The Kin Follow*, *After the Flood*, *Jacob Dreams*, *The Ascension of Elijah*, *The Chalice of Life* and *The Gate of Heaven*. The windows are called *From Earth to Heaven*, *Blue Legend*, *Heaven and Earth*, *The Red Heart* and *The Heavenly Eye*. Controversy has dogged these works since their inception and they are certainly thought-provoking. Along the south aisle, look out for the epitaphs on the walls (all showing *memento mori* symbols of skulls, hourglasses, etc.) and particularly that of Jørgen Pedersen and his wife Anne Christensdatter, and her second husband – they pop up again elsewhere in Ribe. By the pulpit, you can see the highest flood mark from 1634, about 1.8m in height (and remember, this was the highest place in town). Finally, climb the 250 steps up the tower, past the bell and the clock (dating from 1696 and wound every day) for a great view over the town (interesting fact: the flagpole hides the mobile phone masts that allow reception in the area – if they weren't hidden, civic- and historically-minded Ribe would have refused to put them up).

A Walk Around Ribe

Ribe is a lively and delightful town and kept so by the fact that no one is allowed to buy an old property unless they plan for it to be inhabited all year. It's a lovely place for a wander, but if you want a detailed explanation of what you are seeing, take one of the excellent walking tours offered by the tourist board.

The best place to start is on the **Torvet** where the cathedral stands. On the east side (Stenbrogade) stands the **Hotel Dagmar** – the oldest inn in Denmark, built in 1581 after the 'great' fire. Dagmar was a much loved queen, originally from Bohemia, who died at the age of 19 in 1212, giving birth to her second child. (At 12 and 3pm, the cathedral bells play a folk melody 'Queen Dagmar Has Taken to her Bed in Ribe'.) The tourist office is next door in another historic building. The fire of 1580 began just behind the tourist office, on the corner of Stenbrogade and Peder Down's Slippe. The entire area, all the way past Hotel Dagmar and along Grønnegade down to the river, was left in ruins – 11 streets and 213 houses as well as Sankt Catherine's Church.

On the south side of Torvet, if you are visiting between 1 April and 25 August, look up at the roofs and you should see Ribe's stork nest. Traditionally the male stork arrives on 1 April and builds a nest; the female arrives a few weeks later. The eggs must be laid by mid-May if the young are to be ready to leave towards the end of August.

From **Torvet**, wander down **Overdammen** (Upper Dam). Always look up at the buildings. Although it doesn't seem likely from the outside, all the houses in Ribe have courtyards and gardens; don't open gates that are shut, but, if a courtyard gateway is open, you are welcome to go in to have a look; Notice how narrow the house-fronts are. Medieval half-timbered houses were gable-fronted because it was cheaper, and the houses, in effect, ran lengthways down the side streets. The timber frames were filled in with wattle and daub or bricks. Look out for the varied patterns of the brick-work – done on the whim of the brickie to make his job more interesting. Down on the right, look at the **Quedens Gaard** on the corner with Sortebrødegade. This is a four-winged merchant's house. The oldest part dates from 1583 when land was expensive; however, with the 200-year depression, land became cheaper and more space could be used. The extended yellow front dates from 1789. Renovations will be complete in 2005 and the building will be open to the public. Halfway down Sortebrødegade, turn down **Kølholts Slippe** (a slipway) with the river at the end. You will also see buckets, a hook and a ladder on the wall. After the fire, the town council ordered 400 buckets, 30 ladders and 30 hooks to be placed around the town. In the case of fire, men climbed the ladders and pulled the roofs off with the hooks so the fire could be doused at street level and would not spread across the rooftops. Tiled roofs became law after 1580.

At the bottom of Sortebrødegade, you reach Dagmarsgade – the only straight street in Ribe. Originally it was as old and winding as any other, but in 1876 the town council became so excited at the acquisition of a railway – the first progress in over 200 years of stagnation! – that they demolished all the buildings that blocked the view of the station at the east end from the City Hall, now at the west end. Opposite, you will see **Sankt Catherine's Kirke**, which was founded in 1228 as an abbey for the mendicant Black Friars. The current church is the third to occupy this site and was built in the 1470s. The abbey was used as a hospital after the Reformation. The holes in the walls were made for the scaffolding beams when it was built and were never filled in. In the 1920s, the church almost collapsed, but a bold method of 'jacking it up' and tilting it back to the vertical rescued it from destruction. There is a lovely cloister and a pretty abbey garden on the south side.

From here walk across the bridge to **Duck Island** (the little 'houses' in the water are for the ducks to lay eggs in) and the **Ribe Vikinger** (*open April–June 10–4; July–Aug 10–6; Sept–Mar 10–4; Nov–Mar closed Mon; adm*). This amazing museum houses 250,000 items dug up since 1983, when, after years of searching for Ribe's Viking roots, archaeologists finally struck gold. This included two bead-making workshops, an amber workshop and many examples of handicrafts. Many exhibits are interactive.

Further along Sankt Nikolaj Gade is the **Kunstmuseum, t** 75 42 03 62, *www.ribe kunstmuseum.dk* (*open July–Aug Thurs–Sun 11–5; Sept– June Thurs–Sun 11–4; closed first six weeks of the year*). This has some 600 works spanning Danish art from 1750 to 1950, including the lovely Skagen school, Denmark's answer to the Impressionists.

At **Nedderdammen** (Lower Dam) you will see a watermill and eel and salmon ladders. Nedderdammen 31 is the oldest timbered house in Ribe (and possibly Denmark). If the gate is open, enter the courtyard and look at the plaque on the wall listing all the owners since 1490. Here you will see Jørgen Pedersen and Anne Christensdatter – the couple on the epitaph in the cathedral (the second husband did not inherit the house, just the wife).

Nedderdammen runs into **Mellemdammen** (Middle Dam). Have a look at the carving on No.31 where the carpenter has run out of space for all the letters on the second line. Then walk past the Royal Mill where Ribe's first brewery was set up in the 18th century. Finish back at Torvet.

During summer, the **nightwatchman** makes rounds of the town at 8 and 10pm, following a centuries-old tradition. Wait for him at Torvet near Hotel Dagmar.

Ribe Viking Centre

Lustropholm, Lustropvej 4, 6760 Ribe, t 75 41 16 11, www.ribevikingecenter.dk; open May–June and Sept Mon–Fri 10–3.30; July–Aug daily 11–5; autumn school hols Mon–Fri 11–4; adm.

Four km outside Ribe, you will find the charming and fascinating Viking Centre where the Viking age is brought to life in a reconstructed village based on the most up-to-date finds. Everything has been constructed with the same tools as the Vikings would have used (excluding the power saw!) and the whole of Viking life is lived out here, from the manor house with its great central fire (where someone might be cooking if you are lucky), fur-strewn beds and stable at one end, to the townhouses, water mill and market place. You can see the blacksmith at work and falconry displays, as well as Icelandic ponies, cattle and poultry, which are all raised here.

Odense

Odense – named after Odin, king of the Norse gods – on the island of Funen is another pleasant olde-worlde cobbledy town, close to the sea. One of the oldest places in Denmark, it was an important trading, Crown and ecclesiastical centre in the Middle Ages and could just have become the capital as easily as Copenhagen. It regained some of its importance as an industrial centre in the 19th century. These days, its chief claims to fame are as the childhood homes of Hans Christian Andersen (1805–75), and the composer Carl Nielsen (1865–1931) – both of whom were miserable and left fairly rapidly.

The **Hans Christian Andersen Hus**, Bangs Boder 29, **t** 65 51 46 01, *www.odmus.dk*, is said to be where the author was born. The museum chronicles his life with plenty of

Getting There

Trains to Odense leave Esbjerg twice an hour and take 1½–2 hours. If you are visiting from Copenhagen, trains leave every two hours and take 1½hrs.

Tourist Information

Odense: Rådhuset, t 66 12 75 20, f 66 12 75 86, www.odenseturist.dk (open Dec–June 9.30–4.30, Sat 10–1; mid-June–Aug Mon–Fri 9–6, Sat–Sun 10–3).

Odense Adventure Pass

Available at the tourist office, this entitles you to free entry to all museums and attractions and is good value at 110–150kr for a 24/48hr pass.

Where to Stay

Motel Ansgarhuys, Kirkegårds Allé 17–21, t 66 12 88 00, f 66 12 88 65 (inexpensive). Near the centre; a comfortable family-run hotel.

City Hotel Odense, Hans Mules Gade 5, t 66 12 12 58, f 66 12 93 64, www.city-hotel-odense. dk (expensive–moderate). Part of the City chain, this is a comfortable central hotel with mod cons. Check for some good deals.

Eating Out

There are plenty of places to eat in Odense, although the food isn't exceptional.

Den Gamle Kro, Overgade 23, t 66 12 14 33, f 66 17 88 58, dengamlekro@city-hotel-odense.dk (expensive). For a treat, eat in this historic inn, 300 years old, with bags of atmosphere.

photographs, letters, mementoes and room reconstructions. Both this museum and the **Baerndomshjem** on Munkemøllestræde 3–5, t 65 51 46 01, www.odmus.dk, his childhood home where he lived from the age of 2 to 14, have been recently renovated (both open mid-June–Aug Tues–Sun 9–7; Sept–May Tues–Sun 10–4; closed Mon).

The **Carl Nielsen Museum**, Claus Bergs Gade 11, t 65 51 46 01, www.odmus.dk (open Jan–Aug Thurs–Fri 4–8, Sun 12–4), gives a detailed, chronological account of the life and work of Carl Nielsen, and of his wife, sculptor AnneMarie Carl-Nielsen (see p.280). It includes recordings of the composer's music, supplemented by a video show.

Sankt Knuds Cathedral, Flakhaven, t 66 12 03 92 (open Nov–Mar Mon–Sat 10–4; April–Oct Mon–Sat 9–5; Nov–Dec Mon–Sat 10–4, Sun and hols 12–5), is one of the finest examples of elegant high Gothic architecture in Denmark, dating from the end of the 1400s. It is known for its gilded altarpiece, made by Claus Berg in 1521. In the crypt, two coffins contain the remains of King Knud (Canute) the Holy and his brother Benedict, both murdered in Odense in 1086.

The **Odense City Museum** (Møntergården), Overgade 48–50, t 65 51 46 01, www. odmus.dk (open Tues–Sun 10–4), is a museum of urban history and features exhibitions on Odense during the Viking age and the medieval period, and interiors from the 17th and 18th centuries to the 1950s. In the open storehouse of the museum, there are thousands of items exemplifying everyday life from the Middle Ages to the present day.

For a less cultural, more light-hearted couple of hours, visit **Odense Zoo**, Sdr. Boulevard 306, t 66 11 13 60/65 90 82 28, www.odensezoo.dk (open daily 9–4/5/6/7, depending on season; adm), has over 1,000 animals. This makes for a lot of feeding times – choose from the lions, tigers, manatees, chimps, penguins, sealions and piranhas.

Århus

Århus is a very attractive university town by the sea with a pretty old town area that has a small river running through it. It has ancient roots and was an important Viking seafaring town by the 10th century; it is first mentioned in 948 in connection with its bishop, Reginand – only the second Danish town (after Ribe, *see* pp.280–84) mentioned so early in written sources. Towards the end of the Viking period, around 1040, coins were being struck and the characters were in Latin, not in runes, with names such as King Hardecanute and Magnus the Good. It had a coat of arms by 1250 and its earliest known charter dates from 1441. Historically it was prosperous in the Middle Ages, owing much of its wealth to its harbour and its position as an ecclesiastical centre, but it foundered rather when the Reformation took place in 1536 and its church role came to an end. After a stagnant period in the 17th century, its geographical position helped it to recover around 1750, but it suffered severe blockades during the Napoleonic Wars in the early part of the 19th century. However, with the advent of the railway and steamships, it was back on its feet again. Now, it is ranked as Denmark's second city and has a well-deserved reputation for being vibrant and creative, with great nightlife and plenty of delicious cafés and restaurants that stay open until the early hours, especially at weekends. It has a lot of cultural attractions, is close to many others and, if you want a rest, it's all too tempting to flake out on one of several nearby beaches.

The Old Town

Århus's old town is, as you might expect, centred around the cathedral. However, it is thought that the original town was positioned a few streets away around Århus's oldest church building, Vor Frue Kirke (Church of our Lady). Although there is little evidence now, many of the streets in this area have names that relate to its layout in Viking times, such as Borgporten (City Gate), Volden (Rampart) and Graven (the Ditch). Around the Domkirke (cathedral), there are a number of small, interesting museums; otherwise wander the cobbled streets and soak up the atmosphere. A lot of the old town, around Mejlgade, Rosensgade, Graven, Pustervig and Klostergade, is given over to classy clothes shops (including a plethora of shoe shops), arts and craft studios and galleries, cafés and restaurants. Further south, Aboulevarden, which runs across the old part of the city, is on the River Århus, which was hidden under concrete for years. The town council has now decided to open it up again and the area has become a very popular waterfront. Aboulevarden was originally a Viking market area.

Domkirke (St Clement's Cathedral)

Bispetorv, t 86 12 38 45, www.aarhus-domkirke.dk; open Oct–April 10–3; May–Sept 9.30–4; closed to tourists on Sun and hols.

St Clement's Cathedral, like the one in Roskilde, was one of the earliest brick-built cathedrals in Denmark; the first bricks were laid around the year 1200. It was built in

Getting There

From the UK
Ryanair have a daily flight to Århus. British Airways also fly there. Maesk Air flies to Billund (with connecting coach to Århus).

From Copenhagen
You can get a plane (30mins), train (3hrs) or bus (route 888, 3hrs).

Getting to and from the Airport
There is a bus link between Århus and the airport with direct connections to schedule and charter flights. It takes about 45mins. Further information: Århus Airport, t 87 75 70 00, *www.aar.dk*.

Getting Around

Århus is another very walkable city, and you can do the day trips by bus if you want to.

Car Hire
At Århus Tirstrup Airport:
Hertz, t 86 36 36 44.
Avis, t 70 24 77 37.
Budget, t 86 36 39 99.
Europcar, t 86 36 37 44.

Tourist Information

Århus: Rådhuset, **t** 89 40 67 00, **f** 86 12 95 90, *www.visitaarhus.com (open Jan–mid-June Mon– Fri 9.30–4, Sat 10–1; mid-June–Aug Mon– Fri 9.30–6, Sat 9.30–5.30, Sun 9.30–1; Sept–Dec Mon–Fri 9–4, Sat 10–1)*.

Århus Card
The Århus Card is valid for 24hrs, 48hrs or one week and is very good value at under 200kr. It provides free public transport and admission to most attractions and some tours as well as free parking at the Skolebakken car park for up to 5 days.

Festivals

Århus Festival, a week-long city festival, takes pace at the end of August, t 89 40 91 91,
www.aarhusfestuge.dk. The **Århus International Jazz Festival**, now in its 15th year, takes place in July for one week, t 86 12 13 12, *www.jazzfest.dk*.

Shopping

Århus is a very good shopping centre and the largest after Copenhagen. Shopping hours are generally Mon–Thurs 10–5.30, Fri 10–8, Sat 11–2 (some shops open until about 4pm first and/or last Sat of the month), *www.aarhus-city.dk*.

The old town behind the cathedral, around **St Clements Stræde** and along **Volden**, tends to be the especially arty/designer end of town with lots of galleries, studios and independent clothing boutiques and shoe shops. Elsewhere, there are a couple of excellent big department stores in the centre. The pedestrianized **Strøget** (Ryesgade/Søndergade), running up to the cathedral from the station, is the main big shopping street. There is a morning vegetable and flower market in Ingerslev Boulevard on Wednesdays and Saturdays.

Bülow Duus Glassworks, Studsgade 14, t 86 12 72 86 *(open Mon–Thurs 11–5.30, Fri 11–6, Sat 11–1)*. This workshop is a treasure trove of beautiful glass art; come and browse and see glass being made, especially if you don't have the chance to go to the Glass Museum in Ebeltoft *(see p.301)*.

Ulrik Witts Hus, Volden 23, t 23 46 45 08 *(open Tues–Thurs 12–5.30, Fri 12–7, Sat 10–2)*. Ulrik Witts's gallery and studio in the heart of the old town, through a low doorway and up narrow stairs, are a delight of bright colour and expressive forms. If he is working, it's fine to stay and watch.

munthe plus simonsen, Borggade 2, t 86 18 55 77, *www.muntheplussimonsen.dk*. These two are the first ladies of new Danish fashion and were awarded the Veuve Cliquot Business Woman Award of the Year 2004, having been in business for only 10 years. They sell their relaxed, colourful designs in over 200 outlets in 15 countries. Both their men's and women's fashions are on sale in this, one of their flagship stores.

Hørlyck, Vestergade 8, **t** 86 19 73 44. Beware! Gorgeous shoe shop only to be entered with extreme caution or with your hands tied behind your back!

Boutique Marie, Borggade 11, **t** 86 19 74 77. A great shop selling stylish designer fashion for the larger figure. It is their mission to make you look and feel fab.

Trip Trap Traestudie, Carl Blochs Gade 39, **t** 86 13 44 40, *www.triptrap.dk*. This is the place to come if you want to fill your home with authentic Danish design – from home and garden furniture to wooden floors, industrial art and kitchen utensils.

Salling, Søndergade 27, **t** 86 12 18 00, *www. salling.dk (open Mon–Wed 9.30–6, Thurs–Fri 9.30–8, Sat 9–5)*. One of Århus's big stores with 35 different departments.

Magasin, Immervad 2–8, **t** 86 12 33 00, *www. magasin.dk (open Mon–Wed 10–6, Thurs 10–7, Fri 10–8, Sat 10–5)*. In the same chain as Magasin du Nord in Copenhagen, this too is a nice department store with an especially good food department – the organic bakery Emmery's started here.

Where to Stay

Always check for deals, even in expensive hotels. Some of the bigger hotels give better prices if you book on the web. Always ask if breakfast is included – this will make a difference of at least 50kr.

Radisson SAS Scandinavia Hotel, Margrethe Pladsen, **t** 86 12 86 65 *(expensive, but check for moderate deals)*. Everything you would expect from a first-class international hotel.

Hotel Royal, Store Torv 4, **t** 86 12 00 11, **f** 86 76 04 04, *www.hotelroyal.dk*. A classic *de luxe* hotel, this is on the same square as the Domkirke. An 'alternative' entrance gives a sense of Hollywood-style decadence in keeping with the fine art scattered on the walls, the marble fittings and the inhouse nightclub and Royal Casino.

Hotel Guldsmeden, Guldsmedgade 40, **t** 86 13 45 50, **f** 86 13 76 76, *www.hotelguldsmeden. dk (expensive–moderate)*. Whitewashed walls, dark wood, colonial-style furniture, authentic art, Persian carpets, individual rooms, friendly staff, lovely breakfast,

balconies and, if you don't mind being slightly further out of town and walking up a lot of narrow stairs, a fantastic penthouse suite overlooking the harbour.

Villa Provence, Fredens Torv 12, **t** 86 18 24 00, **f** 86 18 24 03, *www.VillaProvence.dk (expensive)* This is an attractive, Provençal-style hotel with stylish décor, a pretty courtyard and good breakfasts. Parking is available but you have to pay extra for it.

Hotel, Café & Restaurant Philip, Aboulevarden 28, **t** 87 32 14 44, **f** 86 12 69 55, *www.hotel philip.dk (expensive)*. This super hotel, run by ex-football player Marc Rieper (he missed the goal in the 1998 World Cup, if you are into these things) is a small intimate, friendly establishment with eight attractive suites and a good restaurant bang in the centre by the Århus River. Although it is in the expensive bracket, you get a full 60m² of accommodation for your money.

Helnan Marselis, Strandvejen 25, **t** 86 14 44 11, **f** 86 14 44 20, *hotel@marselis.dk*, *www. marselis.dk (expensive–moderate)*. If you prefer to be out of the centre with a view over the bay, this nice all-mod-cons hotel (including sauna, fitness centre and swimming pool) is a possible answer. Only 3km from the centre, it also has direct access to the bathing beach and is on the edge of the Marselisborg woods. All 101 hotel rooms have a full view of the city.

Aarslev Kro & Hotel, Silkeborgvej 900, 8220 Brabrand, **t** 86 26 05 77, **f** 86 26 07 65, *www. aarslevkro.dk (moderate)*. A 19th-century thatched inn 10km from Århus. Have breakfast under the open beams in the tap room. This is a nice option for a less relentlessly 'city' trip. Family rooms are also available.

Marselisborg Havn, Havenevej 20, **t** 40 85 44 99, *www.hotelmarselisborghavn.dk (moderate–inexpensive)* A smaller hotel (30 double rooms) on the marina in the bay of Århus in an old warehouse building.

Hotel Cab Inn, Kannikegade 14, **t** 86 75 70 00, **f** 86 75 71 00, *www.cabinn.com (moderate–inexpensive)*. Another in this great chain based on 'ship-cabin' design (i.e. small). Two minutes from the Domkirke in one direction and two minutes from the river cafés and restaurants of Aboulevarden in the other.

Århus City Apartments, Fredensgade 19, **t** 86 27 51 30, mobile **t** 40 27 90 30, *www.hotelaca.dk* (*moderate–inexpensive*). These comfortable 1-, 2- or 3-room apartments with TV, bath and kitchen are very well placed and an excellent budget option, especially if you are planning to stay in Århus a few days.

Eating Out

Århus is chock-a-bloc with delicious, stylish cafés and restaurants and you are never really going to be disappointed wherever you go; sitting out, chatting, eating and drinking and watching the world go by are an essential part of your stay. Cafés are open until the early hours and usually offer breakfast, lunch and supper menus.

L'Estragon, Klostergade 6, **t** 86 12 40 66, *www.lestragon.dk* (*expensive–moderate*). This lovely, intimate candlelit bistro serves up delicious French food with a twist based on seasonal ingredients. It also has a good wine list. An Århus favourite. *Open Mon–Sat 6pm–12am; reservation recommended.*

Prins Ferdinand, Viborgvej 2, **t** 86 12 52 05 (*moderate*). Cosy restaurant in the old town serving very good Danish food with a dash of worldwide inspiration. Large groups are welcome. *Open Tues–Sat noon–3 and 6–late, Sun–Mon by arrangement.*

Restaurant Seafood, Marselisborg Havnevej 44, **t** 86 18 56 55, **f** 86 18 54 99 (*moderate*). You will need to take a taxi as this is 3–4km out of the city, but the great fish dishes and a candlelit view over the harbour are very good incentives. *Open daily 12pm–12am; Sept –Mar closed Sun except for groups of 20+.*

Mefisto Gourmetbar and Café, Volden 28, **t** 86 13 18 13, *www.cafe-mefisto.dk* (*moderate–inexpensive*). In the heart of the old town, this stylish modern restaurant offers good food, décor, service and value for money. Also, a pretty courtyard for *al fresco* dining.

Café Casablanca, Rosensgade 12, **t** 86 13 82 22. The first café in Århus – set up in 1981 near the cathedral – hit a nerve and started a boom. It's still a favourite with the locals and offers live jazz on Wed nights and DJs on Fri and Sat. *Open Mon–Sat 10am–2am, Sun 12–12.*

Bryggeriet Skt. Clemens, Kannikegade 10, **t** 86 13 80 00, *www.bryggeriet.dk* (*moderate–inexpensive*). Surprisingly one of a chain, this is a really cosy, candlelit pub/steakhouse complete with copper brewing kettles, where the beer is brewed using traditional methods on the premises. *Open Mon–Wed 11.30am–11.59pm, Thurs–Sat 11.30am–2am.*

Emmery's, Guldsmedgade 24, **t** 86 13 04 00. Emmery's organic bakery (also in Copenhagen) originated in Århus – this is the restaurant/café/patisserie. Delicious breakfasts, brunches and suppers (tapas, fish, meat and vegetarian dishes). Also sells superior deli produce including chocolates. *Open daily.*

Fredes Flyvvende Tallerken, Østbanetorvet 2, **t** 86 16 92 57, **f** 86 16 92 67, *www.fredeslyvendetallerken.dk* (*moderate–inexpensive*). Minimalist 'Freddy's Flying Saucer' serves up good Mediterranean and Danish dishes and, if you are on the hoof, fabulous sandwiches made with organic home-baked bread. *Open Mon–Sat 11am–12am, Sun 12pm–12am.*

Nightlife

Many cafés offer live music at weekends and/or turn into discos at night. They are usually open until around 2am.

Train, Tolbolgade 6, **t** 86 13 47 22, *www.train.dk*. One of Denmark's largest and most noted music venues. Since its opening in 1998, major artists such as the Cardigans, Bryan Ferry and Iggy Pop have played here. It also hosts the most popular disco in town. *Open Thurs–Sat to 5am; minimum age 23.*

Jazzbar Bent J, Nørre Allé 66, **t** 86 12 04 92, **f** 86 17 93 17, *www.bentj.dk*. Mostly modern jazz at this incredibly cool venue. Free jam sessions on Fridays at 4pm.

Social Club, Klosterpot 34, **t** 86 19 42 50, *www.socialclub.dk*. Popular with students (good discounts!), this club features popular mainstream and chart music as well as R&B at two separate discos. *Open Thurs–Sat 11pm–5am; adm; min. age 20.*

Musikhuset Århus, Thomas Jensens Allé, **t** 89 40 90 00, *www.musikhusetaarhus.dk*. Main concert hall with a programme of classical music, jazz, opera and occasional well-known pop bands.

the Romanesque style and was completed around 1300. However, the church burned down in 1330 and was left in ruins until the end of the century. When reconstruction began, styles had changed and the new cathedral, finished in 1500, was Gothic, although remnants of the original church do still exist. It is 93m high and 93m long – the longest church in Denmark. It can seat roughly 1,200 people.

Inside, the cathedral is whitewashed, with a frescoed vaulted nave and fresco fragments on the walls – all using combinations of red, yellow, green and black. In fact, Århus cathedral has the largest area of frescoes of any church in Denmark, although many of them have now disappeared. They cover many themes and are painted by five different hands. The biggest is on the west wall of the south transept and shows *St Christopher and St Clement* – the patron saint of the cathedral and also of sailors – which measures 220m². St Christopher is dressed as a bearded 16th-century gentleman and St Clement (the fourth pope, who achieved his patron status by virtue of being drowned by the Emperor Trajan with an anchor around his neck – an apocryphal story) wields an anchor and a crosier. In keeping with the ocean theme (hardly odd in a harbour town), there is a votive ship, *Unity*, to the right of the high altar, which dates back to 1720. The story goes that it was made in Holland and sent to Tsar Peter the Great as a working model of the warships that wainwrights in Holland were making for him. However, the ship carrying it foundered and sank in a storm on the coast of Skagen in the north of Denmark (*see* pp.305–306). Miraculously, the model drifted ashore, almost undamaged, and was bought by some fishermen from Århus who donated it to the cathedral. At 2.65m long and 3.50m tall, it is the largest votive ship in any Danish church.

Other frescoes include a lovely *St George and the Dragon*, in which George looks a bit bored and the surprised female dragon (whose baby is left all alone in a nearby cave) draws her last breath while the local damsel says her prayers and the townspeople peer over the battlements to watch the fight. On the vaulted ceiling the *Baptism*, the *Crucifixion*, *Christ as the World's Judge*, and the *Coronation of Mary as the Queen of Heaven* are depicted along with John the Baptist and saints Peter, Paul, James, Bartholomew, Thomas, and Matthias. St Michael, the weigher of souls, appears in an arch near the pulpit and another close by seems to have speech bubbles. Another gem is the *All Souls* fresco in the chancel by the modern organ, in which Christ and the angels are shown in a top tier, the laity and clergy pray on the middle tier and devils and angels battle for souls on the bottom tier; there is a lovely image of angels rescuing souls, feet flailing, from the devil, like a North Sea Rescue helicopter!

The wall-paintings were all made between 1470 and 1520, except the one surrounding the so-called leprosy window in the northwest corner of the church. Painted around 1300, it is the only one left from the Romanesque church.

The high altar is one of the most impressive in Denmark. The elaborate carved, gilded altar piece is the work of Lübeck master Bernt Notke and and was inaugurated in 1479. It is a so-called pentatych that can be folded three times. The Feastday panels (carved and gilded with 23.5 carat gold) are on display from Christmas morning until Ash Wednesday. The Passion-tide panels are visible from Ash Wednesday until Easter morning. On Easter morning the Feastday panels become visible again and the altar-piece remains in this position until Advent. On the first Sunday of Advent the third and last set of panels, the Advent panels, are disclosed; they can be seen until and including Christmas Eve. The central panel shows a fresh-cheeked St Anne (mother of the virgin), St John the Baptist on the right and St Clement on the left (all looking a bit sombre).

Back towards the west end of the cathedral are the font (1481), shaped like an inverted bell and supported by four sculptures representing the four evangelists, and the oak pulpit (1588), a very fine example of Renaissance carving. The nine biblical scenes show the *Fall*, the *Annunciation*, the *Birth in Bethlehem*, the *Baptism of Christ*, the *Last Supper*, the *Crucifixion*, the *Resurrection*, *Pentecost*, and finally the *Day of Judgment*. Have a look at how Judas is depicted in the *Last Supper* – the carver, a Belgian called Michael van Groningen, was of the opinion that the people we love most are also the people we may hurt most.

The cathedral also has six very fine wrought-iron lattice-work portals, all made by the German master smith Caspar Fincke. His mark, a hammer and a key laid across one another, is usually to be found in a corner in one of the large panels that make up the portals. The most remarkable is the golden portal to the chancel, made up of four panels with circles and quadrangles. The quadrangle is the symbol of humanity, and the circle, which is both rounded and indefinite, is the symbol of heaven.

The one stained-glass window is modern and was made by the Norwegian artist Emanuel Vigeland (*see* p.158) in 1926. It is 14m tall and, in keeping with the cathedral's preponderance for having the biggest of everything, is the biggest in any Danish church. In three layers, it shows the grave at Golgotha with Christ's dead body and a tree growing out of the grave at the bottom. The tree then turns into a cross with the crucified Christ, and at the top Christ is risen from the dead.

Around the Cathedral

By the cathedral, there are three small museums of interest. The **Kvindemuseet** (Women's Museum), Domkirkeplads 5, **t** 86 13 61 44, *www.kvvindemuseet.dk* (*open Sept–May Tues–Sun 10–4; June–Aug daily 10–5, Wed 10–8; adm, under 16s free*), is a surprisingly personal collection relating to the changing lives and expectations of women in Denmark over the last century or so. Motherhood and working life, servitude and learning, submissiveness and revolt, isolation and sisterhood are some of the themes under scrutiny, and the collection covers all sorts of objects, from garden tools to sanitary towels, school conduct books to trade licences, snapshots of everyday life to formal portraits, oral stories of beatings and abortions to paintings by women artists. All exhibits give details on the objects, owners and any stories behind them.

The **Vikinge-Museet** (Viking Museum), Nordea Bank, Sankt Clemens Torv 6, **t** 89 42 11 00 (*open Mon–Wed, Fri 10–4, Thurs 10–5.30; free*) is in the basement of a bank because this is an archaeological site where the remains of a 10th-century Viking town wall and several small 'pit houses' were found 2–3m below the current ground level. There were seven houses, some of which also contained objects such as wood-working tools, spurs and harness buckles, flax combs and jewellery.

The **Besættelsesmuseet i Århus 1940–45** (Occupation Museum), Mathilde Fibigers Have 2, **t** 86 18 42 83, *www.besaettelsesmuseet.dk* (*open June– Aug Tues, Thurs, Sat–Sun 11–4; Sept–Dec Sat–Sun 11–4*), in the basement of the old police station, was used as the Gestapo headquarters from autumn 1944. It displays both the peaceful and dramatic events in Århus during the German occupation.

Vor Frue Kirke (Church of our Lady)

*Frue Kirkeplads, **t** 86 12 12 43, www. aarhusvvorfrue.dk; open Oct–April Mon–Fri 10–2, Sat 10–noon; May–Sept Mon–Fri 10–4, Sat 10–2.*

Vor Frue Kirke is, in effect, three separate churches: a crypt church, under the choir of the Church of Our Lady, dating from the 11th century; the abbey church, which was originally the main hall of the abbey, built by Dominicans (Blackfriars) in the second half the 13th century; and the Church of our Lady, also an abbey building.

The crypt (down the stairs from the choir) was the first church on this site and is one of the oldest preserved stone churches in Scandinavia. It was rediscovered in 1956 and reconsecrated in November 1957. Its ceiling has 15 arches supported by eight columns. There are a few remnants of frescoes on the walls and pillars, and the crucifix in the middle apse is an exact copy of the old Roman crucifix from Gl. Åby church near Århus; the original can be seen at the National Museet in Copenhagen.

The present entrance to the abbey church was the original abbey entrance. When somebody knocked on the door to get in, according to the regulations of monastery from 1240, the porter had to make sure that they were not 'women, thieves or other loiterers'. The abbey church is a long barrel-vaulted room and was originally the reception room where monks could meet lay people. Only distinguished visitors were allowed into the main hall. Along the walls were benches and a special seat for the abbot, and all monks gathered here every morning after Prime. This hall was consecrated in 1888 for the abbey residents, and is now an old people's home. The frescoes date from 1517 and the window was painted by Per Kirkeby.

The current red-brick Church of our Lady dates back to about 1250, when the choir and vestry were added. The aisle dates from about 1350 and the side-aisle from about 1450. The tower was built in 1500. The wrought-iron font has a bronze bowl and was made in the first half of the 16th century. The triptych was carved about 1530 in the workshop of Claus Berg in Lübeck. The pulpit, decorated with the four evangelists, the crucifixion and resurrection of Jesus Christ, is later and dates from 1598.

West of the Old Town: Den Gamle By

*Viborgvej 2, **t** 86 12 31 88; open Jan 11–3; Feb and Mar 10–4; April and May 10–5; June–Aug 9–6; Sept and Oct 10–5; Nov and Dec 10–4; adm.*

Den Gamle By (The Old Town) is not an authentic part of Århus's old town – it is the National Museum of Urban History and Culture, founded in 1914, and is situated just to the west of the Vor Frue Kirke and right next door to the **Botanical Gardens**. It is made up of 75 old houses that have been brought from all over Denmark. You can walk into most of them, buy authentic snacks at the bakery and so forth. All the houses are decorated as they were before they were transported to Den Gamle By, and are sometimes accompanied by sounds and smells for effect. Some are home to small museum-quality exhibitions, including ones on clocks and watches, silver and Delftware and toys. During the day, actors in period costume work at different trades, flirt with the girls, play the barrel organ, cook food, lay fires in the grate...everything is intended to make you feel as if you are seeing, smelling and sharing in the past.

The buildings include merchants' houses – the grandest being the mayor's house on Torvet dating from 1597 – a pharmacy, post offfice, school, theatre, custom house and shipyard, as well as shops, gardens, workshops and even 19th-century public conveniences brought from Copenhagen. One of the most recent acquisitions is a house that Hans Christian Andersen used to visit as a child nearly 200 years ago. The building, Eilschou's Alms Houses, was originally located in the street of Munkemøllestræde in Odense, opposite his own home (*see* p.285) and was made up of free apartments for widows of the clergy and respectable spinsters. In one of the flats lived Madam Blunkeflod and her sister-in-law, and it was here, Andersen recounts in his autobiography, *The Fairytale of my Life*, that he was introduced to a lot of books and 'I found a home' and 'learned that being a poet was a wonderful happy thing'. Once the houses close, you can enter and wander round the town for free.

Modern Århus

ARoS

Aros Allé 2, t 87 30 66 00, f 87 30 66 01, www.aros.dk; open Tues 10–5, Wed 10–10, Thurs–Sun 10–5, closed Mon; adm.

ARoS is Århus's gorgeous new art museum, which only opened in April 2004 – the new name is the old Viking name for Århus (which means 'river mouth' and was perverted to Århus in the 16th century) and *Ars*, the Latin for Art (hence the lower case 'o'). The previous museum was by the university but was becoming too small for the collection, and for the role that the museum authorities wanted it to play in the life of the city. The new building, first dreamt up in 1985, is far more central, and completes a triad of modern buildings (along with the Musikhus and the Rådhus), around a green park area running down to Mølleparken and the Århus River (which is being uncovered along Aboulevarden). It was designed by Schmidt, Hammer & Lassen (who also designed the Black Diamond in Copenhagen, *see* p.248). The building itself is a large cube; inside, it opens up into an elegant, white, light-filled interior with galleries running around a central hall, a series of lifts and a wide spiral staircase to move you between the ten floors from the basement to the roof terrace. The collection has been edited and is well presented with good information in English, especially in the modern section. The intention is that only 40 per cent should ever be on view and that the exhibition should change. The collection covers the 'Golden Age' (lots of portraits, landscapes and nationalism), Modernism 1770–1930 (including paintings from the Skagen school), and modern art 1930–80, including masterpieces from the CoBrA group, Warhol, Per Kirkeby, Morgens Gissel and Teddy Sørensen. Have a good look at the mirrored window of the car door by the American artist Edvard Kienholz (1924–94) in the first room and you won't be able to miss the Damien Hirst-like jars of formaldehyde by Bjørn Nørregaad, accompanied by a rather pretentious video – *Horse Sacrifice 1970* – in the second room. Draw your own conclusions. There is also some later work by Asger Jorn, Eljer Bille and Henry Heerup *et al*. The collection arrives at the present day with a gallery on the 5th floor devoted to art from 1980 onwards, covering new media – video installations, photography, etc. as well as abstract expressive images using untraditional materials such as glue, bubble wrap and polystyrene foam. Some of these are humorous and quite a giggle – don't miss Peter Land's portly *Naked Dancing Cellist* cavorting to the strains of Saint Saëns' cello music, *The Swan* and *Carnival of the Animals*.

Downstairs in the basement, a maze of nine rooms houses big installations by artists such as the American Bill Viola. Here, you will also see the highly realistic and psychologically probing *Boy*, a massive sculpture by Australian Ron Mueck, which was first exhibited at the Millennium Dome in 2000 and later at the Venice Biennale 2001; in fact you will already have seen it looking down from other floors, but go down to see it at basement level too.

The Rådhus

Rådhus Pladsen 2, t 89 40 20 00, www.visitaarhus.com; open daily Mon–Fri 9–4; tours (adm) mid-June–early Sept Mon–Fri at 11am, tower only noon and 2pm.

The City Hall was designed by Arne Jacobsen who, with Erik Møller, won a competition in 1937. It was completed in 1942 and the following year Jacobsen, who was Jewish, fled to Sweden to escape the Nazis. Over 50 years old, it is still a modern, functionalistic building and represents Danish design and architecture at their best. The interior is characterized by soft rounded shapes, Danish beechwood panels and a concern for textural effect. Jacobsen also designed the furnishings, fixtures and fittings – with the exception of the lighting – using a total of 2.5km of brass banisters and 15,000 white rails, which typify the internal design. The floors are made of rare bog oak.

Although the building is so forward-, even futuristic-thinking in its design, many elements reflect the period in which it was built. For example, look at the mural *A Human Society* (1946) above the entrance, by Hagedorn Olsen, which symbolically represents the city emerging from the Second World War, and the small civic room in which Albert Naur, who designed it during the Nazi occupation, concealed various Allied insignia in his intricate floral patterns.

From the outside, perhaps the most arresting feature of this building is the 60m-high 'scaffolding' clock tower, which affords a good view, and has become a hallmark of the city. Along with the rest of the building, it is clad with 6,000m² of Norwegian marble panels. The scaffolding has always raised comment. According to Jacobsen, it was there because '...we think the scaffolding looks nice. That is also why it was left in place.'

The clocktower contains 43 bells, which plays the 'May ballad' *In vernalis temporis* by the Danish composer Morten Børup three times a day.

The area immediately surrounding the town hall was established at the same time. The trees were preserved as far as possible and now constitute one of the most important features of the park. The sculptures in the park include a female figure by Svend Rothsack. In front of the building's wing gable, facing the railway station, stands a huge Porsgrunn marble basin, decorated with Johannes Bjerg's fountain *Agnete and the Merman*. The square in front features Mogens Bøggil's *Grisebrønden* sculpture, presented to the city by the local brewery, Ceres.

Other Museums

There are a number of other museums in Århus. Slightly north from the Rådhus is the **Danish Museum of Placards and Posters**, J.M. Mørks Gade 13, **t** 86 15 33 45, **f** 86 15 33 45 (*open Tues–Sun 10–5; adm*), in an extension to the **Århus Art Building** (which often has very good exhibitions). It is based on the private collection by the artist Peder Stougaard, who started collecting posters from all the world 27 years ago. The museum now has about 200,000 posters, which makes it one of the largest collections in the world.

The **Århus Bymuseet**, Carl Blochs Gade 28, **t** 86 13 28 62, *www.bymuseet.dk* (*open Tues–Fri 10–4, Sat–Sun 12–4; free*), is west of the centre, beyond ARoS, in a former railway station, and covers all aspects of the history and development of the city, from its origins as a fortified Viking town to the present day.

The **Steno Museet**, **t** 89 42 39 75, **f** 89 42 39 95, *www.stenomuseet.dk* (*open Tues–Fri 9–4, Sat–Sun 11–4; adm*), in the university park, is fun and explores the history of medicine and the natural sciences; it includes a herb garden with more than 350 medicinal herbs and a planetarium (*performances at 11am, 1pm and 2pm*).

Just north of the Steno Museet is the **Naturhistorisk Museum,** Århus Universitetsparken, Bygning 210, **t** 86 12 97 77, **f** 86 13 08 82, *www.naturhistorisk museum.dk* (*open Sept– June daily 10–4; July–Aug daily 10–5; adm*), which features exhibitions about the Danish landscape and extensive exhibits of animals from all over the world, many in settings displaying the animals' natural habitats.

If you are in the mood, go north out of town to visit the **Museum at the Psychiatric Hospital**, Skovagervej 2, 8240 Risskov, **t** 77 89 36 80, **f** 77 89 36 79, *www.aaa.dk/ musph* (*open Mon–Sat 10–4; guided tours available in English; adm; ring for information*). The hospital is still a working unit. There is a historical section explaining the history of the hospital and that of psychiatric treatment in Denmark, and an art gallery showing art created by inmates both past and present. You can combine visiting this museum with a trip to the **beach** at Den Permanente (take bus 6 or 16 from Risskov).

Day Trips from Århus

Moesgård

Moesgård Museum

*Moesgård Alle 20, 8270 Højbjerg, **t** 89 42 11 00, **f** 86 27 23 78, www. moesmus.dk; open April–Sept daily 10–4; Oct–Dec Tues–Sun 10–4; adm.*

The Moesgård Manor in the woods south of Århus provides the setting for the Moesgård Museum, which houses archaeological and ethnographic collections as well as reconstructed houses from the Iron and Viking Ages. But its star turn is **Grauballe Man**, one of several Roman Iron-Age individuals who have been discovered, tanned like leather, in peat bogs in the area over the last few centuries. Like Tollund Man at the Silkeborg Museum (*see* pp.298–300), this figure has a full head of hair and skin in such good condition that scientists received a good set of fingerprints from him. Also like Tollund Man, he died violently (he had his throat cut). The amount of personal information that has been gleaned 2,000-odd years later is extraordinary: he was in his late 30s, unused to manual work, his last meal was of five different types of grain, he had had his hair cut with scissors, and he is thought to have shaved within three weeks of his death. Computer graphics and explanations make the 1952 discovery very vivid. No one knows why he died, but he was perhaps a human sacrifice – it is known that sacrifices (including animals that had their throats cut and their blood drained into cauldrons) were made to the gods at this time – and the *Gundestrup Cauldron*, now in the National Museet in Copenhagen (*see* p.246), which was found in a peat bog not far from where Grauballe Man was discovered, actually shows a god holding a man head-down above a cauldron. A human sacrifice? It seems likely.

Despite the fascination of Grauballe Man, don't overlook on the rest of the museum, which gives excellent explanations of life in Denmark from the Stone Age to the Viking Age. There is also an attractive 'prehistoric trackway' – a 3km walk that

Getting There

Moesgård is 8km out of town and best reached by car going south from the harbour on Ørmeredevej – it is signposted. You can also reach it on the no.6 bus all year as well as bus no.19 in summer, which goes to the beach.

Eating Out

On a sunny day, it's nice to picnic. There are picnic tables in one of the courtyards of the museum as well as a small kiosk serving the usual crisps, sweets and hot dogs.

Restaurant Skovmøllen, Skovmøllevej 51, Højbjerg, **t** 86 27 12 14 (*moderate–inexpensive*). This is a far more civilized and adult option to crisps and a hot dog up at the museum and is actually on the prehistoric trail. if you're driving, don't turn off to the museum but carry on past. The restaurant is housed in a mill dating from the 16th century, although the half-timbered restaurant building dates from 1824. Next to a babbling brook, it has low ceilings and charming décor and serves good Danish fare and bread made with its own flour. *Open daily 12–6, evenings for reserved groups 6–9pm; 15 Sept–Mar closed Mon–Wed.*

takes you through woodland and fields in which graze Gotland sheep and Icelandic horses – both ancient Scandinavian breeds (the Icelandic is a descendant of Viking horses and is a pure strain) – towards Moesgård Strand (beach). On the way, you walk past authentic ancient sites, including burial cists, a temple, dolmen and an Iron Age house, that have been moved from their original sites to the museum; there are also reconstructions of Viking houses, including a 'pit house' based on excavations of those found in Århus.

A children's playground and various children's activities are on offer, including archery, which can be arranged if you phone in advance between 9am and 12pm.

When you have had your fill, wander along the **beach**, which is the best near Århus.

Silkeborg and the Lake District

If you are expecting wild and woolly grandeur from the Danish Lake District, think again – wild and woolly went out with the Vikings. However, given the flatness and inoffensive dullness of a lot of Denmark's scenery, it is nice to see water, overhanging trees and some gently rolling countryside with a few hills.

Silkeborg is the main town in the region, on the banks of the Gudenå river. It dates from the 19th century and is a popular holiday spot. It certainly merits a visit – even if you don't stay long – for the Silkeborg Museum and the Silkeborg Kunstmuseum. If the weather is good, wander along the harbour or take a trip on the world's oldest operating paddle steamer, still using its original 1861 engine. There are also plenty of opportunities for outdoor activities such as canoeing or fishing. If you are here in the evening, go down to the lake and watch the coloured fountains, which change colour and play until 11pm.

From Silkeborg, you can walk, drive or take the paddle steamer to Denmark's highest point at **Himmelbjerget**, the ironically (we hope) named 'Sky' or 'Heaven Mountain', which rises 147m above sea level (12m higher than the London Eye). Topped by a 25m tower erected in commemoration of King Frederik VII who gave Denmark its free constitution on 5 June 1849, it has a pretty view, overlooking Lake Jul-Sød. If you want to walk, there is a marked regional walking route that takes you from one end of the lake near Silkeborg in the west to the other at Ry, and beyond.

Silkeborg Museum

Hovedgårdsvej 7, t 86 82 14 99, f 87 20 51 90, www.silkeborgmuseum.dk; open mid-Oct–April Sat–Sun 12–4; May–mid-Oct daily 10–5; also winter half-term and Easter week, daily 12–4; adm.

The unmissable highlight of this museum is **Tollund Man**, a bog person dating from the early Iron Age, around 350 BC. Found in Bjældskovdal bog some 10km west of Silkeborg in 1950, he is preserved lying in the foetal position in which he was found, with his eyes closed, apparently sleeping peacefully. But his death was not so calm; he was found with a noose around his neck. Like Grauballe Man (*see* p.297), Tollund Man, aged about 40, was killed and then laid to rest in the bog, probably a sacrificial victim

Getting There

To get to Silkeborg from Århus, take secondary route 195, which will turn into a main road, route 15. **Buses** run between the two towns.

To Himmelbjerget

By car: leave Silkeborg centre going south, either following the tourist 'Margrethe' route north of the lakes, and then turning west at Ry on the 445 for a more leisurely route; or, alternatively, for a more direct route go south on route 52 and turn off on to route 445 at the first opportunity. There are two car parks at Himmelbjerget. Parking charge 10kr (payable when you leave).

By boat: The liner sails frequently during the summer from Silkeborg and Ry to the bottom of Himmelbjerget. From the lake a 1,200m hike leads to the the tower of Himmelbjerget.

By bus: Bus 311 leaves from Silkeborg station and Ry and goes to the car park at Himmelbjerget.

Tourist Information

Silkeborg: Havnen, Åhavevej 2a, **t** 86 82 19 11, *www.silkeborg.com* (*open Sat–Sun and hols all year 10–1 (except mid-June–Aug 10–2); Mon–Fri daily Nov–Mar 10–3; April–mid-June 9–4; mid-June–Aug 10–5; Sept–Oct 10–4*).

Festivals

The Riverboat Jazz Festival, one of the largest jazz events in all Scandinavia, happens in June and the whole town buzzes with jazz music from the boats, tents, cafés and restaurants.

The Hede Rytmer music festival takes place over a weekend in the park area 'Indelukket' in early July, when both Danish and international bands play their latest hits.

The Country Music Festival is staged over a weekend in August in the park. It is characterized by country music, pistol duels, line- and square dance, etc.

The International Puppet festival cheers up November.

For more information visit *www.festival jylland.dk*.

Sports and Activities

Walking

Check out walking routes at the tourist board. One, **Pramdragerstien**, also known as 'the towpath', runs for 23km from Kongensbro to Silkeborg. Here barges were pulled by horses and people.

Canoeing

Silkeborg Kanocenter, Åhave Allé 7, **t** 86 80 30 03, *www.silkeborgkanoudlejning.dk*.

Silkeborg Turistbureau, Aahavevej 2 A, **t** 86 82 19 11 (also prebooked camping/canoe trips.)

Fishing

Fishing permits can be got at the tourist office and also at campsites and inns. Contact the following to hire tackle:

Engholm Lystfiskersø, Engholmvej 1, Kjellerup, **t** 86 87 54 55.

Grønbæk Put & Take, Gl. Kongevej, Ans, **t** 86 87 05 33/40 54 45 33. Hire tackle and pay for your fish at the lakeside.

Eating Out

There are plenty of places to eat, as you would expect, and the tourist board will supply a good guide to restaurants and cafés in the town. But you might like to try one of the following:

Restaurant Piaf, Nygade 31, **t** 86 81 12 55 *www. restaurant-piaf.dk* (*expensive for 2–8 course menu*). Serves gourmet Danish food in a warm, attractive red-walled setting (or outside in the courtyard).

Restaurant Angus, Christian 8 Vej 7, **t** 86 82 28 54, *www.angus.dk* (*inexpensive*). A cosy little whitewashed steakhouse with a three-course menu for under 150kr.

Restaurant Riverside, Papirfabrikken 12, **t** 88 82 22 00, **f** 88 82 22 23, *www.restaurant riverside.dk* (*inexpensive for three-course menu*). The restaurant at the Radisson hotel – it has nice views and you can eat outside on a terrace on stilts over the river.

to the gods whose continued help in peat-cutting was so important. Tollund Man is perhaps the most arresting of the bog people in that his face and skin is in such amazing condition, with clearly visible wrinkles on his brow, stubble on his chin and scars on his feet, as fresh as they were on the day he died. Seeing him is truly a humbling and awesome experience.

The museum has another bog person on display – though less reverently than Tollund Man, which is a pity. In a show case alongside a display on Iron Age fashions lies **Elling Woman**, a tiny body, not as recognizable or in such good condition as her contemporary. She was found in 1938 just 100m from where Tollund Man was discovered 12 years later. She had also been hanged and was, presumably, another sacrifice to the gods. Her red hair (a result of the bog 'tanning' process) is very well preserved and tied in a variety of plaits. The rest of the museum doesn't have good English coverage and is fairly missable, though there is a nice courtyard café.

Silkeborg Kunstmuseum

Gudenåvej 7–9, t 86 82 53 88, f 86 81 51 31, www.silkeborgkunstmuseum.dk; open April–Oct Tues–Sun 10–5; Nov–Mar Tues–Fri 12–4, Sat–Sun and hols 10–5; adm; tours by arrangement (Danish, English, German, French, Russian).

This is an excellent art museum and contains probably the largest collection of works by Asger Jorn, a leading figure in 20th-century European art and the CoBrA group. Most of these were donated by the artist himself over 20 years between 1953 and 1973. His donation of 5,000 works also included pieces by 150 different artists. All the phases of Jorn's own work, including paintings, sculpture, ceramics, tapestries, drawings and graphics, are permanently exhibited.

The Jorn donation contains works by Max Ernst, Picabia, Le Corbusier, Léger, and his Danish contemporaries: Ejler Bille, Bjerke Petersen, Carl-Henning Pedersen, Egill Jacobsen and Heerup. Among the artists from the CoBrA group are Alechinsky, Appel, Constant, Corneille, and Wolvecamp, and from the 1950s and 1960s there are works by Baj, Dubuffet, Gallizio, Lam, Matta, Michaux, Saura, Ting, Wemaëre and Gruppe Spur. For the initiated and the uninitiated alike, these powerful, expressive works are a voyage of discovery, causing bells to ring and connections with other schools of European art to be made.

Ebeltoft

Ebeltoft, in the hilly (by Danish standards) wooded Mols region on the Djursland peninsula 53km (33 miles) northeast of Århus, is a charming market town with medieval half-timbered houses, hollyhocks lining its cobbled streets, a working harbour and a relatively new reputation as a major centre for producing and promoting fine artisanal glass work.

For a wander around the town (whose name means 'apple orchard'), the oldest buildings are in Nygade and Skindergade, north of the old **town hall**, a charming 'playhouse' of a building dating from 1789 with a bell tower (incidentally, the smallest

Getting There and Around

For a quick route, follow route 15 and turn off on to route 21 towards Tastrup and Ebeltoft. Or, for a longer, prettier drive, follow the 'tourist' Margrethe route through Hornslet, Bønde and Lyngsbæk Strand. The town can also be reached from Århus by a regular **bus**.

If you want to walk, there are information points in the Mols Bjerget area, with folders from the National Forest and Nature Agency and maps of signposted footpaths.

Tourist Information

Ebeltoft/Mols: Strandvejen 2, t 86 34 14 00, f 86 34 05 28, *www.visitdjursland.com* (*open Jan–mid-June Mon–Fri 9–4.30, Sat 10–1; mid-June–early Aug Mon–Fri 9–5, Sat 10–4, Sun 10–2; early Aug–Dec Mon–Fri 9–4.30, Sat 10–1*).

Eating Out

For a treat, these are two of the best restaurants in town:

Ane Kirstine, Adelgade 62, t 86 34 44 66 (*expensive–moderate*). Delicious, mouth-watering seasonal food based on Danish, French and Italian cuisine; this pretty restaurant has two dining rooms – one yellow, one white – and is run by one of the region's best chefs, Poul Erik. *Open 12–10; reservations recommended.*

Mellem Jyder, Juulsbakke 3, t 86 34 11 23 (*expensive–inexpensive*). Lovely Danish food in the oldest and most historically evocative restaurant in Ebeltoft (*c.* 1610). There is a popular beer garden at the back. The fixed menu is very reasonable. *Open Wed–Sun 12–8; reservations recommended.*

Rådhus in Denmark). Its **museum** houses an ethnographic collection from Thailand and artefacts from the town's history. You will find more typical crooked, half-timbered buildings in the area south of the town hall.

West of Torvet (the town square), **Farvergårdeb**, an old dyeworks, Adelgade 13–15, t 86 34 13 82 (*open 1 June–31 Aug daily 11–5; adm*), dates from 1772, although the oldest part goes back to 1683. It's an atmospheric exhibition, showing you where the workers lived (the furniture is original), a pressing room, a dye room with boilers, a printing room, and a stable wing dating from the early 18th century.

On Strandvejen, you will find one of Ebeltoft's principal attractions – the lovely **Glasmuseum**, Strandvejen 8, t 86 34 17 99, f 86 34 60 60, *www.glasmuseet.dk* (*open Aug–June daily 10–5; July daily 10–7; adm*), which is located in the old Customs and Excise house. Here, you are left open-mouthed at the talent and craftsmanship on display – how exactly *do* you 'blow' a pair of Cinderella glass slippers, as Silvia Levenson (Italy, 1999) has done? The collection consists of about 1,500 glass artworks (though they are not all on display at the same time) and there are several independent exhibitions a year. But you needn't just marvel at how these beautiful objects are created – there is a glass studio in which young glass blowers practise their craft during the summer months, from May until September. Avoid the shop if you don't wish to be seduced into buying unexpected lovely objects.

The other major attraction in Ebeltoft is the frigate *Fregatten Jylland*, t 86 34 10 99 (*open daily 10–7; adm*). It was launched in 1860 and at 72m is the world's longest wooden frigate. After an eventful life as a man-of-war and a royal yacht, it was beautifully restored and opened to the public in 1994.

If you are here in the evening between mid-June and mid-August, the town crier does his rounds between 8pm and 10pm, calling out to the townspeople and giving you some information along the way.

Touring from Århus

Day 1: Museums and Walking in the Lake District

Morning: Take the 170 route south from Århus to Skanderborg. From here, cross the E45 on to route 445 to **Himmelbjerget**. Park in one of the car parks and walk up to the tower to take in the view.

Lunch: Have an early lunch at the restaurant at the hotel at the base of Himmelbjerget, picnic in the woods or for a gourmet extravaganza eat at Nørre Vissing, *see* below.

Afternoon: Drive on to **Silkeborg** on route 445, turning north (right) on to route 52. Visit the Silkeborg Museum, Hovedgårdsvej 7 (*open mid-Oct–April Sat–Sun 12–4; May–mid-Oct daily 10–5; also winter half-term and Easter week, daily 12–4; adm*), to see the astonishingly well-preserved bodies of Iron Age Elling Woman and Tollund Man, discovered in nearby peat bogs in 1938 and 1950 (*see* p.298). Have a drink in the airy café or its courtyard and then drive a short distance to the Silkeborg Kunstmuseum, Gudenåvej 7–9 (*open April–Oct Tues–Sun 10–5; Nov–Mar Tues–Fri 12–4, Sat–Sun 10–5; adm; tours by special arrangement in Danish, English, German, French and Russian*), to admire the powerful work of Danish pioneer Asger Jorn and his contemporaries (*see* p.300). Then head north on route 52 to the town of **Viborg**, where every Danish king was crowned, from Knud in 1027 to Christian V in 1655.

Dinner and Sleeping: In Viborg, *see* below.

Day 1

Lunch in Himmelbjerget or Nr Vissing

Hotel Himmelbjerget, Himmelbjergvej 20, 8680 Ry, t 86 89 80 45/winter t 86 82 00 68, f 86 89 87 93 (*moderate–inexpensive*). Choose from a café or the nice old-fashioned restaurant, which serves generous portions of international and Danish fare; both have lake views.

Nørre Vissing Kro, Låsbyvej 122, Nørre Vissing, Skanderborg, t 86 94 37 16 (*very expensive–moderate*). Drive north from Ry to Låsby, turn southeast on to the 457 to Nr Vissing. This is one of Jutland's best restaurants and has won several awards. It serves delicious gourmet food in the French, Italian and Danish traditions – *foie gras* with cherry sauce on sautéed summer cabbage, and poached lobster with spinach flan and orange sauce. (The fixed price dinner menu is very good value if you decide to stay; the hotel is charming and moderate in price.) *Open daily 12–3 and 6–9; reservations recommended.*

Dinner in Viborg

See also opposite page, Day 2.

Den Gyldne Okse, Store Sankt Peders, t 86 62 27 44 (*expensive–inexpensive*). This 400-year-old inn is a perfect place for lunch (light *smørrebrød*, salads, fresh-baked rye bread, etc.) or dinner (predominantly steak or fish dishes), for the atmosphere as much as for the food. *Open Mon–Sat 11–3 and 5–10.*

Sleeping in Viborg

See also opposite page, Day 2.

Palads Hotel, Sankt Mathias Gade 5, t 86 62 37 00, f 86 62 40 46 (*expensive–moderate*). Modern on the inside and neoclassical with a hint of Art Nouveau on the outside, this is a nice, comfortable hotel with light, simple décor. Just outside is the Danish showbiz equivalent of the hand prints near Los Angeles's Grauman's Chinese Theater.

Niels Bugges Kro, Ravnsbjergvej 69, Dollerup Bakker, 8800 Viborg, t 86 63 80 11 (*moderate–inexpensive*). Well known for its good restaurant, this inn a few km south of Viborg overlooks a lake, 16 attractive rooms.

Day 2: Viborg

Morning: Visit the winding streets of the old town of **Viborg**, heading first for the twin-towered Domkirke, Domkirkepladsen, Sankt Mogens Gade 4 (*open June–Aug Mon–Sat 10–5, Sun 12–5; April–May and Sept Mon–Sat 11–4, Sun 12–4; Oct–Mar Mon–Sat 11–3, Sun 12–3*), originally built in the 12th century but destroyed by fire in 1876 and rebuilt. Notable features are the biblical frescoes of Joakim Skovgaard (1901–06), the crypt in which there are still traces of the first stone crypt from 1130, and the leather-clad coffin of Valdemar Daa, the alchemist, described by Hans Christian Andersen in his story, *The Wind Tells of Valdemar Daa and his Daughters*. In front of the main altar, the black stone marks the grave of the king Erik Glipping, who was murdered in 1286 when staying at Finderup, southwest of Viborg. A couple of streets away, have a look at the Romanesque Søndre Sogn Kirke, all that is left of the cloisters of the monastery of the Dominican Black Friars, abolished at the Reformation.

Lunch: In Viborg, *see* below.

Afternoon: If you liked the cathedral frescoes, visit the nearby Skovgaard Museum, Domkirkestræde 2–4 (*open May–Sept daily 10–12.30 and 1.30–5; Oct–April daily 1.30–5; adm*), where you can see more of the artist's work, including sketches for the frescoes. For the history of the town since Viking times, visit the Stiftsmuseum, Hjultorvet 9 (*open May–Aug daily 11–5; Oct–Mar Tues–Fri 1–4, Sat and Sun 11–5*).

Dinner and Sleeping: In Viborg, *see* below.

Day 2

Lunch in Viborg

There are plenty of places to picnic in Viborg and many sandwich shops (try Jerbanegade 14). **Arthur's**, Vestergade 4, t 86 62 21 26 (*moderate –inexpensive*). In the main pedestrianized area, this is a small, charming restaurant with a café at the front. It offers a fairly standard choice for a light lunch, including salads, *smørrebrød*, pasta, omelettes, burgers, and marinated or smoked fish, and more imaginative dishes with an exotic international twist for dinner. *Open Mon–Sat 11.30–3 and 6–10; reservations recommended.* **Brugger Bauer**, Skt. Mathiasgade 61, t 86 61 44 88 (*moderate–inexpensive*). Open for lunch and supper, this cellar restaurant, which brews its own beer, is a good, atmospheric gastro-pub, with hearty Danish dishes such as salmon steak with lobster sauce and boiled potatoes and pork filet boiled in beer or fried beefsteak with fried onions and potatoes. *Open Mon–Sat 11–11, Sun 2–10.*

Dinner and Sleeping in Viborg

See also opposite page, Day 1.

Golf Hotel Viborg, Randersvej, t 86 61 02 22, f 86 61 31 71 (*expensive*). One km east of the centre, this is a tasteful, all-mod-cons, spacious hotel overlooking the lake, with big windows, modern art, oriental carpets and leather armchairs.

Restaurant Jagtstuen, Gammel Århusvej 323, t 86 63 90 44 (*expensive–moderate*). This rustic restaurant in the Rindsholm Kro (which also offers 7 cosy but simple, inexpensive rooms) is 5.5km out of Viborg in the countryside and has a Second World War American tank in the garden. From Viborg drive southeast along route 26, following signs to Århus. It serves Danish and international cuisine with dishes as diverse and delicious as wild duckling with port and game sauce, medallions of venison with blackcurrant sauce, fresh plaice with parsley and butter, or catfish with limes. *Open daily 4–8.30 (last orders).*

Day 3: Randers and Aalborg

Morning: Drive east to **Randers** along route 16 and visit the Randers Tropical Zoo, Randers Regnskov, Tørvebryggen 11 (*open Mon–Fri 10–4, Sat and Sun 10–5, hols daily 10–5; mid-June–mid-Aug 10–6*), one of Denmark's most visited attractions, with three domes representing the rainforests of Asia, South America and Africa, complete with free-roaming animals, a snake garden and an aquarium designed to look like an 18th-century Danish frigate. Or you can drive straight to Aalborg on route 13 and join the E45 at junction 32.

Lunch: Early lunch at the zoo, *see* below. Alternatively, lunch in Aalborg, *see* below.

Afternoon: Take the E45 motorway to **Aalborg**. At the harbour Marine Museum, Vestre Fjordvej 81 (*open Sept–April daily 10–4; May–Aug daily 10–6; adm*), you will discover, by climbing inside an authentic submarine, *Springeren* (holder of the Danish diving record of 29 days and nights), that they are nowhere near as big as they look in the movies. There is also a decommissioned warship. The North Jutland Art Museum, Kong Christians Allé (*open Tues–Sun 10–5; adm*), has an impressive modern collection, with works by Warhol, Le Corbusier and Léger as well as important Danish artists, including the CoBrA group. Other sights include the Viking burial site at Lindholm Høje, Vendilavej 11 (*open April–Oct daily 10–5; Nov–Mar Tues–Sun 11–4; adm*), and the Aalborg Historical Museum, Algade 2 (*open Tues–Sun 10–5; adm*), where you can see another Iron Age bog woman. Have a walk round the old town to finish off.

Dinner and Sleeping: In Aalborg, *see* below.

Day 3

Lunch in Randers or Aalborg

Randers Tropical Zoo café (*inexpensive*). Light meals for both adults and children, either in the café or on the terrace with views over Gudenådalen.

Aalborg: Gastronomy, unfortunately, isn't really Aalborg's forte, so don't expect a very wide choice. Try **Jomfu Ane Gade** for lunch (ignore the hype, this street is OK for a very ordinary lunch but disappointing for dinner) or, perhaps a better option, snack at the historic beer cellar, **Duus Vinkjoelder**, Ostergade 9 (also good in the evening but not for food). For convenience, the **Marine Museum**, **Art Museum** and **Lindholm Høje** all have **cafés** on site.

Dinner in Aalborg

Kniv og Gaffel, Maren Turis Gade 10, t 98 16 69 72 (*moderate–inexpensive*). Good French-Danish food by candlelight on old oak tables in a house dating from 1552. Its thick steaks are said to be the best in town. *Open Mon–Wed 12–10, Thurs–Sat 12–11.*

Ristorante Fellini, Vestergade 13, t 98 11 34 55 (*moderate–inexpensive*). Good southern Italian food cooked by southern Italians – a change from all the cold-weather food on offer elsewhere. Lots of fresh fish dishes and delicious marinated vegetables and roast lamb. *Open daily 11am–12am.*

Sleeping in Aalborg

Helnan Phønix Hotel, Vesterbro 77, t 98 12 00 11, f 98 10 10 20 (*expensive–moderate*). Tastefully decorated with dark-wood furniture, this is Aalborg's oldest and most prestigious hotel (1783). Exposed beams in some rooms.

Hotel Scheelsminde, Scheelsmindevej 35, t 98 18 32 33 (*expensive–moderate*). Four km from the centre in large grounds, this is a very popular hotel. Some of it dates from 1808; also a restaurant on site.

Park Hotel, J.F. Kennedys Plads 41, t 98 12 31 33, f 98 13 31 66 (*moderate*). Clean, comfortable modern rooms (though quite small) in an nice 18th-century building.

Day 4: Skagen

Morning: Set off early and drive north to the seaside town of **Skagen**, popular with the rich crowd and famous for its artists' colony in the 19th century. Take route 180 and join the E39 to Hirtshals. Pick up the Margrethe route east, along the coast, and join up with route 597; when you reach route 40, go north. Six km before Skagen, explore the **Råbjerg Mile**, a vast shifting sand dune overlooking the sea (only turn off when signs specifically name it) and then, 11km further on, **Tailsandede**, a church (of which only the tower remains) submerged in the sand. When you reach Skagen, continue on route 40 to **Grenen Point**, the northernmost point of Denmark where the Kattegat and Skagerrak seas meet (you can see one flowing into the other – especially exciting in rough seas). Walk (15mins) or take the tractor bus along the lovely beach. Look for the **grave of Holger Drachman**, a 19th-century artist who loved the sea.

Lunch: In Skagen, *see* below.

Afternoon: In **Skagen**, visit Michael and Anna Ancher's House, Markvej 2 (*open Nov–Mar Sat–Sun 11–3; April and Oct daily 11–3; May–mid-June and mid-Aug–Sept daily 10–5; mid-June–mid-Aug daily 10–6*), home to these famous artists between 1884 and 1935. It is a charming house full of their own paintings and others by their friends who also followed the artistic principles of the French Impressionists. Next door is Saxilds Gaard, now a gallery, showing exhibitions of works belonging to the Helga Ancher Foundation (Helga was their daughter (1883–1964).

Dinner and Sleeping: In Skagen, *see* below.

Day 4

Lunch and Dinner in Skagen

Food here tends to be good (lots of fish!) and most places in town cater for lunch and dinner. Some restaurants are not open all year. *See also* restaurants on following page, Day 5.

Jakobs, Havnevej 4A, **t** 98 44 16 90, *www. jakobscafe.dk* (*moderate–inexpensive*). This is a lively attractive café/restaurant near the harbour with a brunch, lunch and dinner menu. At weekends there is live music, and at night prepare to dance.

Plesner Restaurant, *see* Plesner Hotel, below.

Sleeping in Skagen

If you are staying in the same hotel for more than one night, many hotels have special deals. *See also* hotels overleaf, Day 5.

Brøndum's Hotel – *see* next page (*expensive– moderate*). This is the most historic and poshest place in Skagen but note that, due to its historic standing, the building has not been updated and rooms are not en suite.

Finn's Hotel Pension, Østre Strandvej 63, **t** 98 45 01 55, **f** 98 45 045 55 (*moderate*). The northernmost hotel in Denmark and a delightful find. Run by Finn and his colleague Palle, who live in a house in the garden, this is a Norwegian log-house dating from 1923 originally designed as a summer house for a count. Small and catering to a civilized, relaxed clientele, it has six lovely rooms (most without bath), decorated with antiques, old furniture and a charming clutter of photographs, paintings and ornaments. There is a lovely library (no TV on principle) and a pretty garden. Breakfast is *en famille* in the dining room and, if you would like lunch or supper, tell Finn in the morning and he will rustle up something delicious. No children under 15.

Plesner Hotel and Restaurant, Holstevj 8, **t** 98 44 68 44, **f** 98 44 36 86, *www. hotelplesner.dk* (*moderate*). Friendly and attractive; good-sized rooms not far from the centre. The restaurant is good and has a lovely terrace.

Day 5: Skagen

Morning: Go for a walk and check out some very chic shops, then visit the delightful Skagen Museum, Brøndumsvej 4 (*open June–Aug daily 10–6; May and Sept daily 10–5; April and Oct Tues–Sun 11–4; Nov–Mar Wed–Fri 1–4, Sat 11–4, Sun 11–3*), full of lovely beach scenes by P.S. Krøyer, intimate family pictures by Anna Ancher and many others, including *Drowned Fisherman* (1896) by Michael Ancher, that depict the daily lives of the artists and fishermen in Skagen's white-bright light.

Lunch: In Skagen, *see* below.

Afternoon: Towards **Grenen**, visit the Odde Naturcenter, Batterivej 51 (*open June–Aug 10–10; Sept–May 1–4; adm*), an excellent exhibition, inspired by Skagen's environment, that explains the properties of water, sand, wind and light. Its airy building was designed by Jørn Utson (*see* p.271). The By og Egnsmuseum, P.K. Nielsensvej 8–10 (*open Mar–June and Aug–Oct Mon–Fri 10–4; May, June, Aug and Sept also Sat and Sun 11–4; July Mon–Fri 10–6, Sat–Sun 11–4; Nov–Feb Mon–Fri 11–3*), demonstrates the human side of Skagen, the fishing industry and the fishermen's lives, including reconstructions of homes, one of which has a parlour kept cool in case it was needed to lay out drowned men. Close by are the houses of the artists P.S. Krøyer and Holger Drachmann at Hans Baghs Vej 21 (*open May Sat–Sun 11–3; June–mid-Sept daily 11–3; mid-Sept–mid-Oct Sat–Sun 11–3; adm*).

Dinner and Sleeping: In Skagen, *see* below. If you are flying from Århus in the morning, leave three hours to get to the airport just outside Tirstrup (take route 40 to Frederikshavn, followed by the E45 motorway and routes 21 and 15).

Day 5

Lunch and Dinner in Skagen

See also previous page, Day 4.

Skagen Fiskerestaurant, Fiskehuskaj 13, t 98 44 35 44, *www.skagen-fiskerestaurant.dk* (*expensive–inexpensive*). This fish restaurant on the first floor, overlooking the harbour, can cater to every budget and even does takeaway. Music every evening in summer.

Brøndums Hotel, Anchersvej 3, t 98 44 15 55 (*expensive*). Delicious food in this picturesque hotel where the Skagen artists stayed. It was run by Anna Ancher's parents, the Brøndums, and it is said she was born early while her mother was waiting on Hans Christian Andersen who was being difficult. The original dining room, hung with portraits of and by the group, is in Skagen Museum.

Pakhuset, Fiskerestaurant & Havncafe, Skagen Havn, t 98 44 20 00 (*moderate*). One of the nicest places to have dinner in Skagen. It is on the waterfront, attractively decorated (its walls act as a gallery for a local artist) and boasts a café/bistro and a more expensive restaurant on the second floor. The food is delicious, with fish the speciality, and the company is friendly. There is often live music and the tables are pushed back for dancing.

Restaurant De 2 Have, Fyrvej 42, t 98 44 24 35, f 98 45 07 21 (*very expensive–expensive*). For a treat, this gourmet restaurant on the beach at Grenen has fantastic views. There is also a café, which is nice for lunch.

Sleeping in Skagen

See also previous page, Day 4.

Foldens Hotel, Sankt Laurentii Vej 41, 9990 Skagen, t 98 44 11 66, *www.foldens-hotel.dk* (*moderate*). Rooms vary in size and décor but generally a reasonable option. There is a café and restaurant too.

Villa Skagen, Sankt Clementsvej 3, t 98 44 33 11, *www.villa-skagen.dk* (*moderate–inexpensive*). A pretty hotel close to the harbour, with simple double rooms, shared loos and bathrooms, a kitchen on the first floor if you want to self-cater and a small garden.

Language

Danish is the official language of Denmark, Greenland and the Færoe Islands. Both Greenland and the Færoe Islands have their own language, too, which most people speak, but Danish is used for official purposes and taught in schools.

Danish is also spoken by 20,000 people just south of the German border – going back to the period when this was under Danish sovereignty before 1864. The Danish minority there is very keen on preserving its language. In Icelandic schools, too, the first foreign language to be taught is Danish; it serves as a way of communicating with the other Scandinavian countries.

The Written Language

There are 29 letters in the Danish alphabet – in addition to A–Z, there are æ, ø and å – the latter (used in in Swedish and Norwegian) was introduced in 1948 in the spelling reform, which also abolished the practice of beginning all nouns with a capital letter.

The letters æ, ø and å are the last three letters of the alphabet and they are all vowels. The å was introduced to to replace aa. However, there are many words and places that are spelt both ways – e.g. Aalborg and Århus – which is generally a matter of convention. Aalborg insists on using the double-a even on road signs whereas Århus insists on using the å. (The proper usage of å versus aa is according to Retskrivningsbogen, the Danish dictionary of orthography.)

Besides the æ, ø and å the most important things worth knowing about the Danish alphabet is that the letters c, q, w, x and z are only used in loan words – as, for instance, in check, zoo, weekend – and that the letters v and w are treated as being the same. This is why many Danes have difficulties in the pronunciation of these two letters in English.

Vowels

There are nine vowels in the Danish/ Norwegian alphabet: a, e, i, o, u, y, æ, ø and å. For people who only speak English they are often not pronounced quite the way you would expect.

The five first vowels are pronounced as in most European languages other than English.

æ is pronounced 1) as in hat or 2) as in any or end.

ø is pronounced as in earn.

å is pronounced 1) as awe and or 2) as in no or low.

It is important to distinguish between long and short vowels. A short vowel is often indicated by doubling the consonant after it.

Consonants

b, d, f, h, k, l, m, n, p, s, t and v are pronounced more or less as in English.

g is pronounced as in guess, almost never as in gene.

j is pronounced as the y in yes.

c, q, w, x and z are only used in foreign words.

c is pronounced as s when it comes before e, i, y and æ, and as k in all other cases.

q is pronounced as k.

w is pronounced as v (never as English w).

x is pronounced as s if it is the first letter in a word and is pronounced as ks if it is not.

z is pronounced as s.

Note that Danish does not have the voiced z-sound, so Danish s, x and z are never pronounced as in English.

Useful Phrases

The likelihood of your ever needing to speak Danish is remote as English is widespread and everyone can speak it from the bus conductor to the university lecturer. German and French are also widely understood and spoken. However, in case of need or to show solidarity, here are a few words, phrases and sentences that might come in handy.

Hello *Hej* (informal), *Goddag* (formal)
Goodbye *Hej Hej* or *Farvel*
Please *Vil du være venlig at...*
Thank you *Tak*
How do I get to... *Hvordan kommer jeg til...*
Where is the tourist office? *(Undskyld), ved du hvor turistkontoret ligger?*
What's the weather forecast for the next few days? *Hvordan er vejrudsigten for de næste dage?*
Where is the best club/disco in town? *Hvor er byens bedste diskotek?*
Would you like to dance with me? *Vil du danse?*
May I have a glass of beer? *En øl, tak?*
Where can I rent a bike? *Hvor kan jeg leje en cykel?*
Yes *Ja*
No *Nej*
My name is... *Jeg hedder...*
How are you? *Hvordan har du det?*
I'm very well *Jeg har det godt*
I feel ill *Jeg har det dårligt*
How much does it cost? *Hvor meget koster det?*
Do you speak English? *Taler du engelsk?*
I don't understand *Jeg forstår ikke*
Where is...? *Hvor er...?*
entrance *indgang*
exit *udgang*
danger *fare*
toilets *toiletter*
doctor *læge*
hotel *hotel*
restaurant *restaurant*
beer *øl*
wine *vin*
open *åben*
closed *lukket*
menu *menu*
today *idag*
tomorrow *imorgen*

Days of the Week
Monday *Mandag*
Tuesday *Tirsdag*
Wednesday *Onsdag*
Thursday *Torsdag*
Friday *Fredag*
Saturday *Lørdag*
Sunday *Søndag*

Months
January *Januar*
February *Februar*
March *Marts*
April *April*
May *Maj*
June *Juni*
July *Juli*
August *August*
September *September*
October *Oktober*
November *November*
December *December*

Numbers
one *en*
two *to*
three *tre*
four *fire*
five *fem*
six *seks*
seven *syv*
eight *otte*
nine *ni*
ten *ti*
twenty *tyve*
thirty *tredive*
forty *fyrre*
fifty *halvtreds*
sixty *tres*
seventy *halvfjerds*
eighty *firs*
ninety *halvfems*
one hundred *hundrede*
one thousand *tusind*

Index

Main references are in **bold**. References to maps are in *italics*. (S) = Sweden; (N) = Norway; (D) = Denmark